research IN psychotherapy

research IN psychotherapy

JULIAN MELTZOFF
and
MELVIN KORNREICH

Routledge
Taylor & Francis Group
LONDON AND NEW YORK

First published 1970 by Transaction Publishers

Published 2023 by Routledge
4 Park Square, Milton Park, Abingdon, Oxon OX14 4RN
605 Third Avenue, New York, NY 10017

Routledge is an imprint of the Taylor & Francis Group, an informa business

First issued in hardback 2017

Library of Congress Catalog Number: 2007031520

Library of Congress Cataloging-in-Publication Data

Meltzoff, Julian.
Research in psychotherapy / Julian Meltzoff and Melvin Kornreich.
p. ; cm.
Originally published: New York : Atherton, 1970.
Includes bibliographical references and index.
ISBN 978-0-202-30989-7 (pbk. : alk paper)
1. Psychotherapy--Research. I. Kornreich, Melvin. II. Title.
[DNLM: 1. Psychotherapy. WM 420 M528r 1970a]

RC480.M45 2007
616.89'140072--dc22

2007031520

ISBN 13: 978-0-202-30989-7 (pbk)
ISBN 13: 978-1-138-53192-5 (hbk)

Preface and Acknowledgments

Keeping pace with a runaway literature is one of the major problems of researchers and those in clinical practice. From time to time it is necessary to pause and review the current state of our knowledge about a given area. The area of psychotherapy is in particular need of review. The research literature is there, but few have ever had the opportunity or the incentive to explore systematically its seemingly endless pathways. The function of psychotherapy is to grapple with the conflicts of individuals, but in the process it has become enmeshed in conflicts of its own. We hope that the presentation of accumulated evidence will help resolve some of the conflicts, although we recognize that it may serve to draw attention to others.

This book is written for psychotherapists, researchers, teachers, and students in all of the allied mental health professions. It is designed to be used as a general reference work in this area, as an instructional guide, and as a source of information about specific aspects and problems of research in psychotherapy for those who wish to expand our knowledge through further investigation.

We would like to express our appreciation to those who helped ease the completion of this task. Our greatest debt is to the skill and patience of Mrs. Florence Konz, Chief of the Medical Library Service at the Veterans Administration Outpatient Clinic, Brooklyn, New York, who repeatedly went out of her way to make available to us the scientific literature upon which this book is based. Without her help and cooperation we could have never completed the project. The clerical and typing assistance of Mr. Francis X. Leon, Mrs. Juanita E. Davies, and Mrs. Celia L. Epstein is gratefully acknowledged. Our particular gratitude goes to Mrs. Mary Spellens of Atherton Press, whose outstanding editorial skill, sensitivity to issues, and intelligent guidance through the complexities of manuscript preparation materially enhanced the readability of this book. Finally, we are thankful to Dr. Jerome L. Singer for having encouraged us to undertake this book in the first place.

Introduction

We entered this project in the spirit of free inquiry and with a genuine desire to discover what facts research has established about psychotherapy. Considering ourselves moderately well informed, we had some preconceptions about what the literature contained. Many of them proved to be false. Above all, we were open to having our beliefs supported or negated. We had no particular causes to press—we are both practicing psychotherapists and researchers, have experienced the hopes and disappointments of each, and see the roles as mutually supportive and symbiotic rather than antithetical. We felt that we could learn from and apply whatever facts emerged. Our conviction is that clinical practice should be influenced by research findings and that rigorous research can be done on the subject of psychotherapy. We believe that the difficulty of the subject should not be used to excuse poor research or to exempt it from meeting acceptable experimental standards; nor should research findings be ignored if they run counter to one's own beliefs.

In-depth reading of the research literature on psychotherapy has been a unique experience. We were surprised to find out how much good work has been done, and we were made acutely aware of the staggering amount that needs to be done. The research literature is one of striking contrasts that alternately impress and distress the reader. The high quality of some research projects stands out in bold relief against the glaring deficiencies of others. One cannot but admire the ingenuity and resourcefulness of some researchers in contrast to the half-hearted, pedestrian attempts of others; the respect for data shown by some despite the downfall of their favorite hypotheses as opposed to others' cavalier flouting of data in reiterating an *idée fixe*. We come away impressed with the ability shown by many to reason and to think logically about a subject that is highly charged with attitudes and emotions and whose very subject matter is human feelings. As for those who were unable to meet the challenge, we still feel that the game was worth the candle because others can learn from their errors.

This book consists of three parts. Part I is a general discussion of principles and methods of research as they are applied to investigations of psychotherapy. It is not meant as a "do-it-yourself" manual for home-grown researchers. Nor is it an exhaustive presentation of how to do research and design experiments. It is meant to supply general background material and principles to aid nonresearchers in appreciating some of the important problems that are encountered so that they will be better able to understand and appraise research reports. It is meant to present a perspective and posture on controversial issues surrounding research in psychotherapy and to provide a framework against which new research can be gauged.

In Part II, existing research on the effects of psychotherapy and the determinants and correlates of outcome are clustered and reviewed. Chapters 4 to 7 are concerned strictly with a review and appraisal of controlled studies that were designed to evaluate the effects of psychotherapy. The total number of research reports that had to be read vastly exceeded the number actually reviewed in this book. The winnowing process eliminated a large number of statistical reports of results that lacked control data as well as reports of testimonials and opinions regardless of how authoritative the source. Also excluded are some impressive systematic studies of shaping by contingent reinforcement of specific adaptive behaviors important to institutional living of schizophrenic patients. Despite their theoretical and practical importance, these studies are not included because of their limited focus on the modification of highly specific and restricted behaviors rather than upon broader therapeutic objectives. Case demonstrations by various approaches are not considered. It would be foolhardy to claim that the resulting accumulation of research comprises the totality of existing studies, but we believe that it contains at least a significant portion of the research that has been published and that it is representative of the total. All published controlled-outcome studies that we have been able to track down are reported. No other selection bias of any kind was applied. The appraisal of research evidence is, however, bound to be a subjective matter, and in the final analysis each reader must draw his own conclusions and incorporate what he sees as important into his store of knowledge. We believe that in order to judge the evidence and to be in a position to draw conclusions, the reader would need to have at hand the major aspects of the research, not just the researcher's conclusions or our own. It is for this reason that in our summaries of each research project we have attempted to supply enough essential details for the reader to be able to form his own judgment. We have imposed our own gross evaluative classification of the research as "adequate" or "questionable" evidence, but we do not expect all readers to agree invariably with our judgment. As in any rough classification, each rubric encompasses a distribution, and those projects considered as providing adequate evidence range from weak or borderline to exceptionally strong. Some excellent research is categorized as questionable on the issue of our inquiry only.

Chapters 8 to 13 deal with a large body of research on various factors associated with therapeutic outcome—method, style, and technique variables; patient, therapist, and time variables. As it turns out, more research has been done on these issues than on any other aspect of psychotherapy. Part III is concerned with research on aspects of the therapeutic process and on the effect of many of these same variables on the therapeutic interchange as distinct from the outcome of therapy. Also discussed is research on various therapeutic phenomena and conditions, about which so much has been written and so little really known.

Many studies contain information about several different issues that are discussed in different sections of this book. A certain amount of repetition is therefore required, because this is not the kind of book that is likely to be read in one sitting and the reader cannot be expected to recall the details of an experiment reported in an earlier section. Brief recapitulation of the essentials of the study that bear on the particular issue under discussion are furnished where they are thought to be necessary to facilitate understanding. This should minimize but does not entirely eliminate the need for cross-referral for fuller information. If the book is read in sequence, some studies reported in various contexts will acquire the status of old friends.

Contents

II. RESEARCH ON THE EFFECTS OF PSYCHOTHERAPY

PART I

PRINCIPLES AND METHODS OF RESEARCH IN PSYCHOTHERAPY

Order and simplification are the first steps toward the mastery of a subject—the actual enemy is the unknown.

—THOMAS MANN, *The Magic Mountain*

By faith, and faith alone embrace,
Believing where we cannot prove. . . .

—ALFRED LORD TENNYSON, "In Memoriam"

A bad beginning makes a bad ending.

—EURIPIDES, *Aeolus*

1

Problems and Design in Psychotherapy Research

Almost all aspects of psychotherapy have been subject to extensive controversy. Psychotherapeutic theories and their efficacy, the training of therapists, the various methods and techniques of therapy, the essential nature of the psychotherapeutic process—indeed the very definition of psychotherapy—all have been disputed. Since there is no accepted definition of psychotherapy, it is necessary to specify what we take it to encompass. That this is no frivolous undertaking is attested by a statement in Cushing's (1950) report of the Committee on the Evaluation of Psychoanalytic Therapy of the American Psychoanalytic Association: "In order to evaluate a subject one must first know of what that subject consists, and since apparently there were no two individuals, not only of the Committee but of the society as a whole, who would agree to a definition of psychoanalysis, the Committee was at a loss as to how they were to know just what they were evaluating" (p. 17). Because psychotherapy is a more inclusive term that covers many approaches besides psychoanalysis, no definition is likely to find general acceptance. It is possible, however, to define it at least well enough to delimit the subject matter under review. Psychotherapy is used here as a generic term that includes the entire gamut of specialized approaches. The specific kind of psychotherapy will be designated in any discussion of research that does not allow for generalization to other psychotherapeutic approaches.

DEFINITION OF PSYCHOTHERAPY

The basic concern of our discussion is with the intentional, causal, predictable modification of pathological behavior by methods generically known as psychotherapy. Psychotherapy is taken to mean the informed and planful application of techniques derived from established psychological principles, by persons qualified through training and experience to understand these principles and to apply these techniques with the intention of assisting individuals to modify such personal characteristics as feelings, values, attitudes, and behaviors which are judged by the therapist to be maladaptive or maladjustive.

We imply by the use of the phrase "informed and planful application" of certain techniques that the helping person must possess a systematic body of knowledge and use it in accordance with some specifiable plan. In order for psychotherapy, as conceived here, to take place, the therapist and his patient must have a formalized arrangement, agreement, or understanding about the nature of their relationship and respective roles. Therefore, we exclude from the realm of psychotherapy any chance interpersonal encounters with a qualified person. We also rule out "therapies without awareness," in which one person exerts a beneficial influence upon others in social, business, educational, or any other personal contact. Thus, a school teacher who succeeds in modifying the personality of a pupil incidentally to her primary teaching goal would not be thought of as doing psychotherapy even though some psychological principles were directly applied or formed the basis of her teaching procedures. The teacher is not qualified by training or experience to understand and apply the psychological principles in an informed and planful way, and the arrangement between teacher and pupil in their respective roles is not that of therapist and patient. In the same way, a minister, lawyer, bartender, or any other individual in a personal service relationship, other than those specifically trained in the application of psychological principles, would not be considered to be doing psychotherapy. This is not to say that these people do not modify behavior, effect changes in attitudes, feelings, and values, and exercise beneficial effects upon people, for they often do. The relevant issue is that we are concerned exclusively with research on "psychotherapy," not with the beneficial effects upon personality of other different but related processes. Psychotherapy is not defined by its end product but rather by whatever distinctiveness it may have as a process.

The definition referred to the use of "psychological principles." These are taken in the broadest sense to include the entire systematic body of knowledge that comprises the science of psychology and all aspects of basic and clinical psychiatry exclusive of the so-called organic methods such as chemotherapy, surgical techniques, shock therapy, and the like. The principles are drawn from such fields as learning and conditioning, sensation and perception, emotions, cognition, personality theory, tests and measurements, and abnormal, developmental, physiological, and comparative psychology.

The usual conception of those "psychological principles" involved in psychotherapy is restricted to the verbal exchanges between therapist and patient. However, the great number of variables involved in the most simple relationship between two persons offers much broader possibilities in theory and in practice for the modification of personality. The range extends from simple motor habit conditioning to alterations in value systems. It is possible to intentionally effect changes of one order, or in one dimension, which may, in turn, create changes systematically in other areas or dimensions of behavior which may be superficially unrelated. There does not seem to be any limitation upon the kinds of areas or modalities which may be psychotherapeutic. The issue is what means, systematically applied, create what changes in predictably direct or indirect ways.

In order for someone to be able to apply principles derived from this body of knowledge in an "informed and planful" manner, he must obviously meet some conventional qualifying standards. It is fortunately not our purpose here to attempt to define or specify these standards, but clearly the therapeutic process can best be assessed in terms of the work of "qualified" therapists. Unless this condition is met, no fair appraisal of the process can be made. This seemingly elementary point is stressed because the literature contains so many studies in which the therapists were students still learning the fundamentals of psychotherapy. It is difficult to find another professional field in which this situation exists. Imagine the value of a complex neurosurgical technique being assessed from the experiences of first-year residents or the comparative value of different teaching methods being assessed from the work of a group of student teachers!

The phrase "intention of assisting" implies that the process must be an intentional rather than incidental one. It is not something done *to* a person: it is an interactive process between two people. Although the term "modification" may be taken to refer to any addition, subtraction, or change of behavior, it is, needless to say, change in the direction of improvement that is intended. Certainly germane, if not crucial in outcome studies, is a determination of what constitutes improvement; this determination can best be made in advance by the researcher in relation to the particular patient population under investigation.

The latter part of the definition is concerned with the modification of behavior broadly conceived to include feelings, attitudes, and values and their overt verbal and nonverbal expression. Although it is recognized that much effort is devoted to the purpose of improving the adjustment of already reasonably well-adjusted persons, psychotherapy technically is meant to modify maladaptive or maladjustive behavior patterns. Here again it would be a diversion to attempt to define "maladjustive" or "maladaptive" behavior. It is for this reason that the phrase "judged by the therapist" is inserted. If all the other requirements have been met, the therapist is presumably sufficiently experienced and qualified to be able to make an informed judgment on this issue and not to initiate the process of psychotherapy in instances where behavioral disturbances are not in evidence.

RESEARCH AND SOCIAL RESPONSIBILITY

From its inception psychotherapy has been surrounded by a mystique fed by authoritative if conflicting pronouncements and fostered by its own special vocabulary. The need for research to separate fact from dogma has been repeatedly recognized from almost all sectors. Epitomizing these mating calls to the scientists in our midst is Rogers' (1963) statement:

> There is one final implication of this flowering diversity of psychotherapy. I wish to examine several facets of this implication. It is that of necessity we must move toward looking at the *facts*. And to look at the facts means moving toward research. We are beyond the point where differences will be resolved by the voice of authority or by commitment to an essentially religious type of faith in one point of view as against another. . . . Such fact-finding processes are an inevitable part of the future of our field if it is to move forward. They need not interfere with the subjective personal quality of therapy itself—but they are essential if we are to find our way out of the present confusing Babel of voices, each with its own "truth" [pp. 13–15].

Despite such pleas, it is not uncommon to find signs of ambivalence, anxiety, and preparatory defensiveness against the truths that the researcher might lay bare, truths that might challenge cherished beliefs. Some see research as a threat to established systems of belief and to the validity of their own personal experiences and intuitions. Attitudinal polarization toward psychotherapy and toward psychotherapeutic research has developed.

Among those who believe that there is nothing demonstrably therapeutic about psychotherapy are "hard-liners" who would call a moratorium on the whole practice until there is a scientifically validated method of procedure. Curiously, therapeutic protagonists and antagonists alike are much concerned with the issue of social responsibility and cite it in defense of their position. Protagonists maintain that, regardless of possible lack of established validity, we have a responsibility to society to do our best for human beings in need of help, that we cannot wait for an undetermined number of years until our techniques are perfected. The antagonists argue that it is socially irresponsible to offer the public services whose value has not been clearly established.

The argument about social responsibility has been given as a reason against doing controlled research. It has been maintained that controlled research on the efficacy of psychotherapy cannot, and in fact should not, be done because it is a breach of ethics for members of a helping profession to withhold treatment from people in distress. On the contrary, we believe that it is a matter of far graver ethical concern to refrain from controlled studies. Psychotherapists sell services to a dependent public. The responsibility is theirs to demonstrate conclusively that these services are effective, to modify them so as to make them maximally effective, or to withdraw them if they prove to be ineffective. It should not be a matter of faith, conviction, or testimonial, but of reasonably well-established fact. Not so very long ago, people were equally convinced that bleeding was efficacious in the treatment of assorted diseases. In retrospect, would it have been more unethical to withhold what was considered to be a vital treatment from some sick people so that a controlled study of its efficacy could be carried out, or to refuse permission to make the test?

ART OR SCIENCE?

Attitudes toward psychotherapy range all the way from sincere conviction of its certain validity and almost universal applicability to the view that it is a gigantic hoax oversold by pseudo-scientists to a gullible and defenseless public. Attitudes toward psychotherapy must be considered because they influence the way experiments are conceived, conducted, and interpreted; the way findings are received or even read; and the degree to which they influence clinical practice. Curiously, there are some views about psychotherapy that some of its most active supporters and opponents would both support. Consider, for example, this statement: "Psychotherapy is not a science, does not fall in the realm of science, and is not subject to the usual rigors of scientific scrutiny, appraisal and proof." There are, no doubt, strong advocates of psychotherapy who would embrace this statement on the grounds that psychotherapy is a sensitive interpersonal art involving complex emotional interplay and unusual personal qualities, skills, and techniques that can only be passed on from master to novice and subjectively judged and experienced. Opponents would accept much of the statement and interpret it as a reinforcement of their view that psychotherapy is unscientific, vague, mystical, unproved, and not worthy of serious consideration. Among the former group are those who equate a desire to expand the body of scientific knowledge in this area with prima-facie evidence of a nihilistic and pathological attempt to destroy faiths and beliefs that are to them self-evident and highly cathected. It is not true that convictions about the importance of research are antithetical to a human welfare motive. Yet some feel that to contemplate research on psychotherapy is to question it, to question it is to attack it, and to attack psychotherapy is to be against human welfare.

Supporters who announce that psychotherapy is not a science but an art make it apparent that art or faith cannot be easily questioned by experiments without offense to individual tastes and beliefs. To call psychotherapy an art somehow gives it unchallengeable stature and removes it from the realm of scientific assessment. In our culture, art and science occupy twin pedestals in the hierarchy of values of intellectuals. There are few public references to psychotherapy as a trade, craft, or even as a business. In popular language art and science are often used to connote pinnacles of excellence formerly attributed to magical skill, as in the obsolete definition of art. For example, it is not at all unusual for this kind of sentence to appear in the sporting columns of newspapers: "Mound wizard Lefty Jones has the art of baseball pitching down to a science." The same meaning is conveyed when it is stated that he has the science of pitching down to an art. In either case he is viewed as possessing an almost magical skill. In this way, in almost any field of endeavor expertise beyond the reach of ordinary mortals is semantically graced as artistic or scientific—if not magical. The usage is technically proper, for among the list of accepted definitions Webster's defines art as science, science as art, and both as skill. To come full circle, to maintain that psychotherapy is not a science but an art neither explains, justifies, nor excuses anything.

When references to therapeutic "art" are used to connote "skill in performance acquired by experience, study, or observation," as defined in Webster's, or "systematic application of knowledge or skill in effecting a desired result," the meaning is quite different from "the application of skill and taste to production according to aesthetic principles." It is doubtful if many really see aesthetic implications in this "art" even though clinicians often refer to a patient as a "beautiful case of conversion hysteria." No one actually means it just that way, and no one is really deceived.

When the *practice* of psychotherapy is defended as an art rather than a science, the intent is to say that it is a highly developed set of specialized skills which aim to produce desirable effects, but neither the skills nor the effects are sufficiently predictable, reproducible, tangible, objective, explicit, definable, measurable, or communicable to meet conventional scientific standards. Whether or not this is all true, or true at all, it cannot serve as a rejection of research or as a blanket apology for *research* in psychotherapy not meeting at least minimum standards of scientific acceptability.

Theoretically, principles derived from the science of behavior *should* be applicable to problems of behavior modification, and psychotherapy *should* have a firm scientific base. Of course it is recognized that individual skills will always play a part in administering a scientific procedure as long as a human organism is a variable in the process. This is true whether the procedure involves performing a surgical operation, taking an astronomical reading, preparing a microscope slide, or conducting an experiment in analytic chemistry. In research in psychotherapy, the personal equation is complicated by the fact that at least three people are involved—the patient, the therapist, and the experimenter. Psychotherapy is based upon human behavior and human judgment, both of which are highly variable and fallible. The application of the scientific method can be viewed as a means of reducing errors to a minimum.

REPRODUCIBILITY AND GENERALIZABILITY

Experiments in the behavioral sciences have the same general requirements as those in other fields, and the minimization of errors of observation, judgment, and measurement to permit valid conclusions is a shared goal. Research in psychotherapy is certainly not exempt from the requirements of experimental rigor. As in any other scientific research, the procedures should be reproducible. Another experimenter at another time and another place should be able to repeat the same procedures and obtain similar findings. Dependent and independent variables should be made explicit and all relevant variables that might affect outcome should be controlled, or at least recognized and accounted for. Criterion measures should be objective, reliable, and valid. The experimental design should provide means of demonstrating systematic as opposed to chance effects. If the results are to have real value, the design should permit generalizations to be made from the experimental sample to the population from which it was drawn.

Research in psychotherapy poses its own set of unique problems in each of these requirements. Experiments in the physical sciences are relatively easy to reproduce because different scientists applying precisely the same procedures to equivalent materials under identical conditions with equally accurate measuring devices can expect to achieve comparable results. This degree of exactitude is rarely approached in psychotherapy research for many reasons. One of these is the inherent uniqueness of the particular dyadic relationship between patient and therapist. The unique combination cannot reasonably be duplicated. Some have taken the position that this factor is sufficient to preclude experimentation by making any study essentially nonreplicable. The obvious counterargument is that a sufficiently large sampling of patient-therapist pairs in a study will permit generalizations about therapist-patient relationships that transcend any unique pair. In this fashion one could evaluate or study any aspect of treatment for representative samples of therapeutic dyads.

A supplementary approach that maintains the unique quality of the therapeutic relationship is to study a single therapist-patient pair, within a single session or over a series of sessions, making multiple observations. This is the intensive study of the individual case with an N of one and a large number of repeated measurements. This type of experiment, although potentially useful for some purposes, is limited in its generalizability.

RESEARCH AND PRIVACY

The therapist-patient relationship has traditionally been a confidential and privileged one. Many therapists hold that the introduction of someone other than the therapist would violate this intimate, private atmosphere and significantly alter the therapeutic field conditions. The prohibition against external intrusion also holds for recording devices, obvious or hidden. To hide a tape recorder or motion picture camera or to introduce a one-way screen, they argue, is a breach of faith with the patient in a situation which calls for completely honest mutual faith and trust. By extension, the argument maintains that to expose a patient to any kind of experimentation, with or without his knowledge, is inconsistent with the implicit contract with the patient and jeopardizes and perhaps invalidates the whole procedure.

It is possible, however, to maintain confidentiality in the strictest sense of the word and yet use observational or recorded data for research purposes. There is a long tradition in medicine, for example, of reporting clinical findings and data that may be of benefit to others. In fact, only through a process of free, systematic, and informed reporting and experimentation can a science or an applied field learn from its errors and successes and develop a body of reliable knowledge. A research scientist may have just as strong a human welfare motive as the practitioner, though his concern applies to people in general rather than to an individual patient. The stereotype of the researcher as a cold-blooded, hard-headed, insensitive scientist is often contrasted to the soft-hearted, sensitive, warm, tender clinician. This image, compounded by a series of logical errors, leads to the false conclusion that scientists have no genuine regard for the welfare of human beings. The position that therapeutic relationships are so unique as to make experiments nonreproducible and so private as to make them inaccessible to outside scrutiny tends to discourage research and to prevent acceptance of research findings.

It has been argued that the intrusion of unusual conditions such as recording, observing, or filming into the therapeutic situation for research purposes alters the behavior of the patient and therapist so much that these methods vitiate generalizations about what happens in sessions where strict privacy is maintained. Tape recording is the most commonly used device and the most frequent subject of study. Covner (1942) reported that both experienced and inexperienced counselors reacted to being recorded. Kogan (1950) and Harper and Hudson (1952) concluded that the tape recorder has no important influence on the counseling process and that it does not hamper effectiveness. Lamb and Mahl (1956) found that 40 per cent of their patients and about half of the therapists were affected by it. Since then, people have become more acquainted with and accustomed to tape recorders, and the effect may be diminished. In a later study by Roberts and Renzaglia (1965), graduate students in a counseling practicum saw patients under three randomly assigned conditions: with a recorder present in the room, with a microphone only, and with a hidden recorder. Both client and counselor were affected by knowing that they were being recorded. More favorable self-references were made by clients when they thought that they were speaking off-the-record. The counselors were less client-centered when recorded. This was a well-done, carefully controlled study whose chief limitation is that is was done with student counselors, leaving us in doubt whether similar effects would be shown with more experienced counselors who were more used to the apparatus. It is evident from these studies that the introduction of recording devices can have an effect on the performance of both patients and therapists. Adaptation may take place over a period of time, but this would require demonstration.

Watson and Kanter (1954, 1956) studied the influence of various types of recording during therapy. A total of forty-four analytically oriented sessions held with a single patient were tape recorded and observed through a one-way screen. A polygraph in an adjoining room recorded the EKG of the patient and therapist, and respiration and finger temperature of the patient. Both were given psychological tests before and after each session. The authors concluded that therapeutic progress was made despite the research environment. They observed that anxieties of the therapist and patient could be successfully dealt with in therapy and that the therapist was able to cope with his own anxieties sufficiently to allow him to work with those of the patient. It was noted that transference relationships were established with the unknown and unseen observers, a fact that complicated treatment but may have facilitated some aspects of it.

Sternberg, Chapman, and Shakow (1958) reported impressions from trials of sound filming of hypothetical therapy sessions. Subjects were bothered by the lights, and the therapist was reported to feel much more anxious and threatened than the patients and to be concerned about the breach of confidentiality. Parloff, Iflund, and Goldstein (1960) reported that one therapist found that research methods helped him to review his treatment efforts. Another saw the attention received as ego-enhancing, but felt that the one-way screen and microphone inhibited certain verbalizations. No differences in performance were noted, however, during periods of no recording.

Haggard et al. studied the effects of recording and filming on the therapeutic process (Haggard, Hiken, & Isaacs, 1965). Three psychoanalytic cases were recorded and filmed with the knowledge of the participants; one control case was not. The patients differed considerably in the extent of direct and indirect references to the research context, ruling out generalizations of the effects. References to the research context made by one patient when in the research setting were compared with those made in a nonresearch office setting. There were significantly more references to the research context when the patient was in the research room, but the discrepancy disappeared by the twentieth hour. Interestingly enough, the control patient made frequent references to being observed which were the same as those made by the research patients. One of the therapists who was seen in supervisory sessions referred a great deal to the research context. The conclusions that can be drawn from these studies are quite limited, but there is some evidence that filming, recording, observing, and taking physiological measures have an effect on both therapist and patient which must be taken into consideration in therapy research design and interpretation of results.

THE NATURE OF THE RESEARCH QUESTION

What kinds of questions about psychotherapy can research be expected to answer? Questions about psychotherapy have traditionally been divided into two large categories—outcome and process. The former are questions about the effects of psychotherapy which can be answered by systematic evaluations of outcome and the study of the differential effects of various factors upon outcome. The latter are questions about the inner workings of psychotherapy, its rationale, its methods and techniques. These questions concern the things that go on in the therapeutic session and how they vary from session to session. The question of effectiveness must be considered first, for if psychotherapy does not work there is little point in making exhaustive studies of it as a process except to discover ways of making it work better. The value of process questions is rarely challenged, but the meaningfulness of the outcome question has come under enough fire to make it necessary to defend the wisdom of asking it in the first place.

Sanford (1953) called the question "virtually meaningless" because of variations in patients and types of therapeutic activities. Rosenzweig (1954) stated: "The question is not, then, whether psychotherapy does any good—one might reasonably ask, 'Is life worth living?' " (p. 303). Hyman and Breger (1965) contend that the question "Is psychotherapy effective?" is analogous to asking "Is higher education effective?" without specifying what kind of higher education, practiced by what kinds of teachers on which students. They submit that the experimental paradigm that holds for the basic sciences is not applicable to an applied technology like psychotherapy because "Each patient comes to the therapist with a particular set of problems and symptoms. The set of symptoms as well as the nature and level of the change being sought will vary with the individual patient (as well as the therapist)" (p. 319). In a similar vein Truax and Carkhuff (1967) state: "Thus, to ask whether psychotherapy is indeed therapeutic, and to attempt to answer that question by comparing behavioral or personality change in counseled and 'control' groups, is very much like a pharmacologist asking, 'Is chemotherapy therapeutic?' and then conducting his research by randomly giving unknown kinds and quantities of drugs to one group of patients with various complaints, and no drugs to a similar 'control' group" (p. 18). Kiesler (1966) and Paul (1967) offered essentially the same argument. Kiesler decried the "uniformity assumption myth" that allegedly assumes that patients at the beginning of treatment are more alike than different and that therapists are so homogeneous that whatever they do with their patients may be called psychotherapy. He maintained that patient and therapist heterogeneity precludes the drawing of meaningful conclusions. Paul argued that the question is meaningless because there are so many kinds of therapies. Even the question "Does client-centered therapy work?" was rejected because this approach is too diversified. Individual differences within a diagnostic group were seen as too great to permit asking whether therapy works with that group. Ford and Urban (1967), in reviewing a study that yielded little evidence of effectiveness, offered as a possible reason that "the assumption was implicit that all patients were essentially the same, that they were undergoing an homogeneous set of treatment conditions, and that the treatment would produce the same changes on the same variables in the same direction for all patients" (p. 364). For Paul (1967) the legitimate question becomes "*What* treatment, by *whom,* is most effective with *this* individual with *that* specific problem under *which* set of circumstances?" (p. 111).

This line of reasoning is not very impressive and should not discourage anyone from doing outcome research. The criticisms in no way negate the crucial importance of the question, but only raise problems that stand in the way of finding an answer. Kiesler's "myth that patients and therapists constitute uniform homogeneous classes of actors in the therapeutic encounter" is no myth at all, for who really believes it or assumes it? Clinicians, of all people, are fully aware of the uniqueness of individuals. Experimentalists have known about individual differences for a long time, are cognizant of between-subject differences, and take them into account in analyzing research data. Researchers expect distributions, not uniformity. One can not only talk meaningfully about outcome despite patient, therapist, and method heterogeneity, but with more generality because of it. The validity of psychotherapy in a larger sense is testable and should be demonstrable if it exists. If effects are not general enough to cut across patient, therapist, and method lines, researchers have the tools for setting up these factors as independent variables and studying effects within more homogeneous subgroups. The cry of uniqueness does not rule out the search for communalities. Without this search we would be limited to the level of the individual case and would be unable to draw any general conclusions at all. The more representative the patients are of the population of patients, therapists of the population of therapists, and therapy of the population of therapies, the greater the generality of the findings. With the application of multivariate designs it is quite feasible to study, at the same time, the more specific effects of different therapies, types of patients, and therapists. Rather than eliminating the power of generalization from a study, broad samples, diversification, and randomization can enhance it. If the effect is too restricted to be demonstrable under these conditions, then no general claims ought to be made about the value of psychotherapy.

Such questions as "Is chemotherapy effective in the treatment of emotional disorders?" are certainly worth asking. The test would no doubt be limited to those classes of drugs that are in use and to the way they are used in clinical practice. We would not think of painting iodine on the thumbs of schizophrenic patients as a relevant mode of treatment in assessing the effectiveness of chemotherapy. Drugs and patients could be classified in several large categories and effects studied, or they could be taken systematically, one by one. If, with few exceptions, it were found that drugs had no demonstrable effects, it would seem reason enough to discontinue their use and seek other therapies. In psychotherapy we have not come to the same degree of specificity that has been attained with drugs. There is nothing that enables us to say that seven doses of therapy, consisting of thirty-three minutes of reassurance interspersed at twenty-minute intervals with four deep and two shallow interpretations of the oedipal complex, given by an active therapist functioning at the third level of empathy, are needed for patient X to achieve subgoal Y. We are still saddled with variants of the more general question, "Does psychotherapy work?" Researchers rarely ask it in quite so general a form. They ask, rather, "Is insight group therapy effective with alcoholics?" "Is individual psychoanalytically oriented psychotherapy effective in cases of peptic ulcer?" "Is systematic desensitization effective with severe agoraphobia?" If, in examining a large number of controlled experiments designed to answer such varied questions, positive results were rarely found, we would have reason to doubt the validity of the general hypothesis "psychotherapy is effective." If, on the other hand, positive results with various approaches, samples, and conditions were the rule, we would state with confidence that there is evidence to support the general effectiveness of psychotherapy. If only particular types of therapy with certain types of patients consistently came through with positive results, we would conclude that there is little evidence for the *general* efficacy of psychotherapy, but that benefits accrue from therapy brand X when administered to patient type A and B, from brand Y when administered to patient type A and D, but patient type E is not affected by any therapeutic approach yet tested.

It should be clear that asking if something works is not the same as asking if it is worthwhile. This is in the realm of an individual value judgment. Take the question "Does scientific rainmaking by cloud-seeding work?" Contrary to Hyman and Breger's thesis, the scientific paradigm *is* appropriate for answering such a question of applied technology. The criterion is simple and objective. In designing the experiment, the investigator must take into consideration variations in conditions such as atmospheric pressure, relative humidity, and temperature at different times in different localities, and must control for spontaneous rain in order to prove that any precipitation is caused by the silver iodide treatment. If it can be demonstrated that it rains significantly more often following the treatment than in its absence, we can be confident that the treatment was responsible for it. Even so, it might work only one-third of the time and still be significantly better than no seeding, or work 80 per cent of the time but give only a sprinkle. The decision about whether to use it comes from the answers to the questions "Is rain-making worthwhile?" This is an administrative value-judgment based on how great the need is, and what the odds for success are, balanced against the capacity to pay the price. In the same way, the question "Is psychotherapy worth the time, effort, and expense?" is a matter of personal decision rather than a research question. Research information about the efficacy of psychotherapy can help to make it an informed decision.

HYPOTHESES

Hypotheses are logical derivatives of the question that prompted the research. The researcher, particularly in outcome studies, has a great deal of latitude in deciding on the degree of generality or specificity of his hypotheses. Recognizing the almost unlimited number of specific behaviors that are subject to change, some investigators prefer to state their hypotheses in the broadest and most general terms, making predictions about improvement in adjustment or personality due to psychotherapy or even of its being generally beneficial or effective. Their obligation lies in defining what they mean by "improvement in adjustment" or "beneficial." If they are really successful in defining such terms, stating the criteria, and finding criteria measures, the most general statements about the effects of psychotherapy could be made. Others find it preferable and more expedient to deal with broad behavior systems such as interpersonal relations, or specific categories of behavior within these systems such as relations with authority figures, or with less tangible constructs such as ego functions. The utility and power of a construct of this sort rest upon its ability to predict behavior under specified conditions. A reorganization of ego functions may then have certain detectable results. The adduction of its consequences is the crucial step. A researcher's selection of hypotheses about behavioral subcategories is related to his theoretical position on personality and psychotherapy. It is understood that conclusions will be limited to statements about changes in the category of behavior specified in the hypothesis. We hope that, in the future, there will be enough experiments testing hypotheses from different theoretical bases for us to be able to assess psychotherapy across a broad sampling of systems using a variety of different criteria. Taking it one step further, hypotheses can be made about highly specific symptoms and behaviors. These may include signs such as thumb-sucking or aggressive behavior, or symptoms such as headaches which the therapeutic procedures aim to ameliorate. Here again only limited conclusions that do not go beyond the hypotheses can be drawn.

Many studies are carried out without benefit of hypotheses and findings far outnumber predictions made. Frequently one or two main hypotheses are tested, but there is such an abundance of data available that other interrelationships can be studied as well. This is a worthwhile procedure that can generate further hypotheses for additional research. Sometimes the extra added attractions are more interesting than the main feature. Serendipitous findings, though, are not as convincing as those that are predicted in advance from some sound theoretical position. Cross-validation is usually required to verify them. This is not to minimize the value of replication in studies in which all findings were predicted, for it is always worthwhile. Accidental findings are more subject to reasoning errors in going from known effect to cause. A failure to support the hypothesis may be attributed to the subject (too disturbed, too unwilling and uncooperative, and other *post hoc* findings of unsuitability) or other unforeseen variables. Surveying the data, an investigator may change defeat into triumph by discovering that, although the predicted change did not occur, the patient has fewer quarrels or a better job. Therefore, he concludes, his method is successful. Is it? He has not demonstrated clearly that his method can produce a specified change which did occur. The important step is the next one: to explore the phenomenon systematically—in this situation, to demonstrate with a new sample and with suitable controls for comparison that the new change can be produced.

A special case of this problem, one of the most popular solutions of the problem of choice of criteria, is the "omnibus" approach. Many changes are predicted. A few may be achieved, but chance alone could account for them. The experimenter must demonstrate that these changes are related directly to the experimental procedures and that they can be achieved again.

PSYCHOTHERAPY RESEARCH DESIGNS

Research designs cannot be classified into simple types since they can be characterized along so many different dimensions. Experiments, like people, "behave" differently depending on a variety of intrinsic factors. In this sense the research design is in itself a variable that determines the level of inference and definitiveness of the results, the confidence that can be placed in them, and their generality. The design sets upper limits on the potential of the particular study for yielding facts about psychotherapy, suggesting useful hypotheses for future testing, or merely supplying limited scraps of sample-specific information. A cursory review will permit the mention of some of the main ways in which psychotherapy research designs can be characterized.

Empirical, Inductive, and Hypothetico-Deductive Studies. Psychotherapy research of all three types appears in the literature. Some studies are straight empirical reports in which, for example, an investigator states that in a series of fifty psychoneurotic patients treated at a particular clinic 70 per cent were improved and 30 per cent unimproved, 60 per cent were of high socioeconomic status and 40 per cent low, 55 per cent were treated by method Y and 45 per cent by method Z. No inferences are drawn from the data and no hypotheses are generated. A second investigator looking at the same data discovers that the proportion of successes was greater among patients of high socioeconomic status than among those of low, and that method Z yielded better results than method Y. From these fortuitous observations and supportive clinical data, he reasons inductively and forms a hypothesis for later testing to the effect that people of high socioeconomic status are more responsive to psychotherapy than those of low and that method Z is superior to method Y. It can only be a hypothesis at this stage because the survey data did not permit it as a conclusion. A third investigator, also stimulated by these clues, proceeds in a hypothetico-deductive manner. He relates the clues to theories about personality disorders, social class, and therapeutic methods, and deduces a hypothesis that there should be an interaction between socioeconomic status and the two methods of treatment. He then designs an experiment to provide a test of the hypothesis that low SES patients will respond better to one of the approaches and those of high SES will respond better to the other.

Field versus Laboratory Conditions. Most research in psychotherapy is done under field conditions using actual patients in treatment as subjects, but some is done in the "laboratory" using simulated conditions or analogue situations. Research in naturalistic settings permits more direct conclusions to be drawn but allows far less control over experimental conditions and extratherapeutic events than is possible in analogue experiments. However, extensions and generalizations from simulated situations (which are usually carried out on nonpathological student samples) to psychotherapy are always hazardous. Analogue studies are more useful in experiments that test hypotheses about the therapeutic process than they are in outcome research.

Prospective versus Ex Post Facto Studies. In prospective studies independent variables are systematically manipulated to get at cause and effect relationships. The use of already completed cases rarely permits the same standards of control. The events have already taken place. Self-selective rather than random processes have operated in the sampling. Intervening events about which the investigator lacks information have occurred, and unsystematic records and biased memories have to be relied upon. Some ex post facto studies reason backward from known effects in the search for causes. The likelihood of being able to find the true causes in this way is at best remote.

Controlled versus Uncontrolled Studies. The most common examples of uncontrolled research in psychotherapy are case studies or group data with before and after measures, and surveys of experiences with therapy. Such research cannot supply facts about the outcome of psychotherapy. Controlled studies have been classified according to the type of control group used, such as untreated, waiting-list, drop-out, other-treatment, and behavioral-placebo.

Univariate versus Multivariate Design. Although some experiments are appropriately designed to test for the effects of a single independent variable, more and more multivariate analyses are being done. They require little extra investment from a design and data-gathering point of view, in contrast to that required in setting up a whole new experiment, but they vastly increase the information yield and give knowledge of interaction effects not otherwise available.

Number of Assessment Points. Therapy research designs can be classified as assessing the treatment effects only after therapy (in a before-after design) or in a repeated-measure design at several points along the way. An ongoing picture of progress by trend analysis gives a far more comprehensive view of sequential effects than can a pre-post design. In addition, studies that end arbitrarily at a fixed interval or at termination can be contrasted to those that include provisions for posttherapeutic follow-up to get at a measure of the stability of observed changes.

Sample Size. Therapy research ranges from $N = 1$ studies through small-sample to large-scale investigations. Intensive studies of individual cases can be most useful in generating hypotheses, but they cannot be used to make general statements about psychotherapy. Most therapy research, being prospective and time consuming, is done on relatively small samples. Small-sample statistical techniques enable us to handle the sampling errors effectively. Most large-scale research projects are in the form of surveys rather than controlled experiments, but there are some examples of large cooperative studies. The latter have the tremendous advantage of being able to pool samples from a number of different installations, and the generality of the results is greatly enhanced. In return they usually sacrifice standardization and precision in data collection because of the large number of different people who are involved with the data.

Method of Assigning Ss. Experimental designs are frequently characterized by the method of assigning Ss to groups. This can take many forms such as man-for-man matching, matched groups, randomized group, and random block.

Statistical Design. The statistical method of analyzing the data may serve to describe the research design (for example, factorial design, analysis of variance, factor analysis, correlational analysis).

A research design can thus be described in a combination of these terms. For example: a prospective, univariate field study on a small sample of neurotic Ss randomly assigned to brief supportive therapy or to a waiting-list control group, and assessed before and after therapy in an analysis of covariance design.

THE NEED FOR CONTROLS

Often overlooked yet essential in psychotherapy research is the control of relevant variables that might have an effect upon the outcome or process of psychotherapy. Studies of the effect of a procedure designed to produce change must clearly demonstrate that the observed change is indeed a product of the procedure. It must be shown that nothing other than the intervening procedure could reasonably account for the change. The experimental design must permit the inference that had the procedure not been introduced, the particular change would not have taken place. To produce evidence of behavioral change *coincidental* with psychotherapy is not sufficient indication that the change took place *because* of psychotherapy. Similarly, evidence of no change cannot be taken to indicate that psychotherapy had no effect. In the first instance, variables other than psychotherapy may have accounted for the change; in the second, psychotherapy may have prevented the patient from getting worse. In neither case is an experimenter in a position to draw any definite conclusions about effects of psychotherapy unless suitable controls are introduced. In his critique of a paper by Hartmann, logician Ernest Nagel (1959) succinctly presents this fundamental need for controls. His statement does not deal with psychotherapy, but the issue is the same:

> the fact that some event or attribute B occurs with a certain relative frequency p when some other event or attribute A occurs, is not sufficient to show that A and B are significantly related—unless there is further evidence that the relative frequency of B in the absence of A, or the relative frequency of the nonoccurrence of B in the presence of A, is markedly different from p. Thus, the fact that many men who have certain kinds of

traumatic experiences in childhood develop into neurotic adults does not establish a causal relation between the two, if there is about the same proportion of men who undergo similar childhood experiences but develop into reasonably normal adults. In short, data must be analyzed so as to make possible comparisons on the basis of some *control* group, if they are to constitute cogent evidence for a causal inference. The introduction of such controls is the *minimum* requirement for the reliable interpretation and use of empirical data. I am therefore not impressed by Dr. Hartmann's assertion that psychoanalytic interpretations are based on a great wealth of observations, for it is not the sheer *quantity* of data that is of moment but their probative strength [p. 53].

CONTROL FOR CHANGES NOT DUE TO TREATMENT

The controls introduced in the experimental design to differentiate between changes due to psychotherapy and those that can be attributed to the passage of time offer a number of options. Selection should be made upon consideration of the advantages and shortcomings of each, the question that the research is asking, and the feasibility of using them in the particular setting of the research.

Untreated Controls. For studies attempting to evaluate the effects of psychotherapy, there is no good substitute for a control group consisting of untreated patients who are similar in all important respects to the treated group. This may be difficult to do with outpatients who have the alternative of going elsewhere for treatment. Control patients have to be told why they will not be seen, and their resentment may interfere with follow-up assessments if they are even willing to submit to them. It is much easier to form and maintain an untreated group with institutionalized patients who have few options. The treated and untreated patients should be kept apart so that the untreated group does not feel slighted and the treated group privileged. In this situation the controls cannot realistically get "zero treatment," but it can be kept so minimal that they can be considered, to all intents and purposes, untreated. The failure to be able to assure zero treatment of the controls will not affect the conclusions if significant differences in favor of the treated group obtain, but there is a greater risk of making the error of accepting the null hypothesis when in truth it is false. This is so because even minimal treatment of the controls works against the study's ability to show differences between the groups.

Waiting List Controls. One solution has been to use patients on the regular clinic waiting lists as controls or to tell them that all places are filled at the present but that they will be seen when an opening becomes available. This has several disadvantages that must be weighed against advantages.

In the normal course of events patients move off the regular waiting list and into therapy. The relative shortness of this time interval in contrast to that of a full therapeutic contact may bring about a premature evaluation of the effectiveness of therapy if the waiting and treatment times are kept equivalent.

Being placed on a waiting list is usually preceded by screening and intake interviews, and, frequently, by psychological assessment. While not thought of as psychotherapy, these interviews are often accompanied by reassurance and support, furnish some opportunity for catharsis, and are viewed by some patients as the accomplishment of the first step toward change and as part of the general therapeutic venture. This is true even if the patient is on a contrived waiting list. In addition, follow-up assessments may be mistaken for therapy or serve a therapeutic function.

To keep a patient on a waiting list beyond the normal waiting period or to place him on an artificial waiting list and deny him treatment for experimental convenience has been challenged on ethical grounds. It is, however, easy to justify withholding from a few people a procedure whose value is at best uncertain. In the long run, far more people stand to gain if either the effectiveness or the ineffectiveness of the procedure can definitely be established.

Terminator Controls. Another approach is to use as untreated controls those who reject treatment or drop out after the first few interviews. The principal disadvantage, and a serious one, is that although the subjects are essentially untreated, there is no control over other relevant variables such as motivation for help, motivation for change, and personality characteristics that lead one person to accept treatment and another to reject it. These variables, in and of themselves, could well be determinants of change with or without therapy.

Placebo-Effect Controls. When studying the effect of a particular therapeutic method it is desirable to control for the equivalent of a placebo effect. This refers to the introduction of a neutral placebo process, one that is not designed to be therapeutic. The controls come to see a "therapist" with the same frequency as the treated group, and spend the same amount of time, but the procedures introduced within the session are of a highly different order, consisting of "nontherapeutic" conversation or activities. This will help answer the question of whether it is merely personal contact, belief, faith, or suggestibility that is stimulating behavioral change or whether some more essential therapeutic procedure is involved. The disadvantage lies in our presumption about what is therapeutic and what is not. It could be that the two approaches share identical therapeutic aspects which are quite different from what we presume to be the therapeutic ingredients.

Rosenthal and Frank (1956) correctly argue that if the purpose is to test for the effects of a specific form of therapy based on a particular theory, the only adequate control is another form of therapy in which patients have equal faith. But if that which is therapeutic should turn out to be the placebo effect of faith rather than something specific to a given therapeutic method or technique, then the assessment of "psychotherapy = placebo effect" would require comparison with a group that was not exposed to the process at all.

Other-Treatment Controls. If the experimental question is whether a new therapeutic approach is superior to an old one, the latter is the appropriate control. This is often the question asked before deciding to introduce a new or different approach. It is the point at issue in hospitals where the introduction of a particular kind of therapeutic program is being considered in contrast to one that has been in existence, or in distinguishing a therapeutic from a custodial program. All inpatients receive *some* treatment, and the contrast is of one kind against another, or of "more of" against "less of." In comparing treatment B to treatment A, if B proves to be better than A, and if we either know or can assume that A does not make patients *worse* than no treatment at all, then it follows that B is better than no treatment.

Patient as Own Control. There are some hypotheses that can be appropriately tested by using each subject as his own control in lieu of a control group. This design can be particularly helpful in studies of the comparative effects of various techniques. For example, if the researcher wished to study the effect of reassurance upon patients' verbalizations during the therapeutic session, he could systematically vary his responses and study the patients' verbal output as the dependent variable under the different conditions. The chief advantages of own-control designs are the elimination of the problem of obtaining equivalent samples, reduced error, and smaller total sample required. Another approach, P-technique, offers a way of testing hypotheses during the course of therapy with individual patients. P-technique is a method of collecting a series of different measures from the same individual at many different times. There is no need for extensive controls because the subject is his own control. The technique promises more for the study of process, that is, change at succeeding phases, than for the evaluation of outcome.

There are not too many ways, however, in which a patient can be used as his own control in evaluating the effects of psychotherapy. One way is to give the same patients nonspecific placebo "treatment" and specific therapy in a counterbalanced order for two groups. Assessing each type of treatment before and after would provide data for within-patient comparison. Another particularly useful way for testing highly specific symptomatic therapies is to treat some symptoms but not others. In one study to be described later, cases of bilateral warts were treated on one side of the body only, with the other side serving as a control. In cases of long-standing intractable symptoms that have failed to respond to any other form of treatment and for which a definite baseline has been established, it is tempting to forego the use of an untreated control group in favor of own-controls. It can be done, but the lingering doubts that always remain could be abolished by using other controls.

Combinations. The fullest and most complex exploitation of design potentials lies in the combination of these various control methods. Experiments can be designed in which there is an untreated group to control against changes with the passage of time, a placebo group to control against the simple effects of faith and suggestion, other-therapy group(s) against which to gauge the relative effects of different approaches, and elements of own-control introduced by measurements made before, during, and after each form of treatment and nontreatment. Various combinations can be adapted to the unique needs and interests of a given investigation.

CONTROL OF EXTRANEOUS VARIABLES

Especially in need of control in outcome or process research are patient variables, therapist variables, temporal variables, method variables, and situational or environmental variables.

Patient Variables. Any assessment of change immediately raises the question of the baseline from which the hypothesized change took place. When a control group is used, close attention must be paid to the matching of baselines in the two groups or at least to the determination of these respective baselines so that initial differences can be handled statistically and the relative changes of the two groups compared.

Patient variables that might conceivably influence change without treatment or affect the course of treatment or response to treatment are diagnostic variables including signs and symptoms and length and severity of disorder; a host of personality, intellectual, and motivational variables; and such variables as age, sex, marital status, socioeconomic status, ethnic and cultural background, education, occupation, and employment status. The relevance of the variables controlled depends in part upon the particular hypotheses under investigation.

Therapist Variables. Since the therapist presumably plays a key role in the therapeutic process, he becomes an important variable in the assessment of the efficacy of different therapeutic procedures. Potential determinants of what transpires in therapy or of the outcome of therapy include such variables as length and type of experience and training, theoretical orientation, personality characteristics, personal therapy, interests, values, and the social, ethnic, and cultural background of the therapist.

Method and Technique Variables. If psychotherapy is at all specific as a process, the particular therapeutic methods and techniques that are employed should be major variables in the determination of outcome. As with other variables mentioned, the hypotheses will guide the decision of whether to hold method variables constant, to vary them randomly, or to vary them systematically and to consider them as independent variables whose effects are to be appraised, compared, and contrasted.

Temporal Variables. Any behavioral change that occurs takes place over some time span. The measurement of change consists of the comparison of two measures taken at two different times. The time units are generally large in view of the length of time over which a therapeutic course is sustained. Assessment of change between two arbitrary sets of time intervals may be expected to yield discrepancies unless characteristic curves of change are unidirectional throughout. Unfortunately, this is probably not the case. Recognition of the possibility of markedly different results as a function of selecting different elapsed times emphasizes the importance of controlling temporal variables. This is one of the deceptive factors in the appraisal of outcome. Patients tend to leave therapy when they are doing well, when the change curve is on the rise, or when they are discouraged over doing poorly. If improvement is judged at such times, the ratio of successes is likely to be different from what it would be if the assessment were done after a fixed interval or at many points along the way.

Another temporal variable is the frequency and duration of visits. If it is reasonable to hypothesize a direct relationship between time devoted to therapy and change, then the control of time as a variable is necessary. Should change rate not prove to be a constant within and between people, or curvilinear, it would be desirable to control for differential rates of change.

Environmental-Situational Variables. Regardless of therapeutic intervention, the patient is a dynamic living organism functioning in and interacting with a fluid environment. Changes in the patient's personality and behavior may be caused by changes in the extrapsychotherapeutic environment: a new job, a sympathetic teacher, a new love gained, an old family problem resolved. It is therefore necessary to attempt to introduce controls for important environmental and situational variables in both the patient's life and the entire behavioral field. Invariance of environmental milieu is often erroneously assumed. Regardless of direction, the introduction or relief of unusual environmental stresses or favorable events that have a potential influence upon behavior require control. Most theories of psychotherapy provide for the attempt to modify personality and behavior by altering the patient's experience (within the psychotherapeutic situation). The therapist believes that he is doing this systematically, and further believes that response to these alterations will be generalized. This is the reason for the extremely great interest in behavior within the psychotherapeutic situation. However, the patient's experiences beyond the consulting room are fortuitous. The scientific problem is to study relationships between kinds of situation-experiential variables and intrapersonal processes, and between these intrapersonal processes and behavioral outcomes in situational contexts. To refuse to examine specific kinds of data because of a priori theoretical commitments may result in the avoidance of the central problems in psychotherapy.

RESEARCH STRATEGIES FOR CONTROLLING VARIABLES

So many factors can influence results in addition to those independent variables that are known, identified, and included in the design that the researcher invariably has major strategy decisions to make. Should he match individuals or groups, keep the groups homogeneous, randomize, treat for the effects of as many independent variables as possible? What are the problems, advantages, and consequences?

Sample Restriction by Homogeneity. One way of controlling unexpected systematic effects of extraneous independent variables is to restrict their number by limiting the sample to a group that is homogeneous on variables that might make a difference. Homogeneity can be expected to reduce error variance at the expense of generality. For example, the sample can consist only of employed, middle-class, college-educated, male obsessive-compulsives aged thirty to thirty-five seen for fifty-minute sessions twice a week by male, psychoanalytically oriented therapists with at least ten years of experience. This automatically takes care of eleven variables and tells us with whom we are dealing, but it limits generalizations that can be made to the populations of patients and therapists from which the samples were drawn. There is nothing wrong with this as long as we are not tempted to go beyond the potential of the research and make statements about the effects of psychotherapy in general on people in general. Even though eleven variables have been accommodated, there are enough left to influence the results.

Matching. Man-for-man matching on even a small portion of the variables requires a much larger patient pool than is ordinarily available. To all intents and purposes, it is not feasible unless the investigator limits the matching to a few variables. Advance matching of groups is not quite as difficult but usually cannot be done except in an inpatient setting where the patients are available whenever needed. A much more common practice is to make up groups matched on one or two key variables and then to check for group differences on other variables. Where differences appear, there is still some room for adjustments to improve the match, but the groups are not equivalent in the true sense.

Randomization. Random assignment to experimental and control groups by a table of random numbers or other suitable method is the preferable way to avoid bias, and no deviations from the scheme should be permitted. Subjects can be dropped later from either group to improve the match providing that it is done without knowledge of the patients' progress.

Combinations. These various methods may be combined to give the best match. For example, pairs or triplets, or other clusters of patients, depending on the number of treatments, can be matched and then assigned randomly to treatment or control groups. An experimenter can control some of the variables by limiting the sample of patients and therapists, placing temporal and method variables under direct control, and trusting that environmental variables will distribute themselves randomly.

In the long run, it will be most helpful to find out by research which independent variables really make a difference and then pay special attention to those that do. This will become more and more possible as research knowledge accumulates.

CONTROL OF BIASES

It takes little talent to bias research in psychotherapy, so manifold are the opportunities for the unwary. Many different kinds of biases can be introduced from conception of the research to reception of the completed report. They include biases of investigators, sampling, patients, therapists, criteria, criteria measures, interviewers, testers and judges, data analysis and interpretation, and publication and reader bias.

Investigator Bias. Especially in outcome studies, biases of the investigator may tilt the research machine. This danger is greatest when the investigator approaches the problem intent on proving or disproving a point about which he has a high level of commitment and conviction rather than in the spirit of open inquiry. When the psychological stakes are high for the investigator, his eagerness to find support for his hypothesis may result in glaring errors of design or in the omission of necessary precautions, so that the deck is stacked in his favor. Or the bias may be reflected more insidiously by the accretion of little things, by making a series of minor compromises each so insignificant that it is rationalized and discounted. His biases may influence most of the other biases to be mentioned. Some investigators who are aware of their leanings may bias their research in the opposite direction in attempting to counteract them.

Sampling Bias. The main forms of sampling bias fall in the categories of selective and unrepresentative sampling. Where random assignment is called for in the selection of Ss, the assignment of patients to experimental or control groups, or the assignment to particular therapists, deviations from randomization, no matter how compelling the reason, can introduce a serious bias. It is typical for clinical staff to request exceptions to the randomization scheme so that patients who they feel are in greatest need or most motivated for treatment can be placed in the experimental group. It is easy to see how failure to grant such requests will incur resentment and how capitulation can bias the sample. Selection of patients who look like they "fit" the hypothesis is a serious bias. Selective dropping of patients from the sample can have the same effect. The conditions under which a patient will be dropped, say for nonattendance, should be specified in advance. A decision about a cut-off point that is made *after* the outcome is known can seriously compromise the results. Even when standards for dropping are set in advance they must be made with the greatest care to assure that no systematic bias will be introduced. By the same token, the dropping of particular therapists from the sample of therapists must be fully justified.

Legitimate reasons for dropping subjects along the way are:

1. Therapy may be prematurely terminated by events that are beyond control of the investigator and unrelated to therapy. Such events include hospitalization or incapacitation for a physical ailment, death, or moving out of the area.

2. A patient may be selected for the research project but fail to come in for treatment. Such patients can be dropped without concern, but if as a group they have special characteristics, comparable patients should be dropped from the control group. If, however, a patient drops out after a session or two, the researchers must decide whether the therapy was a failure or whether it is fair to assess a process that never had a chance really to get under way. There is no universally applicable answer, and each investigator has to take a stand on the issue before starting a project. The decision must be a rational one and the reasoning behind it explicit.

3. If the patient does not appear for assessment, he is lost to the project. Precautions to minimize this loss are essential, and require an effective follow-up system.

4. A patient can be legitimately dropped if he proves to have been misclassified and clearly is other than what was initially believed. For example, if a researcher is working with a sample of patients with conversion hysteria and it is later discovered that one was misdiagnosed and really has a physical condition that psychotherapy could not possibly modify, it would be appropriate to drop him from the sample.

5. On occasion it will be discovered that situations existed during the research that altered the experimental conditions for some patients. For example, it might be learned that an untreated control patient has been going for treatment elsewhere. Under these circumstances he should be dropped from the sample.

6. Should one of the therapists leave or be absent for a prolonged period during the project and it is not feasible to replace him, a decision to drop his patients from the research sample can be made.

7. Patients can be dropped from the sample to equalize Ns when that is desirable, but the dropping must be done in true random fashion. If for the same reason cases are added from a reserve pool, this too must be done randomly. Dropping of Ss to improve matching on independent variables or pretest measures can be done as long as full precautions are taken to guarantee that the method precludes knowledge of outcome or predictions about outcome from entering into the choice.

Illegitimate reasons for dropping Ss include the following:

1. A patient terminates therapy for therapy-related reasons. For example, he has an argument with his therapist after twenty sessions, or leaves because he feels he is not making enough progress, or is sent to a neuropsychiatric hospital, or commits suicide.

2. Therapy is interfered with by events that are related to the condition for which a patient is being treated. Thus, he might become worse and his attendance irregular, or an unemployed patient might obtain a steady job which limits his therapeutic contacts.

3. It is not appropriate to drop a patient on the ex post facto judgment that he was not motivated for therapy, was not verbal enough, was not bright enough, or similar reasons.

4. If the patients of one of the therapists are less successful than those of others, it is not appropriate to drop them on the grounds that the therapist is atypical. This should have been determined in advance.

5. Similarly, if a patient is not progressing, he cannot be dropped on the grounds that he is atypical.

Lack of representativeness of the sample can bias it as much as eliminating patients can. The practice of selecting only the "best" therapists and patients will necessarily limit generalizations to the populations from which they were drawn. The exclusive use of unrepresentative samples of therapists, such as graduate students or residents, biases the study at the start. Another type of sampling bias comes from the hopefully infrequent practice of failing to set the sample size in advance, following a series of cases, and stopping only when the results are favorable to the hypothesis.

Patient Response Bias. A variant of the "bias of the auspices" can appear in the responses of patients to evaluation questionnaires or interviews. Some may pick up the investigator's or therapist's bias and give socially desirable responses that are intended to please. Negative response biases can be expected from other patients. These can be controlled somewhat by the selection of the criterion and its measures. Selective nonresponse to questionnaire surveys can also bias the sample.

Criterion Bias. When a single-outcome criterion is used, care must be taken to assure that it is not chosen from among the many available simply because it is the one most likely to support the hypothesis. Of even greater consequence is the use of multiple criteria followed by the dropping of data from those that do not yield expected results. Despite the selection of sound criteria, the choice of measuring devices that are insensitive to change can obscure the results.

Interviewer, Tester, and Judge Bias. When interviewers are used to conduct assessment interviews, testers to administer and interpret criterion tests, or judges to rate patients' behavior or case records, blind arrangements are not always feasible. The possibility of contamination of judgment can be diminished by the use of personnel who are independent of the project and the treatment and have neither knowledge of nor stake in the hypotheses. The use of people who have prior knowledge of both should be avoided. Data from case studies is used most frequently in ex post facto studies. Verifiable factual material taken from such records can be most helpful. The employment of other case data may perpetuate biases present in the records.

Therapist Bias. Studies can be biased by using therapists' case reports as data or therapists' judgments of their own patients and their own work. Objectivity is apt to be difficult under these circumstances. Also, therapists may offer differential efforts with different subject or "methods" groups, thus interfering with a fair and objective test of the hypothesis.

Data Analysis Bias. The main culprit here is the failure to select the most appropriate statistical method in advance and to retain it unless the data reveal unexpected characteristics that make it no longer appropriate. There are many instances in the research literature in which it is obvious that the investigator has tried out several statistical devices and, disappointed by the results obtained from the use of more powerful and precise measures, has made use of less powerful and precise ones that yielded results more favorable to the hypotheses.

Interpretation Bias. Even if appropriate statistical methods are selected and properly applied, bias can be introduced in the interpretation of the data. Confidence levels can be set too leniently after the data has been analyzed. Too much emphasis can be placed on a weak finding and too little on a finding that does not support the hypothesis. Some data may be overlooked and other data stressed out of proportion to their importance. There are even instances in the literature in which the discussion and conclusions completely ignore contradictory evidence in the data. Then there are "alibiases," or extensive alibis that attempt to explain away valid findings.

Publication Bias. This is an old problem that is related to sampling bias. On Hippocrates' island, Kos, in ancient Greece, there was a temple-hospital named after Asclepius, the god of medicine. A patient was admitted at the first of three levels, where his complaints and history were taken. Then he was brought to the second level to await treatment. At night he was honored by a visit from a priest who introduced himself as none other than Asclepius. The priest diagnosed the ailment, prescribed the treatment, and assured the patient that he would recover rapidly. The patient remained at the second level during the acute and intensive treatment stage, and was later moved to the third level to convalesce if he showed signs of recovering. It was here that inscriptions were made on marble tablets of his symptoms and treatment. These "publications" of only successful cases served as texts for medical students at the temple. It is just as true today that if the unsuccessful cases are not recorded, a false legend of success can be created. We will never know how many studies were never submitted for publication because their results were contrary to those anticipated or how many, after submission, were rejected because of editorial bias. We do not mean to suggest that editors of scientific journals intentionally censor views opposed to their own. However, it is a plausible hypothesis that editorial consultants read far more critically when an article is not in accord with their beliefs about a subject and are more likely to find technical flaws in the study and recommend its rejection.

Reader Bias. Finally, the reader brings his own biases to the research report. Even if all the other biases have been exorcised, the reader's receptivity to the conclusions and the extent to which he incorporates the findings into his body of knowledge and practice of psychotherapy may be governed by the strength of his own set of biases.

It should be obvious by now that there is no simple formula for eliminating biases. Disciplined effort on the part of the investigator and everyone else involved in the research is required to anticipate and control as many of the biases as possible. The investigator must be alert to appraise any other distortions that may have drifted in despite all precautions.

2

Change and Its Measurement

THE NATURE OF CHANGE

"Change" implies a deviation from some baseline consistently outside the normal limits of fluctuation of an act, action sequence, or feeling state. The response or set of responses to a given stimulus or complex of stimuli can be expected to vary on successive occasions and distribute themselves normally about a mean for each individual. Behavioral change for that individual would consist of responses that fell outside this distribution and clustered about a new mean. Of course, change is not unidirectional. A distinction must be made between criteria of change and criteria of improvement. Another type of change would be seen in a shift in the variability of an individual's behavior even in the absence of a deviation in the mean of his response values.

Meltzoff and Blumenthal (1966), in describing the properties of change, proposed that change has a content referent, direction, magnitude, a temporal aspect, a degree of importance, and a source. They showed that if change is not linear, appraisal of the amount of change between any two intervals will vary with the points selected. Three kinds of changes were identified: *isolated, enabling,* and *trigger* changes. Trigger changes are those which set off chains or sequences of other changes. Enabling changes are those which permit other changes to take place that would not otherwise have been able to occur. Isolated changes are those that stand alone and do not set off or enable other changes to take place. They postulated that, other things being equal, these types of change form a hierarchy of potential importance in a descending order—*trigger, enabling, isolated*—and that importance is also a function of the proximity of the change to some consequential life threshold (a border point at which a new life pattern or status may emerge, for example, the ability to stay out of a hospital, or obtain a job, or get married). The general principle was offered that the importance of a behavioral change is directly proportional to its relation to a threshold zone and to the degree to which it causes or enables other changes to take place.

In assessing changes in groups of people for research purposes, an investigator may take most of the aspects of change into consideration but run into difficulty in judging the importance factor since this can best be determined individually, in the context of a given patient's life pattern. Informed estimations can be made, however, of the importance of predicted changes for the particular research sample. For example, a small change, that would enable a significant portion of a group of schizophrenic patients on the verge of hospitalization to remain in the community, or one that would enable a group of neurotic patients to remain in gainful employment, could be preestablished as important despite the minuteness of its absolute magnitude. Clearly, the same change does not have the same import or meaning for all individuals, and only the most naïve behaviorist would divest a specific behavioral sequence of its contextual significance. To argue that a specific sequence has the same private meaning for all persons is to ignore our knowledge of psychological ontogeny. However, there are many patterns of behavior within a cultural milieu that have common meanings and broad, commonly understood consequences. This is true for judging individual behaviors as well as for deciding on the importance of change. Within these limits, meaningful research can be done.

A fundamental question in outcome research is whether change is unitary or multidimensional. Is it meaningful to attempt to assess "success" or "improvement" in a general sense, or would it be better to hypothesize and test for specific gains that presumably represent the goals of the particular therapy and sample involved? The unitary or multidimensional character of change is a research question in itself, and has been the subject of investigation.

Parloff et al. tested the hypothesis that improvement is not a unitary phenomenon by intercorrelating four different measures on sixteen neurotic patients before and after twenty weeks of group psychotherapy (Parloff, Kelman, & Frank, 1954). The measures were a symptom checklist, a rating scale of the patient's discomfort by the staff, and Q-sort measures of self-acceptance and self-awareness. The only significant correlations before therapy were between patients' symptoms and lack of self-acceptance, and after therapy between symptoms and lack of self-awareness. They suggested comfort, effectiveness, and self-awareness as useful criterion measures. Gibson et al. gave the Rorschach and Minnesota Multiphasic Personality Inventory to forty-two clients before and after therapy (Gibson, Snyder, & Ray, 1955). Change measures were intercorrelated and factor analyzed, and the factors that emerged seemed to be defined by the instruments used. No psychologically meaningful structure developed.

Nichols and Beck (1960) factor analyzed thirty change scores, including eighteen California Personality Inventory scales, four sentence-completion scores, four client ratings, and four therapist ratings. The measures were obtained on seventy-five students at the Purdue Psychological Clinic for an average of 14.7 interviews by third- and fourth-year graduate students. Six factors were obtained: (1) a CPI factor interpreted as a faking or social desirability factor; (2) a therapist-rating factor; (3) a CPI factor associated with ease of social interaction and comfortableness with others; (4) a client-rating factor; (5) a factor representing change in the ratio of active to passive solutions to a conflict, derived from the sentence-completion test; (6) a factor taken to represent care in responding to test items. There was evidence that the two CPI change factors represented changes in the same influences that were responsible for covariance among the test's scales in the first place. In this study, raw change scores were used despite their correlation with initial level on the CPI.

Cartwright and Roth (1957) applied ten outcome criteria to thirty-one patients whose problems ranged from slight maladjustment difficulties to borderline psychoses. Included were four therapist measures, three client measures, and ratings by diagnosticians and lay observers. Posttherapy measures and pre-post change scores were factor analyzed. Three post-therapy factors were client satisfaction, the therapist's view of success, and the client's response to others. The client, diagnostician, and lay observer agreed on the client-satisfaction factor. The therapist, client, and diagnostician agreed on the response of the client to others, but the therapist stood alone in his views of success. There was some overlap between the first two factors. The change matrix yielded two factors—the client's view of change and the therapist's view of change, with no relation between the two. The diagnostician and lay observer agreed with the therapist factor, and the California E Scale with the client factor. The authors concluded that changes in clients' self-estimate are little related to changes estimated from other vantage points and that the use of multiple criteria which combine estimates from both the client and therapist confuse the issue by summating nonadditive units. Their data countered the notion that outcome could be considered as unitary, but they did not find it as fragmentary as Rogers had suggested earlier.

Cartwright et al. took eighty-four change measures on ninety-three Ss in client-centered therapy (Cartwright, Kirtner, & Fiske, 1963). The measures encompassed fourteen Behavioral Adequacy Scales rated by the client, the therapist, and a diagnostician; and a posttherapy questionnaire, MMPI, Butler-Haigh Q-Sort, and Social Attitude Scales. Other therapist measures included a rating of integration, liking for the client, and a posttherapy questionnaire. Other diagnostician measures were a sentence completion test, the TAT, and ratings of liking for the client. The major change factors that appeared were (1) change in client's perception of adjustment coming mostly from the MMPI, (2) change in adequacy on the TAT, (3) therapist's perception of change, (4) changes in reported symptomatology (largely somatic from the MMPI), (5) length of therapy. They concluded that factors obtained are associated with specific methods of measurement rather than being substantive.

Shore et al. factored thirty variables in their study of delinquent boys (Shore, Massimo, & Ricks, 1965). Their measures included IQ, achievement tests, attitude toward authority, control of aggression, and self-image measures. Pre-post difference scores were used. Six factors emerged: (1) improvement in academic achievement combined with changes in self-image, (2) control of aggression, (3) TAT ratings of attitude toward authority, (4) increase in TAT orientation toward time relationships in attitude toward authority, (5) relationship between guilt and future time perspective, (6) initial IQ. The first three factors appeared to be tied together by self-image.

Lewinsohn and Nichols (1967) employed residual change scores, independent of initial level, derived from eighty measures including several types of ratings of improvement and social adjustment, psychological tests, interview ratings, ward behavior, and length of hospitalization and associated data. Eight factors obtained were: (1) self-evaluation, (2) social adjustment, (3) satisfied patient, (4) assertiveness, (5) a factor negatively loaded on brain damage, (6) introversion-extroversion, (7) psychosomatic symptom, (8) psychotic behavior factor. Only the first three factors were considered method factors because the latter five were constituted from variables representing three or more different methods of measuring change. Lewinsohn and Nichols concluded that change is clearly multidimensional and that "the practice of combining several criteria into a single outcome measure, which assumes a unitary dimension of improvement, does not appear justified. . . ." (p. 502).

The weight of evidence from these studies suggests that change is multidimensional rather than unitary. There is reason to believe that it may also be sample specific, "vantage point" specific, and to a certain extent specific to the method used to assess it. Therefore, change factors that emerge in one study do not match those in another. If therapies of different sorts with different groups have different objectives, it is understandable that change factors should differ.

Change Scores. Therapeutic outcome data almost always consist at least of before and after measures. Many investigators use difference or change scores as a means of contrasting the experimental and control groups. Unfortunately, raw change scores do not have the same meaning at different points along the scale, and the regression of gains on initial scores must be taken into consideration. Among the useful solutions is the use of delta scores, a regression transformation, in lieu of raw change scores. Initial and final scores are transformed into standard scores (z_0 and z_1), with a mean of zero and standard deviation of one. The delta score then equals $\frac{z_1 - r_{01} z_0}{1 - r_{01}^2}$. The effect of the level of initial scores is thus removed statistically and the delta score is independent of it. Another solution is to use analysis of covariance. Many experiments in psychotherapy outcome lend themselves readily to analysis by this technique. Readers who are interested in the special properties and peculiarities of change scores are referred to Thorndike (1924), Thomson (1925), Zieve (1940), Heilizer (1951), Lacey (1956), McNemar (1958), Lord (1958, 1963), McHugh (1961), and Garside (1962). For discussion of methods of assessing similarity between profiles rather than individual scores, see Cronbach and Gleser (1953).

CRITERIA FOR APPRAISING CHANGE

In following the classical experimental model, the researcher starts with hypotheses, selects relevant criteria to test the hypotheses, and applies valid and reliable measures of the criteria. Criteria relevant to test hypotheses about "improved adjustment" would, of course, differ from those relevant to hypotheses about "improvement in nail-biting behavior." An investigator is obliged to specify in advance what criterion of improvement he intends to use to test his hypothesis. A hypothesis about nail-biting dictates the criterion through its specificity, but those about constructs such as "adjustment," "maturity," or "emotional stability" do not. These latter subsume many complex behaviors, and an investigator has to be prepared either to treat them globally or to break them down rationally or factorially into salient characteristics that cluster to form the construct. The items on the list of characteristics then become the criteria. Some investigators follow the dubious practice of starting with a measure and then working backward to establish a criterion and a hypothesis. They are likely to end up with answers in search of a question.

Some studies have relied upon a single measure of a single criterion, and often quite appropriately. This has been done when the goal of therapy has been explicit, such as the removal of a particular phobia or disabling somatic complaint. The criterion should be logically related to the hypothesized goals of the therapy. Goals can be general or specific. Specificity does not imply triviality. In a single case study, for example, a fear of earthworms was alleviated by behavior therapy (Murphy, 1964). This would be of no great consequence to a patient living on New York's Fifth Avenue, where few earthworms are likely to be encountered in the normal course of daily activities. In this case, however, the patient, a woman, lived in a suburban part of England in a home with an outdoor privy. Her phobia was so persistent that her husband was obliged to get up at night with her and lead her with a flashlight, searching the ground for earthworms in her path. By day she was terrified to go marketing. Successful removal of this incapacitating fear was an enabling change that resulted in a marked improvement in her life.

Outcome criteria should be based on sound hypotheses. The two are thoroughly intertwined since criteria are direct derivatives of hypotheses. Unless both are relevant to the goals of the therapy, failures to demonstrate changes that have actually taken place will result. In a study by Seeman (1962), eighteen clients treated for a median of twenty-two client-centered sessions were compared before and after therapy on seven perceptual tasks with eleven controls from the same student population. The tasks administered were the Cube Test, Flicker Fusion, Mirror Test, Stroop Ratio, Pain Threshold, Concealed Figures, and Autokinetic Effect. When re-examined, the treated and untreated groups each did slightly better on half and worse on half. The only significant difference was for Flicker Fusion, a finding which Seeman attributed to chance since one significant result can be expected to arise by chance about 25 per cent of the time in an array of seven variables. When the therapy group was divided into success and failure subgroups on the basis of counselor ratings of outcome, no significant differences in pre-post perception scores were obtained. This, then, was more a study of the validity of perceptual performance as a criterion measure than of the efficacy of psychotherapy. The finding led Seeman to revise his hypothesis that perception should change as a result of psychotherapy into the less general form that for individuals who present an initial disturbance in perceptual organization, psychotherapy will lead in the direction of greater effectiveness.

Hypotheses of positive changes in areas in which individuals show no initial disturbance or malfunction are not likely to be confirmed. Psychotherapy is designed to modify maladaptive and maladjustive behavior, not to make people better in all ways. Many will disagree with this formulation on the grounds that it seems to deny the pervasiveness or intraindividual generality of psychopathology. Therapists, however, have explicit and implicit goals for a given individual that must be related to the very reason for the patient's applying for help, some form of maladaptive or maladjusted behavior that has led to personal dissatisfaction with or without somatic correlates, anxieties, or interpersonal problems. The patient's difficulty may be either more restricted or more pervasive than the patient or therapist knows, but it is this condition that the therapist is attempting to change with his techniques. What is desired, at the least, is change in personal adjustment in those areas where there is a problem. Research that sets the criterion of improvement in terms of reading rate, sleep patterns, motor coordination, problem-solving ability, memory, flicker fusion, or any of an unlimited number of other specifics, would only provide a meaningful test of therapeutic efficacy if the patients had disturbances in these functions and therapy was striving to modify them.

In this connection, reference is made to a study of the impact of psychotherapy on the productivity of psychologists (Wispé & Parloff, 1965). The criterion of productivity was number of publications. There is no indication that psychologist subjects had sought therapy because of any decrement in their ability to publish. The median number of publications of psychologists is very low in any case. Individuals who do not publish can be highly productive in other ways. Failure to publish does not imply that the psychologist is disturbed in that area. It does not appear reasonable, therefore, that psychotherapy which had other objectives would increase this specific form of behavior for the treated group as a whole. The hypotheses, however, were: (1) productivity, so defined, of a sample of psychologists who had received psychotherapy would be higher than for a matched, nontherapy control sample; (2) the correlation between pre- and posttherapy productivity would be negative and significantly different from that of the controls; and (3) the mean of the absolute differences between the quantity of pre- and posttherapy productivity of the treated group would be greater than that of the controls. To test the hypotheses, 1,123 questionnaires were sent out to members of the American Psychological Association; 86 per cent were returned. A sample of fifty-five psychologists who had had a minimum of sixty hours of therapy were matched on a series of relevant variables, including earlier productivity, with fifty-five psychologists who had not received therapy. Each publication was weighted for whether it was a book or an article and whether it was written by a single author or with collaborators. Sixty-five per cent of the therapy group claimed to have entered treatment for personal reasons, and 69 per cent of them had a psychoanalytic therapist. None of the hypotheses received any support at all. Neither the mean nor median number of publications differed in the experimental and control group. The highest and lowest producers before therapy remained so. There was no relation between after-therapy productivity and duration of therapy, reasons for entering therapy, orientation of therapist, or field of specialization.

By way of contrast, Hatterer (1960) studied psychiatric treatment aimed at alleviating creative work block in fourteen patients. He reported a change in all cases from nonproductivity to productivity. Since there were no controls, the study cannot be considered a valid appraisal of therapeutic efficacy. In this instance, however, the therapist selected patients who had, among other things, a known disturbance in this life sphere and attempted to modify their condition with psychotherapy. The hypothesis of change related to one of the goals of therapy and was open to specific test.

It is unrealistic to think that psychotherapy can do all things for all people, that it can make them better and better in every way. To demand the impractical of psychotherapy is to doom it to failure in evaluation; to ask too little is to relegate it to the category of superfluous and trivial self-indulgence. Its *raison d'être* is to help people modify their emotional disturbances and maladjustive behavior patterns in substantive and meaningful ways, not to make them into paragons.

CRITERION MEASURES

Before applying criteria of change, one must obtain satisfactory measures and develop an impartial, unbiased way of using them. Before deciding on specific measures, one must choose from the available sources the kind of data desired. The primary data that comprise the raw material for evaluation may be classified as judgmental, descriptive, performance, or status data. The main sources of these data are the patient, the therapist, outside observers, significant others (friends, relatives, associates, other patients), case records and documents, and therapeutic protocols.

Judgmental Data. Judgmental data are obtained when the primary data are in the form of direct appraisal of the results of psychotherapy. The value judgment can be made via verbal report or questionnaire and then refined by rating scales. When this criterion is used, the sources of primary data and evaluation data are identical since the primary data are themselves in the evaluative form. The risk of uncontrollable bias is high if the patient, the therapist, or "significant others" make the evaluation. In asking a patient to evaluate how much he has changed during therapy, one must expect distortions and inaccuracies that are both intentional and unintentional, consciously and unconsciously motivated. The same considerations apply to therapists' reports. It is especially difficult for the principals in a therapeutic endeavor, each of whom may be intensely ego-involved in the process, to make accurate, unbiased observations and judgments. "Significant others" who play a role in the patient's life can temper the judgment of those who are actually within the therapeutic field, but are certainly not free of their own biases. Evaluative statements that appear in case records may come from or be influenced by the evaluations of the therapist and the patient, and are therefore open to the same biases. Relatively unbiased evaluations can be made by impartial outside observers if they have no knowledge of the treatment received and no relationship to the patient. When this is not feasible (and it usually is not), preconceptions about therapeutic effects introduce a potential bias. When the content of therapeutic protocols is used as the source of the primary data, the evaluator must be heavily influenced by patient and therapist evaluative remarks within the sessions. Judgmental primary data, almost regardless of their source, are therefore sensitive to distortion.

Apparently because of the recognition of inherent difficulties in their use, very few controlled outcome studies, in contrast to surveys, have employed evaluative judgments made by the therapist, patient, or other observer. The question is whether or not the participants see the same things through the same colored glasses. If not, one must determine the nature of any systematic biases that may exist. Neither the patient nor the therapist may be able to judge progress with sufficient objectivity, and the judgment of both may be affected by other considerations no matter how impartial they try to be. This matter of intersource congruence or differences due to vantage points has been studied.

Rogers indicated that the correlation between a client's self-description and the evaluation of him by a diagnostician using the same instrument is generally low, as is the correlation between a client's description of his behavior and a description by his friends (Rogers & Dymond, 1954). Correlations between objective diagnostic pictures by two diagnosticians were described as in the thirties and forties, and between the observations of two friends of the client in the twenties. Agreement on the analysis of client TAT material by two psychologists from different orientations was reported as low. Rogers concluded that statements about the specific changes produced by client-centered therapy would have to be accompanied by an indication of the observer's vantage point.

Storrow (1960) studied the intercorrelations among the ratings of therapists, patients, relatives or friends, and his own ratings based on information abstracted from the patients' charts. The forty-five patients were treated by experienced therapists, residents, or medical students. Judgments of change were made at termination on a series of five-point (much better, better, no change, worse, much worse) rating scales covering areas of symptoms and problems, productiveness, sexual adjustment, interpersonal relationships, and ability to handle stress. The authors' summed rating from the five areas of adjustment was considered the validating criterion and its reliability was established by rerating after a six-month interval. Ratings in the five adjustment areas were found to hang together. Sexual adjustment was judged most resistant to change and symptoms or problems showed the most change. The correlation of the therapist with the judge was $r = .61$, with the patient $r = .57$, and with the relative $r = .32$. The correlation of the patient with the judge was $r = .51$, and with the relative $r = .66$. The correlation between the relative and the judge was $r = .43$. Experienced therapists tended to agree with the judge's ratings ($r = .79$) and student therapists with patients' ratings ($r = .71$). An "index of therapeutic outcome" ($5 \times$ therapist's score $+ 1.5 \times$ patient's score) was derived by multiple correlation for the professional therapists, which yielded a coefficient with the criterion of .81. Since this index was not crossvalidated on another sample, there is no assurance that it would hold up. There is also some question about the judge's rating being used as the criterion measure. The judge's rating was based on case records that were not independent of therapists' ratings since the therapists supplied the information in the charts in the first place. Although there was some agreement among these various sources, it is apparent from this study that intersource agreement is not high enough for reliance to be placed on any of them singly.

In the factor analysis by Cartwright and Roth (1957) there was no relationship between the views of change of the therapist and those of the client. A therapist-rating factor and a client-rating factor were also found to be distinct factors by Nichols and Beck (1960). The therapists stressed self-understanding in their concept of improvement, while the clients stressed how they felt. Therapist and client perception of change also appeared as separate major factors in the Cartwright, Kirtner, and Fiske (1963) study.

The congruence of patient and therapist judgments of the outcome of psychotherapy was appraised in a different way by Board (1959). Questionnaires were sent by mail to psychiatrists who had treated patients at the Mandel Clinic, Michael Reese Hospital, Chicago, asking them to list their five most and least successful cases and to describe the changes that took place. The names of 152 patients were listed as successfully treated. The names of only eighty-six unsuccessfully treated cases could be remembered. Board observed that the memory of psychiatrists for unsuccessfully treated cases failed more and sooner than for the successful cases. Agreement on judgment of outcome by patient and physician existed in 56 per cent of the cases, with 48 per cent agreement on a successful outcome and 8 per cent on an unsuccessful one. Disagreement was present in 27 per cent, with the patient seeing a favorable outcome and the physician unfavorable more than twice as often as the converse. In 17 per cent of the cases the patient was unable or unwilling to arrive at a judgment. Three times as many of these were judged by the physician as unsuccessful than as successful. Despite this statistically significant degree of overall agreement, some of the disagreements were extreme. In one case the patient stated, "A marvelous result was obtained in my case. Kindness and understanding can produce miracles." The physician's comment on this patient was, "Secondary organic brain damage. No capacity for insight or introspection, massive denial of illness—untreatable further." Another patient wrote, "I pray to God that you have more and quicker success with other unfortunate creatures." The physician stated, "Improved—social advances—back to work."

Battle et al. compared therapist and patient ratings of overall improvement in relation to other criteria measures and found a lack of agreement (Battle, Imber, Hoehn-Saric, Stone, Nash, & Frank, 1966). Landfield, O'Donovan, and Nawas (1962) compared improvement ratings of outside judges from interview typescripts with psychotherapists' own ratings and obtained a tetrachoric correlation of .86. The two judges agreed on 75 per cent of the cases when improvement was dichotomized, and on 54 per cent when quartiled. A third judge decided disagreements. Interjudge agreement on a dichotomous classification by chance would be 50 per cent, and a consensus arrived at by using a third judge does not help because agreement of two out of three judges would necessarily be achieved all of the time when there are but two choices that can be made. In short, the ratings of the external judges were not sufficiently reliable for any meaningful comparison to be made.

Robertson (1957) hypothesized that there would be differences in the agreement between patient and therapist depending upon whether or not the patient saw change. A questionnaire consisting of twelve statements relating to changes in feelings or interpersonal behavior was given to twenty-three clients and sixteen therapists in two mental hygiene clinics. When the clients indicated no specific changes, there was a strong trend, though not significant, for therapists to agree with them. However, when clients did indicate a specific change, there was no trend toward agreement. This suggested to Robertson anticipatory exaggeration of slight changes by clients. When both agreed that certain changes had taken place they agreed regarding satisfaction over these changes, but when they agreed that changes had not taken place there was no trend toward agreement about satisfaction over the absence of change.

The study by Brill et al. afforded comparisons of ratings by the therapists, patients, and relatives (Brill, Koegler, Epstein, & Forgy, 1964). Patients tended to consider themselves more improved than did their therapists, and relatives shared their most optimistic view. Bellak et al. reported a significant correlation between patient and therapist judgments, but its magnitude is not given (Bellak, Meyer, Prola, Rosenberg, & Zuckerman, 1965).

Patients in group therapy were rated by their therapists and themselves on changes in symptoms, functioning, and relationship after one year. Correlation coefficients for symptoms (.60) and functioning (.61) were higher than for relationship (.34) (Yalom, Houts, Zimerberg, & Rand, 1967). Dietze (1967) considered the proposition that staff judgments of hospitalized patients might be determined by the staff's specialized roles and patients' judgments by their experiences in hospitals. Forty acute cases were compared with forty-one mild or improved cases. The patients' judgments of improvement were compared with the judgments of fifty-three staff members (residents, nurses, aides, psychiatrists, social workers, psychologists, and psychology trainees). Responses to a reliable scale of improvement were considered. Correlations among the three professional groups indicated general agreement. Acute patients who had been in the hospital for a short time agreed with the aides, whereas patients who had been in the hospital for a longer period agreed more with the professional groups.

Stieper and Wiener (1965) obtained a low but significant correlation of $r = .25$ between judges' ratings of outcome based upon therapists' data at termination and patients' ratings twenty-seven months later. Kraus (1959) found discrepancies in ward physicians' evaluations of hospitalized patients (seven of eight improved), judges' ratings based upon therapists' observations (five of eight improved), and evaluations made by a rating psychiatrist (three of eight improved). Actually the disagreement was more marked than these figures indicate, for the correlation between the rating psychiatrist and the ward physician was $rho = -.51$. They were, however, rating different aspects of the patient's condition. The ward physician was rating ward behavior, the therapist was describing behavior in group therapy, and the rating psychiatrist was looking at psychopathology. This kind of phenomenon may account for rating differences. This was illustrated in the work of Feifel and Eells (1963), who asked therapists and patients to assess the same therapy. The patients stressed changes in insight, attitude, and behavioral alterations, while the therapists emphasized behavior and symptom relief.

Dickoff and Lakin (1963) contrasted ratings of improvement made by a research psychiatrist one to two and one-half years after group therapy with the therapist's earlier ratings. The research psychiatrist rated the patients on improvement in physical symptoms, work capacity, love capacity, interpersonal relationship capacity, level of social activities and interests, and felt anxiety level, and arrived at a summed overall rating. There was a low positive relationship between the rater's and therapist's judgment. Those the therapist saw as markedly improved tended ($p<.10$) to receive higher ratings from the research psychiatrist than those in the mildly improved or unimproved categories, but there was no agreement on the mild and unimproved groups. Volsky et al. obtained low correlations between counselors' ratings of present status and change in test scores of anxiety, defensiveness, and personal problem-solving ability (Volsky, Magoon, Norman, & Hoyt, 1965). The authors felt that the counselors' judgment of change was probably less valid than the test measures.

Amble and Moore (1966) assessed the possibility that knowledge of the fact that the patient had completed treatment might influence a rater's judgment. Fortunately, it did not prove to have a significant influence. Less experienced raters were influenced more by this knowledge. This experiment suggests that it is possible for experienced clinicians to serve as unbiased raters in experiments on the outcome of therapy when blind arrangements are not feasible.

Descriptive Data. Primary data that are descriptive and limited to factual information about the patient can be (but are not necessarily) less open to bias than are evaluative statements. It is only when we are one step removed from actual behavior that can be tabulated or rated, or when one of the principals in the therapeutic transaction becomes a judge of its success, that the criterion measure becomes controversial. In general, distortions are likely to be fewer if the inquiry is more contemporaneous and less reliant on memories of past events, if it is more specific, less complex, and contains fewer judgmental words. For example, contrast the question "Do you drink much?" to the line of inquiry "How many drinks did you have today? What kind? Where? With whom? What time during the day? What about yesterday? . . ." In the first question, the word "much" calls for a relative judgment based on standards that are not known to the interviewer. The interviewer can obtain enough information from the second series of questions to rate the drinking behavior of the patient along a scale whose standards are known to him.

Factual information can thus be obtained through an interview and then placed on a rating scale, rated directly, or gained from a questionnaire or inventory completed by the subject. The same primary sources upon which judgmental data are based can be used. The descriptive data, however, are then processed by someone else, preferably unrelated to the case or the hypothesis, into the form of evaluative data. Biases in the descriptive information are controllable to some extent, but still may not be as accurate and factual as anticipated. A desirable check of the primary source can be made by utilizing more than one source. The risks of bias range from low to high but generally are reduced by the use of descriptive data rather than judgmental criteria.

Performance Data. Performance can be directly observed instead of being reported. The researcher's concern shifts from the accuracy and reliability of the respondent to that of the observers or procedures, and to the adequacy of his sampling of observed behavior. These, however, are under his control to a far greater extent, and bias can be minimized. Trained observers can watch patients function and can measure or rate what they do. Performance, situation, or stress tests can be applied to obtain direct measures. Inferences can be made from psychological test results or therapeutic protocols subjected to various kinds of formal analysis.

Status Data. A fourth class of criteria are those that elicit the physiological, psychological, sociological, or sociometric status of the individual as distinct from performance. The primary data come from the appropriate status examination. As with performance data, criteria can be objective and bias can be controlled.

APPLYING CRITERION MEASURES

The principal methods of applying criterion measures in psychotherapy research are judgments and rating scales, questionnaires and inventories, psychological tests, physiological measures, analysis of therapeutic protocols, and special experimental devices and behavior indices. Needless to say, they do not always agree. Vargas (1954) attempted to discover whether self-awareness and success of therapy are related and ran headlong into the criterion problem. According to the criterion of counselor judgment, there was a positive correlation between self-awareness and success of psychotherapy. With a psychoanalytically oriented TAT analysis as the criterion of success there was a negative correlation. Going by the Dymond Q-Sort Adjustment score, there was no correlation. Judging from other TAT ratings, there was a low positive correlation. Softening the impact of these contradictions is the fact that this spectrum of results was obtained by using rank-order correlations with small Ns of eight to ten and many tied ranks.

Judgments and Rating Scales. The general procedure is to obtain judgments from independent and impartial observers who possess some degree of expertness in observing, judging, and rating the behavior in question. The reliance one can place on a judge is based either upon his established reputation as an authority or upon his being able to meet qualifying standards set up by the experimenter. The degree to which expertise is necessary is a function of the level and complexity of the judgments. It is not required when the task consists simply of counting easily identifiable, noncontroversial, all-or-none behavior. If an observer were required to count the number of times a patient pulled his left ear during a therapy session, the qualifying standards would simply be that the observer take the task seriously, pay strict attention to the task, understand clearly what the experimenter means by ear-pulling, distinguish the patient from the therapist, know left from right, and be able to count or apply a recording system accurately. The ability of the observer to meet these standards and to perform reliably can easily be established in a trial run.

Where more complex judgments are involved, more elaborate steps have to be taken to ensure that all observers understand the criteria in the same way and are capable of applying the measures proficiently. When the situation calls for the judgments of more than one observer, the problem of how best to represent the consensus must be resolved. There are two principal methods, and the selection of the most appropriate is largely a function of whether the data are ordinal or nominal. One method is based upon the mean and the other upon the mode. The former is generally the choice when judgments are theoretically distributed normally, and the latter when the judged material must be placed into discrete categories.

Scaled judgments (rating scales) are used with *ordinal* data. Rating scales are essentially ways of refining, systematizing, and increasing the precision of judgments. The procedure is basically one of quantifying qualitative data by giving numerically scaled values to the observed characteristic or phenomenon, or by assigning numerical values to points along a graphic scale. Suppose an experimenter were studying the effect of a particular therapeutic technique upon the sociability of patients in a specific situation, and had devised a ten-point rating scale to measure it. Let us assume that the numerical units represented a continuous series with equal intervals ranging from a value of one, representing extremely antisocial attitudes, through a value of ten, standing for exceptionally sociable attitudes. Although any single observer might rate the patient's behavior anywhere along the scale, the assumption is that the judgments of a large number of observers would distribute themselves normally around a mean value which would represent his true behavior. Since it is usually not feasible to obtain a large enough sample of judges to obtain either a normal distribution or a highly accurate measure, we are obliged to deal with approximations and calculations of the fiducial limits of these estimates. Enough judges should be used so that a measure of interjudge reliability may be obtained. The mean score of the judges on the rated behavior is taken as the best expression of the consensus.

Judgments of *nominal* data present a different problem. In experiments where judgments are discrete, nonquantitative, all-or-none categories, the modal consensus approach must be used. Consider an experiment in which outcome is classified as "improved" or "unimproved." Here we are concerned with the agreement of skilled judges, and the experimenter must make a determination of how many judges are needed and what degree of agreement among the judges is required. The general principle is that the degree of obtained agreement among independent judges must significantly exceed the agreement that could be attributed by probability to chance alone. With only a "majority rules" rationale, many experimenters accept the judgment of two out of three judges. They do not stop to consider the chance probability of obtaining such agreement. Expansion of the binomial $(A + B)^3$ gives the probability of two out of three or more of the judges agreeing when there are two choices. From the expansion $A^3 + 3A^2B + 3B^2A + B^3$, it can be seen that there are only eight possible combinations, and chance alone will give such agreement 100 per cent of the time. With only two choices, there is obviously no way for all three people to disagree. The probability of all the judges choosing B is one in eight, and of all agreeing on either A or B is two in eight. Thus, even if the experimenter required three out of three agreement, it would not approach the .05 level of probability. Applying successively larger exponents shows sixteen possibilities with four judges, thirty-two with five, sixty-four with six. There would be one chance in thirty-two of five out of five judges saying "improved" ($p<.05$), but only five in thirty-two of four out of five agreeing on the category. To be on safe ground an experimenter would have to demand more than four out of five agreement before accepting a judgment.

As the experimenter introduces other judging categories, the odds change. With three categories (improved, no change, worse) and three judges, the expansion of $(A + B + C)^3$ yields one chance in twenty-seven of all three judges saying C, and one chance in nine of all agreeing on some category. Whatever the combination of judges and categories, requirements can be established which exceed chance. Cartwright (1956b) presents a rapid nonparametric estimate of multijudge reliability for use with varying numbers of categories and judges, and a table for estimation of significance.

There are two primary reasons for disagreement. Either the judges may actually have different opinions or the judges may not understand the judging criteria in the same way. The first is the very reason for calling upon judges to begin with, but the second is under the control of the experimenter. Precautions should be taken to make certain that the judging criteria are clear and explicit, and that all judges understand them precisely in all details. This usually requires training of the judges and preliminary assessment in trials of their ability to understand and apply the criteria. Advance training will improve interrater reliability and prevent the sad discovery, after all data have been collected, that the judgments were not sufficiently reliable. When the criterion is some tangible act or occurrence in the life of the patient, observed or documented, it is usually an all-or-none event of a positive or negative nature that requires no judging. Thus, the patient may have obtained a job, gotten married, become hospitalized, received a discharge, stopped drinking, committed suicide, gone to jail, graduated from school, or stopped wetting the bed. The particular criterion is selected for its relevance to the major treatment goals for the sample under study. The researcher may require the presence of one or more positive outcomes in the absence of negative ones or he may prearrange some weighting scheme. Reliability and validity are not issues if the selected behavior is relevant to the therapeutic goals. The criterion is challenged when it is not relevant to the therapy, when the specific behavior is taken to stand for some broader and more general characteristic (as in Wispé & Parloff's study), or when the behavior is considered of minor importance.

Inventories and Questionnaires. Standard inventories and questionnaires, and original ones devised for specific studies, have both been used in research in therapy. In personal inventories, the patient is the source of the data. Inventories are, in a sense, standardized interviews calling for monosyllabic responses by the patient. They are rather easily subject to dissimulation, although some have built-in reliability checks, social desirability scales, and lie scales. The inventories, in particular, are open to the biases of the respondent, which may take the form of exaggerating complaints on the way into therapy and giving socially desirable answers on the way out (Hathaway's "Hello-Goodbye" effect). Most were designed for diagnostic purposes, and some serve that purpose admirably, but their sensitivity for reflecting change would have to be established. Responses to the many items that refer to past history are revealing for diagnostic purposes. Since they would not be expected to change after therapy, they limit the potential of the inventory for reflecting change and increase the probability of a high correlation between final and initial scores. Other items may be worded in such a way that they cannot pick up nuances that reflect actual change. Inventories originally designed to measure status rather than change may be excellent for their original purpose, but they lack the sensitivity required for this different application. The most frequently used measure of this kind in controlled outcome studies has been the MMPI. There has been some research on its utility as a criterion measure.

Schofield (1950) conducted an elaborate but unsuccessful attempt to validate the MMPI as a measure of change with psychotherapy. One section of the study dealt with twenty-five psychoneurotics who were given the MMPI before and after an average of five therapeutic visits. No significant changes were seen on any of the clinical scales. This did not, however, constitute a fair validation because the patients were seen for a brief period by junior medical students assigned to the psychiatric service for ten weeks. There is no assurance that the results would have been comparable with those of trained and experienced therapists.

Kaufmann (1950), investigating changes in the MMPI as a function of therapy, selected fifty-one improved cases (as judged by the therapist) for comparison with fifty-four normal controls matched for age, sex, and interval between testings. The D, Pt, and Sc scales were found to be most sensitive in differentiating patient and control groups, and most modifiable by therapy. The research limited itself to successful cases, and we do not know if others would have shown similar changes. The nonpatient controls served no useful purpose other than providing a "normal" baseline that was never attained by the successfully treated patients.

Comparable findings were obtained by Gallagher (1953), who appraised MMPI changes concomitant with client-centered therapy. Seven of the scales showed significant differences between pre- and posttherapy scores, but the therapy group remained more deviant than randomly selected college student controls. Feeling or discomfort scales (D, Pt, Hs) showed the greatest tendency to change, and character or behavior disorder scales (Hy, Pd, Ma) the least. Evaluations of progress by the client and therapist were "fairly independent of each other."

Drasgow and Carkhuff (1964) found the Kuder Preference Record to be a useful criterion measure with hospitalized patients. Patients discharged as improved had lower Kuder "escape scale" scores (Musical, Artistic, Literary) than those discharged as unimproved.

Self-Ideal Discrepancy. A derivative of the inventory, change in the discrepancy between the concept of the self and the ideal self, was employed in the Rogers and Dymond study (1954) and became a popular criterion measure. In one phase of this project, Rudikoff studied changes in the concepts of the self, the ordinary person, and the ideal during a no-therapy period, therapy, and follow-up in a small sample of eight own-control cases (Rudikoff, 1954). The Butler-Haigh Q-Sort and Dymond Q-Sort Adjustment Index were used. The perceived self and ideal self became significantly more similar, and the subjects also saw themselves as having become more like ordinary persons. These increases in congruence were greater during therapy than during a control period, and gains were maintained on follow-up. Chodorkoff (1954) compared adjustment ratings of thirty subjects with scores on self and ideal sorts. A significant curvilinear relationship was found. The best-adjusted subjects had the highest correspondence between perceived and ideal self, but the least adequately adjusted did not show the lowest correspondence.

The measure has come under criticism from several sources. Loevinger and Ossorio (1959) maintained that "a high correlation between one's self-description and one's description of the ideal person is probably a better indication of Philistine self-satisfaction than of the success of therapy" (p. 394). Levy (1956) designed an ingenious experiment as a way of testing the meaning and generality of perceived actual-ideal discrepancies. His purpose was to examine the logical justification for inferring that the size of the discrepancy is a measure of self-esteem and for defining maladjustment in terms of this discrepancy. The Butler-Haigh Q-Sort was used to measure self and ideal self. In addition, a "home town" Q-sort was constructed consisting of 100 positive and negative statements about one's home town. It was administered in order to get a Q-sort of the home town as it is and of the ideal home town. The Q-sorts were given to twenty-one students at Indiana University. Actual-ideal self-descriptions and actual-ideal home town descriptions correlated ($r = .70$). Levy concluded, therefore, that there is a tendency to perceive discrepancies that transcend the object of the description and that such discrepancy scores should not be narrowly interpreted as self-acceptance or self-esteem. It would follow that research projects claiming increases in self-esteem with therapy by using self-ideal discrepancy must be looked upon with some skepticism.

Nahinsky (1966) obtained self-ideal Q-sorts from neurotics, inpatient psychotics, outpatient psychotics, and general population controls. The latter showed the highest self-ideal correlation, but most of the between-group variance was attributed to a "generalized set transcending specific traits." This was determined by removing the specific items that accounted for intergroup differences.

Further cautions were introduced by Winkler and Myers (1963). They intercorrelated the Butler-Haigh Q-sort and the Index of Adjustment and Values, both purported to be measures of self-acceptance, with the Taylor MAS, Marlow-Crowne Social Desirability Scale, Couch-Keniston Yeasay–Naysay Scale, and the Bass Social Acquiescence Scale. Self-acceptance did not emerge as an independent trait since response bias and anxiety accounted for more than half the variance. The Taylor Manifest Anxiety Scale was more highly correlated with the two self-acceptance measures than they were with each other.

Kenny (1956) emphasized the need for controlling social desirability factors when testing hypotheses regarding the real self–ideal self discrepancy. On the basis of his data he concluded that the social desirability variable tends to inflate the correlation between the two selves and therefore requires control. According to these data, self-ideal discrepancies are probably not a simple criterion measure of self-acceptance and therefore of adjustment. The discrepancy score is apparently partially a function of broader tendencies in the individual to perceive contrasts between actual and ideal situations and is influenced by a response set of social desirability. The measure is subject to the influences of censorship and bias of other self-report measures which would best be controlled for, balanced by more objective measures, and taken into consideration in interpreting results.

The Q-sort is not the only self-concept criterion to be used. Bowman (1951) developed a rating scale to measure the degree of consistency between "what I am, want to be, and ought to be." Working with a small sample of five cases, he found in three cases an increase in consistency of these three concepts with therapy. He reported that this increase in consistency was associated with decreasing tension as measured by the Discomfort Relief Quotient. Most change was seen in the current self, which was also the most talked about in therapy. Self-satisfaction, as reflected by congruence of these three self-concepts, could be achieved by shifting the wished-for self and proper self and not changing the current self at all. By this criterion, the patient might feel better and view therapy as successful even in the absence of externally observable change.

Luria (1959) and Endler (1961) both reported changes in the concept of the self to be a central aspect of improvement with therapy, and employed the semantic differential technique to measure it. Sheerer (1949) reported increased acceptance of and respect for self and others with successful therapy. Aidman (1951) and Ewing (1954) reported that the present self changed more than the ideal self, and in the direction of greater congruence.

Psychological Test Measures. It is a common procedure in research in psychotherapy to utilize existing objective psychological tests or projective techniques as criteria measures. The main consideration is that the test be appropriate to the situation and provide a valid measure of the criterion. If it does, the investigator's task is greatly simplified, but it is futile and misleading to use a test that was never designed to measure the behavior or characteristic under investigation. Because a test has been validated for one purpose does not mean that it can be used validly for another. It should also be noted that change in test behavior is not necessarily accompanied by a comparable change in general behavior. Particularly questionable are generalizations about behavior from "test signs" that have not been validated. The validity of a standardized objective test, a projective technique, or sets of test signs from either one must be established before any conclusions can be drawn about changes. Otherwise, conclusions must be limited to behavior specific to the test used. The use of test procedures, in contrast to the use of inventories, reduces the risk of censorship or distortion by the patient. However, the level of inference necessary to relate the test performance to life behavior is considerably higher. Projective techniques are subject, even to a greater degree, to the same reservations as objective tests and inventories, with the additional problem of interpreter reliability. The Rorschach has been most frequently used, and its sensitivity to therapeutic change has been investigated. It has been used as a basis for global judgments by some investigators and as a source of individual signs or indices for the examination of change by others. There have been some comparisons of the relative merits of these approaches.

Mintz el al. submitted twenty pairs of Rorschach records to two judges (Mintz, Schmeidler, & Bristol, 1956). One record of each pair was taken early in treatment and one after a mean of twenty months of psychoanalysis. The judges, working blind, were able to sort seventeen of twenty pairs correctly. Mosak (1950) used a global rating scale as well as a quantitative sign analysis for the Rorschach. The Hildreth and Bell adjustment inventories and the MMPI were also used. The Rorschach global ratings of change correlated more highly with the other test changes than did the sign analysis. The correlation of the sign analysis with the MMPI was $r = .09$ in contrast to $r = .44$ for the global ratings. Mosak considered the global ratings to be more sensitive than the sign approach. Which is most valid remained undetermined. Although Rorschach ratings and counselor ratings both showed positive changes for the group as a whole, they showed changes for different individuals.

Employing an empirical sign approach, Watkins (1949) examined twenty-three patients judged to have been helped by psychotherapy. The Rorschach changes obtained were an increase in F+, decrease in F% if it had previously been above fifty, increase in M and FM, appearance of FK and Fc if previously absent, shift from C to CF and FC, and a decrease in content of frightening figures and explosive force. These changes were not cross-validated nor was there any control over the effects of a second test administration without therapy or a comparative group of unsuccessful cases. Also using a Rorschach sign approach, Haimowitz and Haimowitz (1952) reported a series of personality changes differentiating patients treated by client-centered therapy.

Rioch (1949) studied the Rorschachs of fourteen ambulatory and twenty-two hospitalized patients before and after treatment. The average interval between testings was sixteen months for the ambulatory and nineteen months for the hospitalized, representing 150 and 250 psychoanalytically oriented treatment hours respectively. The presence and degree of improvement was completely agreed upon by the therapist and the Rorschach analysis for the ambulatory patients, but there was far less agreement for the hospitalized (mostly schizophrenic) patients. In each case where there was disagreement, it was always the therapist who saw improvement while the Rorschach worker saw no change. The one significant favorable change in determinants was in color responses in line with predicted color dynamics. There was essential similarity between the two tests off most of the patients who were observed. None of the other shifts were clearly significant.

Lipton and Ceres (1952) used the Munroe Inspection Technique, which provides an index of maladjustment. Significant improvement in test signs was found in patients judged improved but not in those judged unimproved. Improvement was judged by the therapists. The Rorschach evaluations were not blind and were open to bias. Piotrowski (1955) applied his Alpha formula, made up of weighted scores for various Rorschach determinants, on fifty schizophrenics reexamined after an average interval of 5.6 years. Change in the patients was independently evaluated in terms of symptoms, work record, family adjustment, level and quality of intellectual processes. The patients were classified as improved, essentially the same, or worse. The Alpha score significantly discriminated among these categories.

Krout et al. used a test-retest procedure with three groups (Krout, Krout, and Dulin, 1952). In addition to nineteen Ss undergoing analytic therapy, there were fourteen in supportive treatment and nine who were untreated. Re-examination took place after about a year for the treated groups and twice that for the untreated. Rorschachs were evaluated by two of the authors, only one of whom was unfamiliar with the case. Judgments were made on a series of variables: anxiety, libido, hostility, guilt, interpersonal relations, integration, approach, reality testing, pathognomic signs, and productivity. The analytic group showed the most change, and the nontreatment group the least. The presumption of the validity of the criterion measure comes from the fact that it favored the group that did best on the second test. The analytic group had 150 hours of intensive therapy compared to forty hours of supportive therapy for the other treated patients and none at all for the untreated. All were initially equal in degree of pathology. Comparison with some external criterion of success would have eliminated the need to assume that the intensively treated group improved the most.

The Barron Es scale derived from the MMPI, Klopfer's Prognostic Rating Scale, and Cartwright's modification of the RPRS have all been presented as measures of ego strength that predict success in psychotherapy. Adams and Cooper (1962) applied all three measures to a hospitalized sample but did not obtain a significant correlation between the Barron Es and the two Rorschach measures. They concluded that the measures tapped different personality variables. Their interest was in prognosis, but the lack of agreement of the two kinds of measures has implications for outcome appraisal as well. It will be recalled that Mosak (1950) obtained no relation between the MMPI and Rorschach sign analysis but did find some relation between the MMPI and a global judgment based on the Rorschach.

Goldman and Greenblatt (1955) attempted to validate the TAT as a criterion measure. Pre-post measures were taken on forty-five schizophrenics who were tested at hospital admission when they were acutely ill and again on leaving the hospital as either improved or unimproved. The improved and unimproved cases could be clearly differentiated. The principal areas that changed were attitudes toward people, perception of the world, and ability to handle emotions. No generalizations can be made about the validity of the TAT as a criterion with less disturbed patients. Watkins (1949) claimed that his sample of successful cases showed alteration of TAT stories. More stable characteristics were ascribed to heroes and there were more successful endings. However, there was no comparison group.

Fiedler and Siegel (1949) used a figure drawing procedure and were able to differentiate successful from unsuccessful cases. They employed twenty-two criteria related to details of drawing of the head and face (taken to reflect interpersonal relations).

Physiological Measures. Physiological measures have been used principally to test hypotheses about the therapeutic process, but there have been some instances of their application as outcome criteria measures. Some of the measures serve as direct criteria measures when they reflect the very disturbance that psychotherapy aims to alleviate, such as blood pressure for hypertension or heart rate for tachycardia. Validity becomes an issue when the physiological measure is assumed to stand for a psychological state. The validity and reliability of a measure such as galvanic skin response, when taken as a measure of anxiety, rest on the evidence from its own somewhat controversial literature. Nevertheless, palmar sweating has been found to be a useful objective criterion measure of outcome over a course of therapy. At the University of Illinois, palmar sweating of a young graduate-student patient was recorded daily (Bixenstine, 1955). Prints were obtained by coating the finger tip with ferric chloride solution, letting it dry, and then pressing it against a paper coated with dried tannic acid. Daily prints were obtained in this manner over a period of six months, and hourly prints were taken every eighth day. A chronology of significant events in four life areas—marital, parental, social, and professional—was kept in addition to subjective self-ratings on tension and sense of well-being. Both diurnal and daily patterns were evident, and palmar sweating gave a good picture of ongoing life experiences. A gradual decrease was seen over the course of interviews. This method of measuring palmar sweating was recommended as a simple and useful tool for the objective assessment of outcome over a course of therapy. Its validation as an outcome criterion awaits application to a larger sample. Hoenig and Reed (1966) reported PGR recordings to contradict patients' reports of relief from phobic symptoms, and suggested it as a superior measure. No real evidence of its superiority, however, was demonstrated.

Analysis of Therapeutic Protocols. The early search for objective criterion measures brought out a number of ways of analyzing therapeutic protocols. It was assumed that utterances of the patient in the interview contained the basic data for the appraisal of change. These could be analyzed in terms of their formal characteristics or by their content. Grummon (1950) for example, tabulated the frequencies of 250 linguistic categories of four patients early and late in therapy. Suggested as useful for assessing improvement were changes in the type-token ratio, increase in clause length, and an increased proportion of adjectives to verbs.

One way of analyzing content for judging outcome was offered by

Raimy (1948). The PNAvQ is a way of classifying the patient's speech units as positive self-reference (P), negative self-reference (N), ambivalent self-reference (Av), no self-reference (O), or nonrhetorical question (Q). Rated responses are then placed in a ratio that reflects the extent of the patient's manifest self-approval or self-disapproval. Extending Raimy's PNAvQ method, Bugental (1952) developed a "conceptual matrix" for assessing self and not-self attitudes in therapy encompassing what the patient says about himself or that which is not himself and the feeling tone expressed. It was offered as a reliable rating scheme that could be further refined and used to test hypotheses about therapeutic effects. Todd and Ewing (1961) had counselors rate improvement of thirty-four student clients on the Hunt-Kogan Movement Scale. The number of positive self-references by the client was significantly related to postcounseling adjustment ratings and to change scores during counseling. As predicted, counseling resulted in a decrease in negative self-references as well as an increase in positive ones, but counselor judgments of success were not associated with this decrease in negative self-reference.

Another way of assessing progress from therapeutic protocols is the Discomfort Relief Quotient (DRQ) proposed by Dollard and Mowrer (1947). It is a ratio of expressed discomfort units to relief units, and is based on a concept of tension reduction. PNAvQ and DRQ were compared by rating typescripts of seventeen nondirective interviews by five different counselors at various stages (Kauffman & Raimy, 1949). The two methods yielded essentially similar results. Cofer and Chance (1950) applied the DRQ to six published cases and noted the expected decline in all of them. However, a single case study by Murray Auld, and White (1954) reported that the DRQ was not useful in assessing change. Mowrer, Hunt, and Kogan (1953) found a low correlation ($r = .20$) between DRQ and case workers' judgments in thirty-eight cases, leading them to conclude that it is probably not a valid measure.

Butler (1952) proposed the use of "context coefficients" in assessing therapeutic protocols in preference to balance coefficients $\left(\frac{A}{A+B}\right)$. For example, in using a measure such as the Discomfort Relief Quotient, the formula $\frac{D}{D+R}$ would equal .5 if there were one relief statement in an interview or if there were fifty, regardless of the other kinds of responses made in the total response context (T). He suggests using the formula $\left(\frac{A}{A+B}\right)\left(\frac{A}{T}\right)+\left(\frac{B}{A+B}\right)\left(\frac{B}{T}\right) = 1.00$. Context coefficients decrease as other responses decrease relative to A and B responses, and increase as the proportion of A + B in the total response context rises.

Experimental Devices. As with test and physiological measures, special devices that are developed specifically for the purpose of serving as criterion measures in a particular investigation should be appropriate to the hypothesis and of established reliability. It is usually necessary to measure reliability and preferable to do so in a pilot study before the experiment proper. It is not necessary to validate simple and obvious behavioral indices, but the burden of proof is on the experimenter to demonstrate that more indirect measures actually measure what they are intended to measure. Face validity can often be deceptive. To clarify these points, consider an experiment on changes in mood as a result of psychotherapy. Should the experimenter simply count up the number of times in a time period that the patient laughed or smiled, this behavior might be literally taken on its face validity, and no elaborate validation procedures required. If the experimenter has reservations about the validity of the direct behavioral expression itself and has reason to believe that it may be masking true feelings, he has the option of using more than one criterion measure. Should he devise a projective technique and use as his sole criterion measure the number of times the patient saw happy or smiling faces, he would be obliged to demonstrate that such responses were actually accurate reflections of the mood in question and that changes in the response pattern indicated changes in mood.

Smith and Johnson's (1962) serial tachistoscope technique for measuring reality construction and Marks and Sartorius' (1967) scale for measuring changes in sexual attitudes are examples of research in criterion measure development. The number and variety of specially prepared experimental devices that can be used are limited only by the imagination and ingenuity of the experimenter, coupled with practical considerations of time, expense, and effects upon subjects.

Comparisons between Other Criterion Measures. Battle et al. studied the use of "target complaints" as criteria of improvement (Battle, Imber, Hoehn-Saric, Stone, Nash, & Frank, 1966). At the end of the screening interview the patient was asked to name the three problems he most wanted help with. After four months of therapy the patient was interviewed. The original target complaints were read to him, and he was asked to rate the amount of change on each problem on a five-point scale. The patient's and therapist's global ratings of improvement, a rating of social interaction by a research sociologist based on an interview, and a pre- and posttherapy fifty-item Discomfort Scale (a checklist of anxiety, depression, and somatic complaints) served as criteria against which the target complaint criterion was checked. It was reported that target complaints correlated with the other four measures to a significant degree, but the validity of none of the measures was assessed.

Brown (1957) compared conditionability with psychometric measures in the evaluation of group therapy. Conditionability of thirty-three psychotics was determined in a simple avoidance situation (faradic shock). Half received intensive group therapy for three months, the other half did not. All were retested. A significant ($p = .001$) increase in level of conditionability for the treated patients was noted, with no change in the untreated. Psychometric evaluation, "including observational and rating scale methods" (no details are given), yielded no significant changes in either group. Brown concluded, therefore, that the conditioning measure was superior. Different it was, but its superiority was not tested.

In an Australian study, Cox (1953) reported sociometric study to be at least as effective an index of changes in adjustment before and after play therapy as was the TAT. Hoenig and Reed (1966), working with outpatients in the Royal Infirmary, Manchester, England, compared PGR with conventional verbal reports of the patient as objective measures of anxiety. The data were obtained from four phobic women. Each S was tested initially and at intervals during therapy. A standard oral word-association list was presented with the key anxiety word (such as "cat") inserted at two points. In addition, the actual stimulus object to which the patient had been desensitized in the previous week's therapy session was introduced (such as "kitten"). The patient was also asked to close her eyes and visualize the anxiety-provoking situation to which she had been desensitized in the previous session. PGR was taken during presentation of the real stimulus, the imaginary one, and the word associations. Lack of congruence between the verbal report and the PGR response was observed. The author concluded that the usual clinical method of assessing outcome by verbal reports cannot be accepted at face value in this any more than in other kinds of therapy. The point is well taken but the examples are not. A dog-phobic patient who reported posttreatment alarm only when in close quarters with fully grown Alsatian dogs had resumed work and could now go out in the street. PGR showed no change during imaginary and real stimulus presentation, although the patient was listed clinically as substantially improved. There is no reason to believe that the PGR reaction is the more valid measure. The experiment clearly needed some objective determination of actual behavioral change to compare with both the verbal report and PGR. The study does raise a doubt about the accuracy of self-reported symptom change.

WHAT CRITERION MEASURES HAVE BEEN USED?

In addition to the criterion measures that have themselves been the subject of research, a great many others have been used. Those that have been employed in the controlled outcome studies that will be reviewed are categorized in Table I, and the percentage of studies in which each category has been used is given.

Table I. Outcome Criterion Measures Used

MEASURE	GOOD STUDIES	ALL STUDIES
Observed behavior	53%	39%
Personality inventory or questionnaire	34%	27%
Rated behavior	30%	27%
Projective technique	18%	19%
Q-sort	13%	10%
Objective performance test	11%	9%
Physical signs	9%	8%

Among the controlled studies considered to be of good quality, the first ranking criterion category is observed behavior (53 per cent), followed by objective personality tests or inventories (34 per cent) and rated behavior (30 per cent). It is notable that ratings of outcome by the patient or therapist are not used. Nor are they at all prominent in studies that are of more questionable quality. In all outcome studies combined therapist and patient ratings rank far down the list (7 per cent are patient ratings and 6 per cent therapist ratings). The principal objective personality test or inventory measure has been the MMPI, with the Rorschach predominating among the projective techniques. About half of the studies have used more than one kind of criterion measure, such as an objective test, behavior ratings, and a Q-sort, ranging as high as six types in a single study. Even those in which one class of measures has been employed frequently have used multiple measures within that class, such as rating of three kinds of behavior or application of several different tests. These are sometimes considered separate dependent variables and are sometimes combined into a single total measure.

PART II

RESEARCH ON THE EFFECTS OF PSYCHOTHERAPY

Our little systems have their day.

—TENNYSON, "In Memoriam"

Most of the change we think we see in life
Is due to truths being in and out of favor.

—ROBERT FROST, "The Black Cottage"

Healing is a matter of time, but it is sometimes also a matter of opportunity.

—HIPPOCRATES, *Precepts*

3

The Effects of Psychotherapy

The dialogue between the psychotherapist and the researcher has been repeated so often that it has become stereotyped. Any therapist who has talked to a researcher, any researcher who has talked to a therapist, or any therapist-researcher who has talked to himself has probably been through it at one time or another. The therapist claims that therapy is effective because his experience tells him so, and he proceeds to describe a case. The researcher wryly observes that barber-bloodletters were just as convinced of the efficacy of venesection and were, no doubt, as adept at citing successful cases. The therapist lets this go by, or interprets it, and goes on to contend that human personality and psychotherapy are so complex and multidimensional that they cannot be evaluated by experiments. The researcher counters that if therapy can alter the complex interlocking network that constitutes personality, positive changes in some of its components or in some global measure of change should be observable and measurable. The therapist insists that the really important things cannot be measured, that one cannot meaningfully translate warm feelings into cold numbers. The dialogue continues in this vein or descends to a more heated exchange. The researcher calls the therapist resistant because psychotherapy has grown as a craft, with its legend and lore, at a more rapid pace than it has as a science. Its spiritual godfathers were witchcraft, voodoo, and other occult and mysterious processes, and its latter-day saints were writers and philosophers rather than scientists. The therapist refers to the researcher as a nihilistic devil's advocate whose resistant attitudes obviously stem from his pathological psychodynamics. At the end, neither of the two is much shaken in his faith.

Any practicing psychotherapist who is convinced of the efficacy of his work should welcome its assessment. Systematic appraisal, however, is looked upon with suspicion by many therapists who see it as a process designed to negate and disprove rather than to uncover and establish the facts. The therapeutic literature abounds in testimonials illustrated by carefully selected, wondrous case reports that boggle the eye and captivate the imagination. Every once in a while, an elder statesman recommends caution, expresses reservations, and calls for evaluation. This may be followed by introspection and ritual cleansing by public confession and analysis of a few failures.

New therapeutic approaches typically generate tremendous initial enthusiasm and attract loyal cohorts. Ardor, fervor, and conviction are mighty lieutenants in the missionary cause. Clinicians who are short on tools and long on difficult problem cases make good converts. Case reports that sound terribly convincing are presented and followed by a survey of a successful series of cases. The hard second look is generally not so optimistic. By the time the controlled research is done (if ever), the therapeutic sun may have already set behind the clinical horizon, replaced by the ascendance of a bright new one.

For example, Rosen (1947) stirred great interest by a report of 100 per cent success in a series of thirty-seven psychotic patients treated by his method of direct analysis. Several years later, he averred that thirty-one were still nonpsychotic and progressing well (Rosen, 1953). These cases were subjected to follow-up by other investigators six years after Rosen's follow-up (Horwitz, Polatin, Kolb, & Hoch, 1958). They were able to locate only nineteen of the original patients for study. They report that the initial diagnosis was schizophrenia in only twelve of the nineteen cases and that six of the remaining seven were psychoneurotic. Following direct analysis, ten of the patients had somatic therapies, four had psychotherapy of other kinds, four continued direct analysis, and one had no therapy. The course of the group of seven nonschizophrenics was what one would "ordinarily expect in a ten-year survey." It was variable but did not involve repeated hospital admissions. The schizophrenics presented a different picture. The authors maintain that by the time Rosen's original report was published, five had already been rehospitalized. Nine of the patients had from two to five admissions and two had undergone psychosurgery. More than half were treated with electroshock, insulin coma, psychotherapy, and chemotherapy. They concluded that direct analysis had failed to lead to a sustained therapeutic result and that the outcome was in line with the usual course of untreated schizophrenic patients. Of course, it is possible, though unlikely, that the eighteen missing cases were startling successes. What this does for us is to point up the limited value of presenting case series in any context other than that of controlled research, objective criteria, and adequate follow-up.

More often than not, surveys have been retrospective in nature. They consist of tabulations of judgments of success and failure, either dichotomized or scaled to reflect the degree of improvement, and are summarized in a percentage of improvement. In most surveys, there is no way of knowing what such terms as "recovered," "much improved," and "slightly improved" mean. There is little constancy in the meaning of these terms from survey to survey. The original data is poor because it usually relies exclusively on the subjective judgment of the therapist or that of the researcher, who depends on case records written by the therapist. The errors are then compounded by a reviewer (see Eysenck, 1952, 1960, 1965; Levitt, 1957a) who takes the improvement percentages (which may be grossly inaccurate to start with) from diverse sources and averages them to arrive at a total estimate of outcome regarded as authoritative because it is based upon so many thousands of cases. The size of the N in such an amalgamation is bound to be impressive but contributes not at all to the validity of the information.

Examination of a large number of surveys convinces us that this kind of study is a blind alley. We could present an exhaustive list of the hundreds of surveys that have been published, but we feel that it would only serve to obfuscate the issues. There is no proof at all that whatever change took place was attributable to psychotherapy. These surveys, in the aggregate, form a vast swamp in which a reviewer could get lost forever. These studies cannot be compared with one another, they cannot be reproduced, they cannot be interpreted, and above all they cannot be averaged. The wisest course is to bypass them entirely.

In derogating the utility of surveys and surveys of surveys for the purpose of evaluating the effects of psychotherapy, we do not mean to imply that they serve no other purpose. The natural progression of appraisal is the selected case presentation, the case survey with gross subjective criteria, the uncontrolled but more objective outcome survey, and finally the controlled experiment. A phenomenon is observed and reported. A series of similar observations is systematically recorded. This is repeated with more careful measurements and the introduction of procedures to reduce error and bias, finally leading up to a rigorous study with appropriate controls. The earlier efforts are, in a sense, pilot studies and necessary preliminary steps before the complex task of designing and conducting controlled research.

There have been many basically adequate researches, designed systematically to measure the effects of psychotherapy on a treated group without bias, with careful before and after measures. However, they have lacked a control group. These studies leave us in limbo, not knowing whether or not the patients would have gotten as much better or worse, as the case may be, without treatment. They leave each reader to form his private opinion in accordance with his own predilections.

The authors of these studies are usually well aware of the limitations of their studies and tell us that, for whatever reason, it was not possible to obtain a control group. Having acknowledged the need for controls and their inability to obtain them, many proceed to interpret their results *as if* they had them. Cappon (1964), for example, in about as honest a self-appraisal of one's therapeutic work as is possible, stated that he was not trying to prove that the results were due to therapy. The title of his paper, however, was "Results of Psychotherapy." Once having gone on record that the results of psychotherapy were not necessarily the results *of* psychotherapy, he stated that he had no "obsessive preoccupation" with controls as the "*sine qua non* dictate of science." Having thus excused himself from meeting minimal requirements, he proceeded to express the opinion that the favorable results were indeed *due to* psychotherapy. The use of controls is simply a method for reducing reasonable doubts to a minimum. They are one of a researcher's occupational tools, not a preoccupational obsession.

Dittman (1966) observed, "To this reviewer the controlled study certainly yields results that can be counted on, but is not the only road to the 'truth.' The large studies which came out of the Veterans Administration during the year, with data collected in such a way that internal comparisons by length of treatment, diagnosis, and the like, can be made, cannot be dismissed simply because there was no control group for comparison" (p. 58). To date, we have not come across any *other* road to truth that can be counted on. The excellent studies referred to are not to be dismissed since they did answer the questions that they were designed to answer. They were not meant to be evaluations of the effectiveness of therapy, however, and cannot be used as such.

The control problem has led to a search for a baseline of expectancies for recovery without treatment, or spontaneous remission. This baseline quest has never met with notable success, and the available results are extremely variable. Since real or imaginary baselines form some of the basic data of some of the most prominent evaluations of psychotherapy, it would be worth examining a few of the investigations that have focused specifically on improvement in the untreated.

IMPROVEMENT IN UNTREATED SUBJECTS

Denker's now-renowned study of patients treated by general practitioners has been cited by Eysenck and others as a kind of baseline for recovery from psychoneurosis without psychotherapy (Denker, 1946). The study does not merit the attention it has received. All of the data came from the files of a large life insurance company. A total of 500 successive disability claims for all types of neurosis were examined.

In order to be eligible for compensation, the claimants had to be judged as totally disabled and unable to carry on any gainful occupation for at least three months. They were paid benefits ranging from 10 to 250 dollars per month until recovery. Their average age at onset was thirty-seven. Many occupations were represented, but the aggregate was weighted in favor of clerical workers, executives, teachers, and professionals. Records contained quarterly statements from physicians and insurance company investigators confirming work disability. The criterion of "cure" was return to any occupation for remuneration or profit and relinquishment of compensation. Within one year, 44.6 per cent were "apparently cured," an additional 27 per cent in one to two years, and reducing percentages thereafter. After five years 10 per cent were still disabled. Thus, 72 per cent were considered to have "recovered" in two years. During the period of disability, the patients were treated by general practitioners with sedatives, tonics, suggestion, and reassurance. Denker assures us that the therapy was "superficial," but was it more superficial than the criterion of cure? The patients were treated for their disability, and we have no idea how they would have progressed with no treatment at all. While return to work reflects change in one important area, there is no way of knowing if the patients' neuroses were actually modified in other respects. Cartwright (1955a) has indicated that the patients were seen during a period marked by national economic recovery, and suggests that this is what the data may reflect.

Denker should have stopped there. Instead, he proceeded to compare the obtained 72 per cent two-year recovery rate with various reports of surveys of the outcome of treatment by psychiatrists and psychoanalysts. Included among others were results from the Berlin Psychoanalytic Institute, London Clinic, Chicago Institute, and Menninger Clinic. The consistent report of 60 to 70 per cent improvement led him to conclude that there was no difference in therapeutic success obtained by general practitioners, psychiatrists, and psychoanalysts, and to hypothesize that psychoneurosis may run a self-limited course. This is certainly a possibility, but Denker has not proved it. He has demonstrated only that insurance disability compensation runs a limited course. His data and the surveys of the literature are just not comparable owing to lack of communality of standards of recovery, definitions of terms, objectivity of evaluations, and comparability of patients. Nothing at all is known about the frequency or duration of the comparison treatments. The data in the surveys that he uses for comparison are just about as useless as his own. This is a case of comparing bad data with bad data and hoping that, because there is a great deal of it, it will somehow turn into good data. If, however, it were possible to reproduce these findings, and if the supportive therapy of the general practitioner is as effective as that of the psychiatrist or psychoanalyst, and if both are equally better than no treatment at all, then there may be an element common to both that is really therapeutic. Only if neither is better than no treatment at all, and all yield the same high improvement rate, could we take seriously the notion that psychoneurosis is self-limiting.

Eysenck (1960) fitted a curve to Denker's questionable data of spontaneous remission as a function of time and came up with the idea that recovery follows a simple exponential curve whose formula is, "roughly": $X = 100(1 - 10^{-0.00435N})$, where X represents the amount of improvement and N the number of weeks that have elapsed. This curve was presented again in 1967 with the outcome of three other studies plotted to illustrate how closely they adhered to it (Eysenck, 1967). The improvement rate after a three-year time lapse, as shown by Wallace and Whyte (1959), was used, and was reasonably close to the curve. Eysenck, however, completely ignored the improvement rates furnished by these authors at the four-, five-, six-, and seven-year points. If these are plotted they can be seen to bear no resemblance at all to this exponential curve. In Wallace and Whyte's data of improvement as a function of time lapse, there was no increase whatsoever in improvement over time. The percentage improved at five years or seven years was no higher than at three years. In their study Wallace and Whyte followed up eighty-three psychoneurotic patients who had been on the waiting list at the General Infirmary, University of Leeds, England. Of this total, forty-nine were successfully contacted and interviewed. They were classified as recovered, improved, or not improved, depending upon their symptoms, employment, and socioeconomic condition. There was no difference in diagnostic distribution between those who were contacted and those who were not. The total improvement rate was 65.3 per cent with the two categories of improvement collapsed into one. By diagnostic group, improvement rates showed 68 per cent for anxiety state, 50 per cent for hysteria, and 75 per cent for miscellaneous diagnoses. When improvement was viewed as a function of time lapse, it was seen that whatever recovery occurred took place in the first three years.

Data from a study by Hastings (1958) were also cited. Some idea of the futility of lumping untreated recovery rates together to get at a baseline can be obtained from this follow-up study of former patients who had been hospitalized at the University of Minnesota Hospital from 1938 to 1944. The 1,638 patients admitted during that period were on a small locked ward for an average of forty-five days. The small staff was diagnostically oriented. Therapy was generally supportive, non-specific, and characterized by good diet, sanctuary, occupational therapy, hydro- and physiotherapy, and some reassurance, explanation, and persuasion. Hastings submits that recovery and improvement reflect more or less "spontaneous" remission. Follow-up from six to twelve years later took the form of a personal contact by a psychiatric social worker to assess posthospital social adjustment. Intervening psychotherapy was considered improbable because of the absence of psychiatrists in private practice in rural Minnesota. Although the remissions were not truly spontaneous, this is a study of adjustment under conditions of minimal treatment. Data obtained on 1,261 of the patients who could be reached were presented for various diagnostic groupings. Good to excellent adjustment was found in 20 per cent of the schizophrenics, 46 per cent of the psychoneurotics, and 49 per cent of those suffering personality disorders. The range extended from 18 per cent of the paranoid schizophrenics to 78 per cent for those diagnosed as having pathological emotionality. Even within the psychoneurotic group, the range for good to excellent extended from 25 per cent for hypochondriacs to 65 per cent for those with anxiety state. Psychotics ranged from 18 per cent of the paranoid schizophrenics rated good-excellent to 43 per cent of the manic-depressive depressed. Thus, baselines are seen to be so varied as to provide unsuitable data for comparison with treated groups. This kind of data is no substitute for a randomly assigned control group. Even so, if we plot Hastings' data, it too is far away from Eysenck's curve and lends no support to his formula. It is as though Eysenck were fitting data to curves rather than curves to data.

The untreated patients in a study by Saslow and Peters (1956) were those who received no therapy because they lived too far from the clinic or because therapy was refused, contraindicated, or not required. The group of 100 included both psychotic and nonpsychotic patients. Time between clinic contact and follow-up ranged between 1.5 and 6.5 years. Information was gained from personal interview, questionnaire, and, in some cases, from relatives. The criteria of improvement involved loss of symptoms, change of basic responses in previously affected areas (work, health, social relations), and less disabling responses in the face of meaningful stress. Although the method of assessment left much to be desired, 37 per cent were judged as improved and 63 per cent unchanged or worse.

Goldstein (1960b) has proposed that the term "nonspecific therapy remission" should be substituted for "spontaneous remission." In this experiment twenty-seven individuals, including fifteen waiting-list controls, received no formal therapy. They did receive ample attention in the form of an initial intake interview and three psychological testing sessions spread over seven and one-half weeks. Fewer and less severe somatic and psychological symptomatic complaints were reported on an inventory by twenty-five of twenty-seven patients. Goldstein attributed this to the therapeutic nature of consultative interventions and stressed the bias that it can create in designs using a no-therapy control group. In this experiment, there were contacts with the patient at two and one-half–week intervals over a seven and one-half–week period. In most no-therapy designs, there is not that much nonspecific contact in relation to total time. Nevertheless, if therapy is to be considered worth the effort, it would have to be demonstrably more effective. It is clearly hard to beat 93 per cent success. However, these figures are out of line with other reports and probably are a function of the self-report inventory measure and the standards of success (in this case merely fewer and/or less severe complaints, not remission).

Endicott and Endicott (1963) furnish another estimate of improvement of untreated psychiatric patients. Their sample consisted of forty soldiers or their dependents (five males, thirty-five females), aged eighteen to forty-five, who applied for treatment in an outpatient facility for Armed Forces personnel. Diagnoses included seventeen psychoneurotics, nine borderline psychotics, eight personality disorders, four psychophysiological reactions, and two schizophrenic reactions. Patients were interviewed, given a battery of tests, placed on a waiting list, and reassessed in six weeks. Improvement was assessed on the Miles Evaluation of Improvement Scale, and 40 per cent were rated as improved after six months of no treatment. There was also a distinct tendency for the least severely disturbed patients to improve the most. Thus, 52 per cent of the patients with neuroses or psychophysiological reactions improved in contrast to 9 per cent of the borderline or schizophrenic patients.

These few studies are sufficient to illustrate the unreliability of baselines of recovery without treatment. Percentages in these studies range from 9 to 93 per cent depending upon the diagnosis, the duration of follow-up, and other variables. The frequently quoted estimates that two-thirds of psychoneurotics get better on their own, or the one that claims that one-third get better, one-third remain the same, and one-third get worse, are myths or hunches, not established facts. Reliable large-scale data are not available that could be safely used for comparison with any selected group of treated patients. There are not now any baselines that could serve as substitutes for untreated control patients matched with a treated group on relevant variables.

EYSENCK'S APPRAISAL APPRAISED

In 1952, Eysenck gave voice to what many had been thinking but few wanted to believe (Eysenck, 1952). He argued forcefully that there was no evidence that psychotherapy with neurotics was any more effective than no treatment at all. Finding no controlled experiments that might reject the null hypothesis, he offered instead a collection of survey data from which he adduced that the expected recovery rate from psychoneurosis without psychotherapy was 72 per cent (Denker's data), compared with 66 per cent with eclectic treatment, and 44 per cent with psychoanalysis. Responses were soon forthcoming: Rosenzweig (1954), DeCharms, Levy, and Wertheimer (1954), Luborsky (1954), Cartwright (1955a), and Strupp (1963) were followed by Eysenck's (1954, 1955, 1964) replies. Many of the criticisms were valid, particularly of his reliance upon Denker's data and his averaging of clusters of poor data to arrive at a nonexisting baseline. Almost all, however, missed the key point. None of the criticisms in any way controverted the main contention that Eysenck kept reiterating in his replies. This was that the null hypothesis had not been disproven and that evidence for the effectiveness of psychotherapy with psychoneurotics did not exist. At the time, Eysenck was quite right on this point.

Eight years later, Eysenck (1960) revised his original report. Again reviewing the literature, he became more firmly convinced of his earlier position, no longer limiting it to neurotics. By then his stance had become even more assertively antitherapy. He stated, "the additional studies which have come to hand since, particularly those making use of a control group, have been so uniformly negative in their outcome that a somewhat stronger conclusion appears warranted. The results do show that whatever effects psychotherapy may have are likely to be extremely small; if they were large as compared with the effects of non-specific treatments and events it seems reasonable to suppose that some effects would have been found in the studies quoted. . . . The writer must admit to being somewhat surprised at the uniformly negative results issuing from all this work." He went on to claim that his motive in 1952 was to stimulate more worthwhile research, and that he had believed then that improved methods would "undoubtedly" disprove the null hypothesis. He now regarded such a belief as untenable and stated, "it rather seems that psychologists and psychiatrists will have to acknowledge the fact that current psychotherapeutic procedures have not lived up to the hopes which greeted their emergence fifty years ago" (p. 720).

The controlled studies upon which these statements were based were four in number: Teuber and Powers (1953), Brill and Beebe (1955), Barron and Leary (1955), and Rogers and Dymond (1954). Three of these provided grist for the negative mill. The Teuber and Powers paper reported on the evaluation of a program of delinquency prevention and has long since been superseded by more contemporary research. The Barron and Leary study had enough design flaws to rule it out as good evidence. The Brill and Beebe study was badly misrepresented. It is an excellent and exhaustive follow-up of war neuroses that was not designed to be a study of the effectiveness of psychotherapy and cannot be used for that purpose. It is a careful and elaborate investigation that stands on its own merits and admirably serves the purpose for which it was designed. The small portion of data dealing with treatment is divided into two sections, treatment in the armed service and treatment since separation. Treatment in the service was categorized as either hospital routine, rest, and sedation or psychotherapy of any type or duration. Treatment of mild cases was usually limited to rest and sedation. Individual therapy was more often given to the more serious cases. Still, a significantly favorable response was shown by 20 per cent with routine hospital care, 31.3 per cent of those with no treatment or rest and sedation, and 40.5 per cent of those who received individual treatment. The authors observe:

An ex post facto study of different treatments is naturally hazardous; the experimentalist requires an element of physical randomization in the allocation of treatments before he is willing to associate differences in outcome with differential effectiveness of therapies. Here the categories of treatment are quite broad and pay little regard to intensity, but in view of the limited resources available for treatment in the military situation only a rough classification is possible. . . . More specifically, individual therapy was given more often to combat than to noncombat cases, to men with a more adequate preservice personality (who were apt to be in combat) and to those whose illness seemed most severe. Those who were given individual therapy responded more favorably to treatment, returned to duty more often, performed more satisfactorily after return to duty, and were less often ill at separation from service [p. 26].

As far as treatment since separation from the service is concerned, Brill and Beebe clearly state, "The effect of treatment cannot be discerned in these data, so confounded is treatment with prognosis" (p. 190). Eysenck takes pains in establishing the credibility of the authors, referring to one as an eminent psychiatrist and the other as an able statistician, but disregards their own statements about the limitations of the data for the purpose of evaluating psychotherapy. It is therefore difficult to understand how he can use this study to build a case for the ineffectiveness of psychotherapy.

Eysenck's appraisal of the effects of psychotherapy relied upon these four studies. In our review of the literature, however, we have found at least thirty controlled studies published by 1959 that were presumably available to Eysenck at the time. Eysenck's 1960 conclusions were based upon a small and unrepresentative sample of the available material. Five years later he again revised his review of the effects of psychotherapy (Eysenck, 1965), citing seven additional controlled studies for a total of eleven. His conclusions about the ineffectiveness of conventional psychotherapy did not change, but new evidence was cited in favor of behavior therapy based upon learning theory. Seventeen prominent authorities were invited to comment. When all was said (and a great deal was), the null hypothesis still stood intact. To cite a few examples: J. D. Frank argued that the remission of untreated cases is not necessarily as "spontaneous" as Eysenck believes. Glover, cited by Eysenck as a leading psychoanalytic authority who had negative views about its efficacy, claimed that he was quoted out of context. Barendregt, whose study was used by Eysenck as supportive evidence of his position, stated that with few exceptions the patients in his research were treated by therapists who had very little experience. Meehl attributed the findings more to the patients and therapists than to any basic invalidity of the process. He argued that, at most, one-quarter of the patients in therapy are suitable cases and that one-quarter represents the upper bound of the proportion of therapists who are much good at their job. The joint probability, therefore, of a suitable patient getting to a suitable therapist is around .06. Wolpe referred to "the still sedulously unpublished" report of the Central Fact-finding Committee of the American Psychoanalytic Association (1958). His own estimate of the success of traditional psychotherapy was 21.5 per cent. Hyman and Breger concluded that, "to try to reduce psychotherapy to the model of a scientific experiment will either result in reasonably objective results that are irrelevant to therapy or outcomes that will be meaningless and ambiguous at their best" (p. 319). They thereby rejected the whole notion of research appraisal. Davidson seemed most convinced, judging from his semiwhimsical comment, "One cannot examine the numerous studies offered by Eysenck without coming to the conclusion that maybe—just maybe—psychotherapy is a kind of a cult. The American Medical Association (II.1 of the 1955 Principles of Ethics) has defined a cult as 'a dogma, tenet, or principle, based on the authority of its promulgator to the exclusion of demonstration and scientific evidence' " (p. 173).

One small voice, belonging to Kellner, approached the Eysenck argument at an entirely different level, at the foundation of the argument itself, the incompleteness of its basic data. In effect, he challenged Eysenck's scholarship by citing a number of studies which Eysenck had missed and which appeared to offer refutation to the null hypothesis. In his own review of the literature he cited other studies and drew conclusions quite different from those of Eysenck. Unfortunately, he too had missed more than he had located, and his review suffered from a failure to evaluate critically the studies cited.

There was no research drought during the thirteen years that intervened between Eysenck's 1952 and 1965 reviews. We are indebted to Eysenck for having thrown down the gauntlet. During the intervening years a large number of researchers had picked it up. By 1964 there had been at least seventy controlled studies on the effects of psychotherapy. But again Eysenck's (1965) conclusions were based upon a small, unrepresentative sample of the available evidence. Eysenck (1967) was still stating, presumably on the basis of the same few studies, "To date, then, there is no real evidence for the effectiveness of psychotherapy—as is now admitted even by leading psychoanalysts and psychotherapists—though with further search such evidence might be uncovered" (p. 40).

It has become almost customary for researchers and reviewers alike to introduce their papers with the erroneous observation that few studies on the effectiveness of psychotherapy exist. Despite the presence of a steady flow of outcome research, Strupp (1963), for example, stated that "relatively scant attention" had been paid in recent years to the outcome problem. No stones can be cast, for Meltzoff and Blumenthal (1966) observed, "One of the unusual features of the history of psychological treatment procedures is the paucity of sound assessments of their efficacy" (p. 28). The widespread myth that controlled, evaluative studies have not been done has been passed along by those of us who relied upon Eysenck's reviews but did not ourselves examine the literature in depth. Other reviewers, for example Truax and Carkhuff (1967), while aware of more of the controlled research that has been done, are convinced that the evidence is overwhelmingly negative. They state, "after a careful review of the relevant research literature, it now appears that Eysenck was essentially correct in saying that *average* counseling and psychotherapy as it is currently practiced does not result in average client improvement greater than that observed in clients who receive no special counseling or psychotherapeutic treatment" (p. 5).

The findings of a large body of controlled outcome research (far more substantial than that upon which Eysenck, and Truax and Carkhuff, based their conclusions) are available and deserve careful appraisal.

4

Review of Controlled-Outcome Studies: I. Adequate Studies with Positive Results

Is it meaningful to consider side by side (without averaging) research projects that use various forms of therapy and types of patients? It has been argued that this is futile. We submit that it is not. The purpose of such a review is to find out if there are any demonstrable effects of any systematic attempts to modify pathological behavior, regardless of kind or type. It is not unreasonable to talk about "psychotherapy" in this sense. One can talk about "going fishing" whether in salt or fresh water; by drop-line, surf-casting, fly-casting, speargun, or net; for guppies or for sharks. The method and the quarry may differ, but it is the same game. It is just as ineffective to try to harpoon a minnow as it is to try to catch a giant tuna with a bent pin. Failure to do so does not mean that people cannot catch fish any more than failure to cure schizophrenia with reassurance indicates that people cannot modify psychopathology. Subsequently we will examine the research on comparative methods, techniques, and populations. For the present, the question, simply put, is whether or not anyone has been able to demonstrate satisfactorily that individuals with emotional disturbances (of any type) can be more benefited by psychotherapy (of any variety) than by lack of it over the same time span. What does the current balance of the evidence reveal?

Experiments in several categories are presented without regard to type or duration of therapy or type of patient. The categories have to do with the adequacy of the research for evaluating the effects of psychotherapy and with the direction and meaning of the outcome. The initial categorization stems from a judgment of whether a particular research is an adequate or questionable study. *Adequate* studies are those considered to fulfill the following criteria: (1) freedom from major design flaws that might invalidate the conclusions; (2) use of an appropriate control group and adequate sampling; (3) relative freedom from bias; (4) employment of reasonably objective, reliable, and valid criteria measures; and (5) presentation of suitably analyzed and interpreted data. We are not seeking perfect studies, but those that appear capable of replication, in which the principal experimental precautions have been taken, and that present results (regardless of direction) which merit a reasonable degree of confidence.

Questionable studies are those that, by design or the vagaries of research happenstance, do not meet the above standards in one or more respects. Included are those analogue studies that may be too limited to be generalized to clinical situations. In addition, there are otherwise good studies that were designed for purposes other than the evaluation of psychotherapy. They may have shortcomings as evaluation studies but present relevant data on the subject. In general, less confidence can be placed in the statements made about the effects of psychotherapy from these studies. In no case does inclusion of any research in this category cast any aspersion on the investigators, all of whom must be considered pioneers who were courageous enough to carry out and publish research in this difficult area.

The second subdivision, applied to acceptable and questionable studies alike, is in terms of results. *Positive* results are those whose balance is distinctly in favor of the treated group. *Null* results are those which show no significant differences between the treated and control groups. Included in this category are studies in which some results are positive and some negative, but the balance of the findings does not show a clear advantage for either side. *Negative* results are those in which the balance is distinctly in favor of the untreated control group. Since studies in this category are practically nonexistent, null and negative results are combined.

The third subdivision is concerned with whether the measured results, regardless of direction, are major-primary-central-multiple or minor-secondary-peripheral-limited in scope. A positive result in the major-primary-central-multiple category would be a study in which the treated group, when compared with the control group, showed significant reduction or loss of major signs or symptoms without the substitution of others of equal import. Another positive result would be improvement in general adjustment or in several important areas of adjustment. In lieu of improvement there could be a demonstration of significantly less decline on these variables than in the control group.

Positive changes in the minor-secondary-peripheral-limited category are seen in those studies in which improvement in treated patients relative to the control group is restricted to one or more limited areas of adjustment that do not demonstrably bear on the central condition. Classification into this subdivision might be a function of criteria measures that do not reflect the extent of the actual changes.

The classification system is summarized as follows:

A. Adequate
- A1 Positive (major)
- A2 Positive (minor)
- A3 Null or negative

B. Questionable
- B1 Positive (major)
- B2 Positive (minor)
- B3 Null or negative

ADEQUATE STUDIES: MAJOR BENEFITS

Chappell and Stevenson (1936) conducted an early, controlled investigation of the effect of psychological training upon peptic ulcer. All of fifty-two peptic ulcer patients received the same medication and dietary treatment. Thirty-two of them, in addition, were given psychological training seven days a week for six weeks. Psychological lectures were given to groups of five to ten patients. One of the principal aims was to teach the influence of thinking upon bodily processes. Patients were advised to prevent worry by thinking about a pleasant period of life when anxious. The assumption was that this would exert a calming influence. This process could be viewed as a precursor of the behavior therapy technique of reciprocal inhibition. The contrast in outcome between the two groups was pronounced. After one month of medication and diet, all the control patients were symptom free. At this point, expansion of diet was suggested to the control patients with the result that all but two of the twenty experienced a full recurrence of symptoms within two weeks. The two patients who did not had serious recurrences within two months. The experimental patients fared differently. After three weeks of group training, diet expansion was recommended because all but one was symptom free. Psychological training was continued for three additional weeks. When it was halted, all but two were eating anything they wished. Of the two who had not responded at the same pace as the others, one gradually recovered. Three years later, twenty-eight of the original thirty-two experimental patients were located and followed up. Ten were found to have been symptom free for three years and had experienced no return of symptoms even for a single day. Five had such mild symptoms that they fell within the range of the normal population. Eleven viewed themselves as healthy, nine had numerous recurrences of mild symptoms, and two had experienced single recurrences of severe symptoms. Only two had recurrences as severe as their original ones. Prior to treatment, the experimental patients as a group had had two- to twenty-one-year histories of severe peptic ulcer, averaging eight years.

The effectiveness of group therapy with ulcerative colitis was clearly demonstrated in a study at the New York Hospital–Cornell Medical Center (Grace, Pinsky, & Wolff, 1954). Three groups of patients were contrasted. Group I consisted of thirty-four patients with ulcerative colitis who were treated by group therapy designed to alleviate life stress. Group II was composed of thirty-four other patients matched for age, sex, severity and duration of illness, age at onset, and x-ray changes. Group III included 109 additional ulcerative colitis patients in the hospital. The patients in Groups II and III were treated by diet and medication. All patients in Groups I and II were observed for at least two years. By the criteria of deaths, operations required, complications, x-ray changes, and time in hospital, those who received group therapy consistently showed the most favorable outcome.

The effectiveness of a single, brief psychotherapeutic interaction with enuretic recruits in the US Marine Corps was evaluated in a controlled study (Harris, Firestone, & Wagner, 1955). The researchers worked with a sample of 200 recruits, aged seventeen to twenty-seven, who were entering training with an admitted history of enuresis during the preceding five years. They randomly assigned 100 to an experimental group and 100 to a control group comparable in age, education, IQ, and degree of apparent neuropsychiatric involvement. For the experimental Ss, the regular psychiatric screening interview was expanded into one brief therapeutic session. The session was designed, through permissive and reassuring discussion of the symptom, to relieve anxiety about enuresis and to provide concrete behavioral suggestions for overcoming the habit. The control Ss merely received a standard screening interview. There were no further therapeutic contacts with either group. The criterion of outcome was admission to the psychiatric observation ward before the completion of recruit training. A rigid set of admission standards were in force. The therapeutic intervention was found to be instrumental in reducing the number of admissions to the psychiatric ward. Twenty control Ss were admitted, in contrast to only eight experimental Ss, a difference significantly better than chance. A third group, recruits who initially concealed their history of enuresis but later proved to be enuretic, had a ward admission rate five times as great as the experimental and control groups combined. This is a clear demonstration of the value of a therapeutic maneuver in controlling a specific maladaptive behavioral sign. Although there is no proof that any of the subjects had in fact been enuretic prior to entering the service, there is strong presumptive reason to believe their reports in view of the fact that they were all voluntary enlistees. It would have been interesting to find out if more prolonged psychotherapy would have brought about any better results than this one-session approach and to discover if it was the allaying of anxiety, the behavioral suggestions, or the combination of the two that made the difference.

Another experiment evaluating very brief therapy yielded clearly positive results (Morton, 1955). Forty students at Ohio State University who desired assistance for severe personal problems were referred by their vocational counselors for psychotherapy. They all displayed inefficient academic effort and impaired personal and social adjustment. They were given the Rotter Incomplete Sentences Blank, the Mooney Problem Checklist, and a diagnostic-survey interview covering fourteen areas of adjustment. Following the interview, each student was given an appointment for a date ninety days later. The students were carefully matched in pairs on the problem area, the seriousness of their problems, the degree and nature of generalization to other areas of adjustment, and prognosis. Within each pair, one subject was randomly assigned to the treatment and the other to the control group. The students in the experimental group only were then called in for an appointment as soon as possible. Therapy was completed in twenty days (four appointments). Rotter's social learning theory of personality was used as a frame of reference for analyzing TATs with the patients and discussing problems revealed. Ninety days after the completion of therapy, each experimental patient was seen by the referring vocational counselor, who made a judgment of his present adjustment. The patient was then interviewed again by the investigator and tested again with the two psychological tests. The control patients were seen ninety days after their initial interview and followed the same procedures. The only difference in the handling of the groups was the presence or absence of the brief period of therapy. The initial and terminal interviews were rated independently in detail by three raters, and a pooled global rating was determined. Morton established that there were no significant initial differences between the groups on the pooled global ratings on either test measure. The matching and random assignment was effective; the absolute differences were very small and the groups clearly equivalent.

According to the ratings of the vocational counselors (who did not have access to any of the clinical material and did not know who was in which group) 93 per cent of the treated subjects and 47 per cent of the controls showed some improvement. The treated subjects improved significantly on the pooled global rating, but the controls did not. The difference significantly favored the experimental subjects over the controls at the time of terminal assessment. Both groups showed improvement on the incomplete sentences, but the treated Ss were significantly better at the end. The difference in favor of the treated Ss on the Mooney Problem Checklist was not quite significant ($p < .10$). The apparent improvement in adjustment of the treated group cannot reasonably be attributed to chance, the unreliability of ratings, the passage of time, or the effects of the initial interview. This was a well-designed and controlled study yielding clear and consistently positive results.

The effectiveness of group therapy in controlling soiling behavior in a sample of male psychotics drawn from a soilers ward was assessed at the Veterans Administration Hospital, Albany, New York (Tucker, 1956). Twenty patients were paired into two ten-member groups equivalent for age, soiling frequencies tallied by nurses, and scores on a brief test of mental altertness. One group was randomly designated to receive forty-five hours of group therapy over a nine-week period. Therapy was oriented toward communication. Ward personnel knew who the treated patients were but did not know the identity of the controls. Since the criterion was an objective count of soiling incidents, it is unlikely that any bias was introduced. The results showed a significant difference in soiling at the end of the experimental period. The controls' soiling behavior actually increased, while the treated patients' decreased. Whether or not the improvement was sustained was not determined, but the experiment convincingly demonstrates the effectiveness of the therapeutic procedure in achieving an important specific objective.

A two-way study to evaluate the effect of psychotherapy on mentally retarded children and those with associated specific defects was carried out at the Fountain Hospital, Tooting Grove, London (Mundy, 1957). In the first part, fifteen children with mental retardation (average age 8.5 years, average IQ 45) received psychotherapy. The approach was individual, nondirective play therapy, modified by an analytically oriented therapist who emphasized transference. Simple but deep interpretations were made. The younger children particularly were given "scientific mothering." A control group of ten (average age 8, average IQ 44.30) received only routine institutional care that did not include psychotherapy. All the children were certified as imbeciles. Following nine to twelve months of therapy, Form 2 of the 1937 Stanford-Binet was readministered. The untreated group showed essentially no change, while the treated group's mean IQ increased nine points. The difference between the final test means of the two groups was at the 10 per cent level of confidence. Since all other conditions remained constant, the change was attributed to therapy. Follow-up after a year was conducted with ten of the treated and eight of the untreated children who were available. Four of the treated group had remained at the final test level, and six showed a significant mean increase of eight IQ points accompanied by improvement in social behavior. (These six had been transferred to a better environment, which may have contributed to the improved social behavior.) Social behavior of the untreated group remained constant except for one who deteriorated.

In the second part of the study, eight complex cases were treated and tested in an own-control design. They included four deaf mutes (one with cerebral palsy and one with epilepsy), two aphasics, and two postmeningitis cases. Since six lacked speech, the Drever-Collins Performance Test was used on four occasions. On the first test the group's mean IQ was 56. After one year, during which there was no psychotherapy, the mean was 58. Therapy was then introduced, and about eleven months later, when therapy was terminated, the mean had risen to 80. About two years later, the posttherapy mean had held up with an average score of 78. The increase of twenty-two points was significant at the 1 per cent level. In terms of readiness for special schooling, alertness, and social conduct, improved adjustment and marked rehabilitation were apparent.

Mundy points out that the change from imbecility to educability "later means the difference between leading an institutional life or being a self-supporting citizen" (p. 8). Some will claim that it is commonplace to make imbeciles out of taxpayers, but the thought that psychotherapy can make taxpayers out of imbeciles is heartening.

Coons (1957) contrasted the effects of two kinds of group therapy with each other and with the condition of no treatment. The experiment took place in a hospital and was conducted on patients (mainly schizophrenics) who met the criterion of amenability to group therapy ($N = 66$). Group therapy was conducted in three half-hour sessions per week by two different therapists for same-sex groups. The number of hours of therapy ranged from eight to ninety for the sixty-six patients. The Rorschach was administered before and after therapy. Each pair of protocols was submitted for blind analysis to a judge who determined which one represented the better level of adjustment. He did not know which set of test responses was taken first. To obtain a reliability check twenty of the pairs were given to a second rater; in nineteen cases his judgment corresponded to that of the first judge. Forms I and II of the Wechsler-Bellevue were administered in a cross-over design before and after treatment to measure intellectual efficiency. One of the two kinds of group therapy yielded a significantly higher number of improved Rorschachs (69 per cent) than the other (43 per cent) and than the control group (37 per cent). The more-improved therapy group also experienced significantly greater improvement in intellectual efficiency, particularly in general comprehension and learning ability.

A study of group therapy with alcoholics by Ends and Page (1957) was primarily a comparison of three different theoretical approaches.

The presence of an untreated control group, however, permits an overview of the effectiveness of psychotherapy. Attrition reduced the original sample of ninety-six to sixty-three, but the proportion of those who terminated treatment voluntarily or were obliged to leave for situational reasons was essentially the same in the treated and untreated groups. Treated patients met in groups of six, three times a week for fifteen weeks for specific psychotherapy, while controls met for social discussion only. The Butler-Haigh Q-sort revealed significantly more positive changes in self-concept in groups treated by two of the three treatment approaches, while controls showed gradual deterioration. Follow-up one and one-half years later by personnel who knew nothing of the therapy revealed that patients who had received these two forms of treatment appeared significantly more frequently in the greatly improved category than did the controls. "Greatly improved" meant that there was no evidence of alcoholic episodes or misbehavior during the eighteen-month period. Seventy-seven per cent of the controls had reverted to their old alcoholic pattern or required rehospitalization, in contrast to 60 per cent of one of the treatment groups and only 33 per cent of the other. The patients treated by the third method showed more negative change than the controls and were no better off at follow-up.

Ends and Page (1959) investigated the effects of Rogerian group psychotherapy. Two groups of twenty-eight randomly assigned subjects participated in a general alcoholic treatment program. One of the groups, in addition, had six weeks of group therapy (thirty sessions). Sessions were held daily and were conducted by experienced therapists. Before and after treatment, MMPI and self-ideal Q-sort measures were obtained. The therapy group showed significant movement on seven of the eight Q-sort indices, the controls on three. Movement was significantly greater for treated subjects than for controls on three indices, and at the $p < .10$ level on two others. There were very few changes on the MMPI that were not present in both groups. Group therapy was considered an effective adjunct to the alcoholic treatment program. The study would be far more convincing if the subsequent drinking behavior of the treated group had been investigated as it was in 1957.

A successful demonstration of the effectiveness of group therapy with defective delinquents was conducted at the Huntington, Pennsylvania Institution for Defective Delinquents (Snyder & Sechrest, 1959). All the patients were chronically delinquent males of below dull-normal intelligence who were nevertheless considered potentially capable of profiting from a rehabilitative program. They were mostly in their late teens and early twenties and were both Negro and Caucasian. The patients were matched on disciplinary status and assigned randomly to three groups of eighteen Ss each. One group met for an hour of group therapy a week over a thirteen-week period. Therapy was structured, directive, at times didactic, and oriented toward improving adjustment. Although discussion topics were predetermined and the material covered was concrete, the climate was permissive. After attrition, the final number in this group was sixteen. A placebo group met for the same amount of time. The members were permitted to talk about similar topics and interest was shown in them. However, the program was not therapeutically oriented. This final group also contained sixteen patients. A third group was a nontreatment control group with a final membership of thirteen.

Outcome measures were objective counts of reports of behavioral violations and a "housing report." The latter consisted of a checklist of thirty-one conduct characteristics and thirty-six personal characteristics which was filled out periodically by officers in charge of the ward. The items were dichotomized into favorable and unfavorable. Data were analyzed by analysis of covariance and chi-square as appropriate. The results were largely positive. There was a significant difference among the three groups in the number of favorable comments on the housing report, but no difference in the number of negative comments. Favorable comments increased progressively in the order: no treatment, placebo treatment, group therapy. Appearances before the behavior court as a result of reported violations included two from the therapy group, six from the placebo group, and eight controls. This was an inconclusive finding ($p < .10$). Two and one-half months after the end of therapy, reports of behavioral violations during the interim involved three from the therapy group, six from the placebo group, and ten controls, suggesting that the beneficial effects of treatment were sustained. There were no differences between the Negro and Caucasian subjects.

A rare opportunity for an effective own-control design was exploited in a study of the treatment of warts by hypnosis (Sinclair-Gieben & Chalmers, 1959). In a pilot study, seven subjects with warts, most of whom had failed to respond to various physical treatments, were treated by hypnotic suggestion. Six were freed of their warts within three months. The one failure in treatment was mentally defective. In the main trial, fourteen patients with bilateral and multiple common warts of at least six months duration were given the suggestion under hypnosis that the warts on only one side of the body would disappear. In each case the side with more and larger warts was selected. The level of each patient's response to hypnosis was graded as light, medium deep, or deep. At least a medium deep (amnesia, partial or complete with effective posthypnotic suggestion) response was considered necessary. Adequate depth of hypnosis was reached in ten of the fourteen patients, nine of whom were cured *on the treated side* in five weeks to three months. One of the patients whose treated side was cured also lost the warts on the control side six weeks after the cure of the treated side. In no other case did the untreated side improve. The lone failure was the only one who did not respond to the posthypnotic suggestion to perform a particular action.

A controlled appraisal of the effectiveness of client-centered therapy with thirty-six students classified as having major behavior problems by both teachers and administrators was carried out in two junior high schools in Massachusetts (Arbuckle & Boy, 1961). The subjects were divided into three groups matched for age, grade, IQ, Stanford Achievement Test averages, teachers' behavior ratings, and proportion of peer groups accepting and rejecting them. The groups were further compared on health, siblings in attendance, socioeconomic status, part-time work, participation in school and nonschool activities, educational-vocational objectives, and Q-sort correlation between actual and ideal-self. No differences among the groups were found on these variables. Group A, the experimental group, was split into two subgroups each with its own counselor. The students were offered individual counseling instead of detention, but their continued participation was voluntary. Group B, the traditional control group, was continued on detention and received no counseling. Group C, the laissez-faire control group, also received no counseling but was released from detention. The experimental design neatly controlled for the presence or absence of detention as well as therapy.

The experimental procedures were in force for twelve weeks. Multiple criteria measures were employed, including: (1) improvement in actual-ideal–self correlations from pre- and posttreatment Q-sorts; (2) pre- and posttreatment comparisons of mean scores of teachers' ratings on a quantitative behavior scale; (3) pre- and posttreatment comparisons of mean proportions of peer groups accepting and rejecting clients as reflected in a sociogram; (4) pre- and posttreatment comparisons of definiteness of educational-vocational objectives as determined by interview.

As assessed by the various criteria measures, it was seen, first of all, that the difference between the mean pre- and posttreatment actual-ideal–self correlations for the group that received therapy was significant at the 1 per cent level of confidence. Neither of the two control groups changed. Teachers' ratings of behavior improved significantly for the treated group but not for the controls. None of the groups gained greater acceptance by peers, but the treated group alone became significantly less rejected by peers. Members of the treated group alone showed a marked improvement in the status of their educational-vocational objectives.

Follow-up period was limited to six weeks, during which continued counseling was offered on a voluntary basis. Eleven of the twelve treated students made fifty-three counseling contacts in that period. The number of postexperimental referrals for discipline among the treated group was less than half that of either of the other groups. In this experiment Arbuckle and Boy have clearly demonstrated the value of short-term client-centered therapy in bringing about significantly positive changes in such relevant areas as self-concept, behavior ratings, peer-group rejection, and status of educational-vocational objectives in a group of young adolescents described as having major behavior problems. Appropriate control groups were carefully and convincingly established and contrasted. There is little doubt that the counseling made the difference. How long the effects were sustained was a question outside the scope of the research, but therapy did achieve tangible, positive results. The appraisal of its effectiveness was exemplary.

A novel experiment was designed by Jensen (1961) at the Veterans Administration Hospital, Salisbury, North Carolina, to contrast the relative efficacy of therapy and consultation in behalf of patients. The subjects were forty-four closed-ward female patients who were randomly divided into three groups, comparable for length of hospitalization. The same physician was in charge of all patients and the ancillary personnel were constant. One group received ninety-minute group psychotherapy sessions twice a week for thirteen weeks. A second group received no therapy of any kind, but consultation was given to nurses, social workers, physical medicine and rehabilitation personnel, and others who had contact with the patient. Such consultation concerned the behavior of the patients and was initiated by the psychologists. Roughly the same amount of time was devoted to the consultation as to the therapy group. A control group not only received no therapy, but any intervention or discussion with personnel about these patients was avoided or evaded if it arose spontaneously. The criteria of outcome were shift from closed-ward to open-ward status and discharge from the hospital. There was no bias in the disposition of patients because neither ward personnel nor any one else knew that the study was going on until it was over.

The hypotheses of the research were that psychological treatment through the medium of consultation and group therapy would lead to open-ward status and hospital discharge and that consultation would be the more effective because it would influence the therapeutic efforts of a larger number of people who had extensive direct contact with the patients. The first hypothesis was supported by the data, as the combined consultation and therapy groups were more successful than the controls on these criteria at the 88-day and 153-day check points. The prediction in favor of consultation was not supported. In fact, there was a nonsignificant trend in the opposite direction. Consultation by itself did not produce significantly different results from those of the control condition, but group therapy was distinctly superior. It would have been good to have had supporting data about specific behavioral changes that led to transfer to open-ward status and to discharge. Even without it, the bold fact that these phenomena took place appears to be a decisive, positive outcome of group psychotherapy.

A large-scale controlled experiment on the effects of hypnotherapy on various dermatoses was reported at a conference on psychotherapy in Moscow in 1956 (Zhukov, 1961). The study was conducted at a sulphur bath, sea, and sunbathing resort in the Caucasus frequented by many people with dermatoses. A total of 600 patients with eczema, psoriasis, neurodermatitis, and other skin ailments were studied. All had a history of psychological trauma and skin conditions dating as far back as twenty-four years. Half received hypnotherapy in the evening hours along with the usual daytime resort treatment. The remainder received resort treatment only. The experimental patients had seventeen hypnotic sessions. Change in skin condition was judged as complete recovery, marked improvement, slight improvement, no change, or deterioration. There were 270 cases of eczema evenly divided into treated and untreated groups. In the combined complete-recovery and marked-improvement categories, the controls had 21.5 per cent so classified and the experimentals 58.5 per cent. Neurodermatitis was diagnosed in 166 patients, and half were assigned to treatment. In the control group 26.5 per cent were judged as markedly or completely recovered, in contrast to 69.8 per cent of the treated Ss. For 144 patients with psoriasis, 20.8 per cent of the controls and 63.9 per cent of those who received hypnotherapy were improved to this degree. Almost all the patients were contacted at a later date by a mail questionnaire and 229 responded. They "overwhelmingly testified to the persistent nature of the improvements." If the ratings of improvement in skin condition were at all accurate, this is a rather dramatic demonstration of the effectiveness of this kind of psychotherapy.

A large group of 400 older juvenile offenders under the jurisdiction of the California Board of Corrections consisted of 200 who had been judged as apt to be amenable to treatment and 200 thought to be not amenable (Adams, 1961). The judgment of amenability was influenced by such characteristics as being bright, verbal, anxious, and possessing some insight and desire to change. These two groups were each subdivided into experimental and control groups of 100 each. The two experimental groups were treated (individually and/or in groups) once or twice a week over a nine-month period. Control patients received no psychotherapy, and all participated in the regular institutional routines. The youths were followed up for thirty-six months after release. The result is an interesting one, although it makes the study difficult to classify by outcome. The boys who were considered not amenable to treatment but who received it nonetheless did the worst. The treated amenables, however, were found less likely to return to prison and had significantly less lock-up time. They also did better on other criteria. This suggests that therapy can have a salutary effect on those who meet certain standards of amenability for it, but it may have a deleterious effect if forced upon those who are not amenable to it.

A six-month counseling program in a minimum-security camp for youthful offenders was evaluated in terms of the subjects' changes in attitude toward others and toward their own role in society (Shelley & Johnson, 1961). The hypotheses were that a six-month experience in a correctional camp with a counseling program would produce a greater decrease in antisocial attitudes than a similar experience without counseling, and that those who showed the greatest decrease in such attitudes would have the highest rate of parole success. The experiment took place in two camps for youthful offenders under the auspices of the Michigan Department of Corrections. Each camp supplied fifty young men under age twenty-five who had been convicted of felonies and sentenced to prison. They were all first offenders with neither sex nor drug offenses. Each had a minimum of three antisocial themes on the TAT, administered as part of the admissions procedure. In one camp, counselors saw clients regularly for thirty-minute weekly sessions and additionally when requested, met with them one hour a month to summarize progress, counseled them in groups of eight one hour a week, and contacted them informally during the day. No counseling was available in the other camp. The TAT was repeated at discharge and scored with high reliability by the researchers. Serious antisocial themes were scored two points and minor ones received one point. The second criterion was parole success, defined as an absence of violations during parole. The counseled group showed a significantly greater decrease in antisocial themes. There was a direct relation between success in parole and reduction in antisocial themes. It is not clear why the relation between counseling and parole success was not directly assessed. The obtained difference was attributed to the organized counseling service. The validity of the conclusion rests upon the assumption that that two camps were equivalent in all other respects.

One of the most convincing demonstrations of the efficacy of a particular type of psychotherapy in removing a specific maladaptive symptom came from the Psychiatric Unit of Witwatersrand University Medical School in South Africa (Lazarus, 1961). The purpose of the study was to compare the therapeutic effects of group desensitization with conventional, interpretive group therapy on matched pairs of phobic patients. Subjects were selected from among volunteers for treatment who, upon being screened, were found to have phobias that severely limited their social mobility, interfered markedly with their interpersonal relationships, and clearly impaired their functioning. None who had had previous psychiatric treatment were included. Altogether, thirty-five middle-class urban South Africans, twelve men and twenty-three women, mean age 33.2, were selected. This total included eleven acrophobics, fifteen claustrophobics, five impotent men treated as sex phobics, and a group of four other assorted phobics (sharp objects, dogs, physical violence, and riding in moving vehicles). The severity of the phobic symptoms of the acrophobics and claustrophobics was pretested with behavioral criteria. The fear of heights of the acrophobics was tested by asking each one to climb an outside fire escape. Few could go higher than the first landing, which stood fifteen to twenty feet off the ground, without being paralyzed by fear. The claustrophobics were seated in a small cubicle-like room with a single French window. A movable screen which blocked the window was pushed toward them. They were urged to remain in the cubicle as long as possible and to refrain from opening the window until the need for air became unbearable. Most of them became acutely uncomfortable as soon as the window was closed, and none could tolerate the screen at less than twenty inches.

Pairs of phobic patients matched for sex, age, nature, and severity of symptoms were randomly assigned to treatment type. An original group of sixteen patients (five acrophobics, six claustrophobics, and five impotent men) was randomly assigned either to desensitization or to interpretive group therapy. Fifteen additional acrophobics and claustrophobics were assigned, seven to desensitization and eight to interpretation. The four mixed phobics were all given desensitization therapy to find out if it could be applied to a heterogeneous phobic group. Group desensitization, modeled along Wolpean lines, involved training in relaxation and the construction and application of anxiety hierarchies extracted from remarks on questionnaires filled out by the various group members. Any imaginal scene that became upsetting to any patient in the group was withdrawn, and desensitization proceeded at the pace of the most anxious patient. Details of session-by-session procedures are reported. Interpretive group therapy in the form of insight with re-educative goals was modeled after Wolberg. It was a conventional group therapy approach with attention paid to the development of a permissive emotional atmosphere, free and open interchange within the group, discussion of phobic symptoms and their relation to emotions and interpersonal relations, personal and historical exploration of the problems of the members, interpretation by the therapist of the relation of the symptoms to feelings, and the like. Interpretation and relaxation was a combination of conventional group therapy with relaxation training but no systematic desensitization procedures. The experimenter was the therapist under all conditions. This immediately raises the question of his possible differential competence and interest in applying the two principal methods. Lazarus was aware of this issue and admitted a preference for doing interpretive therapy, which he finds far less boring for the therapist. From his detailed description of proceedings, he was apparently equally skilled in both approaches.

Turning to the all-important criteria of recovery, the experimenter applied actual stress-tolerance tests instead of relying on personal claims of progress. Acrophobic patients were required to climb to the third landing of the fire escape that they had been unable to ascend in the pretest. This brought them to a height of about fifty feet. They were then required to go by elevator from the third story to the eighth-story roof garden, look out over the parapet, and count the number of passing cars for two minutes. Claustrophobics were required to stay in the cubicle with the window closed and the screen but inches away for a five-minute period. All tests were conducted individually in the presence of a witness. Attesting to the occasional gentility of researchers, change in the impotent men was assessed from verbal reports only. This was also the case with the four mixed phobics. The most rigorous criteria were applied. Any continuation of the symptom in any form or degree was considered a failure. Complete indifference or neutrality toward the formerly anxiety-generating situation was required. Moderate or slight improvement or having learned to "accept his neurosis" was considered a failure. Thirteen of the eighteen patients (72 per cent) treated by group desensitization met this rigid standard. The combined cure rate for the acrophobics and claustrophobics who were subjected to stress-tolerance tests was 67 per cent. None of the nine patients treated by interpretation, and only two of the eight treated by interpretation plus relaxation, recovered. The fifteen patients who had not benefited from group interpretation or interpretation plus relaxation were then treated additionally by desensitization. Ten recovered after a mean of 10.1 sessions, whereas 20.4 sessions had been necessary for group desensitization alone to be effective. This reduction of post-interpretive desensitization time was attributed to nonspecific reciprocal inhibition of anxiety responses evoked by group discussion. Whether or not this is the case, we have a grand total of 71 per cent recovery from seriously handicapping symptoms. To check on the durability of the cure, a follow-up questionnaire was completed about nine months later, on the average. It dealt with the return of symptoms, lists of complaints, handicaps in daily living, and other therapy. A rigorous criterion was again applied, and even a slight recurrence of the phobia was considered a relapse. Ten of the thirteen who were originally treated by desensitization and judged as recovered remained symptom free, as did one of the two who had apparently recovered after interpretation plus relaxation and eight of the ten who had benefited from postinterpretive desensitization. Thus, a total of nineteen of twenty-five recoveries were sustained. This reduces the total of sustained recoveries to a still-impressive 54 per cent. There were no signs of symptom substitution.

Lazarus' study is an exceptionally convincing one. It adheres to the reality of the clinical situation and at the same time maintains scientific rigor. It is direct and ingenious in conceptualization, bold yet painstaking in its execution. Despite the absence of an untreated control group, Lazarus' study can serve our purpose as well as his own. Without an untreated control group, can we be confident that it was psychotherapy that led to the recovery? Would these changes have come about with the passage of time, or because the subjects felt that help was on the way? We think not. In this experiment, the interpretive group is a comparison group which serves the same purpose as a group of untreated controls. It is unreasonable to argue that a group motivated to apply for treatment of a severe phobic symptom of long standing, and seen regularly in a treatment attempt, would do worse than if they had not been seen at all. To put it another way, it is highly unlikely that the group treated by interpretive therapy would have recovered in this short period of time without any treatment any more than did those who received interpretive group therapy. The failure of any of them to recover with interpretive group therapy, coupled with the fact that two-thirds recovered after receiving the desensitization regimen is presumptive evidence (if not proof) that the base rate of recovery for such a symptom, in this time span, is at or near zero. Thus, they provided what can be safely considered an equivalent to an "inert" treatment or placebo control, which was then converted into an own-control design.

Another experiment that has all of the earmarks of a classic was done at the University of Pittsburgh. It also dealt with desensitization of a phobia (Lang & Lazovik, 1963). Here, however, the subjects were not patients, and the symptom was isolated and not truly incapacitating. However, the demonstration of the efficacy of the therapeutic approach was amply clear. Twenty-four college students who had responded to a questionnaire on fears by admitting an intense fear of nonpoisonous snakes were selected. On the basis of an interview, the researchers singled out those who had somatic disturbances accompanying their fears, who always avoided going near live snakes, would not go into the reptile section in the zoo or walk in a field. They admitted having a reaction to the sight of snakes in movies or on television, and would shut their eyes or turn off the set. Even pictures and snake artifacts upset them. This screening produced an experimental group of four males and nine females and a control group of three males and eight females. After administration of Form A of the Stanford Hypnotic Susceptibility Scale, the subjects were placed into experimental and control groups essentially randomly. However, adjustments were made to balance the groups for intensity of fear and motivation to participate in the experiment. All subjects filled out a Fear Survey Schedule (FSS) at the beginning and end of the experiment and six months later. This schedule contains a list of fifty phobias to be rated on a seven-point scale. As a more direct stress-tolerance test, the subjects were confronted with a live, nonpoisonous snake in a glass case, and were asked to approach it, look at it, and if possible touch and hold it. They were then asked to rate their own anxiety on a ten-point "fear thermometer." Based on his observations, the experimenter also rated their anxiety on a three-point scale. An interview about their feelings of fear was then recorded.

Experimental subjects were subjected to five, forty-five-minute training sessions in deep muscle relaxation. Hypnosis was introduced to facilitate visualization of vivid scenes. The Avoidance Test and Fear Thermometer were applied to experimental subjects after the training period, and to the controls. This was followed by eleven forty-five-minute sessions of Wolpean systematic desensitization for the experimental Ss which featured reciprocal inhibition by associating relaxation with anxiety-arousing imagery. Although hypnosis was used at the beginning of the first session, no attempt was made to induce change or alter motivation by hypnotic suggestion. A third criterion test was applied to all Ss following desensitization therapy. Some twenty anxiety hierarchies were prepared. Normally, therapy would continue until all had been successfully mastered, but the experiment was limited to eleven sessions and only four Ss completed the series. Seven completed sixteen or more items and six completed fourteen or less. The therapy was done by the authors and three other therapists. Two were in private practice and one was an advanced graduate student. None had ever done this type of therapy. While it would certainly have been a better test of the hypothesis if all of the therapists were experienced in the technique and if all the subjects had had time to complete the hierarchies, it should be recognized that both of these shortcomings were working *against* the hypothesis. Significant results in favor of the experimental group would therefore have to be considered even more substantial. Inconclusive results would of course leave the question shrouded in doubt. Before examining the results, the exact nature of the criterion tests should be made clear. The Avoidance Test was given on three occasions (before training in relaxation, after training, and after therapy) to the experimental subjects, and at comparable intervals to the controls. There was an absolute measure of touching or not touching the snake and scaled measure of distance in feet of approach to it. Approach-avoidance was placed on a nineteen-point scale, ranging from holding the snake to refusing to enter the room. A change score, consisting of the difference between the pre- and postscores divided by the pretherapy score, was used. Difference scores were used with the Fear Thermometer measure.

On the Avoidance Test, control Ss did not change on three exposures. Apparently, repeated exposure to the phobic stimulus does not relieve anxiety. Nor did pretherapy relaxation training not specifically tied to the phobic stimulus affect the avoidance behavior of the experimental Ss. Following therapy, however, the number who actually touched the snake went up significantly. Among the thirteen experimental subjects, two (15 per cent) were able to touch the snake after training and seven (54 per cent) after therapy. Among the eleven control Ss, one (9 per cent) succeeded at Test 2 and two (18 per cent) at Test 3. While no change was evidenced on the nineteen-point Approach-Avoidance scale during the pretherapy training period, there was significantly greater change on the final posttherapy test for the experimentals than for the controls. Similar results were obtained on the Fear Thermometer and the snake item of the Fear Survey Schedule, with the exception that the decrease in fear alleged by the experimental Ss was greater but not significantly greater than that of the controls. There was a positive but surprisingly low correlation of $r = .40$ between overt avoidance and the subject's verbal report of fear. The authors interpret this as a lag between the subject's report and overt behavior. An important finding was that all of those who completed the hierarchies were observed to hold or touch the snake at the final avoidance test. Those who completed more than fifteen items still did significantly better than the controls, while those who completed less than fifteen differed little from the controls. Those who completed more than fifteen items did significantly better than those who had completed under fifteen. Similarly, there was a significantly greater reduction of numbers of fears listed on the Fear Survey Schedule for those in the over-fifteen-item group that for those with under fifteen items. This result suggests that instead of substitution of other fears for the one eliminated there is some generalization that results in reported reduction in other fears as well.

The question of stability of the therapeutically induced change was approached through a follow-up study six months later. Twenty of the original twenty-four subjects were still available. Among these, eleven had received therapy and six had finally succeeded in touching or holding the snake. After six months two of them declined to repeat the performance but showed no increase in self-rated fear. The mean Avoidance Test change score for the group showed a slight reduction in phobic behavior over the immediate posttherapy test. In addition, even greater gains were shown on the Fear Thermometer, which became significantly different from the controls on the entire schedule as well as on the specific snake item.

Despite its successful outcome, this experiment cannot be generalized to neurotic populations and to more widespread disturbances than those existing in these Ss who showed no evidence of severe generalized emotional disturbance. It does not in any way detract from this experiment to sympathize with those researchers who must struggle with evaluating the efficacy of therapy in more widespread, generalized, and less concrete disturbances. It is much easier to do a convincing experiment (whatever the results) to evaluate the success of a therapeutic procedure in removing one clear-cut, observable, and measurable piece of behavior than it is to modify general adjustment and prove that it has been done.

Looking back again at the work of Lang and Lazovik, the skeptic still might wonder if the therapy itself brought about the reduction of the phobic response or whether there was merely a behavioral placebo effect. This is always a possibility in any appraisal of psychotherapy. Although all the experimental subjects spent the same time in treatment, there was a distinct difference in the success of those who completed all twenty hierarchies, with gradually reducing benefit as the number of completed hierarchies decreased. This could mean that outcome was a specific function of the amount of therapy accomplished, ruling out therapy as a placebo. The interpretation also could be made that those who were unable to master successfully the more anxiety-provoking hierarchies or had to proceed at a slower pace in learning to view anxious images with equanimity were actually more severely phobic to begin with and would require more therapy (or placebo). As a further check on the specificity of the treatment, the same experimenters subsequently reported the addition of a pseudotherapy group (Lang, Lazovik, & Reynolds, 1965). They proceeded in exactly the same way as before, with an additional ten Ss comparable to the prior groups. The same five training sessions were followed by eleven pseudotherapy sessions. The subjects were first hypnotized and then told to relax deeply. During the first fifteen minutes they were asked to imagine a series of scenes that they themselves had described as pleasant and relaxing. The last half-hour was devoted to discussion of nonanxiety-evoking aspects of the Ss life keyed to the hierarchy. Remaining generally nondirective, the therapist tried to prevent the subject from making any phobic responses. The Ss were told that they could overcome their fears by getting to understand themselves better and by learning how to relax deeply. Motivational level was high and the therapists reported that close empathic relationships developed. The results, in brief, were that the mean scores for fear reduction were similar to the pseudotherapy and no-treatment control groups. The subjects exposed to desensitization therapy showed significantly greater fear reduction than controls on all indices of snake phobic behavior (Avoidance, Fear Thermometer, Fear Survey Schedule, and snake item response). Taking a second look at the experimental subjects, the experimenters found all measures of fear reduction to be positively and significantly correlated with the number of hierarchy items successfully completed. Results with the Stanford Hypnotic Susceptibility Scale showed no significant relation between these scores and any fear-change measure among treated subjects, ruling out suggestion as a factor. Hypnosis, training in muscle relaxation, hierarchy building, and their use in a context of therapy do not of themselves change behavior, nor did the therapist-patient relationship and its positive transference effects. The authors conclude that the treatment effect *was* specific to the treatment procedures.

A controlled trial of hypnosis in the symptomatic treatment of asthma revealed it to be more effective than antispasmodic bronchodilatory drugs (Maher-Loughnan, MacDonald, Mason, & Fry, 1962). Two groups of twenty-eight patients each were treated at random for six months either by hypnosis or by a drug new to the patient. Patients kept daily diaries and results were assessed from their recordings. Each patient served as his own control by means of a pre-experimental observation period. By the vagaries of sampling, the two groups were not truly equivalent to start with, but the initial differences appear to have favored the drug-control group. Experimental treatment involved hypnosis, symptom removal by suggestion, and training in relaxation under autohypnosis. The data were carefully tabulated and adequately quantified. The average incidence of wheezing between the third and sixth month differed at the 5 per cent level from the observation month for the hypnosis group, but did not change for the drug-control patients.

It is interesting to note that the trial was carried out in three centers and that the results in two of the centers, where the hypnosis was administered by chest physicians, were better than those in the third, where the patients were referred to the psychiatric department.

An evaluation of group therapy was carried out at the Bordentown Reformatory, New Jersey (Wolk, 1963). Referrals were made for group therapy because of poor institutional adjustment or because it was felt that therapy might help deter future antisocial behavior. A total of 101 men were treated in eight groups led by two different therapists. Seven were conventional therapy groups, and one met for sociodrama. These randomly constructed groups met twice a week, and the average individual received approximately six and one-half months of therapy. To assess outcome, Wolk used data from the disciplinary or infraction report. Infractions of rules were interpreted as indications of maladjustment to the regime of institutional living. Apparently, the aim of group therapy was to improve institutional adjustment since good behavior has a bearing on parole and is received as an indication of readiness for outside adjustment. To evaluate the behavior, the treated group was compared with 518 men who were not in therapy. During the study period, the treated individuals averaged .86 infraction reports and the controls averaged 2.29. The difference was significant at the 1 per cent level.

A comprehensive program of research by Shore and Massimo in a series of five interlocking studies investigated the effectiveness of a vocationally oriented psychotherapeutic program for adolescent delinquent boys at the Newton Baker Project in Massachusetts (Massimo & Shore, 1963; Shore, Massimo, & Mack, 1965). School officials referred twenty adolescent boys aged fifteen to seventeen with IQs ranging from 85 to 110 who had long-standing histories of antisocial behavior, suspension, or dropping out of school. None were observably psychotic or had had previous psychotherapy. They were randomly assigned tc treatment and control groups of ten boys each. The counseling approach was broad and varied and not classifiable as traditional psychotherapy. Counselors made an unusual and maximum commitment to their boys, seeing them at any time of day or night in the field. Contacts were as frequent as eight to ten times a week and extended into all phases of a boy's life. They included helping him to find a job and going with him to obtain health services, shop for clothes, receive driving lessons, and the like. Counselors served as father surrogates or big brothers in pervasive and direct interventions in the activities of daily living. Assessment of progress was made on academic learning, personality variables, overt behavior, and probation records. Academic learning was measured by alternate forms of the Metropolitan Achievement Test administered at initiation of counseling and ten months later. Fifteen thematic apperception–type cards similar to TAT cards were administered at the same times to measure changes in attitude toward authority, control of aggression, and self-image. The stories were rated as better, worse, or no change in before-and-after pairs with randomized order within pairs and with all stories of both groups of subjects presented in random order.

Although analysis of covariance would have been the statistical treatment of choice, pre-post difference scores of the two groups were compared by t-tests. All areas of the Metropolitan Achievement Test—reading, vocabulary, arithmetic fundamentals and problems—showed changes in favor of the treated group at beyond the 1 per cent level of confidence.

Standards of judging were really inadequate because a single judge was used after reaching relatively low (70 per cent) agreement on a sample of responses with a second judge on a three-point scale. The range of possible change on the three-point scale is small. Considering these limitations, it is surprising that such consistently positive results were obtained with a small number of subjects. The results were, however, entirely consistent with the other findings.

Pursuing an inquiry into the nature of the simultaneous changes that took place, in a subsequent paper (Shore, Massimo, & Ricks, 1965), the authors did a factor analysis of thirty variables measured. They obtained six factors dealing with improvement in academic achievement combined with changes in self-image, changes in control of aggression, attitudes toward authority, temporal orientation in attitudes toward authority, a possibly artifactual relationship between changes in guilt and future time perspective, and initial IQ, which was unrelated to other types of change. Subjects were dichotomized into improved and not improved. Chi-square analysis pointed to significant differences in favor of the treated group on self-image ($p < .01$), control of aggression ($p < .05$), and attitude toward authority in the less certain $.05 < p < .10$ range.

Judgment was made on a scale of the degree of differentiation of roles of people in the story, degree of elaboration of the interpersonal situation, degree of flexibility or stereotype in the relationships, and degree of expressed closeness and warmth. Using the difference score approach again, the researchers found that the treated group showed a significant positive change in perception of interpersonal relations for all three areas. The experimental group, with seven out of ten working and the other three having left work for further schooling, had a better employment record. The controls had held more jobs for shorter periods, but the treated group showed more job stability, fewer job failures, and more advancements. As far as disciplinary probation was concerned, of the ten control subjects four were on probation, two others institutionalized and awaiting hearings, and two more had pending hearings. Only three of the treated boys were on probation at the end of ten months, and one of those was for a traffic violation. Attendance and probation officers reported that the behavior patterns of the treated group were distinctly improved. They were arrested fewer times and engaged less frequently in gang and antisocial activities, while the controls became more and more troublesome.

A follow-up study was reported on these same subjects (Shore & Massimo, 1966). At the conclusion of the ten-month period of the original investigation, very few of the boys were seen for other than occasional social contacts. The first five boys of each group were retested after two years and the second five after three years. Interviews regarding job history, legal and marital status, and education were conducted by a new examiner who did not know the status of the boys. Ratings of improvement on thematic stories were done by the same psychologist on coded, randomly paired stories. The rating consisted of judging whether the second story of each pair was worse, better, or no different in quality from the first. The rigorous standard was introduced of considering a rating of "no change" as deterioration since progress had been predicted. T-tests of difference scores for the two groups were done for pre- and posttest, pretest and follow-up, posttest and follow-up. The treated group continued to improve in all academic areas with greatest improvement in reading and least in arithmetic problems. The rate of change was slower than when the boys were in treatment. The average grade level on follow-up was 5.7 for the treated group and 3.7 for the untreated. From the thematic stories it was judged that the treated group continued to show significant improvement in self-image, control of aggression, and attitudes toward authority in that order of magnitude. Overt behavior was consonant with these test findings. One of the treated boys was hospitalized as psychotic and one was unemployed, while five had continued formal education. Among the controls the only two untreated boys who continued formal education were also the only two to show improvement on the test measures. Two of the untreated were serving prison sentences and a third was subsequently sentenced. Six of the untreated group had arrests ranging from disorderly conduct to manslaughter, compared to two arrests for traffic violations among the treated group.

It is evident that the untreated boys showed marked and continued deterioration while those who were treated showed encouraging signs of adapting to society even though initially they gave every indication of becoming hard-core delinquents. The only apparent difference was the ten-month therapeutic intervention, which involved extensive interaction of a type far beyond that of conventional psychotherapy.

Warlingham Park Hospital in Croydon, England, was the setting for an evaluation of psychiatric after-care (Sheldon, 1964). Eighty-three women who had been hospitalized for schizophrenia or depression were randomly assigned to treatment in a day center, outpatient department, or to a general practitioner. In the day center, the primary therapeutic contact was with a nurse, in the outpatient department with a psychiatrist. The patients were followed for six months and then interviewed to confirm information about treatment from other sources. There was no significant difference among the three groups in diagnosis, age, marital status, hospitalization, or previous admissions. There was a nonsignificant tendency for those assigned to general practitioners to be of higher socioeconomic status. Combining those seen in both settings into a psychiatric after-care group, it was seen that 17 per cent required rehospitalization in contrast to 47 per cent of those seen by general practitioners. This significant difference in favor of psychiatric after-care held for both types of treatment and clearly illustrates its value.

Under-achievers in school were the therapeutic targets of a study of three groups: a counseled group, a "placebo" group, and a second control group (Shouksmith & Taylor, 1964). The students were twelve to thirteen years old, under-achievers of above average intelligence. From triplets matched for IQ, age, and achievement test scores, one of each was assigned to each of three groups. The counseled group received individual, nondirective, biweekly counseling sessions and some group discussion. The placebo group took the same psychological and achievement tests as the counseled subjects, while the control group had only initial screening and final tests. After six months the counseled group had improved significantly more on four of six achievement tests than did the other groups. Sixty-seven per cent of the counselees were no longer classified as under-achievers, while twenty-two of the twenty-four nontreated boys remained in that category. Correlated improvement was shown in peer-group acceptance and more favorable teachers' reports of cooperation and improved social adjustment in the treated group alone. The benefits can not be attributed to the passage of time or special attention and appear to be a result of the counseling procedures.

In a study of therapist attendance as a variable in group therapy in a community mental-health clinic, Exner (1966) randomly assigned thirty female patients with psychoneurosis and personality disorders into five groups of equal size. Four of the groups had therapists varying in sex and regularity of attendance, while one group met without a therapist. For our purposes here, it can serve as a no-therapy control group. Before group assignment, all the patients were rated on a fifteen-item scale of symptoms and prognosis by two staff members not associated with the treatment. The ratings were repeated upon discharge or termination. All groups showed improvement except for the no-therapist group, which got worse. Ninety-two per cent of the patients in groups with therapists were rated as showing some improvement in contrast to 33 per cent of the nontherapist group; 75 per cent of the treated patients and 17 per cent of the untreated were discharged. Exner acknowledged the unestablished reliability and validity of the rating scales used, but the evidence that is presented clearly favors psychotherapy.

Dreiblatt and Weatherley (1965) conducted two experiments to evaluate the efficacy of brief-contact therapy with newly admitted, hospitalized psychiatric patients at the Denver Veterans Administration Hospital. Brief-contact therapy consisted of five- to ten-minute friendly, chatty, and informal nondirective conversations beginning with an open-ended question and initiated by the therapist (Dreiblatt) when he happened to meet the patient. At the time of the initial contact, the patient was told that he would be seeing the therapist from time to time. The forty-four patients (twenty-two psychotics, ten neurotics, twelve character disorders) on a psychiatric admissions ward had not been previously hospitalized at this particular institution. None of the patients were in individual or group psychotherapy. The patients were randomly assigned to one of three groups. One experimental group ($N = 16$) received three contacts each week during a two-week experimental period, in addition to their regular ward routine. A second experimental group ($N = 14$) received six contacts in addition to ward routine, while a control group ($N = 14$) received regular ward routine only. All patients received pre- and posttests of self-esteem measured by Hilden's Random Sets of Personal Concepts and of subjectively experienced anxiety measured by the Welsh A Scale. At the end of two weeks, it was determined that both experimental groups showed greater increases in self-esteem than did the control group. The group with six contacts showed greater positive change than the one with three. The six-contact group showed greater decreases in anxiety over the two-week period than the three-contact group or the control group, although the latter two groups did not differ significantly. The patients were followed for length of hospital stay. The three-contact group, with a mean of forty-eight days, and the six-contact group, with a mean of fifty-six days, were not reliably different, but each differed significantly from the control group, which had a mean of eighty-six days.

Dreiblatt and Weatherley were aware of the shortcomings in this promising experiment and replicated it with more elaborate controls and some additional variables. Instead of one, a number of staff members were used to provide brief contacts. The evaluations were carried out by someone other than the one making contacts. The control patients were separated from the experimentals to prevent them from observing patients receiving contacts while they were not. As a control of the Hawthorne effect, a second control group was introduced to assess the effects of contact itself with conversation minimized. Two kinds of foci in conversation during contacts were contrasted, one of general conversation, the other of discussion of symptoms. It was hypothesized that brief contacts involving nonsymptom-oriented conversation would have greater beneficial effect than routine hospital care alone and than essentially nonverbal contacts involving a task administered to the patient. The second hypothesis was that a regimen of nonsymptom-oriented brief contacts would be more effective than one focusing on the patient's symptoms. The rationale was that exchanging friendly small talk with a patient indicates to him that he is an accepted and esteem-worthy person, not just a patient. Conversation about symptoms, on the other hand, reinforces the sick-role.

The subjects in this two-week experiment were seventy-four patients (thirty-five psychotics, twenty-one neurotics, eighteen character disorders) with an average age of 38.5. They were divided into four groups: (1) Group NS-6: six nonsymptom-oriented brief contacts a week ($N = 21$); (2) Group S-6: six symptom-oriented brief contacts a week ($N = 20$); (3) Group C6: a control group contacted six times a week to participate in a five-minute guessing task ($N = 17$); (4) Group C: a control group exposed only to ward routine ($N = 16$).

The last group was admitted at a different time from the others so that its members had no opportunity to observe other patients receiving special contact. Patients were randomly assigned to the other three groups. Within a day or so of admission, all patients received a Self-Esteem Q-sort, Welsh A Scale, Chase Self-Concept Adjustment, an index of similarity of a person's description to normals involving a Q-sort comparing self-sort to a normal standard, and a checklist of symptoms. There were no significant pretest differences among the four groups.

Contacts were made by four different psychologists and testing was conducted by someone other than the one contacting the patients. The type of contact was systematically arranged. Analysis of the data revealed no differential effects among the four therapists. There were however, pronounced differences among the four groups. The group that had six nonsymptom-oriented contacts a week showed significantly more improvement than the uncontacted control group on all the dependent variables with the exception of number of symptoms reported. They showed significantly more improvement on changes in self-esteem, self-concept of adjustment, and length of hospitalization than did the group in which sheer contact was controlled by a task assignment. They showed significantly more improvement on two of the variables, symptoms and anxiety level, than did the group that received symptom-oriented contacts. The symptom-oriented contact group showed no more positive change on any of the five different variables than did the two control groups. Thus the *content* of the conversations was judged to be an important determinant of effectiveness. Neither of the two control groups differed from each other on any of the dependent variables. Length of hospitalization for the control group on ward routine only was 72.6 days; for the control group contacted for tasks, 66.7 days; for the symptom-oriented brief-contact therapy group, 56.2 days; and for the nonsymptom-oriented brief-contact therapy group, 46.6 days. The authors indicate that the results cannot be explained in terms of a placebo effect, catharsis, or insight, and attribute it to the ego-enhancing supportive message to the patient that he is accepted as a person.

This is a good example of investigators replicating an experiment after remedying some of the flaws in design. It ended up as a very well-controlled study. As defined, brief-contact therapy bears little resemblance to intensive long-term individual insight-oriented therapy, but it proved to have very tangible effects in terms of a "hard" criterion like length of hospital stay as well as other measures.

Persons (1965) tested the response to psychotherapy of a group of nonpsychotic sociopaths drawn randomly from the population of inmates at the Federal Reformatory, Chillicothe, Ohio. Their average age was twenty-two, mean IQ 107, mean arrests 5.4, and they had an average of twenty-seven months incarceration. Twelve were randomly drawn as counseiees and forty remained as controls. Eclectic therapy was conducted twice a week for ten weeks. Before and after the experimental period Ss were given a questionnaire measure of psychopathic personality, the Taylor MAS, and the Delinquency Scale. Differences between therapy and control Ss after therapy were highly significant although the two groups were initially equivalent. Posttherapy scores were significantly lower for the treated group on all three tests, while the controls increased their scores on all three tests. This was a striking demonstration of the beneficial effect of brief psychotherapy on the anxiety level and intramural adjustment of sociopaths.

The effects of combined group and individual therapy were carefully assessed in a controlled experiment with delinquent boys at the Fairfield School for Boys (Persons, 1966). Persons randomly divided eighty-two boys, aged fifteen to nineteen, into two equal groups equated for age, intelligence, race, socioeconomic background, type of offense, number of previous arrests, total time incarcerated, and nature of institutional adjustment. The boys of each group had a mean of four offenses and a mean incarceration time of eleven months. The typical offenses were auto theft and breaking and entering, for which the boys were serving indeterminate sentences. Institutional adjustment in both groups ranged from very good to very poor. Each of the boys in the experimental group received forty sessions of group therapy (one and one-half hours twice a week) and twenty sessions (once a week) of individual therapy with the same therapist. The therapists were five psychologists who led six different groups. The control group received no therapy, but participated in the regular institutional program. Pre- and posttesting was done with the Taylor Manifest Anxiety Scale, Delinquency Scale, and MMPI. The postexperimental differences between the groups and the pre-post differences (analysis of covariance was not used) in the experimental group were highly significant for the MAS, DS, and all MMPI subscales with the exception of L, K, MF, and Si. In a more global approach, the entire MMPI profile was judged for improvement by two clinical psychologists with 97 per cent agreement. Thirty treated boys, in contrast to twelve controls, were judged to be improved. Analysis of the delinquent high-point pattern (Pd, Pa, Sc, and Ma) revealed that twenty-four of twenty-eight treated boys who initially had this pattern revealed a reduction, while eleven of twenty-nine controls showed improvement ($p < .001$). Fourteen of the nineteen boys who received therapy had MMPI T-scores dropping from above the critical seventieth percentile mark to within normal range on each of the subscales of the delinquent high-point pattern, in contrast to but three of the eighteen controls ($p < .001$). Turning to relevant behavioral criteria, it was observed that treated boys received passes significantly sooner than controls and had significantly fewer disciplinary reports over the study period. Their improved academic functioning was demonstrated by the presence of significantly more treated boys on the honor roll. A follow-up report (Persons, 1967) on subsequent community adjustment tested the crucial question of generalization of improved institutional adjustment that resulted from therapy. Boys of both groups were released on the average of 2.5 months after the termination of therapy. At the time of follow-up, both groups had been in the community for 9.5 months. A parole officer submitted a standard report twice a month on each boy who had met with him. The officers also had reports from law enforcement agencies as well as employment records. There was a significant difference, in favor of the treated group, in the number of boys returned to penal institutions. The treated group had significantly fewer parole violations and a smaller proportion of boys breaking parole. Of the thirty treated boys who had shown a significant improvement, twenty-five were still functioning in the community one year later. Only three of the eleven boys of the control group who had shown improvement were still in the community. The success of the experimental group also proved to be significantly better than a base rate established on 100 cases from the institution's files. Significantly more treated boys were employed than controls for the entire sample as well as among just those who succeeded in remaining in the community. In order to rule out the possibility that the treated boys as a group were returning to more favorable home environments, the experimenter rated family, financial, relationship, and delinquency variables of each home on a nine-point scale. A second rater reached exact concordance in 73 per cent of the homes rated. The average ratings were equally low for the successful and failure cases in both the experimental and control groups. There does not seem to be any question whatsoever that the combination of relatively brief individual and group psychotherapy brought about important changes in the institutional adjustment of these boys which were clearly demonstrable on psychological tests and "hard" behavioral criteria relative to the adjustment of boys in a control group and to an institutional base rate. Perhaps more important, the change generalized to community adjustment at least for the period encompassed by follow-up.

Truax et al. hypothesized that delinquent girls in a psychotherapy group characterized as high in therapist-offered conditions of accurate empathy and nonpossessive warmth would show more progress than girls in the same institution (Kentucky Village) who received only institutional care without group therapy (Truax, Wargo, & Silber, 1966). Seventy girls were randomly assigned to therapy or control conditions. Forty girls were divided into four groups and were seen by two therapists demonstrated in prior research to be high on these qualities. Each group met over a three-month period for twenty-four sessions. The main criteria were release from the institution and amount of time spent in the community. Analysis of covariance was done for the two groups, with the initial measure being the percentage of time spent out of the institution in the 1,061 preceding days and the final measure, time out of the institution for the 344 days after initiation of group therapy. The difference was significantly in favor of the treated group. A similar analysis was carried out for delinquency proneness as measured by the "C" scale of the Minnesota Counseling Inventory. Again the treated groups were superior, although the girls were still more delinquency-prone than normals in the test standardization. Changes in self and ideal concepts on a modified version of the Butler-Haigh Q-sort also generally favored the treated group, as did attitudes toward parents on the

MCI. Both groups improved on the MCI social and stability scales, but there were no changes on a scale of Anxiety Reaction.

Shattan et al. investigated the value of group therapy for state hospital patients discharged to a mental health clinic for after-care (Shattan, Dcamp, Fujii, Fross, & Wolff, 1966). Ninety conditionally discharged patients (mostly schizophrenic) were randomly assigned to a group of forty-five experimental patients or to a group of forty-five controls equivalent in age, sex, race, marital status, and diagnosis. One group received monthly group treatment sessions while the other received primarily brief, stereotyped, drug renewal interviews. Therapy groups were open-ended for from five to nine members and were conducted by a psychiatrist and a social worker. Nine of the treated patients had to return to the hospital in contrast to seventeen of the controls. There was also a highly significant difference in the number who were granted an absolute discharge (thirty-six experiments vs. twenty-three controls). The mean number of months spent out of the hospital during the conditional discharge period, chronicity, employment after a year, and receipt of medication did not differ significantly. Since the treated group received more absolute discharges and returned to the hospital less, they attended the clinic more and as a group had more contacts. Once-a-month group therapy certainly represents a minimum investment, but this study suggests that even this little effort can help in preventing rehospitalization. While the controls were not totally untreated, they received no systematic psychotherapy and are useful as a comparison group. It is unlikely that they would have done any better had they made no contacts with the clinic whatsoever.

A variant of behavior therapy labeled "implosive therapy" is in a sense the opposite of desensitization by reciprocal inhibition. Instead of associating a hierarchy of anxiety-arousing images with relaxation, the objective is to have the subject experience as much anxiety as possible on the premise that fear learned while experiencing intense anxiety must be unlearned under similar conditions. It is reasoned that the greater the nonreinforced anxiety, the greater the extinction. Implosive therapy was evaluated in an experiment in which forty-three Illinois State University coeds who professed fear of rats were selected from a larger group by a situational pretest in which they failed to pick up a white rat upon request (Hogan & Kirchner, 1967). Subjects were randomly assigned to experimental and control groups. The experimental sessions lasted an average of thirty-nine minutes for the experimentals and thirty minutes for the controls. While their pulses were being recorded as a physiological index of anxiety, experimental subjects were asked to imagine a hierarchy of scenes of the most distressing sort conceivable, ranging from touching the rat to having it claw about in their hair, devour their eyes, being swallowed and destroying their internal organs, being attacked by a man-sized shiny gray sewer rat, and the like. The therapist embellished and elaborated on the scenes that generated the most anxiety for the individual. From the description of subjects' reactions and from pulse measurements, there was no doubt that the therapists succeeded in generating severe anxiety in the subjects. The more fortunate(?) control subjects were exposed to neutral imagery, colors, and relaxed scenes; any cues associated with rats were avoided. The posttest consisted of a second attempt to pick up the rat, scored on a pass-fail basis, and of other indices of approach-avoidance behavior. Following the experimental treatment fourteen of the twenty-one girls (67 per cent) picked up the rat, six were able to open the cage, and one entered the room but could proceed no further. Among the twenty-two controls three refused to try the posttest, four refused even to enter the room, twelve were only willing to stand in the room, one opened the cage, and two (9 per cent) succeeded in picking up the rat. It was concluded that the results supported the "implosive" approach of experiencing intense anxiety in the absence of primary reinforcement in order to extinguish fear. This is a rather startling demonstration with a behavioral criterion of success. The anxiety measure was crude as applied, but the crucial part of the experiment, dealing with the most relevant posttest behavior, yielded striking results after only thirty-nine minutes of "implosion." It would have been most helpful if the researchers had done a follow-up to see if the cure was sustained and if no ill effects were experienced. There is no doubt that the technique worked. The reason for it is open to speculation. Both groups were told that they would be asked to pick up the rat again after the session. The controls had little else to do but try to entertain pleasant thoughts while looking forward to this experience. The experimental Ss were bombarded with such horrible imagery that perhaps an adaptation level was operating, and by contrast, the tame little white rat did not look quite so threatening at the end. At any rate, it is an issue that needs consideration and further cautious research.

ADEQUATE STUDIES: MINOR BENEFITS

Gersten (1951) conducted an investigation of group therapy with institutionalized male juvenile delinquents at the New York State Training School for Boys in Warwick, New York. The boys, all of whom had been reared and trained in antisocial behavior from infancy, ranged in age from thirteen to sixteen and had a mean IQ of 85.6. Each of forty-four boys was matched in age and IQ with another boy. Experimental and control groups were matched as groups on education, socioeconomic status, race, and family background. The groups met once a week for about twenty sessions. All boys were tested before and after the experimental period with the Wechsler-Bellevue, Stanford Achievement Test, Maller's Personality Sketches, and the Rorschach. The Haggerty-Olson-Wickman Rating Schedule was filled out by the staff. After group therapy, it was ascertained that the average IQ of the boys rose three points while the untreated controls remained the same ($p = .05$). The experimental subjects advanced eighteen months in school achievement (S.A.T.) while the controls advanced but three months during the six-month period ($p. = .01$). The treated group was alleged to have made more progress in adjustment as reflected by the Rorschach, but no actual data are presented. Although the study becomes imprecise when dealing with personality changes, the improvement in academic achievement is distinct. Whether or not this had any ultimate bearing on delinquency is not known.

At the North Little Rock Veterans Administration Hospital a controlled research was done on the effect of relatively short-term group therapy on closed-ward patients (Jones & Peters, 1952). The patients were twelve schizophrenics from a continually changing group that met weekly. Therapy consisted primarily of open discussion, without symbolic interpretation, and psychodrama focusing on interpersonal problems. Most of the patients remained for three to four months and were replaced by new ones as they left. Twelve similar patients were alternately assigned to a control group. Patients in both groups continued to receive other hospital treatments. Criterion measures included the Porteus Maze, Mirror-Tracing Test, Rorschach, Draw-A-Man Test, and the Gardner Behavior Chart filled out by four ward personnel (a nurse and three aides). These procedures were given in the first week of a patient's hospitalization and were repeated in four months, or three and one-half months if the patient was about to be discharged. Those released earlier were dropped from the study. Data were treated by analysis of covariance.

The results of this experiment with its five criterion measures were variable. Comparisons of eight Rorschach scoring categories were made. In general, the comparisons favored the treated group, but the differences were small and not significant. Greater improvement was shown on all five of the "least ambiguous" signs by 42 per cent of the treated patients, but by none of the controls. Three judges rated the twenty-four pre-post pairs of protocols according to which of the pair showed more personality stability and less evidence of active psychosis. The second Rorschach was generally rated better in both groups (92 per cent of treated and 67 per cent of control subjects). Similar examination of the Draw-A-Man procedure yielded results that were slightly but not significantly in favor of the controls. The Porteus Maze responses showed no difference in quantitative performance between the groups, but the qualitative features (neatness and regard for rules) were significantly better in the treated group. Differences in mirror-tracing performance was clearly significant in favor of the treated group. Test results, in the aggregate, were thus somewhat equivocal, with some significantly better performance by treated patients on those aspects of the tests that involved overt behavior. The Gardner Behavior Chart scores, consisting of fifteen items dealing with attention to personal appearance, sleep, appetite, sociability, activity control, and cooperation with routine, revealed significant improvement in the treated group while the controls remained unchanged. If constancy of the other hospital treatments can be assumed, group therapy, whatever its meaning to these patients, was apparently responsible for bringing about small but reliable increments in the improved overt behavior of psychotic patients. We do not know if one hour a week of special treatment enabled the patients to leave the hospital earlier or stay out longer, or whether additional psychotherapy would have enhanced the results. Nevertheless, even this minimal effort with severely disturbed patients affected their overt behavior in a positive way.

A cross-over design was used to evaluate group therapy at the New Jersey State Reformatory (Newburger & Schauer, 1953; Newburger, 1963). Sixteen consecutive admissions, aged sixteen to twenty-five, whose offenses ranged from petty thievery to armed robbery with intent to kill, were assigned to groups with the aid of sociometric selection by the participants after a get-acquainted period. Half received group therapy three times a week for three months (sixty sessions), while the remainder met in the library but did not receive therapy. After three months the situation was reversed, with the untreated group receiving therapy for three months and the treated group going to the library. All subjects received tests and interviews at the beginning, at the three-month cross-over point, and at six months when the experiment terminated. Among the procedures used were sociometric tests, the Haggerty-Olson-Wickman Behavior Rating Schedule, disciplinary reports, work marks, attitudes toward the self and others as assessed by two scales of the MMPI, the TAT plus interviews, and the Thurstone Attitude Scales for Law, Treatment of Criminals, Constitution, and Capital Punishment. Group therapy was a mixture of interview therapy and psychodrama.

The varied results included data comparing therapy with no therapy and immediate therapy with delayed therapy. Group therapy increased mutual bonds between patients and increased group cohesion by increasing mutual choices, but there was also an increase in isolation and rejection when therapy was introduced without delay. There was an increase in the number of isolates in the waiting group which went down somewhat with therapy. Rejection was also reduced when therapy was instituted with the waiting group. Scores on the Haggerty-Olson-Wickman showed the greatest gains when therapy was introduced right away. The waiting group declined on this measure. The early-therapy group improved in work marks while the no-therapy group worsened. The early-therapy group also showed more improvement in discipline. Changes in attitudes depended a great deal on the measure used, and no consistent statement can be made about them. On balance, the outcome seemed more favorable than not, with early therapy more conducive to positive change than delayed therapy.

Another attempt to evaluate the effect of counseling activities on chronic schizophrenics was made at Veterans Administration Hospital, Brockton, Massachusetts (Stotsky, Daston, & Vardolk, 1955). Twenty-eight cooperative patients were divided into two groups of fourteen each. The average length of hospitalization of both groups was five years. All patients were pretested with the Harrower Group Rorschach, Bennett Q-sort, Palo Alto Hospital Adjustment Scale, eleven items of the Northport Record for description of psychiatric patients, and an Employment Rating Scale. For eight weeks only the experimental group had weekly group sessions on vocational problems, individual counseling sessions twice a week, attention from rehabilitation therapists, attention from a psychiatric team, and informal visits from the counseling psychologist. The emphasis was on vocational counseling. Comparisons were made of records of attendance and prescribed work activities, changes in level of complexity of assignment, attainment of work privileges and of trial visit to the community.

The counseled and uncounseled groups were not different on any of the five tests and scales before the experiment. After treatment the Q-sort was the only test or rating measure that showed a significant difference between groups. Significant differences, however, were found on four out of five work variables and trial visit. The two groups thus remained homogeneous for psychiatric symptoms, ward adjustment, and personality measures, but the treated group did show improvement in within-hospital work adjustment, Q-sort, and trial visit. Since the focus was on vocational counseling it is not remarkable that benefits were more or less restricted to this area of adjustment. There is not much question that some vocational objectives were successfully achieved, but there is doubt about the generality of the effect.

Group therapy with chronic schizophrenic patients was evaluated at Bryce State Hospital, Alabama (Peyman, 1956). The patients were thirty-two chronic schizophrenic females, aged twenty-one to thirty-nine, who had been hospitalized for at least one year, had IQs of over 70, and were able to cooperate in psychological testing. They were randomly assigned to one of four groups: group therapy plus shock, group therapy alone, shock alone, or a control group. Controls received no special treatment but participated in the usual hospital routines. The Wechsler Bellevue Form I, Bender-Gestalt (Pascal and Suttell's scoring), and the Rorschach (Klopfer's Prognostic Rating Scale) were administered before and after the experimental period. Psychotherapy consisted of one-hour sessions twice a week for six months and involved group discussion and role playing. No changes, either absolute or differential, were displayed on the Wechsler-Bellevue. Results for the Bender-Gestalt and Rorschach were significant and in the same direction. The order of effectiveness was group therapy plus shock, group therapy, shock, and last the control group, which deteriorated. Group therapy plus shock and group therapy alone were both significantly better than no treatment, but shock alone was not significantly better than no treatment. The principal agent was thus shown to be psychotherapy. The design was straightforward and the results clear-cut, but one cannot help wondering whether the Rorschach and Bender-Gestalt changes were reflected in improved hospital adjustment and earlier discharge.

While primarily a study of the comparative benefits of brief against longer interviews, a study at Madison State Hospital, Indiana, contained a control group not seen for psychotherapy at all (Zirkle, 1961). Both forms of therapy were minimal, totaling but twenty-five minutes a week over a period of two months. The thirty patients all averaged about fifty years of age and had been hospitalized for an average of about twenty years. Improvement was assessed on an eleven-factor, ten-point graphic rating scale of social contacts, personal habits, emotional control, spontaneity or naturalness of speech, spontaneity and appropriateness of interests and emotions, willingness to cooperate on ward duties, awareness and concern for feelings or needs of others, participation in activity therapies, capability of handling a hospital job, interest in returning to the community, and change in degree of adjustment. The ward doctor, ward nursing supervisor, and head day attendant (the only one who knew the experimental group assignments) rated the patients. Both treatment groups showed greater improvement than the controls but at an equivocal level of significance. With such minimal treatment and chronically disturbed patients, the results are not lacking in encouragement.

The aim of a controlled study by Shlien et al. was to study the comparative efficacy of time-limited, unlimited, and no therapy. The research was done at the University of Chicago Counseling Center and the Alfred Adler Institute (Shlien, Mosak, & Dreikurs, 1962). Five groups of subjects were compared. Three experimental groups, each with at least twenty Ss, were given client-centered unlimited therapy, client-centered time-limited therapy, or time-limited Adlerian therapy. One control group consisted of an unspecified number of people who applied for therapy but were asked to wait for three months before beginning therapy. A second control group was composed of an unspecified number of "normals" asked to take part in personality research. The dependent variable, or outcome criterion measure, was a modified Butler-Haigh Q-sort yielding a self-ideal correlation. This was initially administered to all subjects, repeated after seven interviews, again at the end of therapy, and after a follow-up period averaging twelve months. The normal control provides, in a way, a validation of the self-ideal correlation as an index of adjustment. The passage of time alone did not change the average correlation for the untreated group, and there was substantially greater congruence between the actual perceived-self and ideal-self for "normals" than for applicants for therapy. Both client-centered groups and the group that received Adlerian therapy showed significant gains (approaching the normal control group in the direction of closer self-ideal congruence) over the course of therapy. The findings were distinctly in favor of psychotherapy as the intervening agent that helped move patients closer to the level of normals in congruence. The research would have been more impressive if the authors had reassured us that the patients were randomly rather than selectively assigned to the different conditions; told us how the drop-out problem was handled; given information about the diagnosis, severity, age, sex, and education of the patients; tested the control patients after the same interval of time and obtained the same interim measures on the controls; and specified the statistical procedures used. Most of these criticisms concern sins of omission and do not necessarily alter the validity of the conclusions. If reasonable precautions were taken, the results must stand as offering support for the hypothesis of therapeutic efficacy in modifying this one aspect of adjustment.

Schwitzgebel and Kolb (1964) tried and evaluated a novel approach to delinquency behavior by bringing their therapy and research directly to the "street corner." The project was described as a test of simple reinforcement, but it obviously became much more than that. The youths were approached individually in their natural hangouts with an opportunity to "make a fast buck," and were induced to come to the store-front laboratory. Once there they were interviewed and rewarded with cigarettes, food, and small change on a variable reinforcement schedule. Subjects were "shaped" to arrive for sessions on time, and most became dependable in fifteen appointments and prompt in twenty-five. The tape-recorded interviews were conducted two to three hours a week. The interviewer was an attentive listener and gave bonuses for "good work," particularly when the subject talked about his experiences with affect. If they asked for it, subjects were given small jobs to perform for pay. Interviews gradually tapered off if the youths took part-time jobs. Separation was natural after nine to ten months as the subjects left for jobs, schools, and the armed forces. It became apparent after about two months that the boys valued the relationship more than the monetary rewards.

The subjects in this experiment were twenty youths, aged fifteen to twenty-one, all with long records of arrests and incarceration in prisons and reformatories. They were matched, man for man, on a series of relevant variables with twenty controls from the records of state correctional agencies. The therapists were a clinical psychologist, a social worker, and a Jesuit priest. Follow-up three years after termination revealed that the experimental subjects had averaged 2.4 arrests in contrast to 4.7 for the Cs ($p < .025$). Time of incarceration for the controls was about twice that of the experimental subjects ($p < .05$). Although the average number of arrests was greater in the control group, the rate of recidivism, 35 per cent of the treated and 45 per cent of the untreated, did not differ significantly. The procedure was therefore seen as "effective in reducing but not eliminating delinquent behavior." Reinforcement technique drew the boys into therapy, but it is not known what the therapeutic agent was—the relationship, the reinforcement of nondelinquent behavior, the recognition of individuality, the self-direction, or the personal freedom and responsibility.

"Body-ego technique," a primarily nonverbal therapeutic approach to the psychotic patient, attempts to rebind ego structure by recreating postures and movements associated with emotions and attitudes (Goertzel, May, Salkin, & Schoop, 1965). It is not viewed as a way of curing schizophrenia, but more as a way of establishing contact prerequisite for other therapies. It is, however, designed to modify psychotic behavior and as such can properly be evaluated as psychotherapy. A controlled evaluation was carried out at Camarillo State Hospital, California, on 115 regressed schizophrenics; sixty were given this treatment and fifty-five served as controls. The groups were equivalent in mental status, sex, age, age of onset of illness, duration of illness, number of mental hospital admissions, and highest level ever achieved on the Menninger Health-Sickness Scale. Total involvement of this group of regressed patients was not feasible; 30 per cent participated only partially and 18.3 per cent not at all. None of these were excluded from the data analysis. Progress was assessed by psychiatrist's ratings, nurses' ratings, psychological testing, and discharge statistics. The psychiatrist who rated the patients on a five-point global rating scale before and after treatment was from outside the hospital, had no knowledge of the treatment, and rated blind in this regard. Ratings were made of total improvement and affective contact. Nurses on the ward rated the patients on scales of motility and general functioning. The Draw-A-Person and Bender-Gestalt tests were administered, but the former was completed by only about three-quarters of the patients and the latter test by slightly more than half. As hypothesized, the psychiatrist's ratings of global improvement and affect contact and the nurses' ratings of motility and general functioning were all significantly in favor of the treated patients. There were no differences on either of the psychological test procedures when the patients were rated on a scale of improvement, and very few of either group were discharged from the hospital. Apparently, then, there were some distinct but limited benefits from the body-ego technique with regressed schizophrenics.

Cooke (1966) did an analogue study of the comparative efficacy of two different desensitization procedures. Since there was an untreated control group, the results throw light on the general efficacy of psychotherapy compared with no treatment. Eight female undergraduates at the University of Iowa were subjected to deconditioning procedures designed to overcome an expressed fear of laboratory rats, while four went untreated. They all took the Bendig Emotionality Scale and a modified form of Lang and Lazovik's Fear Survey Schedule. They were also subjected, under the one-way screen observation of three judges, to a stress test in which they were confronted with a live caged rat. The judges independently rated the girls' fear behavior in attempting to look at, touch, and hold the animal. It was shown that the treated subjects experienced a significant reduction in their fear without any increase in general anxiety level on the Bendig Em Scale, while the controls remained as fearful as before. The time interval between the pre- and post-tests was three weeks. Despite the small number of subjects, the experiment succeeded in its aim of overcoming Breger and McGaugh's (1965) criticism of behavior-therapy research by controlling sampling biases, observer bias, and experimental-control problems. The study does not represent a field trial for curing neurosis, but it certainly shows the effectiveness of this approach in at least temporarily (the final test took place five days after therapy ended) eliminating a specific fear that was not disabling and did not interfere with general adjustment.

In another small-sample deconditioning study, three spider-phobic girls drawn from a larger sample were compared with three controls before and after ten sessions of desensitization and relaxation on an avoidance test and fear-estimate scores (Rachman, 1966). The girls treated by this method had significantly larger change scores on both measures than did the untreated controls. A third group of three treated by a different technique (flooding) did not improve.

Paul (1966) compared the relative effectiveness of three treatment approaches—insight, desensitization, and attention-placebo—against no treatment in reducing the anxiety associated with public speaking of University of Illinois students. The details and results will later enable us to appraise the experiment as a comparative investigation of these various methods. It would be worth our while here, in assessing the efficacy of psychotherapy without attention to method, to sketch the experimental design and place all the therapies together in opposition to no treatment. In brief, ninety-six students in public-speaking courses who were rated as high on performance anxiety and motivation for treatment completed a battery of personality and anxiety and stress tests. Correlation measures were obtained on seventy-four Ss during a test speech. The subjects were assigned to one of a number of groups. One therapy group offered traditional therapy with insight goals, a second provided modified systematic desensitization, and a third non-specific attention and placebo treatment limited to five fifty-minute sessions over a six-week period. In addition, there were two control groups. Control subjects in one group received no treatment but had one telephone contact and a short interview, participated in two test speeches and were promised future treatment. Members of a second control group were never contacted personally. They took the test battery and continued in class, but were unaware of their participation in a study. Cognitive, physiological (pulse rate, palmar sweating), and motoric changes were measured. It was found that psychotherapy (as represented by all these types of therapy) does produce significantly greater reduction of anxiety than no treatment or the mere experience of taking a one-semester speech course. Testing and individual interview procedures apparently produced some degree of anxiety reduction but were in no way comparable in efficacy to psychotherapy. This is not entirely an analogue study, nor is it a test of the clinical efficacy of psychotherapy. The students had genuine, if specific, anxiety, but were not comparable to patients with more generalized adjustment problems applying for treatment. It was, however, a well-controlled experiment with strong implications for psychotherapy.

Paul and Shannon (1966) followed this experiment with another designed to evaluate the feasibility and effectiveness of administering modified systematic desensitization along with re-educative discussion in groups. Both experimental ($N = 10$) and control ($N = 10$) subjects were selected from those in the prior experiment. The experimental subjects were the wait-controls of the prior study and the controls were the former untreated controls. Three groups of the previous study—individual systematic desensitization, insight-oriented, and attention-placebo—were used as comparison groups. The results showed that systematic desensitization could be combined with group discussion without loss of effectiveness. It resulted in a significant reduction of anxiety and increased extra-experimental effectiveness as measured by grade-point averages.

A less elaborate and decisive test of the effects of group therapy and Wolpean desensitization on test-anxiety was carried out with Vanderbilt University undergraduates (Katahn, Strenger, & Cherry, 1966). The Sarason Test Anxiety Scale was administered to students. Forty-three who were in the upper quartile were selected. Two treatment groups ($N = 8$, $N = 6$) were contrasted with twenty-nine untreated controls. The groups met for eight one-hour sessions with a professor as therapist for a combination of group counseling, desensitization, and relaxation training. The criteria measures were changes in Test Anxiety Scale scores and pre- and post-grade-point averages. The mean grade-point average of the combined treatment groups increased from 1.28 to 1.63, whereas the controls went from 1.30 to 1.36. An F-test of these data was significant. The increase of the treated group was statistically significant, with eleven of fourteen showing increases. Six made the honor roll after treatment, in contrast to but one before. Test Anxiety scores for the treatment group decreased significantly from a pretreatment mean of 12.4 to a posttreatment mean of 7.1. It was possible to administer the Test Anxiety Scale to eight experimental and eight control Ss immediately following a final examination. The experimentals showed a significant reduction in anxiety while the controls did not. Because of the design, it was not possible to determine which of the aspects of therapy was most effective. The students thought that both helped, but attributed most benefit to the opportunity to talk about their problem with others with a similar problem and to learn how to organize their study habits. Whether one attributes the benefit to a placebo effect or to specific therapeutic techniques, the treatment was nevertheless successful in bringing about a reduction in a specific anxiety in the contemporary lives of the subjects and a consequent improved level of performance. It is, however, quite different from bringing about a marked change in a generalized psychoneurotic condition.

Schaefer and Martin evaluated behavioral therapy (reinforcement) with chronic schizophrenic adult female patients at Patton State Hospital, California (Schaefer & Martin, 1966). Forty patients on a ward were divided into experimental and control groups of twenty each. The entire ward was on a token economy program. The controls, however, were given tokens at the beginning of each day. Their receipt was not contingent on any particular behavior. The experimental Ss received tokens as reinforcement for signs of reduced apathy. Apathy was operationally defined as engagement in only a single behavior during an observation period. Thirty behavior samples spaced at half-hour intervals were obtained for each patient for three five-day periods—before, during, and after termination of the experiment. At the start, experimental and control patients were equal in apathy. The behaviors to be changed included those concerned with personal hygiene, social interaction, and work performance, and were individually selected for each patient. The treatment lasted three months and the data were analyzed by analysis of variance in a 2 × 3 repeated-measure design. The main effect of "periods" was significant, as was the group × period interaction. The experimental patients showed a steady decrease in apathy over the three time points, but the controls changed little. At the end there was a highly significant difference between the two groups. This was a fine demonstration of modification of intramural adjustment by reinforcement techniques. The crucial question of whether it led to more rapid discharge and generalized to extramural behavior was not answered.

Two variants of desensitization were compared with no treatment in the reduction of test-anxiety in fifty-four volunteers at Stanford University (Emery & Krumboltz, 1967). From the entire freshman class who had taken the Emery Test Anxiety Scale, 260 were identified as "test anxious.' Ninety-six accepted an invitation to participate in a project to reduce test-anxiety and fifty-four were randomly selected from this total and randomly assigned to one of two desensitization groups or to the nontreatment control group. The groups were balanced for sex, age, first-quarter grade-point average, and college entrance scores. Each of nine counselors worked with two students from each treated group on a twice-a-week basis for up to eight weeks. A sixteen-situation standard anxiety hierarchy was given to one of the experimental groups, while the order for the other group was individualized by subject arrangement. Criteria of success were: (1) winter-quarter grades in a course required for all freshmen adjusted for fall-quarter grades, (2) posttreatment anxiety scale administered before winter exams and adjusted for pretreatment anxiety scores, (3) self-ratings of anxiety during and before each exam. Data were analyzed by analysis of covariance. Although there were no differences in grades received, the combined treatment groups had significantly lower test-anxiety scores and self-ratings of anxiety before and during exams than the controls. The authors note that the failure to obtain significant differences in grades may be because academic anxiety in students of high ability seems to have a facilitating effect upon academic performance.

If it is facilitating (adaptive), why attempt to modify it? What was clearly changed was not a measurable endproduct but rather what subjects said about their internal states. Since this is one of the very criticisms that behavior therapists levy against other treatments, it can hardly be considered as major evidence of tangible benefit for this form of treatment.

A preliminary test of the effects of "implosive therapy," a variant of behavior therapy, relied entirely on the MMPI as the criterion measure (Levis & Carrera, 1967). Forty patients with "relatively severe" signs of pathology were subjected to one of four different conditions. Ten of the patients received ten sessions of implosive therapy from two therapists of whom only one had had experience with the technique. Ten had conventional treatment consisting of a combination of insight and support for the same number of hours with four different therapists. This group served as a control on the number of sessions and duration of treatment. A second group of ten patients in conventional treatment were seen for thirty-seven hours by one of the therapists who did the implosive therapy in order to control for the personal qualities of the therapist. A fourth group of ten from a therapy waiting list controlled for commitment to and expectation of professional treatment. All treated subjects were given the MMPI before and after therapy by the therapist. The waiting controls completed the inventory by mail with a three-month interval between.

Pre-post difference scores were computed and analysis of variance of the difference scores accomplished. Analysis of covariance would have been preferable. There were essentially no differences between the two conventional treatment groups and the untreated controls, but there was a persistent trend for the implosive-therapy group to shift away from pathology. The groups were not randomly assigned to treatment or equated on the criterion measure at the start. The implosive-therapy group had the highest (most pathological) scores initially. Inspection of the data reveals what appears to have been a regression toward the mean effect. Wilder's Law of Initial Values applies here. Looking at the sixteen subscales, one can see that on twelve of them the highest initial score reduced on the second administration to the greatest extent —regardless of treatment. This was even true of the nonclinical L, K, and F scales. Nine of these twelve were for the implosive-therapy group and three for one of the conventional-treatment groups. In three of the four instances in which this conventional group had the highest initial score, it reduced more than any other group. On fourteen of the sixteen scales the converse was also true: the *lowest* initial score either went up or was reduced the least. It is a case of the rich getting poorer and the poor getting richer and both winding up in much the same place. The apparent advantage of the implosive therapy is beclouded by this regression effect. This effect might have been prevented by equating or randomizing at the start. The finding that lends most credence to the conclusion of efficacy of implosive therapy is that a substantially greater *proportion* of pretest scores above a T-score of 70 dropped after therapy into the normal range for the treatment group than for any other group. The mean T-score decrease for all scores initially above the critical 70 mark was by far the greatest for the implosive-therapy group. This result is clearly encouraging. From comparisons with the various control groups, the authors concluded that the shift away from pathology in the implosive-therapy group could not be attributed to the number of sessions, the skills and personal qualities of the therapists, the termination of treatment, or the effects of commitment and expectation of treatment.

5

Review of Controlled-Outcome Studies: II. Questionable Studies with Positive Results

Experiments in the categories B1 and B2 showed major or minor benefits from therapy, but are open to more serious reservations. Included are some investigations which, through no fault in design, yielded equivocal results that were interpreted by their respective authors as positive.

QUESTIONABLE STUDIES: MAJOR BENEFITS

A large survey of outcome with 739 patients with somatic disorders provides some useful data on the progress of thirty-four ulcerative colitis patients treated by psychotherapy and thirty-four receiving medical treatment (Berle, Pinsky, Wolf, & Wolff, 1953). Those seen for psychotherapy had fewer deaths and operations; fewer got worse, and more improved or became symptom free. The study was poorly controlled, but it would suggest the value of psychotherapy if the colitis patients with psychotherapy were equivalent in all relevant respects to the controls.

Warne, Canter, and Wizma (1953) designed a study to evaluate the outcome of the treatment of psychoneurotics at the Veterans Administration Mental Hygiene Clinic, Phoenix, Arizona. Clinic-treated patients were compared with those treated by fee-basis physicians (treatment of the veteran by a private physician in his office with reimbursement by the VA) and with untreated patients. Thirty patients in each category were selected at random from among those seen from 1948 to 1951. All those seen in the clinic had available the combined services of a trained psychiatric team (psychiatrist, psychologist, social worker). Of those seen by fee-basis physicians, 25 per cent went to board-certified psychiatrists, 39 per cent to physicians practicing chiefly psychiatry, and 36 per cent to general medical practitioners. The controls received "no consistent program of treatment." The criteria of improvement were work adjustment, social adjustment, marital adjustment, clinical findings, insight, and patient's subjective complaints. Each variable was rated from case records on a five-point rating scale and the ratings of the six variables were combined by averaging. In order to reduce bias, compensation ratings and other examination reports were used as evaluative material rather than therapists' evaluations, but the information was often sketchy and variable. Consensus ratings were made by one staff member with review by two others. At times, one of the raters evaluated his own therapy, but his judgments were watched closely for bias. The intervals between ratings were unequal. Average length of treatment of the fee-basis cases was thirty-three months compared to 8.9 months for those seen in the clinic. The average number of monthly visits to the fee-basis physicians was 3.83, to the clinic 3.03. Examination of total adjustment ratings revealed that 66 per cent of the clinic cases were judged as improved in contrast to 20 per cent and 23 per cent of the fee-basis and controls respectively. Seventy per cent of the fee-basis and 66 per cent of the controls got worse, in contrast to 7 per cent of the clinic cases. Further subdivision of the "improved" category showed 13 per cent of those seen in the clinic to have "significantly improved," but there were none in this category in the other two groups. In terms of social and marital adjustment and subjective complaints, patients in both treatment groups did better than the controls. The clinic group showed the greatest improvement in work adjustment and clinical findings. Insight declined in the fee-basis group.

Thus, clinic treatment was seen to be clearly superior to no treatment and to private treatment. The authors admit that their results may be due to sampling error, but prefer other explanations. We cannot be sure how much of the treatment under either condition consisted of psychotherapy; 36 per cent of the fee-basis physicians were general practitioners who probably restricted their efforts to treating symptoms with medicine. The groups, including the nontreatment group, were not matched or randomly assigned from a common pool at the beginning. Therefore, we have no assurance of their comparability so far as motivation, duration or severity of illness, age, or any of a host of other possibly relevant variables are concerned. The ratings were open to possible bias since they were made by clinic personnel who knew what the conditions of treatment were. In short, while this is a controlled study yielding positive results, neither the nature of the controls nor the sources of data are adequate to permit firm conclusions.

A research project was carried out at Missouri State Hospital to evaluate a form of group therapy in which patients meet as a group without the presence of a therapist (Cadman, Misbach, & Brown, 1954). In this particular approach, despite the absence of the therapist during the sessions, therapists were prominently involved in the general treatment process. Patients were oriented and told to discuss their lives and problems and to make recommendations about the release of patients. Just before each session, each member was given a ten-minute "priming" session; one patient was selected as a "target" for discussion in the session. Patients were elected by their fellow patients to be in the group (a feature that probably biased the sample in contrast to the controls). The remainder constituted the studio audience at the recorded sessions. The sessions were held three times a week in an attractive room equipped with a microphone, signal lights, speaker box, round table, and other accouterments. Everybody was enthusiastic, and patients were made to feel important and responsible. Considerable esprit was developed among the patients on the ward. In short, there was a change in ward milieu that could account for whatever benefits accrued as much as did the sessions per se. There were two experimental groups (seventeen men and twenty-one women) and thirty-two controls (ten men and twenty-two women). Each experimental group had fifty sessions. Sixty-four per cent of the members of the experimental group were rated as improved, and 40 per cent were discharged from the hospital. Only 12.5 per cent of the controls were considered improved, and all of these were discharged. Of the seventeen men in the experimental group, thirteen were rated as improved in contrast to one of ten controls. Eleven of twenty-one female experimental patients improved, against three of twenty-two controls. Twenty months later none of the experimental patients who had been discharged as improved had returned to the hospital, and five more of those rated improved but not discharged at the end of the experiment were now out of the hospital. Only two of twenty-one controls not previously discharged had since been released. It is not known with certainty what accounted for the change, but the experiment suggests that hospitalized patients *can* be moved by other than conventional means.

Cowden et al. did a controlled investigation to evaluate chlorpromazine by itself and as an adjunct to group therapy (Cowden, Zax, Hague, & Finney, 1956). Although the research was designed to evaluate the drug's effect, the design allows for the evaluation of psychotherapy as well. Twenty-four schizophrenic patients at Veterans Administration Hospital, Chillicothe, Ohio, were distributed among three groups. One received chlorpromazine and group therapy, one the drug alone, and the third was given no special treatment. Group therapy, given three times a week for four months, was permissive and was designed to promote group feeling, comfort, and security. All the patients were on a disturbed ward, were withdrawn, uncommunicative, hallucinatory, affectively inappropriate, manneristic, and had previously received ECT and insulin shock without change. The criteria of improvement were attendants' ratings on a behavioral rating scale of relatively low reliability ($r = .66$), decline in the number of wet packs, ECT, fights, and nurses' "disturbed reports," transfer to a better ward, discharge from the hospital, and gains on psychological tests. The drug and therapy groups showed significantly more improvement than the controls on most criterion measures, and the drug plus therapy group displayed more progress than the group that had drugs alone. The authors correctly concluded that no statement could be made about the efficacy of group therapy by itself since drugs were also administered, but the combination did result in the greatest all-around improvement.

A different kind of design is one in which the institution serves as its own control. Here the discharge statistics of an institution before and after the introduction of a particular treatment are compared. The study's validity hinges on the constancy of admission and discharge standards, as well as on equivalency of patients and comparability of staff and other aspects of institutional life. Although no assurance is given of these invariants, an intensive psychotherapy program for sexual psychopaths was introduced at Mendocino State Hospital, California (Lieberman & Siegel, 1957). The year before its introduction 41 per cent were discharged as improved. In the two following years the percentage increased to between 77 per cent and 78 per cent. It appears that psychotherapy made the difference, but far more rigorous controls would be necessary to prove the point conclusively.

Object-relations therapy is a bold approach to repatterning based upon psychoanalytically oriented developmental theory. Adult patients are gradually led through therapeutic stages with activities that reproduce those of the various early levels of development. Thus, in the beginning they are given milk in a baby's bottle and mud to manipulate. They are progressively presented with objects of decreasingly direct resemblance and greater symbolic proximity to the original. Over a period of months they are brought through other childhood stages with such activities as doll play, coloring books, and the like. Psychoanalytic interpretations are given and the therapist maintains a permissive and understanding role. This approach was attempted with a group of severely regressed schizophrenic women with an average age of thirty-five, whose average hospital stay had been ten years (Azima, Wittkower, & Latendresse, 1958). They constituted a patient sample of severe cases including many who were often incontinent, were stool smearers and eaters, were frequently nude and mute, and whose condition had remained unchanged or deteriorated for from three to ten years. Two groups were composed of six each of these markedly regressed patients. One group was designated experimental and the other control. A third group of six moderately regressed patients also received the therapy. The two treated groups were seen for an hour five times a week for six months by a psychiatrist and occupational therapist. Three areas, reality testing, control, and social improvement, were considered. It is reported that incontinence, smearing, and stool-eating behavior disappeared after two months and that five of the six severely regressed patients were transferred to a better ward. Eight months later, three were maintaining their recovery. At a three-year follow-up, however, only one was maintaining improvement. Results with the six moderately regressed patients were even more encouraging. One was discharged at the eighth month and two after the end of treatment. Two mute patients were communicating; one of these was later discharged, and the other was able to work in the hospital. Two years later three had maintained improvement outside the hospital and two inside. In the meantime, the control group showed no appreciable change. Despite the absence of any quantified data or pre-established criteria of improvement, and despite the lack of evaluative procedures and adequate numbers of subjects, it is apparent that important changes did take place.

In the Netherlands, Groen and Pelser (1960), evaluated the benefits of group psychotherapy in the treatment of bronchial asthma. Three groups were compared. Group I consisted of 114 cases treated with symptomatic therapy such as inhalants. This group was compared with thirty-five cases in Group II treated with symptomatic therapy and ACTH and with thirty-three cases in Group III treated with group therapy combined, if necessary, with the former types of medical treatment. The three groups were comparable in social class, sex, and severity of disease, but the psychotherapy group was several years younger. Considered clinically cured or considerably improved were 16.7 per cent of Group I, 28.6 per cent of Group II, and 72.8 per cent of Group III. The difference in favor of the psychotherapy group was highly significant. An "Index of Benefits" was computed (percentage improved minus percentage deteriorated). This index for the three groups respectively was —27.1, —17.1, and +57.6. When a smaller sample of sixty-six subjects was drawn from Group I by matching patients for sex and age, the results remained essentially the same. The criterion of improvement was not clearly defined, and it would have been better had patients been randomly assigned. The authors are very circumspect about attributing the benefits to psychotherapy, but the magnitude of the obtained differences was most impressive. In addition to the improvement differential, it is important to note that a far smaller proportion of those who received group therapy became worse or died than in the other groups. This is reflected in the Index of Benefits, a useful concept in evaluating psychotherapy.

Seeman et al. evaluated the outcome of play therapy in an urban upper-middle-class school (Seeman, Barry, & Ellinwood, 1964). The entire second and third grades were given a modified version of the Tuddenham Reputation Test; the teachers rated the children. Both of these were types of personality assessment that permitted classification of children into high adjustment, aggression, and withdrawal categories. All scores were converted into standard scores and composite adjustment ratings determined. The sixteen lowest-scoring children were divided into experimental and control groups, each composed of eight children. The groups were equivalent for age, sex, total adjustment scores, and type of maladjustment (aggressive and withdrawn). Since the groups were drawn randomly, it was assumed that they did not differ in motivation for treatment. During the study four children moved, but as luck would have it two had been in each group and all in the withdrawn category. This left twelve subjects in balanced groups. Play therapy was given once a week with a median duration of thirty-seven sessions. The mothers of the children in the therapy group were seen on two occasions, once before and once at the end of treatment. Control children's mothers were seen at equivalent time intervals. The teachers' rating scale and the reputation test were given on three occasions, once before therapy, seven months later at the end of the school year, and one year after the second testing. At follow-up, the children were in different classes with new teachers. Two of the children were still in therapy at this time.

Data were analyzed by one-tailed t-tests of differences between change scores of the two groups on the teachers' ratings, reputation test, and teachers' ratings of amount of aggressive behavior. The differences between the experimental and control groups on change from pretest to posttest and from pretest to follow-up were not significant. The difference between them from posttest to follow-up was equivocally ($.05 < p < .10$) in favor of the experimental group. On the reputation test, the two groups did not differ on change from pretest to posttest, but there were significant changes from pretest to follow-up point and from posttest to follow-up in favor of the experimental group. Teachers' ratings of aggressive behavior were compared for four experimentals versus four controls. The change from pretest to follow-up was significant. All eight children had aggression scores that initially exceeded their class mean, while at follow-up all four treated children were below the class mean and all four controls still above average.

The authors concluded that other children perceived treated children as less maladjusted after therapy and that this change in the eyes of others did not come about in the absence of therapy. In addition, there was distinct reduction in aggressive behavior.

The difficulty in interpreting this research, aside from the facts that the very small sample inhibits generalizing and t-tests of raw change scores were used rather than analysis of covariance, is that none of the changes were apparent at the time of the posttest. If this outcome is a reliable one, and not a sampling accident brought about by the small sample, it suggests that the effects of therapy were not immediately apparent but started a chain of events that did not show up until an appraisal point one year after the end of therapy and nineteen months after its beginning.

At the University of Mississippi Medical Center, the benefits of audiovisual confrontation (television) as a therapeutic experience were evaluated (Moore, Chernell, & West, 1965). The authors maintain that watching oneself on television is not psychotherapy, but that the particular arrangement had a psychotherapeutic rationale and intent. Therefore, this study comes within the purview of our inquiry. Eighty consecutive patients admitted to the psychiatric unit, the majority depressive or schizophrenic women, were divided into experimental and control groups of forty each. Within twenty-four hours of admission, each patient was interviewed in a special room with a TV camera concealed behind a one-way mirror. The session was video-taped and the patients knew they were being televised. The interview, about twelve minutes in length, was structured to cover certain broad areas and had no specific therapeutic focus. Immediately following the session, alternate patients were accompanied by the psychiatrist to a viewing room to see the playback. During the presentation the psychiatrist refrained from making any comments, but the patient's remarks were recorded. In four days and at weekly intervals until discharge, five-minute follow-up interviews were conducted on the patient's progress to compare her present condition with that upon admission. At each of these sessions the patient was shown the latest tape and all previous tapes in sequence so that a comparison could be made between her actual earlier status and her reported recollection of it. The control patients also continued to have televised interviews but did not see themselves. All patients participated in regular hospital treatment. Records were kept by the experimenters, who consulted with the resident assigned to the case. He in turn had earlier discussed the case with his supervisor. Neither of the latter was told whether the patient was in the view or nonview group, but twenty-four of eighty patients revealed the information. Results for these cases were comparable to the remainder. At discharge the patients were rated as minimally, moderately, or greatly improved. Despite the fact that the "video-tape therapy" took an average total time during hospitalization of sixty minutes, the differential results were rather startling: 47.5 per cent of the experimental patients were discharged as cured or maximally improved in contrast to 12.5 per cent of the controls. Only 20 per cent of the viewers were considered unchanged or minimally improved, compared to 45 per cent of the nonviewers. The average length of hospitalization was brief, averaging twenty-four days for the view group and eighteen days for the nonviewers. Since the length of stay could have influenced both the ratings and the actual status of the patients, it would have been more conclusive if more objective evaluations had been made for both groups at a fixed time interval. The therapeutic aspect of the patients' audio-visual confrontation with their contemporary and past status came about, in the author's opinion, from patients' being given the opportunity to select "sick" behavior and to try to change it. The technique also produces repeated reality testing and reinforcement of modified behavior patterns.

Shostrom and Knapp (1966) attempted to determine if psychotherapy promotes psychological "growth." The subjects were thirty-seven patients just entering psychotherapy and thirty-nine patients who were in advanced states of therapeutic progress and had averaged 2.21 years of therapy. The groups were fairly equivalent in age and sex but the treated patients were of a somewhat higher educational level. The eight therapists included three who were eclectic, two Gestalt, one nondirective, and one Adlerian. Growth was assessed by the Shostrom Personal Orientation Inventory (POI), offered as a measure of self-actualization, and by the presence or absence of symptoms on the MMPI.

Critical ratios between groups were computed for all subscales of both inventories. All twelve of the POI scales and scores on seven of the MMPI scales showed a significant difference between groups at the 1 per cent level of confidence. The authors concluded that as therapy progresses pathology decreases and positive mental health increases. Unfortunately, the effects of psychotherapy cannot be appraised by this kind of experimental design. The main fault in this design is that it furnishes no proof whatsoever that the differences between the treated and untreated groups were a result of psychotherapy. The experimenters chose to use an entering group as a control against a group that averaged more than two years of therapy. This is an alternative to using patients as their own controls by taking pre- and posttherapy measures. It saves the long wait for patients to complete treatment and is acceptable if the groups are assuredly equivalent (particularly on the criterion measures) at the point of entry into therapy.

Such assurance is lacking in this study, but even had the subjects been perfectly matched, the design would have been equivalent to an own-control pre-post measurement study. The flaw is that there is no way of knowing from this design whether comparable, greater, or lesser changes would have occurred over the two-year period *in the absence of therapy*. There clearly must be a control over the intervening time lapse that could conceivably account for as much or more growth than psychotherapy. An untreated control group evaluated over the same time interval would be required to prove this crucial point in the evaluation of effectiveness.

QUESTIONABLE STUDIES: MINOR BENEFITS

Muench's extensive monograph, designed to evaluate nondirective psychotherapy, lacked a control group against which to compare treatment results (Muench, 1947). Hamlin and Albee attempted to correct this deficit by supplying control-group data that could be used for this purpose (Hamlin & Albee, 1948). Muench's sample consisted of twelve clients who had requested treatment and were seen by five different nondirective therapists at the Ohio State University Psychological Clinic. Hamlin and Albee supplied sixteen students from two classes in abnormal psychology at the University of Pittsburgh. They were considered to be similar to Muench's sample although two years different in age. Students who had the poorest scores on the Bell Adjustment Inventory were selected by Hamlin and Albee, but they differed on the crucial variable of not being candidates for psychotherapy. Muench's clients were given the Rorschach Test, the Kent-Rosanoff Free Association Test, and the Bell Adjustment Inventory. Pre-post differences were tested for significance with no control for initial differences between the groups. The Pittsburgh sample received the Rorschach and Bell at the beginning and end of the semester, five months later. Muench reported significant changes and more improvement than decrement on Personal, Social, and Total scores derived from twenty-two test signs of the Rorschach. The untreated group from Pittsburgh showed no statistically significant positive changes in Personal, Social, or Total Adjustment scores on this test. The difference in improvement between the no-therapy group and Muench's treated group thus measured by the Rorschach was significant.

The results for the Bell Adjustment Inventory were quite different. The improvement of Muench's treated group was equivocal ($p = .09$), but clear-cut ($p = .01$) for the untreated group. The treated group improved 7.92 total score points and the no-therapy group improved an average of 17.00 points. Hamlin and Albee suggest that their subjects, after taking the course in abnormal psychology, were less willing to admit to symptoms of maladjustment on the adjustment inventory, thus questioning the validity of the measure. The Rorschach, they felt, was less susceptible to alteration and tapped more basic aspects of personality. They therefore interpreted their results as evidence of favorable outcome with nondirective therapy. Since Hamlin and Albee's group is a comparison group, but not a true control group, the conclusion must remain in the category of hopeful but not conclusive evidence of psychotherapeutic efficacy.

Studying perceptual changes as reflected in the Rorschach, Jonietz (1950) compared patients in client-centered therapy with "normal" controls. Patients added more percepts than did the controls and increased in the number of human and sexual responses. Responses in which the perceptual object was seen as the passive recipient of often hostile behavior, or was portrayed as attempting to hide or flee from aggression, decreased almost threefold in the treated group while remaining constant in the controls. This was seen as a decrease in feelings of vulnerability. The results indicated that therapy clients move in the direction of normals; without suitable controls, however, we cannot attribute the change to therapy as distinct from the mere passage of time.

An experiment by Kaufmann (1950) was presented as a study of changes in the MMPI as a function of psychotherapy but completely missed the mark. The MMPI was administered before and after therapy to fifty-one student-patients (mostly anxiety states) at the University of Wisconsin, and at the same time interval to fifty-four untreated normal controls matched for age and sex. The treated sample was limited to patients whom the therapist had judged as improved, thereby vitiating the research as a study of the effects of psychotherapy. In addition, the groups were not matched for initial scores on the criterion measure. The patients scored higher on nearly all scales. Positive change was observed in several of the patients' scores but cannot be attributed to psychotherapy. We do not know if untreated applicants for therapy who were to begin at the same level would have shown any different pattern of change over the same time period.

On top of the bedrock of a theory and a tightly packed earthen mound of hope and conviction, Rogers and Dymond (1954) built a monument overlooking a great forest of surveys. Here at last was a coordinated series of controlled research projects designed to appraise the changes attributable to psychotherapy. But as people scrutinized the monument from different angles, the cracks in its base became visible. This research has been analyzed and reanalyzed on enough occasions to make a detailed description of it superfluous. Briefly, the general strategy was to have two groups of patients in therapy, one that began treatment right away and another, designated as "own-control," that was asked to defer the start of therapy for sixty days. Changes in the immediate-treatment group could then be compared with changes that might take place in the equally motivated waiting group, attributable to the passage of time alone. In addition, there was an "equivalent control" group to whom no therapy was given which was subdivided into two groups for comparative appraisal at time intervals equivalent to the treated wait and no-wait groups. Afer dropouts from an initial sample of about eighty, the remainers were twenty-nine treated and twenty-three untreated subjects, equivalent for age (about twenty-seven years), sex, student-nonstudent status, and socioeconomic status. The decision to place a patient immediately in treatment or on the waiting list was *not* randomly determined. The examiner at the initial testing session made the decision and did not put anyone on the waiting list if he felt that waiting would cause the patient "serious discomfort or harm." The assignment was occasionally changed if the client developed anxiety during the waiting period. These procedures, while motivated by humanitarian considerations, may have seriously biased the sample and diminished the meaningfulness of later comparisons between the groups. The equivalent control group was selected from volunteers to participate for payment in research on personality. They were not applicants for therapy, were better adjusted than the experimental group, and, consequently, were not appropriate controls at all.

A test battery was administered on four occasions to two groups and on three occasions to the other two. Waiting-controls were examined before the waiting period of two months, just prior to therapy, immediately following six months of therapy, and at follow-up six months to one year later. Half of the untreated control group was tested at comparable time intervals. The other half of the controls and the immediate-therapy group were tested at the same points, but since no wait was involved there was no prewait testing.

In a critical evaluation of this research entitled "Some misuses of the experimental method in evaluating the effect of client-centered counseling," Calvin (1954) put his finger on the most crucial flaw in the design. He points out that if the control group is not adequately conceived, no conclusions about efficacy can be drawn. If patients show no change in adjustment level during the two-month waiting period and then get well during their six months of therapy, there is no indication that it was the therapy that helped them. The change for the better may be due merely to the passage of the additional six months of time.

Testing was done mostly by two examiners who, in Grummon's (1954a) description, "easily developed warm relationships with their subjects. A leisurely psychological atmosphere was maintained which encouraged casual talk, and not infrequently the subjects felt that they had struck up a real acquaintanceship with the examiner" (p. 51). From the point of view of design, the benign testing atmosphere and the anticipation of getting help could easily have had a therapeutic effect upon the wait group. If so, it would work *against* the hypothesis. In designing the research, the authors considered as necessary factors for control the following: passage of time, important environmental influences, personality characteristics including kind and degree of disturbance, motivation for psychotherapy, client's expectation of therapy, and biosocial characteristics. Calvin correctly maintains that they then proceeded to ignore many of them. He insists that there is no excuse for the omission and states that alternatives to scientific "hard-headedness" are not justified, that the burden is upon psychologists to demonstrate experimentally that they can help patients if they are to substantiate their right to do therapy.

What we have then is research that, by its very design, could not be expected to furnish definitive evidence about the efficacy of psychotherapy. With these major reservations, it is nevertheless worthwhile to look at those specific findings relevant to outcome only while deferring discussion of many intragroup comparisons and criterion measures that are of real value. These include sections by Grummon, Butler and Haigh, Dymond, Grummon and John, Rudikoff, Gordon, and Cartwright and Rogers.

Using the Q-sort correlation between perceived and ideal-self, Q-adjustment score, Willoughby Emotional Maturity Scale, Self-Other Attitude Scale, and two measures derived from the TAT, Grummon found no support for the notion that motivation for therapy (in the waiting group) brings about positive personality change in a sixty-day time interval. Butler and Haigh demonstrated a significantly greater congruence in self-ideal Q sorts after therapy and at follow-up than initially in the treated groups. The change was significantly greater than that shown by the "equivalent controls" who had shown much greater congruence at the start. No change took place in the waiting-list "own controls." Dymond, deriving a Q-adjustment score from the Butler-Haigh Q-Sort, found an improvement in the treated subjects from before therapy to after therapy that was sustained in follow-up. Untreated "equivalent" controls started at a much higher level and did not change. "Own-controls" did not change over the two-month waiting period. Using another technique, she found that controls were significantly better on a TAT adjustment rating than clients before treatment but did not differ after therapy. Grummon and John applied twenty-three rating scales covering a wide variety of variables to TAT protocols. About three-quarters of the scales showed score changes favorable at the 5 per cent level or better by the sign test for the treated group (twenty-three subjects who remained for at least six interviews) while there were no significant changes in the control group (N = 9). When treated and untreated groups were compared on the magnitude of the changes on two summary measures, neither pretherapy to posttherapy nor posttherapy to follow-up differences were evidenced. One measure showed a significant pretherapy to follow-up difference, and the other was equivocal. The absence of significant changes from posttherapy to follow-up were interpreted as not supporting a hypothesis that therapy starts a process of constructive change that continues after therapy has ended. Comparison of changes between therapy and wait-periods was not significant although it was in the expected direction. The most disturbing aspect of the paper was the finding that the TAT scores did not bear any relation to the various other change measures used in the project. The discrepancy may lie in the judging, for there were but two judges who did all the ratings of TAT protocols. All the judgments for the experimental group were made by one judge, while both judges worked on the remaining protocols. What we may be seeing in the data is a difference between judges rather than between treatment conditions. A tremendous amount of effort went into developing the rating categories for this study; it is most regrettable that an adequate number of judges was not used. In addition, the sample was biased by the exclusion of those not seen for at least six interviews (presumably the least successful cases). An attempt to correct for this bias, by excluding other cases still in process at the time of the study, is not convincing without evidence that they were in truth more successful cases.

A small study by Rudikoff of eight of the own-control cases was also limited to self-report measures, as were the other phases of the larger research. In this case, they were the Butler-Haigh Q-sort and Dymond's Q-Adjustment Index. Changes in self-reported self-concept generally increased positively, more with therapy than over the waiting periods. Gains were maintained but not augmented over the follow-up period.

Gordon and Cartwright tested a hypothesis about greater acceptance of and respect for others as a consequence of therapy by comparing twenty-six subjects who had a minimum of six interviews with twenty-six untreated controls. Comparisons were made on a Self-Other Attitude Scale consisting of eight subscales. No significant changes in attitudes toward others were found in any of a series of comparisons that were made. Finally, Rogers hypothesized that, following the completion of client-centered therapy, there would be a greater degree of emotional or behavioral maturity and that it would be evident both to the client and to observers. More specifically, Rogers predicted that the client would behave in ways that were less defensive, more socialized, more accepting of reality in himself and his social environment and that he would show more evidence of having a socialized system of values. Thirteen clients from the wait group and nineteen from the no-wait group were rated by the therapist on a nine-point scale of success and on a scale of degree of integration. The Willoughby Emotional Maturity Scale, with some added items, was administered to the client and mailed to two of his friends to complete about him at pretherapy, posttherapy, and six months after termination. As an added condition, the two friends of the client were asked to choose and rate another person at the same time that they rated the client in order to provide another nontherapy control and a check on reliability. The correlations between the responses of the client and his friends were significant but low ($r = .37$). The correlation between the two friends was not significant ($r = .22$). Despite this unreliability, the data were used. Nonclients rated by friends showed no significant changes in behavior ratings. Clients showed no significant changes either in self-ratings or in the way observers saw them during the waiting period. There was no significant change in the observers' ratings of the clients over the period of therapy, during the follow-up period, or during the combined therapy and follow-up. Observer evaluations were significantly related to counselor ratings of outcome and integration. In other words, there was an observed increase in maturity in successful cases only, but no relation at all was obtained between the degree of change seen by the clients themselves and degree of success in therapy as seen by the counselor ($r = .04$ for the therapy period and $r = -.06$ for the total period). At every point the friends rated clients as being more mature than the clients rated themselves. If ever there were null results, here they were. The hypothesis clearly was not supported. Yet Rogers chose to find that "in a number of respects the hypothesis was upheld" and concluded with the tautology that "where client-centered therapy is judged to have been successful, an observable change in the direction of maturity takes place in the client. Where therapy is judged not to have occurred in significant degree, some deterioration of behavior is observed" (p. 236). It is obvious from the data that treated patients as a group *do not* evidence more maturity as judged by others. The data obtained by friends supplied by the clients were shown to be unreliable. The lack of agreement between observers, clients, and therapists is probably the most important finding.

Taken as a whole, this related series of studies, which lacks suitable controls, relies on self-report data of clients, and contains biased samples, provides little tangible evidence one way or the other about the efficacy of psychotherapy. The main positive findings are of improved self-concept from Q-sorts and improved TAT adjustment ratings, with no assurance that these changes came about because of therapy. These are balanced by a failure to demonstrate changes in maturity or acceptance of and respect for others.

At Maudsley Hospital, London, group therapy was subjected to double jeopardy when its efficacy was tested on a group of delinquents who were also mentally retarded (Yonge & O'Connor, 1954). Three groups were established: a control group that received only routine institutional care, a second control group whose members participated additionally in a work program, and an experimental group that received the work program plus group therapy twice weekly for a total of thirty-two sessions over a six-month period. Attendance was mandatory. Seven adolescent boys whose IQs ranged from fifty-two to seventy-seven comprised the experimental group. All were certified residents of a school for mental defectives, manifested severe behavior problems, and were resistant to discipline in the institution. Five had been processed through the courts for delinquency. Comparable numbers and types of subjects were in the other two groups.

Time samplings of work output in the workshop and checklists of behavior were maintained. Numbers of incidences of unsatisfactory behavior in the workshop, such as idleness, absence, lateness, misbehavior, careless work, and detention, were tabulated by quarters of the experimental period. The treated group was compared with a workshop control group. The other control group apparently was not used for any purpose. The experimental group showed a progressive quarter-by-quarter drop in unsatisfactory behavior from 48, 34, 31, to 15 in the final quarter. The controls showed a marked initial drop and then increased in such behavior. Their tabulation was 39, 10, 27, 44. The improvement in the second quarter for the controls was thus temporary. In testing the significance of these changes, the variation among the experimental group was found to be significant, that for the controls was not. Curiously, however, the data were divided into thirds rather than quarters for the data analysis. The logic of a tabular presentation of the data broken down in one way and a statistical analysis of another (possibly more favorable) breakdown is not revealed. Time sampling of delinquency indicated slight improvement in the experimental group and none in the controls. Since the only large decrease in unsatisfactory behavior for the treated boys was in the final quarter, it would be important to observe follow-up data to see if this was a sustained or transient phenomenon. The authors point out that rivalry between the groups may have been present because one group had been singled out for special treatment. In any event, the results, though generally positive, cannot be considered to be attributable to group therapy beyond reasonable doubt.

Wiener (1955) conducted an analogue experiment of the effects of two counseling techniques upon performance impaired by induced stress. Ninety University of Rochester students volunteered as subjects. Sixty were placed in a stress group and thirty in a nonstress group. Stress was induced by implying that a Rorschach test taken by the students had revealed possible maladjustive features. The stress group proved to be more impaired on a battery of tests that included the TAT, Wisconsin Card Sorting Test, Mirror Tracing, and Attitude Scale. The subjects in the stress group were divided into four subgroups: two groups treated with different therapeutic techniques, a control talk group, and a control rest group. The experimental treatments lasted for twelve to twenty minutes and were followed by repetition of the tests that had been given. The unit of analysis was the difference score between pre- and posttest. Comparison of the two counseled versus the two noncounseled groups showed seven out of eight of the measures to be in the predicted direction (in favor of the counseled group). Two of the differences were at the 5 per cent level, one was at the 6 per cent level, and one was at the 7 per cent level. The probability of seven out of eight differences falling in the predicted direction by chance is three in 100. Other statistical analyses supported the conclusion that experimental counseling helped to reduce impairment in performance. What was done here in twenty minutes or less in reducing effects of induced anxiety cannot be generalized to the effects of real psychotherapy. The obtained differences were not of great magnitude, and the demonstration could have been more convincing if analysis of covariance had been used rather than differences between raw difference scores. At best, the results are suggestive.

Cartwright (1957) reported an experiment to test the effects of psychotherapy upon self-consistency. Posttherapy self-consistency of a treated group was compared with self-consistency of an untreated normal control group. The study was replicated and extended several years later on a larger sample (Cartwright, 1961). In the original study the treated subjects were rated for self-consistency on two occasions, but the controls were tested at only one point in time on the assumption that they would not change. In the second study the controls were also tested twice, but the major defect in the experiment, nonequivalence of the control group, was not corrected. The new sample contained nineteen clients who had applied for therapy at the University of Chicago Counseling Center. They were matched for age, sex, and student or nonstudent status with twenty control subjects who had never had, were not then having, and had no intention of having, psychotherapy. They were not matched for initial levels of the dependent variable. The treated subjects were tested before and after therapy (an average of eighteen weeks) and the controls at a six-month interval on four different Q-sorts. As it turned out, the pre- and posttherapy means for the experimental group differed at the $p = .05$ level, and the first and second testing for the controls differed at the $p = .001$ level.

The second testing of both groups thus showed a significant increase in the consistency of sorting. The control group, however, did not improve in adjustment despite its change in self-consistency, while the improvement in adjustment score of the treated group was significant. Because there was no equivalent control group of nontreatment applicants for psychotherapy, it cannot be determined if the favorable change in adjustment can be attributed to psychotherapy. This is like evaluating the efficacy of a drug designed to relieve headaches by testing it on a group of people who have headaches and a control group of people who have never had a headache.

Wilcox and Guthrie (1957) evaluated the effectiveness of group therapy in an institution for feeble-minded women of child-bearing age. The sample included 114 women, aged fifteen to forty-three, IQ fifty-three to ninety. Ninety-seven were assigned to group therapy and seventeen were controls. Therapy was conducted by four advanced graduate students in psychology, only one of whom had had previous group therapy experience. The goals of therapy were to reduce suspiciousness toward outsiders, release aggressions, encourage feelings of self-confidence and self-worth, and to develop feelings of responsibility for the subjects' own actions. Each woman was rated by three attendants or matrons during the second week of therapy and the week following termination. Ratings were on 128 items of self-care and social responsibility, interpersonal relations, self-control, work, and recreation. Inter-rater reliability was low ($r = .55$). Data were consequently categorized into increase, decrease, and no change without regard to magnitude. Fifty-four per cent of the treated women showed improvement, compared to 23 per cent of the controls. The difference was statistically significant. Although the raters knew which girls were in therapy, the experimenters offered good reasons why this was not likely to be a biasing factor. The relative unreliability of the ratings and the consequent crudity of analysis dictate some caution. Nevertheless, psychotherapy appears to have had genuine beneficial effects upon behavior.

Imber et al. grappled with the problem of suitable controls in evaluation research and rejected no-treatment controls on ethical and practical grounds, dropouts as a self-selected biased sample, and waiting-list controls (Imber, Frank, Nash, Stone, & Gliedman, 1957). Their solution was to compare the outcome of patients who had fewer and briefer sessions with those who received more and longer sessions over the same time span. This is a risky approach. If the results should favor the more intensive treatment, and if one can assume that fewer and briefer contacts are *at least no worse than* no contacts at all, the design can be considered as offering positive evidence of benefit. If, on the other hand, predicted benefits are not obtained, we are left hanging. Assumed in such a design is the belief that if a small quantity of something is good for you, a larger quantity will be even better. Would we say that if one vitamin capsule is good for a patient, two would be better, or that if one tranquilizer pill is good, twenty will be correspondingly more beneficial? If null results are obtained we still would not know if any psychotherapy, regardless of amount, is better than none at all. If, however, negative results were to be obtained, demonstrating the superiority of fewer contacts, it would suggest that too much of a good thing can be harmful. Fortunately, the problem did not come up since this particular study yielded positive results. The experiment, conducted in the Outpatient Department of the Henry Phipps Psychiatric Clinic, involved fifty-four patients who were mostly psychoneurotic and a few with personality disorders. Patients were randomly assigned to analytically oriented individual therapy of at least one hour a week, analytically oriented group therapy once a week for about one and one-half hours, and minimal-contact therapy. Patients in this last group were seen individually for no more than a half-hour once every two weeks. The three groups were equivalent in background variables and the therapists were three second-year resident psychiatrists with equivalent experience in individual and group therapy. The evaluation technique is of methodological interest. A structured interview prior to treatment was conducted by a research psychiatrist and observed through a one-way screen by a research psychologist. Another interview was conducted with a relative or close friend of the patient by a research social worker with a different psychologist as observer. The focus of the interview was the patient's day-to-day relationships with each significant individual in his life. His ineffectiveness during the preceding four weeks was rated on a six-point scale in each of fifteen categories. Each rater made independent ratings and then arrived at a consensus conference rating with his partner. The two interviewing teams met to pool their accumulated information and the ratings in all categories were summed to make a Social Ineffectiveness score. The procedure was repeated six months after treatment began. Analysis of covariance was applied to the data, but the researchers, rather than using initial and final scores as is usually done, partly defeated the purpose of the technique by using initial scores and algebraic change scores. Both group and individual patients improved significantly more than those seen in minimal contact. The authors point out that there was no reason to believe that the minimal-contact patients did not have equal faith in the efficacy of the treatment to which they were assigned. The faith of the therapists is another matter. The resident assigned to minimal-contact therapy may have had less faith and interest in this form of therapy than did the other therapists in their treatments. In order to compare treatments, the therapists should be equally confident and interested in the methods. This would not likely be the case with analytically oriented residents who treat some patients for a half-hour every other week. There was a confounding in this experiment of type, length, and frequency of treatment, leaving us in doubt about what accounted for the beneficial results. At best, then, we have some equivocal support for the value of psychotherapy. This is particularly the case since a footnote reveals that other criteria did not reflect similar changes and implies that only the positive results were reported.

Dorfman (1958) investigated personality changes resulting from client-centered therapy with seventeen elementary-school children each of whom was selected for being among the five most maladjusted in his class. The controls were not therapy candidates but were matched for age, sex, and test scores. Individual therapy extended for a maximum of one school year and ranged from eleven to thirty-three sessions with an average of nineteen. The investigator was both the therapist and principal data analyst, a doubtful procedure, but precautions were taken to control bias. The Rogers Test of Personality Adjustment, Machover Human Figure Drawing Test, a Sentence Completion Test, and follow-up letters from the children were used as outcome measures. The experimental group was tested before a thirteen-week summer vacation (prewait), upon their return (pretherapy), posttherapy (average 28.5 weeks), and at a twelve- to eighteen-month follow-up. Controls were tested before and after a twenty-three week interval. Thus, the controls, who were not true controls since they were not candidates for therapy, were tested on two occasions and the treated children on four. The effects of repeated testing, therefore, were not controlled. The own-control comparisons that were made were questionable because the waiting period was over the summer vacation and the treatment period during the school year. Even the intervals between these testings were grossly unequal.

The therapist rated 59 per cent of the cases as relatively successful (some degree of movement). Two of five indices on the Rogers Test showed significant improvement with therapy (total score and social maladjustment score) and changes during therapy in total score were significantly greater than during the pretherapy wait period. Comparison with the untreated children showed the treated group to have improved significantly more on one scale, social maladjustment. The posttherapy and follow-up scores of the treated group did not differ from each other. There was significant improvement with therapy in an adjustment rating from the Sentence Completion Test. It was maintained on follow-up (own-control), and this improvement was also significantly greater than that found in the untreated group. Treatment of the data was crude and could have been improved by the use of analysis of covariance.

The value of adding group therapy to the hospital care routine of chronic schizophrenics was studied at the Veterans Administration Hospital, Montrose, New York (Sacks & Berger, 1954). The experimental group received one year of group therapy; the controls did not. There were twenty-eight patients in each group. At the end of the year, 46 per cent of the treated patients had been moved to an improved ward in contrast to 4 per cent of the controls; 64 per cent of the controls were unchanged compared to 18 per cent of the treated group. Both of these differences were statistically significant. Movements to more disturbed wards at the one extreme, or discharge from the hospital at the other, did not differ in the two groups. What we have, then, is a marked difference in in-hospital adjustment only. There is no indication that the groups were equated for severity of illness to start with, no information about whether or not the assignment to group therapy was random, and no indication of the way in which the status of the patients was evaluated.

Another attempt to evaluate the effect of group therapy on psychotic patients was made at the New Hampshire State Hospital (Kraus, 1959). In this research, two groups of eight patients on chronic wards were randomly assigned to experimental and control groups equivalent in age, sex, diagnosis, intelligence, education, length of hospitalization, and previous treatment. Primarily chronic paranoids making a good hospital adjustment, the patients were alert and ready to communicate and participate. They were selected because of the ward physician's prognostic estimate that they could benefit from psychotherapy. The experimental group met twice weekly in regular one-hour group therapy sessions with an active therapist for three months, and the controls did not.

The sixteen patients were rated before the experiment on the basis of interviews by an experienced psychiatrist. Patients were rated on appearance, behavior, sleeping and eating habits, stream of talk, mood, affect, thoughts, orientation, insight, and anxiety. Following the three-month experimental period, they were rerated as improved, unchanged, or worse, with the first interview as a baseline. A total rating of improvement was also made. Three of the eight treated patients improved and five remained unchanged. The controls had two rated as improved, five unchanged, and one worse. The ward physician, on the other hand, found seven out of eight in the treatment group improved and the other unchanged, with only one of the controls improved, six unchanged, and one worse. The judgments of the ward physician and the rating psychiatrist correlated negatively (rho = —.51). The Zulliger Ink Blots, administered with both clear and blurred exposure, revealed no consistent changes. The MMPI, however, was the only measure clearly to differentiate between the groups. There was a significant total difference in mean score in favor of the treated group. Eight of nine subscales examined showed improvements in the treated group while six of the nine were in the direction of nonimprovement for the controls. The greatest decrease for the experimental subjects was shown on the D, Hy, and Hs scales.

The general conclusions from this small-sample study are clouded by the inconsistent rating results, which may have come about because of rater bias, the unreliability of the rating procedure, or the possibility that the raters were looking at different aspects of the patients. The fact that the MMPI scores showed clear-cut progress for the treated patients, however, cannot be lightly dismissed. The treated patients thought or reported that they had improved more than did the controls, but professional observers were at odds in their appraisals. At least, neither source felt that the controls had done better than the treated patients.

Using affective complexity as a variable, Greenwald (1959) compared twenty clients at the University of Chicago Counseling Center with twenty nonpatients who answered a call for volunteers for psychological research. He hypothesized that affective complexity as inferred from the TAT would increase as a result of psychotherapy with movement in the direction of bivalent affect and with controlled resolution away from affective inhibition or monotonic affect. Clients averaged thirty-one interviews (range six to sixty-four) over a mean of thirty-one weeks of therapy (range four to ninety-one). An adequately reliable scoring scheme was devised and the TAT was administered before therapy, after therapy, and at follow-up six months to a year later. Controls were tested at comparable intervals. Control subjects were matched with experimental subjects for sex, age, and student status (half were students), but not on the initial level of the dependent variable. In fact, they were significantly different from each other on three pretherapy scores. They were thus not controls at all, but simply a comparison group that could permit no firm conclusions that any increase in affective complexity was a result of psychotherapy.

As it turned out, there were no significant changes in the affective scores of the control group whereas treated clients changed significantly on three out of five affective scores. More pleasant, cheerful, and optimistic moods and fewer unpleasant ones were reported after therapy, and a significant increase in complexity was demonstrated. The only difference from pretherapy to follow-up was an increase in the number of pleasant, and decrease in the number of unpleasant, feelings expressed. There was a slight reduction in complexity from the posttherapy to follow-up period. The fact that treated clients moved closer to controls in the posttest cannot be attributed with confidence to therapy since it is always possible that disturbed subjects without therapy would also move in the direction of the controls with the passage of time. This is the crucial test that was not made in this part of the experiment.

Straight (1960) did a follow-up of an evaluation of group therapy conducted by Vernallis and Reinert. In their eighteen-month study, thirty patients were matched with thirty others on personality organization and were equivalent on a number of other background variables. Both groups had the same hospital routine but one group had group therapy in addition. During the time period, nineteen experimental and sixteen control patients were discharged and seven in each group rehospitalized; two Es and one C were later released again. Therefore, at the end of the study, fourteen treated and ten control patients were in the community, hardly a dramatic difference. However, the treatment group had sixty-one more months in the community. Straight followed up the fourteen treated and ten control patients to assess their comparative social adjustment. A social worker made home visits and interviewed the patients' relatives and close associates. A narrative description and an objective factual report covering the thirty days immediately preceding the follow-up data were prepared. The unidentified reports were rated on the Report of Social Adjustment covering various areas of social adjustment, and summary ratings of "good," "fair," "marginal," and "poor" were made. Social functioning of the Es in four areas (occupational, family, interpersonal, and community) was not found to be significantly better than the controls even though more of the patients in the treatment group were operating on the "good" and "fair" levels. These results are mildly but not convincingly favorable for group therapy. It would have been worthwhile to have used more care to reduce any possible bias and to have established the reliability of the ratings.

Limiting the appraisal of outcome to a simple criterion, Graham (1960) designed an experiment to evaluate the effects of psychoanalytically oriented psychotherapy on levels of frequency and satisfaction in sexual activity. The research was done in an outpatient setting at the Long Island Consultation Center. The experimental group consisted of 142 married men and women who had been in treatment for times ranging from several weeks to forty-nine months. They were compared with sixty-five married men and women who had not yet begun treatment. Information was obtained on levels of satisfaction, percentage enjoying satisfactory coitus, frequency per week, and percentage having coitus two times per week or more. This information was obtained from three subgroups of patients, those in treatment zero to five months (65 per cent women), those in treatment six to eleven months (63 per cent women), and those in treatment twelve months or more (72 per cent women). The controls were 61 per cent women. No information is given in the report about the way in which the data were obtained, the nature of the scale of level of satisfaction, or the other basic measures. Data for men and women were treated separately and controls were compared with experimentals at three intervals of treatment.

With treatment, both men and women showed significant improvement in mean level of satisfaction and frequency. In the six- to nine-month period, there was a drop in all areas except in the percentage of men enjoying satisfactory coitus. This drop was not significantly different from the other two periods. The treated group was still different from the controls; the percentage having coitus twice a week or more continually increased. Graham concluded that psychoanalytically oriented psychotherapy frees individuals for more frequent and more satisfactory coital experiences.

Not knowing how the data were arrived at makes it difficult to evaluate this experiment and impossible to reproduce it. The design called for a 2×4 analysis of variance rather than for the rather incomplete picture of t-values that was given. To complicate appraisal of these results further, the t-values are not shown but are reported to be "significant" at the 10 per cent level. The differences are quite small in an absolute sense, and there is question about how much confidence can be placed in the results. The main shortcoming, however, is that the control group is not truly a control group. There is no indication that the controls were comparable to the experimentals on the dependent variable at the start. They were not reassessed after the passage of equivalent periods of time as were the treated patients. As a group, they merely provide some kind of initial baseline that is less meaningful than the initial level of the experimental group itself.

Hollon and Zolik (1962) evaluated the changes in ego functioning that take place in the initial phase of psychoanalytically oriented psychotherapy. They compared a small group of seven young women patients seen in an outpatient mental health clinic with eight women volunteers. Self-esteem was measured by the self-ideal discrepancy on a Q-sort. The Q-sort and the Mooney Problem Check List were given before treatment and at four-month intervals during treatment. The subjects were asked to underline problems of greatest concern on the Mooney. All patients were seen by the same therapist. The two groups clearly represented different populations at the time of initial testing, and the point of the research was to find out if the treated ones would improve and enter normal range. They still differed after therapy in the number of symptomatic complaints, but the treated group showed a decline in intensity of complaints, making them comparable to the controls. The treated sample significantly reduced the number of complaints on the Mooney and increased their self-esteem. Controls did not change. The subjects in the nontherapy group were not patients and were not functioning at the same level as the patients. They were thus not suitable controls against which to evaluate the efficacy of therapy. They were used as a standard or normative group, but eight people do not make a normative group and are not necessarily representative. All we can tell from this experiment is that the treated patients experienced some measurable changes in the predicted direction. We have no evidence that these changes were attributable to psychotherapy.

At Wichita Falls State Hospital, Kansas, forty-two male patients on alcoholic commitment were randomly divided into two groups of equal size. The experimental groups were split into three smaller groups, each of which received seven sessions of group therapy (McGinnis, 1963). The controls did not receive group therapy, but continued to participate, as did the experimentals, in the regular Alcoholic Anonymous program. Barron Ego-Strength Scale scores were obtained twelve to fifteen days after admission and about a month and one-half later. The treated and untreated groups did not differ significantly on initial test scores. The significance of the difference between initial and final test scores was computed separately for each group. Only the treated patients showed a significant increase in ego strength. A test of the significance of the difference between change scores revealed the change in the treated group to be reliably greater than that in the control groups. Analysis of variance would have been a superior method of assessing these data; nevertheless, the differences appear to be substantial and attributable to the intervening group therapy experience. Whether or not group therapy led to a quicker and more durable recovery from alcoholism is not answered by this research.

Ewing (1964) studied the assessment of change as a function of the client's initial status in certain problem areas. The study was done at the Student Counseling Service, University of Illinois. The subjects were ninety college students who were seen by eleven experienced counselors for an average of sixteen interviews (range three to seventy-eight). A group of about sixty-two students from psychology classes served as a control group, or, more accurately, as a norm group, for they had neither applied for nor were receiving counseling. The counselees completed self-ratings on 100 traits at the beginning and end of counseling; the controls were tested on two occasions twelve weeks apart. An earlier factor analysis of the rating scale yielded seven ways of self-description: dissatisfied, outgoing, contrary, hard worker, conventional, patient, creative. "Normal adjustment" was taken as the mean score of the normal students in each problem area. Counseled students were divided into highest, middle, and lowest scoring thirds on each factor score. An analysis of covariance was conducted for the four groups for each of the seven factors.

Significant F-values for factors labeled "dissatisfied," "patient," and "creative" suggest that counseling is associated with change in these characteristics. The largest change was in the "dissatisfied" score and in the group initially most different from normal. The author concluded that initial status must be considered in evaluating change, and that the mean score of normal students constitutes an inadequate statement of expected change. In a commentary on this experiment, Warman pointed out that the norm group might not be quite as normal as assumed, that the change in the experimental group could be simple regression toward the mean, that the normal group should have been divided into thirds as were the counselees, and that the goals of counseling should have gone beyond working toward the norm. Although this experiment casts some light on the relation of initial status to change, it does not provide good evaluative data because of the absence of a control group of subjects who applied for therapy and whose initial status was comparable to the treated group.

The design of a study comparing the efficacy of three kinds of drugs, a drug placebo, and psychotherapy with a waiting-list control group enables us to restrict our attention to the results of the psychotherapy as against the waiting conditions (Brill, Koegler, Epstein, & Forgy, 1964). Of the fifty patients assigned to therapy, twenty (40 per cent) dropped out, whereas fourteen (41 per cent) of the thirty-four put on the waiting list dropped out. Psychotherapy was basically psychoanalytically oriented and was conducted by psychiatric residents under supervision. The patients were women twenty to forty years of age who were of average or better intelligence and were neither psychotic nor severely depressed. Patients were assigned at random to the control group and told that treatment would be available in four months to a year. The groups were comparable on several measures, and the dropouts were not selective. The criterion measures included ratings by the therapist, the patient, and a close relative and a social worker evaluation and the MMPI. Ratings by the patient at termination showed the psychotherapy group to be somewhat better on all the variables considered. The patients, however, tended to see themselves as more improved than did their therapists. As the statistical analysis did not specifically compare the therapy and control groups against each other, the significance of the difference is in doubt. Ratings by relatives showed the therapy group to have improved somewhat compared with controls, but relatives too rated patients as more improved than did the therapists. No statistical treatment is available. Blind comparisons of pre- and post-MMPI's were made by two psychologists. Controls showed no change on a seven-point rating scale of improvement while members of the therapy group were slightly to moderately improved. Again, there was no specific statistical analysis. The comparative data on psychotherapy and no treatment cannot be clearly extracted from the larger study involving drug treatments. What can be seen is mildly favorable to psychotherapy, but may reflect strong staff biases. The experimenters ran directly into the kind of opposition from residents, staff, and community agencies that researchers in psychotherapy can anticipate. Residents felt that patients to whom they had to administer drugs "were being grossly abused, mistreated, and sacrificed on the altar of research" (p. 591). The researchers were startled by the extent of the bias in favor of psychotherapy even in beginners who had little experience.

Some controlled evaluation data were presented incidentally to an investigation of the prediction of improvement by the use of the Rorschach Prognostic Rating Scale and the MMPI (Endicott & Endicott, 1964). Forty-two patients with mixed diagnoses were alternately assigned to a waiting list or to therapy. After twenty-one had been placed in therapy, additional patients were placed on the waiting list for a total of forty untreated and twenty-one treated patients. Ratings by the therapist on the Miles, Barrabee, and Finesinger Evaluation of Improvement Scale after six months showed 40 per cent of the untreated group as improved, compared to 52 per cent of the treated patients. These data were not treated statistically, but chi-square shows that the difference can be attributed to chance. Although the supporting data are not presented in this report, the authors state that the therapy group improved more on seven of the MMPI scales than did the untreated group. It is unfortunate that the one therapist made all the improvement ratings with no interrater reliability data. However, the authors point out that changes in MMPI scores closely agree with the ratings. At best, the study offers mild support for the benefits of therapy.

A research study evaluating the effects of psychotherapy on the course of ulcerative colitis examined treated and untreated groups observed over a twenty-five-year period (O'Connor, Daniels, Flood, Karush, Moses, & Stern, 1964). Fifty-seven patients with ulcerative colitis who received psychotherapy were matched for severity of illness, sex, age of onset, and use of steroids with fifty-seven patients who did not receive psychotherapy. The control group was not an effective one. The experimental patients were referred for psychotherapy because of obvious psychopathology, but the controls were not referred chiefly because they were less disturbed. For example, nineteen of the experimentals were diagnosed as schizophrenic in contrast to three of the controls. Psychotherapy varied from short-term, psychoanalytically oriented treatment to full psychoanalysis. Psychological response to psychotherapy is crudely estimated and evaluated as highly favorable, but no psychological evaluation was made of the controls for comparison purposes. Surgical and mortality rates over the years were no different for either group. Proctoscopic and symptom changes were thought to be more favorable in the treated group, but the results were not evaluated statistically. The authors' conclusion that "psychotherapy has a demonstrably favorable effect on the somatic course of the disease" must be regarded as largely unsubstantiated.

Among the claimed results of psychotherapy is a general increase in efficiency and productivity in life activities. One approach to substantiating this claim was an attempt to demonstrate that the earnings of patients increase as a concomitant of psychotherapy (Riess, 1967). Since pay rates over time do not remain constant but fluctuate with economic conditions, experience, and seniority, this kind of research is necessarily fraught with pitfalls at the start. Riess surveyed 414 patients at the Postgraduate Center for Mental Health in New York, a psychoanalytically oriented clinic. Each therapist was asked to obtain information from his patients working full-time (except for civil service employees) concerning weekly income before treatment and present weekly income. As a kind of control, information on the wages of 145 additional patients, matched with the study group for occupational category, was collected. These patients began treatment at the time of the completion of the study. It was found that the pretreatment mean income of the study group was eighty-three dollars per week. After a mean of fifty-seven therapeutic sessions, the mean was 112 dollars per week. Comparison with the "control" group shows the treated group to be better off by twenty-two dollars per week than individuals in similar occupations just beginning treatment, but with no significant difference between the initial salary levels of the two groups. Comparison with Department of Labor statistics showed a weekly gain of six dollars for the occupations listed by the department over the two-year period during which most of the patients were treated. It was also noted that more males changed by very large amounts while more females changed at the level of eleven to fifty dollars per week. All this sounds very promising, but it is not at all convincing. The inclusion of only full-time working patients biases the sample. Those who were unemployed at the start (if there were any) and later obtained a job could affect the mean increase inordinately. On the other hand, the initially employed patient who loses his job during therapy, or goes on part-time work, is not qualified for the sample. Both factors could spuriously inflate the true amount of increase. Presentation of the mean without the standard deviation of a variable such as earnings can be misleading. Since some individuals were reported as changed by "very large amounts," the median would probably be a more appropriate measure of central tendency. The accuracy of the information about income obtained from patients is also to be questioned, particularly information from those in therapy for a long time who must recall their income at a specific earlier date, a very difficult task for anyone. Department of Labor statistics may be reasonably accurate reflections of specific occupational groups as a whole, but their utility in research of this sort is dubious. Particularly, they cannot tell us anything reliable enough for research purposes about the earnings of business owners, entrepreneurs, and others not on a wage scale regulated by industry (as it is for the skilled, semiskilled, and unskilled labor force). The hypothesis is an intriguing one, but in order to test it an untreated control group would be mandatory.

6

Review of Controlled-Outcome Studies: III. Null and Negative Results

ADEQUATE STUDIES: NULL OR NEGATIVE RESULTS

One of the pioneers among controlled studies evaluated the effectiveness of therapy in a delinquency prevention program as part of the Cambridge-Somerville Youth Study, which extended from 1937 to 1945 (Teuber & Powers, 1953). This was an ambitious and carefully done long-term project. The names of six- to ten-year-old boys who were judged likely to become delinquent were submitted by teachers, policemen, and settlement workers. All told, 650 boys were matched in pairs on a large number of variables such as age, IQ, grade, delinquency rating, ethnic background, socioeconomic status, and other relevant characteristics. They were then randomly assigned to treatment or control groups, with 325 in each group. Upon selection, each boy in the experimental group was assigned to one of ten counselors (social workers). The kind of treatment was the choice of the individual counselor and ranged from a "big brother" relationship to formal therapeutic interviews. There was a general shift in approach to more orthodox child-guidance-center tactics at the time of World War II. Since this was a study in delinquency prevention, the criterion was the delinquency record of each boy. This was measured by the number of court appearances made from the beginning of the study until 1948 and by the number of appearances before the Crime Prevention Bureau.

The results supported the null hypothesis: ninety-six treated boys made court appearances for 264 offenses as compared to 218 offenses for ninety-two controls. From each group there were forty-nine one-time appearances before the Crime Prevention Bureau. There were sixty-five two- or three-time appearances by the treated group and fifty-two by the controls. The slight differences in favor of the controls were not significant. In the opposite direction, there was a slightly but not significantly greater incidence of serious recidivism (thirty or more offenses) in the control group, and the rating of all offenses according to seriousness slightly favored the treated group. The inescapable conclusion was that treatment did not reduce the incidence of adjudged delinquency.

Of great interest, however, was the finding that the counselors firmly believed that they had substantially benefited about two-thirds of the boys. More than half the boys at the terminal interview said that they had been helped. This dramatically illustrates the importance of a control group and objective measures of outcome. The authors cogently observe that "quantitative indices, where available, are better than professions of faith bolstered by the therapist's prestige and the skillful use of the illustrative case" (p. 140). Significant success had been predicted by all but two staff members, and Teuber and Powers noted that "To some of the counselors, the whole control group idea, and our insistence on an objective description of the counseling process, seemed slightly blasphemous, as if we were attempting a statistical test of the efficacy of prayer" (p. 145).

The program was designed to prevent delinquency. It did not achieve its objective. If other benefits of counseling accrued, they were not relevant to the issue and were not tested. Bergin (1963) has expressed the reservation that we cannot be sure that the effects of extratherapeutic contacts were randomized across the experimental and control groups. In any study that takes place in the patients' natural habitat, this is something beyond the control of the experimenter. Although it is possible, it is highly improbable that one group of 325 should have somehow received selectively more extratherapeutic help than another group of 325 randomly assigned for treatment. The research was concerned with the effects of *therapy* upon delinquency prevention, not of extratherapeutic effects assumed to be randomized. The question that most certainly will be asked is, "Is this therapy?" From the point of view of the counselors, it was therapy by intent and procedure, but the report indicates that the boys did not uniformly see it that way. It was also atypical in that psychotherapy is usually aimed at modifying existing maladjustment rather than at preventing its occurrence in the future. The treatment was so varied and the patient population and preventive goals so restricted that generalizations about psychotherapy cannot readily be made from this study alone.

Working with hospitalized psychotics, King et al. compared two different psychotherapeutic approaches with recreational therapy and no therapy. The patients were forty-eight schizophrenics on a locked ward who had been hospitalized for a mean of nine years and averaged slightly less than thirty-four years of age and ten years of education (King, Armitage, & Tilton, 1960). All were of low verbal and physical activity and had shown no major behavior changes for at least two years. Three varieties of therapy were given in three twenty- to thirty-minute sessions per week for fifteen weeks. The novel therapy, called the operant-interpersonal method, involved an elaborate, multiple operant problem-solving apparatus that dispensed rewards of candy and cigarettes when problems were solved by moving wooden levers in correct sequences. This was individual at first, but the patients were advanced to cooperative problem solving with other patients. Conventional verbal therapy, given to a second group, was individual at first and changed to group therapy when the operant-interpersonal therapy became cooperative. A Recreational Therapy group met for the same number of hours, and a no-therapy group continued mostly to sleep its way through regularly scheduled ward activities.

Three indices of status were used: (1) the Extreme Mental Illness Schedule, a scale for rating low levels of adjustment; (2) Ward Observation Scale; (3) amount of verbalization. Measures of improvement were difference scores from successive ratings on these scales and a Clinical Improvement Scale rated by ward personnel. Patients treated by the operant-interpersonal method improved significantly more than the other groups on most of the measures. Verbal therapy proved to be of no more value than no therapy. The gains from operant-interpersonal therapy were definitely measurable and clinically observable both at the time and at a six-month follow-up, but no patient became well enough to leave the hospital. This was a particularly well-controlled study that yielded a positive outcome for one therapeutic approach and null results for another.

Anker and Walsh (1961) compared the efficacy of group psychotherapy with activity programs for chronic patients (mean duration of hospitalization 9.2 years) at the Perry Point Veterans Administration Hospital, Maryland. The sample of fifty-six male schizophrenics was drawn from the continued-treatment ward and assigned to therapy groups conducted by a psychologist or to a drama group under the aegis of a recreational therapist. The former met twice a week for one and one-half hours. The latter consisted of meetings in the recreation hall to produce plays to entertain staff and patients. The recreational therapist served as a relatively inactive "nondirective resource person" and the groups sometimes met without him. The study was of one year's duration. Ratings were made by nurses and nursing assistants who were unaware of the hypotheses and the constitution of the patient subgroups. Progress was assessed primarily by the MACC Behavioral Adjustment Scale. The activity group improved significantly on motility, communication, cooperation, and total adjustment and at the $p = .08$ level for affect. The psychotherapy patients showed only a reduction in motility. Semantic differential distances between patient self-ratings and those given by him to others in his group showed no changes attributable to any treatment. Changes in choice of luncheon companions did not materialize because social choices remained constant. There were no significant differences in the number of patients released from the hospital. The results of activity therapy were interpreted as being "incomparably better" than verbal therapy. There were distinct signs of improved behavioral adjustment in the activity group and little change in the psychotherapy group.

To test the value of group psychotherapy as an additional therapy in a drug addiction program, Blachly et al. randomly assigned thirty-three addicts to group therapy and an equal number to a routine that did not include group therapy (Blachly, Pepper, Scott, & Baganz, 1961). The addicts were mostly Federal prisoners, aged twenty to thirty-five. Group therapy was compulsory and lasted for only six sessions. Its main purpose was to orient the members to the hospital as a treatment center and to stimulate motivation and self-understanding of their drug need. Examination before and after treatment on the Hill-Monroe Inventory Questionnaire revealed no demonstrable value from group therapy. The change in attitude of both groups of addicts was in the direction opposite to that which the therapists and the hospital in general were trying to foster. Compulsory assignment to a few sessions of group orientation is a far cry from group therapy as it is usually practiced, and generalizations from this study cannot be freely made.

A controlled assessment of remotivation with institutionalized psychotics was conducted at Rusk State Hospital, Texas (Roos, Hayes, Marion, & England, 1963). Mostly schizophrenic, the fifty-two patients were assigned randomly to experimental and control groups on each of three wards. The groups were comparable in age, length of hospitalization, IQ, diagnosis, and somatic treatments. Results of the Kent EGY and L-M Fergus Falls Behavior Rating Scales were obtained on all patients on three occasions: just prior to remotivation, six weeks later at the end of remotivation, and six weeks following its termination. Mean Fergus Falls ratings were compared at each of the time points. No significant differences were found on any of the comparisons between experimental and control groups on the Fergus Falls ratings. Patients exposed to this procedure did not improve more than those exposed to the standard hospital program.

The Palo Alto Veterans Administration Hospital, California, was the scene of a very well-designed study of the comparative efficacy of patient- and staff-led groups with chronic hospitalized patients (MacDonald, Blochberger, & Maynard, 1964). A total of fifty-six patients, forty-eight of whom were schizophrenic, were divided into four groups equated for diagnosis, age, and previous hospitalization (average over five years). The groups were randomly assigned to treatment for a six-month experimental period. Four different approaches were introduced. One group met two times a week with an experienced psychologist and a psychology trainee for traditional group therapy. The focus was on achieving self-understanding and insight. Current feelings and perceptions were discussed and the group interaction was used as the principal subject matter. A second group met twice weekly with the same therapists for *specific* therapy whose content was limited to discharge planning and discussion of problems associated with obtaining jobs and housing. The third group was autonomous. It convened twice weekly with instructions to discuss discharge and related problems for forty-five minutes and was left alone during the period. The fourth group, a no-treatment control group, did not meet at any time.

The outcome criteria were largely objective and behavioral. The number of releases from the hospital totaled ten for the autonomous group, eight for the no-treatment controls, six for the specific therapy group, and only three for those in traditional group therapy. Chi-square for differences among groups in releases was inconclusive ($p < .10$). There were no significant differences in the number transferred to locked wards. The number of rule infractions was tabulated. The groups varied significantly, with the traditional therapy group having the highest number of infractions. Analysis of variance of average weekly minor rule infractions was significant, with the autonomous group showing substantially the fewest infractions. The amount of social interaction exhibited during the morning ward recreation hour, with evening nursing assistants, and with other patients during the evening was tallied or rated. The autonomous group showed markedly more instances of being initiators and recipients of conversation, but spoke least to evening nursing assistancts, while the no-treatment group spoke with them the most. Study of evening patient-to-patient interaction revealed no differences. The autonomous group members tended to choose their own members for social interaction more frequently than did members of other groups. Sociometric study revealed the autonomous group members to have a larger number of choices than any other group. The no-treatment group had the highest percentage of patient-initiated interviews with staff and the traditional group the lowest. These results led the authors to conclude that staff-led therapies failed to promote the two major hospital treatment objectives, favorable dispositions and ward adjustment. A goal-preference test showed that a preference for self-understanding was not acquired as a goal by staff-led groups. Group therapy with an objective of self-understanding was viewed as possibly even impeding the achievement of hospital objectives. The autonomous group, on the contrary, became cohesive and showed marked superiority on ward adjustment and a tendency toward better dispositions. It was noted that traditional therapy with a focus on self-understanding was associated with unfavorable dispositions and more rule infractions, with no enhancement of social activity over the no-treatment group. With hospitalized chronic schizophrenic patients, then, traditional group therapy, with its focus on insight and self-understanding, appears to have no advantage over no treatment at all and is inferior to other approaches.

One of the best designed and most carefully done evaluation studies yielded null results (Volsky, Magoon, Norman, & Hoyt, 1965). The research at the University of Minnesota Student Counseling Bureau was designed to find out if counseling produces beneficial change beyond that produced by mere time lapse, whether different counselors produce different average amounts of movement, whether the client's initial motivations to change or his perceptions or expectations about counseling affect subsequent outcome, and if there is any interaction among these variables. The experimental subjects were eighty male students who sought counseling presumably because of academic problems and twenty comparable controls. The experimental subjects were seen for from one to thirteen sessions (average of three) by eight counselors of varied orientation. All subjects received a screening interview and pretests and were classified as high or low in motivation and as good or bad in perception of counseling. Experimental subjects were assigned to counseling and were retested approximately thirty days after their final interview. Controls received the posttests after an equivalent time lapse without treatment. Measures devised for the study included the Minnesota Manifest Anxiety Scale, Minnesota Defensiveness Scale, and a measure of effectiveness of personal problem solving. Data were treated by analysis of variance and covariance, and thirty-three null hypotheses were tested. Only one of the thirty-three could be rejected, and that in the reverse direction to expectations. The controls *increased* on the problem-solving variable while the counseled subjects did not. This consistent and total failure to demonstrate predicted benefits of counseling led the authors to speculate, after the fact, that a few interviews may not be expected to bring about significant change of the type predicted. No generalizations were made, or could be made, to effects of more extensive therapy on patients with established psychopathology.

A comparison of the effectiveness of five treatment methods with schizophrenic patients at Camarillo State Hospital, California, included the use of drugs and ECT as well as psychotherapy (May & Tuma, 1965). The phase of the investigation of interest to us here is the comparison that it affords between psychotherapy and basic hospital care alone. Twenty patients of both sexes were in each of these groups. They all were schizophrenics on first admission, and assignment to treatment was randomized. Preselection for subjects to be studied was made by three teams of two psychoanalysts who picked those cases in which treatment "might make the greatest difference between success and failure." Individual psychotherapy averaged at least two hours a week. Patients were treated by psychiatric residents under the supervision of a psychoanalyst. Treatment lasted up to one year.

During the two-year period following initial release from the hospital, there were no significant differences in rehospitalizations of the treated and untreated groups. Eleven therapy patients and eight controls were rehospitalized. The total length of time spent in the hospital during the three years following initial admission was slightly but not significantly higher for the treated group. Posttreatment status of the patients was rated on the Menninger Health-Sickness Rating Scale. Ratings were made by eight psychoanalysts who gave consensus ratings in pairs based upon interview of the patients. Since case records were made available to them, the raters were not ignorant of the treatment received by the patients. If they had a bias in favor of therapy it did not show, for there was no posttreatment difference between the two groups. Ward behavior at the end of treatment was rated on the MACC by nurses. The group treated by nurses did not differ from controls. The treatment that consistently yielded the best results was chemotherapy. The addition of psychotherapy to the drug treatment did not bring about results that were different from the drugs alone. Despite the absence of pretreatment data, the results on hospitalization and rating variables are consistent on the finding that psychoanalytically oriented psychotherapy did not increase the benefits obtained from the custodial treatment of hospitalized schizophrenics. Essentially the same results were reported by May & Tuma (1964) in another phase of this project.

DeLeon and Mandell (1966) conducted a comparative study of the effectiveness of conditioning, psychotherapy, and no therapy with cases of functional enuresis. The subjects were eighty-seven children aged five and one-half to fourteen, of whom fifty-six were assigned before the initial interview to conditioning therapy, thirteen to psychotherapy, and eighteen to no treatment. Conditioning therapy was carried out by means of a pad on which one drop of urine closed a circuit and activated a loud buzzer. Both conditioning and psychotherapy were begun three weeks after the initial interview. Psychotherapy was conducted for twelve weekly sessions and consisted of a forty-minute session with the child and twenty minutes with the mother. The controls received no treatment, but nightly data were obtained on them as well as on the rest. The criterion of success was seven successive dry nights on the connected pad, three successive nights on the unconnected pad, and three with the device out of the room. The psychotherapy patients had to remain dry for thirteen successive nights. Failure consisted of not reaching the criterion in twelve sessions (about ninety days), with a similar standard for the controls. Of those who completed treatment, 86.3 per cent of the conditioning group met the criterion in a median of 37 days, compared to 18.2 per cent of the psychotherapy group in a median of 103.5 days and 11.1 per cent of the controls in a median of 84 days. The difference in rate of cure was significant, as was the time it took to meet the criterion. In a follow-up period of at least six months, both of the psychotherapy patients who had succeeded relapsed, along with one of the two controls and nearly 80 per cent of the conditioning group. The criterion of relapse was a rigid one, a single wet night. The mean wetting rate was significantly less during the relapse period than during the basal period. Eleven of those who relapsed were reconditioned and eight succeeded in a median of 22.5 days, significantly more quickly than during the first course. This appears to be a clear demonstration of superiority of the conditioning method to psychotherapy in eliminating this specific symptom. At the same time, it illustrates the ineffectiveness of brief psychotherapy when compared with no treatment at all.

QUESTIONABLE STUDIES: NULL OR NEGATIVE RESULTS

Fiedler (1949) conducted a small experiment to find out if psychotherapeutic methods would be helpful in preventing or reducing the impact of emotionally disturbing experiences, in this case, comprehensive examinations. Twenty-five university students volunteered for the group procedure and were compared with nineteen controls with whom nothing was done. Five groups met for six sessions. A ten-item graphic rating scale of various manifestations of examination anxiety was sent by mail a week following the examination. Only ten of the nineteen controls returned the scale in contrast to twenty of the twenty-five treated subjects. A lower percentage of the students who did poorly in the examination returned the scale than of those who obtained higher grades. With the sample thus biased, Fiedler found no significant differences on the full scale between the respondents in the two groups. Yet, he still persisted with an item-by-item appraisal of four of the five experimental groups. On only one of the ten items were there any group differences. On the strength of this, he concluded that three of the groups benefited. This finding can be most parsimoniously explained as a statistical artifact. Since the experiment really failed to make its point, there is not much that can be said about the value of this kind of "preventive psychotherapy."

An evaluation of group therapy with acutely disturbed patients was carried out at Winter Veterans Administration Hospital, Kansas (Feifel & Schwartz, 1953). Thirty-four patients who received occupational therapy, special services, some ECT, hypnotherapy, and individual therapy were compared with another group of thirty-four who, in addition, received group psychotherapy twice weekly for twenty sessions. The therapy group was open-ended and attendance was voluntary. The experimental and control subjects were matched for diagnosis, IQ, age, education, marital status, race, and rural or urban background. The duration of the present hospitalization was typically less than two months, and most of the patients were schizophrenic. As this was a retrospective study, judgments of improvement had been made by the therapist and supervisory staff prior to the investigation. Change was classified as more disturbed (transferred to a closed ward), no improvement, or improved (discharged, trial visit, or transferred to open ward). The disposition of those who had had group therapy was somewhat more favorable in each of these categories. Seventy-one per cent of the therapy group showed improvement in contrast to 50 per cent of the controls. The chi-square of 2.22 fell at the equivocal 15 per cent level of confidence, and was interpreted as a "trend" in favor of the experimental group. The authors were strongly impressed with the qualitative differences between the groups with respect to ward activities and relations with ward personnel, but they present no data. They acknowledge the limitations of the research and call for more accurate and better controlled studies. What they did was to compare group therapy as an incremental approach with a wide assortment of other types of treatment. It is surprising that it made even that much difference (equivocal as the difference may be) against the therapeutic background shared by all patients. As it stands, however, the results do not refute the null hypothesis.

Barron and Leary (1955) investigated changes in psychoneurotic patients with and without psychotherapy. This study is one of the most frequently cited by disclaimers of the value of therapy. A total of 150 psychoneurotic patients applied for psychotherapy, but a group of twenty-three had to be placed on a waiting list. Eighty-five received group therapy and forty-two individual therapy. All had a minimum of three months of treatment. The experimental and control groups were described as comparable to each other in diagnosis, prognosis, severity of initial condition, age, sex, and education. All patients were administered the MMPI before and after therapy or the waiting period. This interval averaged 7.00 months for the nontreatment group, 8.32 months for the individual therapy group, and 8.63 months for those in group therapy. These means were found to be not significantly different ($.05 < p < .10$) from each other, and the intervals therefore were considered to be comparable. Since the interval between pre- and posttesting is a potentially important variable, it would have been better if the groups had not only been "not significantly different," but significantly *alike*. This was clearly not the case. An examination of the sample reveals that only those in therapy for three months were included. Thus the sample starts off biased (we do not know in which direction) by the exclusion of those who terminated prior to three months. F-tests were done among the pretest scores of the three groups on eleven MMPI scales and the Barron Ego Strength Scale. On none of these scales did the groups show significant variation. The groups were not compared again at posttesting. Instead, raw discrepancy scores between pre- and posttesting were obtained for each scale, and the significance of the difference of the mean discrepancy score from zero was computed. Thus, for example, we are told that the mean discrepancy score between the first and second administration on the Depression Scale for the individual-therapy cases was a discrepancy that differed from zero. Similar information was given about changes in Depression Scale scores for the group therapy patients, and separately for the untreated patients. Improvement was shown by all three groups on most scales, but not all of the changes were significantly different from zero. There were significant decreases in the Depression, Hysteria, Hypochondriasis, and Lie Scale scores for both therapy groups. Scores on the Paranoia and Psychasthenia Scales also decreased with group therapy. Both therapy groups showed a rise on the Ego Strength Scale. Controls showed a significant decrease on the Lie Scale and Psychopathic Deviant Scale, and an increase on the Ego Strength Scale. Tests were also made of the differences between mean discrepancy scores of the individual therapy and nontreatment groups. Only one critical ratio out of forty-eight was significant. It was concluded that therapy patients did not improve significantly more than did waiting-list controls.

The authors acknowledge that therapeutic factors in initial intake evaluations and decisions may complicate the interpretation of the results, and suggest the use of non-waiting-list controls. Some of the Barron and Leary data were further analyzed by Cartwright (1956a). Noting the greater variability of discrepancy scores of the patients treated by individual therapy, he converted the standard deviations of the discrepancy scores into variances and computed variance ratios between the individual treatment and nontreatment groups on all scales. Half of the resultant F-values were significant. He noted that the Barron and Leary conclusion that therapy patients did not improve significantly more than the waiting-list controls is correct but insufficient. He speculated that the variability may have come about because some patients deteriorated more than waiting-list controls whereas some did improve significantly more. This is a reasonable and educated guess, but one for which there is no proof. The facts lie in the original data. The more crucial issues in this report have to do with the sampling, the use of patients on a waiting list, and the use of the MMPI as the sole criterion measure. Barron and Leary were well aware of these limitations and had their own reservations about them.

In the introduction to a follow-up of the Barron and Leary study, Leary and Harvey (1956) observe: "Psychotherapy has existed and flourished during the past five decades in spite of the fact that it remains almost completely unvalidated by scientific standards. Psychotherapy is, in some respects, an implausible procedure offering to the individual the opportunity to learn those things about himself which by definition he does not wish to know. The steady growth in prestige of this intellectual institution in the teeth of these two obstacles—its unscientific status and its inherent threats to the conscious ego—is a remarkable testimony to its basic effectiveness or to the capacity of otherwise intelligent professional workers to deceive themselves" (p. 123). As their contribution, the authors proceed to describe and demonstrate a technique for assessing change before and after psychotherapy based upon the Interpersonal System. The research was designed merely to determine whether or not changes had taken place differentially in the Barron and Leary (1955) sample. By their technique, they were able to show that treated patients *changed* more than controls. The 1955 study, however, claimed that they did not *improve* more. The authors are aware that there is a big difference between change and improvement. This finding lends support to Cartwright's reanalysis of the Barron and Leary data and his contention that if they did not improve more, but did change more, then some must have improved while others were getting worse.

A controlled research project was initiated at the Boston State Hospital to evaluate the effectiveness of group therapy with chronic psychotic patients (Semon & Goldstein, 1957). Thirty-nine schizophrenic patients aged twenty to fifty, who had been hospitalized for at least two years and were receiving no other form of therapy, were divided into five groups matched on general adjustment in the hospital, interpersonal functioning, length of total hospitalization, and age. The measure of general adjustment was the Palo Alto Hospital Adjustment Scale (HAS); interpersonal functioning was assessed by Scale I of the HAS. Ratings were done by a ward attendant. Four of the groups, each with eight patients, were randomly designated as experimental, and one was designated the control group ($N = 7$). T-tests between group means on the HAS and Scale I were not significant, but the control group scored higher on both scales. Two types of group therapy, active-participant and active-interpretive, were conducted. The former was designed to promote interaction, the latter to promote understanding in the patients of their underlying motivations. Two of the experimental groups participated in one kind of group therapy, two in the other. The two therapists, both clinical psychologists, had experience with group therapy in this setting. Groups met for one hour, five days a week for ten weeks, for a total of fifty sessions. All patients continued to receive standard custodial treatment on the wards. The controls received only custodial treatment.

At the end of the ten-week period all patients were rerated. There were no significant pre-post differences on the total HAS score or on any of the three subscales for the control subjects. T-tests were used and two-tailed tests of significance were applied. Similar tests were used on the experimental patients, but for them one-tailed tests of significance were applied. The pre-post difference for the combined experimental group was at $p < .10$ for the total HAS score, $p < .05$ for Scale I (communication and interpersonal relations), $p < .10$ for Scale II (care of self and social responsibility), $p > .35$ for Scale III (work, activities, and recreation). Thus, the only clearly significant improvement was on Scale I.

If the experimental and control groups were truly matched at the start, the appropriate posttherapy test should have been between experimental and control group means. As there were initial differences (even though not statistically significant), analysis of covariance should have been used to adjust for them. It does not seem justified to use a one-tailed test of significance for thirty-two experimental subjects and a two-tailed test for seven controls. It is not sufficient justification to claim that improvement was predicted for one group and not for the other. In fact, no specific predictions were made about subscale scores. The hypothesis called for "clinical improvement" and the total HAS score was taken as its measure. The total HAS score did not show a significant difference even by a one-tailed test. Of the three subscales, two did not yield significant pre-post differences for treated patients even by one-tailed tests. Hence, only one out of three subscales showed significant improvement for treated patients and that result is based upon a questionable statistical approach. Further indication of the doubtful validity of a conclusion about demonstrable benefit of group therapy comes from the report that 43 per cent of the control Ss showed more gain than the average experimental patient, and 56 per cent of experimental Ss showed more gain than the average control patient. With that much overlap, differences are certainly unimpressive. The experiment assumes, but does not establish, the reliability and validity of the behavioral ratings, although they were made by a single ward attendant and are the crucial data. Since the attendant knew which patients were getting special treatment, his own biases could have influenced the results in either way. For these reasons, the results offer no clear support of the hypothesis that group therapy of these types brings about clinical improvement in hospitalized schizophrenics. Perhaps the time was too short, but there was not much to show for fifty hours of treatment.

The Institute for Juvenile Research in Illinois is a child guidance clinic that accepts a substantial number of children annually for treatment by psychiatrists, psychologists, and social workers. Levitt et al. undertook its evaluation (Levitt, Beiser, & Robertson, 1959). The authors discussed the various kinds of controls that could be used and the problems involved. Aware that a defector group could be a biased one, they settled for a group composed of those who had been accepted for treatment but had never availed themselves of it. To survey the ten-year period from 1944 to 1954, 579 treated (at least five one-hour sessions for at least one family member) and 427 controls were drawn randomly. The final study sample was reduced to 237 Es and 93 Cs who could be located. The total sample averaged 5.4 years since closing and had not had treatment since then. Some twenty-six comprehensive follow-up variables were investigated, including psychological tests, parents' evaluation of child, child's own statements, interviewers' judgments, and objective facts. Of the twenty-six variables, nine favored the treated group and sixteen the untreated, but only two of the differences were significant. They were wisely discounted as chance phenomena in an array of this number. This led the experimenters to reconsider the definition of psychotherapy as five or more interviews and to reanalyze the data with cases that had a minimum of ten interviews. This eliminated forty-five experimental Ss. The average number of treatment interviews was twenty-six. Now there were no significant differences on any of the variables, including those that had discriminated earlier. The child guidance clinic emerges as very ineffective indeed. The authors declined to generalize the findings to all child guidance clinics and cautioned against indicting the child guidance movement. The main grounds for caution were that the conditions of therapy were less than optimal. In fact, 35.5 per cent of the treatment was done by students and 13.5 per cent by individuals with a year or less experience. Thirty-four per cent of the patients had to change therapists at least once. Social workers did 76.5 per cent of the treatment of child patients, psychiatrists 15 per cent, and psychologists 8 per cent. Nearly 87 per cent of all parents were treated by social workers. Altogether, only one-third of the therapy was done by therapists with more than three years of experience. If experience and professional discipline were considered to be related to outcome, one wonders why they were not treated as variables. The data were available. It seems to us that the main defense of the clinic lies in the utilization of a poor control group, defectors. If defectors have a poorer prognosis than those who enter treatment, the situation is even bleaker. But if a significant number dropped out before ever starting treatment because of the solution of a minor situational problem, the picture would be quite different. Again, there is no substitute for an appropriate control group.

Walker and Kelley (1960) reported an initial study and three-year follow-up of the effects of short-term psychotherapy upon eighty-two schizophrenic patients in treatment at the Brockton Veterans Administration Hospital, Massachusetts. The design consisted of comparing the progress of forty-four newly admitted patients, who received formal short-term psychotherapy within the first six months of their admission, with thirty-eight other patients who received little formal psychotherapy. Both groups were in the same active treatment-oriented setting. Experimental patients received a median of seventeen hours of therapy (range 4 to 131) in contrast to a median of 1.5 hours for the controls. The groups were equivalent on a large number of variables at the time of admission except for the fact that the psychotherapy group had much less prior hospitalization; were, on the average, three years younger; and were rated slightly less withdrawn and somewhat more cooperative than the controls. Since the patients were neither matched on these critical variables nor randomly assigned to the experimental and control groups, the latter did not constitute a true control group. The research began with a bias seemingly in favor of the treatment group.

The criteria for improvement were symptom improvement, ward behavior, discharge from the hospital, and posthospital adjustment ninety days after discharge. On only one of these indices of improvement was there any difference. By the end of six months 63 per cent of the controls and 36 per cent of the psychotherapy patients had been discharged. The treated patients remained hospitalized for approximately three months longer than the controls. By the end of a year, 68 per cent of the Es and 79 per cent of the Cs had been released. A three-year follow-up revealed comparable readmission rates, 73 per cent for the Es, 60 per cent for the Cs (Walker & Kelley, 1963). The duration of stay in the community was essentially the same for both groups, a median of thirty-one months for the Es and twenty-nine months for the Cs. The same proportion of both groups was rated as comparatively symptom free on the PEP Symptom Rating Scale, and employment was comparable. Community adjustment, as appraised by the Report of Social Adjustment Scale (ROSA), was practically identical. The amount of therapy after discharge was negligible for both groups and there was no significant difference in medication. These related studies certainly lend no support to the hypothesis that formal short-term therapy is efficacious with hospitalized schizophrenics.

Using an own-control design, Cartwright and Vogel (1960) compared changes in twenty-two psychoneurotic patients at the University of Chicago Counseling Center during matched periods of therapy and no therapy. Therapy, averaging 33.4 hours, was conducted by ten experienced and nine inexperienced client-centered therapists. Patients were tested at the time of application (prewait), just prior to beginning therapy (pretherapy), at a point equal in time to the time between the first two occasions (in-therapy), and after the completion of treatment (posttherapy). The measures so repeated were the Dymond Q-Adjustment score derived from the Butler-Haigh Q-Sort and a mental health rating derived from the TAT. For both measures, t-tests between the mean change score from prewait to pretherapy (no-therapy period), and pretherapy to in-therapy (therapy period), were conducted. Change was calculated without regard to direction. The difference in change of Q-Adjustment score between the therapy and no-therapy periods was reported as significant "at about" the $p = .05$ level, with a $t = 1.925$. For the TAT mental health rating it was not significant. It was concluded that therapy affects adjustment based upon self-description whereas equal waiting time does not. The first thing to be noticed about these results is that a $t = 1.925$ is simply not significant at the $p = .05$ level. For twenty-one degrees of freedom a $t = 2.08$ is required. If we go to the trouble of estimating confidence levels by statistical devices, they should be reported accurately. The author or the reader can feel free to decide how stringent he wishes to be before placing his personal confidence in the results, but he needs the actual calculated p value as a guide. Reports of significance "at about" a particular level are apt to be misleading. Further, the authors were treating change *regardless of direction* although it is obvious that concern with positive benefits is implicit in any hypothesis about the effects of psychotherapy. It is true that some patients may improve and some get worse, but increased variablility with therapy was not the issue. The stated purpose of the experiment was "to help clarify the argument that therapy does have some special effectiveness with psychoneurotic patients . . ." (p. 121). When *direction* is examined, it can be seen that thirteen subjects improved in therapy while nine stayed the same or became worse as measured by the Q-score. For the TAT measure, nine improved and thirteen did not. All told, twenty-two measures improved on the Q-scale and twelve out of twenty-two on the TAT, for a combination of twenty-three measures improving, twenty-one not. This directional comparison, which the authors did not make, shows almost identical 50-50 improvement for both wait and in-therapy periods.

The length of the wait (long wait or short wait) was studied by chi-square in relation to direction of change. Direction of change on the Q-sort was found to be unrelated to length of the waiting period, but greater waiting time was reported as significantly related to more positive change on the TAT, contrary to one of the stated hypotheses. The reported chi-square of 4.46 was based on quite small frequencies that were not corrected for continuity. When Yates' correction is applied, it can be seen that the chi-square is reduced to 2.82, which is not statistically significant. Similarly, a reported increase in low scorers and decline of high scorers on the TAT that yielded a chi-square of 4.70 reduces to a nonsignificant chi-square of 3.00 if Yates' correction is applied. This is consistent with a simple regression toward the mean phenomenon. In summary, there appears to be no consistent support for any of the four hypotheses of this research. The closest thing to a positive finding was the equivocal support for the superiority of experienced over inexperienced therapists. If these findings as evaluated are correct, it does not make much difference if a patient waits for a long or short time for treatment or never gets treated at all, except perhaps if he is seen by an experienced therapist. It would seem almost self-evident, however, that if the efficacy of psychotherapy is to be tested, the therapists *must* be experienced for the process to have a fair test. In this study, one therapist who had treated but six cases was placed in the experienced group. The results include the work of nine raw beginners with a mean experience of one case. In addition to these problems, the use of waiting-list controls should be considered. It could be argued that the therapeutic process actually began at the time of the initial interview. The mere fact that applicants had taken the step of seeking help and had been interviewed, examined, and promised treatment may have had a sufficient effect upon some of the patients to obscure the effects of psychotherapy itself. The prologue can be an important part of the play. All things considered, it does not seem that this study constitutes a fair test of the efficacy of psychotherapy.

Dynamically oriented group psychotherapy was evaluated on servicemen and wives seen as outpatients at a US Air Force Hospital (Karson & Wiedershine, 1961). A group of ten male enlisted men who remained in treatment for six months was compared with ten who dropped out within the first few weeks. None had had previous therapy. In addition, a group of officers' wives who had already been in therapy for a year before the start of the study were compared with a comparable group who had just begun. A fifth group, comprised of wives of noncommissioned officers, was compared with the group of officers' wives also just beginning therapy to study the effect of different educational and socioeconomic levels upon outcome. All Ss were tested with the Sixteen Personality Factor Questionnaire, were seen in group therapy by an experienced group therapist once a week for six months, and were then retested. Dropouts were recalled for the second testing. After six months of therapy, no significant gains were shown by the remainers over the terminators, but both displayed some improvement. Comparison of the two officer wives' groups showed little gain that could not be attributed to chance. There were somewhat more net gains shown in the thirteenth to nineteenth month in the group treated over the year and one-half period, but certainly nothing sweeping or dramatic. The outstanding finding was a complete absence of any significant reduction in anxiety in any of the groups. The authors do not feel that this can be attributed to lack of sensitivity in what they consider to be a well-validated instrument for measuring anxiety. The only finding of possible significance seen in several of the groups was an increase in introversion during the early phases of therapy followed later by a reduction. In assessing therapy, terminators are not a good control group. A true test of efficacy would require an untreated control group. None of the groups who remained in treatment, however, had much to show for it after six months. There was some evidence that a longer period in therapy produced more gains, but lacking an initial test from the beginning of treatment of those in treatment for eighteen months, we cannot even be sure of that.

Barendregt et al., at the University of Amsterdam, attempted to assess and compare the relative outcomes of psychoanalysis and nonanalytic psychotherapy with each other and with no treatment (Barendregt, Bastiaans, & Vermeul-Van Mullem, 1961). An original sample of 315 patients was reduced by attrition to 200, forty-seven of whom received psychoanalysis and forty-nine psychotherapy of any kind other than psychoanalysis. Controls were seventy-four patients who remained untreated. More subjects originally assigned to the untreated group were lost to the sample than from the other two groups. Patients were not randomly assigned to treatments, but were, in fact, placed on a highly selective basis. No form of therapy was advised for some of the controls, and others were placed on a waiting list for psychoanalysis. Those who were still waiting two and one-half years later were also included in the control group. This kind of sampling alone would make any results difficult to assess. In addition, however, most of the therapy patients were treated by therapists with very little experience. For many these were a first or second case. A series of eight criterion measures were given initially and patients were retested after approximately two and one-half years. At that time, few of the psychoanalyses were completed.

Measures included a ten-point self-rating scale of "sense of well-being" given at the time of the second testing (the patients were asked how they would have rated themselves at the time of the first testing—a dubious dependence on long-term recall), Wechsler-Bellevue Verbal IQ, neuroticism, lie score and introversion-extraversion as measured by the Two Part Personality Measure, TAT changes as measured by both the Atkinson and Dymond systems of scoring, and the Rorschach with specific predictions made from twelve signs for each subject from his initial record. Six of the eight predictions failed to be borne out at all. The lie score, taken as a measure of self-knowledge, dropped for the therapy groups as predicted, and there were some not entirely firm findings on the TAT (Atkinson scoring). Because of the many design defects of which the authors were well aware, this study cannot be considered as offering reliable evidence on the question.

Feder (1962) investigated the effects of short-term group therapy with newly admitted delinquent adolescent boys at the New Jersey Diagnostic Center. Eighty boys were assigned to two experimental and two control groups of twenty each. Each therapy group had a different leader, participation was voluntary, and the groups were open-ended. One control group had no contacts with the staff beyond about ten sessions with various staff members over an eight-week period for diagnostic purposes. A second control group met with the experimenter for first-aid instruction under conditions otherwise identical with those for the therapy groups. Subjects were administered the Mooney Problem Check List and a Therapeutic Readiness Q-Sort initially and eight weeks (sixteen therapy sessions) later. On the unvalidated Q-sort, which was devised for this study, analysis of covariance revealed greater gains by the experimental subjects. Switching for no apparent reason to a far less precise mode of data analysis, analysis of variance of change scores, the author found differences favoring the experimental group on the Mooney Problem Check List. More critically, there were no differences in institutional adjustment. Neither ward adjustment, sick call, nor disciplinary incidents differed among the groups. Therefore, two months of group therapy was not successful in modifying aggressive and antisocial behavior patterns, but Feder was optimistic about its utility in readying the boys for additional therapy. On the whole, the study must be considered as yielding primarily null results.

Satz and Baraff (1962) undertook an experiment to ascertain whether self-ideal Q-sort discrepancies are characteristic of poor psychological adjustment and self-organization and could be reduced by client-centered therapy. Working with nonchronic psychotics with a mean age of thirty-five, who had been in the South Florida State Hospital for an average of twelve days, they randomly divided their small sample of sixteen patients into three groups. The experimental-experimental group ($N = 4$) received thirteen hours a week of occupational therapy plus two hours a week of group therapy for ten weeks. Experimental-controls ($N = 4$) had the same routine except for the group therapy. The controls ($N = 8$) received neither. They were, in fact, denied the regular occupational therapy classes that were usually held. The average pretherapy self-ideal correlation, in line with expectations, was low ($r = .11$). Half of the experimental-experimental group increased, half decreased in congruence. For the combined experimental groups of eight subjects, therefore, only three improved, in contrast to six of the untreated controls. There was an overall nonsignificant increase in congruence for the controls. The sample was quite small, but the trends were clearly opposite in direction to the hypothesis and did not show the hypothesized benefits of client-centered group therapy.

7

Evaluation of Therapeutic Programs and Overview of Outcome Research

EVALUATION OF THERAPEUTIC PROGRAMS

A distinction must be made between individual or group therapy and therapeutic programs. Therapeutic programs are systematic and extensive efforts to modify the behavior of groups of patients, usually in an institutional setting and usually by means of a combinative approach that utilizes the multiple activity resources and personnel of the institution rather than a single therapist. These programs have been variously described as total push, resocialization, intensive group living, remotivation, heightened patient-staff interaction, therapeutic atmosphere, milieu therapy, and by a variety of other *ad hoc* designations. They have in common intensive activity with patients, often special living arrangements, innovative group structures, and a restructuring of staff attitudes, patient status, and responsibilities, often combined with more traditional group and individual psychotherapy. Some have a special therapeutic rationale that determines their particular form, others an ingenious format in search of a rationale.

Most inpatient programs are designed for chronic regressed patients, mainly schizophrenics. The outpatient programs, starting where they leave off, are generally aftercare programs designed to minimize recidivism and to facilitate community readjustment. Experiments evaluating therapeutic programs have been reviewed in detail (Meltzoff & Blumenthal, 1966). Reference is made to this source for description and critical evaluation of these studies. Table 2 summarizes twenty-one inpatient and four outpatient program results.

Although design flaws make appraisal of some of the studies difficult, it is possible to classify most of them by the scheme previously

Table 2. Therapeutic Programs

AUTHOR	SUBJECTS	TYPE OF PROGRAM	RESULTS
Yoder (1938)	24 chronic schizophrenics, 24 matched controls	Total push for Es; ordinary state hospital treatment for Cs	83% of Es rated improved, 42% of Cs after one year. Results significant for males, not for females.
Sines, Lucero, & Kamman (1952)	54 chronic schizophrenics, 43 matched controls	Total push vs. custodial treatment	Es showed significant increase in Fergus Falls Behavior ratings, Cs did not. Cross-validation failed to replicate results. Males held their gains at one year follow-up, females regressed to pretreatment levels.
Galioni, Adams, & Tallman (1953)	200 chronic mental patients, 200 controls	Total push vs. custodial treatment	After 18 months 18% of Es and 5% of Cs were discharged. Almost three times as many visits to relatives by Es. Rating of improved on Psychiatric Rating Scale in 55% of Es, 33% of Cs. Two years later Cs came abreast of Es in discharges.
Miller & Clancy (1952) Miller, Clancy, & Cumming (1953)	100 hospitalized mental patients, 10 controls	Total push vs. usual hospital treatment	Rating scales and controls were dropped after 8 weeks of 6-month program. Hence results difficult to assess.
Bennett & Robertson (1955)	10 male chronic schizophrenics, 10 controls	Habit training and systematically planned schedule of individual and social activities vs. routine hospital treatment	Es improved after one year on information test, interview behavior, and personal appearance but reverted by end of follow-up; Cs deteriorated in personal appearance.

Baker & Thorpe (1956)	3 groups of 16 patients each	One group received habit training plus exercise, occupational, and social activities; the second had ECT only; the third minimal custodial treatment for 16 weeks	Habit training group showed improvement on 6 of 13 adjustment scales, ECT group on one, custodial group on none. Findings in doubt because of design, sampling, and criterion measure issues.
Merry (1956)	39 female chronic schizophrenics, own-control	Habit training for assaultiveness and bed-wetting	Bed-wetting and assaultiveness incidents fell off as treatment was introduced following baseline period, but assaultiveness later increased again.
May & Robertson (1960)	10 chronic schizophrenics, 10 matched controls	Habit training program, 6 months	No significant differences between groups on Fergus Falls BRS, appearance, performance tasks, and social behavior.
Pace (1957)	33 male chronic schizophrenics; own-control, 4-month baseline	Traditional treatment vs. milieu therapy, 10 months	Increase in social verbal interaction and in social and nonsocial activity. Move towards norm on MSRPP and toward open wards.
Henderson (1960)	18 severely regressed schizophrenic males, 14 matched controls	Activity program vs. usual hospital treatment for one year	One year differences on DAP, Minimum Social Behavior scale, VIBS, and two MSRPP Scales. Data analysis open to question, leaving results in doubt.
Schnore (1961)	One year follow-up of 14 of the 18 Ss in Henderson's study	Es had continued in modified activity program	Improvement shown, but data analysis subject to same reservations.

Table 2. Therapeutic Programs (Continued)

AUTHOR	SUBJECTS	TYPE OF PROGRAM	RESULTS
Fairweather et al. (1960) Fairweather & Simon (1963)	96 hospitalized males, of whom 32 were neurotic, 32 long-term, and 32 short-term psychotics Random assignment to four groups	(1) individual work assignment departure planning (control); (2) individual therapy and work assignment; (3) group therapy, work assignment, and departure planning; (4) group living therapy, work assignment, and departure planning	Significantly larger variance for the 3 therapy groups. Nonpsychotics and short-term psychotics showed adaptive changes in these groups, but long-term psychotics showed maladaptive changes. 18-month follow-up (1963). No difference in community adjustment. Differences between short- and long-term psychotics held. Correlation between 6- and 18-month follow-up high. First 6 months crucial.
Brandon (1961)	72 Es and 62 Cs. Hospitalized, two-thirds schizophrenics	Resocialization vs. regular hospital treatment, 8–16 weeks. Es received after-care for additional year after discharge, Cs minimal follow-up	Significantly higher social adjustment scale rating for Es after treatment and one year later.
Sanders et al. (1962)	10 hospitalized schizophrenics of both sexes in each of 3 treatment groups; 13 equivalent controls	3 types of programs vs. standard hospital treatment: (1) therapeutic community, (2) core interaction program: therapeutic community plus stable activity groups and training in social behaviors and industrial therapy, (3) all of above features plus group therapy and patient government	Significant increase in social participation scores for intensive and core interaction programs. Differences not significant on psychiatric status, motivation, discharge, support on release. Data analysis questionable.

Williams et al. (1962)	26 hospitalized chronic schizophrenics, 26 random controls	Intensive group living, OT, RT, music therapy, group therapy, psychodrama, vs. conventional hospital treatment	42 scores from tests, rating scales, and self-ratings; Es showed more positive gains on 6, Cs on 3; no difference on remainder.
Adams et al. (1962)	78 male chronic schizophrenics and a control group not described	Remotivation, habit training, patient government, paid work, OT, music therapy, RT, activities, 12 weeks	Improvement reported on multiple criteria, but no control data presented.
Appleby (1963)	53 female chronic schizophrenics, 30 randomly assigned to 3 treatment programs and 23 to control	(1) group living conducted by nursing assistant; (2) total push and group therapy, large staff involvement; (3) individual planning with emphasis on management of sexual and aggressive drives; (4) control: usual hospital treatment. Similar to (3) but less intensive	3 treatment groups improved more than controls over one year on Hospital Adjustment Scale and Fergus Falls BRS, but did not vary among themselves. On MSRPP all treatment groups improved. Program (1) produced change at slowest rate of the three treatment groups.
Tourney et al. (1960)	20 male and female chronic schizophrenics, 20 matched controls	Resocialization, OT, patient government, group therapy vs. conventional hospital treatment	Male Es only showed improvement on HAS at end of program and 20 months later. Discharge rate higher among Es but even at 20 months. Ratings of doubtful objectivity and reliability.

Table 2. Therapeutic Programs (Continued)

AUTHOR	SUBJECTS	TYPE OF PROGRAM	RESULTS
Fairweather (1964)	195 psychotic and nonpsychotic hospitalized patients randomly assigned to 4 groups	Small group living and group responsibility; patients moved through 4-step program. Privileges contingent upon performance. Comparison with traditional treatment. 6 months treatment, 6-months in-community follow-up.	Es showed significantly higher rates of conversation, social, and motor activity. Greater acknowledgment of having been helped. Opinions about mental illness did not change. Less time in treatment. Follow-up showed more employed, more with friends and better able to communicate with others. No relation between in-hospital and community adjustment.
Johnson & Lee (1965)	236 female chronic schizophrenics, half matched with controls	Intensive vocational rehabilitation program, 30 months. Privileges contingent on work. Cs in activity programs, but not systematic or intensive	Es improved on MSRPP, but not significantly; Cs declined. Mean difference significant. 31% of Es stayed out of hospital for 6 or more months compared to 17% of Cs. No difference in community adjustment.
Spear (1960)	9 chronic schizophrenics, 9 random controls	Group living, group therapy, art therapy vs. ECT, insulin, drugs, and usual hospital treatment. 6 weeks	No differences in discharge rates or clinical status. On FFBRS the only significant finding favored Cs on ECT. Remainder of Cs deteriorated; Es stayed at same level. Small N, period of treatment short, therapist inexperienced.

Kris (1964)	71 outpatient Es, 70 hospitalized Cs	Day hospital	Median treatment time for discharge of Es 7 weeks, Cs 9 months. No difference in subsequent treatment, employment, social, or community adjustment. As much accomplished in shorter time.
Beard et al. (1963) Fisher (1966)	55 mental patients discharged from hospital	Group-oriented social and recreational program, 2-year follow-up	Rehospitalization rates lower for Es at 8 time points. 64% for Cs and 46% for Es after 2 years. Later report (1966) on 251 Es and 81 Cs: 44.2% of Es rehospitalized in 2 years, 60.5% of Cs. Es better employment.
Vitale & Steinbach (1965)	29 outpatients vs. 23 retrospective controls at a higher level of adjustment	Day Treatment Center vs. MHC. 6 months	17% Es, 26% Cs rehospitalized in 6 months. Patients not comparable to start with.
Meltzoff & Blumenthal (1966)	33 male chronic schizophrenics, 36 randomly assigned Cs	Day Treatment Center vs. conventional outpatient treatment. 18 months	64% Cs vs. 30% Es rehospitalized in 18 months. Job starts 2:1 in favor of Es. Improved adjustment on most adjustment rating variables for Es compared with Cs, and for all 8 variables for initially most poorly adjusted Ss.

used. Among the adequate studies, 62 per cent yield major positive results, 23 per cent minor positive results, and 15 per cent null or negative ones. The corresponding percentages for the more doubtful investigations are 30 per cent, 60 per cent, and 10 per cent. Combined, 87 per cent yield positive results and 13 per cent null or negative, but the proportion of questionable studies is higher than it is for evaluations of individual and group psychotherapy.

Positive results in several of the evaluations were tempered by the fact that the gains of the experimental group were either temporary or later matched by advances in the control group (Galioni, Adams, & Tallman, 1953; Bennett & Robertson, 1955; Merry, 1956). In others, the positive results held for male but not for female patients (Yoder, 1938; Sines, Lucero, & Kamman, 1952; Tourney, Senf, Dunham, Glen, & Gottlieb, 1960). Nevertheless, there is not much question that some of these programs represent a measurable advance over custodial care. Specific outcomes aside, some of the studies not only illustrate that controlled research to evaluate therapeutic programs can be done, but also show that it has been done; it is to be hoped that such research will set a trend for evaluations to keep pace with innovations.

OVERVIEW OF OUTCOME RESEARCH

Success and Goals. It is difficult to attempt to make a value judgment about the *success* of psychotherapy. Success is rarely an absolute even when it can be measured in concrete quantities. It is necessary to talk of *perceived* success, for one man's success is another man's failure. The perception of success is based in part upon goals or levels of aspiration. Success in therapy is especially open to subjective evaluation. Opinions about success held by the therapist are apt to differ from those held by the patient for several reasons. One is that they may not share the same goals. If one has the goal of personality reconstruction and the other desires stabilization at little higher than the entry level of adjustment, both will perceive success if reconstruction is achieved. If only supportive goals are reached, however, one is bound to see failure. Despite their central position, goals of therapy have received scant attention from researchers.

Michaux and Lorr (1961) developed a schema for classifying therapist goals as reconstructive (personality change with insight), supportive (maintaining or strengthening current adjustment), and not classifiable. Therapist statements were classified by four psychologists working independently, and data from ninety-two cases were used. Severity of illness was rated by the therapist on an aggregate of seven scales. At the end of four months of therapy the therapist filled out a ninety-two item checklist of changes covering the interview relationship, positive adjustment gains, and symptom reduction. Reconstructive goals were less frequent in patients seen twice a week and more frequent in those seen biweekly than expected. The greater the rated severity of illness, the more likely was a supportive goal. Goals of psychiatrists, psychologists, and social workers did not differ from each other. Changes after four months were not significantly related to goal type.

In a sequel to this study, McNair and Lorr (1964b) obtained responses to a thirty-item Goal Statement Inventory (GSI) from 259 therapists from forty-four Veterans Administration clinics in relation to 523 of their patients. The therapists included sixty-seven psychiatrists, 103 psychologists, and ninety-five social workers, averaging ten years of therapy experience. The patients were 47 per cent neurotic, 28 per cent psychotic, and 25 per cent personality or psychophysiological disorders. The thirty goals represented a comprehensive list and encompassed those of the reconstructive, supportive, and relationship types. The items were factor analyzed and the analysis revealed that Michaux and Lorr's qualitative goal schema did not fit simple structure criteria and required reconceptualization. Three factors were isolated. Factor I was seen to correspond closely to the reconstructive goal of Michaux and Lorr and represented the conventional goals of intensive therapy with neurotics. Factor II was a stabilization factor representing goals of stabilizing current patterns and preventing worsening. These two sets of goals are incompatible, with a correlation of $r = -.27$. Factor III dealt with situational adjustment goals stressing adjustment in various contemporary life situations. The latter two factors were moderately related and were thought possibly to be components of a second-order supportive factor. Experience (Mensh & Watson, 1950; Anthony, 1967), orientation (Strupp, 1958b), professional discipline (Strupp, 1958a), and therapist personality (Harway, 1959) may be related to therapeutic goals set.

The goals of therapy are central not only to patients' and therapists' perceptions of success but also to the interpretation of the meaningfulness of research findings. In the studies that have been reviewed it can be seen that researchers have usually tested for and, more often than not, found positive changes exceeding mere stabilization at entry levels. At the other goal pole, they have generally by-passed the problem of developing criteria to measure the achievement of such abstract and hard-to-define global goals as personality reconstruction and reorganization. Although therapists are not required to be specific, researchers are, since they have to select distinct and measurable criteria. More typically, therefore, existing research has utilized tangible and definable criteria that have to do with decrease in signs and symptoms, improvement in specified behaviors, or improved adjustment in particularized life situations. These may either be taken at face value or considered to reflect, imply, or be the overt manifestations of, a degree of personality reorganization. Researchers' criteria do not always coincide with patients' or therapists' goals.

Summary of Outcome Research. The "flight into process" that has been alleged to have taken place is not borne out by the facts. On the contrary, every five-year period since 1950 has brought a steadily *increasing* number of outcome studies. From every point of view (design, sampling, criteria, nature of controls, data analysis), the quality of the research has improved along with the quantity. The ratio of adequate to questionable studies before 1960 was 18 to 25; since 1960 the ratio has been 39 to 19 in favor of adequate studies (research on therapeutic programs is not included in this summation). We have reviewed 101 separate investigations exclusive of twenty-five research evaluations of therapeutic programs. Of these, 80 per cent yielded positive results and 20 per cent null or negative results (Table 3). Altogether, 56 per cent were considered sufficiently adequate in design and execution for valid conclusions to be drawn, and 44 per cent were doubtful. Among the adequate studies, 84 per cent showed positive effects of psychotherapy that were statistically significant. Similarly, 75 per cent of the questionable studies reported significant benefits. Among the adequate studies, 54 per cent showed effects that can be considered major, central, or multiple; 30 per cent minor, restricted, or limited; and 16 per cent null or negative. Among those studies subject to a greater degree of reservation, 23 per cent showed major benefits, 52 per cent minor, and 25 per cent yielded null or negative results.

Table 3. Summary of Outcome Research

	ADEQUATE STUDIES	QUESTIONABLE STUDIES	TOTAL
Positive	48	33	81
Null	9	11	20
Total	57	44	101

About one-half of the adequate studies that produced null results were failures of verbal therapies to bring about improvement in chronic schizophrenic patients. Another one-third were failures with delinquency prevention, drug addiction, and enuresis. In one-third of the studies that did not yield positive results with verbal therapy, patients in comparison groups who received other forms of therapy did respond more favorably than untreated controls.

The weight of experimental evidence is sufficient to enable us to reject the null hypothesis. Far more often than not, psychotherapy of a wide variety of types and with a broad range of disorders has been demonstrated under controlled conditions to be accompanied by positive changes in adjustment that significantly exceed those that can be accounted for by the passage of time alone. The therapists represent a cross-section of those who do therapy in the various settings in which the research has been done. As a group, they were not selected for their outstanding ability. Many were indeed quite inexperienced. This does not imply that psychotherapy of any type, when applied by anyone to any given individual, can be expected to be a success. The accumulated evidence that enables us to reject the null hypothesis does not enable us to make any statement about the degree of effectiveness of psychotherapy, expectancy rates, or whether or not it is worthwhile.

The fact that the conclusions from our evaluation are at odds with those that have been drawn by others requires some reconciliation or explanation. First of all, there has been a noticeable lack of comprehensive critical reviews of controlled outcome research. Published conclusions about the state of our knowledge have obviously not come from a careful weighing of the available evidence. Most of them appear to be echoes of Eysenck's (1952, 1960, 1965) inadequate surveys. A more expanded coverage is that of Truax and Carkhuff (1967), even though they readily acknowledge that it is not exhaustive. After examining the literature they state, "Thus the weight of the evidence, involving very large numbers of clients or therapists, suggests that the average effects of therapeutic intervention (with the average therapist or counselor) are approximately equivalent to the random effects of normal living without treatment . . ." (p. 12). They also maintain that "no responsible writer has ever reviewed the evidence of outcome studies and concluded that counseling and psychotherapy as usually practiced have an average benefit beyond that seen in comparable control groups" (p. 13), and, "If all the studies on outcome were to be averaged on the basis of the number of clients involved, it is clear that the overall result would be close to zero effect beyond that observed in comparable clients not receiving counseling or psychotherapy" (p. 14).

What accounts for the difference in our conclusions? Assuming a relative freedom from bias for or against psychotherapy, two reviewers can arrive at different conclusions if they have been examining different sets of evidence or if they do not agree on the probative strength of each of the various studies that contribute to the total body of evidence. There is, first of all, a difference in the scope of the material assessed. Truax and Carkhuff examined a total of thirty-seven studies that utilized some kind of a control group (uncontrolled studies that they cited are excluded). Our conclusions are based upon 101 studies of individual or group therapy and an additional twenty-five evaluations of therapeutic programs. In Truax and Carkhuff's review five of the nineteen null studies had to do largely with educational counseling. These were not included in our review of psychotherapy. Three others (Gliedman et al., 1958; Frank et al., 1959; and Poser, 1966) were presented as negative evidence even though they really were not controlled studies of the efficacy of psychotherapy. The study by Gliedman et al. examined the effects of two weeks of an inert drug placebo on patients who had completed six months of treatment some eighteen months or more earlier (Gliedman, Nash, Imber, Stone, & Frank, 1958). It was observed that the discomfort level of the patients dropped after administration of the placebo just as it had after psychotherapy. The fact that patients improved with psychotherapy, and at a later date improved yet more with a placebo, cannot be used as evidence against the efficacy of psychotherapy. Indeed, the investigators state, "It is not maintained that the help derived by these patients was profound, though it may have been, or that it is as good or better than would have been achieved with intensive psychotherapy. Certainly, the scanty placebo follow-up results indicate that the effects may not be maintained. They do indicate that psychotherapeutic approaches and placebo approaches in this clinic share something in common . . ." (p. 349). Despite this sober statement, Truax and Carkhuff state, "Thus, again, with carefully controlled evaluation of outcome, psychotherapy proved ineffective" (p. 8). The Frank et al. study compared individual therapy and group therapy with minimal contact therapy. All treated patients combined showed a significant drop in discomfort level, and those in individual and group therapy revealed significantly greater improvement in social effectiveness than those receiving minimal contact. Treated patients were compared with early dropouts, but without an untreated control group no definite conclusions about therapeutic efficacy can be drawn. Poser's study compared results achieved by trained and untrained therapists, but also did not include an untreated control group and presents no evidence either for or against therapeutic efficacy.

Further studies considered as evidence for the negative case were those by Teuber and Powers (1953), Rogers and Dymond (1954), Cartwright and Vogel (1960), Anker and Walsh (1961), Walker and Kelley (1960), Levitt, Beiser, and Robertson (1959), Barendregt,

Bastiaans, and Vermeul-Van Mullem (1961), May and Tuma (1964), and a study by Truax and Carkhuff. According to our evaluation (which included all but the last of these studies), the only one that presents adequate evidence in support of the hypothesis that psychotherapy may be ineffective is that of May and Tuma, and that was of treatment of schizophrenics under the supervision of psychoanalysts. Of the eighteen studies that support therapy effectiveness, two are concerned with educational counseling of college students. Of the remaining sixteen, we would consider seven to be controlled outcome studies of sufficiently adequate quality to provide good evidence of positive effects: Shlien, Mosak, and Dreikurs (1962), Shouksmith and Taylor (1964), Lazarus (1961), Paul (1966), Paul and Shannon (1966), Lang, Lazovik, and Reynolds (1965), and Ends and Page (1957).

Although these studies, both positive and null, represent a meager sampling of the experimental literature available for evaluation, from them alone we still arrive at an overall evaluation opposite of Truax and Carkhuff's. The disagreement is obviously due to a difference in our appraisal of the studies that comprise the "evidence." Most of the studies seen by Truax and Carkhuff as presenting proof of the ineffectiveness of psychotherapy fail to meet acceptable standards of evidence from our point of view. We have reviewed these studies and have in each instance given the reasons why we believe this to be the case. Nor do we agree entirely on the evidence in favor of positive effects. As we have seen, there is congruence on only seven of eighteen studies. If we were to limit ourselves, then, to the studies selected by Truax and Carkhuff, we would find the positive evidence outweighing the null seven to one. They, however, found nineteen controlled studies claiming that treated patients do not improve more than controls, and eighteen claiming that they do. Even if we were to accept their appraisal this would hardly constitute "overwhelming" support of the ineffectiveness of psychotherapy.

In short, reviews of the literature that have concluded that psychotherapy has, on the average, no demonstrable effect are based upon an incomplete survey of the existing body of research and an insufficiently stringent appraisal of the data. We have encountered no comprehensive review of controlled research on the effects of psychotherapy that has led convincingly to a conclusion in support of the null hypothesis. On the contrary, controlled research has been notably successful in demonstrating significantly more behavioral change in treated patients than in untreated controls. In general, the better the quality of the research, the more positive the results obtained.

8

Therapeutic Method as an Outcome Variable

Research studies of the effectiveness of psychotherapy were pooled for review purposes without attention to the type of therapy employed. There are two streams of research in comparative psychotherapy that compare and contrast the outcome obtained with different approaches. One focuses on differences between individual and group therapy, and the other on differences among various "schools" of psychotherapy. Examination of these data will provide some enlightenment on the justification for using the generic term "psychotherapy" in the first place and show what progress has been made toward determining what specific types of therapy are most effective with which patients.

INDIVIDUAL VS. GROUP PSYCHOTHERAPY

One major way of classifying psychotherapy uses the categories individual, group, or a combination of the two. Born as an administrative expedient, group therapy quickly acquired a distinctive rationale, a set of specialized techniques, a dedicated cohort of theorists and practitioners, and more than its share of evaluators. Without regard to therapeutic technique, therapist variables, or temporal or patient variables, a simple summation of adequately controlled studies we have reviewed shows roughly 80 per cent of investigations to yield primarily positive results with individual and group therapy alike. This kind of crude comparison does not necessarily have any validity. There are a handful of research projects, however, that make direct comparisons of outcome achieved with these two approaches. Several of these studies are of hospitalized adult patients; others deal with adult outpatients or with children. Some compare individual therapy to group therapy; others compare either one to a combination of the other two.

In the Barron and Leary (1955) study, eighty-five subjects received group therapy and forty-two individual therapy. We are not sure that the subjects were equivalent to start with, although they are described as subsamples drawn from the same psychoneurotic population. Both treatment groups decreased significantly on the MMPI scales of Depression, Hypochondriasis, and Lie scores and increased in Ego-Strength. The group therapy patients decreased on Paranoia and Psychasthenia, whereas those in individual therapy rose on the K Scale. In general, similarities between the two treatment effects were greater than the differences. The study by Frank et al. of fifty-four adults with psychoneurosis or personality disorder featured random assignment of patients to individual or group therapy (Frank, Gliedman, Imber, Stone, & Nash, 1959). Both were conducted by second-year resident psychiatrists for at least six months. Changes on the Discomfort Scale and Social Ineffectiveness Scale were found to be independent of the type of treatment received.

A British study conducted at Belmont Hospital, Sutton, Surrey, examined the comparative effectiveness of the two approaches on patients of varied diagnoses (Thorley & Craske, 1950). The largest categories were anxiety states and depression. Patients were assigned in rotation, with one therapist doing all of the group therapy and the other limiting himself to the individual approach. Group therapy was described as repressive, inspirational, and educational, and individual therapy as non-analytic. Follow-up questionnaires sent to the patients three months after discharge covered the areas of general health, symptoms, further treatment received, and work. The interpretation of results was complicated by the fact that some patients in both therapies received insulin coma, ECT, and other somatic therapies. With these included, half the patients in individual and half in group therapy were judged as achieving favorable outcome; for the rest of the patients, outcome was judged as unfavorable. In a re-examination of the data, sixty-seven patients of the original 216 were found who had group therapy or individual therapy with no somatic therapies (all had occupational, recreational, and educational therapies and social work services). With this reduced sample, 57 per cent were judged to have responded favorably to group and 62 per cent to individual therapy. It was concluded that there was no difference in the effectiveness of the two approaches. It is unfortunate from a design point of view that all of the group therapy was done by one therapist and the individual therapy by the other because any difference in skill was confounded with difference in type of therapy.

A third study was conducted with forty-four mildly disturbed eight- to ten-year-old boys in a community mental health clinic in Westchester County, New York (Novick, 1965). Twenty boys received individual therapy and twenty-four were in groups. The groups were balanced for those judged to be good therapy prospects (high ego strength) and poor prospects (low ego strength), based on psychological test results and psychiatric evaluation. The therapists were three experienced individuals, a psychiatrist, a clinical psychologist, and a psychiatric social worker. They shared a similar orientation, and their common approach in individual therapy was described as warm, friendly, permissive, and flexible in a combination of activity-play and verbal communication. Group therapy was conducted in small groups of three to five and featured encouragement, support, and understanding in both verbal communications and activities. After twenty sessions, there was no significant difference between children receiving group or individual therapy. The groups were equally effective with those who had good initial prognosis and equally ineffective with the poor prospects.

Abstracting a portion of a larger study of systematic desensitization, we can obtain some information on the relative efficacy of behavior therapy applied individually and in groups (Paul & Shannon, 1966). Results with ten test-anxious students treated in groups were compared with those of ten others treated individually. There were no significant differences in anxiety reduction between the two groups. Both were equally effective. It should be noted, however, that the group subjects had nine sessions compared to five for the individual subjects. A strict comparison would require equal time. Although the end result may be the same, it is possible that results were accomplished more rapidly in individual therapy.

Gelder et al. compared behavior therapy with analytically oriented group and individual psychotherapy of phobic patients (Gelder, Marks, & Wolff, 1967). To focus for the moment on the results of individual and group psychotherapy carried out by psychiatrists with some experience, direct comparison is handicapped by the fact that the duration of individual therapy was limited to one year and group therapy to eighteen months. Weekly individual therapy sessions lasted an hour, and group therapy sessions an hour and one-half. Generally there was slightly less improvement with the group than with the individual approach. There were multiple ratings from patients, therapists, and an independent assessor. The results were not entirely consistent. Thirty per cent of the patients in individual therapy were judged as having shown improvement in their main phobia as against 12 per cent of those in group therapy. No patient lost his phobia completely. Patients in group therapy showed somewhat less reduction in general anxiety and depression, but this appeared only in the psychiatrist's ratings, not in those of the patients. Although there was little evident depersonalization, the psychiatrists rated it as more intensive in individual therapy patients.

These six studies, with different types of outpatients and inpatients, with children and adults, and with different types of therapy, all yielded the consistent result of relative equivalence of outcome with group and individual therapy, at best slightly favoring individual therapy. At least one of the authors recommends group therapy on grounds of economy since both kinds produce comparable results.

Peck (1949) compared individual therapy with combined individual and group therapy. The combined group was composed of 153 veterans at the Veterans Administration Clinic, Atlanta, Georgia, who were compared with sixty-eight patients in individual therapy. The latter were described as persons who would have received group therapy except for practical reasons. The "practical reasons" eliminated females, Negroes, persons from out of town, those who could not get away from work, and those who were resistant to attending groups. It is not at all unlikely that they were indeed drawn from a different population and hence were not suitable as a comparison group. Diagnostically the patients were mostly neurotic. Improvement in this retrospective study was rated by the author in five categories: insight, adjustment, symptoms, pathological attitudes, and relationship with physician. Since there was only a single rater of case material, the reliability and validity of his ratings are open to question. Sixty-six per cent of those in combined therapy were rated as improved in contrast to 51 per cent who had individual therapy alone. For each of the five categories, the percentage improved was higher for the patients in combined therapy. Although the statistical significance of these findings was not computed, the differences were described as "astonishing" and "marked." From our calculation of chi-square, neither the difference in general improvement between the two groups nor the difference in such key areas as adjustment and symptoms are statistically reliable.

Using fifty-six subjects, Haimowitz and Haimowitz (1952) reported little difference in effectiveness between individual therapy (seventeen Ss), group therapy (twenty-four Ss), and combined individual and group therapy (fifteen Ss). A Veterans Administration Hospital in Hines, Illinois, was the setting for another attempt to determine the effectiveness of individual therapy, group therapy, and two combinations of these methods (Baehr, 1954). One group of patients received approximately equal amounts of the two types of therapy, whereas one method predominated in the other. The sequence in this study was always group therapy followed by individual therapy. Twelve clinical psychologists served as therapists for the sixty-six hospitalized patients, of whom forty were diagnosed as psychoneurotic and twenty-three as having character and behavior disorders. Both individual and group therapy were nondirective in orientation. Since this was a retrospective study, all the patients had voluntarily discontinued treatment and had been discharged from the hospital. Thus, the sample was too biased at the start for the purpose of evaluating or comparing therapies. Discharged patients represent the relative successes. What cannot be determined from such data is the number who were treated unsuccessfully and not discharged. The criterion measure was a Discontentment Scale, devised by the author, which yielded a measure of the intensity of discontent from 230 potentially discontentment-arousing experiences. Comparing seventeen patients who received predominantly group therapy with sixteen who received predominantly individual therapy and thirty-three who received approximately equal amounts of both, the author obtained no significant differences. When the single methods were considered together and compared with the combined method, the latter was found to be significantly more effective in reducing discontentment. In decreasing order of effectiveness the methods ranked: group plus individual, individual, group. In view of the sampling bias, no conclusions can be drawn about relative effectiveness. There might have been a larger proportion of group and individual patients who failed to improve, remained in the hospital, and therefore did not appear in the discharged sample. The study ideally should have started with an equal number of patients randomly assigned to the three methods of treatment.

Psychodrama was added to individual therapy and routine treatment for an experimental group of twenty-seven patients at the UCLA Neuropsychiatric Institute (Slawson, 1965). Each was matched with a control patient on MMPI profile, age, and sex. MMPIs were given on admission and discharge. Nine computer-programmed comparisons were made on ten of the scales. The psychodrama group met twice a week with a trained director, an actress, a psychiatrist, and a nurse. The reality-oriented content dealt with problems on the ward, with the individual therapist, and with relatives when on pass. The direction of MMPI change was toward the normal for both the experimental and control groups. There were no statistically significant differences between them. Slawson concluded that the zeal and well-intended enthusiasm of practitioners could not "compensate for defective methodology and inadequate data." In a rejoinder, Moreno, the founding father of psychodrama, argued that the MMPI is "utterly useless in assessing psychodramatic experience." From our vantage point it appears that the experimental design itself, the validity of the criterion measure aside, precluded much chance of demonstrating the effectiveness of psychodrama. Both groups were retested *at the time of discharge*. Discharge usually means that the patient has improved sufficiently to leave the hospital. The fact that patients in both groups did improve was reflected (to no one's surprise) in the discharge MMPIs. The test of efficacy of the additional treatment should rather have been made at a fixed interval of time following admission and/or comparative discharge rates examined. The assessment of efficacy in this study was equivalent to comparing two drugs for treating patients hospitalized for the flu and testing all patients for symptoms at time of discharge. One method of treatment may have been far more effective than the other, but we could never discover it this way.

At the Seattle Veterans Administration Hospital, Boe et al. investigated changes in interpersonal variables as a result of group therapy added to a hospital treatment program that included individual therapy, milieu therapy, occupational therapy, and medication (Boe, Gocka, & Kogan, 1966). The thirty-eight patients were schizophrenics, depressives, or had severe character disorders. After two groups were matched for age, education, occupational level, length of hospitalization, severity of illness, individual therapist, and ward assignment, one group was randomly assigned to group therapy. All other hospital treatment continued for both groups. Twelve patients had to be dropped for valid reasons and the final sample consisted of two groups of thirteen patients each. The groups were tested on three occasions, once at the beginning of therapy and two more times at three-week intervals. There were five instructional sets under which Ss were asked to respond to a sixty-four-item interpersonal check list. The sets were "I am," "ideally a person should be," "most patients on your ward are," "most people are," "ideally a doctor should be." Results were factor analyzed by item. Factor scores were computed and then evaluated by analysis of variance. This represents an interesting methodological contribution. Scale structure was abandoned because items were regrouped by factor analysis before consideration of the effects of the independent variables. The authors point out that the method could yield sample-specific factors in contrast to more general scale scores. The results revealed little in the way of effects of group therapy when added to existing hospital treatment. This was a statistically sophisticated approach and a thoughtful appraisal of results.

There is little existing evidence of any systematic difference in efficacy between group and individual therapy. Studies that purport to show advantages of a combination of the two methods are not sufficiently conclusive, either by design or analysis, to permit such a conclusion. Pending contradictory future evidence, we must now conclude that individual or collective treatment, or combinations of the two, are all equally effective or ineffective as the case may be.

VARIANTS OF GROUP PSYCHOTHERAPY

A number of variants of group therapy have been compared for efficacy. The subject population in almost all studies is hospitalized schizophrenics. Most of these researches further included an untreated control group and have already been discussed in that context.

Group therapy employing techniques designed to foster interaction among the group members without concern for imparting insight was compared with group therapy attempting to promote insight while holding interaction to a minimum (Coons, 1957). This research was done in a hospital setting. Experimental patients received three half-hour sessions per week (range eight to ninety sessions) and controls had no group therapy. First, Coons successfully established, through analysis of transcripts of recordings of the group therapy sessions, that the interaction group sessions were characterized by a high proportion of patient-to-patient interactions but that such interaction was largely absent in the insight group. Pairs of pre- and posttherapy Rorschach protocols were subjected to blind global judgment of level of adjustment. Approximately 69 per cent of the interaction group were judged as improved, compared to 43 per cent of the insight group ($p = .04$). The interaction group showed significantly more improvement than the controls while the insight group did not.

Semon and Goldstein's (1957) study, also with hospitalized schizophrenics, compared active-participant with active-interpretive group therapy and with no therapy (controls who received standard custodial treatment). The therapist's aim was to promote interaction in the former therapy and understanding of underlying motivation in the latter. To assure that this had been done, twenty-four ten-minute time samples from each of eight group meetings were judged by two psychiatric residents. They correctly identified the therapist's role in 92 per cent of the samples. The criterion measure was the total adjustment score of the Palo Alto Hospital Adjustment Scale and a measure of interpersonal functioning from one of its subscales. No significant difference was found between the two methods.

A third study compared "traditional" group therapy, which focused on self-understanding and insight, with specific therapy whose content was limited to discharge planning and problems connected with finding jobs and housing (MacDonald, Blochberger, & Maynard, 1964). The same experienced therapists conducted both groups. Their effectiveness was further compared with autonomous group therapy and no treatment. Several criteria were examined. There were more favorable dispositions, such as releases, and fewer unfavorable ones, such as transfers, in the specific than in the traditional group. The autonomous group had the most favorable dispositions. The specific and autonomous groups were equally low in instances of major rule infractions; the traditional group was even worse than the no-treatment group. Average weekly scores on minor rule infractions were, order: autonomous 0.18, specific 1.23, traditional 1.46, no treatment 1.62. The traditional group was lowest in initiating conversation during the social interaction recreation hour. In this regard it differed mostly from the autonomous group. The traditional group had the lowest percentage of patient-initiated interviews with staff and the lowest expressed preference for "being-in-a-group." Not only did these two staff-led groups fail to promote hospital objectives, but group therapy with the objective of insight and self-understanding was seen as possibly impeding these objectives.

The possible superiority of activity groups over what has become the traditional, conventional, or orthodox (either insight, interaction, or both) has also been investigated. DiGiovanni (1958) matched chronic schizophrenic patients for age, chronicity, and performance on a social behavior scale. One group was assigned to intensive orthodox group therapy for one and one-half hour sessions five days a week for seventy-four meetings. The other group was engaged in such activities as playing games and personal care routines for an equal period of time. The criteria of improvement were the Hospital Adjustment Scale and the Minimal Social Behavior Scale. Neither group improved more than the other nor did either improve significantly. Anker and Walsh (1961) compared the relative improvement in hospitalized schizophrenic patients seen twice a week with those in an essentially leaderless activity group organized to produce dramatic plays. Behavioral adjustment was measured on the MACC Behavioral Adjustment Scale. In general, results favored the activity group in terms of improved behavioral adjustment and decreased agitation and restlessness.

The picture is not entirely clear, nor is the weight of evidence overwhelming, but it appears that verbal group therapy aimed at promoting insight and self-understanding is not the treatment of choice with schizophrenic patients. Not only does it seem to have little positive benefit, but there is some reason to believe that it may actually be detrimental. Therapy that promotes interaction and activity group therapy, whatever the therapeutic ingredient may be, have been shown to be at least as good and in some cases substantially better. This tentative conclusion should be viewed in relation to evaluation studies of programs that have gone far beyond simple, formal group therapy and represent programmatic attempts to alter systematically the treatment environment.

"SCHOOLS" OF THERAPY

Many groups lay claim to the superiority of their "school" of psychotherapy over others. Aside from consideration of professional economics and gratification of the needs of some to lead and proselytize and others to follow and identify with movements, the real justification for new systems of therapy is dissatisfaction with results achieved by techniques of the old "schools." Have the Freudians, Jungians, Adlerians, Rankians, Reichians, Sullivanians, Rogerians, Mowrerians, existentialists, gestaltists, rationalists, logotherapists, directivists, behaviorists, or what have you, demonstrated distinct superiority with patients in general or with specific patient groups, or, like the various religious groups, is one neither more nor less effective in saving souls than another? Is it a matter of faith and dogma, or, like the Lions, Elks, Moose, Rotarians, and Masons, are they merely fraternal groups all performing a social function neither better nor worse than the other?

Heine (1950) found that reported changes did not differ among clients from nondirective, psychoanalytic, and Adlerian therapists. What did differ were the factors associated with change. Clients tended to refer to factors that authorities of each school consider important. This did not hold for clients who reported the greatest change, however.

Albert Ellis, the originator of rational-emotive psychotherapy, studied his own effectiveness during three periods of professional practice (Ellis, 1957). He began to do orthodox psychoanalysis under control after seven years of training, experience, and completion of his personal analysis. After three years he gradually abandoned it in favor of an active, interpretive, face-to-face, analytically oriented method. When another three years had gone by, his own form of rational therapy evolved. To compare the three approaches, he took seventy-eight closed cases treated for at least ten sessions from his files of analytically oriented cases, seventy-eight seen in rational therapy, and sixteen treated by orthodox analysis. The groups were fairly comparable for diagnosis, sex, age, and education. Those in orthodox analysis had been seen for an average of ninety-three sessions, compared to thirty-five sessions for the analytically oriented and twenty-six for rational therapy. Improvement was rated *at the time of closing* by the author, using three categories. Under orthodox psychoanalysis, 50 per cent showed little or no improvement, 37 per cent some distinct improvement, and 13 per cent considerable improvement. With analytically oriented treatment the respective figures were 37 per cent, 45 per cent, and 18 per cent. It is of interest that in an earlier paper on the effectiveness of his practice of psychoanalytically oriented psychotherapy with forty individuals who had severe homosexual problems, he reported 64 per cent improvement with males and 100 per cent with females (Ellis, 1956). Rational therapy now had 10 per cent showing little or no improvement, 46 per cent distinct improvement, and 44 per cent considerable improvement. Ellis acknowledges that the outcome ratings could be prejudiced and that he might have devoted different amounts of zeal and energy to the different types of treatment. The data from a single therapist is not representative and lacks generality, especially when he is the sole judge of his own case records and the founder of the approach that shows up best. Just as his method of treatment changed, so may have his implicit criteria of improvement. Cases were seen at three different levels of his experience, and outcome improved as time passed. The results also suggest that, method aside, the greater the number of sessions, the worse the outcome. In short, many things other than the method could account for the results and the case for rational therapy and against orthodox analysis is not advanced by this study.

Forgy and Black (1954) did a follow-up of a study done five years earlier by Barahal, Brammer, and Shostrom (1950). The latter had concluded that client-centered vocational counseling resulted in greater client satisfaction than more highly structured counseling. In the follow-up, seventy-seven of the original ninety-two clients, who had been college or graduate students at the time of the original study, responded to a mail questionnaire. They included equal numbers from both groups. Differences that existed in the initial study were no longer present three years later. There was, however, a counselor × method interaction, suggesting that different methods may be more suitable for different counselors in bringing about client satisfaction. Although this study dealt with vocational counseling, it has implications for psychotherapy.

Direct analysis in the style of Rosen was compared with other therapeutic methods on schizophrenic patients at Philadelphia General Hospital in a five-year evaluation (Bookhammer, Meyers, Schober, & Piotrowski, 1966). All the patients were schizophrenics between fifteen and thirty-five years of age, had no previous history of psychosis or psychiatric treatment, and no physical illness. They were assigned in rotation for either direct analysis or for other therapeutic methods. A second control group was added later. The outcome was evaluated by a committee in a five- or more year follow-up. In arriving at a judgment of improved or unimproved, the committee considered changes in objective signs, self-attitudes, attitudes toward others, thought processes, useful work output, and time spent out of hospital. No significant differences among treatments were found. Fifty-seven per cent under direct analysis were judged as improved, compared to 67 per cent of one control group and 58 per cent of the other. The dimensions and characteristics of the control treatments are not given, nor are the ways in which the judges arrived at their judgments. If we can assume that the committee judgments were valid and unbiased, it can be conservatively stated that no advantage was demonstrated for direct analysis.

In Wiener's (1955) study, reassurance-interpretation was compared with catharsis-reflection in alleviating experimentally induced anxiety in normal subjects. It is presumed that these orientations would be analogous to nondirective and more directive approaches. No consistent differences between the two counseling approaches appeared and both were better than simple talk and rest.

Although it is not a comparison of one type of psychotherapy with another type nor with an untreated control group, one of the few investigations involving "Freudian analytic-type psychotherapy" is worth examining (Harris, 1954). In this instance, thirty-eight psychoneurotic patients in Freudian psychoanalysis were compared with an equal number receiving carbon dioxide therapy. Using social criteria, the author graded the status of the patient. Improvement was judged by evidence of upward shifts. Results were that 16 per cent of the analyzed patients and 29 per cent of the carbon dioxide therapy group were judged recovered. Thirty-four per cent of the analyzed group were judged improved compared to 11 per cent of the carbon dioxide group. In the aggregate, 50 per cent of the analyzed and 40 per cent of the other were either recovered or improved, and the remainder almost exclusively unchanged. The difference between treatments was not significant, but the patients themselves tended to view psychotherapy as more helpful. In this study, however, the method of judging improvement is wanting in many respects, and we know nothing of the objectivity, reliability, and validity of the ratings or the comparability of the patients.

A reflective type of therapy based on the Rogerian approach was compared with a leading therapy based on Dollard and Miller and Fromm-Reichmann (Ashby, Ford, Guerney, & Guerney, 1957). The leading therapy was characterized by directive leads, interpretation, directive structuring, approval, encouragement, suggestion, advice, persuasion, and the giving of information. The clients were twenty-four young adults who were mostly university students with neurotic symptoms and academic problems. The therapists were ten advanced graduate students, aged twenty-four to thirty. Only the data from six therapists were used when it was determined that the other four failed to meet experimental response standards (60 per cent of all therapist responses had to be in the appropriate response family). Clients were randomly assigned to therapists and therapies, and were seen for an average of thirteen sessions. Twenty-one analyses of variance were computed for six client verbal behavior variables, eight relationship variables and seven change variables. Only two of the twenty-one showed a statistically significant difference between therapies. One of these was the therapists' rating of clients in leading therapy as more improved than those in reflective therapy. The authors note that this may be an artifact because all but one therapist expressed a prior preference for leading therapy. The other finding was that clients were more guarded for the first four sessions.

The procedures and design of Ashby et al. were adapted by Baker (1960) in another study of the differential effects of leading therapy derived from neo-Freudian principles (Dollard and Miller, Fromm-Reichmann, Horney, and Sullivan) and Rogerian reflective therapy. Reflective therapists are defined as those who restrict their dealings to the thoughts and feelings in the subject's phenomenological field, whereas leading therapists introduce elements not in the client's present awareness. The clients were twenty-eight mildly to moderately neurotic college students. The seven young therapists had no particular therapeutic allegiance. It was hypothesized that indiscriminate perceptions, personal overgeneralizations, discrepancies between the way a person perceives himself and the way others perceive him, and resistance to analyzing problems would all be reduced more by a leading than by a reflective therapy. No support was found for three of these four hypotheses. There was some support for the hypothesis that leading therapy may be more effective in reducing overgeneralization. On the whole, the differences between the outcomes of the two therapies were minimal. What was perhaps the major finding of the study was glossed over: ten of the eleven dropouts from the project were from reflective therapy.

The experiment by Paul (1966) on the reduction of public-speaking anxiety has been reviewed from the viewpoint of the effects of treatment as compared with no treatment. It also casts light on the issue of comparative psychotherapy in that the subjects were assigned to three different types of treatment all of which were limited to five contact hours over a period of six weeks. Members of the first group were exposed to traditional interview procedures designed to help the client gain insight into his problem. All five of the therapists were highly experienced and of neo-Freudian and Rogerian orientation. Two had completed 500 hours of personal analysis, two had completed ten hours of personal therapy, and one had undergone didactic treatment. They all felt that insight was an important therapeutic goal. Each session was recorded to insure that no noninsight techniques were used. The second group received modified systematic desensitization in imagery and progressive relaxation training. The therapists, unfamiliar with these procedures, received some training before beginning. During the actual therapy session, discussion of dynamics was not permitted, but therapists were asked to maintain a helpful, warm, and interested relationship with the clients. The third treatment group was an "attention-placebo" group who received an inert drug described as a "fast-acting tranquilizer," and a nonspecific task to perform that was ostensibly designed to help Ss to "think under stress." The therapist remained attentive throughout. The fourth group was a no-treatment control. The results of this elaborate study with multiple criterion measures can be summarized as a clear demonstration of the superiority of desensitization in bringing about cognitive, physiological, and motoric changes. These changes were maintained in a follow-up study. Desensitization was significantly better on all measures than either insight or attention-placebo. Whatever the nonspecific factors (attention, suggestion, relationship) in the attention-placebo group may have been, they produced as much reduction of anxiety as gaining insight and self-understanding. Both were far less effective than desensitization. This was evident despite the fact that the entire training and experience background of the therapists was with the insight approach. In terms of percentages systematic desensitization produced 100 per cent success, attention-placebo and insight 47 per cent success, and controls 17 per cent. The findings were extended and further confirmed by subjecting the previously untreated controls to group desensitization combined with re-educative group discussion and then comparing them with the results of the previous study (Paul & Shannon, 1966). Results showed that desensitization could be combined with group discussion without loss of effectiveness and that it was also significantly superior to the insight approach in reducing anxiety.

Lazarus' (1961) study of the effectiveness of group desensitization in treatment of phobias is pertinent to our present discussion of comparative psychotherapy. It will be recalled that one group received group desensitization and a second conventional group therapy modeled after Wolberg, with insight and re-educative goals. Both were given three times a week for the same number of sessions. A third group was treated by interpretation plus relaxation. The combined probabilities for acrophobics, claustrophobics, impotent men, and mixed phobics was significantly in favor of desensitization when compared with interpretative therapy. The difference in favor of desensitization over interpretation plus relaxation was not significant for matched pairs of acrophobic and claustrophobic patients. Of the fifteen patients who derived no apparent benefit from either interpretation or interpretation plus relaxation, ten recovered after a mean of 10.1 desensitization sessions while 20.4 sessions had been necessary for group desensitization alone to be effective. Four of six who failed in interpretation and desensitization recovered after a mean of 9.8 desensitization sessions.

Lazarus (1966), in a subsequent investigation at the Behavior Therapy Institute, Sausalito, California, compared three approaches: behavior rehearsal, advice, and reflection-interpretation. Behavior rehearsal is described as a kind of "behavioristic psychodrama," role playing in which the patient practices desired forms of behavior under the therapist's direction. Its particular applicability is generally with patients who need to develop assertive responses. All seventy-five patients (twenty-five per group) had specific social and/or interpersonal problems. Therapy was limited to four thirty-minute sessions in each group. If by that time (one month) there was no evidence of change, treatment was considered a failure. The sole criterion was evidence of adaptive functioning in the problem area. Lazarus was the only therapist for all patients. At the end of the allotted time 92 per cent of the patients undergoing behavioral rehearsal had shown evidence of learning, as against 44 per cent of those who were given advice and 32 per cent who received reflection-interpretation. All told, thirty-one of fifty Ss did not benefit from reflection-interpretation or advice. They were then treated with behavior rehearsal and 81 per cent improved. The overall effectiveness in the fifty-two cases so treated was 86.5 per cent.

The possibility of experimenter bias cannot be excluded because Lazarus was both the only therapist and judge of improvement. All the patients had circumscribed problems, and role playing was evidently more effective in the brief time allotted in helping them arrive at assertive solutions. The approach cannot be generalized to problems other than those in which an action is lacking on the patient's part. The other approaches might work, too, if given longer time, but as it stands behavior rehearsal appears most efficient for this therapist. It would be essential, of course, to have a more representative sample of therapists and ratings of patient behavior that were objective and free of bias.

Reference is made to another previously described study in which "operant-interpersonal" therapy was compared with verbal therapy, recreational therapy, and no therapy with hospitalized schizophrenics (King, Armitage, & Tilton, 1960). The operant-interpersonal method featured progressively more complex problem-solving situations on a reward-dispensing Multiple Operant Problem Solving Apparatus, and shifted from individual to cooperative effort. Verbal therapy kept pace by shifting from individual to group therapy at the same time the operant-interpersonal therapy became cooperative. The F-value for differences among groups on the Extreme Mental Illness Schedule was significant ($p < .001$), with improvement in the order: operant-interpersonal, recreational therapy, no therapy, and verbal therapy. The operant-interpersonal group improved significantly more than each of the other groups. On the Ward Observations Scale the F was significant at $p < .01$ for differences among therapeutic groups. The order was the same except that, on this measure, verbal therapy ranked above no therapy. The operant-interpersonal method was not significantly higher than recreational therapy, but was reliably better than verbal therapy and no therapy. On the Clinical Improvement Scale, 67 per cent of those in O-I therapy showed minor or considerable improvement, compared to 8 per cent in verbal therapy, 33 per cent in recreational therapy, and 16 per cent with no therapy. Fifty per cent of those in verbal therapy either declined or remained unchanged in level of verbalization. In O-I treatment none declined and 58 per cent improved. Ward personnel, who did not know which treatment procedures were given, recommended 42 per cent of the O-I patients for transfer to a privileged section but only 17 per cent from recreational therapy and none from the verbal therapy or no-therapy groups. A six-month follow-up showed practically no movement to open sections, but ward observation ratings significantly favored patients who had received O-I therapy in terms of pathology and improvement. Ratings of motivation to leave the ward clearly favored the O-I group, and clinical observations paralleled the ratings. Many of those in verbal therapy became worse, several became mute, and there was more evidence of verbal withdrawal behavior. In contrast to some hopeful changes with the operant-interpersonal approach, the gross ineffectiveness of verbal therapy with regressed chronic schizophrenics was clearly shown in this investigation. Verbal therapy, if anything, appears detrimental to this group. A crucial test is needed to determine if an operant but noninterpersonal technique would be as effective. Is it the interpersonal aspect, the operant, the combination, or the special attention and elaborate gadgetry that stimulated interest and change?

Another study that has been discussed concerns the comparison of conditioning therapy, conventional therapy, and no therapy with functionally enuretic children (DeLeon & Mandell, 1966). One group was conditioned to awakening by a loud buzzer activated by a drop of urine on a pad. The therapy group was seen weekly for a comparable total period of time (ninety days). The therapist saw the child for forty minutes and the mother for twenty minutes each visit. The controls received no treatment. The criterion of failure in each instance was not achieving thirteen successive dry nights in the ninety-day period. Results were clearly in favor of conditioning treatment, with 86.3 per cent reaching the criterion compared to 18.2 per cent in conventional psychotherapy and 11.1 per cent with no treatment. The median number of days to reach the cure criterion of those who achieved it was thirty-seven days for the conditioning group, eighty-four days for the controls, and 103.5 days for the psychotherapy group. Relapse was relatively high in all groups except for those who had received conditioning. The reconditioning rate was more rapid than the first trial, being successfully completed in a median of 22.5 days.

Bethlem Royal and Maudsley Hospitals, London, were the settings for a retrospective comparison of behavior therapy with other approaches (Cooper, 1963). The experimental sample, a mixture of outpatients and inpatients, consisted of ten patients with agoraphobia and other specific phobias treated by reciprocal inhibition; five patients with writer's cramp treated by avoidance learning; five patients with obsessive rituals treated by reciprocal inhibition, massed practice, and relaxation under hypnosis; three patients with tics treated by massed practice; three stutterers treated by shadowing, masking, and negative practice; and four miscellaneous cases treated by various behavior techniques. These were matched with five phobics, one obsessional, one writer's cramp, and one stutterer treated by short-term nonanalytic therapy; two phobics treated by occupational therapy and group activities; one phobic treated by individual and one by group analytic therapy; one phobic who received acetylcholine injections intravenously; one obsessional who received ECT; and one leucotomized obsessional. Retrospective assessments were made by two independent judges on two scales at the end of treatment, a month and a year later. One assessment scale dealt with specific symptom-related changes and the other with more general activities not due to changes in the treated symptom. The general assessment scale was less reliable and sensitive because of scanty information. Among those treated by behavior therapy, seventeen were judged to have improved (57 per cent) and thirteen were unchanged. One month after treatment the improvement rate had fallen to 47 per cent; after a year it fell to 43 per cent. Of the phobic patients alone, 90 per cent had improved, but because of relapse the percentage dropped to 60 per cent after one month. There were no further relapses during the year. Comparison of the controls showed a difference only in the phobic cases. Fifty per cent were improved on the symptom scale compared to the 90 per cent treated by behavior therapy. There was no difference between the controls and the behavior therapy cases on the general change scales. There was no evidence of symptom substitution with behavior therapy, but an emotional bond between patient and therapist often appeared. This dissertation was actually too much of a smorgasbord for it to be put to much use. All kinds of patients received all kinds of treatments to the point where one could not tell what was being controlled with whom. The retrospective nature of the data did not help. Even the behavior therapy varied so much between diagnostic categories that no firm and general conclusions can be drawn.

Three experiments on the effectiveness of variants of behavior therapy in the treatment of phobic states were conducted at Maudsley Hospital, London, by Marks, Gelder, and associates. The first was a controlled retrospective study (Marks & Gelder, 1965). Twenty patients with phobic states, who had been treated by psychologists, were matched man-for-man on a number of relevant variables with twenty controls. The patients were chiefly female agoraphobics, 60 per cent of whom were housebound with symptoms of nine to ten years duration. There were also eleven other phobics of different types. Treatment varied and included graded retraining along a hierarchy, relaxation-hypnosis, and desensitization in imagination. Many of the patients in both groups received sedative- or antidepressant drugs, other physical and chemical treatments, and psychotherapy. A detailed summary was made of each patient's history and condition at five time points from the end of treatment to one year later. Follow-up information from psychiatric notes, interviews, and other sources was rated on a Symptom Severity Scale ranging from absent to severe. Rating was done blindly by two independent assessors with disagreements settled by a third assessor. A change in score of one unit was called "improved," and of two units, "much improved." A scale of General Condition was rated as worse, unchanged, improved, or much improved. Analysis of variance showed no significant difference between the groups in symptom scores or in the proportion improved. Fifty-five to 60 per cent improved but none lost all symptoms. The groups remained stationary during the year after discharge and the pattern of relapse was stationary. The scale of general improvement was considered unreliable owing to scanty information, but in 85 per cent of both groups, when phobias changed the general condition improved. When they did not change, neither did the general condition. Those treated by behavior therapy typically advanced ahead of the controls and slipped back to the same level at follow-up. Those in behavior therapy had more treatments (4.1 sessions per week) than the controls (2.4 sessions), of longer duration, and averaged fifty-two sessions in contrast to the twenty-seven of the controls. There was no relationship, however, between number of sessions, duration, and outcome.

Ten of the agoraphobic group were treated by trained staff psychologists, four by postgraduate students under supervision, and six by psychiatric registrars. The latter two groups treated the more severely disturbed patients. It was observed that therapists best acquainted with learning theory (staff psychologists) did no better with behavior therapy than the others, and this was clearly not because they had more difficult cases. This research by Marks and Gelder is highly detailed, but contains a number of serious defects that limit the conclusions that can be drawn. There were far too many other kinds of treatment concurrently involved to enable a real test of behavior therapy. Matched controls do not help a badly confounded independent variable. The use of retrospective data from case records is a procedure that introduces a large source of potential error. Judging outcome from this kind of material is quite risky and calls for particularly high judging standards. In this instance the requirements of rater agreement were quite inadequate. Agreement of two judges on a five-category and a four-category scale was used, with a third rater coming in to settle disagreements. Two judges with a choice of five categories can be expected to agree by chance 20 per cent of the time, and 25 per cent with four categories. Bringing in a third judge does not help a bit. There are 65/125 ways of two out of three judges or better agreeing by chance on five categories and 44/64 ways on four categories. Therefore, the validity of the judgments, because of the materials on which they were based, and the reliability, because of an inadequate number of judges and standard of agreement, cast a pall over the entire effort. Since both experimental and control patients received other treatments, nothing can be said about the efficacy of treatment in general or behavior therapy in particular.

A controlled prospective study, also at Maudsley Hospital, compared behavior therapy with conventional psychotherapy (Gelder & Marks, 1966). The patients, primarily women, were twenty severe agoraphobics, with an average duration of symptoms of seven years. Most patients had been housebound and were treated as inpatients. They were randomly assigned to behavior therapy or conventional psychotherapy. The groups were initially equivalent on a large number of relevant variables. Behavior therapy consisted of graded retraining and Wolpean systematic desensitization in imagination with appropriate use of assertive responses. Controls received supervised, individual therapeutic interviews with a focus on contemporary interpersonal problems related to past experiences. Both groups were seen three times a week in forty-five-minute sessions by psychiatric residents under the supervision of a consultant. Symptoms and social adjustment were each rated on five-point disability scales. Five questions about anxiety, covering physical, autonomic, and psychic symptoms, were averaged to form an anxiety rating. After an interview, independent assessors made these ratings before treatment, two months later, at the end of treatment, and after six- and twelve-month follow-up. Therapists and patients rated symptoms every two weeks during treatment and every three months during follow-up. At the beginning and end of treatment and after six and twelve months of follow-up, the patients filled out a symptom checklist (from the Cornell Medical Index), checklists of phobias and social anxieties (based on the Tavistock Self-Assessment Inventory), a self-adjustment scale (based on the Rogers and Dymond Q-Sort), and the Eysenck Personality Inventory.

To summarize the outcome, seven out of ten in *each* group had improved in the main phobic symptom by the end of treatment. Four in the behavior therapy group and two in conventional treatment were much improved. The difference was not significant, and the course of treatment for behavior therapy patients ran an average of four weeks longer. Most improvement in both groups was shown in the first months. The course of treatment in the two groups was almost parallel. Patients in both groups had a mean score for main phobia at the end of treatment that indicated a definite interference with their lives. None lost their phobia completely. Both groups were left with considerable residual social disability. Whatever gains existed were lost by follow-up. There was little change in symptoms of depression in either group. Those with few symptoms other than phobias did best. There was little evidence of symptom substitution. The sample was small, the agoraphobias were severe, and there was no untreated control group against which to test absolute efficacy. Behavior therapy as applied, however, was not significantly more successful than conventional treatment. Admittedly, the therapists were psychiatrists who, though not lacking in interest and enthusiasm, had little previous experience with the technique of behavior therapy. Wolpe stresses this point in criticizing the study. Otherwise, the experiment was careful and sound.

Another study in this series was designed to compare desensitization, group therapy, and individual therapy in the treatment of phobic disorders (Gelder, Marks, & Wolff, 1967). Patients with one or more phobias were placed in one of three matched groups. Sixteen were treated by desensitization, consisting of an hour a week of Wolpean desensitization in imagination followed, where appropriate, by assertive responses and graded tasks between sessions. The average duration was nine months. Sixteen patients were assigned to analytically oriented group therapy for one and one-half hours a week. The duration averaged eighteen months and was limited in time for the study. Ten patients were seen for an hour a week of analytically oriented individual psychotherapy limited in duration to twelve months. The groups were well matched on age, vocabulary score, initial severity of main phobia, and other symptoms, but there was a significant difference in duration of present illness (12.2 years for group therapy, 8.2 for desensitization, and 6.3 for individual therapy). These imbalances make the results potentially difficult to evaluate but at least partially compensate for each other (the group therapy patients were ill by far the longest, but had the longest treatment period). The group and individual psychotherapists had some, but generally limited, experience. Four of the five psychiatrists who did the behavior therapy had *no previous experience* with it and were supervised by the one who had experience.

Symptoms were rated on a series of five-point scales about phobias, general anxiety, depression, obsessions, depersonalization, and social adjustment. Ratings were made by patients and therapists at the beginning and end of therapy and at follow-up. A second psychiatrist acted as assessor and made independent ratings, at the start, end, and every six months. Reliability was disappointing. It was considered by the authors to be adequate for phobias and anxiety, but less satisfactory for other areas. The patient was also obliged to fill out a number of questionnaires and checklists. Follow-up, averaging seven months after the final rating, was done in an interview of the patient and a relative or close friend by a psychiatric social worker, who rated the patient as much improved, improved, no change, or worse. Only what appeared to be treatment-related improvement was accepted.

Data were treated by a series of analyses of variance. The main phobia improved rapidly during the first few weeks of desensitization, coming to a maximal difference from the other treatments at six months. At the end of treatment, improvement still favored desensitization, but no longer significantly so, as patients in other treatments continued slowly to improve over the whole treatment period. Patients who were rated as much improved totaled 56 per cent for desensitization, 30 per cent for individual therapy, and 12 per cent for group therapy. Only two patients, both in desensitization, lost their phobias completely. Results were generally similar for phobias other than the main phobia. Symptom substitution was not found; on the contrary, loss of main phobias led to the loss of other symptoms. Many of the other ratings and findings are open to question on grounds of reliability, but fell in much the same direction as the data on phobias. Desensitization was shown to be the treatment of choice, but yielded results far below Wolpe's survey claims. This Wolpe attributes to the use of inexperienced therapists, a reasonable point that cannot be disputed without data.

Rachman (1965) compared four groups of three Ss each who reported intense fear of spiders. Four conditions were desensitization with relaxation, relaxation alone, desensitization without relaxation, and a no-treatment control. The only group to show improvement on the outcome measures was the one subjected to desensitization and relaxation. Quite different results were obtained by Wolpin and Raines (1966), who explored the necessity for using either relaxation or a hierarchy in deconditioning with a small group of six patients with fear of snakes. In four deconditioning sessions, two of the Ss were presented with a hierarchy to be mastered with visual imagery but no relaxation. Two others participated in the same visualizations but were told to tense up all muscles to facilitate concentration. A third group of two was started at the top of the hierarchy and asked to visualize the most anxiety-provoking item. All six showed gross reduction in fear and avoidance responses and were able to pick up a snake in a test situation. This suggested the advisability of reconsidering the need for either muscle relaxation or hierarchies in reducing anxiety via practice in imagination. Since there was an opportunity for discussion in each session, there is an evident need to add a nonimagery control treatment to rule out the possible anxiety-relieving effects of unburdening, relationship, or suggestion. The experiment was an ingenious one and should be repeated with this added control on a larger sample. In another approach to behavior therapy, Levis and Carrera (1967) found that conventional treatment featuring a combination of insight and support was no more effective than being on a waiting list for three months but that there was a shift away from pathology for patients receiving implosive therapy, a behavior therapy variant.

One of the most impressive comparative studies contrasted the effectiveness of three types of group therapy with male alcoholics at Willmar State Hospital, Minnesota (Ends & Page, 1957). The generally favorable results of treated vs. control conditions become much more meaningful when the specific comparisons between different therapeutic approaches are examined. Under scrutiny in this research were an approach based on two-factor learning theory modeled after Mowrer, client-centered therapy after Rogers, and psychoanalytic group therapy modeled after Alexander and French. The patients were male inebriates aged twenty-five to forty-five with a median of six years of uncontrolled drinking and a long history of excessive drinking. Sixteen six-man groups were formed. Each of four therapists handled four groups, using a different therapeutic approach with each group. The fourth group in each case met for social discussion rather than specific psychotherapy. Each of the therapists had at least two years of experience and training in psychotherapy and went through a year of elaborate training in preparation for assuming these varied roles. Theoretical biases were considered to be at a minimum. It was hypothesized that the approaches would rank in effectiveness in the order: learning theory, client-centered, psychoanalytic. The Butler-Haigh Q-Sort was the only criterion measure when the MMPI was abandoned owing to a confounding of psychological and physical treatment effects. Ten indices concerning changes in the self and ideal self were utilized. The learning-therapy group showed significant movement on four indices, but not all were beneficial. The main negative finding was an increase, rather than the expected decrease, in self-ideal discrepancy. As Ends and Page describe it, the change seemed akin to "learning the awful truth" about oneself and experiencing increased self-criticism, depression, and loss of self-esteem. In analyzing the verbal interactions in these approaches Rossi reported a withdrawal from the therapeutic endeavor as evidenced by an increase in nontherapy-oriented verbalizations. The client-centered group also showed significant movement on four indices. A lowered self-ideal discrepancy reflected greater self-acceptance, the perceived self became healthier, the ideal was modified in the direction of the changing self, and the ideal moved toward the posttherapy ideal. There was thus a restructuring of the self-value system in which the ideal was realigned with the changing, healthier self. The authors interpreted this as "an integrated, wholesome pattern of therapeutic change." The psychoanalytic group too changed on four indices, but in a different way. Here also there was significantly more self-acceptance, but therapeutic change took the form of a unilateral change of the self to conform to an unchanging ideal rather than an integrated restructuring reflecting sound therapeutic growth.

The control group moved on two indices in a negative direction. The self changed more than the ideal in a gradual downward drift. It was concluded that when the therapist is not actively therapeutic the results are negative and that the learning-theory approach accelerates the deleterious process. Client-centered and psychoanalytic therapy were seen as superficially equivalent in improving the self-concept, but the former was successful in accomplishing a "coordinated reworking" of the self and the ideal while the latter resulted in a one-sided shift in the self. The proof of the pudding with these kinds of interpretations is, of course, whether or not changes were reflected in behavior relevant to the main symptom pattern, in this case alcoholism. Ends and Page were attuned to this and conducted a follow-up study over an eighteen-month period. Personnel engaged in furnishing the follow-up data had no knowledge of the treatment received. A patient was considered "greatly improved" if there was no evidence of alcoholic episodes or misbehavior in the entire period. He was rated "possibly improved" if there had been one or two brief episodes in the first three months after discharge with no signs of further reversion. Those who resumed their old drinking patterns but did not go back to the hospital were rated "apparently no change." Rehospitalizations were also counted. Significantly more members of the client-centered and psychoanalytic groups were found in the greatly improved category when compared by chi-square using the controls as the expected values. Thus, of the patients who were located, 58 per cent of the client-centered and 40 per cent of the psychoanalytic were judged greatly improved, compared to 18 per cent of the controls. The learning-theory group had 7 per cent in this success category. Essentially the same percentages (24 to 36 per cent) of the learning-theory, analytic, and control groups were in the "no change" category, against only 8 per cent of the client-centered. About half the controls and learning-theory patients were rehospitalized, compared to one-third of the analytic group and one-quarter of the client-centered. To summarize these results, it can be seen that 77 per cent of the controls, 86 per cent of the learning-theory, 60 per cent of the analytic, and 33 per cent of the client-centered either reverted to their old pattern or were rehospitalized.

The chief reservation about this study concerns whether or not the therapists were equally "at home" and equally skilled in the various approaches. Ends and Page did take great pains to prepare them for the task, but we would like to have seen data on their actual proficiency in carrying out the various therapies. This admittedly would not be easy, but could have been rated. The attrition rate of about one in three was fairly high. One cannot help wondering what their fate was and if reasons for attrition were selective in any way for the different therapies.

To summarize the present state of our knowledge, there is hardly any evidence that one traditional school of psychotherapy yields a better outcome than another. In fact, the question has hardly been put to a fair test. The whole issue remains at the level of polemic, professional public opinion, and whatever weight that can be brought to bear by authoritative presentation of illustrative cases. People may come out of different treatments with varied and identifiable philosophies of life or approaches to solving life's problems, but there is no current evidence that one traditional method is more successful than another in modifying psychopathology, alleviating symptoms, or improving general adjustment. More recent comparisons of behavior therapy with various forms of more traditional psychotherapy, however, have turned up some consistent differences in favor of systematic desensitization over various verbal therapies aimed at insight and self-understanding. These comparative studies are largely limited to the application of behavioral techniques to phobias, specific focalized anxieties, and habits or behaviors. The comparative utility of behavior therapy with cases of generalized maladjustment has not yet been demonstrated. For phobic states it is now emerging as the treatment of choice, but even within the general category of behavior therapy there is experimental controversy over technique.

THERAPIST STYLE AND TECHNIQUE AND OUTCOME

Some of the research of this type has been considered in comparing the effects obtained by different "schools" of therapy. A few other studies attempt to make direct connections between therapist style of performance, not identified as representing any particular "school," and outcome. Studies of this sort represent the link between outcome and process research. Much of the process research in the literature is limited to what transpires within the therapeutic session. Implications for end results are present, but the direct connection is left untested. Ultimately, when the linkages have been completed, the two lines of research should dovetail.

Rice (1965) set out to construct what she called a "process language" that portrays the lexical and vocal characteristics of the therapist's performance during the session while cutting across content lines. Early and late interviews of twenty clients seen by twenty Rogerian therapists at the University of Chicago Counseling Center provided the research data. Nine were rated by the therapist as successful, four as moderate, seven as little or no progress. Three aspects of therapist style were considered: freshness of words and combinations, voice quality, and functional level (inner exploring, observing, outside focus). Tapes of interviews were divided into thirds, and ten consecutive responses taken for rating from each third. Outcome criteria were a therapist questionnaire at termination, a client questionnaire at outcome, and pre-post difference scores from the Butler-Haigh Q-sort, Taylor Manifest Anxiety Scale, and Barron Ego Strength Scale. Analysis revealed three interview types. In Type I therapist language was commonplace, voice quality even and relatively uninflected, functional level that of reflecting client self-observations, and there were no trends over time. In Type II voice quality was distorted, a few of the responses were in fresh connotative language, and functional level was that of self-observation, with a few responses on the level of exploration. Connotative language and exploration decreased from the first to last third of the interview. In Type III more fresh connotative language was used by the therapist, over two-thirds of the responses featured an expressive voice quality, and more than half of the responses were on the level of inner exploration. Expressiveness of voice quality dropped in the final third of the interview. Therapist behavior classified as Type II, when it occurs early in therapy, is predictive of an unsuccessful outcome, but the other two types are not predictive. These findings are only suggestive. Criteria measures and use of difference scores leave much to be desired. The next step would be to select three groups of therapists who characteristically function in the ways described, assign patients at random, and check the success and failure of their cases. In this study the therapist types were derived from the interviews of an equal number of successful and unsuccessful cases. There is a need to cross-validate the relation of therapist type to outcome on another sample. This is a promising approach and could explain much conflicting outcome data.

Barrington (1961) concentrated on such formal therapist speech characteristics as number of words used, words per minute, rate of therapist-to-client words per minute, latency time in therapist responses, number of words per therapist response, breaks in speech rhythm or content flow, number of responses, percentages of first person wordings, and percentage of emotional words. These nine therapist verbal behavior measures were essentially unrelated to outcome in twenty cases seen at the University of Chicago Counseling Center.

A well-designed experiment at the Veterans Administration Hospital, American Lake, Washington, compared the efficacy of confrontation and diversion in group therapy with chronic schizophrenics (Mainord, Burk, & Collins, 1965). In the latter technique the patient is diverted from strong emotional arousal; the former maintains that he must be confronted with affect if he is to learn to deal with it. One group of twelve patients received three months of confronting therapy followed by three months of diverting therapy. A second matched group was treated in the reverse order, and a third matched group of controls received no therapy. Effects were judged in terms of eleven categories of positive incidents indicating that the patient was closer to discharge. The positive incidents were tabulated weekly from hospital records. Confrontation was accompanied by ninety-five positive incidents, diversion by thirty-five, and no therapy by twenty-four. Confrontation was significantly superior to diversion, but the difference between diversion and no therapy was not reliable. The order of treatments was of no importance. Measures of patient participation and attitudes toward therapy and therapists were not significant. All the patients who were discharged from the hospital during the study were from the confronting groups.

The client's-eye view of the relationship between counselor technique and outcome was surveyed by questionnaire responses of 163 terminated clients of whom fifty-two had personal adjustment problems and

111 had problems of an educational-vocational sort (Grigg & Goodstein, 1957). Clients perceived within-counselor variability in the application of techniques (active participant, inactive participant, inactive-nonparticipant), but did not see success as dependent on any particular approach. They did, however, tend to report getting what they wanted from counseling from counselors who were more active and directive and who took an active interest in them instead of playing the passive role of an interested listener.

Although the literature is replete with therapeutic recipes, very few attempts have been made to find out if they truly have any bearing on outcome. This is a neglected but important area in psychotherapy research. The comparative effects of systematic variations in therapeutic technique must be studied experimentally if they are to be refined. Paracelsus, the eminent Renaissance alchemist and physician, recommended the following salve for burns: "It consisted of the fat of very old wild hogs and bears heated half an hour in red wine, then dropped into cold water, which was next skimmed and the fat rubbed up with roasted angle worms and moss from the skull of a person hung, scraped off during the increase of the moon, to which were added bloodstone, the dried brain of the wild hog, red sandalwood and a portion of a genuine mummy" (Pack & Davis, 1930, pp. 1–3). The remedy may have been effective, for Paracelsus did not get his reputation without cause. But which ingredient or combination of ingredients was therapeutic—the fat, wine, moss, bloodstone, hog brain, sandalwood, or mummy? Or was it really the combination of all of them? If a series of controlled experiments had been done in which all ingredients and combinations were systematically applied, it might have been established that bear grease alone did as well as or better than all the rest singly or in combination. It was not the antiquity of this remedy that caused it to drop out of use; there are far older remedies than this still being applied. For all we know, it might have been discontinued because of a shortage of hangings or old wild hogs. Nor do we know if the remedies that superseded it were necessarily any better. If this concoction now sounds quaint to us, how will descriptions of psychotherapy, as it is now practiced, sound four centuries from now? We are now at the point where we can begin to separate out the bear grease from the roasted angle worms of psychotherapy.

9

The Patient as an Outcome Variable: I. Diagnosis, Severity of Maladjustment, and the Search for Predictors

Of the numerous patient characteristics that may have a bearing on the success of psychotherapy, the two clinical features of diagnosis and severity of maladjustment are among the most prominent. Diagnostic grouping does not lend itself to direct comparative studies, but severity of maladjustment does and can be studied as a variable within diagnostic groups.

DIAGNOSIS

Although direct comparisons of the outcome of psychotherapy with different groups is not too feasible because of inherent sampling problems, we can regroup the studies that have been reviewed along diagnostic lines. In this way we can get a general noncomparative view of the effects of psychotherapy within each of a variety of diagnostic groups.

Psychoneurosis and Personality Disorders. Suitably controlled outcome research is much more difficult to do in an outpatient setting than it is with inpatients. For obvious reasons it is not feasible for a therapist in private practice to have an untreated control group, but controlled research has been done successfully in clinics. Once patients who are frankly psychotic or for whom a diagnosis of brain damage has been established are eliminated, the diagnostic classifications become less clear. There is decreased control over a patient's life outside the experimental situation. Meaningful criteria are more difficult to designate and measures are harder to come by. Patients drop out, miss appointments, and may not be available when the experimental design calls for them. The problem is greatly increased if long-term therapy is being evaluated. All these are problems that, if not insurmountable, have limited the number of acceptable evaluations of the effectiveness of outpatient psychotherapy with individuals diagnosed as being psychoneurotic or having personality disorders.

Among the twenty-three controlled investigations reviewed, three merit the most serious consideration. Morton (1955) demonstrated that students with impaired personal and social adjustment showed more improvement on test measures and global ratings after very brief individual therapy than did untreated controls. Shlien, Mosak, and Dreikurs (1962) reported significant improvement in self-concept with individual time-limited and unlimited therapy. Exner (1966) found forty-two weeks of outpatient psychotherapy to bring about improvement as rated on a scale of symptoms and prognosis.

Sixteen additional studies report various positive results, but there is doubt about the adequacy of their designs for the purpose of evaluating psychotherapy. Improvement following psychotherapy, as measured by tests or ratings, was claimed by Muench (1947), Hamlin and Albee (1948), Jonietz (1950), Warne, Canter, and Wizma (1953), Rogers and Dymond (1954), Imber et al. (1957), Cartwright (1957, 1961), Greenwald (1959), Shostrom and Knapp (1966), Cartwright and Vogel (1960), Hollon and Zolick (1962), Ewing (1964), Endicott and Endicott (1964), and Brill et al. (1964). Graham (1960) and Riess (1967) reported improvements in specific aspects of life performance. Benefits from both conventional and behavior therapy were claimed by Levis and Carrera (1967). In contrast to these reports, four studies yielded no evidence of benefit in comparison with controls: Barron and Leary (1955), Seeman (1962), Karson and Wiedershine (1961), and Wispé and Parloff (1965). All of these latter investigations are subject to serious reservations.

In the aggregate, these controlled investigations were done mostly on nonpsychotic patients who were considered to have psychoneuroses or personality disorders of varying degrees of severity. Therapy was mostly individual, with some group therapy, and lasted from a few weeks to over two years. The type of therapy represented was roughly divided between client-centered and psychoanalytically oriented, although a few other approaches were also used. For the most part, the outcome criteria measures were derived from personality tests, although some more global improvement ratings were also used. In a few instances, the criterion was some life behavior considered to be of central importance in reflecting adjustment.

Evaluative research with psychoneurotics and personality disorders is wanting in many respects. Few good studies are available, although the bulk of studies cannot be rejected out of hand. Reasons why research with these patients has lagged behind investigations with other samples have been discussed, and it is evident that it is much more feasible to do controlled research with institutionalized patients. However, if positive results have been obtained with schizophrenics, antisocial behavior disorders, and other such groups commonly held to be even more difficult to work with, one would presume that equally good or better results could be obtained with psychoneurotics. Clearly there is a current need for well-designed evaluative research with these types of disorders.

Phobias. Phobic patients are special cases of psychoneurosis, and their psychotherapy has been subjected to a number of controlled and uncontrolled evaluations. As is typical of uncontrolled evaluations, the criterion measures are too often subjective and ill-defined, and there is no assurance that the phobic reactions would have persisted without therapy except perhaps in cases of severe reactions of many years' duration. School phobias of recent origin in children might be expected to be more self-limiting than a lifelong dread of heights. School phobias have been treated by conventional psychotherapy with varying degrees of success, depending partly upon the criterion. Greenbaum (1964) reported seven out of eight children returning to school. Rodriguez, Rodriguez, and Eisenberg (1959) claimed 60 per cent success with boys and 93 per cent with girls in a three-year follow-up of brief psychotherapy. Coolidge, Brodie, and Feeney (1964) reported traditional psychotherapy successful in that the majority returned to school, but there were signs of arrested emotional development which were severe in 30 per cent and moderate in 42 per cent. In a longitudinal study of treated neurotic phobic patients with an average follow-up of twenty-three years, Errara and Coleman (1963) determined that phobias persisted at varying levels in eighteen of nineteen patients. On the other hand, Friedman (1950) claimed 70 per cent improvement or recovery in females and 90 per cent in males treated by short-term psychotherapy for travel phobia. Gerz (1966) claimed 76 per cent of phobic patients recovered, 17 per cent improved, and 7 per cent failures with logotherapy.

Uncontrolled clinical trials with behavior therapy are no less variable and form no less difficult a base for generalization. Hain, Butcher, and Stevenson (1966) treated twenty-seven patients with fears and anxieties by systematic desensitization and reported that 70 per cent showed marked improvement. About half were followed up, of whom 20 per cent became slightly worse in about a year and 13 per cent relapsed. Roberts (1964) found 84 per cent of thirty-eight women who were housebound because of phobic anxiety to improve in an inpatient setting, but only 55.3 per cent held up in an eighteen-month to sixteen-year follow-up. Varied phobias in twenty patients responded 100 per cent to relaxation and systematic desensitization as reported by Friedman and Silverstone (1967), but a follow-up less than a year later reduced this to 83 per cent. Wolpe (1961) claimed amelioration or elimination of phobic and other anxieties in 91 per cent of a series of thirty-nine patients, with no relapses or symptom substitutions. The patients were followed up for six months to four years.

Controlled experiments with phobics have been a relatively recent contribution of behavior therapists. They have successfully demonstrated removal of phobic symptoms primarily but not exclusively by Wolpean techniques and have shown that comparable benefits did not accrue from no treatment or from comparison treatments. This growing literature includes the work of Lazarus (1961) with acrophobia, claustrophobia, sex phobia, and other assorted phobias; Lang and Lazovik (1963) and Lang, Lazovik, and Reynolds (1965) with snake phobias; Cooke (1966) with fear of rats; Rachman (1966) with fear of spiders; Paul (1966) with fear of public speaking; and Hogan and Kirchner (1967) with fear of rats treated by "implosive therapy." Percentages of success are not as important as the fact that these experimenters have demonstrated significantly better results with behavior therapy than with other approaches, usually under careful experimental conditions and with rigorous and objective criterion measures. They have been most attentive to the problem of symptom substitution and have not found it to be characteristc of this method of treatment with its focus on symptom removal. Marks and Gelder (1965) and Gelder and Marks (1966) were unable, however, to demonstrate advantages of behavior therapy over other treatments with cases of agoraphobia and other fears.

Psychosomatic Disorders. A great many claims have been made for the beneficial effects of psychotherapy with psychosomatic disorders, but most of the research is in the form of uncontrolled surveys of results. This would appear to be a type of illness that should lend itself readily to good controlled trials, but the quality of many of the existing investigations precludes their usefulness. There are some, however, which are suggestive of the potentials in this area. Of the studies that have been reviewed, four yielded positive results and one was negative. They concern such conditions as peptic ulcer, asthma, ulcerative colitis, dermatoses, and hypertension, approached by a variety of therapeutic methods.

Chappell and Stevenson (1936) clearly demonstrated dramatic benefits of six weeks of daily group psychological training with patients who had long-established peptic ulcers. Berle et al. claimed more improvement and fewer operations and deaths among ulcerative colitis patients who received psychotherapy than among medically treated controls (Berle, Pinsky, Wolf, & Wolff, 1953). Zhukov (1961) reported substantially greater improvement in groups treated for both eczema and neurodermatitis by hypnotherapy than in controls. Maher-Loughnan et al. demonstrated significant improvement relative to controls of asthma patients treated by hypnosis (Maher-Loughnan, MacDonald, Mason, & Fry, 1962). A study by Titchener, Sheldon, and Ross (1959) of changes in blood pressure in hypertensive patients who received group psychotherapy yielded negative results. It was concluded that participation in group therapy tended to nullify a reduction of high blood pressure that could be brought about by medical management alone. Grace, Pinsky, and Wolff (1954) were able to show consistently more favorable outcome in cases of ulcerative colitis treated by group therapy than by diet and medication. Groen and Pelser (1960), working with asthmatic patients, found greater benefits from group psychotherapy than from symptomatic drug treatments. Sinclair-Gieben and Chalmers (1959) demonstrated the unilateral removal of warts on the treated side by hypnotic suggestion in patients with bilateral warts.

Hypnotherapy proved distinctly efficacious in three of the more convincing studies, and a form of group psychological training in another. It is apparent that there is ample room and great need for controlled trials of various forms of psychotherapy with somatic disorders commonly thought to have a large psychic component.

Antisocial Behavior Problems. It is generally believed that individuals with antisocial behavior problems are poor therapeutic risks. Examination of the clinical literature reveals a rather pessimistic attitude toward the value of psychotherapy in modifying such behavior. There is, however, a fairly sizeable collection of experiments conducted both in institutional and community settings that offer refutation of this popular belief. The results of controlled experiments with antisocial behavior problems are overwhelmingly positive. Gersten (1951) reported the effects of group therapy, once a week for twenty sessions, on adolescent juvenile delinquents in a state school. He found improvement in IQ and school achievement, and a trend toward greater emotional security, social maturity, and better adjustment. Newburger (1963) and Newburger & Schauer (1953) reported improved sociometric structure, improved behavior ratings and work marks, and less disciplinary problems with boys seen for group therapy three times a week over three months in a state reformatory. Yonge and O'Connor (1954) found better intramural workshop behavior in adolescent defective delinquents seen twice a week in group therapy over a six-month period. Lieberman and Siegel (1957) reported more discharges as the result of the introduction of an individual, group, and milieu therapy program for sexual psychopaths in a state mental hospital. Snyder and Sechrest (1959) obtained more favorable behavioral evaluations and fewer violations on the part of defective delinquents seen weekly for group therapy over thirteen weeks. Adams (1961) reported that juvenile offenders prejudged to be amenable to treatment had less recidivism and lock-up time following individual therapy one to two times a week for nine months, but those judged not to be amenable were not helped. Arbuckle and Boy (1961) found that twelve weeks of nondirective counseling resulted in improvement in educational-vocational objectives, fewer referrals for discipline, better teacher behavior ratings, improved self-concept, and less peer rejection in junior high school boys with behavior problems.

Shelley and Johnson (1961), working with youthful offenders, reported a correctional camp experience offering six months of individual and group therapy to result in a decrease in antisocial themes on the TAT, which in turn was related to parole success. Massimo and Shore (1963) noted improvement in academic learning, attitudinal and personality variables, employment record, probation record, and interpersonal relations in antisocial adolescent boys subjected to extensive interaction with counselors in their own milieu over a ten-month period. Wolk (1963), working in a state reformatory for men, found that group therapy, conducted twice a week for a year, was associated with fewer infraction reports. Schwitzgebel and Kolb (1964) were successful in shaping behavior of youthful offenders with contacts in their natural surroundings two to three times a week for nine to ten months with a consequent reduction in delinquent behavior.

Persons (1965) found a twice-a-week eclectic individual therapy over ten weeks to improve performance on a delinquency scale, anxiety measure, and attitude questionnaire in a federal reformatory. Persons (1966, 1967) also demonstrated that twenty weeks of group therapy and individual therapy with teen-age boys in a state reformatory resulted in improved MMPI scores, fewer disciplinary reports, fewer parole violations and offenses after release, and a better employment record. Truax, Wargo, and Silber (1966) found institutionalized delinquent girls to improve in self-concept and delinquency scale scores and to spend more time out of the institution one year after group therapy that involved twenty-four sessions over a three-month period.

Ten of these fourteen studies that yielded positive results were with juvenile delinquents or youthful offenders. All but one dealt with males.

The principal approach was group therapy, but individual therapy, milieu therapy, and various combinations have also been used successfully. Treatment time in the various studies ranged from ten weeks to one year, and averaged about six months. Frequency of contacts ranged from once a week to at least ten times a week with a mode of twice a week. The duration of therapy was generally set for experimental purposes rather than as a response to changes in the patient's status. In very few instances was there any voluntary aspect to treatment. In most studies, institutionalized offenders were assigned to treatment whether they wished it or not and were compared with controls not so assigned. Reported outcome was of course partly a reflection of the particular criteria employed and depended upon whether the study took place in an institutional or community setting. There are three classes of criteria: (1) improved intramural adjustment judged from a diminution of antisocial behavior and/or evidence of positive adaptive behavior, (2) improved personality or attitudes revealed typically by psychometric devices, (3) improved extramural adjustment, usually in the form of less recidivism, fewer arrests or parole violations, and a better employment record. Of the eleven positive studies of institutionalized subjects, four extended to extramural adjustment and seven reported improved intramural adjustment, personality, or attitudes. Of the three positive studies with noninstitutionalized subjects, two reflected improved personality plus improved community adjustment and one limited itself to the latter.

One of the two studies that has been placed in the null category (Feder, 1962) was considered by its author as at least hopeful. Group therapy with institutionalized adolescent delinquents in this study was more limited in duration (eight weeks) and amount (about ten sessions) than any of the experiments that yielded clearly positive results. At the end of this period the treated boys did show greater gains than the untreated in "therapeutic readiness" but there were no significant differences in intramural adjustment as measured. Feder was optimistic about the results and stated that the treated group appeared "motivated to recognize their problems more freely" and had become better prepared for therapy, which, if more prolonged, might demonstrably alter aggressive and antisocial behavior. The other study with null results is the best known and most frequently cited of all in this area, the Cambridge-Somerville Youth Study (Teuber & Powers, 1953). Taking place from 1937 to 1945, it was a pioneering controlled study of delinquency *prevention* rather than of treatment of established delinquents. It is outweighed by the aggregate of studies with positive results that have been reviewed.

Conclusions favorable to psychotherapy can be drawn from this collection of experimental evidence. These studies have shown that psychotherapy not sought voluntarily by the patient, whether of the conventional individual or group variety or an approach that involves extensive interaction in the life space of the delinquent, in institutional or community settings, with juvenile delinquents, youthful offenders, adult prisoners, and adolescents with behavior problems, can have a demonstrably beneficial effect upon personality and attitudes, intramural and extra-mural adjustment. This has taken the form of fewer violations and more positive adaptive behavior within the institution and reduced antisocial behavior and recidivism outside of the institution as well as increased adaptive social behavior.

These results are easily subject to misinterpretation. Because the evidence for the positive effects of psychotherapy with delinquents is far more satisfactory than it is for psychoneurotics does not indicate that the former are easier to treat than the latter. No comparisons between the groups can be made from the data. It only means that researchers have been more successful in demonstrating effects with delinquents than with neurotics. Institutionalized delinquents are literally a captive population. They can be treated or left untreated at will. They can be assigned and regulated and their environment controlled. Improvement can be tangibly assessed by objectively counting behavioral transgressions. The chances of being able to design and complete a satisfactory experiment are on the side of the researcher. If antisocial behavior problems are indeed less responsive to psychotherapy than are other problems, the fact that success with them has been demonstrated bodes well for the efficacy of psychotherapy with the others. Then again, clinical impressions could be wrong; it could be that this type of patient is much easier to treat than clinicians believe.

Schizophrenia. More experiments evaluating psychotherapy yield null or negative results with schizophrenic patients than with any other type, yet the balance is clearly on the positive side. Some of the research shows positive results with one therapeutic approach but not with another. It would be well first to gather together those studies that reveal no benefits from therapy and examine them for commonalities.

In one of the therapy groups in Coons' (1957) study, the therapist tried to impart insight to the patient while holding group interaction to a minimum. These patients did not improve more than untreated controls on the Rorschach or on a measure of intellectual efficiency. King et al., working with highly withdrawn schizophrenics, found no benefit from verbal therapy over no treatment on a number of measures. If anything, it was detrimental for some who became mute or more verbally withdrawn (King, Armitage, & Tilton, 1960). Anker and Walsh

(1961) reported far less benefit from a year of conventional group therapy than from a leaderless activity group. Walker and Kelley (1963) obtained no significant differences in a number of outcome and follow-up measures between schizophrenic patients who received no psychotherapy and those who received a median of seventeen hours (range 4 to 131) of formal psychotherapy. MacDonald et al. reported that traditional group therapy, meeting twice a week for six months and focusing on self-understanding and insight, failed to promote, and in fact may have impeded, achievement of major hospital objectives (MacDonald, Blochberger, & Maynard, 1964). May and Tuma's (1965) study revealed that two hours a week of individual therapy for six months to one year, supervised by a psychoanalyst, was no more effective than no treatment in modifying mental health status and preventing rehospitalization. Although not significant, rehospitalization and time spent in the hospital during the three years following admission were greater for the psychotherapy group than for controls or for those treated by ECT, drugs, or drugs plus psychotherapy.

Therapeutic methods in these failures are variously characterized as formal, conventional, traditional, verbal, insight. What they appear to have in common is an attempt on the part of the therapist verbally to promote self-understanding, verbalization of feelings, and awareness of motivations underlying behavior. There is little evidence that this is of much value with schizophrenics, and in some studies it has effects opposite to the intended direction.

There is, however, no dearth of experiments demonstrating *positive* effects of other psychotherapeutic approaches with schizophrenic patients. Tucker's (1956) daily group therapy (forty-five hours in nine weeks) oriented toward communication was successful in reducing soiling behavior. The benefits of Peyman's (1956) group discussion and role playing twice a week for six months were reflected in psychological test performance. Cowden, Zax, Hague, and Finney (1956) observed greater improvement in hospitalized schizophrenic patients treated with group therapy and chlorpromazine than in those treated by the drug alone or in an untreated control group. While Coons' (1957) patients exposed to insight group therapy failed to improve more than controls, a group that focused on interaction succeeded. Jensen (1961) reported that thirteen weeks of group therapy in which the approach is not specified led to more open-ward status and discharge than did no therapy. Feifel and Schwartz (1953), Sacks and Berger (1954), Semon and Goldstein (1957), Kraus (1959), and Straight (1960) all reported more modest successes with group therapy in less clear-cut experiments. Stotsky et al. demonstrated benefits of a comprehensive individual and group vocationally oriented counseling approach (Stotsky, Dastan, & Vardolk, 1955).

Working with schizophrenics has stimulated a number of innovative approaches. These atypical and nonconventional therapeutically designed arrangements have been evaluated and proven beneficial to varying degrees. Cadman et al. pointed to improvement resulting from "roundtable psychotherapy" with no therapist present (Cadman, Misbach, & Brown, 1954). Azima et al. reported distinct behavioral improvement with "object-relations therapy" (Azima, Wittkower, & Latendresse, 1958). King, Armitage, and Tilton (1960) demonstrated clear advantages of an "operant-interpersonal method." Zirkle (1961) showed multiple benefits from either five minutes daily contact or twenty-five minutes weekly contact involving a warm, accepting relationship and friendly talk. Similarly, Dreiblatt and Weatherley (1965) demonstrated clear benefits in the form of shorter hospital stay and improved psychological test performance resulting from "brief-contact therapy" consisting of either three or six sessions of five to ten minutes of friendly, chatty, informal contact per week for two weeks. The contact was designed to indicate to the patient that he was esteemworthy, and it was more effective when not symptom oriented. Goertzel et al. employed the "body-ego technique" with regressed schizophrenics with some success when compared with controls (Goertzel, May, Salkin, & Schoop, 1965). Moore et al. obtained more improvement in treated patients relative to controls from a series of video-tape self-confrontations (Moore, Chernell, & West, 1965). In addition to its efficacy for inpatients, the efficacy of psychotherapy in reducing rehospitalization of formerly hospitalized patients was demonstrated by Sheldon (1964) and Shattan et al. (1966). Reference is further made to the research evaluations of therapeutic programs (primarily with schizophrenic patients) that have been outlined in chapter 7. Altogether, 87 per cent of the experiments evaluating therapeutic programs showed some positive benefits to the patients beyond whatever might accrue from custodial care and routine mental hospital treatment. Psychotherapy of many different kinds, applied individually, in groups or in a programmatic way, in inpatient and outpatient settings, has thus been shown to have demonstrable value with psychotic (predominantly schizophrenic) patients. Its greatest failure has been found in experiments in which the conventional insight approach was used.

Alcoholism. As with studies of other diagnostic groups, the picture obtained from reviewing uncontrolled studies and surveys on the treatment of alcoholism is varied and conflicting. A variety of treatment approaches has been used, ranging from the psychoanalytically oriented, in which alcoholism is considered a symptom of basic conflicts, to strict attention to removal of the symptom by aversive conditioning. For example, Moore and Ramseur (1960) observed effects of three hours a week of analytically oriented psychotherapy in a hospital setting. From among 100 patients, sixty drank consistently throughout their stay in the hospital. By the end of the first admission, seventy-four were drinking as much as when they were admitted and twenty-six were controlling drinking (nine were abstinent). Follow-up averaging 42.2 months revealed thirty-eight to be controlling drinking better than before hospitalization. Rathod et al. reported 50 per cent abstinence in a two-year follow-up after group therapy with eighty-four alcoholics (Rathod, Gregory, Blows, & Thomas, 1966). Glatt (1961) claimed one-third recovered and one-third improved in ninety-four alcoholics treated with group therapy.

Similar variability in success with behavior therapy has been reported. Voegtlin (1940) claimed 64.3 per cent absolute arrest rate with 538 patients treated with conditioned reflex therapy. Blake (1965), using a combination of relaxation and electrical aversion, reported 52 per cent abstinent a year after treatment. Davies et al. claimed 36 per cent of fifty patients abstinent two years after drug aversion treatment (Davies, Shepherd, & Myers, 1956). Anticipatory avoidance learning (ten to forty-six sessions) failed completely in a series of four cases (MacCulloch, Feldman, Orford, & MacCulloch, 1966). All patients resumed drinking, and one began within thirty minutes of leaving the hospital.

When controls have been applied, it has been shown that therapeutic intervention can be credited with effecting change. There are, however, few controlled studies. Ends and Page (1957, 1959) reported personality inventory improvement and a decrease in drinking behavior in alcoholics seen in group therapy as compared with untreated controls. McGinnis (1963) noted a significantly greater increase in ego strength in patients following group therapy than in controls.

Mental Defectives. Another group not usually associated with success in psychotherapy is mental defectives. Psychotherapy, traditionally, has been a verbal-expressive procedure requiring a capacity to introspect, express feelings, undergo cognitive restructuring, profit from past experience, and learn new ways of approaching life problems. At least average intelligence has been thought to be a necessary if not sufficient condition for response to psychotherapy. The trend in the treatment of the mentally retarded, however, has gradually been veering away from the purely custodial in the direction of habilitation. It is recognized that retardates too have personalities and adjustment problems that can interfere with their institutional adjustment and training regimen.

In two of the studies considered, the problem was further complicated by the use of subjects who were delinquent as well as retarded. In all four of the studies reviewed, positive benefits were reported. Three employed group therapy and one individual therapy, with the approaches adapted to the patient population. The outcome criteria were varied. One study focused on changes in IQ, the others on changes in observed personal and social behavior.

Yonge and O'Connor (1954) reported boys with an IQ range of 52 to 77 to improve relative to controls in workshop behavior with thirty-two sessions of group therapy over six months. Mundy (1957) observed a significant increase in IQ and improvement in social adjustment and increased readiness for special schooling in a group of retarded children at the imbecile level following nine to twelve months of individual nondirective play therapy. Wilcox and Guthrie (1957) reported that group therapy with females of IQ 53 to 90 resulted in improvement in such areas as self-care, social responsibility, self control, work, and recreation. Snyder and Sechrest's (1959) study of chronically delinquent males (IQ 50 to 79) revealed that thirteen weeks of structured, directive group therapy was effective in improving institutional behavior.

In view of the magnitude of the problem imposed by mental retardation upon psychotherapy, the fact that these kinds of positive results have been obtained is certainly encouraging. Psychotherapy has helped to achieve goals that are limited in scope but nonetheless important within the institutional context of the lives of these individuals.

SEVERITY OF MALADJUSTMENT

The severity of the patient's disturbance has been thought to be an important variable in predicting the success of psychotherapy. It seems logical that those with minor problems and minimal generalized disturbance should be easiest to help and most likely to improve, but this has not always proven to be the case.

Barron (1953a) found that patients who were better integrated initially were better able to use psychotherapy. Ninety per cent of the clinic patients in his sample whose initial scores were within normal range improved. This prompted him to conclude that the patients who are not very sick in the first place are most likely to get well. Grummon and John (1954) reported a "tendency" for client-centered therapy to be less effective with more disturbed patients. In a like manner, Katz, Lorr, and Rubinstein (1958) demonstrated that patients from thirteen

Veterans Administration clinics who were rated as less severely ill were more likely to improve than were those who were considered to be more severely ill. Schoenberg and Carr (1963) reported that patients whose neurodermatitis was unimproved with psychotherapy had a significantly greater number of initially deviant MMPI scale scores. McNair, Lorr, Young, Roth, and Boyd (1964) observed that patients who were more disturbed before therapy were also more disturbed after, and claimed that the initial scores constituted the best single predictor of later status. Premorbid adjustment as measured by the Phillips Prognostic Rating Scale was found by Query and Query (1964) to be a good indicator of success with schizophrenic patients. Morgenstern, Pearce, and Rees (1965) discovered that those with better initial scores on the Neuroticism Scale of the Maudsley Personality Inventory responded better to aversion therapy for transvestism. This suggested that those who recover have less complex and extensive symptoms to begin with.

A number of other studies offer evidence in support of a null hypothesis. Raskin (1949) found no relation between the starting point on several personality variables and the degree of success judged in terms of interview analysis measures. Page (1953) obtained no relationship between initial maladjustment of college counselees and outcome. Frank, Gliedman, Imber, Nash, and Stone (1957) did not uncover any difference in outcome as a function of initial discomfort scale scores. Klein (1960) surveyed thirty neurotic patients and saw no evidence of differential change in those initially classified as having moderate as against severe dysfunction. Cappon (1964) noted no relationship between severity or intensity of symptoms and outcome. Marks and Gelder (1965) found no difference in response to behavior therapy of phobic patients as a function of symptom severity.

The findings of Gottschalk, Mayerson, and Gottlieb (1967) were more complex. They reported that emergency, brief therapy clinic patients who displayed a high level of malfunctioning at the beginning on the Psychiatric Morbidity Scale were more likely to show malfunction at the end. However, those whose functional level was initially more impaired changed more in therapy than those who were less impaired. The initial level was no longer of predictive value three to seven months after termination. In a five-year follow-up evaluation, Stone, Frank, Nash, and Imber (1961) found initial symptom level to be moderately ($r = .41$, $p < .02$) related to amount of change. The correlation between initial level and outcome for the most improved group was $r = .66$, but of zero order for the least improved. The improved patients uniformly had a high initial discomfort level, while the least improved had either a high or low initial level.

Another cluster of studies suggests that the greatest change can be found in the most severely disturbed patients. Nichols and Beck (1960) noted that the more maladjusted the patient's original score on the California Personality Inventory, the greater the change tended to be. The therapists, however, tended to rate as improved those with well-adjusted initial scores. This suggested that the rating of change may have been influenced by the general level of adjustment while this was not observed in the client's ratings. Meltzoff and Blumenthal (1966) obtained better results with initially more poorly adjusted schizophrenic patients in a day treatment center. Ewing (1964) observed that the largest change in a group of college counselees was in individuals who initially showed the greatest dissatisfaction with themselves. Lessler and Strupp (1967) found more acutely disturbed patients to have a more favorable outcome, and Levis and Carrera (1967) presented MMPI data showing that those with the highest initial scores improved the most. Campbell and Rosenbaum (1967) followed sixty-one outpatients and reported that those with high initial distress reported more relief over four weeks of therapy than did those with low initial distress.

Insofar as duration of illness may be associated with severity, Frank, Gliedman, Imber, Nash, and Stone (1957) reported that patients with illnesses of short duration who remained in treatment did better than those whose illnesses were of long duration. Thorley and Craske (1950) obtained significantly more favorable responses to therapy with patients whose illnesses were of short duration. Miles, Barrabee, and Finesinger (1951), however, observed that the duration of the syndrome was not significantly related to outcome in cases of anxiety neurosis. Swensen and Pascal (1954b) controlled for a large number of variables and found no prognostic importance of duration of illness per se. Marks and Gelder (1965) reported duration of phobic symptoms to be unrelated to outcome.

Other investigators have examined the premorbid state and type of onset of the illness in relation to outcome. Swensen and Pascal (1954a), in a continuation of the same study, controlled for all variables except type of onset and determined that the improved psychotic group had a significantly more sudden onset. A low but significant correlation between outcome and type of onset was obtained. The relationship did not hold for nonpsychotic patients. Stephens and Astrup (1965), in their retrospective appraisal of 236 process and nonprocess schizophrenic patients, classified their status four to fourteen years after discharge. The nonprocess patients were strikingly superior in follow-up status. King, Armitage, and Tilton (1960) obtained a negative correlation between level of prepsychotic adjustment and improvement with a hospitalized sample. Bookbinder and Gusman (1964) assessed the premorbid attainment of sixty-three hospitalized psychotic patients as a determinant of participation in treatment. They obtained modest correlation coefficients for occupational and educational attainment (r = .34) and social relations (r = .28), but not for sex and marriage attainment.

This diversity of findings may be accounted for by several reasons. Severity of maladjustment can be looked at clinically in terms of symptom intensity, duration, pervasiveness, or extent of interference with contemporary life; or it can be viewed more broadly as the balance of functional assets and liabilities in an individual's life compared to some estimate of his potential. Some investigators simply define it operationally in terms of psychometric performance. It is easy to see why different research orientations to the meaning of severity can lead to different results and different approaches to prognosis. There is reason to believe that a relationship that might hold generally for neurotics might not hold for psychotics. Most important, though, is that the question as it is usually formulated is too simple, and lends itself to oversimplified answers. The general possibilities are: (1) The initially better and more poorly adjusted patients both improve, but the rate and/or amount of gain is greater in the initially more maladjusted who do or do not reach the level of the initially better adjusted. (2) Both improve, but the rate and/or amount of gain is greater for those who are initially better adjusted. (3) Only the less maladjusted improve; the more maladjusted remain the same or get worse. (4) Only the more maladjusted improve; the less maladjusted remain the same or get worse. (5) The progress of the groups is parallel and not a function of initial level, with those who are better adjusted at the start still better adjusted at the end.

Those possibilities that concern relative rates of *decline* rather than gain have been omitted, as have possible nonlinear alternatives, for this is meant as an illustrative rather than an exhaustive list of possible outcomes. Researchers have for the most part not conceptualized the question in these terms. Thus, when we are told that those who are least disturbed are most apt to improve, we cannot tell which of the possible outcomes—the second, third, or fifth—actually occurred. It is felt that future research on this issue should posit these more specific questions in the hope of getting more complete and less ambiguous answers.

THE SEARCH FOR OUTCOME PREDICTORS

Ego Strength. Closely associated with the study of severity of maladjustment as a prognostic indicator is the attempt to develop prognostic indices from psychological tests, focusing on a single variable such as ego strength. As a construct, ego strength is sufficiently ill-defined to mean different things to different people. It is no surprise, therefore, that the two principal measures of ego strength are simply empirical extracts of the two major personality assessment procedures, the MMPI and the Rorschach. Neither the Barron Ego Strength Scale nor the Klopfer Rorschach Prognostic Rating Scale was designed or validated as a measure of ego strength. Both were derivatives of prominent assessment devices and were designed to predict the response of patients to psychotherapy. They were then labeled from their content to be measures of ego strength. Implicit in both of these searches for predictors is the assumption that the stronger or better integrated the personality at first, the better the chances for success in psychotherapy.

The Barron Es Scale consists of sixty-eight items from the MMPI that correlated significantly with improvement in thirty-three neurotic patients in outpatient clinic treatment. Improvement was reliably rated by two judges who were not the therapists, and the sample was dichotomized into improved and unimproved groups whose average Es scale score differed significantly (Barron, 1953b). By inspection of the responses of the improved group they were judged to have the following pretherapy characteristics: "(a) good physical functioning; (b) spontaneity, ability to share emotional experiences; (c) conventional church membership, but nonfundamentalist and undogmatic religious beliefs; (d) permissive morality; (e) good contact with reality; (f) feelings of personal adequacy and vitality; (g) physical courage and lack of fear." One wonders why they were in treatment in the first place. The unimproved group on the other hand was characterized by "(a) many and chronic physical ailments; (b) broodiness, inhibition, a strong need for emotional seclusion, worrisomeness; (c) intense religious experiences, belief in prayer, miracles, the Bible; (d) repressive and punitive morality; (e) dissociation and ego-alienation; (f) confusion, submissiveness, chronic fatigue; (g) phobias and infantile anxieties" (p. 328). In three separate cross-validations in different settings, successive correlations of .42 ($N = 53$), .54 ($N = 52$), and .38 ($N = 46$) were obtained. Barron noted that the sample was too small for scale development. Although the correlations do reflect a relationship, the percentage of correct predictions and false positives should be presented with a prognostic device if its utility is to be properly judged.

Several studies have failed to confirm the validity of the Es Scale. Gallagher did not find any relationship at all between success in therapy with thirty clients at the Pennsylvania State University Psychological Clinic and the Barron Es scale. In this study fifteen most and least successful clients were chosen by Tucker's Multiple Criterion Scale (Gallagher, 1954). A significant inverse correlation (rho $= -.41$) between pretherapy Es scores of twenty-six neurotic patients and posttherapy improvement ratings was obtained by Crumpton, Cantor, and Batiste (1960). Getter and Sundland (1962) applied it to fifty-nine therapy candidates fifteen of whom were rated as unimproved, twenty-five improved, and nineteen remained untreated. No significant relationship was found between ego strength, improvement in therapy, or number of hours in therapy. A significant negative correlation existed between Es and age. Males obtained significantly higher Es scores than females. The authors offered the explanation that this was a reflection of a cultural sex role by which males tend to deny psychological and physical weakness whose admission is acceptable to females in our culture. Fiske, Cartwright, and Kirtner (1964) similarly found the Barron Es Scale wanting as a predictor of outcome with ninety-three subjects in client-centered therapy. Endicott and Endicott (1964) also determined that it was unrelated to outcome with forty untreated patients and twenty-one patients in individual psychotherapy. In the light of these studies, the Barron Es scale does not stand up as a promising predictor of therapeutic success.

Klopfer (1951) proposed a rating scale derived from Rorschach determinants to predict success in psychotherapy. The Rorschach Prognostic Rating Scale (RPRS) was offered as a measure of potential ego strength that could be mobilized or made available through therapy. In short order there were many attempts to validate it. Johnson (1953) reported that it clearly differentiated between most and least improved children in play therapy in a residential school for the educationally retarded.

Mindess (1953) investigated the validity of the RPRS using eighty clinic patients including schizophrenics, schizoids, neurotics, exhibitionists, and homosexuals. Half were voluntary patients and half court-assigned cases. The Rorschach was given at the beginning of treatment and therapists rated patients after at least six months of treatment. The correlation between the sum of six Rorschach scores (M, FM, m, shading, color, and average form level) and the final adjustment rating was $r = .81$. By eliminating ten psychotic patients who contributed excessively to the correlation, a coefficient of $r = .66$ was obtained. This was raised to $r = .72$ by application of multiple regression coefficients. Of all the signs, form level and human movement responses were the most effective predictors of success. The efficiency of the RPRS with court cases was no different from its efficiency with patients who sought therapy volitionally.

Another validation attempt utilized forty predominantly neurotic patients at the Veterans Administration Hospital, Long Beach, California, whose closed case records were rated for success (Kirkner, Wisham, &

Giedt, 1953). In this instance only M, m, and shading responses proved to be useful predictors. A multiple R of .70 was obtained using them. The correlation between the sum of the weighted scores and the criterion was .67. The sums of M, Fm, m, and shading responses also correlated .67 with the criterion.

Stutterers at the University of California at Los Angeles Psychological and Speech Clinic were used as a homogeneous group that presented a particular prognostic challenge to the RPRS (Sheehan, Frederick, Rosevear, & Spiegelman, 1954). Thirty-five patients were given the Rorschach at the beginning of therapy, and the prognostic scores of a therapist-rated "most improved" and "least improved" group were compared. As predicted, they proved to be significantly ($p < .01$) different. Significant differences for M, FM, and m were obtained. Patients who continued in treatment were significantly differentiated from dropouts on the total prognostic score, M and FM. Improvement was judged on personality dimensions, not on symptom abatement. As far as the stuttering was concerned, the scale did not predict its symptomatic improvement.

Seidel (1960) reported results with sixty-three schizophrenic patients at St. Elizabeth Hospital, Washington, D.C., who were classified as having attained social recovery or recovery in less than three years, as opposed to continuous hospitalization for at least three years. Point biserial correlation of this dichotomization and RPRS total score was .40. Correlation with form level was .44 and with other determinants .34. All coefficients were statistically significant at the 1 per cent level. The poorer the premorbid social and sexual adjustment as rated on the Phillips Case History Prognostic Rating Scale, the lower the ego strength as measured by the RPRS ($r = .30$).

Cartwright (1958) studied thirteen completed client-centered cases rated on a nine-point scale of success by the counselor. The tau correlation between success and total RPRS was .52, but none of the Rorschach variables correlated significantly with outcome when taken singly or in pairs. From inspection of the data, an *ad hoc* "strength" score consisting of the highest two of M, color, and form level for each subject correlated .73 with the criterion. Further support for this derived strength score was subsequently offered by Cartwright (1959).

Endicott and Endicott (1964) reported on RPRS results with forty untreated patients and twenty-one who were in individual, psychoanalytically oriented psychotherapy. Outcome was determined by therapist ratings on the Miles, Barrabee, and Finesinger Evaluation of Improvement Scale. The mean RPRS score, mean R, mean raw shading, and mean raw color were higher for both the treated and untreated patients who improved than for those who did not. Significant point biserial correlations in the treated group were RPRS (.43), R (.41), raw shading (.40), and color (.40) and in the untreated group RPRS (.38), R (.32), and color (.54). In this study M, FM, m, and form level were not significantly related to improvement.

On the negative side, Schulman (1963) failed to confirm the validity of the RPRS or Cartwright's Strength Scale. Posttreatment Hunt-Kogan Movement Scale scores to evaluate progress in therapy and pretreatment Rorschachs were available for twenty clients at the Illinois Student Counseling Service. The rank difference correlation between RPRS and movement scale scores was .32 (not significant), and the correlation of the Strength Scale and the criterion was of zero order. Another failure was reported by Fiske, Cartwright, and Kirtner (1964). The RPRS was one of a number of predictors that failed to relate to therapeutic gain. In another experiment, a series of pairs (one successful and one unimproved) of pretreatment Rorschachs was given to twelve psychologists for categorizing (Filmer-Bennett, 1955). The group did little better than chance. While not strictly a test of the RPRS, their judgments were reported to be similar to those obtained by the RPRS. Treatment in this study was not limited to psychotherapy, however, but included shock and occupational therapy.

On balance, the RPRS has been found to be successful in predicting therapist-judged outcome of psychotherapy far more often than not. There is a demonstrable association between pretherapy Rorschach signs, alleged to measure ego strength potential, and improvement with psychotherapy. The relationship exists but does not appear high enough for individual clinical prediction.

Three measures, the Barron Es Scale, Klopfer's RPRS, and Cartwright's modification of the RPRS, all purporting to measure ego strength and to be predictors of outcome in psychotherapy, were applied to the same hospital sample (Adams & Cooper, 1962). Since no significant correlations between the Es Scale and the two Rorschach measures were obtained, the authors cautioned that individuals who might be accepted for therapy on the basis of the Es would be rejected on the basis of the Rorschach.

Other Rorschach Prognostic Signs. Other Rorschach-based prognostic scales have been devised and attempts at global predictions made. Some have been more successful than others. Starting with ten signs of "treatability" derived from a subsample of sixteen promiscuous girls, Bradway et al. cross-validated them on a second group of twenty girls. Improvement was judged by the treating social worker (Bradway, Lion,

& Corrigan, 1946). Division of the sample into those possessing five or more treatability signs and those with less than five was successful in predicting improvement. The improvement criterion was weak, the results not treated statistically, and the findings presented as tentative because of the small sample. The ten signs used were: twenty or more responses, average time per response less than forty seconds, two or more FM, presence of FK and Fc, FC equaling or exceeding CF, D% equaling or exceeding fifty, four or more P, R% to last three cards forty or more, no rejections.

Another early attempt at Rorschach prognosis, using fifty-three patients who were in psychotherapy because they showed delay in recovery from physical illness or accident, found no location, determinant, or content scores predictive of outcome (Harris & Christiansen, 1946). The global ratings of a judge were significantly associated with clinical ratings, but since he possessed information about an empirical weighting scheme derived from the scores, not much confidence can be placed in this result. Barron (1953a) applied the Harris-Christiansen Rorschach Prognostic Index to thirty-three Langley Porter Clinic cases and obtained a zero correlation. When test protocols were sorted by four clinicians, only one approached significance, and in a negative direction at that. The Davidson adjustment sign list did not differentiate between therapist-judged improved and unimproved cases in a child guidance clinic (Lessing, 1960).

Piotrowski's long-term Rorschach prognostic index yielded most promising results with schizophrenic patients. Signs were postdictively derived by Piotrowski and Lewis (1952), applied to a 1958 sample of thirty schizophrenics and revised, and then validated on another sample of seventy schizophrenics by Piotrowski and Bricklin (1958). The prognostic index correctly predicted 90 per cent of the cases on follow-up. Prediction on a 1959 sample of 103 schizophrenics, half inpatient and half outpatient, was correct in 89 per cent of the cases (Piotrowski & Bricklin, 1961). The criterion measure for outcome was follow-up statements by experienced clinicians, working independently, using clinical and life-history data alone. To be considered improved, the patient had to improve in three areas: thought processes, psychological relations and work, and attitudes toward self. For the 173 subjects in the combined samples, all twelve prognostic signs predicted outcome beyond chance.

The prognostic value of Koret and Rubin's signs (R, F%, F + %, M, Sum C, Rejections, P, Cards VIII–X%, A%) were tested by Davids and Talmadge (1964) on fifty mothers of disturbed children. The mothers were seen weekly by psychiatric social workers for at least one year, and the Hunt-Kogan Movement Scale was applied by an impartial case worker at termination. For these nine signs, a weighted score devised by the authors revealed a difference at the $p = .001$ level between those who showed therapeutic movement and those who did not. This, of course, would require cross-validation. Most of the individual raw scores were predictive but many were a function of the total number of responses.

Rogers and Hammond (1953) appraised the Rorschach as a predictor on 109 unselected Denver Veterans Administration Mental Hygiene Clinic cases classified as unimproved, slightly improved, or much improved by the therapists in consultation with a senior psychiatric consultant. Three experienced psychologists made both snap judgments and studied assessments with and without knowledge of the name of the therapist. Under one condition, judgments were made on the basis of the therapist's name alone, without reference to the test material. None of these total impression approaches were at all successful even though the judges agreed fairly well among themselves. Application of the Harris-Christiansen scoring method failed to discriminate between criterion groups. In addition, ninety-nine different Rorschach scores and several patterns were applied but did not discriminate. Some evidence was presented that Extensor Human Movement responses, when they appear alone in a record, may be associated with improvement.

Peterson (1954) applied Rorschach sign lists derived from Muench, Haimowitz and Carr to pre- and posttherapy records of forty-two subjects of the Pennsylvania State College psychotherapy research group project and checked them against Tucker's independent objective criterion of success. Obtained correlations were low and did not support the hypothesis that the qualitative aspects of the Rorschach would correlate better with the criterion than quantitative ones.

Another study in which Rorschach indices failed to predict outcome was carried out with fifty-one outpatients at the Veterans Administration Center, Des Moines, Iowa (Roberts, 1954). The pre- and posttreatment psychiatric status of each patient was rated independently by three experienced judges from detailed records of interviews. Eleven different Rorschach indices thought to have predictive value failed to reject the null hypothesis. Bloom (1956) injected a note of caution by finding different prognostic signs for those with productive and nonproductive Rorschach records. This suggests a need for controlling this variable in prognostic research. Gallagher (1954) reported a nonsignificant relationship between Rorschach productivity (number of responses) and outcome. Applying the concept of response variability on the Rorschach as a trait, Rakusin (1953) studied its relation to behavior in therapy. Pretherapy Rorschach variability did not prove to be significantly related to maladjustment and failed to predict behavior variability in therapy. It was not predictive of insight, planning, or variability of approach to the problem shown in therapy by the client. Rorschach measures of rigidity, variability, and productivity were not predictive of discomfort relief or problem resolution. On the other hand, the amount of planning, insight, and variability of approach to problems in therapy was predictive of improvement.

The search for individual Rorschach determinants as predictors has not been too successful. Productivity as measured by the total number of responses (R) has been found to be related in roughly half of the studies but not in the others. Form level has been cited as the most important indicator in a minority of studies but was unrelated to success in the remainder. The Movement response (M) has been reported as related to outcome in at least half of the studies, but there are some clearly dissenting findings. Other determinants taken singly have, here and there, turned up as predictors. Cross-validation of such findings is rare. In brief, no single Rorschach determinant has proven to be a reliable predictor of outcome.

Other Prognostic Measures. Harris and Christiansen (1946) reported five of ten MMPI scales to be prognostic (Pd, PdR, Pa, Sc, Ma), but large sigmas and overlapping made the scores too unreliable for individual use. Global grouping of MMPIs into three prognostic categories (good, indifferent, poor) yielded a significant association with some of the clinical ratings, but again the clinical utility of the procedure is questionable.

Carr and Whittenbaugh (1965) reported outcome ratings to be positively related to pretherapy levels of defensiveness and control as measured by the MMPI K scale ($r = .38$), but to be inversely ($r = -.49$) related to general distress and anxiety as measured by the Welsh A Scale. The authors interpreted this as suggesting that those who rate themselves as improved tend to enter treatment with "less exhibitionistic urges" to confess their weaknesses and display their problems.

Barron (1953a) found only the Pa scale of the MMPI to discriminate between successful and unsuccessful cases. Using the total MMPI, only 62.12 per cent correct predictions could be made, hardly enough to give it prognostic utility. Using the MMPI index of all T scores within the "normal" range of 30–70, predictive accuracy rose to 73 per cent. With this requirement holding except for the D scale score or D + Pt, the accuracy went up respectively to 75 and 80 per cent. These findings were not cross-validated. Endicott and Endicott (1964) reported the

MMPI to be of no value for prognostic purposes. Derr and Silver (1962) were unable to turn up reliable predictors from the Rorschach, TAT, Bender-Gestalt, Sentence Completion, P-F, Draw-A-Person, or Achievement Task. Initial insight, defined as verbalized awareness of deficits, failed to predict length of hospitalization in Eskey (1958).

Morgenstern, Pearce, and Rees (1965) discovered but did not cross-validate differences between successful and unsuccessful cases on the Maudsley Personality Inventory neuroticism scale, verbal conditioning scale, and masculinity-femininity interest scale. Fiske, Cartwright, and Kirtner (1964) saw some promise in the Kirtner Typology as a predictor. Blau (1950) approached the problem differently, by analyzing initial interview verbalizations. Each client statement was classified as reflecting a positive, ambivalent, or negative attitude toward the self, the counselor, and others, or as miscellaneous. The predictive index (PAS% + AmS% − NAS%) correlated .90 with counselor outcome ratings. The small sample of seven cases requires enlargement, and cross-validation is in order for this promising index.

Personality Characteristics as Outcome Predictors. The idea that selected personality characteristics of patients may be associated with response to psychotherapy is an attractive one and has led to many hypotheses. With so many personality variables that could logically be related to outcome, it is no wonder that the arrows have not been clustered on the target. Thus we find under scrutiny an assortment of variables—such as anxiety, hostility, suggestibility, introversion-extraversion, interpersonal and social relations, ethnocentrism and authoritarianism—which yield few reliable predictive indicators.

Anxiety is commonly thought to be not only desirable but also necessary for therapeutic success. Greenfield and Fey (1956) and Greenfield (1958), however, reported that the *degree* of anxiety was not associated with delay in seeking help, and Katz, Lorr, and Rubinstein (1958) found high anxiety not related to improvement. Derr and Silver (1962), on the other hand, found manifest anxiety to be the only one of fourteen measures predictive of outcome; this result, however, is easily attributable to chance. Adams (1961) reported anxiety as one of the elements predictive of amenability to treatment of offenders, but did not isolate the variable. Morgenstern, Pearce, and Rees (1965) were unable to confirm the value of Willoughby Anxiety Scale scores as predictors of outcome of aversion therapy. Level of anxiety was not a strong predictor of improvement ($r = .24$) for Gottschalk, Mayerson, and Gottlieb (1967), nor was it related to length of stay in the study of Affleck and Garfield (1961). While some felt anxiety may be necessary to motivate a patient to undertake psychotherapy, there is no strong case for believing that the level of anxiety has a positive bearing on outcome.

Suggestibility was determined to be related to staying in therapy by Imber et al. (1956) and Frank et al. (1957), but in the latter study it was not related to improvement. Morgenstern et al. (1965) similarly found it unrelated to success. Extraversion may be a consideration in some therapies. Patients who were less extraverted were judged to have made little progress in behavior therapy as reported by Lazarus (1963).

Katz, Lorr, and Rubinstein (1958) ascertained that low antisocial personality patterns are predictive of continuation but not of improvement, while Gottschalk et al. (1967) did obtain an association between a Human Relations Scale score and improvement. Contrary to expectations, Schoenberg and Carr (1963) obtained more improvement in dermatitis cases who showed more overt hostility. Leary and Harvey (1956) found a sex-hostility interaction, with hostile men more likely to change (not necessarily in the direction of improvement) than hostile women.

Ethnocentrism was found by Barron (1953a) to be negatively correlated with improvement, but Tougas (1954) reported that extremes, whether high or low, differed from marginals but not from each other. This suggested that there may be an optimal range of effectiveness. Gallagher, Sharaf, and Levinson (1965) reported that nonauthoritarian patients tend to be given therapy and Katz et al. (1958) noted that low authoritarianism was predictive of continuation but not of improvement. Dana (1954), however, claimed that adequate attitudes toward authority were related to improvement.

The hypothesis that social desirability, as a personality trait, would be related to various behaviors in therapy was tested by Pumroy (1961). The behaviors dealt with were keeping and being on time for appointments, terminating with consent, completing testing, conforming, and outcome. Unfortunately, outcome ratings were made from case notes by the experimenter who formulated the hypotheses. Some hypotheses were supported, others not. The overall picture is that the social desirability scale may predict some gross behavior, but the more specific the behavior the less likely a relationship.

A potentially useful means of predicting client success in counseling was offered by Kemp (1963). Taking extremes on the Rokeach Dogmatism Scale, he experimented with two groups, one "open minded" and one with a closed belief system. His observations led him to speculate that those who had "open" minds would probably benefit more from group counseling, whereas those with "closed" minds would avoid the necessary personal involvement. No data about benefit was provided, but the two types of individuals did perform differentially in a group counseling situation.

Other Predictors. Page (1953) attempted to predict the outcome of counseling from various language measures obtained in the initial phases of the treatment of forty-three college student clients. Four measures of language variability and two measures of productivity were correlated with a Maladjustment Score from the Munroe Checklist applied to the Rorschach and three outcome criterion scores. Variability measures were the spread and shift of content areas used, the type-token ratio measure of vocabulary flexibility, and shifts in feeling expressions between positive, negative, and ambivalent categories. Productivity was gauged from the total words used and the ratio between the number of expressed feelings and content statements. Neither the variability of content and feeling nor the total amount of expressed feeling was related to outcome. The amount of client talk (productivity) was seen to bear a low positive relation to outcome.

Further research on the same sample focused on the hypothesis that behavior variability is related to adjustment and that successful therapy is accompanied by increased variability (Roshal, 1953). The hypotheses were supported using the type-token ratio as the measure of behavior variability. Although the results differed from those of Page, Snyder (1953) points out that Roshal was investigating changes in variability from the first to the last interview while Page was looking at variability at the start of therapy.

Pursuing the import of variability as a trait in relation to therapy, Blau (1953) predicted that early client responses would be stereotyped repetitions of the problem, but would be supplanted by increased response variability as therapy progresses, leading to understanding and insight and discussion of plans for future action and general improvement. As part of the same group research project at Pennsylvania State College, Blau selected the twelve most and twelve least improved cases by Tucker's Multiple Criterion Score. Client responses were classified into seven categories. As Page had also found, the much improved patients had slightly but not significantly more total responses than the less improved. There was no significant difference between the groups in Discussion of the Problem or Understanding and Insight. Both groups made more statements referring to Relief from Symptoms as therapy progressed, but the increase was much larger for the most improved. For both groups there was a tendency early in therapy to use statements of complaints and symptoms and statements reporting situations, facts and incidents, and history and development of complaints. Later in treatment there were more statements about decisions regarding future actions and intentions to change.

The lack of consistency in this conglomeration of studies is probably due to the fragmentation that comes from examining one personality variable at a time without controlling for a host of others. The matter of who will profit from psychotherapy is undoubtedly complexly determined, and examination of any single patient variable in its relationship to outcome is apt to account for only a small portion of the total variance.

10

The Patient as an Outcome Variable: II. Background, Organismic, Demographic, Motivational, and Attitudinal Factors

Background, organismic, demographic, motivational, and attitudinal factors may be associated with the likelihood of improvement in psychotherapy. The roles of such variables as age, sex, marital status, social class, IQ, education, motivation, and the patient's expectancies about therapy have all been investigated.

AGE

Age and Selection. One of the most firmly entrenched beliefs shared by psychotherapists is that younger individuals within a given sample of patients can benefit more from psychotherapy than older ones. This is reflected in the preferential selection of younger patients. Freud believed that those over fifty years of age were not suitable for psychoanalysis, and many clinicians prefer a limit lower than that. Crowley (1950) surveyed the age of patients accepted at the Low-Cost Psychoanalytic Service of the William Alanson White Institute for Psychiatry. Accepted patients averaged twenty-eight years of age against 32.6 years for those rejected, and none of the applicants over age forty were accepted. Knapp et al. reported a survey of 100 consecutive applicants to the Boston Psychoanalytic Institute (Knapp, Levin, McCarter, Wermer, and Zetzel, 1960). Where possible, individuals over age thirty-five were excluded. The mean age was twenty-seven. Half, incidentally, were in work related to psychiatry and psychoanalysis and 72 per cent were from professional and academic fields. Age as a factor in selection or assignment is by no means limited to psychoanalytic institutes. Bailey et al. surveyed 549 patients at the Veterans Administration Mental Hygiene Clinic, New York City, and found that the mean age of those assigned to psychotherapy was significantly lower than that of patients assigned to other forms of treatment (Bailey, Warshaw, & Eichler, 1960). The percentage of those receiving psychotherapy in a public hospital was shown to decrease progressively from 68 per cent for ages sixteen to twenty-five to 25 per cent for ages forty-six to sixty-three. In this investigation a biserial $r = .50$ between youth and receipt of psychotherapy was obtained (Gallagher, Levinson, & Erlich, 1957). In a subsequent study they obtained a biserial $r = .52$ (Gallagher, Sharaf, & Levinson, 1965). Rosenthal and Frank (1958) reported a preference for younger (below age thirty) patients in selection for individual therapy, but age was not a factor in acceptance of therapy by the patient.

Age and Continuation in Therapy. Once the patient has been accepted for therapy, the relationship between age and continuation in treatment has been studied by several investigators, but no firm association has been established. In a variety of different settings, no significant relationship was found by Frank, Gliedman, Imber, Nash, and Stone (1957), Sullivan, Miller, and Smelser (1958), Rosenthal and Frank (1958), Barclay and Hilden (1961), Affleck and Garfield (1961), Beck, Kantor, and Gelineau (1963), or Yalom (1966). Ross and Lacey (1961) reported a nonsignificant tendency for older children to remain longer and Katz and Solomon (1958) a tendency (significance not determined) for younger adults to remain. From the available data age does not emerge as an important determinant of length of stay in treatment.

Age and Outcome. A far more critical issue is the relation of age to outcome of therapy. Information relevant to the hypothesis that younger patients improve more has been furnished by numerous studies. Surprisingly enough, the majority of the studies show no relationship. Seeman (1954), comparing a younger group (aged twenty-one to twenty-seven) with an older group (aged twenty-eight to forty), found the mean success ratings to be exactly equal. Cartwright (1955b) obtained a negligible correlation between age and outcome with another outpatient sample ranging in age from eighteen to forty-three. Rosenbaum, Friedlander, and Kaplan (1956) similarly reported no relationship in an outpatient group whose age was predominantly in the nineteen- to thirty-nine-year category, and Rosenthal and Frank (1958) failed to uncover any relation between age and percentage of patients improved with therapy. With an age range extending higher (twenty-four to fifty-seven years), Feifel and Eells (1963) found no systematic relation between age and patient assessment of change. Examining a still broader range (seventeen to sixty-seven), Cabeen and Coleman (1962) also failed to obtain a relation between age and outcome in their study of the effects of group therapy on sex offenders. Neither Lazarus (1963), Rachman (1965), nor Schmidt, Castell, and Brown (1965) found differences in the success of behavior therapy with adult neurotic patients as a function of age.

Graham (1958) compared outcome statistics for ninety-six adults and forty-four children in a psychoanalytically oriented clinic and found that the percentages considered definitely improved were almost identical. The sample of Kaufman, Frank, Friend, Heims, and Weiss (1962) was composed exclusively of schizophrenic children. Comparing the ten most improved and ten least improved from a sample of forty patients, no significant age difference appeared. The most improved group averaged 8.2 years at the start of treatment, and the least improved 7.6 years.

Less numerous are studies that support the hypothesis that youth favors success, and most of them show differentiations within samples of children. Rodriguez, Rodriguez, and Eisenberg (1959) found more failures in treatment of school phobias in boys older than eleven than in those under this age. Sobel (1962), examining his own private practice, observed an increasingly higher percentage of successful completion in younger children (ten and under) than in those eleven to fifteen years of age, with those from fifteen to twenty-one being least satisfactory. Similarly, Gluck, Tanner, Sullivan, and Erickson (1964) noted the greatest symptom improvement in children under age six, followed by those aged six to twelve, and the least in the thirteen- to seventeen-year bracket. Working with adolescent inpatients, Warren (1965) observed that younger neurotics and psychotics combined did significantly better than older ones.

With adult inpatients, some of whom were receiving physical therapies as well as psychotherapy, Thorley and Craske (1950) reported those with unfavorable outcomes to be significantly older (mean age 38.45) than those with a favorable outcome (mean age 30.14). Feldman and MacCulloch (1965) observed better results from anticipatory avoidance learning with patients under thirty and worse with those over forty. The sample was too small for a meaningful statement about the reliability of the result.

To balance these positive results are some studies reporting that older patients respond better. In Luff and Garrod's (1935) sample of 500 cases the following successful outcomes in five age brackets were reported: seventeen to twenty years, 50.8 per cent; forty-one to fifty years, 57.1 per cent; over fifty years, 60.4 per cent. The significance of these differences was not tested, but middle age appears to present an advantage rather than a handicap. Meltzoff and Blumenthal (1966) demonstrated more success relative to controls in a day treatment center for schizophrenic patients with those over age forty-one than for those under forty-one. Marks and Gelder (1965), reporting on the effects of behavior therapy in phobic patients, noted that those improving were older (mean age forty) than those who were unchanged (mean age twenty-seven).

None of these experiments was specifically designed to test the age-outcome hypothesis. Consequently, many of the experimenters may have unavoidably permitted flaws to cloud the conclusions. The main problem is systematic selection bias. The tendency has been for clinics and therapists to give preferential selection to younger patients. It could be that only those older patients who have some special attributes to compensate for their age get selected while younger patients with poorer prognoses might be selected chiefly *because* of their age. If this were the case, the dependent variable of age would be confounded with prognosis. Age may also be confounded with other variables, such as education and its correlates. Older people in our era tend not to have had the formal education increasingly demanded of younger persons. A well-designed experiment, therefore, would require assignment to therapy of patients of different age groups who were matched as far as possible on other background and prognostic variables. Change may have different meanings at different stages of development. For example, change in occupational choice or in ability to socialize has different intrapersonal and extrapersonal significance and consequences at eighteen than at thirty-eight. Pending more definitive tests of the hypothesis and judging from the weight of experimental evidence that presently exists, age (at least through middle age) does not seem to be a particularly potent outcome variable.

IQ

The belief that IQ is positively related to success in psychotherapy is so firmly entrenched that it is typical for researchers to deal with it as a side issue and to explain away their findings should the relationship fail to obtain. Verbal therapies, in particular, involve learning, mastery of new concepts and cognitive patterns, capacity for introspection and self-exploration via linguistic media, and translation of feeling states into meaningful verbal communication. Since these kinds of activities would seem to require a high order of intelligence, intelligence is usually considered to be a necessary but not sufficient condition for success in psychotherapy. This idea has received experimental support in a variety of different settings. A positive relation between IQ and therapeutic outcome was reported by Thorley and Craske (1950), Barron (1953a), Rosenberg (1954), Ellis (1958), Miles, Barrabee, and Finesinger (1951), Rioch and Lubin (1959), and McNair, Lorr, Young, Roth, and Boyd (1964).

The relation has not always proven to be a simple linear one. Thorley and Craske reported that those with superior intelligence had more favorable than unfavorable results, but the finding was not statistically reliable. Those of below average intelligence, however, showed significantly more unfavorable results. Superior intelligence was thus not seen so much as a boon as below average intelligence was seen as a handicap. Rioch and Lubin similarly noted that the accuracy of prediction increases as the IQ decreases. Indications that the connection is not as clearly established as psychotherapists believe are found in a number of other investigations. Harris and Christiansen (1946) reported IQ not to be prognostic in a group of fifty-three patients in brief psychoanalytically oriented psychotherapy. Shore, Massimo, and Ricks (1965), dealing with delinquent boys with IQs in the range of 85 to 110, found the initial IQ to be unrelated to other types of change. The therapy employed focused on vocational counseling, academic assistance, and concrete experience. The authors suggest that IQ may only be of importance with verbal therapies aimed at the acquisition of insight through language.

Similarly, Cabeen and Coleman (1962), working with incarcerated sex offenders ranging in IQ from 90 to 143, obtained no relation between IQ and outcome. In fact, they observed that intellectual defenses slowed progress by keeping the interchange at an abstract rather than a feeling level. Fiske, Cartwright, and Kirtner (1964) found that the WAIS failed as a predictor of change during therapy. Phillipson (1958) discovered no relation between IQ and group therapy outcome, nor did Rachman (1965), Schmidt, Castell, and Brown (1965), or Morgenstern, Pearce, and Rees (1965). In many of these studies attention to IQ is an afterthought, and the experiments were not designed for the purpose of answering the question.

In view of these disparate results, experiments evaluating different types of therapy and different therapeutic goals across the range of IQ, with IQ as the independent variable and outcome as the dependent variable, would be most helpful. Such research would help clarify the limits of effectiveness of different approaches with patients of various levels of intelligence. Benefits of psychotherapy have been demonstrated even with mentally retarded children classified as imbeciles (Mundy, 1957). To be sure, they did not receive psychoanalysis, but therapeutic techniques were successfully adapted for use with them. A high level of intelligence is clearly not a *necessary* condition for success in psychotherapy, even though some therapies may be more handicapped by the patient's lack of it than others.

EDUCATION

The reasoning applied to IQ and socioeconomic status also applies to level of education. IQ is one of the principal determinants of educational level as, in turn, educational level is of social status. Education has often been assumed to be a factor in therapeutic success but has not frequently been the subject of direct test. Neither Frank, Gliedman, Imber, Nash, and Stone (1957) Karson and Wiedershine (1961), nor Rosenthal and Frank (1958) found it to be significantly related to improvement. Lorr and McNair (1964a) obtained a not very impressive correlation of $r = .22$ between education and self-ratings of improvement, and Sullivan, Miller, and Smelser (1958) reported that the higher educated show more improvement. In none of these research projects was educational level systematically varied without selection bias so that its relation to outcome could be appraised. Bailey, Warshaw, and Eichler (1960) showed an assignment differential, with patients assigned to psychotherapy averaging 12.5 years of education in contrast to 10.5 years for those assigned to somatic therapies. Bloom (1956) reported that those with good treatment outcome show higher grade attainment than those with poor outcome, but the dependent and independent variables would have to be reversed if we would test the effect of education upon outcome.

Educational level does seem to make a difference in the expectations of the patient regarding therapy, his acceptance of it, and his remaining in it. These, in turn, may all be related to the attitudes, valuation, and approach of the therapist toward the patient and the amount of effort expended in his behalf. Clemes and D'Andrea (1965) found that those with a higher educational level have more expectations of participation than of guidance. Rosenthal and Frank (1958) found an equivocal tendency for those with lower education not to accept psychotherapy. Frank, Gliedman, Imber, Nash, and Stone (1957), Rosenthal and Frank (1958), Katz and Solomon (1958), and Sullivan et al. (1958) all reported a greater tendency for better educated patients to stay longer and less educated ones to drop out sooner. On the other hand, Affleck and Garfield (1961) and Garfield and Affleck (1959) found education unrelated to terminating or remaining. Meyer et al. offered a possible clue to the inconsistency of these results by obtaining a nonlinear relationship (Meyer, Spiro, Slaughter, Pollack, Weingartner, & Novey, 1967). In their data 81 per cent of high-school educated patients completed a time-limited course of therapy. This percentage was significantly higher than that for patients who were either *more* or *less* educated. An interaction between sex and education was present, with college males tending to drop out and college females to stay. Apparently education is no sure guarantee either of remaining or succeeding in psychotherapy, and probably interacts with other variables in a complex fashion.

SEX

There is no clear relationship between the sex of the patient and the outcome of psychotherapy. Most studies that have investigated sex as a variable report no differences. It too is typically an incidental finding rather than one upon which research has focused. Much of the data comes from surveys with fallible criteria measures and uncertain experimental conditions.

Cartwright (1955b), Rosenbaum, Friedlander, and Kaplan (1956), and Rosenthal and Frank (1958) found no differences in outcome as a function of sex in adult outpatient clinic patients treated by conventional psychotherapy. Neither Lazarus (1963), investigating the results of behavior therapy with severe neurotics, nor Katahn, Strenger, and Cherry (1966), applying group counseling and systematic desensitization to test-anxious college students, obtained any sex differences. There was little difference in reported symptom improvement in children in studies by Gluck, Tanner, Sullivan, and Erickson (1964) or Levitt, Beiser, and Robertson (1959). Hamilton, Varney, and Wall (1942) found little difference in average length of hospitalization of male and female neurotics. Neither Esterson, Cooper, and Laing (1965), studying hospitalized schizophrenics, nor Kaufman et al. (1962), investigating schizophrenic children, revealed any sex-linked differences.

Frank et al. (1957), Katz and Solomon (1958), Affleck and Garfield (1961), and Yalom (1966) all reported no difference between the sexes in terminating or remaining in therapy.

Some studies have reported better results with females. Luff and Garrod (1935) noted a higher percentage of improvement in neurotic females (58 per cent) than in males (50.2 per cent) three years after discharge in a survey of 500 cases. Females diagnosed as anxiety state, hysteria, obsessional state, and delinquency, all did somewhat better than men with these diagnoses, but men diagnosed as "depressive state" fared better than similarly diagnosed women. Counselor judgments and adjustment changes measured by self-sorts both reflected greater improvement in female than in male patients in Rogers and Dymond (1954). Ellis (1956) claimed that female homosexuals responded significantly better than their male counterparts. Several studies with children reported somewhat better results with girls than with boys (Rodriguez, Rodriguez, & Eisenberg, 1959; Sobel, 1962; Warren, 1965; and Hare, 1966).

A few studies favored males. Friedman (1950) found males to respond better to short-term psychotherapy for travel phobia. Rachman (1965) obtained more improvement in males with behavior therapy. Schmidt, Castell, and Brown (1965), in a retrospective study of forty-two cases of behavior therapy, found that significantly more males than females showed marked improvement.

On balance, the sex of the patient does not seem to be a crucial variable in the success of psychotherapy. If there really are any differences, women and girls appear to have a slight edge except in behavior therapy. There may be some differences in attitudes of patients in therapy. Garfield and Wolpin (1963) pointed to a "tendency" for women to expect more advice and direction, to emphasize emotional factors more, to take a less serious view of therapy, to stress their own role more, and to feel less guilt about coming.

MARITAL STATUS

Marital status has frequently been linked negatively to incidence of mental illness and positively to hospital discharge. There have been a few attempts to observe it as a variable in psychotherapy. Lorr and McNair (1964a) obtained a correlation of .41 between marital status and increase in self-other acceptance. Unmarried patients were more likely to view the therapist as cool and critical. Rosenbaum, Friedlander, and Kaplan (1956) and Tolman and Meyer (1957) found marital status to be unrelated to improvement. Luff and Garrod (1935), however, showed an interaction between sex and marriage, with single women doing slightly better and single men slightly worse. The reliability of the interaction was not established. Diener and Young (1961) determined that male patients taking the adult life role (living with wife and/or children) are more likely to apply for treatment than those taking the child role (single, separated, or divorced and living with parents). The relationship to outcome, however, was not assessed. As far as terminating or remaining in therapy is concerned, neither Frank et al. (1957) nor Yalom (1966) found any relationship. Katz and Solomon (1958) reported that patients who were married or single remained longer than those who were divorced or separated.

Insofar as it has been studied, being single or married does not appear to be an important outcome variable.

SOCIAL CLASS

One of the patient variables that has received the greatest attention as a determinant of various aspects of psychotherapy is socioeconomic status or social class. The schemes for classifying people that have been most frequently used in psychotherapy research are the Hollingshead Two-Factor Index of Social Position and Warner's Index of Status Characteristics. The latter divides individuals into upper class, upper middle class, lower middle class, upper lower class, and lower lower class. The Hollingshead method is also a five-category arrangement. Class I contains families of wealth, education, and top prestige. Class II consists of families in which adults generally hold college degrees and husbands have executive, high-level managerial or professional occupations. Class III, composed mostly of high school graduates, contains proprietors, white collar workers, and some skilled workers. Members of Class IV are semiskilled workers with less than a high school education. Finally, Class V consists of nonskilled or semiskilled workers with no more than a grade school education who live in the poorest areas.

Research has been done on differences among classes in source of referral for therapy, expectations about therapy, selection and acceptance for therapy, acceptance of therapy by the patient, assignment to particular therapists, type of therapy received, duration and amount of therapy received, and outcome of treatment.

Social Class and Source of Referral. Differences in patterns of referral for treatment have been found to be a function of social class. In a New Haven, Connecticut, sample of schizophrenics, 85.9 per cent of the lowest class were referred by legal sources compared to 27.6 per cent for the two highest classes (Hollingshead & Redlich, 1954). Referrals by medical sources contributed 55.2 per cent of the upper class group, while 12.3 per cent of the lowest class came from this source. Self-referrals and referrals by friends and relatives accounted for 17.2 per cent of the highest classes and 1.8 per cent of the lowest class.

Studying outpatients of varied diagnoses, Schaffer and Myers (1954) found that the family physician made referrals from all classes and that patients of all classes referred themselves. Referrals from medical and other clinics in the hospital were greatest among lower class patients, and referrals by psychiatrists and different psychiatric clinics and hospitals greatest among upper class patients. As would be expected, there were more referrals from social agencies of lower class patients. At the Medical Center of the University of California Hospital, a significantly greater percentage of upper than lower class patients were self-referred (Albronda, Dean, & Starkweather, 1964). A survey of children seen in outpatient clinics in Philadelphia revealed that parents of higher status tended to bring their children in for treatment at an earlier age than did lower status parents (Tuckman & Lavell, 1959).

Social Class, Expectations, and Attitudes. A number of investigators have hypothesized that expectations about the form of treatment to be received and about the way it would be administered would vary with social class. Redlich et al. found Class V patients to express an organic bias, with expectations of pills and shots mixed with sympathy; to have little understanding of or confidence in the "talking" cure approach; and to be resistant to emotional exploration (Redlich, Hollingshead, & Bellis, 1955). Jones and Kahn (1964) assessed attitudes of fifty-five inpatients on a factor-analytically developed scale. Analysis of the data revealed that the higher the social class the more psychologically oriented the attitude and the lower the class the more rigidity and resentment toward hospital procedure.

It is an overgeneralization to state that lower class patients as a group are merely seeking symptom relief when they enter treatment. Gliedman et al. determined that situational or environmental reasons for seeking treatment, as contrasted with the desire for self-modification, were *not* distributed according to social class (Gliedman, Stone, Frank, Nash, & Imber, 1957). In one survey of 250 patients in the three lower classes, the investigators were surprised to find that 52 per cent indicated a desire to solve their problems by talking about their feelings (Goin, Yamamoto, & Silverman, 1965). They expected this view to be far less prevalent among lower class patients. Aronson and Overall (1966) found no difference between lower and middle class patients in the degree to which they expected the therapist to focus on emotional and dynamic material. Where they differed was in the greater expectation of lower class patients for action, direction, and support from the therapist. The lower class group was found to expect a medical examination and attention to current complaints. Unfortunately, many other background variables were confounded with social class in this study. The lower class patients were referred from medical clinics and the middle class patients were mostly self-referred for psychiatric help. This sampling bias could well transcend the variables investigated. If the lower class patients were seeking help for a physical problem and were then sent for psychotherapy, it is understandable that they would focus more on medical problems and expect to be told what to do in accordance with the medical model. The differences could just as easily be attributed to the nature of the problem and source of referral as to social class.

The most systematic appraisal of the hypothesis that the lower the socioeconomic status the more the tendency to view presenting problems as physiological illness was carried out at the psychiatric outpatient clinic of the Grace–New Haven Community Hospital (White, Fichtenbaum, Cooper, & Dollard, 1966). Transcripts of tape-recorded interviews were divided into sentence units and classified into content categories. The average amounts of physiological focus were not related to social class. There was a tendency for those who had been treated by drugs for their current symptoms to refer to present physiological symptoms.

Related indirectly to expectations is the finding of Gallagher et al. of a significant positive correlation (r = .34) between social class and score on the Gilbert and Levinson Custodial Mental Illness Ideology Scale (Gallagher, Levinson, & Erlich, 1957). In addition to the more custodial orientation of the lower class patients in their sample of 120 inpatients, the researchers obtained a comparable correlation (r = .38) between social class and authoritarianism as measured by the California F Scale.

Social Class and Selection and Acceptance for Therapy. Crowley (1950) reported high selectivity according to social class even in a low-cost psychoanalytic clinic and even higher selectivity for those seen in private practice. Rosenthal and Frank (1958) examined the disposition of 384 patients assigned to individual therapy at the Henry Phipps Psychiatric Clinic. They reported that psychiatrists tend to refer for individual therapy those who are most like themselves. They referred significantly more whites than Negroes, the better educated, and those in the upper income range. Of those eligible for treatment in this setting, more neurotics than psychotics were referred and more patients with at least moderate motivation. There was almost a straight-line relation between educational level and frequency of referral. The psychiatrists showed a decided preference for self-referral patients and those referred from psychiatric sources.

Gallagher et al. (1957), working in an inpatient setting, found that the percentage of patients receiving psychotherapy steadily declined with class level from 86 per cent in Classes I and II to 35 per cent in Class V. Biserial correlation was .38. Myers and Schaffer (1954) studied the pattern of acceptance in a community clinic oriented around long and intensive expressive psychotherapy. A significant relation was found between acceptance for therapy and social class of the patient. Treatment was not recommended for 64 per cent of the lowest class. At the University of Utah Medical School 322 consecutive applicants for outpatient treatment were investigated (Cole, Branch, & Allison, 1962). In this clinic, which offers dynamically oriented psychotherapy, there was somewhat lower acceptance only of the lowest social class in contrast to the remainder. In Freeman's (1967) report of a psychoanalytic clinic, thirty-two of the thirty-three patients chosen for individual treatment were from Class I or II.

Differential selection on a social class basis is apparently not a localized phenomenon. A study of 195 consecutive applicants to the psychiatric outpatient department of the Hadassah-Hebrew University Hospital, Jerusalem, revealed a tendency for the offer of psychotherapy to be related among other things to the patient's social background (Shanan & Moses, 1961). The longer the patient had lived in Israel and the higher his occupational level the more the offers. A latent bias against women and patients of Afro-Asian origin was apparent. When one background factor was held constant in relation to another, a favorable decision was apt to be made when a patient had some asset to counterbalance some liability. Thus, older people got preference only if of a high occupational level, while younger people were selected regardless of occupation. Class selectivity seems to dwindle as a factor with younger patients. At the Child Psychiatry Clinic of the University of Washington Hospital no significant differences in the proportions of accepted or rejected were found among different social classes (Baker & Wagner, 1966).

Social Class and Acceptance of Therapy by the Patient. Just as acceptance of a patient for therapy may be in part class determined, there could also be a class linkage in acceptance of therapy by the patient. Imber et al. found that almost all the patients in their sample who failed to return after initial screening were lower class members (Imber, Nash, & Stone, 1955).

In addition, they offered an interesting relationship between class membership, suggestibility, and acceptance of treatment (Imber, Frank, Gliedman, Nash, & Stone, 1956). Using the body sway test as an indicator of suggestibility, they found class membership and suggestibility to be relatively independent but both to be related to the patient's acceptance of treatment. Suggestible individuals accepted therapy regardless of class. This did not mean that therapy was rejected by nonsuggestible patients, but that lower class status increased the chances of rejection (63 per cent of the nonsuggestible lower class patients terminated early).

Rosenthal and Frank (1958) reported a greater tendency ($p = .10$) for patients with less education not to accept therapy when offered and a significant negative relation (rho $= -.83$) between coming in for treatment and income. Failure to accept (63 per cent) was highest in patients referred by a social agency, and these were predominantly lower class members. Yamamoto and Goin (1965) also reported less follow-through among lower class patients.

Social Class and Therapist Assignment. Once the selection has been made, the patient's social class plays a substantial role in determining who treats him. This is an issue only in clinics and hospitals since private psychotherapists are for the most part beyond the means of lower class patients. In their census of psychiatric patients in the metropolitan area of New Haven, Redlich et al. found that 63.3 per cent of those in treatment in the two upper classes were seen by private practitioners (Redlich, Hollingshead, Roberts, Robinson, Freedman, & Myers, 1953). This percentage was reduced to 39.6 per cent in Class III, 18.9 per cent in Class IV, and only 2.8 per cent in Class V. Lower class patients predominated in state hospitals and higher class patients in private hospitals.

Assignment within a clinic in that same community was also found to be class-linked (Schaffer & Myers, 1954). Therapists were ranked according to their "status positions" within the clinic—senior staff, residents, medical students, other therapists (social workers, students). Assignments of patients in various social classes were examined, and striking differences were observed. Senior staff treated mostly patients from the higher social classes represented in the clinic (Classes II and III). A few Class II patients were treated by residents, but most of their patients were in Classes III and IV. The medical students treated predominantly Class IV and V patients, and were the only group that had no choice of assignment. The "other therapists" were able to arrange a distribution of cases.

On the contrary, Cole, Branch, and Allison (1962) reported that in their setting staff psychiatrists treated no Class I or II patients; 80 per cent of their caseload came from Classes IV and V. Residents had 19 per cent of their cases from Classes I and II and 61 per cent from Classes IV and V. Medical students had 78 per cent from the two lower classes and 8 per cent from Classes I and II. Baker and Wagner (1966) found a trend for lower class children to be more frequently assigned to social workers and students. All those in Class I went to psychiatrists or residents. A greater portion of Class III patients were assigned to students. Assignment is a function of attitude of the staff, and Carlson et al. found therapists generally to regard lower class psychotic patients as uninteresting and uncooperative (Carlson, Coleman, Errera, & Harrison, 1965). They observed that the help required by these patients runs counter to the resident's usual conception of his psychotherapeutic role. In addition to selectivity of assignment it was noted that lower class patients experienced more delay in getting assigned (Kamin & Caughlan, 1963).

Social Class and Type of Therapy Received. A number of investigators have studied the effect of social class upon the type of therapy received by the patient. In the schizophrenic sample of Hollingshead and Redlich (1954), 83.3 per cent of Class I and II patients received individual psychotherapy, none group therapy, and 16.7 per cent organic therapy. By contrast, 70.2 per cent of Class V patients received organic therapy, 8.8 per cent individual therapy, 8.8 per cent group therapy, and 12.3 per cent no therapy at all. In the total New Haven census of Redlich et al. (1953), 79.1 per cent of Class I and II patients received psychotherapy, 11.8 per cent organic treatment, and 9.1 per cent no treatment (custodial). Among Class V patients the reverse was true, with 51.2 per cent receiving no treatment, 32.7 per cent organic therapy, and 16.1 per cent psychotherapy. Classes III and IV were ordered between the other classes. Further elaboration of these data by Robinson, Redlich, and Myers (1954) revealed similar breakdowns, with some variations in percentages, for psychoneurotic, schizophrenic, and paranoid disorders and for intoxication and the addictions. In general, the higher classes received significantly more psychotherapy than the lower classes, who received more organic treatment or custodial care. Within the category of psychotherapy, there was a clear linkage between method employed and social class. Of those receiving psychoanalysis 90.5 per cent were in Classes I and II, 9.5 per cent in Class III, and none in the two lower classes. Analytic psychotherapy, as distinct from formal psychoanalysis, was offered to decreasing numbers down the socioeconomic classification with 45.8 per cent going to Classes I and II, 33.3 per cent to Class III, 16.7 per cent to Class IV, and 4.1 per cent to Class V. Eclectic psychotherapy was fairly evenly distributed among classes except for a lesser percentage in Class V. Relationship therapy, including supportive, directive, and suggestive methods, increased progressively moving down the class hierarchy, but the lowest class received relatively little of it. The psychotherapy given to Class V patients was group therapy. About 85 per cent of the group therapy was reserved for Classes IV and V, with 13.5 per cent allotted to Class III and only 1.6 per cent to Classes I and II. Kamin and Caughlan (1963) also found more lower class patients in the categories of group therapy or "intake only."

Whitehorn and Betz (1957) noted that 88 per cent of their sample who were treated by active personal participation on the part of the therapist were middle or upper SES but only 55 per cent of those treated by other tactical means were middle or upper class. Group and individual therapy, however, were not applied differentially in accordance with social class at the Boston Evening Clinic, where group therapy is the predominant form of treatment (Gallagher & Kanter, 1961). Results were similar in a Veterans Administration Mental Hygiene Clinic as well (Winder & Hersko, 1955). There were no Class I patients in the sample of 100 drawn randomly from the total clinic population. Classes II and III were combined and considered middle class and IV and V were considered lower class. Middle class patients received significantly more analytic psychotherapy and less relationship therapy than did lower class patients.

General confirmation of the New Haven findings was reported in a survey of the 172 patients in the Hillside Hospital, New York, although such social factors as cultural background, education, and place of birth rather than socioeconomic status were studied (Kahn, Pollack, & Fink, 1957). Years of education, being native or foreign born, and being of eastern European birth were all significantly related to treatment received. Psychotherapy was more frequently given to better educated, native born patients, and shock therapy more to the less educated and foreign born, particularly those of eastern European origin. Moore et al., in a study of 200 schizophrenic patients at the University of Michigan Medical Center, present no data but report that lower class patients were significantly more likely to be treated with physical therapies and less likely to be treated intensively with psychotherapy (Moore, Benedek & Wallace, 1963). A study of inpatients at Massachusetts Mental Health Center also revealed that patients in higher social classes were more likely to receive psychotherapy than lower class patients. The correlation between social class and receipt of psychotherapy was "moderate" but statistically significant (Gallagher, Sharaf, & Levinson, 1965).

In diverse locales and settings, both inpatient and outpatient, there appears to be a consistent relation between type of treatment (psychotherapy vs. physical treatments) and social class, with psychotherapy going to those of higher status. If psychotherapies are placed in a hierarchy, there is then a tendency for the more intensive, individual, dynamically oriented therapies to be applied to those of higher class status. It is not simply that these therapies cost more and are not available to individuals of lower socioeconomic status, for the pattern was present in studies in which the fee was held constant or no fee was charged. It is also not just a function of different distributions of diagnoses in different class groups, for the finding is obtained within single diagnostic groups.

Social Class, Duration, and Amount of Therapy. Schaffer and Myers (1954) found a marked relationship between social class and duration of clinic contact. Among Class II patients, for example, 11.8 per cent were seen for a week or less (one visit) in contrast to 47.6 per cent of Class V. On the other hand, 29.4 per cent of Class II patients and only 4.8 per cent of Class V patients maintained contact for twenty-five weeks or more. Winder and Hersko (1955) reported that middle class patients received significantly more therapy sessions than did those considered lower class. Imber et al. (1955) determined that the average number of interviews for lower class patients was 11.6 and for middle class patients 16.4. Only 11.1 per cent of the middle class patients left before five interviews, in contrast to 42.9 per cent of lower class patients. Correspondingly, the number of middle class patients who remained in treatment beyond the twentieth interview was double that of the lower class groups. Rosenthal and Frank (1958) found social class to be an important determinant of length of stay, with the higher classes remaining longer. Cole, Branch, and Allison (1962) showed the greatest loss of the lowest classes in the first ten interviews. Past twenty interviews 55 per cent of the upper classes and 32 per cent of the lower classes remain. Past thirty interviews 40 per cent of the upper and 12 per cent of the lower classes remain. Albronda, Dean, and Starkweather (1964) noted that those who dropped out after the initial contact were less affluent.

Several other investigators found no significant relationship between social class and duration or amount of therapy (Hollingshead & Redlich, 1954; Tuckman & Lavell, 1959; Ross & Lacey, 1961; Lowinger & Dobie, 1966; Strickland & Crowne, 1963; Baker & Wagner, 1966; Yalom, 1966). In several of these studies there were some essential differences in settings and patient populations. The investigations that show a relation between length of stay and social class were mostly conducted in psychoanalytically oriented adult outpatient clinics that were training centers for psychiatric residents. The patients were primarily psychoneurotic. Remaining in therapy is considered desirable and positive with this population in this type of treatment. Hollingshead and Redlich's sample was composed of schizophrenics. Duration of treatment for less than a year was twice as high for Class V as for Classes I and II, but there were thirty-one times as many lower class patients among those who remained in treatment for twenty-one years or more. Here a longer stay is considered an undesirable or negative factor indicative of failure rather than of cooperativeness. Lowinger and Dobie's sample of 300 included seventy-eight schizophrenics, twenty depressives, and sixteen patients with organic brain syndrome. The samples of Baker and Wagner, Ross and Lacey, and Tuckman and

Lavell all consisted of children rather than adults. The sample of Strickland and Crowne included some psychotics, but more closely resembled the samples showing a relationship between social class and length of stay. The correlation of r = .19 that they obtained between the two variables, however, was quite low.

Remainers had more education and higher SES than terminators in a study by Rubinstein and Lorr (1956). At the Phipps Clinic, the proportion of lower class patients who dropped out was twice that of middle class patients (Frank, Gliedman, Imber, Nash, & Stone, 1957). More lower class patients dropped out before the sixth interview in the investigation of Kamin and Caughlan (1963). Education and occupation significantly differentiated stayers (nine interviews) from non-stayers for Sullivan, Miller, and Smelser (1958), but the effect was not as strong on cross-validation. Katz and Solomon (1958) claimed that higher status patients stayed longer, but the data were untreated. Lake and Levinger (1960), as predicted, found more continuers among middle than lower class children in a child guidance clinic. Gallagher and Kanter (1961) also found this relation to hold. Although there was not much variation at the onset, differentiation between the classes became increasingly marked at later stages.

In a treatment arrangement limited to ten visits, Meyer et al. reported that most of the patients who never returned after the initial evaluation were in Class V, and a higher percentage of those in the upper classes completed the allotted course of therapy. Those in Classes I, II, and III who had physical complaints did not drop out, in contrast to their counterparts in the lower classes (Meyer, Spiro, Slaughter, Pollack, Weingartner, & Novey, 1967).

Social Class and Outcome of Therapy. In view of the findings about social class that have already been surveyed, it would be risky to draw any conclusions about the outcome of psychotherapy as a function of social class membership from any experiment that did not control such variables as selection, diagnosis, assignment, type of therapy, and duration. Inconsistencies among the results of those investigations that do report differential outcome statistics may well be due to confounding of these variables.

Rosenbaum, Friedlander, and Kaplan (1956) reported more upper class patients than lower class patients in the much improved category. Freeman (1967) found that only 14 per cent of those in his sample receiving psychoanalytic psychotherapy who were rated as recovered and improved were from Class IV or V. Strickland and Crowne (1963) obtained a correlation of .36 between social class and satisfaction with the results of therapy received. Cole, Branch, and Allison (1962) reported that upper class patients had a 65 per cent chance of being terminated with a rating of socially improved, irrespective of length of stay, compared to a 52 per cent chance for the lower classes. In a study by Kamin and Caughlan (1963) a smaller percentage of lower class patients felt better. Albronda, Dean, and Starkweather (1964) found no significant difference between upper and lower class patients in their chances of being improved based on the subjective impression of the therapist. An initial bias in favor of the upper class was lessened by twenty-one interviews, and after thirty interviews both groups showed an increasingly better chance of being considered socially improved by their therapists. Rosenthal and Frank (1958) found no significant relation between education, income, or race in the percentage of patients cited by therapists as improved. Despite more frequent dropouts, the lower class patients who remained in therapy did as well as middle class patients in the study by Frank et al. (1957). Baker and Wagner (1966) reported no social class differences in outcome as rated by the therapists despite an initial assignment bias. Karson and Wiedershine (1961) found no differences in outcome of group therapy as a function of socioeconomic status.

With hospitalized schizophrenics, Moore, Benedek, and Wallace (1963) found significantly poorer treatment results with lower class patients. Gottschalk et al. found that Class IV and V patients improved significantly more than did Class II and III patients with emergency brief psychotherapy, even though five of the six therapists liked the latter better (Gottschalk, Mayerson, & Gottlieb, 1967). Meltzoff and Blumenthal (1966) reported that lower class schizophrenics treated in an outpatient day treatment center benefited more in terms of avoiding rehospitalization than did patients of higher socioeconomic status. With conventional treatment lower class patients were more apt to be rehospitalized.

Obtained differences among social class groups on therapeutic variables have been attributed to therapists, patients, and their interaction. No single explanation predominates in the speculations that have been given in the literature on the subject. The reasoning is logical, if not usually validated, and the most common explanations can be summarized. It has been maintained that middle class therapists approach lower class patients with a bias or negative set. They are alleged to have preconceptions (possibly erroneous) about these patients and an anticipation of failure from the start. There is nothing new about this bias. It has been vividly described by Bockoven in his exceptionally enlightening summary of moral treatment in American psychiatry (Bockoven, 1956). Moral treatment, which sounds remarkably like modern social and psychological approaches to treatment in institutional settings, achieved survey results that would be admired today. At Worcester State Hospital in the twenty-year period from 1833 to 1852, 71 per cent of the patients were discharged as recovered or improved. Decline began after the Civil War, when the increasing impetus of the industrial revolution led to a wave of immigration and an influx of lower class workers to the cities. This in turn resulted in the building of large, impersonal asylums, an intensification of class attitudes, and the end of a promising form of psychotherapy.

Middle class therapists are thought to like middle class patients because of shared values and cultural background. Redlich et al. (1955), for example, surveyed the attitudes of seventeen therapists working with lower class patients and recorded expressions of the therapists' dislike for them. Therapists experienced frustration stemming from their inability to do insight therapy with these patients and their having to work against the handicap of desperate environmental conditions. They expressed liking for 61.5 per cent of Class III patients, but for only 16.6 per cent of those in Class V. It is interesting to note that the male therapists were more tolerant of lower class female patients than they were of males. It has been suggested that therapists feel uneasy with lower class patients and have difficulty understanding and empathizing with them. The therapists may have little appreciation and comprehension of, or respect for, the values, standards, reality problems, and way of life of lower class patients. The educational disparity is thought to create difficult problems in mutual communication since language usage, meaning, and facility are basic to verbal, expressive therapy. The concepts and insights that the therapist feels it necessary to impart may be beyond the scope of comprehension of the patient and he may be unable to conceptualize in the manner and at the level that some therapies require. There may also be culturally based differences in goals and expectations between classes that interfere with psychotherapy. It has been posited that lower class patients are primarily seeking symptom relief and direct solutions to their problems and that they start off with different styles of disturbance, symptoms, and reaction and defense patterns. So far as their orientation to psychotherapy and receptivity to different therapeutic approaches are concerned, upper class patients are thought to be better informed, more "psychologically minded," and to have a greater readiness for psychotherapy and better "mental health values." The lower class patient, conversely, is thought to bring his experiences with physicians concerning physical ailments to psychotherapy and to expect a more authoritarian, advice-giving solution. White et al. (1966) found that the less the physiological focus in initial psychiatric interviews the greater the amount of content focused on emotional involvement with others. It may well be the case that it is the *therapists* who focus more on physiological issues with lower class patients because they find communication difficult. This topic may be an easy peg upon which to hang their treatment and may set the tenor of things to come. Others maintain that lower class patients' rebelliousness to social institutions interferes with therapy while the conformance, repressive tendencies, docility, and emphasis on responsibility of the middle class are rewarded in the therapeutic institution. Finally, it has been observed that there is less financial or other reward for the therapist who treats lower class patients, with a consequent diminution of interest in them and sympathy for them.

These formulations by middle class authors are available for verification. Some of the evidence from psychotherapy research that bears on them has been cited. Experimental literature in social psychology and sociology is highly relevant to these issues, particularly in assisting the development of insightful hypotheses that can be tested within the context of psychotherapy. Overgeneralizations come easily in this area, and testing is needed. For illustration, the desirability of giving lower class patients direct advice in accordance with their expectations has been frequently stressed and applied. The research of Goin, Yamamoto, and Silverman (1965) is particularly pertinent here. They submitted a questionnaire to 250 applicants to the Psychiatric Outpatient Department of Los Angeles County General Hospital. The group consisted predominantly of Class III, IV, and V patients. The questionnaire asked if they wanted the doctor to do something to make them feel better and to give them advice or whether they wanted to solve their problems by talking about their feelings and past life. Of the original 250 surveyed, eighty-six stated that they wanted advice but more than half expressed a desire to solve their problems by talking about their feelings.

Forty patients who expressed a wish for advice were selected for further study and were asked to respond to another questionnaire at termination. In therapy, roughly half of the patients were given advice and half received no advice, but interviews focused on "discussion of feelings in an attempt to achieve self-understanding and insight." On the terminal questionnaire 72 per cent of the "advice" patients and 57 per cent of the "no advice" group were pleased with the results even though the majority had abruptly terminated treatment before the ten visits allotted to them. The obtained percentage difference between the groups on satisfaction with treatment outcome was not statistically significant. All those who completed the therapeutic course reported that they were better. There were no differences between the improvement rates of the "advice" and "no advice" groups in the total sample as judged either by patient or therapist ratings. Interestingly enough, the patients tended to rate themselves as more improved than did the therapists.

Review of the information in the whole area of social class and psychotherapy points up a need for further hypothesis testing with the possible result of establishing what therapist attitudes are and of modifying them and the relevant therapeutic methods to meet the needs of the large numbers of patients for whom psychotherapy as we know it was not designed in the first place.

MOTIVATION

One of the axioms of psychotherapy is that an individual has to be motivated for it and want to change if any change is to take place. Psychotherapy is seen as a dynamic process in which the patient willingly plays an active role rather than a process in which the patient endures something done *to* him, like surgery, whether he wants it or not. It is analogous to academic accomplishment: a child who does not want to go to school, absents himself frequently, makes no effort, and does not attend to what is going on in class is not apt to learn much. Lack of motivation is commonly used as an after-the-fact explanation for failure in psychotherapy. There is ample evidence that therapists prefer well-motivated patients and select them where possible. The term well-motivated not only refers to a desire to change but also implies a desire to change in ways congruent with the aims of the therapist and assumes that the patient shares the therapist's expectancies with regard to general approach (psychotherapy vs. physical and medicinal therapy) (Raskin, 1961). Motivation has frequently been inferred in circular fashion from the patient's remaining or withdrawing from therapy. It remains to be explained why therapeutic gains have been successfully demonstrated in nonvolitional institutional settings where there is no dropout option and in instances where patients are obliged to see a therapist by the nature of the referral. The various studies already cited in which patients were assigned without choice to psychotherapy, yet benefited from it, suggest indirectly that initial motivation is not a *necessary* requirement for improvement.

Some investigators have specifically looked into the matter of motivation and have obtained varying results. For example, Cartwright and Lerner (1963) obtained a significant initial difference on the "need to change" variable between those judged improved and unimproved. Schoenberg and Carr (1963), on the other hand, found that motivation, as inferred from initial interviews, was not related to outcome in cases of neurodermatitis. Ross and Mendelsohn (1958), working with homosexuals in college, reported that initial signs of high motivation for change were not ordinarily present in successful cases. Rosenthal and Frank (1958), with Phipps Clinic outpatients, found improvement in 54 per cent of those with low motivation, 22 per cent of those with moderate motivation, and 43 per cent of those with high motivation. Volsky et al. were unable to find support for the idea that motivation of student counselees is related to outcome (Volsky, Magoon, Norman, & Hoyt, 1965). The most plausible present explanation of this seeming paradox is given by Ends and Page (1959) from their experience with alcoholics. The need for therapy and the desire for change via therapy do not necessarily have to be understood or accepted by patients at the onset of treatment but can develop as therapy proceeds. Motivation is not fixed but is subject to modification, just as are other aspects of the individual. It is just as possible for highly motivated patients rapidly to lose their desire for therapy after their initial experiences as for poorly motivated patients to increase theirs. The school analogy can be applied here just as well. Initial motivation is apparently not a necessary or sufficient condition for success, but the emergence and fostering of motivation during the educational process is thought to be of considerable importance.

Related to the question of motivation is the patient's view of the source of his troubles—specifically, whether he accepts responsibility for them or ascribes the difficulty to external sources. Schroeder (1960) hypothesized that those at the extremes would prove more difficult than those who accepted moderate responsibility. Difficulty was defined in terms of taking a long time in treatment or terminating early because of resistance or lack of motivation. Acceptance of responsibility was measured by the Gilbert Self-Interview Test, and movement in therapy was judged by the therapist at the end. Three different scoring devices for the responsibility variable were used and yielded different results. The main result seems to be that high responsibility is associated with difficult (long) therapy and high movement. The finding that high responsibility cases take more time and show more change may be partly confounded by the tendency for therapists to rate those who stay longer as more changed. On the face of it, the variable of perceived responsibility appears to be an important one whose parameters merit further study.

ENVIRONMENTAL FACTORS, CONDITIONS, AND SETTINGS

A few investigators have focused their attention on the effects of various extrinsic factors upon aspects of psychotherapy. For the most part these factors concern such things as the effect of distance from the clinic, size of the clinic, climatological conditions, daily and seasonal variations in applications for treatment and in attendance, and economic conditions upon requesting and coming for therapy. The matter of fee is also involved. To a large extent, some of these variables appear to be linked to motivation for treatment.

The congruence between patients' and therapists' evaluations of the importance of topics discussed was found to vary with the day of the week in a study by Parloff, Iflund, and Goldstein (1960). Congruence was far greater on Mondays, Tuesdays, and Wednesdays than later in the week. On eighteen Fridays 72 per cent of the correlations between patient and therapist were negative. On twenty Mondays 80 per cent were positive. The two patients used as subjects were schizophrenic, and the results were interpreted partly in terms of anxiety over the approach of the weekend and relief upon the return of the therapist on Mondays.

Hyman and Wohl (1958) examined daily and monthly variations in application for treatment and explored possible connections with the weather and with employment situations. Examining the intake pattern at the Veterans Administration Mental Hygiene Clinic, Detroit, they found the heaviest intake most likely to occur on Monday and least likely on Wednesday. They speculated that the Monday influx might be due to a weekend backlog, and they associated the Wednesday slack with the custom in Detroit that private physicians do not work on Wednesdays. The heaviest intake days were in September, November, and March, and the least heavy in June, February, and December. Temperature was curvilinearly related to intake, which was heavier when temperature was moderate and lighter in either very cold or very warm weather. The presence or absence of rain, snow, or sunshine, however, was not related to intake. There was a zero order correlation between intake and the number unemployed during the year or the number of claims for unemployment compensation. For these findings to have any generality, they would have to be cross-validated in other places. It was concluded that, at least in this particular setting, applicants apparently come because of a need for help that is not related to situational factors such as weather conditions and unemployment.

This conclusion received general support in a study at the Mental Hygiene Clinic of the Veterans Administration Hospital in Denver (Diener & Young, 1961). A survey revealed that 63 per cent of veterans eligible for treatment in Colorado did not avail themselves of it, and the purpose of the study was to determine how those who applied differed from those who did not. Eighty treated and eighty-one untreated cases were selected by random sampling, and it was ascertained that the untreated had never been seen in any facility. The findings that interest us here are those concerning distance from the clinic, compensation rating, and urban or other residence. The hypothesis that more of those who came would reside in urban communities was not supported. The degree of disability as reflected by compensation rating was significantly ($p < .001$) related to obtaining treatment even when those who had been hospitalized were excluded. The degree of disability correlated $r = .40$ with the criterion, and distance from the clinic correlated with the criterion to a lesser extent ($r = .19$, $p < .05$). Combination of these two variables in a multiple correlation increased the coefficient to $R = .44$. It was concluded that the greater the disability and the closer the patient to the clinic the more likely he is to come in, but that the extent of disability is the crucial variable. Those whose need is most pressing are the ones who attend. Pursuing this inquiry further, the sample was expanded to include all of the 2,130 veterans in Colorado (Dworin, Green, & Young, 1964). Distance from the clinic was divided into four categories: 0–50 miles, 50–100 miles, 100–200 miles, and more than 200 miles. A biserial correlation of .33 was obtained between degree of disability and the criterion. A significant chi-square between distance and the criterion was converted into a phi-coefficient with a value of .37, considerably larger than that obtained with the smaller sample. Combination of the coefficients for distance and disability into a multiple R to predict the criterion yielded a value of .52. It was now concluded that the closer a patient's residence to the clinic the greater the probability that he will seek treatment, although there were patients living close to the clinic who did not avail themselves of it. Distance became especially important when large. They were dealing here with distances that make coming to the clinic on a regular basis almost prohibitive. The authors, however, do not differentiate between coming to the clinic once or twice and pursuing a regular course of treatment. It is important to make this distinction in appraising the overall effect of distance.

The effect of distance on frequency of attendance of ambulatory schizophrenics at the Day Treatment Center of the Veterans Administration Outpatient Clinic, Brooklyn, was examined (Meltzoff & Blumenthal, 1966). Here all of the patients lived in a limited area within the boundaries of Brooklyn and were able to use public transportation. Distance was measured in terms of miles and separately in terms of travel time required. There was no relationship between miles ($r = -.14$) or travel time ($r = .02$) and attendance.

Obvious and commonplace environmental factors, conditions, and settings are readily cited in explanations of intake and attendance patterns. The available research suggests that it is not general economic conditions so much as personal distress and various personal needs that bring patients in. Motivation for treatment apparently surmounts environmental factors except in those instances where excessive distances or extreme weather conditions make the trip impractical.

A variable external to the patient that may have a bearing on treatment received is the size of the clinic attended (Feldman, Lorr, & Russell, 1958). These investigators surveyed a random sample of 5,367 cases drawn from twenty-one small, twenty-five medium, and seventeen large Veterans Administration Mental Hygiene Clinics. The average number of weeks a patient is seen was found to be directly proportional to the size of the clinic. Similarly, the number of interviews increases with the size of the clinic and the length of the interview decreases somewhat. The percentage of patients seen more frequently rises significantly with the size of the clinic. There was no difference, however, in judged patient improvement.

Wenar et al. compared the relative effectiveness of three contrasting settings in changing the behavior of autistic children (Wenar, Ruttenberg, Dratman, & Wolf, 1967). The three settings were a large long-established state institution, a large modern state institution combining a school and therapeutic program, and a small psychoanalytically oriented day care unit emphasizing the emotional relationships between staff and children. Children were rated on the Behavior Rating Instrument for Autistic Children for relationship, communication, mastery, psychosexual development, and socialization. Ratings were made by seven trained observers at one-year intervals, with a different rater making the second rating. They were based on six hours of observation as well as on supplemental information. The day care unit was the only one with a demonstrated therapeutic effect on the variables of relationship, mastery, and psychosexual development. Communication and vocalization did not improve. Unfortunately, the patient samples in the three settings were not directly comparable. The average age of the children in the day care unit was 5.9 years, compared to 9.6 and 8.6 years in the other two settings. Other uncontrolled variables leave the findings in doubt.

Fees. There are many references in the literature to the importance of paying a fee for psychotherapy. Wolff (1954) surveyed forty-three leading psychotherapists of various schools on a variety of therapeutic practices. Among other issues, he delved into the question of fees. In this group, 56 per cent expressed the belief that payment was not an essential factor in therapy, while 44 per cent considered it as an essential symbol of sacrifice or self-assertion. Private psychotherapeutic services are necessarily costly, and a highly trained and skilled professional is entitled to place a valuation upon his time even though he can make no guarantees of the outcome of his efforts. Need and motivation for treatment, capacity to pay, effects of the economic burden on the individual and his family, and the guilt and hostility it can arouse are all interwoven, become part of the psychotherapeutic process, and may directly affect outcome. The options are greater in clinics that can afford to offer low-cost treatment and sliding-scale fees and in free public institutions. Policy in these institutions has been influenced by this common belief among therapists that fee payment is therapeutically essential or at least highly desirable. The whole issue is one that has been discussed a great deal but about which little research has been done or is likely to be done.

Rosenbaum et al. examined the fees paid by patients in three low-cost clinics that charged from nothing to three dollars per visit (Rosenbaum, Friedlander, & Kaplan, 1956). It was determined that 48 per cent of those who were rated as much improved paid fees, compared to 27 per cent of those improved and 33 per cent of those considered essentially unchanged or worse. The percentage who paid fees in the much improved category was significantly higher than in the two less successful categories combined. The authors acknowledged that the results could have come about through an association between financial security and improvement, in that those who could afford fees may have been under less economic stress and thereby better able to profit from therapy. They also surmised that the fee may have been charged out of respect for the patient and his strengths, and that those with greater strengths may have had a better prognosis. The hypothesis that fee-paying cases in child guidance treatment could be more likely to remain in therapy was not supported (Ross & Lacey, 1961). In his assessment of his own private psychoanalytic practice, Schjelderup (1955) reported that size of fee was not a consideration in outcome and that some of the best results were obtained without payment.

Experimental evidence regarding the importance of fees is lacking, but payment is obviously not necessary for a successful outcome. At the current state of our information on the question it would be erroneous to attempt to justify the size of the fee on the grounds that it facilitates outcome. Fees for professional services can be justified on other than therapeutic grounds.

THERAPY READINESS

The concept of therapy readiness has been around for some time, but has never really caught on and achieved widespread applicability. We suspect that the reason is that it has been ill-defined and conceptually unclear and has been confused with other concepts. Although it undoubtedly includes motivational variables it should be a broader concept than "motivation for therapy," since one who is motivated is not necessarily "ready." It should also differ from "possessing pretherapy characteristics of successful patients" or having a "good prognosis." The term does imply temporal variation in receptivity and suggests that a potential of benefit exists and that there is an optimal time for introducing the process. Studies on the subject have really not come to grips with the distinctive meaning of the term; they have not clearly defined it, but have attempted to measure it and discover its correlates.

Therapy readiness of nine patients was independently rated by two raters from transcribed interviews (Grant & Grant, 1950). Each used his own criteria, yet a rank-order correlation of rho = .92 was obtained.

Burnham (1952) thought of it as an initial set and attempted to discover if it could be judged by psychologists from standard pretherapy psychological testing procedures. Six psychologists independently evaluated 28 patients' readiness for therapy by rating and ranking them on the basis of their test performances. The patients were rated on a four-point graded scale of emotional involvement after at least six months of psychotherapy. Agreement among psychologists was low but significant (average correlation .40), and there was slight but positive agreement of psychologists' evaluations with the psychiatric criterion of performance in the therapy relations ($r = .20$). Standards for what constitutes "therapy readiness" and "emotional involvement" were not established in advance, and there was not too much agreement on either concept or on this relationship.

Fey (1954) dealt with expressed attitudes of readiness for therapy not of a patient group but of sixty members of a freshman class. Expressed readiness for therapy was correlated with scores on scales of acceptance of others and self-acceptance. Expressed self-acceptance was not significantly related to therapy readiness ($r = -.25$), nor was expressed acceptance of others ($r = .18$). Those least interested in therapy had high self-acceptance and low acceptance of others. This study cannot be construed as casting much light on the concept of therapy readiness or as demonstrating its validity. Skinner and Anderson (1959) found that clients who were judged to be ready for therapy appeared on objective tests to be more anxious, less defensive, less comfortable, and less satisfied with their self-concept than those judged as not ready. Those who were judged as ready verbalized more realistic perceptions of counseling during a standardized interview and were judged by their counselors as having a more successful outcome.

Heilbrun and Sullivan (1962) set out to devise and validate a counseling-readiness scale, using staying more than five interviews or dropping out as the criterion. An attempt to validate it on clients seeking vocational and educational counseling showed the scale to differentiate significantly between terminators and remainers for males but not for females. Low counseling readiness was associated with insufficient psychological problems and/or defensiveness. The most interesting finding was that counseling-ready males and females tend to ascribe cross-sexual characteristics to themselves. Males see themselves as inhibited, weak, timid, softhearted, and the like, and females as aggressive, bossy, independent, unemotional. Further validation data on the Counseling Readiness Scale showed that it differentiated significantly between terminators and remainers and other categories of disposition (Heilbrun, 1964). The differences, however, were not pronounced, and questions were raised about its practicability. This time it was more accurate with females. It was determined that the scale was more accurate in identifying those who would stay than those who would leave. In another study, the scale was given, along with the California Psychological Inventory, to 261 male and 126 female college students who had solicited help for personal adjustment, vocational, or educational problems (Heilbrun, 1962). The counseling readiness scores were correlated with each of four CPI scales; Responsibility, Psychological Mindedness, Self-Acceptance, and Good-Impression. The *low* counseling-ready individual turned out to be more self-accepting, sensitive to social appearances, responsible, and psychologically minded if male, and more sensitive to social appearances, responsible, and psychologically minded if female. In his discussion, Heilbrun referred to counseling readiness as synonymous with continuation in therapy despite the fact that it is far from a valid measure of remaining. In this study personal adjustment counseling cases are grouped together with educational-vocational cases. It is not at all certain that the concept of counseling readiness has the same meaning in these different groups.

Jacks (1963) devised a scale to measure accessibility to group therapy of adolescent offenders and found it to be a better predictor of the criterion than were judgments based upon psychiatric interviews, psychological testing, or therapists' pretherapy interviews. The eighty-three items on the scale were derived empirically from the experimental sample and require cross-validation.

EXPECTANCY

Expectancy has long been thought to play a part in psychotherapy, but its parameters have not been thoroughly explored. As Cartwright and Cartwright (1958) have pointed out, expectancy has frequently been confused with faith, belief, credulity, anticipation, confidence, and conviction, and we might add such terms as set, trust, reliance, promise, hope, and wish. Goldstein (1962) has made expectancies the subject of a comprehensive monograph and has differentiated between prognostic and participant role expectancies of both patient and therapist.

A prognostic expectancy is an outcome that is looked for with the belief, faith, confidence, or conviction of being found. It is essentially a prediction anchored in belief that may or may not be warranted. Therapeutic expectancy has an object, a direction, an instrumentality, and a temporal schema. The object is symptom relief, conflict resolution, or attainment of some positive state, or the expectation can be of failure. Its instrumentality is that which brings about the anticipated goal. It is the person or process in whom the belief or faith is placed. It may be the patient himself, the therapist, the therapeutic process, or external forces alone or in combination. The patient who sees *himself* as the instrument says, "I have faith in myself, I can snap out of it with perhaps a little guidance," or "no one can help me, I have to do it myself." For him therapy and therapist may actually be seen as intruders. Another patient has expectancies characterized by faith in the *therapist* as the instrument. Regardless of the approach, "the right doctor" is expected to be able to cure him. The same techniques in the hands of another would be expected to have little chance of success. The next patient is therapy oriented. His expectations are that the techniques of *therapy* will bring about relief. The last places his faith outside therapy—in time, circumstances, environmental conditions, other people in his life, or spiritual forces. Another characteristic of expectancies is their time dimension, how long it should take to obtain the object. Since both the patient and the therapist have expectancies, they may complement each other, influence each other, or conflict with each other. This should hold for both prognostic expectancies and role expectancies in therapy. It is also clear that expectancies are fluid and subject to change, making it important to distinguish between expectancies at the beginning of therapy and the modified expectancies at a later point.

A patient enters therapy with one set of expectancies, but others can be engendered or induced. This is particularly true for role expectancies since a certain amount of role learning is expected in the initial stages of therapy. It also holds for positive placebo reactions, which are thought to dovetail with pretreatment expectations. Placebo responsivity is not necessarily related to initial expectancy since it may be the therapist who engenders expectations in the patient that the placebo will work. Experiments on the placebo effect, such as that of Frank, Gliedman, Imber, Stone, and Nash (1959), imply but do not demonstrate that expectancy is involved. As Goldstein has hypothesized, partly on the basis of level of aspiration data, expectation and change may be curvilinearly related, with those possessing moderate expectations likely to show more improvement than those at either extreme. To look at it from another angle, the expectancy of success may help more than the expectancy of failure may hurt, or the converse may be true. With all of these variables in mind, research on expectancies is obviously no simple matter.

Lipkin (1954) based ratings of outcome on before and after therapy TAT protocols of patients in client-centered therapy. His data on nine cases led him to conclude that more successful clients entered therapy with more favorable feelings toward therapy and therapist than did less successful clients.

Goldstein examined the relationship between client and therapist expectations of personality change and perceived change due to therapy (Goldstein, 1960a). Thirty clients, drawn from a homogeneous college sample, were randomly assigned to therapy or to a nontherapy control group. The treated clients were seen twice a week for a median of fourteen sessions, and controls remained on a waiting list for seven and one-half weeks. Client expectations of personality change were obtained from Q-sorts of present versus expected self, with items drawn from the Mooney Problem Check List. Perceived change was measured from differences in Q-sorts made by the client and therapist before therapy and at three spaced intervals. None of the correlations between expectations (client, therapist, or combined client and therapist) and client-perceived changes differed significantly from zero, nor did those for the controls. The expectations of the therapists of patients who perceived their problem as improving ($N = 11$), however, were significantly different from those who saw their problems as becoming worse ($N = 4$). The possibility that therapist expectations may be more important than those of the client and may be communicated to him was suggested. There was also some association between therapist expectation and duration of therapy. Generalizations are limited by the fact that the study dealt with short-term client-perceived changes in a small sample of students.

In a study of "nonspecific therapy," Goldstein reported on fifteen waiting-list control patients who received an intake interview and several testing sessions but no formal therapy. Correlation between expected and perceived improvement was $r = .65$ at two and one-quarter weeks, $r = .86$ at five weeks, and $r = .86$ at seven and one-quarter weeks, indicating the presence of a significant relationship between expectation and improvement associated with nonspecific interventions (Goldstein, 1960b). These experiments were followed up by a study on thirty psychoneurotic outpatients in treatment with thirty inexperienced senior medical students (Goldstein & Shipman, 1961). Patient expectancy of symptom reduction was gained from the difference between responses to a symptom-intensity inventory given before treatment under present-self and expected-self test-taking sets. The inventory was repeated under perceived-self conditions immediately following the first therapy interview. Confidence in the clinic was assessed from the mean rank assigned to the clinic as a source of help for fifty symptoms when presented along with five alternate sources (friend, parent, no one, clergyman, clinic). The patient's expectation of symptom reduction was found to be curvilinearly related to perceived symptom reduction (epsilon = .41) and linearly to pretherapy symptom intensity (r = .53). Moderate expectations were most closely related to symptom reduction in the initial interview. Again, there must be reservations about the generality of these findings. The experiment dealt with symptom reduction in the initial interview only and the therapists were inexperienced medical students.

Heller and Goldstein (1961) obtained partial support for the hypothesis that a favorable expectation of improvement by the therapist can function to maintain therapeutic relationships. The relation held only for expectations measured after the fifth session but not after the tenth or fifteenth. In another study, a linear relation between expectation and reported reduction in symptom intensity was reported for forty-three patients (Friedman, 1963). Expectancy was obtained from a discomfort schedule consisting of ratings of twenty-six symptoms. At his first visit to the clinic, the patient was asked to rate how he felt at the moment and how he expected to feel after six months of treatment. Following a structured fact-finding interview, the inventory was repeated, and reported reduction in symptom intensity noted. It was found that the greater the expectancy the greater the reported reduction of symptoms. Friedman commented that both expectancy and the reported symptom reduction could be determined by the patient's desire to make a good impression and appear consistent by reporting predicted symptom reduction. As in the other studies, this one dealt with reported symptom reduction, not objective behavioral change. The social desirability response set cannot be discounted, nor can a general characteristic of optimism or pessimism that would color the expected-self and present-self outlooks alike.

In a study by Heine and Trosman (1960) lack of complementarity of patient-therapist expectations was proposed as a disruptive factor in the early stages of therapy which could lead to termination. The forty-six patients, whose complaints were largely somatic, were lacking in psychiatric sophistication. A questionnaire sought their reasons for seeking help, their expectations of help to be received, their views on how help would be given, and their degree of conviction that treatment would help. There was no relation between the degree of conviction expressed that treatment would help and continuance, nor was there any difference in this regard between those who saw their primary complaint as somatic and those who saw it as emotional. Those who saw the means of obtaining treatment goals in terms of active collaboration tended to continue; those who expected to play a role of passive cooperation tended to terminate, as did those who expected medication or diagnostic information in contrast to help in changing behavior. The authors concluded that an important role could not be assigned to hope, faith, or conviction about being helped or to acceptance of a psychological basis for discomfort. Although no supporting data were presented, they claimed that mutuality of therapist-patient expectations is important. The therapists were alleged to expect shared responsibility and active participation from the patients. It was suggested that patients with complementary expectancies are rewarded and those with contrary ones rejected and discontinued. Lennard and Bernstein (1960) also reported lack of compatibility of expectations to be associated with greater strain in the interview.

Clemes and D'Andrea (1965) tested the effect of compatibility and incompatibility of patient and therapist expectations upon patient anxiety in an initial interview. Expectations were classified on the Heine and Trosman questionnaire into Guidance ($N = 26$), Participation ($N = 33$), or Mixed ($N = 25$). The group expecting participation had a significantly lower mean age and higher education. Anxiety during the interview was measured by two self-rating devices. Therapists found compatible interviews to be less difficult and less anxiety-arousing for themselves. According to one of the measures, patients too felt less anxious during compatible interviews. Differences between the two types of expectations were not significant, but those with participation expectations tended to remain longer in therapy, to terminate on a mutual rather than nonmutual basis, to have had more previous experience with therapy, and to be closer to the therapists' ideal patient. The data suggest that since therapists preferred those with participation expectations and found the others more difficult to work with, this may have had much to do with the latter dropping out sooner and without mutual consent. It must be remembered that the researchers were dealing only with the initial interview and that expectations can shift in the course of therapy and adaptations take place. In this experiment, it is not clear why analysis of variance was not used to test the main hypothesis of an interaction between roles and expectations although it was used to test other hypotheses.

Another study tested the proposition that client satisfaction is in part a function of conformance of the counselor's role to the client's expectations (Severinsen, 1966). The findings, based upon a single interview, suggested that dissatisfaction is related to dissimilarity of expected and perceived counselor behavior. Since the clients were entering college freshmen seeking preregistration educational counseling, the study's applicability to psychotherapy is doubtful. Overall and Aronson (1963), studying expectations in lower socioeconomic status patients, hypothesized that therapists are less active and medically oriented than the patients expect and that patients with less accurate expectations would be less likely to return for treatment. In an interview, a psychiatric social worker gave each of forty new patients an oral questionnaire about a therapist's possible behavior, presenting varying expectations that he would be active, medical, supportive, passive, or psychiatric (focus on emotional or dynamic material). This was followed by a therapeutic interview with a medical student–therapist. The questionnaire was repeated at the end of the interview with additional questions about feelings and attitudes toward the therapist. A comparable questionnaire was completed by the therapists about the patients. As predicted, patients who failed to return for the next scheduled interview showed greater discrepancies between their expectations and their view of the interview than did those who did return. Most of the discrepancy between expectation and observation was in the categories of active, medical, and supportive; that is, the therapist's behavior in each was less than anticipated.

Expectancies of outpatients applying for treatment at the Nebraska Psychiatric Institute were surveyed by questionnaire (Garfield & Wolpin, 1963). Most of them expressed attitudes that were congenial to psychotherapy. They thought that psychotherapy was the best type of treatment for their condition, felt positively about discussing their personal problems, had an appreciation of the patient's active role in therapy, had confidence in the therapist's ability, and were motivated for treatment. As far as duration is concerned, 73 per cent anticipated some improvement by the fifth session and 70 per cent expected treatment to last ten sessions or less. No attempt was made to relate expectancies to outcome. Expectancies of this sort are apt to be sample specific, and few general statements about what people in general anticipate can be made.

Not all studies have shown the connection between expectation and outcome. Brady et al. explored the relation between expectation of improvement and actual improvement in 135 patients at the Hartford Institute of Living (Brady, Reznikoff, & Zeller, 1960). Expectation was measured by Pictures Attitudes Test and Sentence Completion Test, which were given soon after admission. The degree of improvement was rated by the therapist on an eight-point scale four to six months after admission. Not the slightest hint of a relationship emerged. Volsky et al., in their research with eighty student counselees, also obtained no evidence to support the idea that expectations about the counseling process or patient and counselor roles have a bearing on outcome (Volsky, Magoon, Norman, & Hoyt, 1965).

Getting at some of the theoretical underpinnings of expectancies, Block studied the applicability of achievement-motive theory to patient expectations (Block, 1964). The adaptive nature of expectations was stressed as the key to applying achievement-motive theory to the understanding of therapeutic phenomena. Two alternate theoretical positions were tested. Experimental results did not support McClelland's Unidirectional Theory, which predicts that the *size* of the discrepancy from the expectancy level determines the primary affect and secondary motive. Instead, support was obtained for Helson's Bipolar Theory, which proposes that the *direction* of the discrepancy is the determinant. Block thus concluded that when the direction of the discrepancy from the prevailing adaptation level of expectations produces positive affect it leads to an approach motive, and vice versa. Approach motive in therapy was considered to include such in-therapy behaviors as presenting new associations and dreams, taking the initiative in talking, making productive use of silence, and exhibiting actions and attitudes that reflect deeper movement into therapy. Avoidance motives were thought to be reflected by evasions, forgetting of dreams, angry silences, thwarting of associations, switching of topics, coming late, threatening termination, and generally withdrawing from involvement in therapy.

Assuming the importance of expectations, several plans for influencing them early in treatment have been evaluated. Hoehn-Saric et al. introduced a pretherapy "role induction interview" covering a general exposition of psychotherapy, description and explanation of the behavior expected of patient and therapist, preparation for such typical therapeutic phenomena as resistance, and induction of improvement expectation within four months (Hoehn-Saric, Frank, Imber, Nash, Stone, & Battle, 1964). Therapy was explained as a learning process, and expectations of ups and downs were discussed along with the meaning of the unconscious, the importance of self-expression and expression of feelings toward the therapist, the role of daydreams and fantasies, the role of the therapist as a listener rather than a giver of advice, and the importance of keeping appointments. Control patients were simply given an appointment with a therapist and told to try to terminate in four months. Those who underwent the preparation proved to have better attendance patterns and higher relationship ratings as rated by research staff from taped interviews. There was some evidence of more favorable outcome for the prepared group, but the results were far from being consistently positive. The general result suggests that the procedure was probably worth the effort.

Yalom et al. evaluated a technique of twenty-five-minute preparatory lectures prior to group therapy that were designed to "enhance faith" in group therapy, increase the attractiveness of the specific group, and orient patients to the confrontation process (Yalom, Houts, Newell, & Rand, 1967). Controls were seen for a comparable amount of time, given factual information, and urged to stay for at least twelve sessions. The two groups were equivalent in faith in group therapy as determined by a two-item questionnaire given after the orientation, but the experimental group showed significantly higher scores after the twelfth session. Hypotheses of greater group cohesiveness in the experimental group, better attendance, and fewer dropouts were not supported, but there was more interaction during the sessions of the experimental group. Perhaps the twenty-five-minute orientation was too short to attain the desired ends.

Munzer (1964) described and tested a variety of group-therapy warm-up procedures designed to promote and facilitate early therapeutic interaction. Some of the aims were apparently achieved, but there was no evidence of lasting effect. The most practical applications were thought to be for short-term group therapy. Procedures included predicting the roles of the other members; sharing memories, dreams, and fantasies; and employing "draw-a-problem" and life-space drawings.

In summary, little work has been done to relate expectancy to outcome. The usual criterion of outcome has been the patient's evaluation of improvement, and the results have been inconclusive. Some data suggest curvilinear relationships; others imply that the variable of social desirability, translated into psychotherapeutic terms, may influence both the patient's expectancies and his reports of improvement. Moreover, it is possible that the therapist's expectancies may, over the course of treatment, modify the patient's expectancies. More promising have been those studies that have explored the function of patient expectancy (or its compatibility with therapist expectancy) in the development or maintenance of the therapeutic relationship in its early phases. Other interesting investigations have looked into the effect of influencing patient expectancies before therapy has begun. There have been few, if any, studies of the change of expectancies over the long course of therapy. What knowledge we have serves best to suggest hypotheses in an area that may be crucial to the fate of the therapeutic endeavor.

11

The Therapist as an Outcome Variable: I. Qualifications

At least as much effort has been devoted to studying the therapist as a variable in the outcome of therapy as to studying the patient. One series of investigations deals with what may be regarded as the formal qualifications of the therapist. These concern his professional affiliation, formal training, and experience rather than any basic personal qualities. They represent, in a sense, those aspects that can be taught or added to enhance a therapist's effectiveness. The research asks whether or not they in fact contribute to successful outcome in the therapeutic endeavor.

PROFESSIONAL DISCIPLINE

There is a noticeable lack of direct studies on the efficacy of the therapist as a function of his professional discipline. The antecedent issue, as has been stressed before, is whether or not psychotherapy itself, in any form, is efficacious. If therapy is not beneficial, there would be no more point in arguing about who should do it and how it should be done than in trying to determine who is best qualified to teach photography to the blind. If, however, it is accepted that psychotherapy has positive effects, the question has scientific, professional, legal, and social implications of more than passing interest. Definitive answers should have an impact on program planning and administration, training models, case assignment and therapist selection, legislation, and endless related issues. This question has been the subject of speculation and debate; of attitudes, opinions, pronouncements, and position papers; of offensive and defensive maneuvers; of polemics, politics, testimonials, and indictments. Hopes, aspirations, prejudices, tradition, prestige, influence, vested interests, economics, the professional labor market, and social needs are all confused in a way that makes it difficult for those who are concerned with the matter to view the situation objectively.

The question is: Do psychiatrists, psychologists, or psychiatric social workers (to limit the discussion to the three major groups in the "mental health" field) achieve differential results in performing as psychotherapists? It is easier to raise the question than to find the answer. Proper planning of such an investigation would require control of at least such variables as experience, professional generation in which training was received, setting, type and difficulty of cases, and frequency and duration of therapy. It would be misleading to compare outcome results obtained from unrelated studies without control of these variables. As far as we can determine, the question has not been answered simply because it has not been tested. Consequently, there is no satisfactory evidence to indicate that one professional discipline is any more or less effective than another. This null hypothesis will stand or fall when, and if, pertinent evidence accumulates. Since neither individual nor collective opinion is determined exclusively by the weight of evidence, particularly in areas of ego involvement and faith, no genuine resolution is visible on the horizon.

PERSONAL THERAPY OF THE THERAPIST

Many words have been written and many assumptions made about the desirability of some form of personal therapy for the therapist himself. There is no need to repeat the arguments here. Simply stated, proponents affirm that the therapist must go through the experience of having been a patient and become aware of his own conflicts if he is to help others. Antagonists maintain that within broad limits of "normal adjustment" such personal experience is not at all necessary. Opinions on the matter range all the way from those who consider personal therapy a *sine qua non* to those who view it as irrelevant. Again, interwoven into the fabric of the issue is the prior question of whether or not psychotherapy itself is an efficacious process. If it is not, it would obviously be superfluous to consider the desirability of therapy for therapists. Even though positive effects of psychotherapy with emotionally disturbed patients have now been demonstrated, it still remains to be shown whether the personal adjustment or personal therapy of the clinician facilitates or interferes with the successful outcome of his therapeutic work with patients.

Seeman (1950) surveyed the opinions of seventy prominent therapists, most of whom were outstanding writers in the field of psychotherapy. They received a nine-item questionnaire on the importance of therapist adjustment and personal therapy for the effectiveness of the therapist. The greatest agreement was on the question of making therapy *available* to prospective therapists. There was consensus, however, that we lack evidence indicating that the best-adjusted therapists are necessarily the most effective. In the many years since the publication of the results of this survey, we still lack such evidence. Psychoanalytically oriented therapists tended more than others to hold to the view that personal analysis is necessary to prevent therapists from working out their maladjustment on patients. Whatever the question, whether pro or con, psychoanalysts tended to take stronger positions than nonanalysts; 41 per cent of the analysts' responses were in the strong category in contrast to 13.6 per cent of the nonanalysts.

Despite its importance, there have been few direct investigations that would help us resolve this controversy. Holt and Luborsky (1958) hypothesized that psychiatric residents who received psychotherapy during training would be more likely to rise in the level of their performance than those who did not. The residents, from the Winter Veterans Administration Hospital, Kansas, received training and supervision by the staff of the Menninger Clinic, an outstanding psychoanalytic training center. A total of 218 residents were divided into four categories: those who had received therapy, those who had had more than brief therapy, those who had applied for but had not received therapy, and those who had not applied. Changes in level of competence, as measured by supervisors' ratings, bore no relationship to the presence, absence, or duration of personal therapy. As for the type of therapy, a comparison for those who received psychoanalysis as distinct from psychotherapy is not given, although the data were apparently available. It is interesting to note that for all categories only about one-quarter of the residents were judged as improving in competence. The fallibility of supervisors' ratings as a criterion was, of course, considered. A more direct test was made of the relationship between improvement in the patient as rated by the therapist and personal analysis of the therapist (Katz, Lorr, & Rubinstein, 1958). Little or no relation was found between the two variables. Here too the authors acknowledge the weakness of the criterion measure.

Peripherally connected to outcome is a study of patient and therapist influences on quitting therapy (McNair, Lorr, & Callahan, 1963). No differences were found between therapists with and without personal therapy. Working with a subsample of this same group drawn from three of the seven Veterans Administration clinics studied in this investigation, the researchers discovered that therapists with more personal therapy tended to keep patients for a longer period (McNair, Lorr, Young, Roth, & Boyd, 1964).

At this point there is obviously not enough evidence to permit drawing any firm conclusions. So far, personal therapy does not seem to make any critical difference. The null hypothesis certainly has not been rejected. If personal therapy makes one a more or less proficient therapist, it has yet to be demonstrated. The need for personal therapy for the therapist is neither a self-evident truth nor an established fact. Research on the two related questions of the effect of therapist adjustment and personal therapy upon outcome is certainly feasible. The question of whether the therapist's adjustment affects outcome could be approached by selecting therapists of varying degrees of personal adjustment, with other relevant therapist characteristics controlled, assigning cases randomly, and objectively assessing comparative outcome. A similar experiment could study the effects of personal therapy of the clinician upon his success as a therapist both while he was still in treatment and after he had completed his own therapy. It would be difficult but necessary to avoid confounding therapy and experience.

EXPERIENCE OF THE THERAPIST

In almost any conceivable field of endeavor it is axiomatic that improved performance is a by-product of experience. Is it not curious, then, that even this has become a subject for research in the field of psychotherapy? Would anyone seriously undertake research to ascertain whether experience improves the performance of a surgeon or a plumber? The fact that experience has been a subject of research seems to be a reflection of deep-seated doubts about psychotherapy. If, however, an experiment were to demonstrate convincingly that experience makes no difference in the success of psychotherapy it would create only a minor dilemma. Some would maintain that if a process itself is ineffective, more experience in performing it could not make it any more effective. Others would argue that some people have the peculiar talents required to be a successful therapist while others do not, and no matter how much additional experience either receives the increments in performance will be minimal. Still others would disregard the research on the grounds that it is the *type* of experience that is important, not the amount. No matter how the charge might be answered, however, inability to show beneficial effects of experience upon case outcome would severely indict the therapeutic process.

Myers and Auld (1955) conducted a direct investigation of the effect of therapist experience upon outcome at an outpatient clinic at Yale University. The experienced therapists were senior staff psychiatrists of the rank of instructor or assistant professor, while second-year psychiatric residents served as the inexperienced group. All data came from examination of case records. The reasons for termination were placed in four categories: patient quit, therapist discharged patient as unimproved, therapist discharged patient as improved, therapy continued elsewhere. Comparison of the disposition of sixty-three patients revealed that for those who attended fewer than ten interviews the experience of the therapist was not related to outcome. None of these patients were considered improved; 21 per cent continued elsewhere and 71 per cent simply quit. For those patients seen ten or more times, however, there was a significant difference between the experienced and inexperienced therapists in dispositional categories. The more experienced and better trained staff tended to have more successful terminations and fewer failures. None of the patients seen by experienced staff for ten or more interviews quit, in contrast to 28.5 per cent of those seen by residents. For patients considered improved, the improvement rate of those seen by staff (64 per cent) was twice that of those seen by residents (32 per cent). It is of interest to note that, even though the therapists were judges of outcome, the total improvement rate for all patients was only 25 per cent. The authors themselves raise the main critical issues in this retrospective study. They acknowledge that since cases were not randomly assigned, senior staff may have selected cases judged more likely to be successful and left the less promising cases to the residents. They also point out that observed differences in case termination may have been a result of different *conceptions* of improvement (as opposed to veridical change) stemming from different training and experience.

A similar caution is raised by Katz et al. in analyzing data on 116 patients from a cooperative study involving thirteen Veterans Administration clinics (Katz, Lorr, & Rubinstein, 1958). In two samples they obtained significant positive correlations between therapists' ratings of patient improvement and years of experience. They were unable to ascertain without other external criteria whether increased experience actually leads to greater success or whether the standards and perceptions that determine ratings of improvement change with additional experience.

The question of experience was also approached in the client-centered setting of the University of Chicago Counseling Center (Cartwright & Vogel, 1960). A total of twenty-two clients were treated by nineteen therapists, ten of whom were considered experienced and nine inexperienced. The experienced therapists had seen six or more cases, with an average of 25.8 and a range of six to sixty. The inexperienced had worked with an average of only one case, with a range of zero to five. Change was assessed by a repeated application of the Butler-Haigh Q-Sort, from which an adjustment score was obtained, and a mental health rating derived from the TAT. The data were analyzed in two ways. Chi-square analyses of change revealed experienced therapists to be no more effective than inexperienced ones in effecting changes reflected in Q-scores but significantly more effective in producing positive change in TAT mental health ratings. T-tests between pre- and posttherapy were significant for Q-scores and TAT ratings for experienced therapists, but not for the inexperienced ones. The authors concluded that an experienced therapist is effective in improving the patient's adjustment as revealed both by the TAT and by self-descriptions on Q-sorts but that the inexperienced therapist is ineffective in improving the self-picture and may actually bring about a decrease in adjustment as revealed by the TAT. The obtained t of 2.19 between pre- and posttherapy TAT scores is reported as "significant" even though it does not reach the $p = .05$ level of confidence. There is reason to believe, however, that the results would have been more consistent and more conclusive had the standards for experience been more stringent than the median split that was used. In this study, a therapist who had seen six cases fell in the experienced category. Certainly a therapist who has seen six cases is more experienced than one who has only seen one, but he can hardly qualify as experienced. Inclusion of such beginners in the experienced group along with others who had seen sixty cases may have attenuated the effect.

Another investigation in the same clinic was an elaborate factor analytic study, one small phase of which dealt with therapist experience in relation to a host of variables (Fiske, Cartwright, & Kirtner, 1964). The authors were frankly puzzled by the absence of any significant relationships. The measure of experience used was the square root of the number of clients seen (a transformation to normalize the distribution). The authors suggest that a better measure might have been the combination of this with number of sessions and years of experience. Another reservation expressed was uncertainty whether client difficulty was comparable across experience levels.

Still another study from the University of Chicago Counseling Center touched upon the issue of experience and outcome (Barrett-Lennard, 1962). Eight therapists classified as experts had completed at least two years of internship, had a minimum of three years of experience at the Center (mean 5.4 years), and had been appointed to staff positions on the recommendation of a selection committee. Five nonexperts were first-year staff interns and one was a research assistant. The nonexperts had a minimum of one-half year of experience (average one year) and averaged seven years younger than the experts (35.4 to 28.4 years). Therapist-client sex ratios were comparable in the two groups. The experts treated twelve clients and the nonexperts fifteen, for a total of twenty-seven. Length of stay was taken as an indirect approximation of outcome, and the quality of the patient-therapist relationship was measured by a questionnaire covering five relationship variables that was given to both therapist and patient. Length of stay was found to be significantly greater for the patients of the expert group than for those seen by nonexperts. A two-fold index of change was also applied. A rating was made on a ten-point scale of the client's general adjustment level after the first therapy interview and again at termination of therapy. This first change index was the pre-post difference score. The other index, made by the therapist at termination, was a four-point rating of the degree of change ranging from "not changed" to "changed a great deal." These two indices were combined by dichotomizing each index and including in the "most changed" group only those who fell in the upper category on both indices.

When patients of experts and nonexperts were compared on the resulting two-fold index, it was observed that nine of the patients seen by experts were in the "more changed" and three in the "less changed" category, in contrast to six and eight respectively for the patients of nonexperts. Thus, 75 per cent of those seen by experts and 43 per cent of those seen by nonexperts were in the "more changed" category. The difference, as measured by Fisher's Exact Test, fell at the $p < .10$ level. Results for the client-centered relationship variables of regard, empathy, congruence, and conditionality as seen by the client were also in the predicted direction in favor of the experts. They were equivocal, however, as only one difference reached the $p = .05$ level of confidence with a one-tailed U-test. The groups did not differ on the variable "willingness to be known." From the therapists' vantage point the only significant difference was in "level of regard." The author interpreted the results as "provisional confirmation" of the hypothesis. F-ratios revealed the experts to be more homogeneous (but not significantly so) than nonexperts on empathy and congruence. It should be noted that in this study the pretherapy adjustment levels were so high that there was concern about a ceiling effect. Generalizations to a more maladjusted population cannot be made. The "experts" in this investigation can in no sense of the word be considered experts, but they were clearly more experienced than the nonexpert group. Because of the lack of any external criterion of outcome, the research is limited by the validity of client and therapist ratings.

In their study of terminators and remainers, McNair et al. found that therapists with more than four years of experience held 72 per cent of their patients while those with less than four years held 60 per cent (McNair, Lorr, & Callahan, 1963). Since the sample was fairly large, this difference was statistically significant. The degree of relationship, however, was low, with a phi of .12. The finding, although minimized as *post hoc* by the authors, is consistent with other studies. Baum et al.

reported that resident psychiatrists with more clinical experience in various fields of medicine or psychiatry before entering their residency (average 11.7 years) had 16 per cent dropouts compared to 46 per cent for those with less (average 1.1 years) clinical experience (Baum, Felzer, D'Zmura, & Shumaker, 1966).

Grigg (1961) studied client response to counselors at three levels of experience. Over 200 cases were seen for a median of 4.2 interviews (range two to sixteen), roughly one-third for personal counseling and the remainder for vocational-educational counseling at the University of Texas Counseling Center. There were six Ph.D. counselors, six experienced trainees, and four inexperienced trainees. Data came from a client-observation report filled out after the final interview. Among the variables considered was client satisfaction with counseling, expressed in the categories very helpful, moderately helpful, and minimal to not helpful. Grigg reported that feelings about improvement were independent of the experience of the counselor but he questions the reliability of the criterion. The finding could be questioned on other grounds as well. First there is the matter of possible case assignment bias. He reports that the distribution of cases was "routine," but the routine might involve assigning easier cases to beginning students. The distribution of cases in the categories vocational-educational and personal to the various experience groups was reported as not significantly different ($p = .11$). The breakdown of assignments should have been equivalent, not merely not significantly different. As it stands, we can observe a shift in assignment from vocational-educational cases to personal adjustment cases as experience level increases. For example, the percentage of personal adjustment cases rose from 23 per cent to 28 per cent to 39 per cent as we progress through the three experience levels. This shift could be a factor in all results. The standards for "experienced" were not very rigorous, and the length of experience was not specified. The levels of experience of the experienced and inexperienced groups were not clearly differentiated. In addition, client satisfaction with counseling is not impressive as the sole criterion of outcome. Generalizations from this study to psychotherapy with emotionally disturbed patients cannot readily be made because the sample appears to be comprised mainly of minor situational college adjustment problems.

Thus, inquiry into the effect of therapist experience is limited to a handful of studies that do not yield a strikingly definitive picture. As the studies were generally not specifically designed to answer the question, experience levels were not always sharply delineated nor other relevant variables well enough controlled for us to say with confidence that obtained differences were due to experience alone. The preponderant weight of evidence, nonetheless, is that experience *does* seem to make a difference. In no instance did the inexperienced do better, in a minority of studies experience did not differentiate, and in most studies it tended to promote more favorable results. A lower dropout rate appears to be a consistent result of experience. Most of the investigations originated in the same client-centered setting. The clients were relatively well-adjusted individuals with minor problems and considerable presumptive growth potential. It is not unlikely that experience could be shown to have even a more decisive effect with more difficult and acutely disturbed patients. A well-designed study would require therapists of clearly differentiated experience levels and would take length of experience, number of cases, and type of experience into consideration. Relevant therapist variables other than experience would have to be controlled, patients would have to be assigned randomly or systematically without selection bias, and convincing measures of outcome would have to be applied.

TRAINING OF THE THERAPIST

At one time or another, practically everyone becomes involved in informal, unsystematized, and noncontractual attempts to help other people with their problems of adjustment. Since everyone has had a variety of personal problems, people usually feel no great reluctance in giving others advice drawn from their own life experience. There are probably more self-proclaimed experts on human behavior than on any other subject. Few hesitate to admit that they know nothing about physics or plumbing or parakeets, but as people they are convinced that they know about people. Having lived, they feel they know life and its vicissitudes, at least up to a certain point. When that point is reached, the *formal* psychotherapeutic task becomes the function of highly trained professionals. There is some disagreement on the form that training should take, its nature, content, extent, and timing, but train we must to meet rigorous professional standards.

Psychotherapy, in one shape or another, has been in existence for many years. An untold number of therapy sessions have been conducted with a vast army of patients. Specialized training programs have been greatly expanded as has the establishment of licensing, certification, and similar requirements designed to limit the field to "fully qualified" practitioners. It is therefore a most curious phenomenon in the mental health field that it is still not considered frivolous for a researcher to attempt to determine if training has an effect upon the outcome of psychotherapy. It would be considered patently absurd to consider the proposition that any other than an extensively trained master could do the job in most of the other learned professions or highly skilled technologies or crafts. One exception is the profession of teaching at the college and graduate school level, where experts in a given subject matter are employed even though they are not trained as teachers. Another is the nonperforming arts, where many untrained or at best self-trained artists achieve great success with their painting and sculpture. Teaching, art, and psychotherapy are all fields in which objective standards of effective performance are generally lacking.

Some believe that a mature nonprofessional who has had enough of the "right kind" of real life experiences to qualify him as an expert in living might be able to transmit his skills to the less fortunate. Others see a skilled psychotherapist as a kind of artist (perhaps with innate talents) who can recreate or reconstruct people with troubled lives much as a sculptor molds a clay figure. Underlying both of these beliefs is the notion that there is such a thing as a "therapeutic personality" and that contact with this charismatic person brings about change. The personality of the therapist is seen as cutting across methodological lines. Whereas expertise can be acquired in many ways, training can at best elicit, not transmit, innate talent.

Uncertainty about the essential nature of psychotherapy and the necessary and sufficient conditions for bringing about behavioral change opens to scrutiny the issues of the optimal type of training and even the value of specialized training itself. If the crucial ingredient of psychotherapy is some monolithic variable such as sympathetic listening, the giving of sound advice, guidance in social interaction, or the formation of a positive interpersonal relationship, full professional training would not be a necessary prerequisite for success. If emotional disorders are either self-corrective or run a more or less unalterable course, the training of the therapist is immaterial. If psychotherapy is ineffective in modifying behavior regardless of who does it, training would obviously be superfluous.

Advocates of specialized training are guided by quite different postulates. They maintain that it is possible to alter the course, direction, and rate of behavioral change. They see the process as a complex one and the methods as varied rather than simple and unitary. They hold specialized training to be essential for the development of therapists who will be adaptable to multiple roles and knowledgeable about what, when, how, and how much to do or not to do to achieve objectives. Despite the existence of these antithetical positions, it is doubtful if the heretical challenge to the value of training would have become a serious research issue if it were not for a critical shortage of psychotherapists. Manpower needs stimulate searches for substitutes and researches to justify them. Financially well-supported community mental health services are handicapped by lack of trained personnel. With increasing pressures to use subprofessionals and nonprofessionals to take up the slack there are several questions that need to be answered: (1) How well can untrained or minimally trained personnel perform in contrast to fully trained professionals? (2) With what kinds of cases and levels of difficulty can they function effectively? (3) What are the comparative consequences of their errors and failures? (4) Under what circumstances and settings, and with what kind and amount of supervision, can they perform well?

All of these questions can be answered by controlled research before taking the risk of staffing community mental health centers with untrained therapists or giving relatively brief training courses to aspiring nonprofessionals. The logic of maintaining high standards of training instead of lessening training requirements is buttressed by the experiences of other fields. It would seem socially irresponsible to advocate any substitute for training until such time as research clearly supports another position. What, to date, has the research revealed on this subject?

Ten studies bear directly on the issue of the training of the therapist. In most of the studies, the patients treated were severely disturbed. Eight of the ten studies conclude that untrained therapists can do an effective therapeutic job. Five researchers reported success when untrained "therapists" treated chronic hospitalized schizophrenics; two studies reported failure. Two investigations claimed success with psychoneurotic outpatients treated by those who were not trained psychotherapists, and one investigation alleged that therapeutically untrained graduate students in psychology were as effective as experienced and fully trained Ph.D.s when working with college counseling cases. Of these ten studies, only four made direct comparisons with professional psychotherapists as controls. The results favored the nonprofessionals in two studies, and showed them to do as well in the other two. If these studies are taken at face value, one sees developing an apparent validation of the view that nonprofessionals of various backgrounds can be effective psychotherapists, in some cases without supervision and in others without any training at all! Several of the studies suggest that nonprofessionals can do as well and perhaps even better than highly trained professionals. These conclusions, if valid, have profound implications for the mental health field. This outcropping of evidence, which goes against the grain of common sense and threatens so many reasoned convictions, merits closer examination.

The case for the untrained therapist is based on a collection of independent studies involving a combined total of more than 1,000 patients. The first of these investigations, Denker's (1946) study of the effectiveness of general medical practitioners in contrast to psychiatrists and psychoanalysts, has been reviewed in some detail in our discussion of spontaneous recovery in chapter 3. Denker reported that psychiatric patients seen by general practitioners recover at a rate at least comparable to recovery rates achieved by trained professionals as reported in the literature. Within the limitations of the validity of the data, the study casts doubt on the need for specialized training in order to achieve positive behavioral change. As we have indicated, however, the design of the study and the assumptions that it makes exclude it from consideration as strong evidence.

Beck et al. designed a research project to assess the effectiveness of nonprofessional case-aid volunteers in bringing about significant and practically important changes in the clinical and social status of hospitalized patients (Beck, Kantor, & Gelineau, 1963). The volunteers, Harvard University undergraduates, were each assigned to work with one of 120 patients on a one hour a week basis. The patients were predominantly chronic schizophrenics with an average age of 43.5 years. The students selected their patients after reading case histories. The therapy given did not follow a stereotyped pattern; it consisted of activities as well as verbal interaction and included direct participation with families when patients attempted to leave the hospital. Although they were untrained, the volunteer "therapists" did not proceed completely on their own. They received hour-for-hour supervision in groups of eight to ten by a psychiatric social worker and had biweekly individual supervisory conferences. Each student worked with his patient throughout an academic year. Two criteria of effectiveness were employed. The first was the number of treated patients who were discharged from the hospital. The second was a rating in the categories "sick as ever," "marginal adjustment," "considerably improved," and "apparently well." These ratings were based upon examination of student records and a follow-up telephone interview with relatives of patients who had left the hospital. Although it is not stated, the ratings were presumably made by the authors. There were no controls, and the data bearing on the main issue were simply tabulated since no hypotheses were subjected to test. The results in terms of discharges were compared with those of a report in the literature that cited a 3 per cent discharge expectation. This rate was contrasted to the 31 per cent (37 out of 120) who left the hospital while being seen by the students. Twenty-eight patients were still out of the hospital 3.4 years later and the remainder stayed out for an average of 1.4 years. An additional seven patients left the hospital subsequent to their period of working with the students. As for the clinical status of the thirty-five discharged patients who were still out at the time of follow-up, two were judged as sick as ever, ten marginal, eighteen considerably improved, and five apparently well. The 31 per cent discharge rate was considered highly favorable compared to the alleged 3 per cent discharge expectation. The authors concluded from their data that the treatment program was a successful one.

The major limitation of this study is the absence of any kind of controls. In a hospital setting it might have been feasible to have a control group seen by professional staff and another receiving no special treatment. As it is, there is no way of knowing whether the work of the students was less, equally, or more effective than either no special treatment or highly specialized treatment given by professionals. Without absolute standards or control data, the answers to the experimental question were not forthcoming. We are left not knowing whether or not there actually was either a "significant"or a "practically important" change in the clinical and social status of the patients attributable to work with case-aid volunteers. For comparative purposes, reliance on a 3 per cent discharge expectation reported in a single study seems an inadequate standard to go by. Clinical status ratings were made only on discharged patients. Thus the twenty-three patients who were reported as considerably improved or apparently well actually constitute 19 per cent of the total sample of 120 patients. What happened to the clinical status of the eighty-three patients who were not discharged is not reported. Nothing is said of the discharge criteria or procedures, nor is it stated who made such decisions. As subject as discharge judgments are to bias, this information should have been explicitly presented. Gross ratings of data obtained from relatives, collected unsystematically through telephone interviews, are questionable at best. There is no assurance or even mention of any efforts to eliminate or counteract the possibility of rater bias. As far as can be determined from the report, the ratings were neither blind nor made by impartial and uninvolved observers.

In a study by Poser (1966), the theme was the same but the therapeutic mantle was passed on from Harvard men to young lady undergraduates in Montreal. Patients were seen in groups rather than individually, and experienced therapists were introduced as controls. The patients were 343 male chronic schizophrenics, with a median age of forty-seven years, who had been in the hospital for at least three continuous years. The median length of hospitalization was fourteen years. The untrained therapists were eleven women ranging from eighteen to twenty-five years of age. They had no prior psychological training or mental hospital experience, and served as paid volunteers. Two inpatients, an alcoholic and an hysteric, were also used as therapists. Their professional counterparts were seven psychiatrists, six psychiatric social workers, and two occupational therapists. The psychiatrists were all male, aged thirty-five to fifty, with five to seventeen years of experience. Three were specialists in group therapy, and all but one had experience in conducting therapy groups. The social workers, aged thirty-six to forty-three, two male and four female, had at least five years of experience. All but two had done group therapy. The occupational therapists were twenty-seven and thirty years of age, with five and seven years of experience including some mental hospital work. All the professional therapists were from outside the institution in which the study was conducted and were paid for their services.

The patients were divided into thirty-four groups of ten patients each, matched for age, severity of illness, length of hospitalization, and test performance on the criteria measures. Of these thirty-four groups, twenty-eight were randomly assigned to trained and untrained therapists, while the remaining six groups served as untreated controls in the sense that they received usual hospital care rather than specialized group therapy. Each treatment group met with its therapist one hour daily, five days a week for a five-month period. Even though an attendant assembled the patients for each group, some refused to attend. Forty-eight patients who failed to attend two-thirds of the sessions were dropped from the study. Groups were conducted in accordance with each therapist's determination, and therapy varied from verbal interaction alone to games, parties, dancing, painting, and other activities. The criteria measures consisted of two psychomotor, two perceptual, and two verbal tests administered before and after the treatment period. The data were treated by analysis of covariance.

Poser reported that the patients treated by lay therapists did significantly better on four of the six tests, whereas only two of the six were in favor of the controls. A comparison of the inexperienced and the experienced therapists yielded results in favor of the former on three of the six tests. No difference in effectiveness was reported between psychiatrists and social workers. A follow-up study, three years later, was done on only sixty-one of the patients using but four of the six tests. This sample consisted only of control patients and those treated by lay therapists. The treated group did better on all tests than they had done before, while the controls exceeded their earlier performance on only one test. A scale of hospital adjustment was administered before and after treatment only to eighty patients treated by lay therapists. Ratings made by an attendant and a nursing supervisor were not in agreement with each other. There was no difference between the treated and untreated groups in discharge rate and presumably none between those treated by professional and lay therapists. The author concluded that the lay therapists did somewhat better than the professionals in facilitating their patients' test behavior. Although cautioning against generalization, he observed that the study gave some support for the conclusion that "traditional training in the mental health professions may be neither optimal nor even necessary for the promotion of therapeutic behavior change in mental hospital patients" (p. 289).

In this investigation the training of the therapists was supposed to have been the independent variable upon which behavioral change in patients was to depend. Age, sex, and therapeutic method, however, remained uncontrolled. The experienced and trained therapists were considerably older and predominantly male. The eleven young college girls were compared with a group of fifteen trained individuals, nine of whom were male. The trained therapists apparently did traditional group therapy. Whatever the lay therapists did is not clearly indicated but was obviously something different. The results might reflect an age × sex × method interaction as much as or more than training. That is, the improvement rate may reflect the response of middle-aged male patients who had been long institutionalized to the attention given by a group of young college girls coming in with dancing, parties, and other social activities in contrast to their response to conventional group therapy conducted by middle-aged professional men. But if this were the reason for differential change in patients, it would give us cause to pause and re-examine just what *is* therapeutic!

Looking further, we see that the criteria measures are crucial. The tests given—tapping rate, reaction time, verbal fluency, digit-symbol, Stroop Color Word Test, and a word association test—have been found to distinguish between schizophrenics and normals, but it was not established that they validly differentiated levels of adjustment within a chronic schizophrenic population. There are real questions of the practical importance of these measures and doubts about just what the changes in test performance measure. It is not clear how increases in tapping rate or reaction time, for example, are related to significant change in adjustment. The measures of adjustment that *were* used showed nothing. Most of the patients were still in the hospital three years later, and the results concerning hospital adjustment were in no way conclusive. Changes in discharge or hospital adjustment would have been far more impressive than changes in tapping rate.

Two occupational therapists were used as trained professionals in this study, but there is no indication that they were group therapists either by training or experience. Their inclusion might have to some degree diluted the results. This is not a major point since the data for psychiatrists and social workers are separately presented. In discussing the placebo effect, Poser states that there is no reason to believe that patients had more faith in trained than in untrained therapists since they were largely unaware of this distinction. This seems highly unlikely because experienced patients are usually not so naïve as to be unable to distinguish middle-aged gentlemen with the title of "doctor" from college girls. Poser rules out placeboid effects of prestige and sees the untrained therapists as contributing an "inert" placeboid effect with the experience of the trained therapists as the "active" ingredient in therapy. It should be noted that professionals in mental hospitals can also be seen negatively as a result of the past experiences of the patients.

From the basic data, it is claimed that the patients of lay therapists did better on four of six tests even though one of the four was not statistically significant ($p = .10$). The difference of improvement on three of six tests for one group and two of six for another is not impressive. Analysis of covariance was used, but F-values are not mentioned. Why t-tests were reported rather than Fs is not explained. Poser makes a point of the fact that the standard deviation is smaller on all tests for patients treated by professionals, but he was not concerned with or did not deal with this apparent violation of the assumption of homogeneity of variance in his statistical analysis. The three-year follow-up is of limited value since it only included data for patients treated by the lay therapists. It is hardly credible that five months of group activity discontinued for three years could be the variable accounting for whatever changes in test behavior were shown. There were also twenty-six fewer patients than in the original sample who were not accounted for.

All of these matters aside, there is one central flaw that in and of itself would be sufficient to raise doubts about all the conclusions. There were forty-eight dropouts of patients who could not be induced to attend enough sessions. These dropouts were, it seems reasonable to assume, the least motivated and least cooperative patients. The dropout rate was not equivalent in the groups conducted by the two types of therapists. The thirteen lay therapists treated eighty-seven patients and had 6.7 patients per group after forty-three had dropped out. The professionals treated 145 patients, with 9.7 patients per therapist and only five dropouts. This is the largest and probably the most significant difference of all, but it was neither noted nor commented upon. The difference in group size might have been a factor, but most critical is the fact that the professionals had a dropout rate of less than 4 per cent in contrast to the 33 per cent lost for the untrained therapists. This introduces an obvious bias to the two samples. It is likely that the more highly motivated, "better" patients excessively weighted the groups of the untrained therapists, inflating their end results, and/or the results of the professionals were lowered by the presence of all the poorly motivated, "worst" patients. In effect, the patient samples were no longer comparable. The single most stable finding of the study might well be that experienced, trained therapists are able to "hold" their patients while untrained beginners are not.

The relationship of training and experience to therapeutic outcome formed one phase of a study by Grigg (1961). The major portion of this investigation dealt with aspects of counselor performance. A total of 219 clients out of 249 sampled at the University of Texas Testing and Counseling Center completed that aspect of a Client Observation Report dealing with their judgment of whether counseling had been helpful to them. Their ratings were made at the end of the final counseling session in three categories of help including "very," "moderate," and "minimal to none." They were told that the ratings would be withheld from their counselors. The counselors were six experienced individuals who had Ph.D. degrees and had completed training and internship, six experienced trainees who had finished a year of internship, and four inexperienced trainees who had either not completed their internship or had had no prior experience. Cases were routinely assigned following an intake interview, and the median number of interviews was 4.2 (range two to sixteen). The results showed that 80 per cent of the clients of the Ph.D. counselors felt that they had been considerably or moderately helped, in contrast to 89 per cent of those seen by the more advanced trainees and 85 per cent of those seen by the beginners. The breakdowns within the three categories of help were quite comparable for the three levels of training and experience, and no significant differences were obtained by chi-square analysis of the data. This led to the conclusion that feelings about improvement are independent of the counselors' level of experience.

The distribution of case assignments was described as "routine," but the meaning is not explicit. Did the routine involve assigning "easier" cases to the students? Cases were of two types, vocational-educational counseling and personal counseling. The ratio of the former to the latter increased as experience and training level decreased. Thus, the Ph.D.s had a 61% : 39% ratio of vocational-educational to personal problems to deal with, the beginning students had a 77% : 23% balance, and the advanced trainee group had an intermediate ratio. This shift in type of cases assigned could have influenced results, and assignments should have been made on a random basis to obviate this possibility. The distribution was reported as not significantly different ($p = .11$), but the experiment would have been launched from firmer ground if the groups had been truly equivalent.

The percentage of nonresponse to the section of the rating scale calling for evaluation of the counselor can be reconstructed from Grigg's data. Nonresponse ranged from 5 per cent of the clients of the Ph.D.s to 14 per cent for the advanced trainees and 17 per cent for the neophytes. These percentages suggest the possibility of a sampling bias in response. If clients tended to hold back negative appraisals, the greater nonresponse rate by the clients of the student counselors would reflect to their advantage. The chief reservation about this type of experiment, however, is its reliance upon client satisfaction as the sole criterion of outcome. In his commentary following the paper, Robinson observed that client satisfaction may not be a good criterion of outcome at all. He also calls attention to the fact that while the N is in the 200s in the data analysis, the experiment involved sixteen counselors. He states, "Chi-square assumes complete independence of all ratings: to fulfill this assumption every client would need a different counselor" (p. 222) and proposes that the data might better have been treated by analysis of variance. There is no indication of the severity of the disturbances of the clients, but by inference one would assume that they were mainly minor problems of college adjustment that could be handled in an average of four interviews. The author does not generalize beyond the scope of his data, and this counseling procedure is not to be confused with psychotherapy. No generalizations to psychotherapy with neurotics can be made from these data.

Another study, whose focus was on the therapeutic method, touches peripherally on the issue of therapist training and outcome (Anker & Walsh, 1961). The relevant finding was that chronic hospitalized patients participating in drama group activity under the guidance of a recreation therapist improved more than a comparable group receiving formal group therapy led by a trained psychologist. The conclusion of the authors that "this inexpensive technique produces results which, in this study, were incomparably better than the more 'expensive' and time-consuming group psychotherapy requiring a highly trained therapist" (p. 480) does not necessarily impugn training. It is quite possible that had the psychologist conducted the activity group he might have gotten equally good or superior results.

Mendel and Rapport (1963) studied the effectiveness of an existential approach in treating chronic schizophrenic outpatients. One hundred sixty-six patients were distributed among fifty-eight psychiatrists, thirty psychologists, thirty-one social workers, and forty-seven untrained aides. Each treated one patient once a month for twenty to thirty minutes. Psychiatric supervision was furnished. The hospital return rate over a fifty-one-month period was 36 per cent for the aides, 34 per cent for the psychiatrists, 23 per cent for the social workers, and 20 per cent for the psychologists. Since the cases were not of equal difficulty and were not randomly assigned to begin with, variations in return rates were attributed to case selection. The authors' conclusion that the favorable return rate was "brought about" by this very brief and infrequent contact with nonprofessionals is clearly unwarranted. Causality has in no way been demonstrated. It would first have been necessary to show the effectiveness of *this* form of treatment by comparison with some other form of treatment, monthly nontreatment visits, or no contact at all. Within this structure, unselective assignment of patients would be necessary to test the hypothesis of the effectiveness of nonprofessionals.

The case for the negative is presented by Sines, Silver, and Lucero (1961), who set out to evaluate the effectiveness of therapy by psychiatric aides in a state hospital setting. The patients were 117 female schizophrenics with a mean age of forty-eight who had been continuously hospitalized for at least two years and had an average length of stay of thirteen to fourteen years. The therapists were forty female and twenty male aides who were randomly selected from the hospital staff. All had been at the hospital for at least one year. Patients were randomly assigned to an experimental or control group, with the former again being randomly assigned, one to an aide. The mission of each therapist was to try to improve his patient's psychiatric and behavioral status. Verbal, recreational, and other activity procedures were optional. The aides met with their patients twice weekly for fifty minutes over a twelve-month period. Periodic seminars were held and the patients' progress was reviewed and the treatment plans guided. Nevertheless, the aides were given considerable latitude in the management of their patients. Thirty-seven of the patients were treated by female aides and eighteen by males. The control patients received routine hospital care.

The L-M Behavior Rating Scale and MMPI were administered before and after therapy, and the data were assembled on fifty-one control and fifty-five experimental subjects. An additional criterion measure was an eleven-category forced Q-sort of improvement performed by two clinical psychologists. The major finding was that there was no significant difference in L-M ratings between the experimental and control groups, or within the experimental group before and after therapy. There were no significant differences between experimental and control groups on the fourteen MMPI scales or between the pre- and posttherapy clinical ratings. Statistically reliable changes were reported for controls before and after therapy on four MMPI scales (L, D, Hy, and D). As both the initial and final means on the L scale were 7, both were 63 on the D scale, the mean on the Hy scale increased from 59 to only 61 and on Pd from 68 to 72, and all sigmas were comparable, it is hard to understand how these changes could have been construed as reliable. The point, however, is not crucial to the conclusions of the study. The authors concluded that beneficial results did not accrue from the random assignment of psychiatric aides to chronic psychiatric patients for the purpose of psychotherapy.

The fact that the authors did a controlled experiment with random selection and assignment of both therapists and patients is refreshing.

Despite questionable methods of statistical assessment, the conclusion seems entirely justified when one inspects the data. The intent of the study was limited to the single question of the effectiveness of aides as therapists and yielded data relevant only to this question. Since the authors did not purport to contrast the effectiveness of trained and untrained therapists, the study sheds no light on whether professionals would have done any better with this patient population.

Eliseo (1964), in a controlled experiment at Lebanon Veterans Administration Hospital, demonstrated a clear failure of psychiatric aides to affect "social interaction habits of chronic psychiatric patients" by remotivation techniques. There was no attempt in the experiment to find out if trained therapists would have done any better.

The most widely quoted and most often misinterpreted study of all is the research done by Rioch et al. The objective of this investigation was to test the effectiveness of training nonprofessionals to do psychotherapy, not to appraise their effectiveness in doing it without training (Rioch, Elkes, Flint, Usdansky, Newman, & Silber, 1963). It was hypothesized that carefully selected, mature individuals could be trained to do therapy under limited conditions in two years. The eight trainees were selected from a fairly large group of initial applicants who were winnowed down to forty-two and ultimately to the final handful on the basis of tests and interviews designed to assess their intelligence, perceptiveness, integrity, and emotional maturity. The trainees were all forty- to forty-four-year-old mothers with professional or executive husbands. Three-quarters had themselves held professional-level jobs in other fields at one time, and all were at least college graduates who had majored in behavioral or biological sciences or the humanities. The training was planned for four semesters, but the study took place when the period was half completed.

The women were trained by eclectic professionals in a wide variety of practices and theoretical information. They had training in interviewing normals and patients, in group therapy with supervision and playback of recorded interviews, and in observation of group, individual, and family therapy. Teaching methods included lectures, seminars, outside readings, writing reports, and work in the community in courts, clinics, counseling centers, and related settings. Thus, their training was both intensive and extensive, and in many respects equivalent to an internship of the sort that clinical psychologists (without the assessment training) or psychiatric social workers receive. The only difference was an absence of formal academic training in a graduate school setting. Sixty-nine per cent of the patients assigned to them were judged as difficult or very difficult to treat. Efforts were made to screen out schizophrenics and those likely to act out or to become too demanding. Most of the forty-nine patients were college students and their parents who were being seen in outpatient treatment. Each trainee saw an average of seven patients once a week. The length of treatment averaged ten weeks but ranged up to six months.

Four outside raters made blind ratings of tape-recorded interviews and of the trainees' autocriticisms of their interviews. Interview performance was rated on a five-point scale from excellent to poor. A reference interview by a professional therapist was given an average rating score of three by six judges and served as a standard for comparison purposes. The data received no analysis per se, but average ratings on interview and autocriticism variables were tabulated and gross estimates of changes in patients were made. The ratings of the trainees on interview variables ranged from 2.7 to 4.0, which was considered "good," and on autocriticism from 3.6 to 4.0. The patients were rated as 6 per cent markedly improved, 20 per cent moderately improved, 35 per cent slightly improved, and 39 per cent no change. There was no category for "worse." Thus, slightly more than one-quarter of the patients were judged as having improved more than slightly. It was concluded that the trainees had done a good job in the work assigned and had made progress that was good to excellent.

The rating scales employed in this study were weak in that points were not defined and may have had different meaning to different judges. In this investigation to determine whether mature women could be trained to become effective therapists, there is no really adequate measure of their effectiveness in terms of outcome. The interview variables they were rated on included such things as respect for the patient, interest and understanding of the patient, success in drawing out affect, starting and ending the interview, professional attitude, and skill in using patient cues. The trainees were nonprofessionals but were highly motivated, intelligent, and adaptable people who received intensive training in the craft under close supervision. "Effectiveness" was not assessed except against other untested standards of effectiveness. The appraisal was really of whether people can be trained to do things the way trained therapists would like to see them done. There were no controls in the study, and all it really tells us is that bright, motivated, educated, mature, and carefully selected women can be trained to apply techniques in a way that mimics their mentors. This is no surprise since it has been done successfully in all those fields that have apprentices, and it is clearly a craft approach. The really important variable is not their adaptability in learning technique, but the outcome of their work. Even without any external criterion of outcome, only one-quarter of their patients showed improvement judged as clear-cut. Would a group with full training background going into this sort of internship do sufficiently better to make the extra training worthwhile? Would far less carefully selected trainees do any worse?

A series of papers by Carkhuff and Truax contended that the therapeutic conditions of empathy, unconditional positive regard, genuineness, and depth of self-exploration could be easily taught to nonprofessionals (Carkhuff & Truax, 1965a, 1965b). In the first study the aim was to demonstrate that these conditions could be taught, and it was implied that therapists so trained would produce favorable results. In the second, the effectiveness of the training methods in the hands of lay group counselors was tested. The therapists were three aides, a volunteer worker, and an industrial therapist, and only the latter was college educated. The seventy-four experimental patients and seventy controls were mostly long-term psychotics at Eastern State Hospital, Lexington, Kentucky, who were not participating in any form of psychotherapy. Didactic and experiential training was accomplished in less than 100 hours. Three counselors were assigned to two groups of ten patients each and the other two counselors each had one group. Six of these eighty patients dropped out within six sessions, leaving the total of seventy-four experimental subjects. The groups met twice a week for twenty-four sessions over three months. Outcome criteria were discharge rates and pre- and posttherapy ratings of ward behavior made by nurses and attendants on three nine-point scales (degree of psychological disturbance, degree of constructive interpersonal concern, and degree of constructive intrapersonal concern). Posttherapy ratings were made of the degree of general improvement over the three months. Data were analyzed for each variable by 2×3 chi-squares comparing experimental and control groups on the categories "improved," "deteriorated," and "unchanged." The authors interpreted significant chi-squares for ratings of general improvement, psychological disturbance, interpersonal and intrapersonal concerns as proof of the success of the lay counselors. They concluded, "The evidence points to uniformly significant improvement in the patients treated by lay group counseling when compared to control patients. The suggestion is that a specific but relatively brief training program, devoid of specific training in psychopathology, personality dynamics, or psychotherapy theory, can produce relatively effective lay mental health counselors" (p. 430). They proposed this type of training as an economical and effective solution to the professional manpower shortage. There are too many weaknesses in this study for these optimistic conclusions to be accepted. Aside from the fact that no validity checks of the ratings or information about the rating scheme and inter- or intrajudge reliability are presented, the rating of general improvement is inconsistent with the other three variables. This is the only one not derived from pre-post ratings and stems from a global impression based upon a fallible memory of how a patient was three months ago. The measures give only the direction of change, not its magnitude, and the standards for categorization are undefined. The design seems appropriate for analysis of covariance rather than the method employed. More important, the conclusions reached are either not supported by the data or are actually contradicted by it. In the data on degree of psychological disturbance, for example, 38 per cent of the Es improved in contrast to 16 per cent of the Cs, but 26 per cent of the Es *deteriorated* compared to 10 per cent of the Cs. For the interpersonal concerns variable, 45 per cent of the Es and 32 per cent of the Cs improved (1.4 times as many Es improved), but 19 per cent of the Es deteriorated and only 4 per cent of the Cs declined (4.8 times as many Es deteriorated). A similar breakdown exists for the third variable. For all three variables the ratio of per cent improved to per cent deteriorated shows a greater deterioration balance for the treated patients. This greater deterioration rate is disregarded and simply referred to as variability. The significant chi-squares that are presented included and were heavily contributed to by the differential deterioration rates in the two groups. When the data are recast and reanalyzed for improvement and deterioration separately, we find that in two of the three variables there is no significant difference in improvement between the two groups but that in *all three* there is significantly more deterioration among the patients treated by the lay therapists. The discharge data revealed chance differences, and not much of a case can be made from these results. Besides, the six dropouts, possibly the "worst" patients, were excluded from the experimental group while their counterparts remained in the control group.

From a design point of view, no changes can be attributed to the specific *type* of training given without a control group of lay therapists receiving no training or different training. It would also have been well to compare the results with those of professionals working with the same type of patient. The results suggest that when one takes a group of chronic custodial cases and gives them attention, some will show at least transient improvement in ward behavior (it is not known if the changes are sustained), but in the process lay therapists will also stimulate deterioration in significantly more patients than if they were left alone. This does not sound like an effective solution to the problem.

To summarize, the majority of investigators in this area conclude, though usually with some cautions and reservations, that various groups of people without extensive prior specialized training can do as well or better than trained and experienced professional psychotherapists. Closer scrutiny of these studies reveals shortcomings in experimental design, mainly in the form of inadequate or absent controls, sampling biases, and unsatisfactory criteria of effectiveness. After examining these studies as a group, we have concluded that the point is not only unproven but essentially untested. A good controlled comparison of the effectiveness of trained and untrained therapists has yet to be made. Not only is there no good current evidence that people untrained as therapists are as effective as trained professionals, but there is no resolution of the question of the comparative effectiveness of therapists with different *amounts* of training. Some data suggest that there are risks in using untrained therapists because they are less successful in holding patients and may contribute to the deterioration of more patients than they help. It would seem reasonable to continue to believe that training does not hamper therapeutic effectiveness, but we can still not be certain that it does any good. We do not know if the rigorous pre- and post-doctoral training requirements really make people better psychotherapists in terms of outcome rather than merely more skillful in the application of techniques. We could consider it a straw man issue and disregard it, but too many studies have called attention to it and the findings are likely to influence public policy and practice in the mental health field.

The answers to the question are feasible to obtain. The experimental design in its simplest form calls for a covariance design with some clear-cut criterion of outcome as the dependent variable. There would be two groups of psychotherapists, one trained and one untrained. The therapists should be equated at least on variables that might be relevant, such as age, sex, verbal ability, and selected personality variables. The therapeutic approach should be held constant in its gross form (individual, group, verbal, activity). Patients should be randomly assigned to therapists of both types, a reasonable interval to effect change allowed, and before and after criterion measures taken. In such a design the only important independent variable would be the training background of the therapist. Additional valuable data could be obtained by making the design more complex. Trained therapists at two or more *levels* of training could be introduced. Similarly, to get at the issue of limits or breadth, several different types of patients (diagnostic or personality variants) and different levels of difficulty could be brought into the design as variables.

THERAPY WITHOUT THERAPISTS—PSYCHOHERESY?

Our definition of psychotherapy required as a minimum one individual designated as the therapist and another as the patient. Many arrangements have been tried, ranging all the way from one therapist and many patients to one patient and multiple therapists. The inventiveness of psychotherapists has extended even beyond these possibilities. The arrangement of one patient and no therapist was formalized by Freud in his own self-analysis and was extended by Horney. A group of patients with no therapist present has variously been called a leaderless, autonomous, self-directed, patient-led, or roundtable group. Not only has it been tried, but efforts have been made to evaluate it. We will therefore have to broaden our concept of psychotherapy to include patient-led groups that meet under the aegis of a therapist who at least initially convenes the group, helps to give it structure by defining its mission, and keeps himself available as a resource person even though not physically present. Entirely self-initiated discussion or activity groups could conceivably be just as therapeutic, although we prefer not to believe it. By the arbitrary prerogative of definition we will limit ourselves to groups that at least have an authentic therapist in the wings.

Cadman, Misbach, and Brown (1954) devised and evaluated what they referred to as round-table therapy at Missouri State Hospital. Patients met three times a week for fifty sessions without the therapist present. They were first oriented by the therapist and told to discuss their lives and problems. Each meeting was preceded by a ten-minute "priming" session. In this research, thirty-eight patients who participated in the round-table sessions were compared with thirty-two controls who did not. The number of experimental group patients who were rated improved and discharged greatly exceeded those in the control group.

MacDonald, Blochberger, and Maynard (1964) compared the relative efficacy of different forms of group therapy with hospitalized patients. Four groups were used, including a traditional group led by a psychologist and a trainee which focused on self-understanding and insight; a specific therapy group led by the same individuals with content limited to discussion of discharge planning, job, and housing problems; an autonomous group that met without a therapist and was instructed to discuss discharge and related problems; and a no-treatment control group. All groups except the controls met twice a week. The autonomous group had the most favorable dispositions (release from hospital), the fewest rule infractions, by far the highest amount of social interaction during the recreation hour, and the most sociometric choices. The autonomous group developed a considerable degree of cohesiveness and achieved the two major hospital treatment objectives, favorable disposition and improved ward adjustment, while the staff-led group did not.

Rothaus and his associates compared autonomous and therapist-led groups at the Houston Veterans Administration Hospital (Rothaus, Johnson, Hanson, & Lyle, 1966; Rothaus, Johnson, Hanson, Brown, & Lyle, 1967). Both groups showed similar patterns of growth and development over a four-week period, but there were differences in the distribution of power and influence within the two settings with greater stratification and differentiation of leadership in the autonomous groups. The autonomous groups were apparently successful in inducing leader-follower polarizations, but the relevance of this to therapeutic gain is unclear. It was demonstrated that leaderless groups can function effectively as groups, but it has yet to be demonstrated that the groups can attain therapeutic objectives.

Berzon and Solomon (1964) explored the feasibility of self-directed therapeutic groups but did not assess their effectiveness. Two voluntary groups met weekly at the Western Behavioral Sciences Institute, La Jolla, California. They were told that the leader would observe them through a one-way window and would be available to join them at any time the group unanimously requested it and summoned him by a buzzer. Feasibility was assessed by absenteeism and attrition, willingness and ability to get along without a leader as judged from the frequency of his being summoned, and self-reports from the members. Unmet leaderships needs were judged from tape-recorded discussions about whether or not to call the leader and by a postmeeting questionnaire. There was a slight decline in attendance in all groups; one subject dropped out of each group for non-group-related reasons. The groups demonstrated willingness and ability to get along without a leader by the fact that each group called him in on but three occasions. The questionnaire revealed that members of the first group hoped for increased self-awareness, improved communication, and a chance to test their own leadership ability. Most felt that these expectations were fulfilled in a limited way. The members of the second group sought an opportunity for deep, honest, and meaningful personal encounters and increased empathy and self-awareness; they also expressed an interest in their own problems and maladaptive behaviors. All felt benefited. A follow-up interview disclosed that members felt it would have helped to have a leader to focus activity, clarify issues, give support, and prevent wasting time. The authors concluded that self-directed groups were feasible, but there was no control condition of a therapist-led group for comparison of efficacy in this exploratory study.

In lieu of dispensing with the therapist altogether, several experimenters have tried an alternating schedule in which the therapist is present on some occasions and absent on others. Exner (1966) had two groups in a community mental health clinic in which the therapist was regularly present, two groups in which he attended a random half of the meetings, and one group with no therapist. The groups met for a maximum of forty-two weeks. The greatest improvement was shown in the groups whose therapist attended irregularly. Those with a regularly attending therapist improved to a lesser degree, and the group with no therapist was the only one to get worse rather than better. The irregular-therapist group had the most rapid discharges, and the no-therapist group took the longest. Thus, 92 per cent of patients in the irregular-therapist groups were discharged by staff recommendation in contrast to 58 per cent of the regular therapist groups and 17 per cent of the group without a therapist. Study of recordings of the sessions suggested that the discussions in the therapist-absent sessions were more "revealing"; the groups were more reserved and dependent upon the therapist when he was present. Exner speculated that group therapy may be facilitated when there is no chance of establishing a "behavioral habit routine" protected by the presence of an "omnipotent therapist." This study is of double interest because it not only yields negative results about the efficacy of proceeding without a therapist but also demonstrates an advantage and a rationale for irregular over regular therapist attendance. Irregular attendance is offered not as an expedient but as a device that facilitates beneficial self-expression and interaction among the members in a way that aids the group process if coupled with therapist-led sessions.

Truax and Carkhuff (1965a) compared results of treating two groups of hospitalized patients with alternate sessions and two groups with regular meetings. Alternate sessions (one session with the therapist and the next without) were introduced after the tenth regular meeting and continued until the end of twelve weeks. Thus, these patients had twenty-four sessions with the therapist and fourteen without. The regular groups had twenty-four sessions with the therapist. The MMPI was given prior to the first session and again at the end of the three-month treatment period. The doubtful procedure of comparing raw change scores of each subscale was employed. Three of the twelve subscales and the sum of the clinical scales were in favor of the groups that had regular sessions only. The patients were considered to have derived no benefit from the fourteen additional alternate sessions. In fact, they led to a less favorable outcome than regular sessions alone. In a hospital there are opportunities for behavioral criteria measures, and these seem preferable to exclusive reliance upon a self-report inventory by psychotic patients. In any event, twelve weeks may be too short a time to expect significant changes to be reflected on an inventory given to psychotics. Exner's data were obtained on outpatients who were diagnosed as psychoneurotic personality disorder, which alone might account for the discrepant results.

Salzberg (1967), at the Veterans Administration Hospital, Augusta, Georgia, designed an experiment to determine whether spontaneity and problem relevance of patients' verbalizations when the therapist was present in a group differed from those during sessions when he was absent. The majority of the patients had less than a high school education, had been unable to work steadily, were unskilled or semiskilled, and were of low socioeconomic status. The group was open-ended, and thirty-five patients participated over a sixteen-week period. Meetings were held three times a week, two of the sessions with the therapist present and one with him observing through a one-way mirror with the patients' knowledge. All sessions were taped. Patient verbalizations were scored from the tapes by the therapist, a methodological shortcoming. He judged the verbalizations as spontaneous or nonspontaneous, environmental, personal (reference to own problems), or group (reference to problems of fellow members). The therapist-led sessions had fewer spontaneous responses than did the leaderless ones but more relevant (personal and group references) comments. It was therefore concluded that leaderless sessions are not of much therapeutic usefulness. The assumption was made that personal and group references are therapeutic.

Stollak and Guerney (1964) requested twelve adolescent delinquents to spend up to seventeen half-hour sessions alone in a room recording comments on their backgrounds, problems, and feelings. Raising the question of whether a therapist is really necessary, they noted that the subjects were generally cooperative, eager to come, and regular in attendance. Some of the phenomena of therapy were evident, including introspections, positive transference to the experimenter, resistance, and the expression of negative emotions. This experiment is a start, but before any judgments about efficacy can be made, it would be necessary to have a control group seeing a therapist and one without any therapy.

The general assessment of this subject remains blurred. Cadman et al. and MacDonald et al. show advantages of autonomous groups of schizophrenics within the therapeutic structure of a hospital setting. Exner found the autonomous group approach to be ineffective with nonpsychotic outpatients, but groups attended irregularly by the therapist gained more than those whose therapist was in regular attendance. His patients engaged in more revealing communication without the therapist, while the remarks of Salzberg's patients were more spontaneous but less relevant to the group's therapeutic objectives. Truax and Carkhuff saw no personality changes in hospitalized patients as the result of additional alternate sessions without the therapist. Obviously, no definitive statement about therapist-less therapy can be made without further work. At present, the technique can apparently be used efficaciously with selected patient groups when a specific purpose is intended (for example, when it is applied within a broader therapeutic atmosphere with dependent schizophrenics of low self-esteem and little feeling of belonging for the purpose of stimulating interpersonal relationships and developing feelings of independence and responsibility). Specific hypotheses of this sort could be tested for particular patient groups for whom concrete therapeutic objectives are specified. The characteristics of patients who can and cannot profit from varying degrees of autonomy need to be explored. Systematic investigation of the optimal levels of autonomy is required in terms of the extent to which the therapist should have to give structure to the group, help define its goals, and guide its directions and operations. Optimal schedules of therapist irregularity with different patient populations and at different phases of therapy could be systematically tested. In short, the question remains open for appraisal and innovation.

12

The Therapist as an Outcome Variable: II. Personal Characteristics and Attitudes

Another series of investigations has examined the effect upon outcome of more inherent characteristics and qualities of the therapist. These include studies of interaction effects of therapist-patient characteristics where such studies exist. Such variables as therapist sex, therapist-patient sex pairings, therapist interests, therapist liking for the patient, therapist personality, and therapist-patient personality similarity have been subjects of fairly extensive research, as have therapist-offered conditions.

EFFECT OF SEX OF THE THERAPIST

In view of the intimacy and emotional investment that exist in psychotherapy and the way sex-determined subrole behavior can influence technique, transference, and countertransference relationships, the sex of the therapist has frequently been considered as a variable that can affect the outcome of treatment. It is certainly taken into consideration by patients in choosing a private psychotherapist and by clinics in making case assignments. Several related questions are actually encompassed within the broader issue. Do males or females as a class, with all other things equal, do equally well, better, or worse as therapists? Do same-sex therapist-patient pairings do better, worse, or equally well as opposite-sex pairings? More specifically, do male or female therapists perform differentially when paired with patients of the same or opposite sex? Are there any particular kinds (other than sex) of patients with whom male or female therapists have noteworthy success or difficulty? Do personality, style, and approach affect the success of therapists working with same- or opposite-sex patients? All these questions are eminently researchable. Nevertheless, direct experimental work that could put speculations to rest is meager. More often than not, sex pairings are treated as a side issue of other research for which data are available more by happenstance than design. Information obtained this way is no less valuable, but experiments not specifically designed for the purpose are not as likely to control for all variables relevant to the question.

Cartwright and Lerner (1963) studied improvement in fourteen male and fourteen female patients averaging 27.7 years of age. Improvement was measured by changes in rating scales filled out by the therapist after the second and the last interview. Therapists obtained significantly higher empathy scores with patients of the opposite sex than with those of the same sex, but this difference disappeared by the end of therapy because empathy for clients of like sex increased significantly over the course of treatment (average forty interviews). There were no differences in improvement rate.

In a study on the effectiveness of therapy, forty female and twenty male psychiatric aides worked with 117 chronic hospitalized female patients (Sines, Silver, & Lucero, 1961). The aides worked closely with assigned patients twice weekly for a year in verbal, recreational, and off-ward activities. Their treatment plans were guided and supervised, and the goal was to improve adjustment. No differences between male and female aides were found on outcome measured by behavior rating scales, MMPI data, or pre- and posttherapy clinical ratings.

In the course of their study of client-counselor personality type similarity, Mendelsohn and Geller (1963) examined client-counselor combinations of sexes (male counselor-male client, male counselor-female client, female counselor-male client, and female counselor-female client) in relation to length of counseling. A total of forty-one female and thirty-one male clients were seen by six female and four male counselors. Analysis of variance yielded a nonsignificant F-value among the four sex combinations. When grouped into two categories, same-sex and opposite-sex pairs, there was no difference whatsoever. This led the authors to conclude, justifiably, that sex matching has little or no effect on length of counseling. In a subsequent investigation with 201 subjects (111 male and 90 female) seen in counseling by six female and five male professional staff psychologists, it was again found that neither the sex of the counselor nor any of the four possible sex pairings had any differential effect on the duration of counseling (Mendelsohn, 1966).

Several researches on the premature termination of psychotherapy have dealt peripherally with the issue of the therapist's sex. A reanalysis of the data of the last study cited revealed that a significantly higher proportion of continuers (91 per cent) than terminators (46 per cent) was paired with a counselor of the same sex, but in a subsequent sample the difference was found to be reduced to 76 per cent against 55 per cent (Mendelsohn & Geller, 1967). Sex of the therapist was one of a variety of possible influences on quitting therapy examined by McNair, Lorr, and Callahan (1963). The sample consisted of 282 male outpatients in seven Veterans Administration mental hygiene clinics whose therapists were a broad sample of the psychiatrists, psychologists, and social workers working in these installations. No relation of therapist sex to duration of treatment was found among predicted terminators and remainers. For these two groups combined, more patients were held by female therapists than by males (about 83 per cent to 62 per cent). The authors did not place much stress upon the finding because of its *post hoc* character.

An investigation carried out at the Veterans Administration Mental Hygiene Clinic, Detroit, Michigan, attempted to determine if different types of therapists tend to lose or hold in treatment different types of patients (Hiler, 1958). Forty male patients seen by female psychologists and social workers were compared with forty seen by male psychologists and social workers. The patient sample included forty terminators and forty remainers. Hiler concluded that productivity (the number of Rorschach responses) is not related to continuance in therapy with female therapists but is with male therapists. Thus, while female therapists keep unproductive patients in treatment, they lose highly productive ones. The experimental question here is that of the interaction of sex of the therapist and productivity of the patient in bringing about the outcome (terminating or remaining). In this experiment no direct answer to the question is ever given. Instead, there appears to be a reversal of the dependent and independent variables. Terminating-remaining is treated as an independent variable and Rorschach productivity prior to therapy as the dependent variable. It is illogical to conceptualize this problem in terms of the Rorschach reponses *prior* to therapy depending upon whether the patient *subsequently* terminates. The conclusion reached about the differential effect of therapist sex upon termination of productive and unproductive patients cannot therefore be accepted with confidence.

In a particularly comprehensive, methodologically sophisticated, and carefully done dissertation, Fuller (1963) surveyed client preferences regarding the sex of the counselor and studied the interaction of the sex of the client and counselor and the verbalization of feeling. This dependent variable was thought to be related to both outcome and process. It was hypothesized that female clients would express significantly more feeling than male clients regardless of the sex of the counselor but that male clients would express more feeling in the presence of male counselors than in the presence of female counselors. Preference for a counselor of a particular sex was surveyed on 534 clients and 588 nonclients drawn from the student body of the University of Texas. Male students preferred male counselors, and female students preferred male counselors more than male students preferred female counselors. There was less frequent preference for female counselors among clients than nonclients. In fact, it was a rare male client (1 per cent) who preferred a female counselor. The main hypotheses were tested on a sample of thirty-two student-clients balanced for sex and preference. Half preferred male counselors and half had no preference. The study excluded clients with personal problems and dealt only with those with problems of an educational or vocational nature. At the onset, it must be recognized that this greatly limits the generality of the findings because the process is, strictly speaking, not psychotherapy. For whatever association with psychotherapy it may have, however, the study merits attention. There were nine counselors, one of whom did intake interviews. The remainder, four males and four females, were in the same age range and balanced for experience. Each counseled four clients, one male and one female, in each of the two preference categories. Client statements were reported in casenotes. Although they were found in a preliminary study to compare accurately with tape recordings, these reports remain the greatest weakness in the study. Scores for the amount of feeling expressed were obtained from a revised Kelly and Fiske Relationship Index. Client statements were independently categorized into topics by two trained judges, one male and one female, and topics were weighted and scored for feeling with satisfactory reliability. A check for assignment bias revealed none.

In the intake interview conducted by a male interviewer, it was found that female clients expressed significantly more feeling than males, but no difference was associated with client preference or the sex × preference interaction. During the counseling interview, female clients expressed significantly more feeling than males regardless of the sex of the counselor. Clients with no preference for a counselor of either sex expressed significantly more feeling than those who preferred male counselors, with no client preference × counselor sex interaction. There was, however, a significant client-sex × counselor-sex interaction. More feelings were expressed when the dyad contained a female, *whether client or counselor*. Fuller also did an analysis of variance of the shift that took place from intake to counseling and took care first to transform the difference scores into delta scores. The analysis revealed that expressions of feeling by clients who expressed no preference increased significantly more than scores of those who preferred male counselors. Females with no preference increased more than males with no preference. There was a greater increase in pairs that included females regardless of whether the female was a counselor or client. The author recognized that the conclusions were limited by the validity of casenotes and observed that women may use more emotionally toned words in recording than men. The sex of the counselor-as-counselor may have been confounded with the sex of the counselor-as-recorder. The use of video tapes was suggested so that nonverbal reflections of feeling could also be noted. It was also acknowledged that the lack of clients who prefer female counselors limited the completeness of the study. The major reservation, of course, is that personal adjustment counseling might produce different or even opposite results.

A study by Campbell (1962), dealing with the effect of counselor personality and background upon his subrole behavior in the interview, touched on the sex of the counselor as one of the background variables. The author worked from tapes of first and second interviews of fourteen male and ten female counselor-trainees each seeing at least three clients who presented a range of study and adjustment problems. Three trained judges classified the various subroles used by counselors, such as friendly discussion, listening, information gathering, and reflecting. It was found that females made significantly more use of friendly discussion, information gathering, and supporting. The study is suggestive only, since client variables were not controlled, counselors were beginners, and the findings were ex post facto and require cross-validation.

As a side issue of a study of the effects of training on psychotherapists' responses, a group of graduate students wrote out the responses they would give to a series of transcribed client statements at three different points in their training (Barrington, 1958). The part of this investigation relevant here is that the five female members of the class consistently used more words per response (29.9 to 24.2) than the males, but the difference was not statistically significant. There is nothing here that can be generalized to the behavior of trained female therapists in actual therapeutic situations. A final study to be considered was concerned with professed therapeutic techniques (McNair & Lorr, 1964a). Working with a large sample of experienced therapists representing psychiatry, psychology, and social work, they found that more women than men endorsed an impersonal directive approach. Since the social workers were mostly women, possibly confounding the variables of sex and profession, the outcome within the social work group was examined. The results showed that more men than women (21 per cent to 9 per cent) endorsed the personal-nondirective approach while more women than men (33 per cent to 13 per cent) endorsed the impersonal-directive approach. It was noted that the more impersonal approach of women in this sample may be due to the fact that they were working with predominantly male patients. Other sex pairings might have yielded different results.

In summation, we find that the very few studies available on patient improvement showed no differences between male and female therapists, nor do those that deal with duration of therapy as the dependent variable. Studies of terminators and remainers yield inconsistent results. There is some evidence, far from definitive, that like-sex dyads continue more than opposite-sex pairings and that females hold more patients than males. In subrole behavior and professed technique, female therapists appear to differ somewhat from males, but there is no indication that this affects outcome systematically. Expression of feeling within the interview is increased if *either* the patient or therapist is a female, but the relation of this to outcome is not established and the phenomenon has not been tested on personal adjustment interviews. The best we can say at the present time is that the question has not been subjected to rigorous and systematic research. In the majority of studies cited the information emerged peripherally to the main purpose of the experiment. Therefore, appropriate controls were not usually exercised.

At present there is no clear basis for preferential assignment of a patient of either sex to a therapist of either sex. No statements can be made with confidence about the relative benefits of selected sex pairing with given types of patients. At the least, it would seem that the four like- and opposite-sex pairings would have to be systematically varied and controls introduced for such variables as the nature of the therapeutic problem, diagnosis, type of therapy, patient and therapist age, expectations and preferences of patients as regards sex of therapist, and therapist training, experience, and discipline. Effects of the sex of the therapist upon outcome, if any, could then be systematically ascertained. A finding of particular like- or opposite-sex combinations that would be reliably more effective with patients of either sex could be of substantial value in improving therapeutic batting averages. There is no reason to believe that such a combination exists, but it would be well worth finding out.

THERAPIST'S INTERESTS AND OUTCOME

For more than a decade, Whitehorn and Betz conducted a series of related and sometimes overlapping investigations of the therapist as a crucial variable in the outcome of psychotherapy with schizophrenic patients. They were particularly concerned with those aspects of the therapist's personality that they early discovered to contribute to success with this type of patient. The studies took place at the Henry Phipps Clinic, in an inpatient treatment setting. The purpose of the initial study (Whitehorn & Betz, 1954) was to explore the patient-physician relationship and its effect on clinical progress as well as upon the types of relationships, diagnostic perspective, goals, and tactical patterns employed. The study was retrospective, and all data came from analysis of case records. The therapists were fourteen resident psychiatrists drawn from a sample of thirty-five. All had had experience treating at least four schizophrenic, four depressed, and four neurotic patients. Schizophrenic patients of the therapists were classified as improved or unimproved, and therapists were ranked in accordance with their rate of success. The improvement rate ranged from 0 to 100 per cent with an average of 50.6 per cent.

Two extreme groups of seven therapists each were selected from the pool of thirty-five therapists. The resulting therapist sample thus consisted of a high success group (Group A) with a range of 68 per cent to 100 per cent improvement and an average of 75 per cent, and a low success group (Group B) with improvement rates ranging from 0 per cent to 34 per cent and an average of only 26.9 per cent success. This differential success rate did not hold for these same therapists in their work with depressed or neurotic patients. In a later study, Whitehorn and Betz (1960), the original sample of therapists was extended to make a total of fifty. Upon administering the Strong Vocational Interest Blank to twenty-six of them, it was empirically determined that four vocational interest scales (Lawyer, CPA, Printer, and Mathematics-Physical Science Teacher) differentiated between fifteen Type A (successful with schizophrenics) and eleven Type B (unsuccessful with schizophrenics) physicians. Type A physicians were found to have interests like those of lawyers but not like those of mathematics-physical science teachers, and Type Bs resembled printers and mathematics-physical science teachers. A "predictive screen" of items was cross-validated on the remaining twenty-four physicians. The original 400 items were reduced to twenty-three and finally to ten items that the authors claim predicted Type A physicians with 83 per cent accuracy and Type Bs with 78 per cent accuracy. In order to check the generality of the findings to physicians in other settings, they sampled eleven physicians from a neighboring psychoanalytically oriented hospital. They reported that the direction of prediction was 67 per cent accurate with a five-point screen and 80 per cent to 100 per cent accurate with an eleven-point screen. The finding is accompanied by a purely intuitive and speculative characterization of putative personal characteristics of lawyers, printers, and mathematics-physical science teachers. At best, the study is useful in stimulating hypotheses for further test.

In order to assess the possibility that Type A therapists were assigned easier patients and were therefore more successful, seventy-three patients of the earlier sample were classified as "process" or "non-process" (Betz, 1963). The two samples were comparable in size. The therapists of these patients were divided into Type A or B on the basis of their Strong scale scores for Lawyer and Mathematics-Physical Science Teacher, with a scale score of 40 as a cut-off point. Earlier studies used different classification standards on the Strong, but the reason for the shift was not mentioned. As before, the discharge status of "improved" or "unimproved" was obtained from the medical records. A reliably higher rate of success was reported for Type A than Type B therapists with the more serious "process" patients, but not with those classified as "nonprocess." The principal finding of the investigation was that 71 per cent of the "process" patients seen by Type A physicians were rated as improved in contrast to 18 per cent of those seen by Type Bs. The improvement rates for Type A and B therapists with "nonprocess" patients were 68 per cent and 56 per cent respectively, a difference attributable to chance. The data reveal no significant difference in improvement rate among Type A therapists with "process" patients, Type As with "nonprocess" patients, and Type Bs with "nonprocess" patients. The only therapist-patient combination that yields markedly different rates of improvement is that of the Type B therapist with process schizophrenics. Eighty-two per cent of their patients failed to improve. The classification of patients into the categories "process" and "nonprocess" was made by C. Astrup, who was not directly associated with this study. He had access to, and indeed used, the discharge rating of improved or unimproved in making his determination from clinical records of whether each patient was "process" or "nonprocess." Their improvement or nonimprovement played an important role in the judgment of whether or not they were "process" patients. The data relating to the "process" variable is thus fully confounded with the improvement variable. The study, however, does reaffirm the previously discovered relation of selected vocational interest patterns to outcome—at least in terms of the failure of one type of therapist with the more difficult process patients. It should be recalled that the purpose of the study was to rule out the notion that in prior studies Type A therapists might have had easier patients to work with. This purpose was not realized because no direct attempt was made to answer the question.

It is of interest to compare the outcome of this study with another that dealt with virtually the same issues (Stephens & Astrup, 1965). Working in the same institutional setting, the authors sampled records of 334 patients of whom ninety-eight had been in Whitehorn and Betz's sample. Some 138 patients were retrospectively classified from case records as "process" and 196 as "nonprocess." The therapists were sixty-three resident psychiatrists classified as Type A, B, or neither by four methods all derived from the Strong Vocational Interest Blank. The methods were Whitehorn and Betz's three-, five-, and eleven-point scales and a fourteen-point scale devised by McNair, Callahan, and Lorr. Patients had been classified as improved or unimproved at the time of discharge, and were followed up four to fourteen years later and reclassified as recovered, improved, or unimproved. Follow-up data were obtained on 236 patients (70 per cent) with an average follow-up period covering 7.3 years. The follow-up consisted of information obtained from letters, phone calls, and personal contact with patients and relatives. Those classified as recovered were judged to have no residual symptoms of psychosis. Those listed as improved were no longer overtly psychotic despite some residual signs but were working or taking care of a home. The unimproved patients were mostly in mental hospitals. The "nonprocess" patients clearly did better than the "process," with 96 per cent judged as recovered or improved in contrast to 47 per cent of the "process" patients. The main question here, however, is how this relates to therapist interest patterns. The data revealed no significant relation between either discharge or follow-up status of those treated by Type A or B therapists as classified by any of the four methods. When patients were classified into "process" and "nonprocess," the same high relation between this classification and follow-up remained *regardless of therapist type*. There was also no relation between A and B status and the process-nonprocess distribution.

Therapist interest patterns thus did not prove useful as predictors of success with schizophrenic patients. This failure to replicate earlier findings is particularly puzzling since it was done in the same place with overlap of the patient and therapist samples. The results regarding "process" and "nonprocess" patients and follow-up data appear to be decisive. The authors were aware of the fact that an observed significant relation between this variable and *discharge* status may have been contaminated since the classification was made from the study of charts containing the discharge information. As in the Whitehorn and Betz studies, the research would have been more convincing if patients rather than their charts had been assessed and if all ratings had been blind.

A well-designed check of a variant of the Whitehorn and Betz hypothesis was carried out in a different setting (McNair, Callahan, & Lorr, 1962). They set out to ascertain if the comparative success rates of Type A and B therapists could be confirmed in a nonschizophrenic sample. Patients were forty male veterans drawn from seven Veterans Administration outpatient clinics. The therapists were forty males, twenty-one psychologists, ten psychiatrists, and nine social workers. The total therapist group averaged five to six years of experience, although five were trainees. Thirteen had had personal therapy. The therapists were given a twenty-three-item A-B scale drawn from the Strong Interest Inventory and classified into Type A or B by a median split. Twenty of the highest and twenty of the lowest, matched for profession, level of training, and competence, were selected. Competence was rated by three psychologists from an audit of therapy recordings.

The patients, all nonschizophrenic and actuarially equivalent, were seen weekly for the purpose of personality change rather than support. They were given reduced versions of the Taylor Manifest Anxiety Scale and Barron Ego Strength Scale, a symptom checklist, and a series of sixteen five-point graphic rating scales of self-satisfaction. Their therapists rated them for severity of illness on seven four-point graphic rating scales and also completed an inventory of interpersonal changes and a symptom reduction scale. A social worker rated the patients independently on the same scales. After four months, greater total change was observed in patients of Type B therapists, and this was sustained after twelve months. Since the finding was opposite that of Whitehorn and Betz, the authors hypothesized that Type A therapists might be more successful with schizophrenics and Type B with neurotics. One plausible alternate explanation of the results was in terms of sampling differences. Patients of lower or lower-middle class socioeconomic background comprised 70 per cent of the McNair sample but only 30 per cent of the Betz sample. A cluster of interest inventory items reflect interest of the Type B therapists, who were the most successful in the McNair study, in skilled labor and technician activities. The authors speculated that their greater success could be attributed to similarity of interests and greater familiarity with the daily life problems of the patients. In another study, McNair et al. found no relation at all between therapist A-B type and duration of stay in therapy for 106 terminators and 176 remainers selected from seven clinics (McNair, Lorr, & Callahan, 1963). The Strong interest patterns of twenty-seven psychiatrists, forty-six clinical psychologists, and twenty-six psychiatric social workers of varying experience were checked by

Klein, McNair, and Lorr (1962). Essentially no differences in interests were obtained between competent and poor therapists and between psychologists with and without personal therapy.

Draper (1967) studied the effect of twenty-eight intern therapists' Strong patterns on the discharge rate of their 389 schizophrenic patients at Kings County Hospital, Seattle. Contacts with the patients were brief and transitory. The therapist group was dichotomized into high and low discharge categories. The Betz and Whitehorn findings were reversed, with the high discharge groups tending to have lower scores on the Lawyer and CPA scales and higher Mathematics-Physical Science Teacher and Printer scores.

Kemp (1966) performed an intricate analogue experiment with sixty-eight Duke University undergraduates as "therapists." They constituted the first and fourth quartile of a distribution of 178 subjects on a modified A-B Scale. Tape-recorded interviews with actors playing the roles of patient and therapist were prepared in such a way that one "patient" was characterized as "turning-against-self (intropunitive-type psychoneurosis) and the other as "avoiding-of-others" (schizoid). The subjects were asked to make "therapeutic interventions" from a multiple choice listing at interruption points during the recording and to complete a post-recording questionnaire. Findings were contrary to expectations. Of the many variables assessed, the only significant finding was that Type As, when listening to the "schizoid" patient, and Type Bs, when listening to the "neurotic," found it more difficult to choose therapeutic interventions and were less comfortable during the recordings than were subjects in the other two conditions. According to the Whitehorn and Betz hypothesis opposite results would have been predicted.

Pollack and Kiev (1963), in an experiment one step removed from psychotherapy, studied the spatial orientation of forty psychiatrists and 136 college students. The psychiatrists were classified by the Strong into Type A or B, and all were tested with the Witkin Rod and Frame apparatus. The psychiatrists as a group oriented themselves in a more field-independent manner than the students. Contrary to the hypothesis, the most field-independent psychiatrists shared interests with vocations allegedly requiring a precise and mechanistic approach (Type B). The Type A group was less field-independent. This experiment was replicated by Shows et al. with twenty-nine undergraduates (Shows & Carson, 1965). Type As were neither field-dependent nor independent, but were more variable than Type Bs, who differed in mean score but not in variability from controls. (Controls were individuals with intermediate A-B scale scores.) The Bs were extremely field-independent and were considered to show more psychological differentiation in their perceptual approach and to be more homogeneous in cognitive style.

Carson et al, performed two analogue experiments on the A-B variable (Carson, Harden, & Shows, 1964). In the first, sixty introductory psychology students were classified on Kemp's modification of the A-B scale and were asked to answer rigged "letters" from three types of "patients." Their responses were rated on six scales (psychopathologic-personalistic, passivity-activity, conformity–self-expression, coldness-warmth, depth directedness, and anxiety–self-confidence). Analyses of variance for each of the six scales revealed no therapist type or patient type main effects. The only significant interaction was on the scale of depth directedness. In the second experiment with sixteen Type As and sixteen Type Bs, eight of each were paired with eight interviewers who were set to anticipate help, trust, and friendliness and eight set to expect harm, distrust, and hostility. The task of the interviewers was to elicit self-disclosure information in a twenty-minute interview. Again there were no main effects for interview or interviewee types, but Type A interviewers obtained more information from subjects expecting harm and Type Bs more from those set to expect help. They suggest that it is only when the characteristics of the other person are considered that differences emerge in the performance of Types A and B, and offer this as an explanation of the discrepancy between the findings of Whitehorn and Betz and McNair, Callahan, and Lorr. The authors acknowledge that "the difference between actual psychotherapy relationships and the experimentally created relationships studied here are so manifold that it would seem pointless to argue any direct correspondence between them" (p. 432). They are quite right. There is nothing "quasi-therapeutic" about the situations. "Patient types" did not exist in the personality of the "patients" but in the instructional set. The students were neither therapists nor patients, letter writing and interviewing are not therapy, and little can be gleaned from this exercise.

In summary, Whitehorn and Betz discovered that two types of therapists, one successful in treating schizophrenics and the other not, could be differentiated by selected Strong Vocational Interest Blank items. They were able to reproduce the finding several times but with much overlap of patients and therapists and a shifting of predictive measures. Stephens and Astrup were unable to confirm their finding regardless of which measure was used, even though they sampled many of the very same patients and therapists. McNair, Callahan, and Lorr obtained opposite results to Whitehorn and Betz with neurotic patients. Subsequent investigations, in the aggregate, fail to provide affirmative support.

Owing to the lack of clear reproducibility of the finding, the hypothesis of a relation between the vocational interests of the therapist and the outcome of therapy with schizophrenics and other types of patients remains a hypothesis. The hypothesis would have to be tested in a variety of settings and with more rigorous procedures. If the hypothesis can be supported, it would seem likely that underlying these interests one could find personality, social class, and other background variables that were primary determinants of the interest patterns. It would be of value to examine the direct similarity of patient and therapist interests in successful and unsuccessful cases.

THERAPIST'S PERSONALITY AND OUTCOME

The psychotherapeutic relationship is so personal that "who" the psychotherapist is may be confounded with what he does. Is there a "psychotherapeutic personality"? A psychotherapist who has this kind of personality, many believe, may obtain positive results no matter what he does. To describe it more carefully, what he does is guided by what he is. In other hands his techniques may be not only unsuccessful but actually harmful. In everyday life, those who influence others to change their opinions, attitudes, or behaviors leave impressions of personal power. Professional psychotherapists are deeply impressed by the personalities of the great leaders and innovators of psychotherapeutic "schools": the Freuds, Rogers, and Adlers. The charisma may not fall upon faithful disciples. Occasionally some untrained maverick appears and develops a reputation as a "therapeutic personality." Are these characteristics innate? Do they, in fact, yield favorable psychotherapeutic outcomes? Related issues, considered in other contexts, are these: are these characteristics augmented or developed by particular courses of training, by personal psychotherapy, or by particular experiences?

The central problem is to identify "therapeutic personality" or its traits and to demonstrate that their possessor does achieve favorable outcomes with his patients more frequently than his less gifted colleagues. We must demonstrate that his reputation is based upon performance rather than on the rationale that he is a possessor of these traits and must, therefore, be a successful psychotherapist. If we can identify these therapists, then we will be able to study their personalities and techniques. Unfortunately, more is known of prominent psychotherapists as writers, teachers, and publicists than as psychotherapists. There are no systematic studies of the great innovators or of contemporary "therapeutic personalities." If we are able to identify them, we would then have to control the conditions of therapy and establish specific criteria of outcome in addition to the judgments of the therapist or patient involved. Patients of supposedly gifted and ungifted therapists would have to be equated for all relevant variables. However, there is always the chance that the therapist's specific personality organization may be therapeutic for a specific kind of patient, one who may have certain complementary (or contrasting) social, ethnic, cultural, personal, or psychopathological characteristics. No studies exist that demonstrate the existence of the "therapeutic personality" or its general or specific applicability to psychotherapeutic problems.

Many experts offer lists of personality traits that are supposed to be either characteristic of the "good psychotherapist" or prerequisite to one's becoming a good psychotherapist. Still others suggest that what is important in the personality of the effective psychotherapist may not be a group of miscellaneous attributes but a few central characteristics relevant to the task of the psychotherapist. Rogers (1957) believes strongly that among the necessary conditions for personality change in psychotherapy are therapist characteristics of genuineness, empathy, and unconditional positive regard for the client. It is not clear whether these are considered prerequisite characteristics to be augmented in training or a total product of training. They will be considered elsewhere as "therapeutic conditions."

Two studies begin with measures of therapeutic competence and attempt to discover those personality traits that discriminate between the more and less successful therapist. Holt and Luborsky (1958) combed the literature for lists of traits that the experts believe to be characteristic of the good psychotherapist. They selected thirty-two traits. The researchers eventually assembled data on about sixty-four of 238 psychiatric residents being trained at the Winter Veterans Administration Hospital by the staff of the Menninger Clinic. Supervisors rated the competence of each resident. Two judges, reviewing the assessment data on each resident, made ratings on the thirty-two personality variables. Correlations between the personality ratings and the judgments of therapeutic competence were computed separately for the ratings of each of the two personality trait raters. The data of one judge yielded sixteen significant correlations of low magnitude; the other judge's data gave no significant results. There are no substantial results despite the promise, effort, and sponsorship of the study. Supervisory ratings of competence were subjective and were open to possible contamination from some of the traits studied (for example, social adjustment and self-confidence). This should have augmented the chance of good results. The ratings of personality traits were based upon secondary evidence and were made in retrospect. We have learned nothing of the competent resident's personality nor of the personality of the resident who becomes the successful psychotherapist in professional maturity.

Burdock, Cheek, and Zubin (1960) attempted to discover the characteristics of successful students at a psychoanalytic institute. The inference is that successful completion of the course is the sign of a good psychotherapist. The criteria were rapidity in completing the course and retrospective ratings of the student's therapeutic skill by the faculty. Despite the authors' conclusions, there are no outstanding differences between their successful and unsuccessful groups, possibly because the criteria are remote from the actual operations of psychotherapy. Aronson (1953) studied the effects on client-judged outcome of student-counselors' personalities and understanding of themselves and their clients and found no systematic relationships.

Knupfer, Jackson, and Krieger (1959), studying the personality traits of psychiatric residents, concluded that almost nothing is known about those who obtain the best results in psychotherapy. They used two criteria of competence: ratings of competence in psychotherapy with schizophrenics and ratings of general competence in all aspects of the residents' work in and out of the hospital. The researchers relied upon expert judges' interpretations of Q-sort personality items. They reported that residents with high ratings in therapeutic skill were self-confident, passive, and expressive and that residents high in general competence are "self-disciplined." There is some item overlap in other traits. The hypothesis that personality traits related to one criterion are not related to another would have received more support if a direct statistical test of this hypothesis had been made. In addition, the criteria used were based upon a few supervisory sessions (specific) and upon a mass of heterogeneous data (general).

Levine, Marks, and Hall (1957) compared the success of two therapists, one outgoing, relaxed, and enthusiastic and the other distant, critical, and compulsive after both therapists had presided over two kinds of "activity" groups. Although patients in all four groups improved, those in the groups of the first therapist achieved significantly higher improvement scores. We are not sure which aspect of the therapist—his personality, experience, liking for people, or interest in the activities—determined the difference. A future experiment calls for a larger sample of therapists and a greater number of relevant controls.

Bare (1967) studied different dimensions of the therapeutic relationship (counselor helpfulness and empathy and knowledge of each other by client and counselor). Criteria were judgment of these four variables by both participants. Correlations of the variables with an interesting series of personality traits of social involvement yield several significant correlations of very low magnitude. This study promises to provide a model for the investigation of therapist traits hypothetically related to different criteria or different aspects of complex criteria.

Some researchers limit their inquiry to a small number of traits that they assume to be of particular importance to the psychotherapeutic situation. Of these traits, empathy is easily the most discussed. Cartwright and Lerner (1963) measured empathy by discrepancies between patient and therapist responses to Kelly's Role Construct Repertory Test. The criterion of improvement was change in the therapist's pretreatment and posttreatment rating of the patient. There were no differences in empathy for improved and unimproved patients at the beginning of treatment. By the end of treatment, differences in therapist empathy between these two groups were significant. At the beginning of treatment, therapists were significantly more empathic to members of the opposite sex, but there were no final differences. The evaluation of sex-role adequacy, and hence severity of disturbance, may influence empathic responses. The study answers no questions. The same therapists who gave empathic responses also rated the improvement of the same patients. "Experienced" therapists were those who had treated more than five cases of unknown difficulty. However, the study points to the possibility of variables (such as sex role) that may influence the empathic response of the therapist.

Lesser (1961) found that change in treatment, measured by the Butler-Haigh Q-Sort, was not related to empathic understanding whether this was rated by counselor or client. Further, the best "understood" group made less progress. Of course, the counselors were not rigorously described. The clients were a small number of students and the treatment was limited to a maximum of twelve sessions. Measures of empathy are difficult to design and validate. The results indicate the need for more complex hypotheses and experimental designs.

Streitfeld (1959) did not confirm his hypothesis that successful therapists are more accepting of themselves and others. His therapists were students. He regards his instruments as fallible. Bandura's (1956) study of self-insight and anxiety yielded no relation between the therapist's insight and his competence (by supervisor's rating). However, there were significant, high, and negative correlations between the measure of competence and peers' ratings of the therapist's anxiety about sex, hostility, and dependency. Although the therapists were students and the measure of competence not objective, the latter finding should be investigated more rigorously. Combs and Soper (1963) studied the "perceptual organization" of effective counselors. Twelve hypotheses concerning adequate attitudes toward self and others were confirmed by a global judgment of faculty supervisors, many of whom may not have had direct knowledge of the student.

We know little about the personality of successful psychotherapists. Most researchers have not studied experienced psychotherapists and the experience of the therapist-subjects has usually been neither measured nor varied. One of the few studies that presents an adequate number of experienced subjects (Rubinstein and Lorr, 1957) does not present measures of experience or measures of success. Another central issue is the selection of traits to be studied. Blunderbuss methods have not been successful. Traits indicating the adequacy or "mental health" of the therapist have been much discussed but little studied. Holt and Luborsky, working in a psychoanalytic training center, seem to have had an opportunity to clarify this issue but they did not have relevant data. There may be therapist traits having particular relevance to the therapeutic situation (empathy, for example).

Still other traits have to do with the therapist's behavior in any complex social situation (dominance, attractiveness, and so on). Hardy's (1948) attempt to demonstrate that dominant individuals do not become adequate nondirective therapists was not successful, perhaps because her subjects were novices or because her measures of dominance were fallible. There is some reason to believe that therapists tend to minimize the importance of the role of their personalities. The fact that staff do not see themselves as patients see them was brought out in two related studies (Simmons & Tyler, 1964; Tyler & Simmons, 1964). Staff generally conceptualized themselves in terms of the nature of their skills, duties, functions, and professional identity with less emphasis placed on their personal characteristics. Hospitalized patients, on the other hand, were found to conceptualize therapists largely in personal terms.

The implication of most of the studies is that traits deemed important are generalized characteristics. They apparently apply to the therapist's commerce with all patients in all therapeutic modalities and in all settings. Are all successful individual therapists successful with groups, and are those successful with groups of separate individuals also effective with family groups? Clinical experience offers hints to the researcher that this may not be so. Therapists who do well with schizophrenics frequently do not succeed with neurotics. Those who succeed with adults find that children are difficult patients. The researcher's question becomes: what traits of the therapist are useful with what kinds of patients under what circumstances? One begins with at least three sets of variables.

As all personality studies, studies of the personality of therapists, have to deal with the selection and measurement of personality variables. Global or unitary assessments may mask important traits or interactions. They also present problems of validity and reliability. The use of devices designed to measure psychopathological traits in the patient may not be relevantly applied to the therapist. These traits may not be important to his performance. Standard measuring instruments also may be inappropriate. Their use implicitly makes their authors usurp the place of the researcher as the creator of hypotheses for his experiment. The researcher is responsible, as always, for the selection or creation of measures suitable to his own hypotheses. There is no lack of hypotheses about the personality of the "good" psychotherapist. There is a need for relevant studies.

THE EFFECT OF THERAPIST-PATIENT PERSONALITY SIMILARITY

It has often been pointed out that individual psychotherapy is essentially a relationship between two individuals each with his own unique personality. A therapeutic relationship is a special case of dyadic relationships in general and subject to the same laws, or at least the same folk lore. The infinite wisdom of folk lore is often attained by presenting equally plausible but opposite alternatives. "Opposites attract" as everyone knows, but "it takes one to know one." These proverbial truisms have been applied to the therapeutic dyad. The logic that patient-therapist similarity should maximize the chance for success is no more or less compelling than the logic in favor of dissimilarity. It is reasonable to expect that therapists who have personality characteristics similar to those of their patients and who have experienced similar feelings and conflicts would be more understanding and empathic. It is also reasonable, however, to expect that shared characteristics might interfere with effectiveness by making the therapist too involved, nonobjective, and unable to help the patient to cope effectively with his problems in new ways. For these reasons, the curvilinear hypothesis has been advanced. It maintains that either excessive similarity or dissimilarity will interfere and that the greatest benefit can come from conditions of medium similarity.

For the sake of conceptual clarity in talking about personality similarity, a researcher should specify whether he is referring to global personality as reflected in, let us say, a complex pattern of personality test performances, broad personality types, or similarity in specific traits or factors. All of the speculations about similarity are based upon the assumption that something inherent in the dyadic relationship is the key to that which is therapeutic and that the therapeutic potential of this relationship is a direct function of the interaction of the two personalities who are partners to it. Most therapists today accept this as a truism rather than as a hypothesis subject to test. Suspending axiomatic beliefs for a moment, one must admit (as heretical as it may sound) that if indeed the dyadic patient-therapist relationship is not crucial to behavioral change in the patient, then similarity or dissimilarity of the two personalities should make little difference at all. Failure to support a hypothesized connection between similarity or dissimilarity and success would not rule out the crucial importance of the dyadic relationship, but a clear demonstration of a differential effect attributable to similarity or dissimilarity would greatly strengthen the belief in the importance of the patient-therapist relationship for outcome. The similarity-dissimilarity hypothesis is an intriguing one with profound implications for case assignment. It is a tempting thought that success ratios could be improved by informed and systematic matching of the personalities of therapists and patients. In recognition of its potential importance it has become a moderately popular subject for experimentation.

A number of investigators claim to have demonstrated a positive relation between similarity of patient and therapist personality and therapeutic progress. One of the earliest attempts tested the hypothesis that patients in dyads in which there was greater similarity would show more progress (Axelrod, 1952). The research was done with ten staff psychiatrists and forty psychoneurotic patients of average or better intelligence at the Veterans Administration Regional Office, New York. Each psychiatrist was asked to select his two most and two least improved patients. Three judges rated the subjects on a seven-point scale on twelve traits. Patient-therapist pairs were compared on each trait individually and on all combined. Of the twelve traits, only one, "ideation," significantly differentiated between the improved and unimproved groups, although the combined characteristics yielded a significant result. The Rorschach test was given to patients between the second and fifth interviews and to the therapists. Based upon a global evaluation, patients were categorized into the two of each psychiatrist's four patients who were most like him and the two who were least like him. Results showed only chance agreement between similarity and improvement. When Rorschachs were classified qualitatively into three characterological categories it was found that psychiatrists in only one of them (those who were orderly, controlled, self-critical, and tended to intellectualize) achieved success with similar patients. It appears that the author found more support for the hypothesis than is revealed in the data. There is at least as much to support a null hypothesis as a conclusion that patient-therapist similarity leads to a more successful outcome. Since the therapists made the original judgment of success on their own, the two variables may have been contaminated. In view of the possibility that therapists may have selected as successful those patients who most resembled themselves, success should have been independently assessed.

Gerler (1958) investigated the relation between client-counselor personality similarity and therapeutic improvement in fifty-seven college students with emotional problems at the University of Illinois Counseling Center. The students were in treatment with five clinical and counseling staff psychologists. Personality similarity was assessed by the Ewing Personal Rating Form given to both clients and counselors. Difference scores between client and counselor were classified as high, medium, or low and were compared with judged improvement. Gerler's hypothesis that a medium amount of similarity would be more conducive to favorable outcome than either high or low similarity received partial confirmation. Although no difference was found between the medium and low similarity groups, there was significantly more improvement in the medium than in the high similarity group. A second hypothesis predicted that low or medium similarity would be more conducive to favorable outcome than high similarity on those traits where a therapist's self-rating is different from the way his colleagues rate him. Differences between self and ideal ratings for clients and between self and pooled colleague ratings for therapists were derived. This hypothesis was also partially supported with the finding that medium similarity was more conducive to favorable outcome than high similarity, but there was no difference between high and low similarity. The author believed that he had demonstrated a basis for patient assignment, but the establishment of a distribution of conflicts and similarities based on a much broader sample of therapists than the five who were used would be necessary.

In a series of studies, Mendelsohn and his associates explored the effect of client-counselor similarity in cognitive and perceptual style on length of stay in counseling, failure to keep appointments, and client attitudes toward the counseling experience. The initial investigation (Mendelsohn & Geller, 1963) involved seventy-two clients seen by ten counselors of varied experience at the University of California Counseling Center. Client-counselor similarity, the independent variable, was assessed by the Myers-Briggs Type Indicator (MBTI), which had been administered to all students at the time of college admission, and to the counselors after treatment had terminated. The device purports to measure cognitive-perceptual orientation in Jungian life-style terms on four dimensions: judgment-perception, thinking-feeling, sensation-intuition, and extraversion-introversion. Measures of similarity were obtained by summing the absolute difference scores between client and counselor on the four scales. Outcome, the dependent variable, was evaluated by length of stay in counseling, which was construed as a limited indicator of success and taken to reveal the willingness of the client to permit himself to become involved in counseling. The total combined difference score as well as the difference scores on each dimension were correlated with the number of sessions the clients remained. It was found that as the total difference scores increased (client-counselor dissimilarity) the mean number of sessions decreased ($r = -.308$). This relationship was significant for male clients but not for females. On the extraversion-introversion dimension, the correlation between similarity and length of stay was $r = -.463$ for males, with zero order correlations for females, and males and females combined. The variable sensation-intuition showed no relation between similarity and length of stay for males or for males and females combined, but yielded a significant correlation of $r = -.316$ for females alone. On the thinking-feeling dimension there were no significant correlations of any kind. For judgment-perception, the correlation of similarity and length of stay for all subjects was $r = -.229$ and for males $r = -.378$. The correlation for females separately was not significant.

The authors observe that the greater the client-counselor dissimilarity for each dimension the shorter the duration of stay, but the only correlation that reaches significance for the group as a whole is on the judgment-perception dimension. Despite the alleged importance of feeling to therapy, the only dimension that yielded no significant correlations of any kind for either sex was that of thinking-feeling. The significant correlations in this study were of low order. Length of stay, a doubtful criterion of success, cannot really be taken as an indicator of either success or failure without a determination of reasons for termination. It is obvious that clients may terminate because they feel that the problem has been resolved, because they feel they are not being helped, or for a host of other reasons. It is certainly not a good criterion of positive behavioral change. The use of raw difference scores is open to question. The generality of this study is limited to those aspects of similarity tapped by the MBTI. Taken as a whole, this research can be viewed as providing minor support for the hypothesis of a relation between counselor-client similarity only if the questionable assumption is made that length of stay is an indicator of outcome.

This study was followed up and some of its flaws corrected in a subsequent paper by Mendelsohn and Geller (1965). The subjects who had participated in the first study were mailed a rating scale of attitudes toward the counseling process and outcome some three to twelve months after completion of the interviews, and 62 per cent responded. After the returns were analyzed into clusters, the questionnaire was revised and sent to 178 additional undergraduate and graduate students three months after their last interview. Seventy-two per cent responded, of whom fifty-eight were freshmen and seventy-one more advanced students. A cluster analysis was done and a cluster correlation matrix derived. As an advance over the prior study, which employed absolute difference scores, Cronbach's D^2 method (square root of the sum of the squared client-counselor differences on each MBTI dimension) was used to assess counselor-client similarity. Subjects were then divided into high, middle, and low similarity groups and analysis of variance was used to examine the effects of similarity on the cluster scores on same and opposite-sex dyads. Three major clusters emerged from both analyses: evaluation, comfort-rapport, and judged competence. The portion of this investigation of interest to us here is the finding of a significant curvilinear relationship of evaluation to similarity in the nonfreshman group only, with middle similarity producing the highest scores. The authors point to a curvilinear relation (nonsignificant) in the two freshman groups even though the error variance was larger than the source variance in each analysis. The results for comfort-rapport were somewhat ambiguous, with a linear relationship for one of the groups of freshmen and a curvilinear one for nonfreshman. The effects of similarity were more pronounced in opposite- than in same-sex matchings of therapist and patient, although this finding was of questionable reliability. In general, Mendelsohn and Geller did a careful, competent, and at times methodologically sophisticated study. The results, however, vary from group to group and variable to variable. If we merge all the data into one group the curvilinear relationship appears to be present for both evaluation and comfort-rapport, but the same-opposite sex differences wash out.

Mendelsohn (1966) reported a third study, which was an attempt to replicate the 1963 report of a positive linear relation between counselor-client personality similarity and duration of counseling, with control of counselor and client personality and sex introduced. The counselors were six female and five male professional staff psychologists, and the clients 111 male and ninety female clients. The majority of the clients sought assistance with vocational and educational problems while a small minority came for help with personal difficulties. As before, the client and counselor took the MBTI. Similarity was measured by the D^2 method on the same four scales as before, and duration by the number of sessions before the client terminated. The number of sessions attended ranged from one to six, with a mean of 2.36. Data were examined by analysis of variance. There were no significant differences in duration as a function of client or counselor type, sex of client, or dyadic sex-pairing. There was, however, a significant effect due to counselor-client similarity between high and low similarity groups. The scatter plot was mildly curvilinear but not U-shaped (the significance of this curvilinearity was not assessed). The authors concluded similarity to be a necessary but not sufficient condition for clients remaining in treatment. The study itself was well designed but limited in generality. It must be recognized that most of the clients were not psychotherapeutic patients. The duration of counseling was particularly restricted.

These data were reanalyzed in a subsequent investigation (Mendelsohn & Geller, 1967) of similarity, missed sessions, and early termination. What appear to be contradictory results were obtained. A client was considered to have failed a session if for any reason he did not appear for a scheduled interview. Continuers were those who missed an appointment but continued treatment. Terminators were those who did not return. Chi-square analysis contrasting all failers (those who terminated and those who missed sessions but continued) and nonfailers was highly significant. Frequency of missed appointments was greatest in the high similarity group, whereas more of the nonfailers were minimally similar to their therapists. Rank-order correlation between the proportion failing and the mean difference score of therapists from clients was rho = —.83. Thus, the less similar the counselor to his clients the lower the proportion of his cases that miss appointments. Examination of individual case loads revealed that in seven out of nine comparisons, failers were more similar to their therapists than nonfailers. These data were taken as evidence that it is similarity and not counselor characteristics that determine failure. With counselor personality ruled out, the possibility remained that it was client personality that produced the effect. Client scores on the individual scales, however, were not found to be associated with failure. For further evidence, combinations of scores on the four scales were examined. A client who had not failed at all (control) was matched on MBTI pattern with each client who had failed (experimental). With personality pattern held constant, investigators could test for the effects of similarity. A t-test for the difference between controls and experimentals was clearly significant for the upper third of the client-counselor similarity distribution but was not significant for the lower two-thirds. The effects of counselor-client similarity summate across the four scales to yield a reliable result, but are significant for only one scale—thinking-feeling. When taken individually, the results are interpreted as possibly meaning that similarity may facilitate communication but may also encourage the premature exploration of personal and conflictual material. This may lead to excessive involvement at the expense of concrete objectives by the therapist and generate ambivalence on the part of the client because counseling is at the same time attractive and anxiety-provoking. Missed sessions may reflect this ambivalence.

Lowinger and Dobie (1966) obtained a factor of patient-therapist similarity from their factor analysis of the questionnaire responses of sixteen resident psychiatrists. The questionnaires were evaluations of

300 patients of varied diagnoses. There was a significant positive relation between the initial patient-therapist similarity (as perceived by the therapist) and case outcome in terms of the number of visits made by the patient.

A study frequently cited as providing positive evidence for the similarity hypothesis was reported by Tuma and Gustad (1957). This is an important study not only because it has been quoted so frequently but also because it is a striking example of how misleading research reports can be if only the conclusions are read. There were two hypotheses. The first proposed that different counselors, using the same tests and interpretation methods, would obtain significant differences in the amount of learning about the self shown by comparable groups of clients. The second hypothesis, of principal interest to us here, is that there would be a systematic relation between the amount of client-counselor similarity and the amount of learning about the self that takes place in the client. The clients were fifty-eight male undergraduates at the University of Maryland Counseling Center, and the counselors were three graduate students with one to three years of experience. Client learning about the self was assessed before and after counseling by administration of the Dressel-Matteson Self-Knowledge Inventory and a series of graphic rating scales estimating the self on a number of ability, aptitude, and interest variables. Administered at the same times were the ACE, Cooperative Reading Comprehension Test, and Strong VIB. The measure of learning was the sum of the differences between the initial and final discrepancies between self-ratings and the tested position on all scales.

Similarity, the independent variable, was based on the Taylor MAT, California F Scale, and eight scales of the California Personality Inventory administered to both counselor and client. There were three methods of introducing the dependent variable tests and four methods of test interpretation, none of which proved to have differential effects on client learning. Therefore, any effects were assumed to stem from similarities and differences between client and counselor on personality traits. Product moment r's were computed between similarity indices on each of ten personality areas and criterion measures for academic ability, reading comprehension, and vocational interests. Of the thirty correlation coefficients, *only one* was statistically significant, though modest. This indicated even less of a relation between counselor-client similarity and criterion performance than might be expected by chance, and should have led the authors to abandon their experimental hypothesis and accept the null hypothesis. Instead, clinging tenaciously to their hypothesis, they decided that perhaps the background of one of their three counselors was interfering with the results. He was foreign born, and it was felt that cultural differences might obscure or confound results. (If they really felt this to be an issue *before* the experiment he should not have been used, but the chances are that they decided this after inspecting the data.) Eliminating this counselor and reanalyzing the data, they now found three out of the thirty correlation coefficients to be significant, still hardly better than chance. Despite this convincing demonstration of *lack* of effect of counselor-client similarity, their conclusion was essentially a restatement of their hypothesis. They claim that a close resemblance between client and counselor on personality traits is associated with relatively better criterion performance by clients. There is no point to collecting and analyzing data if they are then to be completely disregarded. The findings related to the first hypothesis do not bear on the issue of similarity, but here too their conclusion is almost entirely contradicted by their own data as they find nonexistent support for their hypothesis. This study stands as a prime example of how to draw erroneous conclusions from experimental data. Unfortunately these unwarranted conclusions have been cited and accepted uncritically in reviews of this issue.

Another approach to this question is to study similarity perceived or experienced by the patient rather than actual similarity. Sapolsky (1965) proposed that greater improvement would be found in patients who felt that they were similar to the therapist. This was conceived as a study of compatibility and mutuality of perception and outcome, and bears more on identification and rapport than it does on the effects of similarity. The subjects were twenty-five female patients hospitalized at Hillside Hospital, New York, in treatment with two first- and one second-year psychiatric resident (one of the three was female). Similarity scores were derived from semantic differential measures, and improvement measures were based on eight-point ratings by supervisors. Greater improvement was observed in those patients who thought of themselves as more similar to their therapists on two of three semantic differential factors. An important issue is that no correlations were done between therapists' self-ratings and patients' self-ratings. It is interesting that there was only a nonsignificant "trend" toward greater improvement in patients whom the therapist saw as more similar to himself. The author notes that felt similarity might be too difficult for beginning therapists to accept, while more experienced ones might be freer in revealing it. This touches one of the main shortcomings of this research. Only three therapists were used and they were all relatively inexperienced psychiatric residents. Very little can be said about therapist-patient similarity in general from this limited sample.

A study by Cook (1966) at the Testing and Counseling Service, Missouri University, is indirectly related in that it deals with client-counselor similarity in values rather than personality. He was concerned with the influence of value similarity on changes in the client's responses to four concepts: own-self, ideal, education, and future occupation as measured by semantic differential scales. Ninety university students who requested counseling were seen by forty-two advanced counseling trainees for two to five interviews (mean 2.48) over an average of twenty-six days. All clients and counselors completed the Allport, Vernon, and Lindzey Study of Values. Similarity in values was measured by comparing profiles with Cronbach's D Statistic. Change in meaning for clients was assessed by direct raw change scores on each concept, and differences in change scores were tested by analysis of variance across high, medium, and low similarity groups for each of the four concepts. The results indicated a curvilinear relationship between value similarity and changes of concept. Medium similarity was associated with more positive change than either high or low similarity. A more positive change here means that the concept is now held in more value. Aside from the fact that this study does not cast light on personality similarity and improvement, it has many limitations, most of which are acknowledged with refreshing candor by the author. He points out that the index of similarity used may be too global and that the measure seems to be a mixture of interests and values. The appropriateness of the criterion instrument used to measure change has not been established for brief counseling. More critically, he submits that the semantic differential may be contaminated by a social desirability factor since subjects tended to use the positive end of the scales. There was a variable number of clients assigned to counselors, ranging from one to five. Cook wisely suggests that the study be done with noncounseled controls as well. In addition to these observations, it can be pointed out that graduate student trainees represent a poor choice of counselors for these research purposes. The range of client-student values was too narrow and undoubtedly too similar to those of graduate student counselors at the start. The use of raw change scores presents problems that have been discussed elsewhere. The period of counseling was too brief to expect real change to take place anyway. Incorrect F-values observed in tables of his results fortunately do not alter the conclusions.

In summarizing the studies that purport to offer positive support for the hypothesis of a significant relation between patient-therapist similarity and improvement, we can find no convincing support of any kind. One showed a weak linear relation between personality similarity and improvement, and another showed a similar relation for patient-perceived as distinct from actual similarity. One showed partial support (and more nonsupport) for a linear relation of similarity and duration of stay in therapy and another a curvilinear one. Still another study reported a curvilinear relation for value similarity and conceptual changes. The result of one study presented as positive was a better demonstration of support for the null hypothesis. If there are any trends in these data, they suggest that curvilinearity, with a medium degree of patient-therapist similarity on selected and as yet not clearly defined or explored personality variables (and, more likely, cognitive style and value system similarities), is conducive to somewhat better results.

Not a single study was found in which the hypothesis was tested on dyads in an intensive, individual psychotherapy relationship with an adequate sample of experienced therapists, suitable criteria of outcome, and delineation of important areas of similarity either predicted on some rational, theoretical ground or derived empirically. On the other side of the coin, there are studies that claim to demonstrate that patient-therapist *dissimilarity* is conducive to a more favorable outcome.

As part of a study on the relation between empathic understanding and the counseling progress, Lesser (1961) investigated the effect of client-counselor similarity of self-concept on counseling progress. The clients were twenty-two students and wives seen for counseling at Michigan State University Counseling Center for a maximum of twelve hours. Change in self-concept was measured by change in self- and ideal-self perception on the Butler-Haigh Q-Sort, filled out by the client after the first hour and at the final session. Similarity was appraised in terms of actual similarity between self Q-sorts filled out by counselor and client, and "felt similarity" was appraised on a seven-item scale devised to rate the counselor's feelings of similarity toward the client. Actual similarity of self-concept was significantly and *negatively* related to counseling progress (positive change in self-concept in the direction of ideal self) and was unrelated to client and counselor ratings of empathic understanding. Counselor feelings of similarity, overestimation of similarity to client, and unwarranted similarity all proved to be unrelated to progress in counseling. There was, however, a positive relation between a counselor's accurate awareness of his similarity to his client and counseling progress and no relation of counselor feeling of similarity to empathic understanding. Counselor's overestimation of similarity to client was *negatively* related to counselor ratings of empathic understanding but not to client ratings of this. Neither counselor's correct awareness of similarity nor counselor's unwarranted assumed similarity were related to empathic understanding. It was therefore concluded that an incorrect perception of similarity may hinder counseling progress and empathic understanding. The greater the counselor-client dissimilarity of a single aspect of personality (self-concept) the greater the improvement as measured by self-ideal discrepancy.

A negative relation was also suggested by Snyder (1961) as one of the findings of his detailed report on the psychotherapy relationships of twenty patients with a single therapist, all of whom took the Edwards Personal Preference Schedule. The findings can only be considered suggestive since this was not a focal point of the study and the data were not fully analyzed. It is interesting to note, however, that three of the four patients whose PPS scores were most similar to the therapist's at the start of therapy were rated by the therapist as among the most difficult and unsuccessful cases. The four who were least like the therapist in PPS need structure in the beginning were considered to be the most successful and had the best rapport during therapy.

A further scrap of indirect evidence comes from a study of countertransference effects in psychotherapy (Cutler, 1958). In this research, two therapists dealt with five patients, of whom three were students in counseling and two were patients in a Veterans Administration facility. Subjects received three to four interviews. Therapist conflicts were ascertained by significant discrepancies between own-self ratings on sixteen personality traits and ratings of the therapist by judges. Recorded interviews were coded on the sixteen traits and the adequacy of therapist behavior was judged. The conclusion that interests us here is that the appearance in the patient of conflict-relevant behavior for the therapist prevents the therapist from functioning at maximal efficiency. It seems difficult to justify the assumption that discrepancies between self and others' judgments necessarily reflect conflicts. In addition, the two therapists differed markedly in formal training, personal therapy, and experience. None of these variables were controlled in any rigorous way. It is, therefore, impossible to evaluate their effects. Since there were only two therapists, both of whom were relatively unskilled and dealing with entirely different patients, generalization of the findings is not warranted.

A direct assault on the problem of similarity and success in therapeutic dyads was undertaken by Carson and Heine (1962) and served as a prelude to two other studies that together make a unique contribution to the literature of psychotherapy research. The authors measured personality similarity of patient-therapist dyads using the MMPI. They used as subjects fourth-year medical-student therapists and thirty-five female and twenty-five male patients seen once a week for individual therapy for up to eighteen weeks. The criterion of success was a composite of outcome ratings made by the supervising psychiatrist of the degree of patient satisfaction, the rater's own judgment of outcome, occupational adjustment, and adequacy of interpersonal relations and symptomatic status. The experiment was limited in scope principally by the notable inexperience of the therapists. The results showed a curvilinear relation of dissimilarity and success. That is to say, success increased as dyads became more dissimilar up to the point of marked dissimilarity when success markedly declined. The authors speculate that overidentification with the patient and his problems might make excessively similar dyads ineffectual and that excessive dissimilarity might hamper the therapist in understanding the patient. The authors modestly brand their own reasoning as "inelegant," but it sounds eminently logical and seems to be supported by the data. The paper was followed up by Lichtenstein (1966) in an attempted replication of this intriguing result. Using third-year medical students as therapists for fifty-four patients (fourteen men, forty women) and the same instruments and procedures, he found no relation between measures of similarity and success. In addition, a similarity index based on Welsh's Anxiety and Regression scale was found to be unrelated to success. Carson's response to this was to attempt himself to replicate the original findings, using sixty-five patients and twenty-two therapists and the same similarity index and outcome rating devices as in 1962 (Carson & Llewellyn, 1966). The total number of interviews was added as an outcome criterion. There were no relationships whatsoever between similarity and number of interviews or outcome. The authors concluded that the original curvilinear relation was "at best a rather ephemeral phenomenon" and doubted that global personality similarity was a fruitful, workable concept. The notable thing about this series of studies is that when Lichtenstein reported a failure to reproduce Carson's findings, Carson himself repeated his own work and forthrightly withdrew his original finding when replication failed. This is a most laudable display of the orderly process of science, of the greater attachment to fact than to entrenched position, and of the importance of replication in psychological research where truths are expressed in terms of probabilities as opposed to certainties and invariants.

Bare (1967) examined forty-seven counselors in a graduate training program and 208 of their clients at the beginning of counseling. The Gordon Personal Profile, Gordon Personal Inventory, and Edwards Personal Preference Schedule were included. Clients were seen weekly for ten weeks and then rated the helpfulness of counseling, how well they had gotten to know the counselor, and counselor empathy. In general, dissimilarity of client-counselor personality was more often associated with rated success of counseling, although correlations were of low magnitude. In particular, dissimilarity on the variables of original thinking, vigor, and responsibility were related to criterion scores.

A departure from examination of global personality similarity in favor of directly hypothesized dyadic interaction concepts encompassing specific aspects of personality was undertaken by Swensen (1967). He focused on client-counselor complementarity on the dimensions of dominance-submission and love-hate, predicting that it should be possible to select client and therapist dyads on these variables so as to maximize the probability of profiting from therapy. Carson and Heine's (1962) data were rescored on Leary's dominance-submission and love-hate dimensions because, for both therapists and clients, the original MMPI data and results were suggestive enough to encourage Swensen to pursue this approach in two related studies. In the first, clients from the Purdue University Psychological Service Center and practicum graduate students in clinical psychology serving as therapists were given the MMPI, which was scored on the Leary system. Improvement in therapy was measured by indices of behavioral change based on therapists' final summaries. Two raters judged improvement or no improvement. Greater improvement was found when therapist and client were complementary on dominance-submission, but whether they were the same or opposite on the love-hate dimension made little difference. Swensen concluded that the hypothesis was not conclusively confirmed, but merited further investigation. The use of student therapists, few cases, and tests of low power argue against a conclusive demonstration.

Accompanying studies supporting similarity and dissimilarity are others that find essentially no relation between either similarity or dissimilarity and criterion measures. Two such studies, Lichtenstein (1966) and Carson and Llewellyn (1966), have already been reviewed. Schopler's (1958) dissertation, using the Leary Interpersonal Checklist to get at similarity in the affiliative-hostile dimension, long preceded Swensen's 1967 study. Fifteen therapists and fifty-eight patients were given the checklist. Patients described themselves, their fathers, and an ideal person on the checklist. Therapists described themselves and five other therapists. The dependent variables were therapist's judgment of success and the number of interviews attended by the patient. Only statistically nonsignificant curvilinear trends were obtained for similarity and judged outcome. No relation was found between similarity and number of interviews. Similarity of the patient's self-description and the therapist's rating by others was not related to either criterion. It is also of interest to note that there was no relation between similarity of the therapist to the patient's father or father image and either outcome criterion. The one finding of substance was a positive relation between the degree to which a therapist differentiated others' affiliative behaviors from his own and average success and time in treatment.

This suggests that therapists who can make such a differentiation may be less likely to use themselves as a frame of reference for reacting to patient behavior. In this study both outcome criteria are fallible. Therapist judgment as a criterion is subject to the usual reservations and may be related to duration of treatment and contaminated by the independent variable, affiliative-hostile behavior.

As a side issue of an evaluative study on the efficacy of psychotherapy with sociopathic offenders, the effect of similarity on a number of measures was investigated (Persons, 1965). Twelve inmates in a federal reformatory were counseled twice a week for ten weeks and compared with forty controls. Therapist and clients completed Snyder's Client Affect Scale. The Personal Experience and Attitude Questionnaire, Taylor MAS, and Delinquency Scale were administered before and after treatment. At the initiation of the project the therapist took the same scales. Subjects were ranked from most to least similar to the therapist on the three tests. Rank-order correlations were computed between affect scores of both inmate and therapist as measured by Snyder Scales and similarity to the therapist's personality. Rho in every case was less than .1, showing no relation between therapist personality and positive affect. No attempt was made to relate similarity to the outcome of treatment in terms of the behavioral adjustment data that were used in determining treatment efficacy, but similarity was an incidental part of this study.

Vogel (1961) concentrated on the therapeutic relationship in equalitarian, authoritarian, and mixed dyads on the hypothesis that similarity in this trait would facilitate therapy. Two groups were used: thirty-two patients seen by thirty-two senior medical students at the University of Chicago Hospital and thirty patients seen by seventeen therapists (ten of whom were experienced staff) at the University Counseling Center. Authoritarianism was measured by the California F Scale, administered before therapy. An Authoritarian-Equalitarian Therapy Sort (AET), constructed for the study and filled out by patient and therapist, was designed to measure pretherapy preferences for an authoritarian or equalitarian therapist relationship. A therapist-rating scale was developed to elicit the quality of the relationship (poor to good) and to estimate the satisfaction of the patient in the relationship. The California F Scale and AET were given prior to therapy and the therapist-rating scale after the second interview. In addition, beginning and end recorded segments of one of the groups were rated on quality of relationship, patient satisfaction, therapist behavior (aggressive-submissive, directive-nondirective, high-low anxiety, dominating-equalitarian, rigid-flexible), patient behavior (aggressive-submissive, dependent–self-sufficient, high-low anxiety, dominating-equalitarian, rigid-flexible), and other factors. Observer-rating scales had a significant but uselessly low reliability of .38 with two judges, one of whom was the author. The hypothesis that authoritarian patients would form better relationships with authoritarian therapists was not supported, nor was the notion that equalitarian patients would tend to form better relationships with equalitarian therapists. Two of the therapist ratings were, in fact, in the opposite direction. The notable absence of results argues against the importance of patient-therapist similarity along the authoritarian-equalitarian dimension insofar as the quality of relationship and estimates of patient satisfaction are concerned.

Thus, the case for patient-therapist dissimilarity rests on two studies of global personality (one of which could not be replicated in two attempts), one study that found the presence of conflict-relevant behavior in the therapist to hamper efficiency, one finding of a negative relation between similarity of self-concept and counseling progress, one that found complementarity of traits of dominance-submission to lead to greater improvement, and one in which similarity led to failure to keep appointments. The intermediary position supporting the null hypothesis is found in five studies with varying measures of similarity ranging from a general measure like the MMPI to specific therapist-patient characteristics like authoritarianism. Looking at all of these studies in the aggregate, we can find no solid evidence that patient-therapist similarity or dissimilarity either aids, abets, or hampers effectiveness. Hopes for matching patients and therapists along personality dimensions dwindle. No strong, consistent effects have been found with a variety of aspects of personality, and some clear failures to find any relation lead us to conclude, pending a truly definitive study, that the null hypothesis is the most tenable.

Having examined the evidence that currently exists, we should pause to consider why such an attractive and plausible hypothesis should not be easily verifiable, or why some distinct trend has not evolved in twenty-one studies. It is not at all unlikely that some similar or dissimilar global personality patterns facilitate success while others are predictive of failure.

As an illustrative sample, and nothing more than that, the model presented below portrays one possible set of outcomes from pairings of patients and therapists based on some system of personality typology. It is an imaginary schema of pure cases of a four-category typological system.

In this schema, Personality Type A patients would succeed with any type of therapist whether similar or dissimilar in personality type, and Type B patients would fail regardless of therapist personality type. Type C patients would succeed only with similar (Type C) therapists

		Therapist Type				
		A	B	C	D	Outcome
Patient Type	A	S	S	S	S	Succeeds with any type therapist
	B	F	F	F	F	Fails with all types
	C	F	F	S	F	Succeeds only with similar therapist
	D	S	S	S	F	Fails only with similar therapist

S = Success; F = Failure

and Type D patients would succeed only with dissimilar therapists. If this kind of phenomenon is operating, research that has been conducted on global or typological classifications could be expected to yield confusing positive, negative, or null results because of the particular combinations unwittingly sampled. If there is any validity to this schema, establishing it would require a good system of typology, accurate prior classification of therapists and patients into personality types, and systematic assignment of all types of patients to all types of therapists; furthermore, it would be necessary to hold techniques and all other relevant variables constant and examine the relative effectiveness of each combination.

Those who see more promise in trait or factor theories of personality might hypothesize or empirically demonstrate that specific aspects of personality similarity or dissimilarity, singly or in combination, have a bearing upon outcome. Perhaps similarity or dissimilarity in some selected aspects, or even special combinations of similarity in some traits and dissimilarity in others, facilitates success.

The latter possibility is illustrated below.

Trait or Factor				
1	2	3	4	
S	S	D	D	Success Pattern
D	D	S	S	Failure Pattern

S = Similarity
D = Dissimilarity

Here a success pattern would require similarity of patients and therapists on traits or factors 1 and 2, and dissimilarity on traits 3 and 4. A researcher proceeding from this theoretical base would have to develop an exhaustive matrix from all combinations of trait or factor similarity and dissimilarity in a large number of therapeutic dyads. If degrees of similarity—high, medium, and low—were to be added as a variable to this schema, the problem would become far more complicated but probably much closer to the true state of affairs. It is no wonder that different researchers have come up with different results.

LIKING FOR PATIENT AS A DETERMINANT OF OUTCOME

Since psychotherapy is a two-way interpersonal relationship, it can arouse personal feelings ranging from intense liking through neutrality to marked dislike of the patient on the part of the therapist. Liking for another person does not develop *in vacuo*, and countertransference attitudes are a function of the past experiences of the therapist. A distinction is here being made between a therapist-offered condition such as Rogers' unconditional positive regard and a personalized feeling that a therapist has for a particular patient along the like-dislike continuum. That such feelings exist is a reality, but how they come about, how they can be identified, how they shift over the course of therapy, the determinants of such shifts, their correlates for both the patient and the therapist, their influence upon the process of therapy and its outcome—all are open to investigation. Our concern here is limited to research that has been done on the effect upon outcome of liking for the patient.

It is difficult to define liking for a patient. Does it mean a preference for taking him into therapy on prognostic grounds, enjoying his company, under other circumstances desiring him as a friend, feeling an affective bond with him, feeling comfortable with him, admiring his assets, finding him physically attractive, seeing a resemblance to someone liked in the past, sharing his values and opinions? Is it some ill-defined global attitude that leads one to state affirmatively, "I just like the cut of his jib," without being able to specify what or why? There are obviously many ways in which a person can be liked or disliked, and a complex arrangement of factors contribute to the feeling. Most studies do not attempt to do more than operationally define liking as a point along a rating scale. Others use it as almost synonymous with "preference for" the patient by the therapist. A review of the literature reveals very few experimental investigations of this subject.

Strupp et al. found positive correlations between ratings of successful outcome and feelings of warmth (.61) and liking for the patient (.53) (Strupp, Wallach, Wogan, & Jenkins, 1963). Mills and Abeles (1965) reported a significant relation between counselor needs for nurturance and affiliation and liking for clients only for beginning practicum students. Advanced graduate students and senior staff showed no such relation. In a study by Lowinger and Dobie (1966), liking for the client by resident psychiatrists in the initial interview was not found to be systematically related to diagnosis, age, sex, marital status, race, religion, social class, referral source, or extent of treatment.

Psychiatric residents, in a study on emergency brief psychotherapy, showed a significant preference for patients who were initially less impaired (Gottschalk, Mayerson, & Gottlieb, 1967). Despite the greater liking for higher class and less impaired patients, Class IV and V patients improved most with this type of treatment. There were no consistent correlations between how well a therapist initially liked a patient and how much the patient improved in therapy. The degree of liking a therapist had for a patient at the start was positively correlated with his liking for him at the end of therapy. Improvement did not depend upon liking for the patient, and posttreatment liking for the patient was more dependent upon initial attitudes than on the degree of improvement. The therapist's positive attitudes toward the patient were concluded to be of no demonstrable benefit in short-term therapy, although their importance in long-term therapy remains to be explored.

Redlich et al. provide some consistent data that at first glance appears contradictory (Redlich, Hollingshead, & Bellis, 1955). In their study of fifty psychiatric patients representative of the New Haven census, attitudes of three private practitioners, nine residents, two medical students, and three psychologists revealed that they tended to dislike lower-class patients. They described it as frustrating to work with a "bad case" whose great environmental difficulties made gains from therapy unlikely. The value systems of the Class III patients were understood, if rejected, but they found themselves at a loss even to understand the values of Class V patients. They were left with a feeling of disappointment from being unable to carry out insight therapy with these patients. With these kinds of attitudes, success with insight therapy would be unlikely. Gottschalk et al. (1967) have shown, however, that with different goals and approaches in mind, liking for the patient is of no relevance as far as limited-goal outcome is concerned.

Caracena (1965) obtained liking ratings by thirty counselors for sixty undergraduate clients and found that those who were liked were more apt to remain in therapy than those who were disliked. Only six of the counselors were experienced staff members, the remainder quite inexperienced. Contrary results were obtained in a study of the relation of liking to duration of stay (Garfield & Affleck, 1961). Subjects were twenty therapists, representing three disciplines, and twenty-four outpatients. Positive personal feelings toward the patient and positive interest in accepting him initially as a patient were unrelated to duration of stay in therapy. In this study, positive feelings toward the patient, prognosis, and interest in accepting the patient were all intercorrelated.

Stoler (1963) viewed liking for the client more in terms of a patient trait of likability. He attempted to determine if a global personal reaction to some clients led therapists to feel immediately more compassionate and optimistic toward them, and studied the relation between likability and success in therapy. More successful clients received significantly higher mean likability ratings from judges who listened to short taped interview segments. Agreement on likability was considerably greater ($r = .58$) among raters who had prior familiarity with the patients than among raters to whom the cases were new ($r = .30$). In a subsequent study, Tomlinson and Stoler (1967) reported that judges' ratings of client likability remain constant over time, early interviews not differing from late ones. They did not confirm the earlier finding that more successful clients are better liked than less successful ones.

Liking for clients has also been investigated from an entirely different point of view, that of its relation to the therapist's personality (Abeles, 1967). The therapists were twenty-eight inexperienced doctoral candidates in clinical and counseling psychology who were either in an internship or taking a practicum course. They were asked to tape a fifth interview with a client. Typescripts of two five-minute portions were coded, randomized, and returned for each other therapist to rate on a four-point Liking Scale ranging from "easy" to "difficult to like." Each therapist-subject was administered the Holtzman Inkblots, which were scored for anxiety, hostility, human movement, and form appropriateness. Contrary to the hypotheses, form appropriateness was negatively correlated ($rho = -.39$) with liking for patients (in general) and therapists who liked clients were found to be more anxious ($rho = -.41$) and hostile ($rho = -.36$). All these coefficients were significant at the 5 per cent level. There was no relation between M responses and liking. The study suggested that liking of clients may be associated with personality qualities of the therapist. These "therapists" were young, and as yet untrained, and one cannot generalize the findings to skilled practitioners. Also, it has not been established that indicating a liking for someone else's patient from reading a short typescript is equivalent to liking one's own patients.

The few studies on liking for the patient and outcome have yielded results that are not sufficiently consistent to permit firm conclusions. Liking has not meant the same thing to all investigators nor has it been measured in the same way. The importance of the variable may also be a function of the type of therapy (brief or long-term) and the point at which the feeling is measured. Further and more comprehensive research on liking for the patient is indicated.

THERAPIST-OFFERED CONDITIONS

In a growing number of studies, certain characteristics of the therapist's behavior are regarded, somewhat ambiguously, as conditions offered by him to the patient. Rogers (1957) believes strongly that among the necessary conditions for personality change in psychotherapy are the therapist's qualities of genuineness, empathy, and unconditional positive regard for the patient. Working with these hypotheses, Barrett-Lennard, Truax, and their collaborators have studied these "conditions" and have added some related variables: nonpossessive warmth and a more specific version of "genuineness," willingness to be known. Truax considers "unconditional positive regard" and the therapist's "genuineness" as most basic in a successful psychotherapeutic relationship. These traits are sometimes called "therapist's responses" and sometimes "therapist-offered conditions." Are these "conditions" techniques, to be offered or withheld from the patient according to the best judgment of the psychotherapist? In some of Truax's studies, the attempt to vary these "conditions" is made. However, these investigators suggest that different therapists offer different levels of these "conditions" and each generally maintains the same level despite differences in patients. The maintenance of high levels of these "conditions" is believed to be the important determinant of outcome. Truax and his associates also believe that it is possible to increase a therapist's ability to offer these "conditions" in a relatively brief period of time. One important implication of this set of hypotheses and assumptions is that a psychotherapist may not require lengthy professional training. Instead, his ability to offer these "conditions" may be augmented. Rogers (1957) describes the conditions as "qualities of experience" that must be acquired through experiential training rather than through professional training. Martin, Carkhuff, and Berenson (1966) emphasize that these qualities are personality or attitudinal traits in an unconvincing experiment. Student volunteers were interviewed once by a "best friend" and once by one of two experienced counselors. The student subjects were urged to discuss any problems they might have had. Interview samples and questionnaire scores yielded significant differences between friends and counselors and between the counselors themselves in empathy, positive regard, genuineness, and concreteness. Interestingly, there were no significant differences in interviewee self-exploration. Perhaps these volunteers had little to explore. The authors' point of view is that the possession of the facilitating traits is a crucial condition for their future development.

Whatever the source of these "conditions" offered by the therapist, do they, by themselves, produce successful outcomes? Halkides' dissertation (1958) was one of the earliest of a growing number of attempts to demonstrate the importance of these therapeutic conditions. Three judges rated randomly selected extracts from two interviews of each of twenty cases for the degree of the therapist's empathic understanding, genuineness, and unconditional positive regard. The clients were divided into "more" or "less" successful cases on the basis of a multiple criterion composed of several change and outcome measures. Halkides found highly significant associations between success and the three therapeutic variables. One other, the therapist's affective intensity, yielded ambiguous results. Truax (1963) reported that an attempt by Hart to replicate this study was a failure.

Barrett-Lennard (1962) followed Halkides with a more complex study that we have discussed in reviewing studies on the effect of therapist experience upon outcome. He attempted to relate the therapist's empathic understanding, his level of regard, the unconditionality of that regard, his congruence (the degree to which one person is integrated functionally in the context of his relationship with another), and his willingness to be known, to the client's personality change after counseling. Forty-two clients were counseled by twenty-one counselors, some expert, some not. Using the therapist's judgment of improvement, Barrett-Lennard reported significant differences between the more and the less improved clients in the five therapist characteristics measured initially, whether reported by clients or therapists. The two exceptions were client-reported "therapist-willingness to be known" and therapist-reported "therapist's unconditionality of regard." The author had some difficulty in using the clients' judgments of improvement as a criterion. Pretherapy measures of adjustment were so high that little positive change was possible. Correlations were computed only for the eighteen clients who were less improved by client judgment. Correlations with therapist reports of therapist traits were low and insignificant; correlations with client reports of therapist traits ranged from $r = .29$ to $r = .47$ and were significant. In the same way, Barrett-Lennard compared differences between the more changed and the less changed (by the client's criterion) in therapist traits measured at termination. There were significant differences between these patient groups on all therapist traits as reported by the therapists. As reported by the clients, the groups differed significantly in therapist empathy and congruence.

The study is one of the earliest to deal with the several variables that Rogerians regard as crucial therapist traits. It grapples with most of the central issues, the very same issues that must be faced by later researchers. Like them, Barrett-Lennard has had varying success. First in question is the psychotherapy studied. Psychotherapy is customarily used to effect some major change in the personality, motivation, and/or behavior of the patient. The pretherapeutic adjustment of many of the clients was so good that little change was needed or obtained. This caused the researcher some difficulty in examining results and raises problems of generalizing any results obtained to patients who are significantly disturbed. Another issue involves the nature of these traits of the therapist and their measurement. Accepting the Rogerian definitions of these traits, we are doubtful that questionnaire responses by therapist or patient are valid measures of them; it is impossible to be certain that responses are not influenced by attractiveness of personality or the halo of the person rated. Can the patient believe that the therapist making some uncongenial request really understands him? Some observer's report of these traits would be more convincing. Finally, there is the problem of a criterion of improvement. Here, separately for each, several measures of the therapist's judgment and of the patient's judgment are combined. Each measure can be considered to indicate a different aspect of improvement or adjustment. However, it is clearly to the best interests of the experimenter as well as his interested reader that the experimenter examine each criterion measure separately and present the specific contribution of each to any total criterion. It may be that different traits of the therapist result in different kinds of improvement. In Barrett-Lennard's study, the criteria are aspects of the therapist's and the patient's opinions. They are "interested parties," with various and uncontrollable investments in the outcome. Perhaps nothing has changed and the members of the dyad are merely reporting their favorable opinions of each other. It would have been more certain that these traits of the therapist had helped to determine the client's improvement if an outside observer, using some objective criterion, had made the judgments of improvement.

Barrington (1961) studied the relation between the therapist's willingness to be known, empathic understanding, and congruence, measured early in therapy by the therapist's verbal behavior, and outcome. A fourth variable, unconditionality of regard, proved profitless. Barrett-Lennard's Relationship Inventory measured clients' perceptions. The variables measuring therapists' "conditions" yielded better predictions of the clients' perceptions of the therapist than they did of the case outcome. Therapists' "conditions" were measured early in treatment, success perhaps a year later. Neither clients nor therapists are described. The investigator, attempting to demonstrate similarity of the therapist's behavior with more than one client, concludes from his results that the behaviors measured are a function of the dyad and are "minimally influenced" by the therapist's habitual verbal response patterns.

Truax and associates and van der Veen studied the effect of these facilitative "conditions" upon the outcome of treatment and made some important changes in research arrangements. The patients were seriously disturbed: neurotics, psychotics, and delinquents. Therapists' traits were derived not from questionnaires but from three-minute samples (four minutes in van der Veen's studies) taken from tape recordings of therapeutic interviews. The samples were rated by judges, frequently naïve with respect to psychotherapy and psychopathology, who were trained to high levels of rating reliability. The ratings of therapists' congruence, positive regard, and accurate empathy did not always correspond to either the therapist's or the patient's report of these traits measured by Barrett-Lennard's Relationship Inventory. Correlations between the two sets of measures are low, from $r = .06$ to $r = .26$ (Truax et al., 1966a). Nor do the two sets of measures yield the same results when correlated with the same measures of case outcome. Truax believes that the ratings and questionnaire scores measure different aspects of these therapist traits.

Despite some problems of reconciling the two principal measuring devices, the authors of this growing number of studies believe that they are demonstrating that these traits are crucial for personality change in psychotherapy, that the "conditions" originate with the therapist, that they may be augmented in a relatively short time, that their absence in the therapist leads to deterioration in the patient. The studies have been done with psychoneurotic outpatients (Truax et al., 1966b), hospitalized schizophrenics (Truax et al., 1965), institutionalized male and female juvenile delinquents (Truax, 1966a; Truax, Wargo, & Silber, 1966). Groups of patients have been studied and the course and outcome of treatment in particular patient-therapist dyads have been followed. Both group and individual therapeutic methods have been used. In these studies, the criteria of outcome have been most varied. They included complex criteria combining test and questionnaire scores, behavioral measures, and rating scales into one score; clinical judgments based on test scores; single patient-derived measures of self-concept; single tests like the MMPI; judgments of improvement by the patient and the therapist; and such "hard" criteria as the disappearance of "target" symptoms and the amount of time delinquents spend outside of an institution after therapy. Surely, in this assortment, there are criteria for all preferences. These researchers have provided promising tools for the measurements of the traits they study.

Each succeeding study reveals a growing sophistication of experimental technique (witness the complex model for determinants of therapeutic behavior designed by van der Veen, 1965b). In spite of this, the central variable, the therapist himself, has been sadly neglected. Usually the therapists are students or fairly young in their profession.

They work with few patients. Truax studied four psychiatric residents (Truax et al., 1966b), four "relatively experienced" therapists (Truax, Carkhuff, & Kodman, 1965), one, not described (Truax and Carkhuff, 1965b), and four senior resident psychiatrists (Truax et al., 1966a). Each therapist saw one or two patients, or perhaps, one group. The therapist's experience, training, and possession of these traits were not controlled or systematically varied. The patients vary widely in personality, attractiveness, and degree of disturbance. If on no other grounds, the results of Barrett-Lennard, Truax, Carkhuff, and van der Veen cannot be generalized. On occasion, one of the studies reverts to the study of pseudoclients in a pseudotherapeutic situation. For example, Kratochvil, Aspy, and Carkhuff (1967) tried to show that the clients of high functioning counselors gained more than the clients of low functioning counselors. Results were inconclusive. Clients seemed to have few problems.

What are the positive findings? These researchers conclude, with certain exceptions, that patients improve who receive therapy from therapists high in accurate empathy, nonpossessive warmth, and genuineness. Patients of therapists low in these traits do not. In one study, however, delinquents who received these desirable therapeutic conditions improved more than control subjects who received no therapy, proving the efficacy of psychotherapy over none, not of high conditions over low (Truax, Wargo, & Silber, 1966). In another study (Truax et al., 1966b), after one discounts positive findings obtained with "one-tailed" analysis of variance, the most numerous findings concern the positive effect of role induction (therapeutic orientation) upon outcome. In a study of schizophrenics and juvenile delinquents who received varying therapeutic conditions in group therapy, criteria are somewhat different for each group and dropouts (a definite outcome) seem to be ignored.

There are many exceptions to the positive results. Barrett-Lennard's (1962) questionnaire yielded no results for patient-reported "therapist willingness to be known" and for therapist-reported "unconditionality of regard." With neurotic patients, Truax's scales revealed no relation of outcome to therapist warmth (Truax et al., 1966b). Truax's attempt to demonstrate that the therapist alone contributes these traits concludes reluctantly that in first interviews and screening interviews the patient as well as the therapist may influence the therapist's nonpossessive warmth (Truax et al., 1966a). Van der Veen's (1965a) study, despite limitations of number and choice of patients, suggests that levels of both therapist and client therapeutic behavior may influence outcome.

Waskow (1963), in her excellent study of the counselor's acceptance, interest, expressiveness, and nonjudgmentalness, found no positive relation between discussion of feelings and counselor's judgment of success. The principal hypothesis, that the studied counselor traits were related to the client's feelings of safety, was confirmed only of nonjudgmentalness. Acceptance was negatively and significantly related to the client's discussion of feelings. There were no significant findings for the client's expression of feelings. Some other criterion of outcome is necessary. However, the investigator exercised great care in her study, which was done at a Rogerian center. The findings are a challenge to the Rogerian position.

In summary, the Rogerian hypothesis that these traits of the therapist are necessary and sufficient for patient change has not been tested adequately. Obvious flaws in research design, hopeful rather than valid conclusions from the evidence, and contradictory findings lead to a verdict of "not proven." These studies are exploratory rather than conclusive. They provide new tools for the measurement of therapeutic behavior and open the way for the examination of more complex hypotheses. The patient may contribute personality or other variables that evoke responses from the therapist (van der Veen, 1965b). Questions of all-or-none traits or optimal levels of traits in the therapist arise. Which therapist traits are beneficial for which patients and how much of them is it best to possess? The "therapist-subjects" are usually students or neophytes. What are the effects of experience and varying amounts and kinds of training upon these traits? Finally, do measurably successful professional therapists possess these traits?

THERAPEUTIC RELATIONSHIP

Many psychotherapists have suggested that a favorable outcome may depend not upon traits or other characteristics of the therapist but upon the relationship between the therapist and his client. Few researchers have attempted to study the issue directly. Fiedler (1950a) derived a concept of an "ideal" therapeutic relationship but did not test its association with outcome. Parloff (1961) measured the difference between the obtained therapeutic relationship in group therapy and Fiedler's ideal one. As the relationship approached the ideal, successful outcome significantly increased. However, of the three groups, the one with the poorest relationship remained intact and the one with the best lost 38 per cent of its members. Gonyea (1963), in a reasonably well-done study, asked two supervisors to rate eight counselor-interns who saw 208 clients. The supervisors compared the relationship obtained with Fiedler's ideal relationship. Outcome was measured by the client's response to a self-description form. There were few differences between counselors and these were not related to the quality of the relationship.

Lorr (1965) studied the client's perception of the therapist and found five dimensions of perceived therapist behavior. These were: accepting, understanding, authoritarian, independence-encouraging, and critical-hostile. They were similar to those of Fiedler, possibly because Lorr drew some of his inventory items from Fiedler's items. Switching the emphasis to the client, Lorr and McNair (1964b) began with statements descriptive of client behavior. They emerged with five factors: hostile-resistive, active involvement, blocking, controlling-resistive, dependency. Factor B (active involvement) was significantly related to the follow-up sample of 500 patients' ratings of improvement, their feelings of warmth and understanding in therapy, and also to therapists' ratings of their improvement. Patients described as hostile-resistive were rated by themselves and their therapist as unimproved. These categories make therapeutic "sense" and should be related systematically to other therapeutic variables.

Gendlin, Jenney, and Shlien (1960) found that outcome ratings correlated significantly with the counselor's report of the client's spontaneous communication, his realization that the therapeutic relationship is either new or an instance of his general problems. There were no correlations with reports of the client's discussion of the relationship, the counselor, or present events. Both the outcome ratings and reports of client behavior were made by the therapist.

A distinction has been made between the therapeutic relationship, which is a two-way interaction, and such variables as therapist-offered conditions and therapist liking for the patient, on the one hand, or patient attitudes and behavior on the other. Both may affect the relationship and the outcome. It is interesting that most of the research in this general area has originated in the client-centered framework but has dealt with *therapist*-offered conditions. It is true that these conditions are offered to make the therapist client-centered, but they are therapist-oriented nonetheless. Much less research has been done on the relationship itself, half of which comes from the client. There is no talk of client-offered conditions. One would think that there might be in a truly client-centered therapy. Future research on the therapeutic relationship will have to take into account the interaction between the conditions brought into therapy by the two principals in order to study the consequences of their various combinations.

13

Temporal Variables and Outcome

TIME-RESTRICTED THERAPIES

Time-limited Therapies. Traditionally the length of the individual therapeutic session has been fixed to an hour or a fraction of it, but the length of the course of therapy has been left indefinite. One approach to the problem of interminability has been to set a limit on the number of sessions in advance. Two streams of thought have converged to stimulate this idea. One is derived from the hypothesis of diminishing returns. After a certain point, it is reasoned, the limited gains anticipated do not warrant the effort, and the danger of the patient becoming excessively dependent upon therapy increases. The other is the notion that the therapeutic pace for both parties will be accelerated if they are obliged to reach their goals within a set time limit. The urgency imposed by the time limit, it is maintained, will reduce the amount of time wasted and the number of sessions frittered away during the more leisurely pace of therapy without limits. The idea of time limits is particularly appealing to clinics with large case loads and long waiting lists. It is doubtful if the idea is very popular with therapists. The comparative effectiveness of setting limits is a "natural" for research appraisal, but very little has been done with it.

At the University of Chicago Counseling Center, Henry and Shlien (1958) limited a group of fourteen clients to twenty sessions on a twice-a-week schedule by telling them that the time was clinic policy. A time-unlimited group of twenty-six clients averaged thirty-seven sessions in contrast to the average of eighteen for the former group. Both groups showed significant improvement on self-ideal Q-sorts that was maintained in a six- to twelve-month follow-up. The therapist's assessment on a counselor's rating scale was 90 per cent successful for the time-limited group and 66 per cent for the unlimited. Attrition for the time-limited group was only 5 per cent as against nearly 50 per cent for the unlimited. Twenty per cent of the limited group and 40 per cent of the unlimited group returned for therapy in two years. All these measures favored the time-limited procedure. On the other hand, an unvalidated composite index derived from several TAT signs of affective complexity was unfavorable to the time-limited group. On balance, time-limited therapy is at least as effective as unlimited.

The theme was pursued and other experimental and comparison groups added in a subsequent investigation (Shlien, Mosak, & Dreikurs, 1962). A client-centered time-unlimited group of twenty all voluntarily terminated after an average of thirty-seven interviews. Members of a client-centered time-limited group of twenty were restricted to twenty interviews and averaged eighteen. A third group, similarly limited, was seen by therapists of different orientation in a different setting, the Alfred Adler Institute. One untreated group consisted of an unspecified number who applied for treatment, were tested, and were then asked to wait for three months. A second untreated group was composed of an unspecified number of "normals" asked to take part in personality research. In summary, there were a normal and disturbed untreated group, a time-unlimited group, and two time-limited groups each receiving a different type of therapy. The mean self-ideal correlation for the waiting controls was zero both at the start and end of the waiting period. The passage of time alone, therefore, did not alter the average correlation for the group. The two correlations of the normal controls were both $r = .55$, also reflecting no change over time but indicating that they started and remained at a significantly higher level than the untreated therapy applicants. The client-centered time-unlimited group, similar to the waiting controls, initially had a zero order self-ideal correlation ($r = -.03$) that rose to about $r = .32$ at termination and held up to yield a final $r = .29$ at the end of the follow-up period. The improvement for this group was statistically significant. The client-centered time-limited group fared even better. They began at $r = .05$, rose to $r = .23$ after seven interviews, and to about $r = .44$ at termination. The rise continued to $r = .54$ at follow-up. Thus, they not only showed a significant gain but ultimately reached the level of normal controls. The Adlerian time-limited group, similar to the client-centered group, also started at $r = .05$, rose to $r = .12$ after seven interviews, to $r = .36$ at the end, and maintained this level at follow-up. These two time-limited groups were unique in showing increments in the first seven interviews. In contrast to therapy in which no time limits were set, the limited groups tended to start showing improvement earlier and rose to a higher level.

Muench (1965) investigated the effectiveness of time-limited psychotherapy at San Jose State College Counseling Center. The initial plan of informing clients that they would be limited to eight sessions in any one semester was abandoned because the staff became too uncomfortable and insecure with the arrangement. The experiment involved three groups of thirty-five clients each. *Short-term* therapy consisted of termination in less than eight sessions; *time-limited* therapy involved setting a prearranged termination date, with the clients told that they were restricted to ten interviews. The range was actually eight to nineteen sessions. *Long-term* therapy was not limited and lasted twenty or more sessions. Clients were seen by twelve experienced staff therapists whose general goals were to promote self-understanding and self-acceptance. The Rotter Incomplete Sentences Blank and Maslow Security-Insecurity Inventory were given before and after therapy, and at termination a therapy movement scale was completed by the therapist, who had no knowledge of the test data. A significantly greater number of clients improved than declined on both test measures in short-term and in time-limited therapy but not in the long-term group. There was no great degree of congruence between test measures and therapists' judgments.

There is room for far more systematic exploration of variants of time-limited therapy with limits set at different intervals and with different kinds of problems. The preliminary work that has been done should encourage further attempts.

Brief Psychotherapy. Brief therapy is a very ill-defined procedure; when one examines the literature it becomes apparent that brevity is in the eyes of the beholder. One man's brevity is another man's longevity. Survey of a sizeable number of studies of brief or short-term therapy reveals a range from one to well over 100 interviews for some patients, extending in time from one day to over seven months. About half the therapies designated as brief or short-term were found to have means or medians of twelve or less sessions, and half had more. This may be compared to surveys in the literature of the length of stay in treatment in general. Rogers' (1960) survey of 10,904 referrals in six states showed an average number of 12.9 interviews. Garfield and Kurz (1952) reported a median of six to seven interviews with only 8.8 per cent of patients seen for twenty-five or more interviews. Garfield and Affleck (1959) found a median of twelve visits in screened and selected cases. Median duration reported by Affleck and Mednick (1959) was three visits, Sullivan et al. (1958) nine, Rosenthal and Frank (1958) six, and Albronda et al. (1964) ten to nineteen. What is usually described as brief or short-term therapy equals or exceeds the median of treatment in general. As often as not, therapy *is* of the brief or short-term variety.

Distributions of length of therapy are badly skewed, and the range of sessions extends into the thousands for some individuals. Five hundred hours of psychoanalysis is not at all uncommon. When we talk about twelve sessions compared to 1,200 sessions are we discussing the same process? Is the yield from one 100 times greater than from the other, ten times greater, or no greater at all? Is the length of therapy correlated with degree of improvement? A number of investigations have been addressed to this question. In reviewing them certain distinctions have to be made between various kinds of temporal variables.

TEMPORAL VARIABLES

Among the more obvious, elemental, and tangible aspects of psychotherapy that could be related to outcome are its total and unit duration, amount, frequency, and regularity. These look like simple independent variables that are quantified by their very nature and easy enough to vary systematically. They are of exceptional practical importance to all parties in the therapeutic transaction. Yet the daily decisions that are made about them by therapists are based more upon custom, dogma, personal predilection, availability of the patient and the therapist, and of course economic considerations, which include the ability of the private patient to pay or of the public clinic to handle the caseload. It is easy to rationalize almost any arrangement, but it is wiser to be guided by facts to the extent that they are known.

The five variables mentioned require definition because they have been confounded in many experiments. "Total duration" refers to the elapsed time between onset and termination of therapy; "unit duration" is the length of a single session. "Amount" concerns the total contact time between patient and therapist measured in units of time or sessions. "Frequency" is the number of treatment contacts in a given unit of time, and may be "regular" or variable by prearrangement or by the vagaries of attendance. Numerous questions immediately come to mind concerning the effect upon outcome of each of these variables singly, jointly, or in interaction with each other. With five temporal variables, the possibilities for experimentation are manifold. When one adds other variables, such as different types of therapy with different patient groups, the task no longer looks quite so simple.

Total Duration of Therapy. There is a collection of studies in which the investigator studied total elapsed treatment time (usually in months) as an independent variable. In most instances, duration was studied as a small side issue of a larger project. A few investigators have obtained a positive relation between total duration of therapy and outcome.

Dymond et al., for example, found change patterns on the TAT to be related to length of therapy (Dymond, Grummon, & Seeman, 1956). In Karson and Wiedershine's (1961) study of group therapy, one group had been in treatment for a year before a second group began therapy. At that point, they both underwent group therapy with the same therapist for six months. The group that had been in therapy for eighteen months showed a greater number of changes on a personality questionnaire than the group with only six months. As the differences were not striking and the groups not necessarily equal to start with, the finding must be considered only as suggestive.

In evaluating the effectiveness of psychotherapy with ulcerative colitis patients, O'Connor et al. (1964) compared short-term psychoanalytically oriented therapy with full psychoanalysis. They reported that duration bore no relation to physiological improvement but was clearly related to psychological improvement. The purpose of the therapy was to modify the colitis condition, however, and whether long or short, it did not accomplish that end. Duration and frequency were confounded with therapeutic approach, and no statement about duration *per se* can really be made with confidence.

Schreiber (1966) attempted to evaluate family group treatment in a family agency. Seventy-two families who had requested help with a child were seen, and those who continued treatment beyond three months showed more improvement in selected areas than those who only remained for three months. Therapists were the evaluators. No information is given about how or when the judgments were made, and the data were not evaluated statistically.

In the process of evaluating his own private practice, in which he used a modified psychoanalytic technique, Cappon (1964) carefully reviewed results with 160 consecutive patients who had completed treatment. His rating at the end of therapy was found to be significantly related to duration. The longer the duration, the better the rating. Of course, the therapist's rating might be influenced by greater familiarity. However, the same relation held for loss of one symptom and loss of main problem. The relation of duration and outcome was not a simple linear one, however. Six months was found to be the critical period for loss of one symptom, and six to seven months the peak of change for loss of main problem. This represented an average of fifteen sessions and led Cappon to conclude that most patients who are going to change begin to get better about this time by first losing one symptom, followed about a month later by loss of the main problem. He states that after the optimal time (up to one year) diminishing returns set in, which "dwindled to a dribble after two years of therapy."

One of the few studies in which length of therapy was specifically established as an independent variable considered both number of weeks of therapy and number of interviews (Cartwright, Robertson, Fiske, & Kirtner, 1961). The average length of therapy of the eighty-seven patients was 29.5 interviews over 31.9 weeks. Three outcome criteria were employed, all based upon therapists' ratings. The first was a post-therapy estimate of change, the second a difference score between adjustment ratings made after the first interview and after the final one, and the third a counselor's rating of success on a nine-point scale. The correlation between log number of weeks of therapy and pre-post difference in adjustment score was a nonsignificant $r = .10$. Correlations with posttherapy estimate of change and counselor ratings of success were $r = .22$ and $r = .29$ respectively, both statistically significant but low. The authors point out that counselors' judgments could have been influenced by length of acquaintance with clients. Even more caution is required in interpreting correlations of this magnitude when a rating bias could exist. This point was confirmed in a study of ninety-three clients seen by thirty therapists for a median of twenty-six interviews (Fiske, Cartwright, & Kirtner, 1964). Seven factors of change were checked, but log length of therapy related only to changes in ratings of diagnosticians who listened to the last interview with the patient, and to therapists' ratings of success.

Studies failing to turn up a relation between duration and change are more abundant. Rosenbaum et al. investigated results of psychotherapy with outpatients generally seen by psychiatric residents on a weekly basis (Rosenbaum, Friedlander, & Kaplan, 1956). The patients, having completed therapy, were divided into six groups ranging from worse to apparently recovered. These six categories were subsequently collapsed into three: much improved, improved, and insignificant change. These three subgroups did not vary significantly in duration of therapy in months. Kaufman et al. examined a number of variables in an attempt to differentiate between the ten most improved and the ten least improved of forty schizophrenic children at the Metropolitan State Hospital, Waltham, Massachusetts (Kaufman, Frank, Friend, Heims, & Weiss, 1962). Data came from interviews with children and their parents, psychological tests, and observations by ward personnel, teachers, and community agencies. Length of treatment in months was not positively correlated with improvement. The least improved averaged more months in treatment, but the distribution was skewed because of long institutionalization of some of the least improved cases. Both of these studies demonstrate that retrospective investigations of this sort, particularly where institutionalization is involved, are almost meaningless on the question of duration. The duration of the long-term failure cases is bound to bring about this kind of a result. To study duration, it is necessary to keep duration as the independent variable instead of dividing the group into its success and failure components and considering duration as a dependent variable.

Marks and Gelder (1965) reported that phobic patients treated by behavior therapy for more than six months did not improve significantly more than those treated for shorter periods. Nor was there any relation between duration and outcome in various control therapies used. In a later comparison of behavior therapy and conventional psychotherapy with agoraphobic patients, the investigators found most of the improvement in both groups to take place in the first month (Gelder & Marks, 1966). Another study on systematic desensitization with twenty-seven anxious patients also showed no relation between duration and outcome as rated on several scales from case summaries (Hain, Butcher, & Stevenson, 1966).

The major study on duration was planned specifically to examine correlates of length of psychotherapy (Lorr & McNair, 1964a). The sample of 416 male cases with varied diagnoses was drawn from forty-three Veterans Administration clinics. Patient and therapist measures were obtained. In this sample, 51 per cent of the patients were found to be in treatment for two years or less, but the distribution ranged beyond eight years. Correlates of duration differed in neurotics and psychotics. Therapists reported that the greatest reduction in somatic complaints of neurotics took place in the first year, while the largest interpersonal changes were reported after the first year. Reduction in hostility, increased acceptance of others, insight, and total improvement were reported between the first and fifth years. Therapists' techniques and goals changed with time. Insight as a goal dropped steadily after the first year. Analytic techniques increased in frequency for the first five years and dropped significantly thereafter. Rapport reached a peak after the first year. These findings all came from therapists' reports. Neurotic patients reported little that was associated with duration. Symptom distress and self-reported change were not associated with duration. For psychotic patients there were few correlates of duration. Therapists reported increases in self-acceptance and acceptance of others after the second year and greatest gains in insight from the second to the fifth year. The patients reported the greatest gains after the second year. The authors believe that a minimum length of treatment is required to produce some change, but do not estimate what this minimum might be. They speculate that those who find therapy worthwhile come for more sessions and continue longer, and conclude with the observation that the definitive assessment of duration, amount, and frequency has yet to be made.

One of the most comprehensive investigations of psychotherapeutic change considered frequency of visits, duration, and amount (Lorr, McNair, Michaux, & Raskin, 1962). Designed primarily as a study of frequency of visits within specified periods, this research did not separate duration and amount. Data were obtained on 133 patients from seven Veterans Administration clinics who were "moderately" disturbed individuals assigned to intensive therapy. The patients were randomly assigned to three treatment schedules, twice weekly, once weekly, or once biweekly, and were evaluated at four time points. The initial evaluation was made on the basis of an interview conducted by the intake social worker and a psychiatrist, a test battery by a psychologist, and a rating by the therapist after the first session. All procedures were repeated at sixteen weeks, with the exception of the rating by the intake psychiatrist, and were repeated again at thirty-two weeks with the omission of the social worker's interview. The patients were retested and rated by the therapist if they were still in treatment. The test battery included fourteen inventories, rating scales, and checklists from which eight hypotheses could be tested. Therapist measures included a Severity of Illness score, a Change Inventory, an Interview Relationship score, an Interpersonal Changes score, a measure of Symptom Reduction, and several other assessments. The main social worker measures were social adjustment and severity of illness ratings.

To by-pass the results on frequency for the moment, the combined frequency groups showed no significant gains on patient measures at four months, although both therapists and social workers reported a decrease in severity of illness. At eight months, with fifty-eight patients remaining, only two of the ten patient measures considered—gain in ego strength and decrease in dependency in self-description—reflected improvement. As at four months, the therapists saw a significant decrease in severity of illness and also significantly more interpersonal change and symptom reduction. Those who were still in treatment after a year showed differences on three of eight patient measures (manifest anxiety, number of symptoms, and ego strength) and two of four therapist measures in comparison to pretreatment measures. The therapists saw more interpersonal changes and symptom reduction than at four months. The pattern of change was "somewhat broader" than the eight-month pattern and "considerably broader and more consistent" than the four-month pattern. In a sequel to this study, McNair et al. conducted a three-year follow-up of eighty-one patients (McNair, Lorr, Young, Roth, & Boyd, 1964). The mean number of therapy sessions was sixty, with a range from nine to 206. Nineteen of the patients were still in treatment at the time of follow-up. The log duration of therapy did not relate to any of the multiple outcome criteria.

In the research of Frank et al., comparisons were made on discomfort and social ineffectiveness with outpatients who were psychoneurotic or had personality disorders and were in treatment with psychiatric residents (Frank, Gliedman, Imber, Stone, & Nash, 1959). Patients were followed for two years. Those who left treatment before the fourth session showed an average drop in discomfort comparable to those who stayed in treatment for six months or two years! In general, there was no consistent pattern after six months for the group as a whole on the discomfort scale. Half of those who returned for more treatment improved and half became worse. The same was true for the dropouts. The persistence of a lowered discomfort score did not depend on whether or not patients remained in treatment. The authors suggest that diminution of discomfort is a function of the patient's expectation of help activated by contact with the therapist and that it is independent of duration of treatment. The improvement in social effectiveness, however, was related to duration of treatment to a limited degree. This aspect of the data was not treated statistically and the reported continued improvement is not convincing.

Stieper and Wiener (1959) examined the problem of interminability in psychotherapy at the St. Paul Veterans Administration Clinic. Four patient groups were contrasted. Group A consisted of fifteen veterans treated privately on a fee basis for three years and six months to ten years (mean 7.9 years). They were seen once monthly. The eighteen patients in Group B were seen on a monthly basis at the clinic. They had been in treatment from two years and eight months to seven years and eleven months (mean 5.3 years). Group C consisted of fifteen patients seen by the clinic staff about once every ten days for an average of fourteen months. Group D contained eighteen patients who had already terminated in the clinic after having been seen an average of once every ten days over 7.1 months. Treatment settings, duration and frequency, and closed or active status were thus all confounded. In addition, Groups C and D were significantly younger. However, the data afford a rough comparison of treatment of long duration measured in years and shorter duration measured in months. The main finding, as assessed by the MMPI, was that no greater benefit accrued from several years of therapy than from several months. This conclusion was arrived at without any direct comparison between long- and short-term groups. The fact is that none showed any notable improvement on the criterion measure. Confounding of treatment setting and length of treatment also appeared in another comparison between clinic and fee-basis treatment (Warne, Canter, & Wizma, 1953). For psychoneurotics treated by fee-basis physicians over a thirty-three-month period, 70 per cent were classified as worse and 20 per cent as improved. Similar patients treated in the clinic over 8.9 months had 66 per cent improved and only 7 per cent worse. It is not known whether this negative result for duration was due to sampling error, differences in treatment setting, or the detrimental effect of prolonged psychotherapy.

Thus, we see very little good evidence that time in therapy past some undefined point brings commensurate additional benefits. Admittedly, the question has not been studied in a way that meets adequate standards of experimental design. It would be worthwhile to examine the effects of duration in a repeated measure own-control design to determine the characteristics of the curve of change.

Amount of Therapy. Results on duration need to be viewed in relation to studies of amount of therapy measured by the number of treatment sessions. Although not equivalent, they are correlated. Cartwright et al. obtained a correlation of $r = .85$ between log number of weeks of therapy and log number of interviews (Cartwright, Robertson, Fiske, & Kirtner, 1961). Number of sessions is a much more common way of measuring the length of therapy than is total duration. Direct positive relations (of varying degrees of strength) between number of interviews and some criterion of outcome have been reported in numerous studies.

In a large-scale survey at Tavistock Clinic by Luff and Garrod (1935), outcome was classified by the therapist as much improved, improved, slightly improved, or not improved. Five hundred cases were sampled. Of those seen for less than twenty interviews, 58 per cent were considered relieved three years after discharge, compared to 51.2 per cent for those seen from twenty to sixty interviews and 54.5 per cent for those seen beyond that. The data were not treated for reliability, but there seemed to be a decline in outcome with increased therapy for cases diagnosed as hysteria or obsessional states. Not much can be gleaned from this kind of data since amount of treatment was not established beforehand as an independent variable. These data may merely indicate that the more difficult cases took longer.

Evaluating the result of brief therapeutic counseling with 498 veterans, Bartlett (1950) obtained a correlation of .24 between the number of interviews and improvement as rated by referring rather than treating personnel. Those rated as much improved had 5.2 interviews, some improvement 4.0, and no improvement 2.0. Miles, Barrabee, and Finesinger (1951) conducted a follow-up evaluation of sixty-two patients with anxiety neuroses two to twelve years after intramural psychotherapy at Massachusetts General Hospital. Contemporary adjustment was rated on the basis of interviews and compared with ratings of prehospital adjustment judged from hospital records, at best a shaky procedure. The number of therapy interviews was significantly related to the degree of rated improvement. Examining the records of 1,216 patients (63 per cent psychoneurotic, 21 per cent psychotic, 16 per cent other) at the Veterans Administration Clinic, Milwaukee, Garfield and Kurz (1952) obtained data on the results of treatment and number of interviews for 142 patients for whom adequate evaluative information was available. The evaluation standards were haphazardly dependent upon what appeared in the records, and were of doubtful validity. The final sample was not considered to be representative. Number of interviews was broken down into the categories 1–4, 5–9, 10–14, 15–19, 20–29, and 30 or more. There was a tendency for a relatively higher percentage of improvement to be associated with increased length of treatment, but it was noticeable that 30 per cent of those who improved at all did so in less than five interviews, and over half in less than ten. In the Rogers and Dymond study, Seeman (1954) reported that variability of ratings was significantly lower for long-case groups. There was a "trend" in favor of higher success ratings for longer cases. He concluded that if a client is in therapy for at least twenty interviews there is a strong assurance of gain from therapy as judged by the therapist.

Dana (1954), at the Danville Veterans Administration Hospital, Illinois, compared forty-four patients in individual therapy for six to nineteen sessions (mean 12) with forty-six others in therapy for twenty to 153 sessions (mean 51). This was a retrospective study, and outcome was judged as improved or unimproved by the experimenter from case summaries. If such judgments can be relied upon (no evidence of validity or reliability was presented), 70 per cent of those seen longer improved in contrast to 46 per cent of the short-term group. Patients were classified before treatment on the adequacy of their responses to Rorschach Card IV, taken as a measure of their attitudes toward authority. From the description of scoring standards, inadequate responses appear to reflect psychosis. What may have been measured was not so much attitudes toward authority as diagnosis and severity of personality disturbance. In any event, patients with adequate responses improved with either short or long therapy. Those with inadequate responses (poor form, contamination, confabulation, for example) showed chance improvement with long-term therapy but failed badly in short-term. Those with negative responses (reflecting hostility, threat) did significantly better in long-term than short-term therapy. If the judgments are accurate, the main contribution here is that of a *differential* relation between number of sessions and initial severity of disturbance.

Myers and Auld (1955) followed the therapeutic progress of sixty-three patients treated by senior staff and residents at Yale University and found that the fewer the number of interviews the greater by far the chance of failure. The categories of termination from examination of case records were: patient quit, discharged unimproved, discharged improved, therapy continued elsewhere. Among those seen for less than ten interviews, 79 per cent quit or were discharged unimproved. None were discharged as improved. In the category ten to nineteen interviews, 50 per cent quit or were unimproved and 39 per cent were considered improved. For the twenty or more interviews group, the failure categories had dropped to 15 per cent, and 42.5 per cent were discharged as improved. Again, as the authors caution, we are dealing here with success and failure by therapists' definition rather than by objective criteria, and we do not know what percentage of those who quit did so because they felt better. As twenty or more interviews is the highest category, the relation of improvement within this category is not known. It is just here that the real question of the added value of prolonging treatment begins to arise—the question of whether 200 or 500 interviews bring about sufficient benefits appreciably beyond those obtained at twenty or fifty to make the added expenditure worthwhile for a given individual.

Another retrospective survey, at the Los Angeles Veterans Administration Clinic, covered 354 patients who had been seen for five or more sessions including intake (Tolman & Meyer, 1957). Here again the experimenters depended upon data from case records. They found that the group rated unimproved contained a significantly greater proportion who had fewer than fifteen sessions (67 per cent) than those who were considered slightly improved (34 per cent) or much improved (10 per cent). The converse was equally true.

Standal and van der Veen (1957) studied length of therapy in relation to counselor estimates of integration and other case variables. The independent variable was the number of interviews and there were ten separate dependent variables all stemming from the therapist's before and after ratings. The researchers concentrated on the one variable (degree of personal integration of the client) which they felt least likely to be affected fortuitously by circumstances outside therapy. They nevertheless predicted that the other nine case variables would also be positively related to length of therapy. The subjects were seventy-three clients seen by sixteen experienced therapists. Case length ranged from two to more than seventy-two interviews in a skewed distribution that was logarithmically transformed for purposes of data analysis. The reliability of the ratings was either not good or doubtful on six of the ten rating variables in a small test-retest study, and the validity of therapists' ratings was not established despite the authors' extensive research of the literature to justify it. Patients seen for longer periods may be rated as better integrated or more successful whether they are or not. Impartial measures not subject to bias from knowledge of case length or to influence by it are obviously required. With these limitations and reservations in mind, the findings were that most case variables were slightly related to length of therapy, with level of integration showing the highest relation.

An incomplete study lacking a control group and limiting itself to patients' ratings of outcome, or ratings by parents in the case of children, presented some useful comparative data on the relation between the amount of therapy and outcome (Graham, 1958). The sample of 140 (96 adults, 44 children) was seen at the Long Island Consultation Center in limited psychoanalytically oriented psychotherapy. Among the adult neurotics seen for four to nineteen sessions, 19 per cent reported definite improvement, compared to 52 per cent of those seen twenty to thirty-seven times and 74 per cent of those seen thirty-eight to 135 times ($p < .01$). Similarly increasing percentages of improvement as a function of the number of sessions were seen for child neurotics ($p < .05$). The results for adult psychotics, however, showed no such trend; rated improvement did not increase with the amount of therapy.

Garfield and Affleck (1959) appraised correlates of length of stay at the Nebraska Psychiatric Institute in a retrospective study of 135 closed cases. They used the therapist's judgment of improvement. Forty-four per cent of the patients were psychoneurotic, 25 per cent had personality disorders, and 21 per cent were psychotic. Slightly over half the patients were judged improved before the ninth interview, and 91 per cent of those who remained beyond the twelfth interview were judged improved. The authors acknowledge that therapists' judgments about outcome may have been influenced by length of stay, thus confounding the two variables. They correctly caution that judged improvement does "not automatically" indicate that an improvement in behavior or personality has taken place.

Cabeen and Coleman (1961, 1962), in studies of the effectiveness of group therapy with institutionalized sex offenders, employed no controls. The patients were treated by Slavsonian analytical group therapy for a mean of thirty-four sessions by three psychologists and two psychiatrists. Staff ratings and MMPI changes were used as improvement criteria measures. On the basis of both of these criteria, those who participated in the greater number of therapy sessions improved significantly more than those participating in fewer. McNair et al. reported a small but significant relation between the number of interviews and outcome on four of thirteen criteria (McNair, Lorr, Young, Roth, &

Boyd, 1964). Greater symptom reduction and more insight were reported by interviewers for patients who had made a greater number of visits.

Another series of investigations has uncovered a curvilinear relation between the number of visits and outcome, with the number of patients improving either leveling off or declining as the amount of therapy increases past a critical zone. Feldman, Lorr, and Russell (1958) drew a representative sample from 20,000 cases seen in sixty-three Veterans Administration clinics. The random sample included 4,892 open cases and 475 closed cases for a total of 5,367. An improvement questionnaire filled out on each patient by the therapist included a judgment of general improvement. In addition, the therapist was asked to indicate the degree of change in the patient on nine scales, each representing common problems and complaints of outpatients. The mean level of rated improvement was observed to show a sharp initial rise and then to level off by the end of forty-five sessions. The curve shifted to a downward trend between the fifty-fifth and sixty-fifth interview, possibly because some of the more improved patients had discontinued therapy by that time. The correlation between rated improvement and number of interviews was .31 for large clinics and .23 for medium-sized ones.

Cartwright (1955b) drew seventy-eight patients from the research files of the University of Chicago Counseling Center who had been seen by seventeen therapists. The criterion measure of outcome was counselor ratings of success on a nine-point scale. A significant curvilinear relation was found between success and number of interviews. The most intriguing finding was the presence of a "failure zone" ranging between the thirteenth and twenty-first interview. Cartwright suggests that there may be two kinds of processes, short (one to twelve interviews) and long (thirteen to seventy-seven interviews). He offers the possibility that short-term clients might come in with situational problems and long-term ones with personality problems. The failure zone, he maintains, could be associated with resistance that prevents the individual from continuing in long-term therapy. Taylor (1956) corroborated this idea of a failure zone in a psychoanalytically oriented clinic. A total of 309 case closings with varying diagnoses and therapists at the Outpatient Clinic of the Denver Veterans Administration Hospital was evaluated for number of interviews and outcome, rated by the therapist and a consultant as mildly, moderately, or greatly improved. The curve of improvement as a function of the number of interviews appeared to be quite similar to Cartwright's.

The failure zone appeared much earlier in a study by Johnson (1965) in a university counseling setting. Two samples were appraised. The first consisted of 175 students with vocational problems and sixty-four with emotional problems. The second sample contained 246 vocational and sixty-three emotional problems. Success was defined as graduation or senior-year status during the graduating year. This is obviously not equivalent to relief from emotional disturbance, and certainly many other variables in addition to the interviews could have contributed to the outcome. The relation between severity of presenting problem and length of treatment and success was not assessed. Too many uncontrolled variables were present, and the counseling too limited in scope for this study to have any generality. Nevertheless, it was found that the failure zone for vocational cases appeared between the fifth and seventh interviews for one sample and the sixth and eighth for the other. There was a significant relation between number of interviews and success for emotional problems but not for vocational problems.

Pruit (1963), working with more seriously disturbed patients, attempted to determine if there was an optimum period for vocationally oriented group therapy. Thirteen patients were schizophrenics, five had character disorders, and one was neurotic. The patients were seen for an hour twice a week over an eighteen-month period for a range of sixteen to 108 sessions. The Palo Alto Group Psychotherapy Scale was filled out biweekly by the therapist and covered the behavior of each patient over units of four sessions. The scale evaluated eighty-eight items of group participation. Mean ratings for individual subjects in four-session units were computed through forty-eight sessions and correlated with time in therapy. An increase in ratings up to the twenty-fourth session was followed by a decline thereafter. Rank-order correlations between mean ratings and total number of sessions were a perfect 1.0 for the first twenty-four sessions and —.89 for the next twenty-four. No generalizations about this "satiation effect" were made beyond vocationally oriented group therapy with restorative goals, but the definite nature of the result encourages taking a hard look at amount as a variable with other kinds of therapy. Rosenthal and Frank (1958) also found that the percentage of patients judged improved increased up to twenty sessions and then declined. Cappon (1964), working psychoanalytically with a varied patient load, reported his ratings of his own patients to be significantly related to the number of sessions. The relation held up when a more rigorous index, loss of main problem, was used as the criterion. The critical period was thirty-five sessions, beyond which there were diminishing returns. There was no reliable difference in improvement between patients seen for thirty-five sessions and those seen for a greater number ranging up to 217 sessions.

These studies are from diverse sources and are characterized by different therapeutic approaches with different patient groups and different treatment goals. Two things are apparent, however. The first is almost self-evident—sooner or later in psychotherapy there is a point of diminishing returns. If this were not the case, all therapy would be interminable. The point at which this occurs is of paramount importance. While this is certainly an individual matter, it would be well worth knowing what the range and central tendency of this point is. Such knowledge would have a profound effect on patient and therapist expectations and planning. These varied studies suggest that it takes place sooner than most therapists imagine. The optimal point has been found to range anywhere from the fifth to the sixty-fifth interview, depending on the type of patient and the type of therapy. The controversial issue comes about from the discovery in some studies of a failure zone followed by successful continuation on the part of some patients who are able to weather it. Other studies report a constant decline after reaching the optimal point. This is an issue of substantial implications that requires careful reappraisal. It is quite possible that neither the failure zone nor the optimal point was found in many investigations because the experimenter did not treat the data with this in mind but simply looked at the correlation between the total number of interviews and outcome. In Pruit's study we saw a highly positive correlation in the first twenty-four sessions balanced by a highly negative correlation in the next twenty-four, yielding an overall correlation of zero order.

Contrary results that do not reject the null hypothesis are also in the literature. In a retrospective study at the University of Tennessee by Pascal and Zax (1956), no differences were found in the number of behavioral changes in the predicted direction for patients seen for at least 100 interviews, those seen at least thirty sessions, and those seen for at least five. Dorfman (1958) found therapy gains not to be related to the number of sessions of client-centered child therapy. Nichols and Beck (1960) found that the number of interviews correlated with only one of six derived factors. The correlation, $r = .29$, was with the therapist's posttherapy success rating. Rogers (1960) conducted a large-scale survey and obtained statistics from five state departments of mental health and one Veterans Administration clinic. Information was based upon 10,904 patients from fifty-three clinics. Populations varied on many characteristics from state to state. The methods of reporting lengths of treatment varied as did definitions of an interview. Only 4,081 (37.43 per cent) of the 10,904 referrals were actually treated. Of the treated patients, 71.04 per cent were reported as improved. The average number of interviews ranged from 9.0 in Texas and Iowa to 17.2 in California, and the mean for the entire sample was 12.9 sessions. There was no relation between the percentage reported improved and the average number of treatment interviews in a state. The large number of subjects is impressive, but in all probability percentages of improvement have no consistency from state to state and bear no relation to what a rigorous appraisal of the patients would show.

Lazarus (1963) reported on 126 severe neurotics treated by systematic desensitization and other behavior therapy techniques who remained in treatment at least six sessions. The 20.6 per cent who were rated as unimproved averaged 11.3 sessions, 17.5 per cent rated as slightly improved averaged fifteen sessions, 42.9 per cent who were considered markedly improved had 14.2 sessions, and 19 per cent rated completely recovered had 15.9 sessions. It can be seen that the unimproved averaged three to four fewer sessions, but it is doubtful that the difference is reliable. Marks and Gelder (1965) found no relation between outcome and number of sessions in their retrospective study of behavior therapy in phobic patients.

In Cartwright and Lerner's (1963) research, twenty-eight patients at the University of Chicago Counseling Center were seen for up to 116 interviews (mean 40) by sixteen client-centered therapists. The outcome was arrived at by change scores obtained from pre- and post-therapy rating scales administered to the therapist. The mean number of interviews for the improved patients was 37.33 and for the unimproved 43.69. The difference was not a reliable one. Heilbrunn's (1966) study of three variants of psychoanalysis included thirty-seven patients seen for over 300 hours, fifty-four seen for 100 to 300 hours, and seventy-five seen for up to 100 hours. The therapist's judgment of his own cases revealed no difference among the three. Improvement percentages were respectively 38 per cent, 43 per cent, and 45 per cent. The number of interviews is confounded with frequency and duration is not given.

In summary, interpretation of the relation between amount of therapy and outcome is handicapped by failure to control for severity of illness in the experiments and by the fact that judgments of outcome, particularly when made by the therapist, may be influenced by the amount of therapeutic contact. About half the studies show a positive relation between outcome and amount of therapy, and the remainder report either a curvilinear relation or no association. Two conflicting phenomena that may play havoc with the data have been reported. Many of the patients who are going to improve apparently show the lion's share of their gains early. Others terminate early as therapeutic failures. The two tend to nullify each other in group data. When there are more early failure dropouts than early successes, a positive relation between amount of therapy and outcome is more apt to be obtained. The relation between amount of therapy and outcome fades as we ascend to the realm of those relatively extensive courses of therapy that are measured in hundreds of hours.

Frequency and Outcome. A patient seen five times a week will have 260 sessions a year, if seen one time a week fifty-two, and if seen once a month only twelve. The total duration of treatment in each case is one year. If the first patient is seen for five-minute daily visits he will have about twenty-two hours of therapy a year, equivalent to the second patient being seen once a week for half an hour and the third for two hours once a month. A direct comparison in which duration was held constant and frequency varied is available in the Ends and Page (1959) study of group therapy with alcoholics. Two groups of twenty-eight patients each were seen for six weeks of psychotherapy, but one received thirty sessions and the other fifteen sessions in that period. Using pre-post MMPI and a self-ideal Q-sort, the authors reported that doubling the number of sessions without increasing the total elapsed time results in significantly greater therapeutic gain.

Zirkle (1961) held total contact time to a constant twenty-five minutes a week but confounded unit duration and frequency by comparing five five-minute contacts with a single twenty-five minute contact. The patients were chronic hospitalized schizophrenics. The finding in favor of shorter, more frequent sessions against longer, less frequent ones was equivocal ($p = .10$). What we do not know from this experiment is whether one five-minute contact a week would have been less effective than one twenty-five-minute contact. Within the framework of brief-contact therapy with newly admitted hospital patients, Dreiblatt and Weatherley (1965) compared the effects of three contacts a week for two weeks with six contacts a week for the same period. The groups seen more frequently showed greater increases in self-esteem and greater decreases in anxiety, but did not ultimately differ in the amount of time spent in the hospital.

Ramsay, Barends, Breuker, and Kruseman (1966) compared massed to spaced desensitization of a fear at the University of Amsterdam. Twenty students who admitted to various fears on interview were seen by three advanced undergraduate psychology students. The various fear stimuli—such as spiders, cockroaches, and snakes—were collected and fear hierarchies constructed. The subjects were treated by Wolpean reciprocal inhibition. An avoidance test and fear thermometer were used as criterion measures. Two conditions were contrasted. In the first, each subject was asked to imagine the feared situation twenty times in a twenty-minute period each day for four days. In the second (massed practice), the schedule was forty times in a forty-minute period with the second treatment four days later. The two groups were thus balanced for the total amount of time spent in treatment, the number of visualizations, the number of presentations of the actual feared stimulus, and the time between the presentations of the actual stimulus (before and at the end of treatment). Fear ratings showed the spaced-practice group to start a little higher and end a little lower than the massed-practice group, although the total difference between the two was not significant. Differences before and after treatment for both groups were highly significant. A significant interaction between Massed-Spaced $\times$ Before-After was extracted by an inappropriate one-tailed test and used as evidence of superiority of spaced practice. Not much confidence can be placed in this finding. The use of trained therapists instead of undergraduates would have been more suitable.

In Graham's (1958) study with psychoanalytically oriented therapy, which used self-report as the lone outcome criterion, it was reported that 43 per cent of the adult neurotics seen once a week improved in contrast to 64 per cent of those seen twice a week ($p < .05$). The opposite result obtained for adult psychotic patients. Again, 43 per cent of those seen once weekly improved, but among those seen twice weekly, improvement dropped to 25 per cent ($p < .05$).

A number of other studies yield null results on frequency and outcome. Rosenbaum, Friedlander, and Kaplan (1956) found no difference in average visits per month at various improvement levels. McNair and Lorr (1960), working with therapists' judgments of suitability of treatment frequency rather than absolute frequency, found it independent of the response of patients to therapy. The therapists' reasons for showing preference for one treatment schedule over another with a particular patient were found to be related more to such variables as liking for the patient, clinical judgments about severity of the patient's illness, and practical and theoretical considerations than to any change in the patient that could be established. Kaufman, Frank, Friend, Heims, and Weiss (1962) observed that frequency of treatment made no difference in their study of schizophrenic children. Lorr, McNair, Michaux, and Raskin (1962), in their study of intensive therapy with outpatient adults, found that treatment frequency made no difference in patient or therapist measures in four or eight months of therapy. Garetz (1964) analyzed questionnaire data from psychoanalysts as well as from non-psychoanalytic therapists. He found that there was no difference in "treatment-oriented behavior" between patients seen once a week and those seen more frequently by psychoanalysts, or between those seen less than or more than once a week by nonanalytic therapists. Cappon

(1964), reporting on his own private practice involving 160 patients, claimed that a treatment "density" of less than once a week is reliably less effective than once or twice a week, but there was no difference between once a week and more than once a week on any index he used. Marks and Gelder (1965) noted that cases treated more frequently with behavior therapy tended to be rated much improved, but the finding was not statistically reliable. Hain, Butcher, and Stevenson (1966) reported no relation between frequency and outcome with systematic desensitization. Similarly, Heilbrunn (1966) obtained no difference in outcome between those seen one to three times a week, two to three times, or three times.

In summation, there are more null than positive results regarding frequency of visits and outcome. Frequency greater than once a week is apparently not accompanied by comparably greater benefits. Although research has not yet conclusively confirmed it, there are suggestions that one visit a week is a working optimum that is noticeably better than less frequent contacts and no less effective than more frequent ones. Diagnostic considerations may be important in deciding on frequency, but they have not been examined. There is an absence of research on variable frequency schedules. The comparative benefits of greater initial frequency followed by spacing or of "demand" scheduling based upon fluctuating needs governed by life crises have not been systematically explored.

Unit Duration and Outcome. Few studies touch on unit duration. By and large, the time of the treatment session is based more upon custom as modified by experience than anything else. The traditional fifty-minute hour dwindles to forty-five minutes or half an hour as a matter of expediency. Practice is as often followed as preceded by theory and research. In Garetz's (1964) survey of psychoanalysts, respondents reported no differences in treatment-oriented behavior of those seen for less or more than thirty minutes. It would help to know if a half-hour session is more or less effective than an hour session. If it makes no difference, fees could go down and case loads could go up. This might not be too popular with therapists in institutional or private practice, but it would fulfill a social need. If indeed it does not help to see patients so frequently and for so long (total and unit time), the practices of therapists should be overhauled. The need to determine optimal temporal arrangements, while not a very attractive research enterprise for most investigators because of its "bread and butter" nature, is nonetheless waiting to be done in some definitive fashion.

An overview of temporal variables and outcome leads to the tentative conclusion that psychotherapy, when successful, achieves its major gains relatively early. Failures, too, soon make themselves apparent. A failure zone, according to Cartwright, lies between the thirteenth and twenty-first interviews. Some patients go on profitably, but beyond a certain point, therapy has been reported to yield diminishing returns. Precisely when this occurs is no doubt a unique function of the particular patient-therapist pair. General knowledge awaits comprehensive, longitudinal, repeated-measure research that may provide more information about expected curves of progress. It is clear that there is no simple one-to-one relation between duration or amount of therapy and outcome. Increasing frequency beyond once a week does not seem to have the desired additional effect. Length of therapy in terms of number of sessions bears a more consistent relation to outcome than do other measures that have been considered.

There is some evidence that setting time limits may facilitate and accelerate the therapeutic process. Once the notion of diminishing returns is accepted, time-limited therapy becomes more palatable. Research on optimal time limits needs to be done even though talk of time limits and of termination of long-term cases tends to make therapists anxious. Patients in long-term supportive therapy have been referred to as "interminable" and continued indefinitely in treatment for fear of serious repercussions if terminated. The therapist is fearful of breaking a long-established relationship that is assumed to be the glue binding the fragile ego of the patient and preventing its fragmentation. If treated in a clinic, such patients often have had a long series of therapists, easily making the transition from one to another as therapists move on. They may be thought of as having a relationship with the clinic or with therapy rather than with the therapist; treatment over the years becomes part of their life pattern. Wiener (1959) asked if arbitrary termination of such patients would truly result in dire consequences. When a therapist left the clinic at the St. Paul Veterans Administration Center, forty-eight of his patients were told that they could call if they felt they needed further treatment rather than being reassigned to another therapist. All their incoming calls, letters, and visits were followed up. Those who requested clinic service within six months were considered as returning patients, and those who did not were called nonreturning. Neither age, education, intake diagnosis, number of interviews, or somatic vs. psychic orientation was associated with returning. However, more of those with a year or more in treatment did return than those with less time. Apprehensions about termination proved to be groundless. In no case was there any dire consequence.

TERMINATORS AND REMAINERS

The problem of who survives in treatment is linked with many other issues in the study of psychotherapy. It is concerned with criteria of success, with the characteristics of the patient and therapist, with the effects of different settings and kinds of treatment, with prediction problems, with the ultimate fate and state of those who do not remain and of those who do, and with the issue of duration of treatment.

Terminators are patients who unilaterally decide to leave therapy at any point. Most commonly they are considered to be patients who have been accepted for treatment and have usually begun treatment but who have ended it prematurely. Some authors consider patients to be terminators if they have been accepted for treatment but do not appear. Levitt et al. referred to those who voluntarily terminate before the onset of treatment as "defectors" (Levitt, Beiser, & Robertson, 1959). The members of their treated group were required to have had at least five interviews. In another study, Levitt (1957b) again considered as defectors those patients who failed to appear for treatment, and as remainers those patients who attended at least twenty interviews. In a third study, Levitt (1958) classified as defectors those who did not begin treatment after having been accepted, and as remainers those who attended at least five interviews. The definition of "terminators" is consistent: those who avoid treatment after having been accepted. Other investigators regard as defectors those who end treatment after a small number of interviews. Terminators are separated from remainers at the fourth session by Frank et al. (1957) and Gliedman et al. (1957), at the fifth session by Katz and Solomon (1958) and Heilbrun and Sullivan (1962), at the sixth interview by Heilbrun (1961a, 1961b). Hiler (1959a, b), like Levitt, used separate time criteria; terminators were those who attended five or less interviews and remainers attended twenty or more. Some investigators employ an aspect of patient distribution, such as a cut-off point at the median (Sullivan et al., 1958) or some convenient division of subjects. Finally, some investigators study chosen therapeutic variables of patients who remain or leave treatment at successive time intervals (Lorr et al., 1962; Lorr & McNair, 1964a).

It is frequently impossible in reviewing published reports to distinguish between patients who are truly dropouts and those who have left after completing brief courses of therapy. The typically low median duration of therapy in most studies makes brief therapy the mode. It is not true that all patients who terminate treatment after the first six to twelve interviews have been unsuccessful. Rosenthal and Frank (1958) studied 384 patients accepted for psychotherapy by the Henry

Phipps Clinic, Baltimore. Of those accepted, 65 per cent attended at least one session. Of those attending, 42 per cent were discharged as improved, and of this number 32.5 per cent attended one to five sessions, 20.5 per cent attended six to ten sessions, 28.9 per cent attended eleven to twenty sessions. In summary, 82 per cent of those patients considered improved attended no more than twenty sessions. The expectations of the patient, the therapist, and the clinic administrators determine who is labeled a "dropout." The designation "dropout" or "terminator" may indicate a disagreement between patient and therapist about the goals to be achieved.

Some representative data from varied settings give a somewhat clearer picture of the extent of early termination, much of which is presumably premature and indicative of failure. Katz and Solomon (1958) reported that one-third of the patients at the Yale University Outpatient Clinic came only once, and one-third less than five times. Gallagher and Kanter (1961), reviewing 633 patients of a low-cost evening clinic, found that 23 per cent dropped out after one session. Of all applicants to the clinic, treatment was offered to 48 per cent, of whom 44 per cent remained for four or more interviews and 30 per cent for nine or more sessions. Frank et al. (1957) reported that 31 per cent leave treatment before the fourth session at the Henry Phipps Clinic. Lindsay (1965), discussing data from the outpatient service of a hospital in New Zealand, found that 982 of 1,056 patients (93 per cent) had nine or less interviews, and 707 of these 982 (72 per cent) had four or less interviews. Garfield and Kurz (1952) found that 27 per cent of 768 veterans to whom treatment was offered refused it, and 42.7 per cent had less than five interviews.

Some conspicuous exceptions to these high dropout rates, or very brief treatment series, have been reported. Lief et al. recorded a 6 per cent dropout rate of those accepted for treatment at the Tulane University Psychiatric Clinic (Lief, Lief, Warren, & Heath, 1961). Gundlach and Geller (1958) claim that 6 per cent of the cases of the Postgraduate Center for Psychotherapy terminate after one to five sessions. They report that of 129 patients entering treatment in 1958, thirty-two (25 per cent) had terminated by May, 1958, and that only eight had fewer than six sessions. These studies seem to present a different order of data. To place them in the context of the other studies, it is necessary to know the composition of the samples studied, the "stage" during which rejection of treatment takes place, and the intentions of the patient, the therapist, and the clinic. Sample and "stage" variables frequently may be closely related. Williams and Pollack (1964) specify the different "stages" of rejection of therapy. Their "closure" groups arrived for evaluation, but lost contact with the clinic before the treatment decision could be made. The "refuser" group rejected treatment after being accepted by the clinic. The "failure" group did not come for treatment after being accepted and, presumably, after accepting treatment. "Defector" patients dropped out of treatment after having started. The "treatment" group remained for treatment until the clinic decided that it was no longer necessary. Comparison of these functional groups may yield useful information when the sources of the patient samples are known. The characteristics of the terminator may be closely related to the experience he is rejecting. In the Lief et al. (1961) and Gundlach et al. (1958) reports, the 6 per cent of the patients who dropped out were patients who had selected themselves for treatment, had been selected by the clinic for treatment, and had experienced treatment, at least briefly. Both reports reveal specific and rigorous criteria for admission. The Lief et al. study records that 664 of 1,291 applicants (about 50 per cent) were rejected by the clinic for treatment. Apparently, such rigorous selection helps to reduce the risks of early termination and to insure that the patient will accept the clinic's view of the nature of treatment and its duration.

A few investigators have examined the problem of termination in a broader time perspective. Lorr and McNair (1964a) investigated the correlates of length of stay in psychotherapy instead of designating a fixed criterion for terminators. Their data, from forty-three Veterans Administration outpatient clinics, indicates that 28 per cent of their 500 patients dropped out before the eleventh month of treatment, and an additional 23 per cent before the twenty-third month. By the thirty-fifth month, a total of 64 per cent had left treatment. The range of treatment studied was from three to ninety-six months. No correlation of length of stay with either background or treatment measures was great enough to be important. One clue to problems of later termination may be the finding that the therapists reported that the greatest reduction in somatic complaints and the largest interpersonal changes occurred in the first year.

The characteristics of the terminated, those applicants rejected for treatment, will probably depend upon the type of patients served by a clinic or hospital and upon the criteria for the kind of treatment offered by the clinic. Institutions specializing in a particular treatment method may be highly selective. Most public clinics, serving any applying citizen, are able to reject relatively few. Of the fifty-three clinics studied by Rogers (1960), one was a Veterans Administration clinic required by law to serve veterans with disabilities incurred in military service. It had the highest percentage of remaining patients with the smallest possibility of being selective. Rosenthal and Frank (1958) reported that 45 per cent of 3,413 new patients were accepted for various kinds of psychotherapy at the Henry Phipps Clinic. Comparing a sample of 384 patients referred for individual psychotherapy to the 3,413 new applicants, they found the preferred patients were more usually white, better educated, and of upper rather than lower income levels. The Psychoanalytic Clinic at Columbia University recorded data on 1,348 patients who had completed treatment (Weber, Elinson, & Moss, 1967). Of these, 54.6 per cent had at least some college education, 33.8 per cent had professional occupations, and at least 73 per cent were below thirty-five years of age. Williams and Pollack (1964) compared several groups accepted for treatment with the population of which they were part. The clinic was a free outpatient clinic for children that accepts 20 per cent of its diagnosed cases for treatment. The accepted children differed from the general sample in several respects: they were usually of school age, more were white than Negro, more came from families with less than four children, more were referred by parents or the school, more were from Jewish families, and more were from families with two parents present. Williams and Pollack presented in one group those patients who lost contact with the clinic before a treatment could be made. They were most like the general sample and least like those patients accepted for treatment. The clinics in these studies selected patients who met psychological criteria for the kinds of psychotherapy offered. The interplay of clinic selection and self-selection is revealed in the Williams and Pollack study. The patients who refused treatment when it was offered and those who did not report when treatment was offered differed from those who did begin treatment principally in the religion of the children's parents. Clearly, the more important and extensive differences are between those accepted and those rejected.

Patient Characteristics. Williams and Pollack found no differences in demographic variables between those patients who failed to report and those who defected once treatment had started. Both kinds of patients possessed characteristics associated with their acceptance for treatment. Investigators have studied many demographic variables and have turned up some socioeconomic differences between terminators and remainers. Bailey, Warshaw, and Eichler (1959) found significant educational differences in favor of the outpatients who remained more than two months. Rubinstein and Lorr (1956) discovered that an index of education, occupation, and vocabulary differentiated between those who left before five sessions and those who remained for at least twenty-six. Sullivan, Miller, and Smelser (1958) reported significant differences in education and occupation between terminators and remainers, using nine sessions as a dividing point. Stieper and Wiener

(1965) offered their firmest predictor of a patient's remaining beyond the fourth session: his mother being a housewife.

Studies of patients in other clinics yield similar results. Of the many variables studied, the few significant differences are of socioeconomic variables. Garfield and Affleck (1959) at the Nebraska Psychiatric Institute and Frank et al. (1957) at the Henry Phipps Clinic found no demographic differences. Rosenthal and Frank (1958), studying another Phipps sample, reported significant differences between those who stayed for more than six hours and those who did not in sex (more males stay), in race (more whites stay), and in education (the more educated stay). Gallagher and Kanter (1961), at the Boston Evening Clinic, divided patients at the ninth session and found Hollingshead's socioeconomic index to be a significant discriminator. Katz and Solomon (1958) presented unanalyzed percentages that indicated that the younger, better educated patients of higher occupational status tended to stay beyond five sessions at the Yale University Outpatient Clinic. Studies of child patients, after the examination of many demographic variables, yield no significant differences (Levitt, 1957b; Tuckman & Lavell, 1959) or report that remaining in treatment is associated significantly (Lake & Levinger, 1960) or tentatively (Ross & Lacey, 1961) with some aspect of parental socioeconomic status.

Socioeconomic variables do not seem to be of importance by themselves. What would seem to be significant are the psychological implications of the social position of the patient: his learned behaviors, roles, attitudes, expectancies, and traits. Therefore, in any inquiry about the personality of terminators and remainers, the composition of the sample studied is of the greatest importance. Dymond's (1955) study of a very small sample found terminators to be "rugged individualists." The remainer group had nearly twice as many males and students as did the terminators. Heilbrun (1961a, 1961b, 1962) obtained data from students applying to the University of Iowa Counseling Service. The client who conforms most to the expected cultural stereotype of masculinity or femininity tends to terminate early. Immature, inadequate males tend to remain as do independent female clients. The orientation of the center is to encourage independence. The dependent female client may, then, find that her expectations are realizable more easily outside the counseling situation since female dependency is more congruent with cultural expectations. A desirable addition to the Heilbrun study would have been the systematic variation of the sex of the counselor. However, the developmental, educational, and adjustment problems of college students are not necessarily a representative sample of behavioral disorders. The Heilbrun findings should be examined in other therapeutic contexts.

In studying patients who apply to Veterans Administration outpatient clinics for treatment, Rubinstein and Lorr (1956), in a well-designed study bearing its own replication, found terminators to be more impulsive, restless, and nomadic than remainers. The terminators (patients with five or less visits) were more conventional, uncompromising in their views, and less dissatisfied with themselves. In a closely related study, Lorr, Katz, and Rubinstein (1958) sought to confirm the findings with a new sample of nonpsychotic patients. They found that terminators do not report anxiety, are lacking in psychological sophistication and "insight," and are authoritarian. Remainers are anxious, dissatisfied with themselves, and willing to explore their problems with others. These results are based upon the significant differences between the two groups on several personality questionnaires and inventories.

Taulbee (1958), dividing terminators from remainers at the thirteenth session, found differences in personality obtained by Rorschach and MMPI responses. Continuers were higher on MMPI symptom scales (D, Pa, Pt, Sc) and gave significantly more Rorschach responses, rejecting fewer Rorschach cards. Taulbee interprets these findings as an indication that continuers are less defensive, more persistent, anxious, and dependent than those who leave. His claim that remainers are more like normals in their Rorschach and MMPI scores is somewhat belied by the remainers' elevated MMPI patterns and the absence of an actual normal control group. Nevertheless, his results are congruent with Lorr's findings. Sullivan, Miller, and Smelser (1958), with another Veterans Administration sample, found no significant differences on the MMPI between those who stay in treatment and those who leave.

Other studies of the personality traits of terminators are more fragmentary. Katz and Solomon (1958) characterize continuers as more hopeful and fearful and regard this attitude as the best indicator of length of contact. However, all data were abstracted from case histories and none were evaluated statistically. Yalom (1966), at Stanford's Outpatient Clinic, found four of thirty-three variables to differentiate between those who stay and those who leave. One of these was a personality characteristic, curiosity about others. Dropouts had significantly less curiosity than those who stayed. Frank et al. (1957) reported that suggestible patients tend to remain in treatment. Finally, in a carefully executed study with a replication sample, Strickland and Crowne (1963) demonstrated their hypothesis that patients with a high need for approval are more likely to terminate treatment early, presumably because of their defensiveness.

So far as child patients are concerned, most studies deal with a mixture of socioeconomic, case historical, and the child's and his parents' personality characteristics. Levitt (1957b) found no significant differences. Ross and Lacey (1961) reported some significant differences. Of those predicted, child remainers have reduced social responsiveness; of unpredicted characteristics, terminators tend to run away. Lake and Levinger (1960) found that parents of remainers, significantly more than parents of terminators, wish to change themselves or their families. The weakness of these studies and many other studies of terminators is that the cases surveyed are closed cases. The data are patient reports and interviewers' records, neither necessarily complete nor accurate for future research purposes or accurate researcher coding.

Predictors. The obvious benefit of being able to tell in advance who is likely to terminate prematurely has spurred many efforts to find predictive patient characteristics. Some researchers advance prediction variables by hypothesis; some explore differences between terminators and remainers. The explorations yield differences that are then offered as predictors. A validating study is then required in which the "predictor" is the independent variable and stay in therapy the dependent variable. Some investigators do not follow an exploratory study with one in which the discovered predictor functions as a predictor. Studies of both kinds are fairly abundant.

Many kinds of variables have been investigated for their potency as predictors. Psychiatric diagnosis usually proves a poor predictor of dropouts (Gallagher & Kanter, 1961; Katz & Solomon, 1958; Garfield & Affleck, 1959; Rosenthal & Frank, 1958). One exception to this summary is the Frank, Gliedman, Imber, Nash, and Stone (1957) study. This study of dropouts reports that those diagnosed as having anxiety or depressive reactions remained significantly longer than others. Studies of symptoms or initial complaints have yielded more promising results. Bodily complaints are believed to be associated with early termination; psychological complaints, with the implication of dissatisfaction with self and some willingness to change, have been thought to be associated with remaining in therapy. Hiler (1959a), establishing rather than predicting group differences, found that both terminators and remainers complain of bodily symptoms. Terminators are more likely to complain of them. Remainers more frequently complain of psychological disturbance. Terminators have complaints of assaultiveness, irrationality, and paranoid ideation. Lorr, Katz, and Rubinstein (1958) report that terminators have complaints of frequent trouble with the law because of antisocial acts. Ross and Lacey (1961) report the unpredicted result that remainers have a higher incidence of somatic disorders. Their primary subjects were children. Children are likely to express anxiety in somatic terms. The terminators in this study more often had histories of truancy, a finding congruent with results of studies on adults.

Of the psychological tests studied for predictive purposes, the Rorschach test has been the most popular. Rogers, Knauss, and Hammond (1951) asked three psychologists to evaluate the Rorschach in a "total impression" manner and to predict which patients of a group of eighty-seven would not return after less than five interviews. There were unequal numbers of terminators and remainers. The predictions were not better than chance. Tests of significance of differences were calculated for ninety-nine Rorschach categories. These, too, proved failures. Kotkov and Meadow (1952) derived a weighted Rorschach index on a sample of ninety-eight patients in group therapy that correctly classified 69 per cent of the terminators and remainers. Applying their prediction formula in individual therapy, they again achieved 69 per cent correct predictions (Kotkov & Meadow, 1953). Gibby, Stotsky, Miller, and Hiler (1953) found that a number of Rorschach signs discriminated between terminators and remainers. Upon application of a derived prediction formula involving R, K, and m to another sample, their predictions of who would terminate or remain proved 67 per cent accurate (Gibby, Stotsky, Hiler, & Miller, 1954). As in the Kotkov-Meadow formula, the terminators were predicted with greater accuracy (87 per cent). It was also discovered that the number of Rorschach responses (R) by itself classified 69 per cent of terminators and remainers successfully. Auld and Eron (1953), using the Kotkov-Meadow formula on a sample of thirty-three patients, obtained correct predictions in 52 per cent of the cases. The only promising Rorschach variable, number of responses, was found not to be significantly associated with continuance.

Affleck and Mednick (1959) developed a discriminant function formula on a sample of seventy-five patients and cross-validated the formula on a new sample of fifty terminators (three or less interviews) and fifty remainers (more than four interviews). Taking base rates into account, they obtained 63 per cent correct predictions, a 13 per cent improvement over calling every patient a terminator. The number of responses contributes heavily as a predictive variable. Taulbee (1958) divided terminators from remainers at the thirteenth interview and compared each group with fifty "normal" members of the community. His principal Rorschach finding was that those who continue give more responses than those who leave therapy. The finding, a common result of Rorschach studies, indicates the greater willingness of the remainer to behave and to verbalize in the therapeutic situation. This characteristic requires further exploration with instruments designed for any variables hypothesized as its determinants.

Studies using both standard and newly assembled scales of the MMPI have been inconclusive. Sullivan, Miller, and Smelser (1958), with 268 cases divided at the ninth session, found no significant differences on any MMPI scale. Taulbee (1958), separating eighty-five patients at the thirteenth session, reported a significant increase in scores on some of the symptom scales (Depression, Paranoia, Psychasthenia, and Schizophrenia). No cross-validation was made. Hiler (1959b) found that fifteen items of the Michigan Sentence Completion Test discriminated between terminators (five sessions or less) and remainers (twenty sessions or more). Five items discriminated with 71 per cent accuracy. A clinician using protocols globally predicted with 68 per cent accuracy.

Libo (1957) examined liking or attraction of a therapist by the patient in relation to return or failure to return for treatment. For this purpose he developed the Picture Impressions technique, a projective device consisting of four picture cards each portraying a patient-therapist situation for which the patient is asked to tell a story. A reliable scoring system was established, and the technique was applied to forty consecutive incoming patients. A prediction of return was made if attraction was expressed in the stories. A significant chi-square between predicted and actual attendance led Libo to the unfounded conclusion that the technique was a more accurate predictor than would be expected from knowledge of the clinic's total return rate. Of those who returned, 77.4 per cent were correctly identified (the number of valid positives). The percentage of false positives (return predicted when patients actually did not return) was 33.33 per cent. The actual base rate of return was 77.5 per cent. If Bayes' rule for calculating inverse probability is applied, it can be seen that the test yields more erroneous classifications than would be made by proceeding without it. If the prediction "will return" were made for all cases, it would have been correct 77.5 per cent of the time. The test made correct predictions 75 per cent of the time.

If a single test does not enable one to predict well, an investigator could use several tests in a battery to improve prediction. Lorr and his colleagues have conducted several well-designed studies employing differing batteries. Usually the subjects have been divided into two sizable subsamples. In one study (Lorr, Katz, & Rubinstein, 1958), scoring by an a priori test key was unsuccessful in differentiating terminators from remainers. In another study (Rubinstein & Lorr, 1956), the separate tests of the battery, two personal inventories, a self-rating scale, a brief modification of the F (authoritarianism) scale, and a vocabulary-education-occupation index all differentiated significantly for one or both subsamples. Using ten predictors, eight of which were personality tests and questionnaires, McNair, Lorr, and Callahan (1963), obtained significant differences for all ten. Using scores of the three terminator-remainer questionnaires in a multiple regression equation, the investigators were able to predict with 69 per cent accuracy. The three terminator-remainer questionnaires contained items from the Manifest Anxiety, Behavior Disturbance, and F scales. Heilbrun and Sullivan's (1962) Counseling Readiness Scale discriminated between male terminators and remainers but not females, but in Heilbrun (1964) it was more accurate with females. The scale was better at selecting remainers than terminators.

In many clinical situations, evaluation of the patient and the likelihood of his early termination is made by judgments of the staff. The following studies concern such judgments made from patient behavior, records, or ratings by the judges or others. White, Fichtenbaum, and Dollard (1964) attempted to predict the return of patients for three additional interviews. The predictor was a ratio of favorable to unfavorable statements about therapy and the therapist. Using the unscored, transcribed interview, two staff therapists predicted no better than chance. The investigators obtained 81 per cent correct predictions when the scores were applied. The question is whether or not ratings of this intratherapeutic behavior can be predictive of therapy of longer duration. Garfield and Affleck (1961) required thirteen therapists to rate each patient after presenting the patient to the staff. Ratings were made of anxiety; defensiveness; patient's assets, deficiencies, and goals; and rater's feelings, interests toward patient, and view of prognosis. Only the ratings of prognosis were significantly related to duration of stay (median interviews kept were seventeen). Dividing patients at the seventh interview, Affleck and Garfield (1961) asked three staff members, five residents, and four student social workers to rate fifty-seven outpatients after their presentation to the staff. There were no significant differences between terminators and remainers on any of the fifteen variables rated. Garfield, Affleck, and Muffly (1963) asked three experienced therapists to listen to recordings of first sessions. The judges, the patients, and the therapists completed various rating scales. Predictions of therapists and judges of patients terminating before the fifth interview did not exceed 14 per cent accuracy. Some significant differences between terminators and remainers emerged as the extreme thirds of the sample were compared on the therapist's judgments of the patient's intelligence, achievement, acceptability, and adequacy of communication.

The exploratory nature of many of these studies suggests the need for hypotheses and replication in studies of prediction. Evaluation requires the investigator to select a relevant base rate for comparison with his own prediction especially since there is no established point at which a terminator becomes a terminator. Beyond these considerations, complexities abound. Many investigators have arranged their studies as if there were a characteristic of "terminating" inherent in the patient. Prediction, except in large-scale terms, is meaningless unless all the variables in the therapeutic situation are taken into account. What are the patient's goals? Are they congruent with those of the therapist? Is the patient who reluctantly or *pro forma* attends therapeutic sessions in order to obtain his tranquilizer truly a remainer? Should the patient who quickly experiences catharsis and leaves be considered a dropout? In many studies students and inexperienced therapists are given the task of interviewing and evaluating new patients. These preliminary meetings may very well determine whether or not the patient believes that he will be able to reach his goals. The little evidence now available suggests that the inexperienced therapist is less able to retain patients. Whether the patient drops out or is dropped is a most relevant issue. Any prediction of termination will have to take into consideration not only the terminator but also the characteristics of the assistance that he is rejecting.

Therapist Characteristics. What contributions do characteristics of the therapist make to remaining in therapy? McNair, Lorr, and Callahan (1963) divided 282 patients into remainers or terminators, the latter being those who refused or ended therapy by the sixteenth week. No significant differences were found in therapists grouped according to profession, personal therapy, judged competence, or Whitehorn-Betz Type A or B. Experienced therapists held 72 per cent of their patients, the less experienced only 60 per cent. Therapists with high liking for their patients retained 72 per cent, those with low liking 59 per cent. If the therapist was interested in the patient's problem, he kept 77 per cent, if not, 54 per cent. Female therapists held significantly more patients than did male therapists. Several of these findings were *post hoc*, but they are certainly worth pursuing. Hiler (1958), using varying numbers of patients and therapists, also found that female therapists kept more patients. Evaluating patient productivity from Rorschach performance, he reported that female therapists retain the unproductive but lose the highly productive patients. This kind of productivity is associated with the retention of patients by male therapists. "Warm" therapists keep both productive and unproductive patients; "cold" therapists keep mostly the productive ones. Therapists rated "competent" lose significantly fewer productive, well-motivated patients. Neither the profession nor the passivity of the therapist yielded any significant differences in Hiler's study. Sullivan, Miller, and Smelser (1958) found no significant differences in patient retention when the training, experience, and sex of the therapist were considered.

Garfield, Affleck, and Muffly (1963) divided remainers from terminators at the median number of interviews, between six and seven. The twenty-four patients and the six therapists, two experienced psychologists and four second-year residents, rated the first and fifth interviews and completed various scales. The therapist's attitude scale responses and rating of the patient's behavior yielded no significant differences between terminators and remainers. The data "suggest" that a discrepancy between therapist's and patient's view of the first interview may be related to early termination. Therapists rated more competent by judges tend to hold more patients (although the relation was not statistically significant). The congruence of the patient's and therapist's regard for each other may be related to remaining in therapy. Six or seven interviews do not make a remainer. However, the study is carefully done and full of variables for future investigation.

An earlier study (Garfield & Affleck, 1959) reported on the initiation of termination. The therapists of 135 patients were inexperienced psychiatric residents. Patients initiated 61 per cent of terminations before the ninth interview and 39 per cent after the twenty-first; therapists initiated 82 per cent of terminations between the ninth and twenty-first interview. It is impossible to interpret these data. No criteria are reported. One patient leaves because he feels better, another because he feels worse. Inexperienced therapists may be pleased with a casual improvement or may become disheartened during Cartwright's "failure zone." Several investigators have studied the effect of therapist experience on the retention of patients. Baum, Felzer, D'Zmura, and Shumaker (1966) compared seven therapists with from four to twenty-one years of experience with thirteen therapists of from zero to three years of experience. The less experienced had a 46 per cent dropout rate, the more experienced 16 per cent. This confirms the finding of McNair, Lorr, and Callahan (1963), and was also seen in Poser's (1966) study.

Caracena (1965) studied six counselors with four to ten years of experience, twelve counselors with one year of supervised experience, and twelve practicum students. Staff therapists approached client dependency statements more than the less experienced, but approach to dependency did not differentiate the remainers from the terminators. Clients who were liked by the therapists were more likely to remain in therapy than clients who were disliked. Winder, Ahmad, Bandura, and Rau (1962) also studied the responses of therapists to patient dependency. The therapists were seventeen graduate students in clinical psychology. The patients were twenty-three parents of children in treatment. Termination was significantly higher when the therapist avoided dependency and remaining was higher when the therapist approached dependency. Terminators and remainers did not differ on other related variables. There is no doubt that the therapist's management of dependency is the determinative variable in this careful study. The study of this variable should be extended to more disturbed subjects.

Heilbrun (1961b) explored the effects of high and average dominance in counselors upon male and female student clients. The counselors were graduate students. For counselors high in dominance, the more autonomous females tended to continue, the less autonomous to terminate early. The reverse was true of counselors of average dominance. No such interaction was true of male clients. The males who remain are the more immature and inadequate clients. The differing results by sex remain an interesting problem for further study.

The issue of counselor-client similarity was studied in relation to termination by Mendelsohn and Geller (1963) and by Mendelsohn (1966). The earlier study yielded low but significant correlations between dissimilarity on the Myers-Briggs Type Indicator and early termination. The second study was a replication and confirmed the findings. Dissimilarity seems to be a limiting condition. Sex matching of counselors and clients gave no significant results. The findings are interesting but should be confirmed on longer therapeutic series with more disturbed subjects and with variables more closely related to the psychotherapeutic situation than the Jungian typological questionnaire employed here.

These studies offer central problems to the investigator. Which therapists retain which patients? Do female therapists retain more patients? If so, do they retain the more or less productive patients? The studies summarized here, except for the Mendelsohn and Geller studies, do not provide for systematic variation of patients and therapists by sex. Therapeutic experience has not been studied carefully. The therapist's behavior in initial interviews as a determinant of patient retention has scarcely been studied. This important area in psychotherapy remains to be more thoroughly investigated.

Other Contributing Factors. The effect of therapeutic setting, goal, and kind of therapy upon early termination tend to be closely associated in research as in clinical practice. There is little systematic research. Most studies of terminators have been conducted in large public clinics. Private practitioners offer virtually no data. In Gundlach and Geller's (1958) study, they report 6 per cent termination during the first five sessions at their psychoanalytic clinic. They believe that their patients are much like those of other outpatient clinics in age, social status, and problems, but data are not presented. What are the goals of the patients? Does referral or self-referral function selectively? What are the consequences of screening procedures, the waiting period, and the fee schedule? No current research answers these questions or offers exact comparisons with other kinds of settings. Michaux and Lorr (1961) present data on treatment intensity and the therapist's goals for the patient. Patients were scheduled for biweekly, once weekly, or twice weekly sessions. The goals of the therapists of sixty dropout cases were agreed upon by judges. Seventy per cent of these cases had reconstructive goals, 12 per cent had supportive goals, and 18 per cent had relationship goals. The therapists' initial goals were not independent of scheduled treatment frequencies. However, reconstructive goals were less frequent in twice weekly and more frequent in biweekly patients than expected.

Clinics offer differing modes of treatment. There are few studies of the termination rates of these different kinds of treatment, and certainly no studies of the influence of differing modes by kinds of clinics upon termination rates. Frank, Gliedman, Imber, Nash, and Stone (1957) compared termination rates of group therapy, individual therapy, and minimal individual therapy. Patients were assigned randomly to therapists and type of therapy. Dropout rates were 44 per cent for group therapy, 27 per cent for minimal individual therapy, and 14 per cent for standard individual therapy after the fourth session. Unfortunately, more complex analyses of data were not made.

Gallagher and Kanter (1961) compared dropout rates of patients attending group and individual therapy. Most patients (83 per cent) received group psychotherapy. There were no significant differences in termination rates from the first to the twenty-first interview. Yalom (1966) reported a termination rate of 33.8 per cent for middle-class, fee-paying patients in group treatment after twelve sessions. Scher and Johnson (1964) found a 25 per cent loss of patients attending group therapy after a month in an "aftercare" clinic. These studies are exploratory and reveal the need for more detailed and sophisticated comparative research.

Follow-up. What of the ultimate fate of patients who reject or prematurely leave therapy? Some clinicians hold an informal hypothesis that this early retreat from psychotherapy is followed by an eventually successful stay in therapy. The tooth that stops hurting in the dentist's waiting room must finally be treated. Tolman and Meyer (1957) surveyed 431 clinic outpatients who were judged "not treated" because they came fewer than five times. Of these, 5.8 per cent returned to the clinic later. These patients did not differ from the clinic's usual patient on initial application. Brandt (1964) studied 155 patients who applied for treatment at a psychoanalytic clinic but did not come for an appointment arranged within four months of application. Follow-up reached one hundred. Sixty-three patients had entered treatment elsewhere, and twenty-eight were still in treatment at the time of the survey. The variable waiting period, the patient's choice of a particular kind of therapy, and the socioeconomic characteristics of the patients render it difficult to generalize from this study. Yalom (1966) reported on thirty-five dropouts from group therapy. Following them over a three- to six-month period, he found that fifteen had no subsequent therapy. Another ultimate issue is the effect of terminating or remaining after treatment has ended. Of the twenty dropouts who later returned to treatment, 40 per cent reported subsequent benefit. There is no comparison with remainers who completed a course of treatment.

In summary, despite extensive research on terminators and remainers there are wide gaps in our knowledge. It is an area that presents central therapeutic issues for the systematic investigator. If terminators are considered to be patients who have ended treatment prematurely, by whose standards is the termination premature? To interpret much of the data, one must have information not only of the goals of the therapist and the clinic, but also of the purposes of the patient. Available evidence indicates that most courses of treatment are shorter than twelve sessions. There are some indications that patients who accept long-term treatment have been carefully selected for their agreement with the purposes of the therapist or clinic. Patients who reject treatment or are rejected by treating institutions seem to differ from remainers in socioeconomic variables. These fairly consistent findings may not indicate the importance of these socioeconomic variables but do have implications for the patient's understanding of his problems and the appropriate remedy. Hostile, independent, somatically oriented patients tend to leave early; anxious, curious, and not too defensive patients tend to remain.

Good predictors would save time and increase therapeutic efficiency. Interest in bodily symptoms and socioeconomic status are not invariant predictors of stay in treatment. Of test variables, the number of responses on the Rorschach test seems the most promising. It seems to reveal the patient's willingness to verbalize in the therapeutic situation. Perhaps a more direct test of this characteristic would be profitable. Multitest batteries have yielded interesting results. However, they involve time-consuming procedures and may present sample-specific problems. A more sophisticated approach to premature termination involves the exploration of the therapist and treatment situation to which the patient may be responding. The experience, sex, and regard of the therapist may, pilot studies suggest, influence the early success or failure of the therapeutic relationship. The kind of treatment offered and the "climate" of the clinic may modify patient response. For the ultimate fate of terminators and remainers, we must again return to the patient's goals rather than to unevaluated lists of percentages.

PART III

RESEARCH ON THE PROCESS OF PSYCHOTHERAPY

In this world, second thoughts, it seems, are best.

—EURIPIDES, *Hippolytus*

Analogies prove nothing, that is quite true, but they can make one feel more at home.

—SIGMUND FREUD, *New Introductory Lectures on Psychoanalysis*

In the fields of observation, chance favors only the mind that is prepared.

—LOUIS PASTEUR, in VALLERY-RODOT, *Life of Pasteur*

14

The Therapist as a Variable in the Therapeutic Process

PROFESSIONAL DISCIPLINE, ATTITUDES, AND PERFORMANCE

Opinions have often been expressed about similarities and differences in therapeutic attitudes and practices of members of the different professional disciplines who render psychotherapy. Such considerations serve as guides in therapist selection by patients and referral sources and in matters of case assignment in institutions. Whether or not professional identity and the training that leads to the establishment of this identity have a bearing upon the therapeutic function is a question that has been approached by a handful of researchers.

Eells (1964) surveyed the views and preferences concerning intake cases of a group of eighteen staff members at the Veterans Administration Clinic, Los Angeles. The group consisted entirely of experienced therapists and was relatively homogeneous, with mainly a psychoanalytic or modified psychoanalytic orientation. The sample consisted of seven psychiatrists, six clinical psychologists, and five social workers. They were presented with sixty thumbnail sketches of various kinds of patients who might be referred to this kind of clinic and were asked to Q-sort them in terms of the importance of having such patients accepted for treatment. In addition, they were requested to specify the order of importance of principles they used in arriving at the decision and to indicate the point at which they would recommend that treatment be denied even if it were available. A second Q-sort was performed in which they were asked to arrange the sketches in order of their personal preference for taking on such a patient in therapy. The scores for each therapist were intercorrelated with those of every other therapist, and linkage analysis was applied to the resulting matrix to determine the extent to which they tended to fall into homogeneous groups. There were no differences among the three professional groups in judging either the importance of accepting different kinds of patients or their preference for particular types of cases. There was a difference, however, in the degree of concordance between views and preferences, with psychologists being most concordant, social workers least, and psychiatrists distributed over the entire range. The discrepancies shown were chiefly in the acknowledgment that a particular kind of patient should be seen, but in the indicated preference that the assignment be made to someone else. The sample from each professional discipline was small and homogeneous and could hardly be considered sufficiently representative of the views and preferences of these disciplines to permit generalizations about either the observed similarities or differences.

As one phase of his larger study employing the technique of having subjects respond as the therapist would at pause points of interrupted filmed interviews, Strupp (1955b) was able to contrast the technique of twenty-five psychiatrists, seven psychologists, and nine social workers. Techniques were classified into twelve Bales interaction categories. The professional groups contained varying percentages of experienced and inexperienced persons. Strupp could not separate out the exact effects of professional discipline by the statistical technique used. Of the twelve technique categories, the only one that he feels was a function of professional affiliation was the greater use of reassurance by social workers. Again, the lack of representativeness of the sample prohibits generalization.

Using the same interrupted film technique, Strupp (1958a) contrasted hypothetical therapist responses of fifty-five psychiatrists and an equal number of psychologists matched in experience and personal analysis and obtained data from a questionnaire about such things as diagnostic impressions, treatment plans, and goals. No significant differences between the two professional groups were reflected in diagnosis, description of defense mechanisms, formulation of dynamics, prognosis, or attitude toward the patient. There was a significant difference in their judgment of therapeutic goals for this particular patient. The psychologists stressed goals such as insight and self-acceptance, but the psychiatrists entertained the more modest goal of symptom relief. They were similar on many aspects of therapeutic approach and technique. Among the relatively few differences that appeared were that the psychiatrists expected more acting out from their patients and would discourage it, would be stricter, and would discourage free association. The psychologists advocated a more intensive form of therapy. From the responses to the film it was seen that psychiatrists asked more exploratory questions whereas the psychologists reflected feeling and were more likely to go along with the patient's frame of reference. Otherwise, psychologists and psychiatrists were quite similar in modes of communication.

Approaching the issue from the point of view of differences among professional groups in professed rather than measured technique, McNair and Lorr (1964a) surveyed a sample of sixty-seven psychiatrists, 103 psychologists, and ninety-five social workers. The group averaged 10.1 years of experience. The researchers constructed a series of eight-point statements on which therapists were asked to indicate their degree of agreement. These were empirically pared down to forty-nine variables in number. When the variables were factor analyzed, three hypothesized technique factors were extracted. Factor A represented a psychoanalytically oriented treatment approach with emphasis on such variables as childhood experiences, interpretation, dream analysis, resistance and transference, free association, and emphasis on the unconscious. Those high on Factor I endorsed a detached, objective, impersonal mode of relating, while those low on this factor endorsed relationship therapy characterized by a close personal and human interaction with the patient. The two poles of Factor D contrasted directive techniques and active therapist role with an inactive approach that left the goals and direction to the patient. Psychiatrists were found to be concentrated in high Factor A patterns, with one-third endorsing a preference for psychoanalytically derived techniques couched in an impersonal relationship in which the therapist controlled the therapeutic course. Psychologists, apparently more influenced by the Rogerian position, endorsed techniques that featured a personal, affective relationship with the goals and direction left to the patient. Social workers revealed two main preference patterns, both of which were nonanalytic and controlling of the course of treatment. Nevertheless, one-fourth showed preference for personal-directive techniques and another one-fourth for impersonal-directive. It was pointed out that since the social workers were predominantly female and the patient population mostly male, sex and profession may have been confounded. This is a good study of professed therapeutic approaches based on an unusually broad national sample of Veterans Administration clinic therapists. The types of therapeutic techniques and attitudes surveyed were the kind that could be objectively reported by therapists and appear likely (although not necessarily) to correspond to actual practice.

In their study on patient and therapist influences on quitting therapy, McNair et al. found no general difference between psychiatrists, psychologists, and social workers in the number of patients who remained or terminated therapy in less than sixteen weeks without the advice or consent of the therapist (McNair, Lorr, & Callahan, 1963). Excessive length of time in therapy has also been studied in an investigation of the problem of interminability in outpatient psychotherapy (Stieper & Wiener, 1959). Sampling 130 patients of eight experienced therapists, they uncovered no concentration of long-term patients in any one discipline. Only three psychiatrists, two social workers, and two psychologists, however, were represented in the sample.

In summary, there is hardly enough research from which to draw conclusions of any scope or definitiveness about whether the professional discipline of the therapist is a significant determinant of either the outcome of therapy or the approaches employed. As groups, there is essentially no differencee in their views and attitudes and preferences for patients. There is some slight indication that psychiatrists as a group lean more toward impersonal, psychoanalytically derived techniques in which they control the course of therapy; that psychologists prefer more personal, affective, and patient-directed relationships; and that social workers tend toward either personal or impersonal but nonetheless more directive approaches. There is a great deal of overlap between the groups, and these preferences can be considered group tendencies that may reflect something more basic than professional affiliation, therapeutic orientation, or "school."

EFFECT OF "SCHOOL" OR ORIENTATION OF THERAPIST ON PRACTICES AND ATTITUDES

Fiedler's (1950a) investigation of the concept of an ideal therapeutic relationship utilized four psychoanalytically oriented therapists, two nondirective therapists, and two eclectic ones. A second study sampled seven different subjects including an Adlerian. It was concluded that description of an ideal therapeutic relationship is not a function of the "school" of the therapist, but the sample was small and unrepresentative. Raskin (1965) obtained similar results with a much larger sample of fifty-two experienced therapists of whom seventeen were Freudian, sixteen client-centered, eleven eclectic, and eight other (existential, experiential, Sullivanian, Adlerian, gestalt, and transactional). Also sampled were twenty-six graduate students in clinical psychology with Freudian, client-centered, and eclectic viewpoints. The Freudian, client-centered, and eclectic therapists showed high agreement on the characteristics of the ideal therapist even though the dimensions supplied cut across specific technique lines.

In another small-sample study by Strupp (1955a) eight Rogerians were compared with seven non-Rogerians. The subjects were asked to supply the responses they would give to twenty-seven patient statements, and these responses were categorized by the Bales system. As expected, the two groups differed across most categories. In a subsequent study (Strupp, 1958c), utilizing the sound film interruption technique, no differences between sixteen orthodox Freudians and sixteen neo-Freudians were found when the communications were analyzed. Using the same technique, Strupp (1958b) compared fourteen Rogerian psychologists with sixty-four psychoanalytically oriented psychologists. Sixty-seven per cent of Rogerians' responses favored reflection of feelings. Analytically oriented therapists preferred exploratory questions (40 per cent of the total). Insofar as clinical evaluation of the patient was concerned, the two groups did not differ. The Rogerians, however, saw the prognosis as significantly more favorable, and more professed a positive attitude toward the patient. Considerable differences in attitudes and therapeutic strategies emerged. Rogerians were less concerned with poor motivation, excessive dependency, acting out, countertransference, and problems of technique. They were less apt to designate areas for focus or particularize attitudes and behaviors to be encouraged or discouraged. Analytically oriented therapists favored inducing changes by such means as interpretation while Rogerians left things to the patient in the hope of arriving at a corrective emotional experience. As previously noted, there is no assurance that performance in this simulated situation duplicates the way the therapists would behave in an actual encounter, but the responses of the Rogerians seem to characterize their approach.

Wrenn (1960) asked fifty-four counselors of varying orientations (phenomenological, analytic, eclectic) to respond by mail to thirteen excerpts from counseling interviews in which the counselor statement was left open. Responses were compared on nine Bales categories and on degree of lead, assignment of responsibility, response to the core of the client remark, and response to content or feeling aspects. The core of the client's remarks was responded to 85 per cent of the time regardless of the theoretical orientation of the counselor or the particular counseling situation; counselors responded to the feeling aspects 83 per cent of the time. The client was given primary responsibility most of the time, and the degree of lead was low. The only category that showed a significant difference was the less frequent use of reflection by analysts than by phenomenologists or eclectics. Theoretical orientation thus had little influence on mode of counselor response.

Wallach and Strupp (1964) factor analyzed a seventeen-item scale of therapeutic practices. Twenty-one orthodox Freudian, 116 general psychoanalytic, twenty-eight Sullivanian, and thirty client-centered therapists were compared on four of the factors that were found. The four factors were (I) maintenance of personal distance, (II) preference for intensive psychotherapy (psychoanalytic, uncovering), (III) preference for keeping verbal interventions to a minimum, (IV) view of therapy as a flexible artistic and artful activity. Significant F-values for Factors II, III, IV across the four orientation groups were reported and interpreted. The authors acknowledged that they were unsure of the meaning of the factors. The most variable array of means of the four groups, on Factor IV, was 7.87, 7.78, 7.87, 8.30. These means were reported as varying significantly at the .01 level. If the F-values are of statistical significance they are surely of insufficient practical importance to permit statements about how activities of therapists of various orientations differ.

Sundland and Barker (1962) received responses to their 133-item Therapist Orientation Questionnaire from 244 psychologists of 400 solicited by mail. As a group, they pictured themselves as slightly more passive and noninterruptive than not, yet fairly interpretive. Only 7 per cent claimed to be nondirective. The emotional tenor of the relationship was evenly divided between personal and impersonal objectives. The majority tend to set goals, plan the strategy of treatment, and reject the spontaneous approach. As many as 95 per cent attempt to figure out the nature of the therapeutic relationship. Half felt it important to discuss childhood with the patient. Freudians claimed to place more emphasis on discussions of childhood, the use of interpretation, unconscious motivation, and conceptualizing, and believed that the therapist should be more impersonal, follow plans, and inhibit spontaneity. Sullivanians, on the contrary, placed less emphasis on childhood unconscious motivation and interpretation and stressed the personality of the therapist more. In contrast to Sullivanians, Rogerians placed still less emphasis upon childhood, interpretation, conceptualizing, planning and goals, and unconscious motivation.

Factor analysis revealed six first-order factors and a general factor with "analytic" and "experiential" poles. Analytic here refers to a way of attending and responding that stresses conceptualizing, therapist training, planning of therapy, unconscious processes, and control of therapist spontaneity. Experiential emphasizes the therapist's personality, spontaneity, and the unplanned approach, and de-emphasizes conceptualization and unconscious processes. Sundland and Barker note that this type of factor has been described elsewhere as objective versus subjective, cerebral versus visceral, impersonal versus personal, planned observer versus unplanned participant, science versus art, analysis versus holism, mechanism versus organism, rationalism versus intuitionism, theology versus mysticism, nomothetic versus idiographic, positivism versus existentialism. At the extreme analytic pole they placed Freud, Fenichel, Thorne, Ellis, Miller and Dollard. At the midpoint were Sullivan, Adler, Alexander and French, Horney and Fromm-Reichmann. Rank, Jung, Perls, Reik, and the existential analysts were toward the experiential pole. Whitaker and Malone and Rogers were placed at the extreme experiential pole.

Available research indicates that there are apparently genuine differences in approach and technique as a function of "school" or orientation of the therapist. Therapists tend to conceptualize therapeutic problems, steer a course, and use strategems that reflect their orientation.

PERSONAL ANALYSIS OF THE THERAPIST AND PERFORMANCE

Just as there is little research on the effect on outcome of personal analysis of the therapist, there is little on the way it affects his performance. Strupp (1955c) explored the effect of the therapist's personal analysis upon his techniques as part of a larger study. Therapists included forty-one of the fifty used in the larger study. Of these, thirty had received a personal analysis. Among the analyzed group 77 per cent were considered experienced in contrast to only 18 per cent in the nonanalyzed group. The two variables are thus badly confounded. The procedure consisted of presenting subjects with twenty-seven cards containing patient statements including examples of suicide threats, transference reactions, and complaint statements. Strupp acknowledged that therapist responses were obtained by a method whose validity remains to be tested, that patient statements were brief and out of context, and that background information was lacking, as was any therapist-patient relationship. With these limitations in mind, detailed consideration of results is not warranted. The general finding was one of increased activity on the part of analyzed therapists. In a subsequent study, using his interrupted film technique, Strupp (1958a) reported, in opposition to his earlier finding, that analyzed psychiatrists gave more silent responses than did those who had not been analyzed. This did not hold for psychologists. Analyzed psychiatrists tended to be more empathic at the higher experience levels, but again this was not true of psychologists or social workers.

McNair and Lorr's (1964a) study of professed therapeutic techniques revealed that those with considerable personal therapy (particularly psychologists) endorsed psychoanalytic techniques such as interpretation, free association, dream analysis, analysis of resistance, and transference.

THERAPIST PERFORMANCE AND ATTITUDES AS A FUNCTION OF EXPERIENCE

Aside from its effect upon outcome, therapist experience has been studied as a determinant of therapeutic role and technique, the quality and form of the relationship established, and such matters as the evaluation of the patient's strengths, weaknesses, and motivation for therapy, goals and expectations for treatment, and various therapist attitudes relevant to psychotherapy. The purpose of these studies is to find out if, and how, psychotherapists at various levels of experience differ in their performance of the therapeutic task. Rarely stated but usually implied in such research is the value judgment that there are certain preferred modes of performing that are associated with successful outcome. This judgment is the outgrowth of a logical error that fosters incomplete research and premature conclusions. The initial assumption is that experienced therapists are better (more successful) therapists. The researcher then demonstrates that experienced therapists perform differently than inexperienced ones and attempts to delineate some of the specific ways. He then concludes or implies that the differences in technique *account* for the assumed success. Unfortunately, the research that we have reviewed does not confirm anything resembling the close one-to-one relation between success and experience that would be desirable for the first assumption to be made. But even if it were a certainty that experience equals success, we could not say that the demonstrated differences in technique or performance account for the success of more experienced therapists. This would have to remain a hypothesis and not a conclusion. To test it would require research with a group of therapists of equal experience with technique systematically varied and outcome the dependent variable.

The concept of an ideal therapeutic relationship could serve as a standard against which to judge performance. Fiedler's (1950a) concept of an ideal relationship was based on the pooled ratings of four "expert" therapists from Q-sorts of 119 qualitative statements describing patient-therapist relationships. On the basis of two studies, one with eight and the other with seven subjects, Fiedler concluded that the ability to describe the concept was probably more a function of expertise than theoretical orientation. He also concluded that the concept could be described as well, and in the same manner, by nontherapists as by therapists. This seems paradoxical, for if naïve raters are indistinguishable from therapists, it is odd that expert therapists are distinguishable from inexpert ones. The only logical explanation of this finding, if it is not an artifact due to confounding of experience and other variables or due to the very small samples, is that early training and therapy experiences temporarily color the outlook of beginners who then return to their pretraining attitudes with added experience.

Fiedler's study was challenged by Behar and Altrocchi (1961) in an investigation of the concept of the ideal therapist as a function of experience. They maintained that Fiedler did not take into consideration exposure to academic training, theories, and practices, but limited himself to therapeutic experiences. They suggest that the lack of large statistical differences between the expert and nonexpert groups may have resulted in part from similarity in the amount of academic training. They also pointed to what they regarded as important weaknesses in the Q-sort items themselves. They attempted to improve the method by constructing and pretesting a Q-sort and by using groups differing in amount of academic training as well as amount of therapeutic experience. Unfortunately they obscured the issue by investigating the concept of the "ideal psychiatric nursing therapist" and by using four groups of nurses varying in this experience. The nurses were also asked to describe the control concept, the "ideal female high school teacher." They found agreement to increase significantly with experience except for those tested immediately following an intensive training period. There were no differences on the control concept. The results suggested that changes in the concept of the ideal psychiatric nurse were not a result of age or general life experience. A substantial increase in agreement on the concept was found for two of the groups who had no psychiatric nursing experience and differed only in academic experience.

The next step for Fiedler (1950b) was to test the hypotheses that relationships created by experts would approximate more closely the concept of the ideal therapeutic relationship than would those of nonexperts. He also retested the hypothesis that the relationship is determined more by expertise than by the "school" variable and made predictions about ways in which the experts and nonexperts would differ. Specifically, he hypothesized that the experts would show greater ability to understand and communicate with patients, to maintain an emotionally proper distance, and to eschew status concerns by considering patients more as intellectual and social equals. These dimensions were defined by clusters of items in the initial study. Three judges with some training and one who was untrained listened to ten recorded interviews, five conducted by experts and five by nonexperts. Four of the therapists were psychoanalytically oriented, four were nondirective, and two were Adlerian. The judges assessed the interview by Q-technique on seventy-five statements in three sections: communication, status, and emotional distance. The ratings of each judge were correlated with the rating of the ideal therapeutic relationship from the previous study. Support was found for the first two hypotheses. The ability to understand, communicate, and maintain rapport with the patient was found to be more closely associated with expertise than was the ability to maintain distance. Unfortunately the validity of these results rests on the shaky foundation of the concept of the ideal therapeutic relationship as Fiedler established it. Criteria of expertise are not given, the judges were not particularly well trained for the task, the experimenter served as a judge (introducing a possible bias), and interjudge reliability was poor. Judgments were subject to contamination by recognition of the voices of the therapists by the judges. The author is careful to state that the study does not evaluate the effectiveness of therapeutic schools, but he implies that it does evaluate the effectiveness of individuals. He equates the therapeutic relationship with good and poor (successful and unsuccessful) therapy and states, "This investigation, in other words, supports the theory that relationship *is* therapy, that the goodness of therapy is a function of the goodness of the therapeutic relationship" (p. 443). The statement, however, cannot be deduced from any data in this study. The logical error is that of equating relationship and expertise with successful outcome in a circular manner. At no point is it demonstrated that the kind of relationship recommended and established by experts leads to a more successful outcome. The point was pursued in a factor analysis of the same data (Fiedler, 1951a). Here it was suggested that the factors that differentiate experts from nonexperts are ability to communicate with and understand patients, security, and emotional distance from patients.

Sommer et al. approached the issue in an experiment on therapeutic listening (Sommer, Mazo, & Lehner, 1955). A tape recording of a therapeutic interview, with the original therapist responses deleted, was played to a group of nine graduate students in clinical psychology and to ten experienced clinical psychologists and psychiatrists. Subjects were asked to respond to statements made by the patient with "What has the patient told you?" These responses were then classified into seven content categories and as either descriptive or interpretive. Analysis of the data revealed that the experienced therapists did significantly more interpreting than trainees, but none of the content categories differed. The inexperienced tended to describe what the patient said; the experienced tended to go beyond the explicit material. Although this does not prove that the experienced therapists would do more interpreting to the patient in an actual therapy siutation, or that if they did it would lead to a more successful outcome, it does indicate that experience encourages one to "listen with the third ear" and get at the latent meanings of manifest verbalizations.

Phillips and Agnew (1953) employed a hypothetical counseling situation in which each of twenty client statements were responded to by a choice of one of five possible counselor statements. Choices were understanding (reflection of feeling), evaluative, interpretive, supportive, and probing. As predicted, untrained people responded primarily with nonreflective choices while trained clinicians used predominantly reflective responses. The trained clinicians were not necessarily Rogerians. One response category used by all respondents, trained or not, was probing, a way of getting more information when desired. It was concluded that clinical skills cannot be viewed simply as extensions of general knowledge of interpersonal relations that mature and intelligent people possess.

Strupp's dissertation (1954), comparing theoretical orientation, experience level, and professional affiliation, was published in the form of a series of papers. One phase of the study (Strupp, 1955a) involved four experienced and four inexperienced Rogerians and three experienced and four inexperienced psychoanalytically oriented psychologists. Some in each group had had a personal analysis, others did not. The experienced group had more than five years of experience. They were asked to state the responses they would make to twenty-seven patient statements taken from early interviews of neurotic patients. Their responses were categorized by the author. Reliability was tested on a stratified random sample of 20 per cent. Responses were classified by the Bales system of interaction process analysis into such categories as shows solidarity, shows tension release, agrees, gives suggestions, gives opinion, gives orientation, asks for opinion, asks for suggestion, disagrees, shows tension, shows antagonism. Data were analyzed by t-tests of the significance of the difference between uncorrelated percentages. There was a total of 553 responses by the fifteen therapists. Statistical comparisons were made between various therapist groupings (such as experienced non-Rogerian versus inexperienced non-Rogerian) on the percentage of the total number of responses that fell in a particular response category (such as "gives orientation"). Thus, although Strupp was working with an average of seven subjects in one group against eight in the other, he was testing the significance of the difference between proportions with an N of 553 (responses). The test was of the difference between proportions of responses rather than of the proportion of people who responded in a certain way. Pooling all the responses disregards interindividual variability, or sampling error, the main source of error in the experiment. To test his hypotheses as stated we believe he should have tested the significance of the difference between the mean number of a particular type of response in the two small subject groups. As it stands, very small differences in total proportions of responses that are of no practical significance are found to be statistically significant because of the very large number of responses actually given by a small sample. The conclusions, although they sound most reasonable, still require a true test. Strupp concluded that differences between experienced and inexperienced analytically oriented therapists are due to chance. Rogerians, however, showed a decline in reflective responses with increasing experience and a corresponding use of more exploratory responses. He concluded that reliance on one specific technique is a product of inexperience. In another phase of this study he used twenty-five psychiatrists, of whom fifteen were experienced; seven psychologists, four of whom were experienced; and nine social workers, of whom seven were experienced. Using the same kind of statistical analysis he found that experienced psychiatrists used more interpretations and a larger number of passive rejections than inexperienced ones, whereas inexperienced psychiatrists showed a predilection for exploratory responses. No difference was apparent between experienced and inexperienced psychologists, and the hypothesis was not tested on social workers because there were only two in the inexperienced group. He concluded that experience leads to a diversification of technique. The experienced therapists of all disciplines could have been pooled and compared with the inexperienced, but were not. From inspection, all differences could have washed out if this had been done. Again, although the conclusions are reasonable ones, they remain in doubt. In addition to the statistical issues, there is no assurance that responses given in this type of artificial situation would correspond to actual performance in a therapeutic interaction with real patients.

In a particularly well-analyzed study, Fey (1958) examined the influence of doctrine and experience on therapeutic practices. He mailed questionnaires about therapeutic practices to thirty-six therapists representing the total population of therapists in a midwestern university city. Responses were returned by 94 per cent. Included in the sample were seven Rogerians, five analysts, eight young eclectics with less than ten years of experience, and fourteen older eclectics with ten or more years. Of the four factors that were derived, the young and older eclectics differed significantly on two. One reflected the broad, resourceful, supportive approach to patients and the other the therapist's "expedient virtuosity" in moment-to-moment dealings with patients. The split was observed to correspond to pre- and post-World War II training in psychiatry, with the younger group relying more on psychodynamics and the older group more on diversification of technique. The latter finding is similar to that offered by Strupp, but his suggestion that experienced psychiatrists tend to interpret more was not confirmed.

In their survey of professed therapeutic techniques, McNair and Lorr (1964a) found that therapist experience did not relate to technique pattern or factor scores. In Caracena's (1965) study, therapists at a university counseling center were of three levels of experience. Six were staff members with four to ten years of experience, twelve were interns with an average of one year of supervised experience, and twelve were practicum students working on their first to fourth case. The focus of the investigation was on the elicitation of dependency expressions in the initial stage of therapy. A total of forty-eight initial and twenty-four second sessions were recorded and tapes classified into the content categories of dependency, hostility, and "other." A therapist's response was scored as "approach," if it was designed to elicit further verbalization, or "avoidance," if it was designed to inhibit, discourage, or divert further verbalization on the subject. Unfortunately, the judging was done by the author. A reliability check was done with an independent judge, but it was not particularly high. The basic data were thus opened to the possibility of rater bias. It was noted that the experienced staff therapists approached dependency more than the interns or practicum students. The author carefully noted that he was dealing with therapist technique and that persistent leading behavior on the part of the therapist did not seem to increase the tendency of the client to follow.

Experience has also been suggested as a variable that affects a therapist's evaluation of his patients. Storrow (1960) noted that student-therapists tend to view results in the same way as their patients, but experienced professionals agree more with external judges and less with patients. Wallach (1963) looked into assessments of motivation for psychotherapy. His therapists were seventy-one medical students who interviewed 151 patients and twenty psychiatric residents who interviewed 182 patients. Both groups completed questionnaires about the patients after the interviews, giving clinical estimates, proposed treatment plans, their personal reaction to the patient, and their judgment of the patient's motivation for psychotherapy on a seven-point scale. They also gave the basis for their judgments. The medical students were reported as accepting patients more at face value and tending to rate motivation higher than did residents. There were no tests of the significance of these differences or any attempt to validate whose predictions were the most accurate.

Strupp (1958a) examined the performance of therapists to determine how their approach in a simulated interview varied as a result of a number of therapist variables. Experience was one of the variables, but was confounded with presence or absence of personal analysis. Some 235 therapists responded in writing with the response they would make to the statements of a neurotic patient in a sound film. They were also given a comprehensive questionnaire on diagnostic impressions, treatment plans, goals, and the like. Experience was found to have a negligible effect on evaluation of patients by psychiatrists although the more experienced psychiatrists and psychologists rated patients' ego strength as lower than did their less experienced counterparts. Psychologist experience also correlated positively with more unfavorable estimates of social adjustment and negative attitudes toward patients. Both warmer responses and communications in which the therapist emerged as an authority increased with experience. There was also a tendency for the more experienced analyzed therapists to be more empathic. It must be remembered that this was a simulated rather than a real therapy situation. Artificiality is one of the objections to vicarious therapeutic situations in which "therapists" write responses that they would make to a patient statement from a sound film. Jenkins et al. compared speaking the responses into a microphone with the written technique and reported a strong preference by subjects for the verbal approach and the impression that it yielded a closer approximation of actual interview behavior (Jenkins, Wallach, & Strupp, 1962).

Bohn (1965) used a simulated therapy technique to study counselor behavior as a function of counselor dominance and experience on the one hand and client type on the other. Thirty experienced counselors were matched with thirty inexperienced ones on dominance scores of the California Personality Inventory and the entire group was dichotomized into high and low dominance groups. The standard of experience was wholly inadequate; the "experienced" group consisted of graduate students whose experience was limited to one course in counseling and one semester of experience. The subjects listened to recordings of simulated initial interviews with actors playing both parts. The three "clients" were meant to portray a "typical," a "dependent," and a "hostile" client, and the subjects responded via a forced multiple-choice questionnaire about what they would say at ten interruptions. They were given directive and nondirective response options to select, thus making the situation into a kind of intellectual exercise not necessarily related to what they would do if they found themselves in an actual therapy interchange. In any event, the directiveness scores of the high and low dominance group did not differ. The more experienced counselors, however, were less directive, indicating only that the graduate students had learned their lessons. No generalizations can be made from the study. The technique was again used with eighteen students at the beginning and end of a semester in a course on theories and techniques of counseling (Bohn, 1967). Shortcomings in design and data interpretation permit little but the obvious conclusion that a therapist varies in his approach to different types of clients.

Rice (1965) examined style of participation as a function of experience level. The twenty clients were seen at the University of Chicago Counseling Center by twenty Rogerian therapists ranging from highly experienced to relatively inexperienced. Style of participation was classified for freshness of therapist's language usage, voice quality, and functional level (inner exploring, observing, outside focus). Rice discovered that the style of the inexperienced was characterized more by distorted voice quality, few fresh connotative responses, and a functional level that featured self-observation and a little exploration. The experienced therapists were characterized more by fresh connotative language, expressive voice quality, and inner exploration.

Grigg (1961) noted a shift with experience from being more verbal, active, and prone to interpret and advise to being a more careful listener. Russell and Snyder (1963) found that hostile client behavior made experienced counselors no less anxious than inexperienced ones. This does not mean that they handle the situation in the same way, however. In fact, Gamsky and Farwell (1966) demonstrated that more experienced counselors showed less avoidance of client hostility than did less experienced ones. Fuller (1963) reported that counselor experience interacted with client preference for a male or female therapist to produce increased expression of feeling. When opposite preference assignments were eliminated, expression of feelings increased with counselor experience alone.

Counselor experience was studied in relation to counselor needs and counseling style at Michigan State University Counseling Center (Mills & Abeles, 1965). The therapists were thirteen full-time staff members with doctorates, fourteen advanced graduate students, and ten beginning students seeing their first clients. The fifth interviews were recorded and scored for the percentage of time the counselor approached the client's dependency and hostility bids. Liking for clients was obtained by the semantic differential technique from the differential between responses about an ideal client and about the actual client. This seems to be a rather indirect measure whose validity has not been established. Data were treated by correlational analysis, which revealed a relation between counselor's needs for nurturance and affiliation and liking for clients. This was present only in beginners. Similarly, a direct relation between need for affiliation and approach to hostility was seen only in beginners. The authors interpret this in terms of people coming into the field with high need levels and learning to inhibit them for the good of the client. Another possible but less flattering explanation could be that the need to help others gets satiated with experience or that other therapist needs take precedence.

Mensh and Watson (1950) surveyed psychiatric opinion at different experience levels about treatment goals and factors expected to change. Given a list of seventy personality terms, the psychiatrists were asked to indicate which changes would be expected in therapy, which characteristics would not change, and treatment goals. Residents were more in agreement than experienced therapists on factors expected to change with therapy, but experienced therapists were in more agreement on treatment goals. Other therapist attitudes, particularly those concerning methods and practices, are apparently not so much affected by experience. Using two sample groups of therapists, Wallach and Strupp (1964) investigated therapists' preferences for and attitudes toward some of the basic therapeutic practices. Sample A consisted of fifty-nine medical psychotherapists with an average of 5.3 years of experience. Sample B was composed of 248 therapists from throughout the United States (91 psychiatrists with 8.5 years of experience and 157 psychologists with 8.2 years of experience). A seventeen-item scale dealing with major instances of the usual practices of a therapist was administered, and the responses were factor analyzed. Hardly any differences appeared between experience levels in preferences for or attitudes toward therapeutic practices. A correlation coefficient, $r = -.15$, for Sample B alone, was interpreted as showing a tendency for more experienced therapists to prefer intensive psychotherapy. The modest size of the coefficient, the fact that it accounts for little more than 2 per cent of the variance, and the zero order correlation in Sampie A lead us to place little stock in this as a tendency. An earlier study by Sundland and Barker (1962) yielded similar results. Responses were received from 139 psychologists to a mail survey that called for completion of a Therapist Orientation Questionnaire composed of 133 items designed to reflect both poles of thirteen scales of therapeutic attitudes and methods. Only one of the thirteen scales differentiated between experience groups. This scale, which had to do with the therapist's theory of personal growth, showed that the less experienced groups were more in agreement with the idea of innate self-actualization. In general, professed therapeutic attitudes and methods were not found to be a function of experience.

Sundland and Barker's groups of inexperienced Freudians, Rogerians, and Sullivanians were followed up four years later in a unique longitudinal study (Anthony, 1967). Thirty-eight of the original sixty responded and completed the Therapist Orientation Questionnaire. Freudians, who were initially least talkative, became significantly more talkative. Therapists of all orientations became more interpretive. Freudians shifted from being least to most probing, and Rogerians from most to least interpretive. There was a significant shift in the emotional tenor of the relationship toward the personal pole, with Rogerians changing from being most objective to most personal. Rogerians increased in spontaneity, while Freudians and Sullivanians decreased. All became more concerned with conceptualizing how the client was relating to them. All increased in setting goals, with the Freudians shifting from least to most. All groups became less secure and less certain of themselves in the therapy situation, or, as Anthony notes, became secure enough to admit their insecurity. Respondents shifted in regarding client self-understanding as an increasingly important goal. For all, the belief that therapy is a verbal and conceptual process declined in favor of viewing it as an affective, nonconceptual one. On the other hand, all assigned less importance to unconscious processes, with Freudians adhering to it least. Freudians became more convinced of the need for discussing childhood experiences, and Rogerians less. All told, Freudians changed on nine of sixteen attitudes, Rogerians on eight, and Sullivanians on four.

Few of these studies used data obtained from actual performance of a therapist with a patient. The remainder were either surveys of therapists' opinions and attitudes about therapeutic techniques, methods, and practices, or were simulated by having therapists respond to pauses in films or taped interviews. The latter is an appealing research technique in that it presents standard stimuli to all therapists, something that real therapy cannot do. Its shortcomings are numerous. What many consider to be the vital aspect of psychotherapy, the relationship, is missing. The consequences of the therapist's response are certainly not the same, and the therapist cannot modify his response in accordance with the reactions of the patient. The demands for immediacy and spontaneity of response are not the same. An experimental therapist can pause, reflect upon, and think through his answers before writing them down, an opportunity not available in a genuine verbal interchange. The burden is upon the experimenters who use the technique to demonstrate its close relation to a therapist's actual performance in therapy. Similarly, surveys of opinions and attitudes about therapeutic practices are a step removed from what the respondent actually does in therapy and may or may not be accurate reflections of practice.

However, if we accept the findings as they are offered, we are told by some studies that experience is not related to professed techniques, attitudes, methods, and practices, and by others that it does make a difference. The latter maintain that experience generates a less literal, more critical, and less optimistic view of patients. The relationships of experienced therapists with patients are believed to approximate more closely a consensual ideal. Their technique is said to be more diversified, less reliant on monolithic approaches, and more versatile and adaptable. Their experience enables them to deal with, rather than back off from, patient demands and reactions. They are alleged to come across to patients more as authorities and to show more warmth and empathy without letting their own needs interact with their liking for the patient to affect outcome. They seem to agree with each other more on what the goals of therapy ought to be for a patient, but their expectations of what will be accomplished vary more than do those of inexperienced therapists.

For the reasons given, very few of these differential statements can be accepted as firm conclusions. Some of the inconsistencies may be due to varying standards of experience from research to research. Therapists who are considered experienced in one study are in the inexperienced group in another. Experience is frequently confounded with other variables such as age of the therapist, life experience as opposed to therapy experience, era in which training was received, and personal therapy.

THERAPIST-OFFERED CONDITIONS

From their beginnings, nondirective therapists have been deeply concerned with the process of psychotherapy. Their interest in what actually transpires in the psychotherapeutic hour led them to attempt to identify and label the characteristic behaviors of counselor and client. This very specificity encouraged early research in the psychotherapeutic process. Eventually, the search for the determinants of change in personality and behavior led Rogers (1957) to the conclusion that there are necessary and sufficient conditions of change and that these are principally conditions offered by the counselor. Both client and counselor have to be in "psychological contact." The client initially is in a state of incongruence, being vulnerable or anxious. (The last point is important, for in many studies that bear on Rogers' hypotheses, the clients seem in no way vulnerable.) The most important conditions are the therapist's alone. The therapist has to be congruent or genuine (that is, integrated into the relationship); he has to experience unconditional positive regard for the client; he has to experience an empathic understanding of the client's internal frame of reference and to communicate this to the client. The client has to perceive, if only to a minimal degree, the therapist's genuineness, positive regard, and empathy for him, and he, himself, will experience constructive change.

Upon Rogers' designation of these "therapeutic conditions" researchers stimulated by these concepts began to forge instruments to measure these variables in the therapist and the related variables of the patient's responses. At first, these devices took the form of questionnaires of both the counselor's and the client's behavior and attitudes (for example, Barrett-Lennard's questionnaire). Later, Truax and others developed rating scales of these interview behaviors designed to be applied to samples from tape-recorded interviews by judges who were usually naïve in psychotherapy and trained to acceptable levels of judgment realiability. The hypotheses suggested by Rogers, implemented by increasingly suitable measuring instruments, inspired a rapidly growing number of studies of outcome and process.

An initial problem in this body of research was to establish differences in levels of these facilitative conditions in different counselors and to discover the determinants of these differences. Martin, Carkhuff, and Berenson (1966) evaluated the differences between counselors and "best friends" of clients. The clients were sixteen volunteer college students, and the counselors were two trained counselors with over five years of clinical experience. Each client was interviewed by a counselor and by his best friend, each counselor interviewing four "first" and four "last" clients in the series. Following the interview, the clients completed questionnaires on the empathy, positive regard, genuineness, and concreteness of the counselor (or friend), and on their own self-exploration in the interview. In addition, three trained graduate students rated these five variables on Truax and Carkhuff's five-point scales using three four-minute excerpts from each taped interview. There were no formal criteria, although client self-exploration seemed to be dependent upon the other four variables. The counselors differed significantly from the friends on all rated variables. Differences on these traits measured by the questionnaire scores were significant except for the client self-exploration variable. The counselors obtained a mean of 3, claimed by Carkhuff to be the minimal level of facilitative functioning; the friends obtained a score of 2. There were differences between the two counselors on the four counselor variables. The authors conclude that "while professional experience may be of primary value in the development of receptive and communicative skills, other factors such as the personality and attitudes of the individual counselor may be crucial" (p. 358). A volunteer college student does not a patient make, nor a friend a psychotherapist. The basic point, directly opposite to the authors' conclusions, is that the counselors obtained higher ratings on facilitative conditions than did the friends. The difference was training and experience, not personality or attitude, here neither measured nor studied. Significantly enough, there were no reliable differences in client self-exploration. Perhaps these clients had little to explore.

Truax and Carkhuff (1965b) studied the effect of manipulating therapeutic conditions within one therapeutic hour upon the intrapersonal exploration of three hospitalized female schizophrenics. There seems to have been one therapist, not described. During the first twenty minutes, a base-line level of the patient's intrapersonal exploration was established with the use of a ten-point scale. The therapist was interrupted, thus obtaining a reason for later preoccupation. For the next twenty minutes, he "deliberately" lowered his empathic understanding and positive regard for the patient. He "lowered conditions" by "withholding the best response." During the last twenty minutes, he restored his empathic understanding and his unconditional positive regard of the patient. It was not intended that genuineness be altered during the entire interview. Empathy, positive regard, and genuineness were measured by the respective scale ratings of fifteen three-minute samples from each of the three therapeutic hours. Analysis of the data indicated that these conditions were lowered during the experimental middle third of the interview as intended. These changes in therapist-offered conditions served to lower the patients' depth of self-exploration. The descriptions of the procedure suggest that there was restriction of the therapist's behavior and indication of his disinterest. That this should lead to a parallel reduction in patient response is not surprising. A more cogent demonstration of the researchers' point would have been the reduction of the "conditions" without reduction of level of participation. These were initial interviews, and any findings cannot be generalized to the entire therapeutic process.

Another attempt to demonstrate that it is the counselor who determines the level of conditions he offers was also characterized by the manipulation of these conditions (Holder, Carkhuff, & Berenson, 1967). In this study, the clients were six female college students, selected from a sample of eleven who had enacted the role of counselor. The three highest and lowest functioning students were selected to be the clients. The counseling hour was divided into thirds and an "experienced" counselor lowered the therapist-offered conditions during the middle third of the interview. With each client, the difference in the offered conditions (here empathy, respect, genuineness, and concreteness) between the first and third periods, on the one hand, and the second period, on the other, was significant. During all periods, the high-functioning group functioned at higher levels than did the low-functioning group. For the high-functioning group, there were no differences in level of self-exploration between the middle third of the interview and the other portions. For the low-functioning group, however, this difference was significant. These findings suggest to the researchers that, contrary to Truax and Carkhuff's belief, "high-level" clients may make good use of counseling despite the low levels offered by a counselor. Only "low-level" clients seem to require high levels of these therapeutic conditions from the counselor. The clients in this study were obviously pseudoclients, and the therapeutic process scarcely therapy. Moreover, do the characteristics that make for a good counselor also make for a good client?

As part of a larger study Truax et al. tried to demonstrate that the therapist alone determines the level of accurate empathy, nonpossessive warmth, and genuineness that he offers to the patient (Truax et al., 1966a). Forty psychoneurotic outpatients of the Henry Phipps Psychiatric Clinic were randomly assigned to four senior psychiatric residents. Half the patients of each therapist were screened by two screening interviewers. Furthermore, half the patients screened by each interviewer were given a Role Induction Interview (orientation to psychotherapy) and half were not. Each patient was then seen once a week for a four-month period by the assigned psychotherapist. Two three-minute segments were recorded from the first, the tenth, and the fifth from the last therapeutic interviews. The segments were randomly selected from the middle and final third of the interview with the provision that both a patient and therapist verbalization had to be present in each sample. The investigators reasoned that one would expect differences attributable to therapists in these variables for all patients if the therapists indeed offered different levels. If the patients elicited different levels from their therapists, one would expect significant patient variation and totally insignificant therapist variation. The results indicated significant differences by analyses of variance between the screening interviewers in accurate empathy and in genuineness, but none in nonpossessive warmth. In a similar way, in the segments from the first interview, the therapists differed significantly from each other in genuineness, inconclusively in accurate empathy, and not at all in nonpossessive warmth. When the data from the first, tenth, and fifth from the last interview were averaged, however, the therapists differed significantly on all three variables. The conclusion was that the therapist alone determines these conditions even though the design of the study did not deal with any patient characteristics—such as degree of pathology, diagnosis, personality, sex, attractiveness—that may have contributed in some way to the therapist's responses. One available variable, the Role Induction Interview, was not treated in any analysis.

Kratochvil, Aspy, and Carkhuff (1967) conducted a study of "growth in counselor functioning." Twenty-four college students, in groups of six, were oriented to discuss any personal problems or experiences they might share with the counselors. Two of the counselors were functioning at minimally facilitative levels and two were functioning below minimal levels. Two excerpts from each of the ten sessions were rated. One high-level and one low-level counselor were considered to have shown "constructive growth." The counselees of the high-functioning counselors did not gain significantly more than those of the low-functioning counselors, nor did the clients of the counselors who showed the most growth gain more. Neither hypothesis was supported. Nevertheless, the investigators conclude optimistically that the counselor's direction of growth is potentially a more important source of effect upon the client than the counselor's absolute level of functioning. The clients were not bona fide clients, and these results scarcely warrant the conclusion.

In what can only be called a pilot study, Alexik and Carkhuff (1967) attempted to vary the relevant behavior of a "client" to demonstrate that a low-functioning counselor would be manipulated by the degree of the client's self-exploration but that a high-functioning counselor would not and would continue to offer high levels of the facilitative variables. Two counselors, both with doctoral training, similar orientations, and eight years of experience, interviewed the same graduate student separately. The counselors believed that they were seeing a regular client for the first interview. The "client" was instructed to explore herself fully during the first and last third of each interview, but to be impersonal and irrelevant during the middle third of each interview. The counselors had been scored in previous studies on the facilitative variables; Counselor A had scored low on all, while Counselor B had scored at minimally facilitative levels on all but one. For both counselors, the "client" explored herself significantly more during the first and last periods than during the middle phase. Counselor A, as expected, functioned lower than his colleague during all periods and dropped significantly during the experimental middle period below his own level in periods one and three. For Counselor B, there was no such change. The researchers were themselves aware of the need for replication with larger numbers of clients and counselors. This was an initial interview conducted under highly atypical "therapeutic" conditions. It would be more reasonable to conclude that the hypothesis remains unconfirmed.

A study done early in this series (van der Veen, 1965b) provides the most sophisticated model for the determinants of therapeutic behavior and the most complex design. Van der Veen's general hypothesis was that the patient and the therapist influence each other's behavior and that these behaviors are positively related to each other. More specifically, for patient variables, the patient's levels of experiencing and problem expression are a function of both himself and the therapist, and also a function of the particular patient-therapist combination. For therapist variables, the therapist's levels of congruence and accurate empathy are also a function of both persons, and the therapist's functions are also determined by the particular therapist-patient combination. For the relation between these two sets of variables, therapist and patient variables are positively related to each other.

In van der Veen's study, eight therapists saw twenty-five hospitalized patients for almost 600 interviews varying in length from a few minutes to over one hour. The researcher selected three hospitalized chronic schizophrenics who had seen the same five therapists at least two times. Three four-minute segments were taken, one from each third of each interview, with the safeguard that both participants spoke at least twice during the segment. These were tentative therapeutic contacts arising by chance during the therapists' visits to the wards. For the therapist variables, van der Veen used Hart's Congruence Scale and Truax's Accurate Empathy Scale. For the patient variables, he used a seven-stage Experiencing Scale and a seven-stage Problem Expression Scale, each of relatively low interrater reliability ($r = .58$ and $r = .46$ respectively). A complex analysis of variance yielded support at the author's pre-established confidence level of $p = .025$ or better for all of his hypotheses about patient and therapist except for the therapist's functions being determined by the particular dyad. So far as the relation between patient and therapist variables is concerned, the researcher obtained intercorrelations of from $r = .36$ to $r = .54$, which were of moderate size but all significant at the 1 per cent level. He is aware that neither patients nor therapists were selected randomly and that they were not exposed to systematically varied conditions. These two interviews did not constitute a true therapeutic series, another reason for the marked lack of generalizability of the findings. However, the model presented by van der Veen offers great promise for further and broader research.

Mills and Zytowski (1967) attempted an interesting psychometric critique of Rogers' "necessary and sufficient conditions." They administered Barrett-Lennard's Relationship Inventory, which purports to measure these conditions and which has been used in many studies, to seventy-nine female undergraduate students. On one form the subjects assessed their relationship with their mothers; on another, they rated their perception of their mothers' feelings about them. The investigators performed a factor analysis on these data, and an identical one on the two series of intercorrelations reported by Barrett-Lennard (1962). They hypothesized that there might be a general factor that accounts for much of the variance of the entire instrument. Three components that accounted for 93 to 96 per cent of the variance were found. The largest component accounted for 63 per cent of the variance of the students' mother-relationship answers and 70 per cent of their perceptions of the relationship; it also accounted for 65 per cent of the client responses and 72 per cent of the therapist responses of Barrett-Lennard's data. In ranking loadings on this factor, the authors give the following order: congruence, empathy, level of regard, unconditionality of regard. A second component accounted for 15 per cent of the variance in each analysis and had high positive loadings on unconditionality of regard and negative ones on level of regard. The third component, accounting for 10 per cent of the variance, was marked by positive loadings on level of regard and unconditionality, and negative ones on the other conditions. The authors conclude that the multiple characteristics of the helping relationship may well be differential manifestations of a single overriding characteristic. This may explain some of the contradictory results sometimes obtained in this series of studies. However, neither the present sample nor that of Barrett-Lennard seemed to be very maladjusted. The procedure should be repeated with a disturbed sample and not only with the Barrett-Lennard Questionnaire but also with the interesting scales actually designed to measure the interview expression of these facilitative conditions. One unimpressive experimental contradiction to Mills and Zytowski's study is Zimmer and Park's (1967) factor analysis of counselor warmth verbalization in two interviews with one high school volunteer. Although the authors find ten principal factors of warmth, the data are too inadequate for the study to be an answer to Mills and Zytowski.

Two other studies are concerned with facilitative conditions in the Rogerian sense as these apply to the training of therapists. Allen (1967) tested the hypothesis that "psychological openness" helps predict the counseling effectiveness of counseling trainees. Twenty-six students in counseling viewed a filmed interview. The film was stopped in twenty-eight places to elicit "counselor" response. Counselor "openness" measures were obtained from the Rorschach Index of Repressive Style (RIRS) and a Group Supervision Report Scale (GSRS), which evaluated the trainee's own feelings as opposed to external events. Measures of response to the interview were: Response to Feeling Scale (RFS), a Q-sort, a Response to Client Affect Scale (RCAS), and a seven-point scale of the supervisor's ratings of the student's competence. Significant rank-order correlations of competence with RIRS and with GSRS were the most promising. Rho's of these two measures of "openness" with the two scales measuring response to the filmed interview were lower. The only one of significance was the correlation between GSRS and RFS. Despite the author's firm conclusion, his actual findings are that supervisory ratings (which may be based on considerations other than therapeutic skill) correlate moderately with measures of openness. The students' openness does not seem to be closely related to even this remote approach to actual psychotherapy.

Carkhuff and Truax (1965a) too were concerned with therapeutic conditions and the training of psychotherapists. Twelve graduate students and, separately, five volunteers from the nonprofessional hospital staff, received a training program lasting two hours a week for sixteen weeks. They were taught about the facilitative conditions (unconditional positive regard, self-congruence, and accurate empathic understanding) and about the scales that measure them. They heard tape-recorded samples of psychotherapy, were taught identification of the levels of the facilitative conditions, and practiced role-playing. They then interviewed schizophrenic patients. The lay volunteers, the graduate students, and eleven experienced staff therapists were compared on the three scales and on the patient's self-exploratory response. Although the order was generally experienced therapists, graduate students, lay personnel, there was only one significant t-test, that between the lay and the experienced therapists in therapist's self-congruence. Interrater reliabilities were not high, between $r = .40$ and $r = .60$. The implication, of course, is that lay therapists with very brief training can master the process of psychotherapy. However, this is training in one genre of interview for one interview. One wonders how the various samples would do if they continued, armed with knowledge of this single technique and their present general knowledge of personality, psychopathology, and psychotherapy.

Pierce and Mosher (1967) dealt with only one of the facilitative conditions, empathy. They divided sixty male students at their median on the General Anxiety Questionnaire into high and low anxiety groups. Half of each group was assigned to a fifteen-minute interview during which there was appropriate or inappropriate timing. In both conditions, the experimenter had a repertory of fourteen nondirective remarks. In the appropriate condition, he did not interrupt the subject and did not allow five seconds to elapse without making a remark. In the inappropriate condition, he interrupted the subject and, at one point, did not respond for fifteen seconds. The criteria were the Post-Interview Anxiety Questionnaire and the Barrett-Lennard Perceived Empathy Questionnaire. Results indicated that the subjects in the appropriate condition perceived the interviewer as more empathic than did the subjects in the inappropriate condition. Perceived interview scores correlated inversely with perceived empathy scores. The results from this analogue study may not be applicable to actual patients, but they do suggest what the components of "empathy" may be.

The facilitative conditions proposed by Rogers and the experimental means created to demonstrate their existence and meaning from the process of psychotherapy are interesting. However, this group of studies presents problems for theoretical and experimental examination. In process studies, for the most part, the various facilitative variables are related only to the patient's self-exploration. The implicit, and sometimes explicit, argument is that the facilitative conditions lead to self-exploration, which in turn leads to favorable outcome. Both hypotheses remain to be firmly established. There are clues that indicate that self-exploration may not be the only road to change, and, indeed, may not necessarily lead to change. Some of the studies suggest that the "conditions" may be accounted for by one major variable; others offer the possibility that some simple and specifiable therapist behaviors may underlie these conditions (silence or the restriction of behavior, for example). It would be a mistake to freeze therapeutic research in process into the current versions of these facilitative conditions when the results are ambiguous and much remains to be explored.

15

Verbal Processes and Techniques

RESEARCH PROBLEMS AND METHODS

Hypotheses should stimulate the creation of appropriate methods of analyzing various aspects of psychotherapy. The therapeutic process is so complex and the problems of its analysis so general that many researchers have devised methods of study that they believe to be of general applicability. Formal verbal characteristics of the therapeutic process, such as duration of utterances, number of adjectives used, and the like, can be measured objectively, but content analysis is dependent upon more easily biased judgments. The farther the categories are from observable or countable items, the more difficult it becomes to obtain reliability.

The practice of using the judgments of experts to test hypotheses relevant to the diagnostic and therapeutic process has come under scrutiny. One report, originating at the University of California School of Medicine, began with an attempt to develop a device for assessing clinical skill in psychiatry by evaluating a patient for psychotherapy (Stoller & Geertsma, 1963). It turned out that experts were unable to agree on a sufficient number of items to make up an examination. The psychiatric experience of the twenty-seven instructors sampled ranged from one to twenty-two years since residency, with a mean of 9.7 years. Eleven had had classical psychoanalytic experience. Some 565 psychiatric statements were assembled that allowed for clinical description of a wide assortment of patients. The subjects were shown a filmed interview and required to rate the appropriateness of each statement as descriptive of the patient. The statements included items concerned with diagnosis, prognosis, psychodynamics and theory, psychopathology, direct observation, empathic intuitive observations, treatment, and nonsense items. The latter were absurd statements, such as, "At this point, the patient's depreciation of introjected father's penis is revealed."

Interrater correlations between pairs of raters over all statements were computed. The mean coefficient, $r = .37$, differed significantly from zero but was low. Judges with less than seven years of experience agreed to a greater extent than those with more. Next came analysts, nonanalysts, and last those with more than seven years of experience. No trend toward agreement was found on specific categories of items whether they dealt with psychodynamics, prognosis, patient's feelings, or empathic intuitive observations. The nonsense items received an even spread of ratings from not characteristic up to extremely characteristic. This study casts a long shadow on the reliability of clinical judgments and the expectation of consensual validation among experts.

Walton and McPherson (1964) went farther, and checked the reliability and validity of clinicians' naturalistic observations of a therapy session. Five psychiatrists were asked to write a narrative account of a group therapy session. A therapist and observer were in the meeting and three additional observers watched from behind a one-way screen. The session was recorded and two judges counted the number of separate incidents (a unit of verbal communication by a patient on a given theme) that took place. Altogether, there were ninety-one incidents in the typescript, only six of which were reported by all observers. About 32 per cent of the content was reported by the majority of observers, 42 per cent by a minority, and 25 per cent was not mentioned by any. New topics introduced by a member ("initiatory incident") received most attention, continuation by a second member of a topic raised by another ("reciprocal incident") was observed less, and interpretations by the therapist were least observed. Initiatory incidents were most lengthy and therapist statements shortest, and the longer incidents were reported most. Neither the phase of the session in which the statement was made nor its content determined whether it would be reported. Content categories were symptoms, sexual topics, attitudes and beliefs, dreams and fantasies, treatment, and behavior in the group. The therapist was in less agreement with the observer who was present in the group than with the others, but the two who were present reported a higher percentage of incidents than those who were concealed. The therapist reported the most. This study emphasizes the danger of relying upon observational reports of naturalistic events and the need for rigorous, if laborious, recording procedures of events as they take place.

Forer et al. tried to determine how well observers could agree on what was perceived, the kinds of clinical material that could be judged most reliably, and the best methods of enhancing agreement. Six experienced psychologists who had worked together for a long time observed three patient-therapist pairs through a one-way screen for a total of twelve sessions (Forer, Farberow, Feifel, Meyer, Sommers, & Tolman, 1961). A checklist of observational and inferential items was rated for their presence or absence. Although ratings were made independently, after each series of three sessions items were discussed, refined, and replaced in the hope of increasing agreement. The authors reported that significant agreement among judges was obtained on very few items. Although the total amount of agreement exceeded chance, it was not enough to warrant confidence in the judgments. Agreement was not affected by the apparent objectivity of the item (even an item such as "thirty seconds or more of silence" was not agreed upon consistently). Neither practice, greater familiarity with the patient, nor discussions to clarify items helped. The experiment was worthwhile in pointing up the need for extreme care in designing experiments in which judgments are made about what goes on in therapy, but the task is probably not as hopeless as this study would lead us to think. With six judges and two choices, perfect agreement of all six is required to exceed chance, and this properly was their standard of agreement. In some areas, such as hostility, reaction formation, and rationalization, there never was perfect agreement. Even something like the presence of gestures was significantly (unanimously) agreed upon only once. It is obviously difficult to get unanimous agreement among a group of six judges on anything. The proportion of observational items that showed significant agreement varied from 31.3 per cent to 54.5 per cent among the twelve observational periods. The range was 28 per cent to 54 per cent for inferential items. This does not mean that it cannot be done. The implication for researchers is that they should keep only those judged data for which agreement exceeds chance and discard the unreliable ones. The poor results obtained may have been in part due to the fact that more than forty items had to be judged, making the task far too complex. The results might have been quite different if the rating task had been limited in scope to judgments about a small number of variables. The authors acknowledge that the clinicians may have had too much data to process and that the large mass of heterogeneous data may have created interference with the evaluation.

Many schemes for analyzing interviews have been developed. They have ranged from ways of analyzing single units of speech such as adjectives and verbs to methods of analyzing series of interviews. The relative effectiveness of using larger units rather than single speech units was studied by Muthard (1953). The units studied were *discussion topic* (conversation of patient and therapist about the same topic), *problem area unit* (all the contiguous statements dealing with the same kind of problem), and *fraction* (percentage of total remarks within a series of interviews). All three could be rated reliably. Both problem area and discussion topic units were more effective than quintiles of the interview series, and provide an opportunity to study changing client and counselor roles.

Strupp (1957abc) proposed a multidimensional system for analyzing the verbal technique of the psychotherapist. Analysis is done by trained raters from typescripts of recorded sessions, and requires two to four hours for each session. Major categories include type of therapeutic activity, depth-directiveness, dynamic focus, initiative, and therapeutic climate. Type of therapeutic activity refers to the subcategories of facilitating communication by minimal activity, exploratory operations, clarification, structuring, direct guidance, activity not relevant to the task of therapy, and unclassifiable. Depth-directiveness is classified on a five-point scale anchored at one end by deep interpretations. Dynamic focus involves accepting the patient's formulation without introducing a new frame of reference or directing him to new channels. In redirecting, the therapist may call for additional information, focus on dynamic events in the past or the present, or elicit comment on the therapeutic relationship. Therapist initiative is rated on a four-point scale from absent to authoritative. Therapeutic climate is assessed on a five-point scale from cold through neutral objectivity to warm. Strupp illustrated the applicability of the system for the longitudinal study of a single case and for comparison of two different therapeutic approaches. In the former (Strupp, 1957b), nine interviews of a patient by Wolberg were rated. Some of the dimensions varied significantly across the interviews. In the latter (Strupp, 1957c), Wolberg's interviews were compared with those of a series of interviews by Rogers. The method successfully differentiated between the techniques used by the two in ways that agreed with the theoretical position of the therapists and reflected what they claim to do in therapy.

Walker, Rablen, and Rogers (1960) developed a scale to measure process changes with the focus on the patient rather than on the therapist. The direction of change was conceived to be from stasis or fixity to change or flow in the areas of relations to feelings and personal meanings, manner of experiencing, degree of incongruence, communication of self, construing of experience, relationship to problems, and manner of relating to others. The scale was reliably judged on twenty-four samples from six cases of client-centered therapy. Tomlinson and Hart (1962) checked the reliability and validity of the Process Scale on ten client-centered cases. As a test of validity they hypothesized that the overall process level would be higher for more successful cases than for less successful ones, for later than for earlier interviews, and for the second half than for the first half of a single interview. The latter two differences were expected to hold especially for the more successful cases. Second and next to last interviews were selected for each case, and nine two-minute samples taken from each type were rated independently by the experienced raters. The correlation between judges ($r = .65$) was considered "adequate" but not high. Judges differed significantly in ratings assigned to a given segment despite this general agreement. Five cases were considered successful and five unsuccessful on a multicriteria success score comprised of therapist and patient ratings of outcome and a self-concept Q-sort. As predicted, the more successful cases had significantly higher process scores than less successful ones. The scale differentiated between early and late interviews; however, the finding was interpreted as of little practical value. None of the other hypotheses were supported. Since the more successful cases uniformly started at a higher initial process level than the less successful ones, there may have been some confounding of initial level and success criteria. The authors speculated that there may be personality characteristics that a patient must possess to a minimal degree if he is to profit from psychotherapy.

Various other methods of classifying and systematizing aspects of therapy sessions have been tried. An early study by Seeman (1949) represented a naturalistic classification of responses designed to contribute understanding about the process of nondirective therapy. The content of sixty interviews was classified into various client and counselor categories. Over the course of therapy, statements of the problem declined and insight and understanding increased, and this shift was correlated with counselor judgment of outcome. Positive attitudes of the client (with increasing concentration on self rather than others) increase, negative attitudes decrease, and there is a shift in tense. Early in therapy, positive attitudes tend to be expressed in the past tense and negative ones in the present, with the situation reversing itself as therapy proceeds. Individual differences in both process and attitudes increase as time goes on.

Butler (1951) proposed a method, Rank Pattern Analysis, for analyzing interviews. It is a way of clustering frequency data so that hypothesized comparisons can be made. Pepinsky, Siegel, and Vanatta (1952) constructed a scale to measure the effectiveness of participation in group activity in terms of the extent to which members initiate, define, sustain, or direct activity leading to goals thought to be important. Fine and Zimet (1961) used a Participation Rating Scale for research in group therapy. Observers scored all the responses of patients for the quality of the theme and evaluation of the interaction. Hogan (1952) presented a method of studying defensive behavior by analysis of statements made during the interview. Nunnally (1955) proposed and demonstrated a factor analytic method for systematic study of the therapist's impressions during the process of therapy.

Eldred et al. devised a promising method of analyzing communication in therapeutic interviews (Eldred, Hamburg, Inwood, Salzman, Meyersburg, & Goodrich, 1954). Their focus was on distinct changes in the content of communications by either participant in terms of reference to a different kind of experience, a different person, or a shift in time reference. Judges, using recorded and transcribed material, were able to identify fifty-eight changes that met two or more of these three criteria from a series of interviews of three patients with three different therapists. There was an average of three drastic changes per interview. Five categories of changes were arrived at empirically. The *direction* of change was classified as leading to more or less direct communication or having no determinable effect. *Awareness* of change by the subject was rated as conscious, unconscious, or undetermined. The *initiator* of the change, either patient or therapist, was identified. Ten different techniques of changing the subject were isolated, including: (1) shifting the time reference, (2) introducing emotionally laden material about another matter, (3) silence, (4) shifting from a topic of unestablished communicability to one of previously known communicability, (5) the converse of this, (6) introducing self-recriminatory material, (7) shifting from conventional pleasantries to the work of the session and the converse, (8) indication by the therapist of disapproval or disinterest in the topic, (9) therapists' too rigid interpretation of unconscious material, (10) reintroduction of a previous topic. The *causes* of change were classified as: (1) one of the participants becomes anxious about the topic, (2) desire to introduce more relevant material, (3) insight, (4) free association, (5) poor wording by a participant causing it to be heard as a change, (6) one party doesn't understand the other, (7) existing topic seems exhausted, (8) need to communicate on another topic of greater immediacy, (9) one becomes anxious about his relationship with the other.

When the fifty-eight changes were classified according to these categories, thirty-one tended to lead toward more direct communication, suggesting that a change of topic is not necessarily a defensive device. More of the changes were patient-initiated (a ratio of 2.6 to 1) although there was marked variability among patients and therapists. Much more so than unconscious shifts, conscious changes led to far more direct than less direct communication. Changes of topic by patients led to more direct communication almost four times as often as not. Therapist shifts varied in effect. One therapist changed the topic three times, all consciously, and each time it led to *less* direct communication. Another changed five times (four unconsciously) and all led to less direct communication. This variability was present even though all therapists were highly trained and experienced psychoanalysts. The ratios of patient's changes leading to more as against less direct communication were 2:1, 4:1, and 10:1 for the three patients. There is an obvious need here for more data on different patient-therapist pairs to determine whether these categories are sufficiently inclusive and can be judged reliably. If so, it could be a most useful method for testing a variety of hypotheses.

Howe and Pope (1961b) conducted a complex, interwoven series of studies to develop a parallel pair of scales to assess therapist verbal activity level, defined in terms of ambiguity, lead, and inference. Responses, classified as simple facilitation, exploration, clarification, interpretation, and supportive reassurance, showed successively increasing activity levels. Reliability of the scales was demonstrated and differences in activity level were obtained in published interviews by Wolberg, Gill, Rogers, and a Finesingerian. Howe and Pope (1961a) obtained three factors from psychiatric ratings of ten therapist verbal responses. From most to least important, the factors were: professional evaluation, precision/potency, and subjectivity/objectivity. The universe is, of course, extremely limited, but the tendency to judge principally in evaluative terms (skillful-unskillful, good-bad, wise-foolish) is of interest. In a later study Howe (1965) used the same subjects and technique. Subjects rated the therapist's statements from two interviews. Independence of the three dimensions was not confirmed for both interviews. Anxiety arousal was correlated with all three dimensions.

These various approaches represent a sampling of the general approaches that have been applied to the study of verbal processes in therapy. Other techniques are described in discussions of specific areas of inquiry.

VERBAL CONDITIONING

A considerable amount of work has been done on verbal conditioning, and efforts have been made to extend it directly to the interview situation with psychiatric patients. Taffel (1955) showed that hospitalized patients could be operantly conditioned to use personal pronouns in an experimental situation by saying "good" as a reinforcer, but reinforcement by flashing a light was not effective. Scores on the Taylor Manifest Anxiety Scale were related to the amount of conditioning, with the high anxiety group showing the greatest amount of conditioning. There is other evidence of differences in verbal conditioning as a function of diagnosis. Cohen and Cohen (1960) found verbal reinforcement to have negligible effects on verbal task performance of schizophrenic patients, whereas neurotic patients showed significant acquisition curves. In another experiment, conditioning of verbal affective responses was accomplished in a nonpsychiatric sample that showed greater resistance to extinction than did schizophrenics (Salzinger & Pisoni, 1960). Slechta, Gwynn, and Peoples (1963), comparing verbal conditioning in schizophrenics and normals, found that schizophrenics did not change significantly from conditions of nonreinforcement to reinforcement, while normals changed in both direction and magnitude. Marlowe (1962) was successful in operant conditioning of self-references of seventy-six undergraduates in an interview setting but found that subjects with a strong need for social approval produced significantly more positive self-references than those with low need for approval.

The crucial question for psychotherapy is whether altered verbalization generalizes to bring about more fundamental change. Rogers (1960) approached this question with student subjects who were asked to talk about their own personality characteristics. One group was reinforced by "mm-hmm" and a head-nod for positive self-references, a second group was reinforced for negative self-references, and a control group was not reinforced at all. The results showed clear reinforcement of the negative self-references, while the group that was reinforced for positive self-references did not increase their output of positive responses. The group that was reinforced for negative self-references and the control group both showed a significant *decrease* in positive self-references. This suggests that positive self-references can be maintained by reinforcement but extinguish without it. Further study revealed that there was no generalization of self-references to situations outside the interview as ascertained from pre- and postreinforcement scores on an Adjective Self Description Test and a Sentence Completion Test, nor were there any significant changes on the Taylor MAT or Q-Sort Adjustment Test.

Instead of applying reinforcement to self-references, Ullmann et al. reinforced emotional words that represent the kind of material produced in therapy (Ullmann, Krasner, & Collins, 1961). Subjects were hospitalized patients. Those in one group were given a head-nod and "mm-hmm" whenever they used emotional words while telling a story to pictorial stimuli. A second group was reinforced by a mechanical signaling device, and a third group was not reinforced. Patients' interpersonal behavior in group therapy was rated before and after reinforcement sessions on the Palo Alto Group Therapy Scale. Only the group that received the positive-personal reinforcement gained significantly. Wimsatt and Vestre (1963) reanalyzed these data, claiming that the statistical analysis was incomplete, and failed to obtain significant differences. At best, in-therapy verbal behavior was marginally influenced, and there is no way of knowing whether these results were due to reinforcement of a class of words or simply to personal acknowledgment.

Schwartz and Hawkins (1965), also working on the assumption that affective expression is necessary in group therapy, attempted to elicit such expression in a group of hospitalized schizophrenics. Patients in three groups all received positive reinforcement of affective statements. In one group, however, two patients whose verbalizations mostly took the form of affective statements served as models in the group. A second group had two models who used primarily nonaffective statements, and in the third no models were provided. In each group there was significantly more expression of feelings in late than in early sessions. The only group that did not increase in affective statements was the one with models who were nonaffective verbalizers. This group actually declined.

An experiment by Moos (1963), which dealt with the retention and generalization of operant conditioning effects in an interview situation with college students, bears on the issue. Statements of independence or affection were positively reinforced for the experimental group, and statements of the control group were reinforced every thirty seconds no matter what the content. Conditioning of the reinforced categories did occur in the experimental group and was retained over a twenty-four-hour period, but generalization did not take place.

Wimsatt and Vestre (1963) also failed to obtain a generalization effect with seventy-four inpatients at the Veterans Administration Hospital, St. Cloud, Minnesota. Subjects were randomly assigned to one of two experimental groups or to a control group. The task was to read aloud and respond to thirty-five MMPI Si Scale (introversion) items and fifteen filler items. In one group, responses in the introverted direction were verbally reinforced by the word "good." In the second, only extraverted responses were reinforced, and the controls received no reinforcement. Two sessions were held two days apart, and the final session was followed by administration of the Guilford-Zimmerman Temperament Survey on scales known to be significantly correlated with the Si Scale. All patients were rated before, after, and three weeks later on the Withdrawal Scale of the Lorr Psychotic Reaction Profile by a ward attendant. Results showed that conditioning took place, but there was no generalization. While acknowledging that more conditioning trials might have brought on a generalizing effect, Wimsatt and Vestre concluded that the technique was "of no more psychological consequence than if such elevation or depression were produced by a mischievous test scorer, and it seems in effect as if the thermometer has been tampered with while the furnace remains untouched" (p. 403).

The verbal conditioning sessions were likened to a problem-solving task in which the patient figures out how to make the experimenter say the word "good." Therapists' judgments of patients may too often be based on how well the patient has learned to make the desired in-therapy verbal responses rather than on extratherapeutic behavior. A further clue to this was offered by Sarason (1958), who found that patients rated by their therapists as being very compliant were found to perform in the verbal conditioning situation at a significantly higher level than those rated less compliant.

Another failure to obtain generalization was found in an excellently controlled University of Iowa dissertation (Lanyon, 1967). Ninety undergraduates were randomly assigned to six groups and asked to describe important childhood experiences for twenty minutes. Members of one group received response-contingent social reinforcement for references to parents, and a second group received reinforcement for affect responses. Those in the third and fourth groups were given approval at constant time intervals regardless of response, and two other control groups were not given the interview task. Immediately following the conditioning task, a transfer task was given, which consisted of orally completing 100 incomplete sentences. The group that received response-contingent approval for parent words increased significantly in such content responses during the interview. Members of this group also increased significantly more than a noncontingent constant-interval approval group with which they were contrasted. The frequency of affect responses, however, did not increase with contingent social approval. The increase in content responses did not transfer to the sentence completion task even though conditions had been set up to maximize the possibility of transfer.

Waskow (1962) worked with students to test the hypothesis that selective responding by a "therapist" would reinforce content or feeling aspects of a subject's communication. Matched subjects were assigned to a group in which feeling aspects were reflected, to another in which a combination of feeling and content was reflected, and to a third in which only content was reflected over four interviews. The content group clearly showed the effect of reinforcement, but the other two groups did not. The major effects of the successful reinforcement in the content group occurred within the first third of the initial interview. Content reinforcement was also attempted by Ullmann et al. with hospitalized schizophrenics (Ullmann, Forsman, Kenny, McInnis, Unikel, & Zeisset, 1965). Interviewers reinforced either "sick talk," "healthy talk," or plural nouns during a structured interview. In addition, Welsh A and R Scale items were administered before and after reinforcement. The percentage of "sick talk" emitted changed differentially under the various conditions and correlated with changes in the Welsh R scores. The authors noted that the popular idea that "as the bad feelings come out the good feelings sprout" not only is ineffective but actually works in the opposite direction.

In an analogue experiment, Dinoff et al. were successful in increasing references to the environment, the self, or the experimenter by verbal reinforcement (Dinoff, Rickard, Salzberg, & Sipprelle, 1960). These experiments leave little doubt that the content of a patient's verbalizations can be shaped by verbal reinforcement techniques. A therapist has the option of subtly shaping the content of a patient's discussion in this manner or of shaping it more directly by suggesting that he discuss specific topics. It is likely that the latter would produce an even higher level of the desired type of verbalization. Of greater interest is the possibility that therapists may be unaware that they are reinforcing selected topics, unwittingly taking their emergence as proof of a theoretical position. Quay (1959) asked thirty-four students to recall events from their early childhood and established a baseline during an initial operant period. Subsequently, sixteen of the students were reinforced for memories concerning their families by the experimenter saying "uh-huh," and eighteen were reinforced for nonfamily memories. The reinforced category increased in both groups compared with the operant period. This may well happen in therapy; if it does, it would explain why therapists tend to evoke the kinds of material they are seeking and then make erroneous generalizations.

An experiment by Truax (1966b) lends further support to the notion that reinforcement may play more of a role in client-centered therapy than has hitherto been supposed. The possibility that reinforcement, with or without the therapist's awareness, plays a role in shaping patient responses was approached by intensive analysis of twenty transcriptions of interviews with a patient successfully treated by Carl Rogers. Forty therapist-patient-therapist interaction units drawn from these interviews were rated on nine patient scales and three therapist scales by five experienced psychologists. Internal controls in rating were applied with great care. Patient behaviors considered were: learning of discriminations about self and feelings, ambiguity, insight, similarity of expression to style of the therapist, problem orientation, catharsis, blocking, anxiety, and negative feeling expression. Considered as therapist reinforcers were empathy, unconditional positive regard, and directiveness. Levels of these three therapist reinforcements were then intercorrelated with the nine patient behaviors, yielding a matrix of twenty-seven coefficients of which eleven were statistically significant. Therapist acceptance and empathy were associated with patient discrimination learnings. Therapist directiveness was positively associated with patient ambiguity, but the latter was negatively related to therapist empathy and acceptance. Patient insight was positively associated with therapist empathy and acceptance. Similarity of patient expression to therapist style was positively related to therapist empathy and acceptance, and negatively to therapist directiveness. These were interpreted as a tendency on the part of the therapist to respond selectively with different levels of these conditions to different patient behaviors. Unfortunately, it is not clear from the correlation analysis whether it is the therapist, the patient, or both who are responding selectively. There was evidence, however, that patient behavior reinforced by the therapist increased over time in therapy. Interestingly enough, therapist verbalization of "mm-hmm's" occurred primarily during patient expression of high negative feeling and was absent during low negative feeling expression, suggesting a conscious or unconscious pattern of selective therapist response. From these data Truax concluded that reinforcement effects occur even in client-centered therapy.

REINFORCEMENT OF DEPENDENCY RESPONSES

Winder et al. studied the effects of reinforcement of verbal expressions of dependency upon further expressions of dependency and continuation in treatment (Winder, Ahmad, Bandura, & Rau, 1962). There was a higher termination rate when dependency bids were avoided by the therapist and a higher rate of remaining when dependency was approached. Approach to dependency (positive reinforcement) led to further patient dependency, and avoidance (negative reinforcement) led to a decrease in dependency. Similarly, the proportion of aggressive response following approach of aggression exceeded that for aggression following its avoidance by the therapist.

Caracena (1965) examined the elicitation and verbal reinforcement of dependency expressions in the initial stage of therapy. Clients were sixty students with no previous psychotherapy seen in a university counseling center. Recordings were made of forty-eight first and twenty-four second sessions, and the tapes were scored by Winder's system. The thirty therapists were at three levels of experience, ranging from raw beginners to those with up to ten years of experience. For all levels of therapist experience, approach to dependency (attempt to elicit further verbalizations by the therapist) was associated significantly with immediately following expressions of dependency by the patient and avoidance of dependency on the part of the therapist by nondependent expressions by the patient. The frequency of dependent statements did not increase in the second half of the interview, and there was no evidence that approach or avoidance had a reinforcing value. The percentage of approach to dependency did not differentiate the remainers and terminators. More experienced therapists approached dependency statements more than less experienced ones, but it was apparent that attempts to lead did not encourage the patient to follow. Schuldt (1966) confirmed the finding that approach leads to continuance of dependency responses and avoidance to their decline. He also determined that therapists approach dependency directed at themselves more readily than dependency directed at others.

DEGREE OF LEAD

Dependency of client responses was also examined as a function of counselor style and induced set (Rottschafer & Renzaglia, 1962). In this experiment, forty-one students were given instructions to expect a leading or reflective counselor and were randomly assigned to a counselor previously classified as one or the other type. There were no differences in dependency responses of clients seen by counselors who made predominantly (65 per cent) leading responses and by those who were mainly reflective. When the counselor response distribution was cut into thirds, however, leading counselors produced more dependent behavior in the clients. The conflicting results, which depend on how the distribution of counselor responses was cut, enables us to place little confidence in the conclusion. The main point of the experiment, according to Moos and Clemes (1967), is that counselors use a mixture of styles depending on the client seen and that patient behavior cannot be predicted from a general classification of counselor style. Danskin and Robinson (1954) assessed interviews of thirty-five experienced counselors from counseling centers in five universities known for their different points of view and discovered a continuum of "degree of lead" rather than a directive-nondirective dichotomy. Counselors were found to vary their techniques from client to client, but the data were not really analyzed.

In another therapy analogue study with college student volunteers, Gordon (1957) found no significant difference between leading and following techniques in lifting hypnotically induced repression and hostility, although leading had a slight edge. Generalizations to real therapy with patients cannot be made. The interaction between the personality of the patient and technique of the therapist was examined by Tolor and Kissinger (1965), who hypothesized that responses would be more favorable if patients with high dependency needs were exposed to more structured and directive comments, with the converse true for less dependent patients. Accordingly, forty-eight chronic hospitalized patients were selected for extreme (high or low) Succorance scores on the Edwards Personal Preference Scale. Three quasi-therapeutic half-hour sessions were held a week apart, and patients were informed that it was a new experimental procedure to help people talk to the therapist. The patient spoke into a microphone and pressed a button whenever he wished a therapeutic intervention. A predetermined type of intervention was applied each session—either "positive mental health" based on Norman Vincent Peale (by which the therapist advised the patient to think calm thoughts), rational-directive based on Ellis, or nondirective. Responses were given from a tape recording, all by the same person. An anxiety checklist, a rating scale measuring general satisfaction with the therapy, and a semantic differential of meanings assigned to the concepts "my therapist" and "me" were given before and after therapy. Data were carefully analyzed, but no differences appeared.

The effect of other related therapist techniques on patient responses have been investigated. Bergman (1951) reported that therapist's structuring and interpretation were followed by a decline in self-exploration; in contrast, self-exploration continued after reflection by the therapist. The exceptional analogue study of Kanfer and Marston (1964) produced findings with implications for psychotherapy. Subjects in general preferred interpretation to reflection. Half the subjects were told that the interviewer would try to influence the conversation and half were not. Among those who were informed, the more they allowed themselves to be influenced, the more negative their attitude toward the interviewer became. In addition, half the subjects received emotional topics to discuss and half were given neutral topics. Subjects were classified earlier for their tendency to give socially desirable responses. Those low in this tendency decreased significantly over time in their requests for comments from the experimenter while the high social-desirability group continued to seek the social response of the interviewer. Those high on social desirability resented having to talk about personal topics. The study revealed a number of interacting determinants affecting verbal responses and subject attitudes. The nature of the comments by the interviewer affected both the attitudes of the subject toward him and the way the subject talked. Favorable attitudes are related to minimal threat in the interview. Solicitation of advice or information by the subject increases when the therapist gives agreement, support, or avoids threatening material, but negative attitudes may develop.

OTHER TECHNIQUE AND STYLE EFFECTS

D'Zurilla (1966) evaluated the effects of persuasion and praise on the rate of verbal participation. While the research took place in the group setting of a university classroom, there may be some extension to group therapy. Verbal participation under the reinforcement conditions (persuasion, praise, and neutral) differed significantly from a control condition but the various reinforcement conditions did not differ among each other. D'Zurilla attributed the result to generalized nonspecific reinforcement.

An attempt to manipulate verbal behavior was carried out in group therapy sessions with chronic, inactive, hospitalized schizophrenics (Drennen & Wiggins, 1964). In the first phase, using persuasion, direct questions, redirection, suggestion, criticism, and other verbal reinforcements, two therapists attempted to stimulate interaction among the patients and between patients and therapists. Fourteen semiweekly sessions were held. In a second phase of the experiment four therapists worked in two teams. One team was gruff and hypercritical and chastised the group for being inactive and not interacting. The other pair was congenial, supportive, praised the group, and passed out candy, cigarettes, and chewing gum. Total verbal activity increased during the first phase along with patient-to-patient and patient-therapist interaction, but the increase was limited to a portion of the group. The "negative" therapists elicited much less patient-therapist interaction in the initial session but rates were similar by the fifth session.

Heller et al. studied the effects of interviewer style in a standardized interview (Heller, Davis, & Myers, 1966). Interviewers were twelve actors trained to play five roles: active-friendly, passive-friendly, active-hostile, passive-hostile, silent. Interviewers were 120 students. Before the interview the subjects took a battery of tests and listened to a tape of a model fifteen-minute interview. In the interview they were asked to talk about the tape, about themselves, and about the counseling situation. An interview-reaction checklist revealed that subjects preferred friendly interviewers. Active-friendly interviewers were best liked and passive-hostile ones least liked. The silent ones were in between. Subjects with active interviewers used the time available for speaking more than those with passive interviewers. Talk time was lowest when interviewers were silent. The therapist activity level rather than the friendliness led to the greatest increases in verbalization. The fact that therapist silence apparently inhibited talk is of methodological interest, and argues against using silence to establish operant levels. The authors offer several cogent cautions against generalization. The interviews only lasted fifteen minutes. Normal interviews rely not on one type of role behavior indiscriminately applied, but make use of a series of reciprocally contingent interactions. This was, however, an interesting and well-done analogue study, aspects of which could be repeated in live therapy situations.

Various investigators have focused on the effect of formal characteristics of the therapist's verbalizations upon aspects of patient responsivity and upon the patient-therapist verbal interaction process. Frank and Sweetland (1962) distinguished between forcing insight (either by placing focus on a particular cause or effect and asking for the missing element, or by giving the client both elements of a cause-and-effect relation and asking for a connection), interpretation, clarification of feeling, and direct questioning. Forcing insight was reported to lead to tentative striving ("I'm going to try . . ."; "Maybe I ought to . . ."). Interpretation, clarification of feeling, and direct pointing to cause and effect relations led to increases in understanding and insight, while direct questioning and forcing the topic led to a decrease in understanding and insight and increased statement of the problem.

Dibner (1958) reported that more structured interviews with hospitalized patients created less anxiety than less structured ones. Clemes and D'Andrea (1965) were unable to confirm this finding on an outpatient sample of higher educational level. Pope and Siegman (1962) investigated the effect of the verbal activity level and specificity of the therapist on patient's verbal productivity and speech disturbance (anxiety). Ratings were made from twelve transcripts of initial interviews. All therapist remarks were judged for activity level and specificity, and each patient remark that followed immediately was rated for productivity (clause units) and speech disturbance. Predicted negative correlations between activity level of the therapist and the two patient speech variables were not found. On the other hand, significant negative correlations were found between the specificity of therapist remarks and patient clause units and speech disturbance. The authors speculate that high specificity on the part of the therapist may reduce anxiety when the content is neutral but arouse anxiety when the content is emotional. Howe (1962) reported that *deep* specific statements arouse anxiety. It is possible that as long as the therapist is specific (as opposed to ambiguous) and remains within certain limits of depth, anxiety will be relieved. This fits in with research findings on depth of interpretation and could account for some of the success of directive therapists.

In a similar vein, Truax and Carkhuff (1964) proposed concreteness as an important process variable. Concreteness was defined as specificity of expression of feelings and experiences, and was thought to be directly under the therapist's control. The investigators sampled three-minute sections of verbal interaction from more than 100 recorded group therapy sessions involving thirty-nine hospitalized patients. To digress for a moment, an important technical point in process research that involves analyzing recorded interview segments is the matter of length of the segments sampled. Kiesler et al. had judges rate segments whose lengths ranged from two to sixteen minutes on one dimension of process (experiencing); no important difference between shorter or longer segments appeared (Kiesler, Mathieu, & Klein, 1964). For research purposes, short segments, as used by Truax and Carkhuff, apparently introduce no distortion. In their experiment, therapeutic approaches varied widely. Thirteen judges rated the material on the Process Scale, designed particularly to measure changes in self-exploration, the Insight Scale, and the Personal Reference Scale, which measured the number of personal references per word emitted. The authors claim that of sixteen different therapist-influenced variables, concreteness was the most highly related to the criteria measures. It correlated significantly with all three and was negatively correlated with the sociability of the relationship. Therapy sessions in the nature of a social hour apparently lack specificity, self-exploration, and insight. It was concluded that concreteness is of "overwhelming importance in effective psychotherapy if the importance of the change indices is conceded" (p. 267). Unfortunately, the concession cannot be readily made without knowledge of the extent to which self-exploration, insight, and personal reference are correlated with behavioral change or other evidences of positive improvement in adjustment. Specificity of expression and the three criteria measures may merely reflect modes of verbal responses in the group therapy situation. It can be stated that specificity of expression is related to other in-therapy variables that some observers hold in high esteem. Intuitively, the variable makes good sense, for if a verbal therapy is to have an effect, discussion in "anonymous generalities" (the lowest level of concreteness) should logically do less than expression of specifics. This could be a key variable, and calls for research that attempts to clarify the association between in-therapy concreteness and improved adjustment.

INTERPRETATION

Interpretations are designed forcibly to bring to the patient's conscious awareness the causal relations between aspects of his current behavior, attitudes, and feelings and their antecedents and motivations. If the interpretations are to have the desired effects of cognitive restructuring and affective and behavioral reorganization, it is assumed that they must "hit home" by dint of their "truth status." In practice, the *veridicality* of an interpretation is often gauged by the immediate effect it has. This idea was put to the test by Noblin et al., who hypothesized that when the content of an interpretation lacks "truth status," verbal behavior may nonetheless be modified (Noblin, Timmons, & Reynard,

1963). Schizophrenic patients in an acute hospital treatment ward were presented with a stack of 120 cards each having a first- and third-person pronoun at the top and a sentence fragment at the bottom that made a complete sentence when merged. The first twenty-four cards were used to establish the operant level for using the first-person pronoun. The next sixty cards were the experimental treatment phase, and the last thirty-six constituted the extinction phase. For one group (N = 24), the experimenter read back an interpretation designed to relate to the content of the stimulus after each statement in which the personal pronoun was selected during the experimental treatment phase. A second group (N = 12) was given random interpretations by the experimenter, who shuffled cards containing the same interpretations and drew the one that happened to be on top. A third group (N = 24) received reinforcement for use of the personal pronoun by such affirmatory expressions as "good" or "OK." The control group (N = 12) showed no consistent change in the use of personal pronouns in going from the operant level to the first and second halves of treatment and extinction. The single reinforcement group showed a rapid rise during the treatment phase and a drop during extinction. The performances of the paired interpretation group and the random interpretation group were very much alike. The random interpretation group had a near chance distribution of first- and third-person pronouns in the operant phase, and increased the use of first-person pronouns during the first thirty treatment trials and again during the second thirty. There was a pronounced upward trend during the extinction phase. Thus, relevance of the interpretation was clearly not the central factor in determining the systematic modification of verbal behavior in this verbal conditioning situation. "Any old interpretation" was effective. While not strictly a test of what happens in psychotherapy, and particularly in the psychotherapy of nonschizophrenics, the study does raise reasonable doubts.

In another indirect test, Ulrich et al. used fifty-seven college students in one experiment and seventy-nine in another (Ulrich, Stachnik, & Stainton, 1963). A psychology instructor administered the Bell Adjustment Inventory and H.T.P. A week later each student was given what he was told was an individual interpretation, although all interpretations were the same general, vague statements. Students were asked to rate the interpretations on a five-point scale from very poor to excellent and to make comments. To control for the prestige of the person making the interpretations, in the second experiment the tests were given and "interpreted" by students to roommates or friends of their choosing. In both experiments most of the Ss accepted the standard interpretations. Thus, fifty-three of fifty-seven rated the psychologist's interpretations as good or excellent, and fifty-nine of seventy-nine so rated the student's interpretation. Many of the comments were laudatory, such as, "For the first time things that I have been vaguely aware of have been put into concise and constructive statements which I would like to use as a plan for improving myself" (p. 833).

Forer (1949) obtained a similar result but reported a higher degree of acceptance of the interpretations when made by a person with more prestige. These experiments strongly suggest the need for research that will substantiate or further negate the importance of the truth status of interpretations. Is it the insight that comes from truth that is therapeutic, the patient's *belief* that it is true, or the anxiety that is aroused and dealt with?

With veridicality assumed, the *depth* of interpretation has been considered as a fundamental variable in the therapeutic process. Some of the investigations are methodological, with a focus on devising measures of the depth variable, and others study the impact of different degrees of depth upon patient in-therapy performance. Collier (1953) attempted to quantify the verbalizations of the therapist on a continuum of "uncovering or interpreting." Descriptive items representing a variety of therapeutic approaches were rated and a Thurstone Scale constructed. Items were discriminable, but scale distances did not provide equal intervals because too few initial items were used. In constructing the items, Collier inadvertantly varied the length of the items excessively so that there is a very high correlation between scale value and item length. However, this kind of quantification of formal aspects of the interview is of considerable utility in process research.

In an exceptionally well designed, conceived, and executed study, Harway et al. developed a seven-point graphic rating scale of depth of interpretation and studied results obtained under various conditions of measurement (Harway, Dittmann, Raush, Bordin, & Rigler, 1955). They used both experienced and naïve judges to sort statements in the original scale development. In so doing they demonstrated the importance of taking this variable into account, for naïve judges were significantly more variable and placed significantly more items at the deeper end of the scale than did experienced judges. In the experiment proper, sixteen raters evaluated four therapy interviews from different cases with different therapists in different settings, thus maximizing generality. Independent variables were the *unit* of the interview (individual therapist response versus interview as a whole), *method of presentation* (typescript versus tape recording), and amount of information given or *context* (therapist response in the context of the preceding interview material versus only the therapist's sequence of responses). The study was designed to control systematically or evaluate the influence of raters, interviews, and practice in the use of the scale.

The scale was able to differentiate among the interviews. For each interview, the evaluation based upon the entire interview as a unit was "deeper" than the mean of individual response units. It made no difference whether the material was presented in the form of a typescript or tape recording, and ratings of depth of interpretation are apparently based only upon the words spoken. Appraisal of context as a variable suggested that it is not necessary for a rater to possess knowledge of both the therapist and patient activity, although variations in certain conditions of context led to changes in depth ratings.

Further study of this Depth of Interpretation Scale by Cutler et al. considered the possibility that the generally low interjudge reliability of the scale would be improved by using raters who were more sensitive to subtle aspects of the therapeutic relationship (Cutler, Bordin, Williams, & Rigler, 1958). The four interviews were therefore given for rating to four psychoanalysts and four analysts-in-training. The raters were able to distinguish between interviews. The amount of contextual information and the method of presentation had no effect. On the question of reliability, it was found that this group of raters agreed even less among each other than the group of psychologists who had done similar ratings in the prior study. Agreement was higher within the analyst-trainee group when the information furnished was limited to the therapist responses.

Raush et al. explored the dimensions of depth of interpretation and attempted to determine if it is a unidimensional variable (Raush, Sperber, Rigler, Harway, Bordin, Dittmann, & Hays, 1956). Interpretation was defined as any therapist behavior that expresses his view of the emotions and motivations of the patient. Depth was defined in terms of the disparity between the therapist's expressed view and the patient's awareness. The greater the disparity the deeper the interpretation. Judges were inexperienced psychologist-therapists at the University of Michigan. In the first study, ten judges were guided only by the definitions of interpretation and depth that were given. At least three dimensions were required to account for the results. When given a graphic rating scale, three judges had unidimensional judgments, but three dimensions were still needed to account for all the judgments. In a second study to determine if the improvement was due to the improved frame of reference furnished by the graphic scale or to prior practice, it was found that both helped. Three dimensions were again isolated, one of which was depth of interpretation. Subsequent studies showed that depth of interpretation was consistently the primary dimension. The other dimensions varied with the judges and stimuli used. The authors recommended the pooling of judgments to maximize the contribution of the primary dimension and to minimize secondary factors specific to individual judges. They cautioned that the assumption of unidimensionality underlying rating-scale construction could mask the influence of additional factors.

Fisher (1956) hypothesized that judgments of depth of interpretations are implicitly derived from estimates of their plausibility, with those that are more plausible rated as more shallow. Sixty therapist statements covering the entire range of depth were presented along with a fictitious case history to be rated on seven-point scales of depth and of plausibility from the patient's point of view. Ratings proved to be reliable and intercorrelated in the predicted direction. Fisher concluded that inferences regarding depth may be based upon similar cues used in drawing inferences about plausibility. Depth may be related to perceived rather than actual truth-content. If depth is a function of the patient's awareness, Fisher points out, the same interpretation made late in therapy would be more plausible to the patient and hence not as deep as if given early in therapy. Fisher's findings on plausibility were substantiated.

To examine the rated correlates of depth of interpretive statements, Howe (1962) had forty-eight experienced psychiatrists rate sixty-two interpretive statements along one of five annotated seven-point scales. Judges rated the material for either depth, generality-specificity, potential for anxiety arousal in the patient, therapeutic skillfulness of response (likeliness of being helpful to the patient), or plausibility from the patient's point of view. Reliability for depth was $r = .52$, for specificity $r = .30$, for skillfulness $r = .11$, for anxiety arousal $r = .29$, and for implausibility $r = .43$. The intercorrelations of the mean ratings of depth, specificity, anxiety arousal, and implausibility were moderate to high, ranging from $r = .45$ to $.75$. Ratings of skillfulness showed only chance departure from zero correlations with the other four. Statements rated as deep by therapists were also seen as relatively implausible, specific or sharply focused, and anxiety arousing. As therapists see it, interpretations that are not too plausible to the patient or are not understood or accepted by him are likely to arouse anxiety.

Other researchers have studied the effects of depth of interpretation on the patient. Grossman (1952) investigated the comparative degree of improvement in ten pairs of mildly disturbed college student patients treated under conditions of recognition of explicitly expressed feelings and attitudes or of interpretation of deeper feelings inferred from verbal or motor behavior. The criterion of improvement was the therapist's rating of insight gained and therapeutic progress and two insight inventories designed by the author. Although the groups were initially matched on motivation for treatment, verbal and reasoning abilities, and prognosis and insight, it unexpectedly turned out that the "deep" group had a majority of the less inhibited and less resistant individuals. They participated readily in the three interviews held while most of those in the "surface" group were more interested in the test results or claimed they had no problems to explore. This, of course, reduces the meaningfulness of any comparisons. Still, there were no differences between the groups following the interviews on the insight inventories even though significant gains over pretherapy scores were obtained. The therapist (whose judgment in this case must be discounted) claimed that the deep group acquired more insight. On the basis of rating scales given four weeks after the interview, it was ascertained that deep interpretations did not produce more anxiety. The groups felt equally well understood, did not differ in their perception of the authoritarianism of the therapist, felt equally that the therapist was accepting, and equally claimed freedom to express personal material. The surface group felt that more responsibility was placed on them to work out their own problems.

Typescripts of 965 therapist responses in thirty therapeutic interviews of a single patient were rated by three judges on a number of variables including an interpretation continuum ranging from superficial to deep (Dittmann, 1952). The judges were also asked to evaluate therapeutic movement from the patient's responses on a five-point scale ranging from rapid movement toward improvement to rapid movement away from improvement. Progressive movement was found to be associated with therapist responses that were "slightly deeper than pure reflection."

Speisman (1959) investigated verbal resistance as a function of depth of interpretation. Working from transcriptions of actual cases, teams of three raters judged depth of interpretation on the scales of Harway et al. (1955). Interpretive responses were classified as superficial, moderate, or deep. Other raters judged resistance with therapist statements deleted. The categories of exploration (positive) and opposition (negative) were used. In support of the hypothesis, both superficial and moderate interpretations were followed by more exploration and less opposition, taken to indicate lower resistance, than were deeper interpretations. More resistance was encountered to superficial than to moderate interpretations. Thus, deep interpretations evoked most resistance, moderate least, and superficial intermediate. Shifts from moderate to superficial levels were followed by increased resistance, and shifts from deep to moderate by lowered resistance. While the interpretations of the therapist had a systematic influence upon the patient responses, the converse was not true. Speisman concluded that a moderate level of interpretation is most effective for maintaining mimimum levels of resistance. This is a particularly interesting result in the light of Dittmann's earlier finding that movement in therapy is associated with an intermediate level of interpretation. Auld and White (1959) reported that interpretation did *not* produce more resistance than other types of intervention.

Frank and Sweetland (1962) developed a 9 × 14 table of frequencies of types of client statements in response to therapist statements obtained from the first four hours of interviews of four Rogerian therapists with forty clients. They determined that therapist responses had a direct influence on client responses. Interpretation was followed by an increase in understanding and a decrease in statement of the problem. The technique just short of interpretation, in which the client is given both elements of a cause-and-effect relation and asked if he can make the connection, also led to an increase in understanding and insight, as did clarification of feelings. By contrast, direct questioning and forcing the topic resulted in an increase in statements about problems and a decrease in understanding and insight.

Howe (1962), as previously indicated, found an interrelation among implausibility, specificity, depth, and anxiety arousal. As far as specificity is concerned, Pope and Siegman (1962) reported that more specific therapist remarks in an initial interview tended to *reduce* the patient's anxiety as reflected by speech disturbance. They suggested the possibility that specificity is anxiety reducing when the content area is neutral, but anxiety arousing when the content is emotional. This is consistent with the finding of increased anxiety-arousal with deep and specific interpretations.

In addition to these investigations, there have been a few studies comparing the relative effects on patient in-therapy performance of interpretations and other interview techniques such as reflection and interrogation. Kanfer et al. checked the comparative effects upon the duration of the interviewee's utterances of interpretations as opposed to exploratory or information-seeking statements (Kanfer, Phillips, Matarazzo, & Saslow, 1960). The study was not done in the context of psychotherapy. Data were obtained from standard interviews with a group of nurses. The interviews were divided into three periods. During the first and third periods the interviewer made only exploratory and information-seeking remarks, while twelve interpretations were made during the second period for experimental subjects. Exploratory statements were continued for control subjects. All interactions were recorded by the interaction chronograph. During the interpretation period the experimental subjects showed significantly lower mean duration of utterance while controls did not change over the three periods. The interpretation period was followed in the next period by a significantly higher mean duration of verbalizations. The authors speculated that interpretations might be considered as punishing, aversive stimuli, and therefore lead to reduced verbal output. This is in keeping with cited findings that relate interpretation to anxiety arousal. On the other hand, an alternative, more mechanical explanation was offered, to the effect that exploratory questions could, by their nature, call for more extended verbalizations whereas interpretations call for a simple yes or no answer. This may have been an artifact brought about by the interrogative way in which interpretations were worded in this experiment. The interviewer apparently asked, "Do you think that . . . (interpretation)?" Interpretations worded as statements rather than questions might well stimulate different verbal outputs. In this connection, Colby (1961) compared the "amplifying power" (increase in free association) of causal-correlative inputs with that of interpretations offered in causal terms such as "You felt this way because of . . ." and interrogatives (questions asked by the therapist). Normal subjects in a controlled interview situation were seen four times a week for three weeks in thirty-minute sessions. The subject lay on a couch with the experimenter behind him and was asked to free associate. The experimenter's statements were restricted to either interrogatives or causal correlatives referring to immediate antecedents. The subject's response unit following the experimenter's statement was scored for presence or absence of the personage or topic indicated in the input. A significantly greater number of sentences were noted after the causal correlative than after interrogative inputs.

Kanfer and Marston (1964) performed a superior analogue study on the characteristics of interactional behavior. In one phase of the study, an experimenter behind a screen was assigned an interpretive role and another a reflective role. The subject pressed a "ready" switch to produce a topic in a window and another switch to select one of the interviewers. At a signal the subject was expected to begin talking and to continue until the light went off. At this point, the selected interviewer made a comment. The topics were MMPI statements. The rather farfetched interpretations were extremes of the Harway Depth of Interpretation Scale. Fifty trials were given to each college student volunteer. Measures were taken of choice time (latency between ready signal and choice of interviewer), incubation time (posttrial delay from end of interviewer's comment to the next ready signal), starting latency (time from interviewer selection to start of S's verbalizations), talk time (duration of the subject's verbalizations during the thirty-second period), and silence time obtained by substraction. Subjects were randomly assigned to three groups: R-R (both switches yield reflective statements), I-I (both yield interpretive statements), I-R (one of each). After the session the subjects were given a fifty-item questionnaire reflecting positive or negative reaction to E. Attitudes toward Es were significantly more positive when they used reflection (R-R group) than when they used interpretation (I-I group). There was no significant difference in the amount of silence, starting latency, or choice time between the groups, but the interpretation group had a longer delay after E's comments. When given a choice, the subjects selected about twice as often the interviewer who would interpret. These findings raise questions about the aversive character of interpretations, but the authors stress that the initial interview material was not threatening.

In research on interpretation, the problem is in part a lack of absolute standards of depth levels that are external to the reactions or estimated reactions of the patient and the frame of reference of the judge. If depth is defined in terms of the awareness of the individual patient, it is obvious that what may be deep for one may be shallow for another, and what is deep early in therapy may be superficial later on. Lack of conceptual clarity in the measuring of depth handicaps its use as a research variable. Its operational definition as the disparity between the expressed views of the therapist and the patient's awareness assumes its truth status. For if the therapist's formulation is wide of the mark it must perforce be outside the patient's awareness. The concept of depth implies the existence of strata. The hierarchical arrangement of these strata is a function of the personality theory that guides the therapist and the judge; it is also a function of how well oriented the patient is to the particular conceptual schema. Nevertheless, these studies have shown that something operationally defined as depth can be identified (even though it is closely associated with implausibility, specificity and anxiety arousal), scaled, and judged—if not as reliably as we would like. Other studies have shown that interviewees respond differentially to its systematic variation. The work that has been done suggests that there is more of what therapists see as movement, less resistance, and greater patient preference for intermediate-level interpretations that go beyond mere reflection of feelings yet are plausible to the patient (whether or not they are true). When too "deep," abstruse, or beyond the patient's present ability to understand, accept, and be influenced by it, the interpretation may serve as an aversive stimulus that arouses anxiety and resistance to a degree that interferes with the therapeutic process. Much more work is needed to clarify the concept of depth, define the other parameters of interpretation, and test hypotheses within actual psychotherapy situations.

SILENCE AND RESISTANCE

Psychotherapy has traditionally taken the form of a verbal interchange with most of the burden for talking on the patient. Periods of silence on the part of the patient are usually interpreted as resistance, and on the part of the therapist as a therapeutic tactic. The phenomenon of silence has intrigued researchers, who have attempted to verify its meaning for patients. In addition to investigating a number of different forms of speech disturbance, Mahl (1956) obtained measures of the "patient-silence quotient," consisting of the ratio of the number of seconds of silence to the number of seconds available to the patient to talk. These were measured accurately with times from recordings. Applying the measure to a single patient, Mahl found that the mean silence quotient increased by 35 per cent during phases independently judged as anxious for the patient and also became more variable.

Auld and White (1959) investigated internal interdependent sequences in psychotherapy. Each of four patients was seen by a different therapist, two of whom were psychoanalysts. In three of the cases the free association rule was insisted upon. Silence was found to occur more often after talk judged by two psychologists to be resistant than after nonresistant talk. Silences were also likely to be *followed* by resistant talk. They concluded, therefore, that silence was equivalent to resistant speech. Since the raters were working from transcripts, their judgments could have been affected by the context in which the silences appeared. This design flaw was corrected in a subsequent experiment in which the raters did not know where the silences occurred (Goldenberg & Auld, 1964). Data were obtained from six cases. The probability of a silence after a resistant statement was .23; after a nonresistant one it was .06. After silence the probability of resistance was .50, of nonresistance .16. Longer silences were no more resistant than shorter ones. Neither longer nor shorter silences occurred systematically early or late in a session.

The assumption that silence is negative behavior in psychotherapy has even led to research on methods of eliminating it by conditioning (Heckel, Wiggins, & Salzberg, 1962). In this experiment, a continuous unpleasant tone of eighty-five decibels at 4,000 cycles per second was used successfully to reduce the number and duration of silences during the first fifteen minutes of group therapy. The group was told that the sound was due to malfunction of the recording apparatus. Following discontinuance of the stimulus, silence did not reach the former operant level. Other investigators have challenged the relation between silence and benefit. Bassin and Smith (1962) obtained zero order correlations between the amount of talking of fifteen individuals in two group sessions and the extent of changes measured. They concluded that for some participants in group therapy "silence may be golden." Cook (1964) explored the relation of silence to movement in individual client-centered therapy by examining interview recordings from early and late interviews in five more successful and five less successful cases. The patients' performance in the interviews was rated on Rogers' Process Scale from random two-minute segments. Silence was counted only if it extended for five or more seconds and was terminated by the client. Seventy per cent of the silences were client-terminated and 30 per cent were therapist-terminated. Contrary to the view that silence is antitherapeutic, the more successful cases had higher proportions of silence (4 per cent and above). Lower process ratings were associated with silence extremes in both directions, but higher process ratings were found in segments with 4 to 20 per cent silence. Silence was independent of the early-late dichotomy. Cook suggested that the silence ratio may be largely a therapist variable reflecting the therapeutic relationship. Simply from the point of view of what transpires, Cook's data on who terminates silences is supplemented by some information about who initiates them. Analysis of sixty-one transcripts of nondirective therapy by twenty-two counselors uncovered 708 pauses (Tindall & Robinson, 1947). Of this total, 52 per cent were judged by one of the authors to be counselor initiated, 40 per cent counselee initiated, and the remainder unclassifiable. Therapist silence is here regarded as a technique.

In an ingenious experiment, Salzberg (1962) measured the comparative effects of silence, talking, directing, and redirecting on the verbal responses of nineteen patients on a privileged ward at the Veterans Administration Hospital, Augusta, Georgia. The composition of the group varied; new members were admitted when old ones were discharged. Under the condition of redirection, in answering a question from a patient, the therapist would mention other patients. Under the condition of direction, he would speak directly to the patient without referring to other group members. These two conditions were combined with either silence or talking, yielding four combinations. The two silent conditions were necessarily the same. Each session was divided into four fifteen-minute periods during each of which a different combination of conditions was applied. The order was rotated systematically, with one order prevailing for the first five sessions and a different order for each succeeding block of five sessions until the twentieth session was completed. The patients were reported to be not consciously aware of the therapist's differential responding, and the progress of the group did not seem to be hampered. Each patient's responses in the four treatments were classified as referring to himself, other group members, or other objects or persons, and it was noted whether he spoke only to the therapist or to another group member. For total responses of patients, there was no significant difference between silence and talking, directing or redirecting, or in the silence-talking–directing-redirecting interaction. There were significantly more environmental responses (references to objects or persons outside the group) when the therapist was silent, and more personal responses when the therapist was talking (particularly when directing). There were more group responses (references to other group members) under therapist talking-redirection. More patient interaction responses appeared when the therapist was silent, and therapist talking (particularly when directing) elicited more noninteraction responses. Since therapist silence elicited the more environmental responses (assumed to be least therapeutic), it was not recommended. It was suggested that a talking-directing role would be a good way to start a group if personal patient responses are desired, with redirection applied later. From these data it appears that patient behavior in groups follows lawful principles. The only doubtful aspect of this study is the nature of the arrangement of conditions within sessions and across series of sessions. A systematic rather than random order was used in five-session blocks. As a result, two of the conditions were not applied until the eleventh session. Order may have been a variable, but its possible effects were not tested. With the composition of the group changing as patients left and were replaced, it is likely that some never experienced several of the conditions.

Heller, Davis, and Myers (1966) reported that silence on the part of the therapist seemed to inhibit interviewee speech, as talk time was lowest under this condition. However, Bandura, Lipsher, and Miller (1960) reported that silence by the therapist in response to patient expressions of hostility tended to elicit further expressions of hostility. Silence, an ambiguous cue, seemed to be interpreted as encouragement. Pierce and Mosher (1967) conducted a therapy-analogue experiment that offered some evidence to the effect that interviewees are made to feel uneasy by interviewer silences and interruptions and perceive the interviewer as less empathic than when responses are made promptly but without interrupting. Taking therapeutic advantage of pauses, Toman (1953) introduced a technique of pause analysis consisting of the review of pauses made by the subject in a brief recording of his life history. Many of the pauses were found to be linked to hidden or suppressed material.

The purpose of a study by Gillespie (1953) was to develop a technique for locating and classifying verbal resistance signs and to determine the relation between counselor errors and resistance and between resistance and success. Counselor statements were coded by seven raters into accurate clarification of feeling, inaccurate clarification of feeling, clarification of unverbalized feeling, interpretation, or restatement of content. Signs of verbal resistance were defined, and raters were trained to identify them reliably. The frequency of resistance following each category of counselor statements was obtained, and ratios of resistance per interview and per counselor statement type were correlated with Tucker's (1953) Multiple Criterion Score of outcome and with length of treatment. Resistance was grouped into resistance toward the therapist, toward the therapeutic process, or within the client. Counselor statements were classified as error (interpretation, inaccurate clarification of feelings and clarification of unverbalized feelings) or nonerror (accurate clarification of feelings and restatement of content). Some of the "errors" here defined, such as interpretation, are only errors in the nondirective framework of this study. In the 218 interviews that were coded, there were 5,003 signs of resistance, of which nearly 60 per cent were classified as resistance within the client. These took the form of pauses, short answers, blocking, excessive verbalization or intellectualization, changing the subject, and stereotyped repetition. The most frequent of these (41.5 per cent) were short and monosyllabic answers. Resistance toward the therapist accounted for 13.8 per cent and included rejection of the therapist's statement, criticism of the therapist, or frank antagonism. Resistance toward the therapeutic process comprised 13.3 per cent, and client-initiated long pauses 13.3 per cent. The most frequent signs, then, were client-initiated short answers or long pauses.

Analysis of the data revealed a significant positive relation between the number of counselor statements, *regardless of the counselor statement category*, and the amount of resistance following these statements (r's from .90 to .99). The mean resistance for what were herein considered nonerror categories were, counter to expectations, *larger* than for error categories, although resistance directed toward the therapist and therapy process did run higher for the error categories. Counselor directiveness or nondirectiveness was not significantly related to resistance. Insofar as outcome is concerned, there was no relation between the resistance measures or resistance change and success even though verbal signs of resistance did diminish.

Many aspects of a patient's behavior other than silence are interpreted as resistance to therapy. One such behavior, retaliatory resistance, is cancellation of appointments by patients after an unexpected cancellation by the therapist. McCue (1954) studied this phenomenon using forty-seven patients who were notified on the day of the appointment of the therapist's cancellation; subjects were matched with an equal number of control patients. The data did not support the hypothesis of retaliatory cancellation. Following the canceled appointment, six patients canceled, compared to seventeen cancellations of the next appointment by controls. There was, in fact, a negative correlation (phi coefficient = — .88) between therapist and patient cancellation. Another related phenomenon is the view that failure to return for treatment after testing is a form of resistance. McCue et al. reported that tested clinic patients did not differ in percentage of returns from nontested patients (McCue, Goodman, & Rosenthal, 1954). There are reservations about the method of selecting controls in this study.

In summary, the available data suggest that neither the therapist's nor the patient's silences always have the same significance. For some patients, silence tends to be associated with "resistant" statements; for others, responses of silence seem to be related to either short-term or long-term benefits. Sometimes the therapist's silence inhibits patient speech; sometimes it encourages patient responses. Context, that most unmanageable variable, matters. Investigators have to exercise great care in spacing of silences, controlling their order in the interview, and above all, in specifying the meaning of the silence in view of its potential ambiguity.

PHYSIOLOGICAL MEASURES DURING PSYCHOTHERAPY

Research on physiological correlates of verbal and other in-therapy behavior and processes provides an important bridge to the understanding of underlying feeling states. Although all these studies do not concern verbal behavior, they are kept together because of their special methodological interest. Recording of physiological changes during the therapeutic session can provide particularly valuable objective data about the process of therapy and about the emotional and somatic concomitants of change.

Change can be studied in relation to variations in therapist technique, interview form, or content. Much of the research so far has consisted of studies of individual cases. These have been more demonstrations of a method than tests of hypotheses.

Boyd and DiMascio (1954) found an increase in sympathetic tension at the beginning of the interview of a single case, using polygraphic measures of heart rate, skin resistance, and face temperature. Social interaction was simultaneously classified by the Bales system and shown to reflect high "neutral" productivity. This was followed by sympathetic relaxation as the interview progressed. Several studies have concentrated on galvanic skin response measured from palmar surfaces. Dittes (1957a) reasoned that fear of punishment accompanying embarrassing sex statements should lead to GSR changes and that these changes should decline when the therapist responds to the statements with a nonpunitive attitude. A thirty-five-year-old neurotic patient was seen for thirty recorded sessions by an experienced therapist, and a continuous GSR record was kept. Embarrassing sex statements were subsequently selected by judges from typescripts. In support of the hypothesis, the percentage of such statements on which a GSR change occurred declined from 100 per cent for the initial two or three sessions to 10–20 per cent by the thirtieth session. Extending this technique, Dittes (1957b) studied GSR as a measure of the patient's reaction to the therapist's permissiveness during the final forty-three hours of a course of therapy. Judges rated typescripts of the therapist's remarks on four aspects of permissiveness: attentiveness, understanding, gentleness, and general acceptance. GSR was scored whenever there was either a rise at the rate of 4,000 or more ohms per second with an amplitude of at least 6,500 ohms or a rise of at least 10,000 ohms amplitude at the rate of 1,333 ohms per second. The change was approximately 3 per cent of the basal resistance level. The frequency of changes of this magnitude in each session was counted. Frequency of the GSR was shown to be inversely related to the judged permissiveness of the therapist. The GSR was interpreted as a measure of the patient's anxiety or mobilization against cues threatening punishment by the therapist. The GSR, however, was related to the emotional significance of the patient's speech as well. Since there has never been much doubt that the therapist (or anyone else for that matter) can bring about emotional responses in a patient, the most important contribution is the demonstration of an objective method of gauging patient reactions to in-therapy stimuli.

In an analogue experiment, Gordon et al. explored the relation between anxiety, operationally defined as skin conductance, and the lifting of repression through the stage of awareness without verbalization (suppression) to overt verbalization (Gordon, Martin, & Lundy, 1959). Under hypnosis the subjects, ten University of Wisconsin students, were instructed to recall conflicts with their parents, and were given post-hypnotic suggestions not to think about them (repression), to think about but not talk about them (suppression), or to talk about the conflicts (verbalization). Each condition occupied fifteen minutes of a forty-five-minute nondirective interview. The order was varied—repression-suppression-verbalization or repression-verbalization-suppression—among the subjects. Skin conductance was continuously recorded and attitudes toward the therapist assessed on a scale at the end of the interview for comparison with a separate control assessment of attitudes. Change in GSR was measured by differences in slope over two-minute intervals. Regardless of the order of conditions, there was a total increase in anxiety throughout the session. The increase was most rapid under repression, but there was no significant difference between suppression and repression. The slopes tended to flatten during verbalization. There was a nonsignificant tendency for attitudes to become more positive when the final condition was verbalization rather than suppression.

Panek and Martin (1959) checked the relation between GSR and speech disturbances in therapy since both have been shown to reflect changes in anxiety level. The psychogalvanometer and the tape recorder were synchronized for four therapy clients. It was demonstrated by a careful analysis that speech disturbances in the form of both "Ah's" and repetitions co-varied with maximal GSR deflections. The investigators concluded that an index based on the combined measures would be a reliable and valid indicator of momentary anxiety changes during therapy.

Martin et al. did an analogue experiment with twenty-seven student volunteers assigned to one of three groups (Martin, Lundy, & Lewin, 1960). The first group talked to a tape recorder with no therapist present; in the second group the therapist was present but responded only by nonverbal means; in the third group the therapist responded in client-centered fashion. Continuous GSRs were synchronized with a tape recording. Content of the interviews was rated for avoidance and levels of approach behavior to therapeutically meaningful behavior. The client-centered therapy group tended to increase its approach to emotional material as the interviews progressed; the tape group showed the opposite trend and the nonverbal group was intermediate. GSRs of members of the client-centered group revealed an increase in anxiety as they approached emotionally important material in the initial sessions, but such increases diminished progressively with time. The group that talked to the tape recorder, on the other hand, showed a decrease in approach behavior as sessions progressed but a marked increase in anxiety as measured by GSR. This suggests that there is less of an increase in anxiety when conflict areas are approached than when overt discussion of these areas is avoided. Generalizations must be made with considerable caution. Any interpretation rests on the validity of GSR data as an accurate reflection of anxiety.

Another analogue experiment done with students concerned GSR correlates of different modes of experiencing (Gendlin & Berlin, 1961). Three sets of instructions were carried out with content that was personally disturbing and nondisturbing. Under the first condition, the subjects were requested to think about a particular feeling. The second involved attending continuously to some external object, and the third required speaking. More tension reduction on GSR accompanied silence than speech. Silences during which the subject concentrated on troublesome feelings were also tension reducing. This encouraged the inference that disturbing content can be referred to in tension-reducing ways in therapy.

Kaplan (1963) explored social interaction and GSR activity during group psychotherapy at the Houston State Psychiatric Institute. A therapist met with two schizophrenic patients in thirty-seven group sessions at which continuous synchronous GSRs were recorded for each participant. The mean number of GSR deflections and mean amplitude per minute for each session were correlated with each person's total responses. Response categories were: positive responses, answers, questions, negative responses, and tension. The correlation between the number and the amplitude of GSR responses was $r = .50$ for the therapist and $r = .19$ for the patients. The two measures failed to correlate significantly with the same social parameters. Autonomic activity was associated with different specific categories for different individuals. There were too few subjects for any general patterns to emerge, but the approach is of potential value. This particular therapist showed greater autonomic reactivity in sessions during which there were more answers, questions, and negative responses by the therapist and more questions, more negative responses, and fewer positive responses by the group.

The therapist's reactions were also investigated by Rigler (1957), who coded verbal responses of participants as conflictual or conflict-free and obtained scores on therapist ambiguity and inferred anxiety from the therapist's skin resistance when he listened to the playback of sessions. The data revealed that conflict did not arouse therapist anxiety when therapist responses were concerned, but did when the patient's responses were involved. There was no consistent relation between anxiety and ambiguity.

Studies of therapist reactivity by DiMascio and his associates tapped measures other than GSR. In one study, various measures were continuously recorded from both patient and therapist during interviews (DiMascio & Suter, 1954). During a period of high rapport, their heart rates were observed to fluctuate together, but the fluctuations were in opposite directions during a period of low rapport. Emotional involvement on the part of the therapist that was as great as that of the patient was adduced from the therapist's cardiac reactivity. Interviews judged high in anxiety were associated with higher and more stable heart rate but lower and more unstable finger temperature. Major shifts in importance of the clinical material discussed were associated with similar finger temperature reactivity. More subtle variations, however, corresponded to shifts in heart rate and lability. Differential effects of therapists on patients were seen when one therapist consistently brought on a lower mean heart rate in each of three subjects. In a further study, DiMascio et al. related physiological measures to Bales interaction categories of disagreement, tension, antagonism, and tension release obtained during twelve therapy sessions (DiMascio, Boyd, & Greenblatt, 1957). Tension scores for the patient were directly related to his heart rate, and tension release was inversely related. The greater the patient's tension, the higher the therapist's heart rate, the pattern following that of the patient. Antagonism in the patient was accompanied by a slowing of his heart rate, but the therapist's rate accelerated. It is of interest that in this particular patient tension was reflected more in heart rate than in skin temperature, with the reverse true for antagonism.

Milton (1961) factor analyzed correlations between blood pressure and therapy interview content in a single hypertensive patient. Fluctuations in blood pressure were related to patterns of hostility and identification. Anderson (1956) demonstrated a relation between physiological and verbal behavior during client-centered therapy. Ten interviews were held with one client and his cardiograph was recorded simultaneously with his verbal interactions. He was given the TAT before and after the counseling period. Client communication was analyzed in terms of topical orientation, time reference, and direction and intensity of verbally expressed affect. Physiological measures used were the mean heart rate for each interview, standard deviation of the heart rate, and index of the heart rate in variation. It was predicted that the client would experience an increase in threat and tension as therapy proceeded to the midperiod, with a decrease in tension at the end of counseling. Cardiographic data did not support this hypothesis even though the TAT reflected that the patient was less anxious and better organized at the end of treatment. Increases in physiological tension were found to be associated with many different changes in verbal behavior.

At McGill University, electromyographic recordings were related to psychodynamic themes in another approach to the investigation of physiological correlates of the therapy process (Shagass & Malmo, 1954). Continuous EMG recordings were synchronized with second-to-second voice recordings. Three separate cases were studied in depth. In the first case, a twenty-five-year-old female patient, leads from the forehead, right neck, right forearm extensors, and right and left leg yielded three miles of tracings for analysis. There was no relation between the amount of talking by the patient or therapist and the mean muscle tension in the interview. Muscle tension was found to be related (high when depressed, low when cheerful) to nurses' notes at the end of each day on the patient's mood, activities, and complaints, but the therapist's assessment of mood from interview transcripts did not agree with the nursing notes. Tension in the last five interviews was significantly lower than in the first four, reflecting progress. There was a significant increase in muscle tension of the right leg only, associated with sex content in the interview, and a significant relation between hostility and tension for the right forearm extensor only. Interestingly, there was an inverse correlation between forearm tension and statements involving movement. In seven of the nine interviews the patient complained of a headache but did not show an increase in neck muscle or forehead tension at these times. In a second case, seen in a single interview, muscle tension was similarly not related to amount of talking, and again it was the right leg that showed higher muscle tension accompanying sex content. While the first patient had experienced increased tension in the right forearm during expressions of hostile content, the second patient had higher tension in the left forearm extensor and right forearm flexor and neck areas, but only the increase in the left forearm approached significance. Both patients were right-handed. Furthermore, headache in this patient was paralleled by neck muscle tension. The third patient, a seventeen-year-old male, showed greater tension when talking, and references to his father were accompanied by forearm extensor tension. Other sensitive topics were associated with left forearm and leg tension. All things considered, this promising exploratory methodological study points toward a relation between interview content and muscle tension. No conclusions can yet be drawn about correlations between sex and hostility and specific muscle potential alterations.

Kanfer (1960) tried to relate verbal rate, content, and eyeblink during structured interviews with thirty-eight schizophrenic patients. Four questions covered current attitudes toward home, family, and sex, and reasons for hospitalization. Analysis of variance revealed that the mean blink rate did not differ among topics ($F = .88$). Instead of stopping here, Kanfer plunged ahead to find support for the hypothesis. Performing a one-tailed t-test of one topic against the mean of the other three, he strained to find a "tendency" ($.05 < p < .10$) in the hoped-for direction, but it cannot be accepted with any degree of conviction.

In summary, studies of physiological correlates of response to variations in therapeutic technique and to therapeutic progress usually have been exploratory and have dealt with a handful of patients. The emphasis has been upon devising measures that will yield results. GSR, heart rate, EMG, and other such measures have been used and their relation to various therapy processes examined. General emotional disturbances are known to be reflected by physiological changes. The important problem in this area is the determination of specific relations. What aspects of the therapeutic situation are being used as cues? Does the specific physiological change have a universal meaning or an idiosyncratic one? These are researchable questions of potential value to the therapist in gaining an understanding of the therapeutic process and in assessing change.

16

Patient-Therapist Interactions and Relationships

The proof of the therapeutic pudding lies in what actually happens between the participants. Therapist variables may induce patient behaviors; patient behaviors may elicit therapist behaviors. Both actors may simultaneously influence each other in a transitory or permanent way. These possibilities require ways of categorizing what may be important dimensions of these interchanges and hypotheses about the immediate and long-range consequences of different modes of interacting and relating.

PATIENT-THERAPIST INTERACTION

One of the earlier and better-known systems for classifying interactions in small groups was offered by Bales (1950). It has since been applied to the therapeutic interaction. Observers classify interactional behavior into six social-emotional and six task areas. Positive social-emotional behavior occurs when the individual shows solidarity, tension release, or agreement; negative behavior occurs when he disagrees or shows tension or antagonism. Task areas are the individual's giving or asking for suggestion, orientation, or opinion. Detailed definitions and guides for rating are furnished.

Lennard and Bernstein (1960) modified the Bales categories to descriptive, evaluative, and prescriptive. The descriptive category involves asking for or giving information, and the evaluative includes requesting or offering value statements. Prescription has to do with giving or asking for direction or suggestions. Longitudinal classification of treatment revealed a decline in description and an increase in evaluation. In other words, less and less time was spent in orientation, transmittal of information, and discussion of the treatment, and more time was devoted to references to feelings and evaluations. Lennard and Bernstein (1967) attributed this to role learning of appropriate behaviors and expectations within the therapeutic transaction. They point out that discussion of this primary role system occupies an important part of early treatment sessions, and must be dealt with by role induction if the sequence is to be an orderly one. Very disturbed individuals fail to assume the patient role and require special efforts by the therapist. This is illustrated by data on verbal output of the primary role system in interviews with neurotics and schizophrenics. The latter show far less attention to role establishment.

Application of the Chapple Interaction Chronograph to therapeutic interviews has been helpful in charting some of the formal characteristics of the interchanges that take place. Hare et al. analyzed the content of initial interviews of twenty-four adult outpatients with both Bales and Chapple measures (Hare, Waxler, Saslow, & Matarazzo, 1960). The two correlated highly enough to be considered interchangeable. Studies of the stability of interaction patterns have made a methodological contribution. In one such investigation, twenty outpatients were interviewed independently by two different interviewers (Saslow, Matarazzo & Guze, 1955). The interviews were standardized in that particular rules were followed for prescribed time intervals during each of five predefined segments of the interview. Free give-and-take interviewing was interspersed with silence during one of the segments and with interrupting during another. Such categories as the frequency and duration of actions and inaction on the part of the interviewer and interviewee, as well as initiative, dominance, and synchronization (failing to respond to or interrupting the other), were included. Marked stability of interaction patterns was reflected by high correlations between the interviewers, and intrainterviewer flexibility by variations in pattern in accordance with predetermined conditions. The experiment was replicated and the findings cross-validated on another group of subjects (Matarazzo, Saslow, & Guze, 1956). Taking it a step farther, the investigators studied the relation between interaction behavior and descriptive content in the interview (Phillips, Matarazzo, Matarazzo, Saslow, & Kanfer, 1961). Subjects were thirty mixed psychiatric patients who were given a partially standardized interview by the same psychiatrist. Seventeen content categories were intercorrelated with the interaction chronograph variables. All told, twenty-eight of 336 coefficients were statistically reliable (seventeen could have been by chance alone). The sizes of the coefficients were actually low, and the authors point out that they account for little of the variance. Two main results appeared, however, for tentative consideration. Patients who speak less frequently, respond quicker, talk longer, and are more dominant produce content that is more oriented toward others and interpersonal interaction; these patients see themselves as assuming more dominant (paternalistic or hostile) social roles. Those who are less active verbally, more hesitant, and submissive to interruptions produce more noninterpersonal content and describe themselves as more submissively hostile.

In a related study, Matarazzo et al. studied the connection between nontherapeutic interview content and speech durations of the interviewee (Matarazzo, Weitman, & Saslow, 1963). Twenty applicants for police and fireman jobs were interviewed by the same individual and speech patterns were recorded on the Interaction Chronograph. Each forty-five-minute interview was divided into three fifteen-minute periods. In each, the interviewer steered the focus onto a different area—family, educational, or employment history. The duration of utterances of interviewees was found not to be a function of the content topic, and it did not vary among the beginning, middle, or final third of the interview.

Some indication of counselor consistency was provided by Ellsworth (1963) in his appraisal of feeling verbalizations of counselor trainees. Tapes of counseling sessions and judgments of feeling verbalizations in nonclient situations were obtained. Consistency from the social to the therapeutic situation was shown. The phenomenon would be worth further exploration with experienced counselors. Goldman-Eisler (1952) also showed consistency in discovering that the duration of a psychiatrist's silent pauses are characteristic for him and remain constant with different types of patients.

Temporal factors in verbal interaction in therapy were studied by Lundy (1955) using the Interaction Chronograph technique. A total of thirty-eight interviews of a client who was seeing two therapists alternately were analyzed. Factor analysis revealed three factors: speed of response, duration of therapist response, and dominance. Further examination of the interview suggested that a pattern of slow therapist response and rapid client response signaled approach to meaningful material, and the duration of the therapist response appeared to be related to his reaction to the material brought up by the client. The same factors existed for both therapists but varied in time of occurrence and were judged to be a function of the client-therapist relationship. The technique would have to be applied to other therapist-client pairs before any general conclusions could be drawn.

Data from Pope and Siegman's (1962) study did not support the view of the interview as a reciprocal information-exchange system. When the therapists' remarks immediately following those of the patients were examined, no significant relations were found for these variables. Moos and Clemes (1967) viewed psychotherapy as a system in the hope of determining the aspects of the process that are therapist determined, patient determined, or an interaction between the two. They also used their systematic approach to study the consistency of patient and therapist behaviors across different interpersonal settings. Accordingly, four therapists saw four patients in a counterbalanced order for interviews held a week apart. Each interview was taped, transcribed, and divided into four equal segments. For both patients and therapists a count was made of the number of words spoken, percentage of feeling words, percentage of action words, number of questions asked, and number of reinforcements (um-hmm's). The number of words used and the number of reinforcements varied significantly among therapists, and all the therapist variables except number of reinforcements varied from patient to patient. All the patient variables varied significantly among patients, and three of the variables showed a significant patient × therapist interaction. The therapist asked more questions and the patients used more action words in the first half of the interview. In the last quarter of the interview the therapists used more words and the patients correspondingly spoke less. There was a significant positive correlation between the percentage of feeling words emitted by the therapist and the overall number of words ($r = .49$), percentage of feeling words ($r = .57$), and number of reinforcements ($r = .52$) emitted by the patient, but a negative correlation ($r = -.67$) with the percentage of patient action words. The percentage of action words of the patient also correlated negatively ($r = -.71$) with the number of questions asked by the therapist. Of particular interest was the fact that therapist reinforcements did not correlate significantly with any patient variables, while patient reinforcements correlated positively ($r = .52$) with therapist feeling expression and negatively ($r = -.52$) with therapist action. This experiment demonstrated the initial influence that takes place as the patient and therapist interact. The techniques of the therapist are apparently determined by both the situation and the patient with whom he is interacting. The particular patient to whom the therapist was talking had as much to do with how much the therapist talked as did his general trait of talkativeness. The patient emerges as the major determinant of therapist technique while the patient is more consistent from therapist to therapist. In view of the limited sample, generalizations from this provocative study are not in order. Kiesler et al. obtained further evidence of patient constancy (Kiesler, Mathieu, & Klein, 1967). Little difference was found in self-exploratory verbalizations of patients and formal communication factors assessed by interaction chronograph measures.

Grater (1964) reported that clients who place greater importance on affective characteristics of counselors are more apt to focus their discussion on personal-social problems in the initial interview than are those who prefer cognitive characteristics. Counselor personality effects were studied by Brams (1961). He found little support for hypotheses relating trainee counselor personality characteristics and the ability to communicate effectively with clients except for a not-too-sturdy linkage of effectiveness with tolerance for ambiguity. Counselor constancy was explored by Hoffman (1959), who classified counselor verbal technique in communicating with clients into fifteen "subroles." These included asking for elaboration, information gathering, participating, friendly discussion, structuring, advising, listening, reflecting, tutoring, supporting, diagnosing, rejecting, administering, and relating. A large number of interviews of forty-six clients by twenty counselors from five different university counseling centers were rated by judges. Most of the counselors were seen to use more than 60 per cent of the subroles. The most important finding was that counselors utilize a similar pattern of subroles with different clients even though the clients and the nature of their problems differ. There was pattern similarity among counselors within settings and differences from center to center. Pursuing this work, Campbell (1962) reported that inexperienced counselor trainees were similar to experienced counselors in their subrole behavior, but there is no way of knowing if they would have used the same subroles with the same clients at the same times.

Dipboye (1954), in an analysis of fifty-one interviews by six counselors with seventeen counselees, found that most counselors varied their styles according to the topic. Such topics as interpersonal relations, family relations, educational and vocational problems, and others were considered, and responses were classified into such categories as questions, responses, interpretations, suggestions about either feeling or content, or simply giving information. There was similarity among counselors in similar units, but some individual variation. Despite uncontrolled and unanalyzed counselee variance this was a good early attempt at inter- and intracounselor differences in technique.

Anxiety arousal in therapists of different levels of experience as a function of hostility or friendliness of clients was appraised in a dissertation by Russell (Russell & Snyder, 1963). Ten more and ten less experienced graduate students interviewed two actors trained in playing the roles of hostile and friendly clients. The counselors believed them to be genuine clients. Counselor anxiety measures were palmar sweating, eyeblink rate, clients' scale of counselor anxiety, and judgments of verbal anxiety by six judges. In general, the hypothesis that hostile client behavior would arouse significantly more anxiety in the counselors was supported, but there was little support for the hypothesis that more experienced counselors would be less affected.

Earlier, Bandura (1956) had found partial support for the hypothesis that therapist anxiety is negatively related to therapeutic competence. Anxiety was rated by colleagues and competence by supervisors. The experiment was done with exceptional and elaborate control of artifacts and unusual rigor of design and execution, but the "experienced" therapists were really novices. It is not known how truly experienced therapists would react. Bandura et al. examined the patient-therapist interaction around the expression of hostility and the effect of therapist anxiety (Bandura, Lipsher, & Miller, 1960). Subjects were seventeen parents in therapy at a parent-child clinic and twelve student therapists. Patient-therapist-patient interaction sequences were randomly selected from a large number of taped interviews. Patient responses were rated for expressions of hostility and the referent of the hostility. Therapist responses were rated as approach, avoidance, or unclassified. In addition, personality characteristics of the therapists were judged by staff psychologists on eight five-point scales, three of which concerned hostility. Only two therapist characteristics had any effect. Therapists judged to be individuals who characteristically express hostility in direct forms were found to be more likely than those low on direct hostility to approach (attempt to elicit further expressions) patient expressions of hostility when it was directed toward extratherapeutic objects. The two types of therapists did not differ, however, when the therapist was the object of the patient's hostility. Therapists high in need for approval were more likely to avoid the patient's hostility when it was directed toward the therapist or others. Therapists generally were less likely to approach hostility when it was directed toward themselves than when it was directed toward others. Approach to hostility by the therapist was usually followed by continuation of its expression. Avoidance tended to lead patients to change the object of the hostility. Silence and mislabeling were the therapist avoidance responses that were most likely to draw further expressions of hostility.

Heller et al. studied interviewer behavior as a function of standardized client role (Heller, Myers, & Kline, 1963). Four actors were trained to play the roles of dominant-friendly, dominant-hostile, dependent-friendly, and dependent-hostile clients. The actors were carefully selected and extensively trained, and their performance was pretested. Thirty-four graduate students at the University of North Dakota Counseling Center interviewed them, believing that they were testing the efficacy of a thirty-minute interview in reducing the waiting list with real clients. The consistency of the actors in maintaining their roles was carefully checked, and all but the "dependent-hostile" client were found to be performing the specified roles. Each interview was observed through a one-way screen and was rated for control and affect on a modified form of the Leary Interpersonal Check List. The hypothesis that client hostility would evoke interviewer anxiety was not supported, but other hypotheses were. Dominant client behavior evoked more dependence in the interviewer than did dependent client behavior. Client friendliness evoked more interviewer friendliness than did client hostility. This was technically a good study in most respects. The fact that one-tailed F-tests were used does not alter the findings since the Fs were large enough to be significant by the conventional test anyway. The relative inexperience of the interviewers detracts somewhat from the generality of the results.

Gamsky and Farwell (1966) examined the effect of client hostility upon counselor verbal behavior. Four actors were trained to perform the roles of a friendly male, friendly female, hostile male, and hostile female. Under the hostile conditions they at first directed their hostility at others, and later directly toward the counselor. Three groups of ten counselors each were used, half of whom were male and half female. One of the groups was composed of "experienced" individuals with a minimum of one year of experience. The "moderately experienced" group had completed all courses for their master's degree and had a semester of supervised field experience. The "inexperienced" group had limited course work and no field work or experience. Each "client" was interviewed by the thirty counselors, who thought that they were seeing real clients at the University of Wisconsin. Each interview was recorded and scored by a modification of the Bales System of Interaction Process Analysis. Three raters trained to rate reliably judged segments of each recorded interview. By analysis of variance, the experimenters examined the main and interaction effects of counselor experience, sex, focus of hostility, and client sex. Counselor experience had a significant effect on only two of the fourteen Bales categories, agreement and avoidance, with the more experienced agreeing more and avoiding less than the less experienced. No effects of counselor sex were obtained, but there were several effects of client sex that the authors feel may have been due to uncontrolled variables. The main issue, that of client focus of hostility, significantly affected eleven of the fourteen categories. When client hostility was focused on the counselors they used more reassurance, suggestion, and information, but also showed more avoidance, disapproval, and antagonism. In the face of hostility, counselors also used less agreement, interpretation, reflection, elaboration, and requests for information. The general conclusion was that counselors responded in a negative manner when hostility was directed toward them. The use of more reassurance was suggested as an effort of the therapists to reassure themselves. Although the range of counselor experience was limited, those with more experience still showed less avoidance of client hostility in this realistic though contrived research. The investigators began to go beyond trying to ascertain whether counselors are made anxious by client hostility to the more important issue of how it is handled and how it affects the therapeutic process. It would have been more enlightening if the data obtained from the "friendly" role had been included in the analysis for comparison. The use of actors as imitation clients has its shortcomings, yet it has the advantage of providing more or less standardized roles for study and was probably the only feasible way of submitting the same interviewees to thirty different interviewers. All things considered, the experiment is an impressive one.

Isaacs and Haggard (1966) reported a series of studies covering several important aspects of patient-therapist interaction. They hypothesized that affect verbalizations by interviewers elicit more meaningful responses by the patient. Scales were devised to classify the content of therapist and patient statements into affect words (direct expression of subjective feelings), emotionally toned words (mixture of affective and cognitive elements), and nonaffective words. The meaningfulness of patient statements was rated by psychoanalysts, clinical psychologists, and social workers. Within-profession group variation was greater than between-group, with psychoanalysts agreeing least among themselves. The general coefficient for all raters, however, indicated a high degree of consensus. Ratings were factor analyzed and three components of meaningfulness identified: (1) the extent of the patient's concern with himself and his problems, (2) his concern with and ability to relate to others, (3) his current motivational state. The meaningfulness of patient statements was then related to the preceding interviewer statement. Interviewer interventions of the affective type were followed by significantly more meaningful patient statements than were nonaffective ones. When the interviewer's intervention was affective, 39.7 per cent of the immediate responses of the patient were affective. When the interviewer's intervention was nonaffective, only 12.8 per cent of the patient responses were affective. The interviewer's and patient's levels of affectivity were highly related (rho = .80). A high percentage of interviewer affect was accompanied by fewer and longer patient responses, and shorter patient statements followed low interviewer affect. It was also determined that in affectively toned interviews patients tended spontaneously to return more often to previous interviewer content. In summation, regardless of the therapist's orientation, response to the patient's affect verbalization tends to lead to more meaningful affective responses by the patient that are fewer but longer and to more spontaneous returns after a time lag to the content of the interventions. This is achieved with no loss of factual information. By "following the patient's affects," Isaacs and Haggard suggest that one can obtain meaningful responses from the patient "because they are elicited as part of a totality of affectively oriented discourse" (p. 238). What we may be getting is a reflection of the biased opinion on the part of professionals that affective statements by patients are meaningful ones. It is then shown that the judged meaningfulness of the patient's following statement is a function of the therapist's preceding remarks. All that this may mean is that when the therapist focuses on affect the patient tends to pick it up and follow the theme with affective (judged to be meaningful) statements. By implication this should lead to a more successful outcome. Since this remains to be demonstrated, it is all rather circular. What the study does clearly tell us is that affect begets affect.

Glad et al. were able to show that the therapeutic technique employed interacts with the personality of the patient, so that a technique may be good for one patient but bad for another (Glad, Hayne, Glad, & Ferguson, 1963). They used an ingenious experimental approach consisting of systematically varying therapist technique in group therapy and studying its effect upon different types of patients. As described by the authors, techniques used were: (1) Relationship Feelings, in which the therapist emphasizes the patient's feelings toward other group members or the therapist ("You like me today"); (2) Relationship Roles, emphasis on immediate interpersonal behavior ("You are trying to be friendly to Mrs. T."); (3) Self-Feelings, focus on patient's feelings without reference to interpersonal context; (4) Self-Roles, a reference to social meanings of patient's behavior without regard to personal context ("You're pretty critical"). The differential effects of these techniques on disturbed antagonistic and affectively blunted types, as typified by two patients each, were illustrated. A larger sample would be necessary before any definite recommendations could be made. If it were repeated on a much larger scale with a greater variety of patients, the study could lead to tailoring of the technique of the therapist to the personality of the patient so as to maximize therapeutic benefit.

Tourney et al. checked patient behavior correlates of therapist errors of commission (overactivity) and of omission (inactivity) (Tourney, Bloom, Lowinger, Schorer, Auld, & Gusell, 1966). In neurotics and schizophrenics, therapist overactivity was positively associated with patient anxiety and hostility, and additionally for schizophrenics there were negative correlations with verbal productivity, negative arousal, and depression. Correlation coefficients of patient variables and therapist inactivity were generally lower, but the effect was more marked for schizophrenics. Therapists were overactive when anxious and hostile. In general, neurotics tended to reciprocate the feelings of the therapist, whereas schizophrenics reacted more diffusely. The sample of patients was small and the therapists were all residents, but the approach to studying differential effects of therapist technique is of value.

A variety of within-therapy arrangements have been employed to structure the interaction, and some have acquired the status of essential components of particular therapeutic approaches. The effects of these innovations have rarely been tested. Zielonka (1951) examined three therapeutic arrangements. In the first, the patient and therapist were face-to-face. In the second, the patient was lying on a couch with the therapist sitting out of his sight. In the third, the two sat near each other with an opaque screen between them. Patients' dominance-submission behavior did not vary from condition to condition. Fewer expressions of feeling were emitted in the face-to-face situation, and more negative feelings were expressed when the participants were separated by the screen.

Verbal Processes in Group Therapy. The verbal content, amount of participation, and the nature of interactions in group psychotherapy have been subject to research scrutiny in attempts to understand better the therapeutic process. Differences of opinion about the importance of overt content as opposed to more subtle feeling relationships led Talland and Clark (1954) to evaluate the significance of group therapy discussion topics in seven groups undergoing group analytic psychotherapy at Maudsley Hospital. The participants were mostly psychoneurotic patients of above average intelligence. Patients were asked to rank a list of fifteen topics selected from records of forty group meetings. Topics were childhood memories, dreams, reactions to others in the group, feelings and thoughts about the therapist, people outside the group, psychological or somatic cause of illness, marriage problems, money troubles, problems at work, quarrels and angry feelings, children and child rearing, symptoms and anxieties, social position and class feelings, sex, shame, and guilt. The purpose was to discover which of these topics were thought by the patients to be helpful, unhelpful, disturbing, or a hindrance to treatment; patients were asked to consider the progress of the entire group as well as their own. All seven groups showed significant concordance on the usefulness of the various topics. The patients did not distinguish between the value of topics to themselves as individuals or to the group as a whole. Topics judged as helpful were also judged as disturbing to the individuals. Topics were judged by thirty-five psychologists as items that could only be brought up in an intimate setting, and there was a correlation of $r = .69$ between patients' ranking of helpfulness and judges' ranking for intimacy. Some of the topics seen as most helpful were judged as appropriate for a non-intimate group setting. Most helpful in the opinion of the patients were discussions directly relating to areas of maladjustment such as sex, symptoms and anxieties, shame and guilt, and the effort to relate these to early life experiences. Judged as least helpful were topics related to money problems, people outside, and social and work problems. It is evident that the particular choice of topics may be sample specific and would not necessarily hold for groups in general. The important thing is that the specific content of the topics was seen as being of differential importance even though no topic was seen as hindering progress and that the bitterest medicine was thought to be the most beneficial. Lest conclusions be prematurely drawn, there was no attempt to relate these beliefs to objective measures of help received, and there is no necessary correspondence between the two.

Corsini and Rosenberg (1955) sought to develop a general taxonomy of concepts basic to group therapy. A total of 166 distinct statements of dynamics were culled from the group therapy literature and clustered into categories. Nine identifiable classes of statements were: acceptance, altruism, universalization, intellectualization, reality testing, transference, interaction, spectator therapy, and ventilation. These were then regrouped to form three large categories called an intellectual factor, an emotional factor, and an actional factor. Different therapists stress different factors.

In another study, the dimensions of interaction between patients in group therapy were classified by factor analysis. Lorr (1966) analyzed data from observations of 194 patients from forty-five therapy groups. Behavior was rated on a schedule of seventy-five statements descriptive of interpersonal behavior. Identified factors were called: hostility, attention-seeking control, leader role, supportive role, succorance, submissiveness, withdrawal, and disorganized behavior. The method was offered as a means of studying changes in group behavior over time and for contrasting groups differing in leadership and composition.

Patient-perceived benefit was the criterion in a well-done study of its relations to degree and kind of participation in group therapy (Sechrest & Barger, 1961). Samples from group sessions conducted by four therapists of varying orientation were analyzed for nine measures of verbal participation and seven measures of benefit. Of the resulting sixty-three relations, twenty-one were statistically significant in predicted directions and none in the opposite direction. Patients generally most valued those sessions in which they participated at what for them was a relatively high level. They reported that sessions in which they were most verbally active were most helpful and relevant to their problems, and permitted them to make the greatest contributions to the group. Ratings of the comfortableness of the session did not relate to any participation measures, and subjective mood following the session and understanding of people and personal problems were largely unrelated to verbal activity.

The degree of verbal participation was related in another study, not to patient perception of benefit, but to independent measures of attitude change in fifteen adult offenders in two psychotherapy groups (Smith, Bassin, & Froehlich, 1960). Participation was rated according to the amount of time each patient spoke during fifteen sessions. Changes in attitudes toward authority were tapped by a modification of the TAT administered before and after treatment, and changes in social conformity by the Human Relations Inventory, a projective questionnaire. Zero order correlations led to the conclusion that the most articulate person is not necessarily the one who gains the most nor the quiet one the one who changes the least. For no apparent reason, the same paper was republished in a different journal two years later (Bassin & Smith, 1962).

The effect of self-disclosure upon the group process and liking between people within the group was examined by Query (1964). In view of the fact that the subjects were nursing students rather than patients, generalizations must be limited. Some support, however, was obtained for the hypothesis that groups composed of individuals of high self-disclosure output would have greater attraction of their group for them than groups who disclosed themselves less. However, individuals higher in self-disclosure did not necessarily show a liking for one another, and a person who withholds personal information may be preferred over one who reveals a great deal about himself.

Hannon et al. hypothesized that the introduction of nonrecognition of patients by the therapist in a group would increase patient-to-patient interaction accompanied by decreased patient-to-therapist interaction (Hannon, Battle, & Adams, 1962). Under one condition the therapist answered patients' questions directly. In the second, he remained silent for at least five seconds after a patient's question or comment and refrained from looking at the patient. If no other patient spoke, he redirected the statement to another member of the group. Although there are questions about the error terms selected and other details of the analysis of variance, patient-to-patient interaction did appear to increase in the face of nonrecognition by the therapist.

Eisenman (1966) uncovered an interesting relation between the birth order of the patient, anxiety, and verbalizations in group psychotherapy. He conducted and replicated an experiment, each with twenty-four Milledgeville State Hospital, Georgia, patients, to test the hypotheses that (1) more speech will occur in group therapy among first-born and among highly anxious patients than among later-born and less anxious ones, (2) first-born will ask more questions than later-born, and (3) first-born will talk more than later-born when highly anxious. All hypotheses were supported.

McPherson and Walton (1964) demonstrated that over a course of group therapy there are changes in communication patterns. Discussion of formal roles and responsibilities within the group declines, while recognizing, verbalizing, and expressing feelings for one another increases. The therapist's responsibility for identifying and analyzing links to other social situations is gradually taken over by group members. The effort to understand what really goes on in the group process in group therapy led Krieger and Kogan (1964) to formulate hypotheses in group dynamic terms. They predicted that there is an emerging consensus in the conception of social roles among group members and greater consistency and stability in role conception over time. Neither hypothesis was supported, but the authors cited design weaknesses that made the study a questionable one.

Effect of Formal Arrangements on Group Therapy Interaction. It has been suggested that verbal interactions in group therapy vary with the therapist and the size and composition of the group. At the Indianapolis Veterans Administration Hospital, 146 patients were assigned at random to five different open-ended therapy groups (Grosz, Stern, & Wright, 1965). The groups varied in size with changes in membership. Groups were composed of four patients in twenty-nine sessions, five patients in twenty-three sessions, and six patients in twenty-two sessions. Therapists were a psychiatrist with training and experience in analytic therapy, a trained clinical psychologist, and three psychology trainees with little group therapy experience. All aimed at fostering patient-to-patient interaction. The number of verbal responses emitted by the therapist and each group member, and to whom they were directed, were recorded. Each therapist's group developed a unique pattern of verbal interaction despite their common aim. The experienced psychiatrist obtained more patient-to-patient interaction than the three trainees but not significantly more than the staff psychologist. Therapist-to-patient and patient-to-therapist verbal response frequencies varied significantly among therapists. A trend toward increase in patient-to-patient responses with group size was shown by a significant difference between the four- and six-man groups. The idea was worthwhile but design problems make it difficult to attribute the increases in communication to any one variable with confidence.

Size of group aside, much has been written but little done on the matter of homogeneity of patients within groups. Neither Anker and Walsh (1961) nor Phillipson (1958) found that it made any difference. In the former, there was no difference in outcome in group therapy with hospitalized schizophrenics. In the latter there was no reported variation in the efficiency of psychoanalytically oriented group therapy as a function of homogeneity or heterogeneity along the severity of disturbance dimension.

Nonverbal Interaction. In addition to the verbal exchange of the usual psychotherapy session, a variety of nonverbal communication takes place. This communication may be observed and/or interpreted by the therapist. The therapist's nonverbal communications, in turn, may elicit responses from the patient. All this subtle exchange is lost to the research that relies for its data on tape recordings and typescripts. Renneker (1960) reported that an average hour of therapy contained 325 units of relevant information and the therapist made over 1,000 body movements. Thus, the patient talks and the therapist wriggles. Charny (1966) conducted a frame-by-frame viewing of a sound film of a therapy session and analyzed both therapist and patient posture in relation to their verbal behavior. More and more time was spent in "upper-body mirror congruent" posture as the interview progressed. This was taken as a manifestation of rapport, for during mirror-congruent periods, the content was interpersonal, positive, and specific. During non-congruent periods, the lexical content tended to be more self-centered, negative, and nonspecific.

Haggard and Isaacs (1966) studied "micromomentary" (fleeting) facial expressions as indicators of ego mechanisms during psychotherapy. Expressions were observed to change dramatically within three to five frames of film (one-eighth to one-fifth of a second). Two and one-half times as many changes in expression were observed when the film was viewed at slow speed than at the normal speed. From films of two patients in treatment with a training analyst, the researchers discovered that "MMEs" tended to occur in a context of conflict. In an examination of fourteen content themes, they found an association between MMEs and both statements of denial and instances of verbal blocking. MMEs were recommended as valuable indicators of aspects of the therapeutic process.

Berg (1954) tested the hypothesis that clients who were counseled for sexual conflicts would display more sexually symbolic gestures than counselees with nonsexual problems. Accordingly, fourteen university student clients with sexual problems were contrasted with twenty-one who had financial problems. Gestures taken to have a sexual meaning were: rotating, sliding, clasping, wrapping, inserting, pressing, or licking.

General restlessness was also noted. Because of recording problems, data on the frequency and duration of gestures were not available. Analysis was limited to the presence or absence of gestures. With this limitation in mind, the investigator reported that gestures were not different in the two groups but that the sex-problem group showed more general restlessness. The experiment must be considered inconclusive, with a more careful analysis of gestural behavior in order.

Fretz (1966a) requested thirteen undergraduate observers, viewing first, third, and sixth interviews, to describe all movements physiognomically and to maintain a continuous record of these movements on a tape recorder. The counselors were twelve graduate students, and the clients seventeen undergraduates. The observers listed 131 separate movements, only sixty of which were used by three or more subjects. Some low but significant correlations were reported between the criteria (Barrett-Lennard Relationship Inventory, Cundick Charisma Healing Scale, and the author's Satisfaction Scale) and movements. The best indicator of satisfaction for both participants were vertical hand movements. The client's leaning backward and forward was the best indication of Barrett-Lennard client variables; the counselor's clasping was the best indication of these counselor variables. All hand movements, smiles, and laughs were significantly correlated with the majority of Barrett-Lennard variables. Head movements had the fewest significant correlations with the criteria. In another study with the same subjects, Fretz (1966b) attempted to relate the movements observed with five other questionnaires. Of the 176 correlations, the sixteen significant ones could easily have arisen by chance. The counseling situation was somewhat removed from a live psychotherapeutic encounter. The lack of definitive results after the use in both studies of a variety of standard questionnaires emphasizes the need for hypotheses suitably related to the psychotherapeutic situation.

The use of gestures, postures, and facial expressions seems to offer a great deal to the study of what transpires minute by minute in psychotherapy. The present small number of studies is no more than suggestive, and this is somewhat surprising in view of the promise of an earlier literature on expressive movement in personality psychology.

THE THERAPEUTIC RELATIONSHIP

What are the important aspects or dimensions of the relationship between patient and therapist in the psychotherapeutic situation? There have been few systematic studies of the entire therapeutic relationship, few attempts to map the important connections between patient and therapist. The next question is: important for what reason? Since the ultimate issue is outcome, many of the studies do have outcome referents, implicitly or explicitly. However, within the immediate psychotherapeutic situation, there may be a host of variables that are intimately related to relationship variables. It is possible that these complex relationships change at various stages in a psychotherapeutic series. Most studies have been limited to the investigation of some specific variable or aspect of the relationship.

The first group of studies discussed here is concerned with what the investigators believe to be determining the important dimensions of the therapeutic relationship. Using ten interviews by therapists of various schools that were judged by others of various schools, Fiedler (1951a) obtained different sets of factors. The psychoanalytic judge identified insecurity and immobility, poor communication, security, and empathy. The nondirective judge presented other factors of the relationship—esteem of the patient, emotionally estranged, dominant-aloof-cold. A psychotherapeutically naïve judge identified the following factors: self-confidence and sincere interest in the patient, inability to cope with the patient because of lack of insight, poor rapport, emotionally close relationship. Most of Fiedler's factors have to do with the therapist's contributions to the relationship. Lorr and McNair's (1964b) factorial study of 150 male outpatients and fifty-nine therapists concerned the patient's contribution. They obtained five factors: hostile-resistive, active involvement, blocking-frequent silences, controlling-resistive, and dependency. These seem more specific and behaviorally oriented.

Snyder and Snyder (1961) attempted a global assessment of the therapeutic relationship. They studied twenty cases (immaturity problems, character disorders, hysterics, schizoid personalities, and one depressive), all but one of whom were graduate students in psychology. The therapist clearly was the senior author who describes himself as a guiding, advice-giving, warm, protective, and nurturant therapist. After each interview the client completed a questionnaire about his reactions to the therapy and the therapist. The therapist also filled one out as he believed the client would and responded to a questionnaire designed to measure his own feelings toward the client. After every fifth interview, the client answered the Edwards Personal Preference Schedule. The therapist took the same scale twice, with a one-year interval between. The client also completed the MMPI early in therapy. All tests were returned to the therapist's coauthor. The therapist also estimated the patient's progress in therapy (the last estimate at the end of therapy, therefore, became an outcome measure). He also ranked the patients on personality traits and value variables, once at the end of therapy and once from one to three years later.

From the ensuing factor analyses of the affect-scale items from both client's and therapist's scales, the authors obtained the following factors: client's active resistance or hostility, client's passive resistance or withdrawal, therapist's impatience with the client, and therapist's anger or irritation with him. There were no significant correlations or differences between correlations of therapist's and client's responses to the Edwards PPS. There were complex and confusing analyses of MMPI and Leary personality trait scores. The therapist reports that he succeeds (by his own judgment) with patients whose personal characteristics he likes, are complementary to his own, and who are least disturbed. The results of the study are difficult to assess. There is constant shift in emphasis from process to outcome. The therapist was the designer of the study, the rater of his own and the client's session-by-session behavior, the judge of client personality and of client progress. There is need for external criteria, uninvolved judges, and, at many points, an adequate control group. The crucial lack is of a set of suitable hypotheses; the mass of frequently useless data from conventional instruments is not an adequate substitute. Relevant data, such as patient-therapist complementarity on the Leary circle of social traits, is partially or wholly absent. The factors so laboriously derived are representative only of this therapist in these specific circumstances.

A few studies of the therapeutic relationship deal with the evaluation of the relationship. Orlinsky and Howard's (1967) appraisal of "the good therapy hour" is such a study. The researchers have investigated the experiential correlates of both therapists' and patients' evaluations of therapy sessions. The subjects were sixty female outpatients (55 per cent neurotics, 29 per cent personality disorders, 15 per cent schizophrenics) and seventeen therapists averaging six years of experience. From eight to twenty-six consecutive sessions were evaluated. The patient and therapist each completed a questionnaire, the Therapy Session Report (TSR), immediately after each session. The items covered topical content, the nature of the relationship, feelings experienced by both participants, the exchange process, and the development of the session. The first item on the questionnaire was an evaluation of the session. Product-moment correlations were computed separately for each therapist-patient pair for each TSR variable. Positive and negative correlations were counted and the proportion evaluated against an expected chance distribution.

Eight topics were found to be related positively and negatively respectively to patient's and/or therapist's positive and negative evaluation of the session. The one topic that both participants associated with a good session was the discussion of childhood experiences with family members and the accompanying feelings. So far as the relationship was concerned, both patient and therapist valued sessions in which the patient was emotionally involved; neither valued sessions in which the patient was unresponsive and in which there was no mutuality. In sessions judged as good, therapists were seen by both as friendly although therapists did not deem friendliness essential. Sessions in which therapists were neutral or uninvolved were judged poor. There was mutual agreement that, in good sessions, patients received, generated, and emitted positive affect. Patients believed that in bad sessions they felt irritable, frustrated, and inadequate. Therapists did not agree, for to them good sessions included those in which patients expressed some of these feelings. In an analysis of the exchange process, patients' good sessions were those in which they expressed desire to collaborate and to achieve insight, and therapists saw them as seeking insight and cooperation. The therapist's satisfactions in the exchange were his experience of efficacy, competence, and involvement in his work. Almost all phases of session development (patient's task in communicating, therapist's in responding helpfully, progress toward resolution of problems) were associated by both participants with global session evaluation. The investigators did not intend to relate their findings to any theory or to therapeutic effectiveness. They were aware that their samples of patients and therapists were not good random ones and that their patients were highly sophisticated in psychotherapy, occupationally as well as by profession (many patients were members of mental health professions). The study is an interesting one, analyzed with care and restraint, and presents a promising technique.

A different aspect of the evaluation of the therapeutic relationship was explored in Peterson, Snyder, Guthrie, and Ray's (1958) study of therapists' preference or rejection of clients' statements of gain. A Q-sort of clients' statements was given to thirty-five psychologists, all with Pennsylvania State University training. The statements concerned direction of gain, attitude (self- or other-orientation), mode of change, and area of conflict. Two factor analyses of the data revealed five identifiable factors describing the counselor's concern with dependency, conformity, sex problems (client as overcontrolled), aggression and undercontrol, aggression and overcontrol. A much smaller and less direct study than that of Orlinsky and Howard, this research emphasizes the therapist's concern with content variables.

An exploratory study of unconscious feelings in fifteen therapist-patient pairs was conducted by Fiedler and Senior (1952). Both participants were asked to describe themselves on a seventy-six-item Q-sort as they were, as they would like to be, and as the other member of the pair described himself. Eighty-four correlation coefficients were computed, of which nine were significant. The authors interpreted their results as hypotheses. Better therapists (by supervisor rating) tended to predict their patients' self-sorts more accurately than did poorer therapists. Better therapists tended to be less satisfied. The better the therapist, the more the patient tended to see him as an ego ideal. The greater the similarity of the therapist to the patient's ideal, the less the therapist tended to empathize with his patient. The more the patient resembled the therapist's ideal, the more the patient tended to see the therapist tended to empathize with his patient. The more the patient he felt that the therapist was better adjusted than he and the more the patient resembled the therapist's ideal. The more the therapist resembled, to the patient, the patient's ideal, the less the patient felt the therapist to be maladjusted. The number of subjects is very small for a correlational matrix. The authors note that correlations may be spuriously high because they were based upon correlated variables. The sex, experience, and orientation of the therapist, and the severity of illness and frequency of treatment of the patient, are all uncontrolled. We must reiterate the authors' request that the findings be regarded as hypotheses.

Parloff (1956) tried to relate the therapist's ability to form social relationships to his ability to establish therapeutic relationships. Nineteen ambulatory psychoneurotic patients were randomly assigned to three groups for treatment. Two equally expert therapists saw all groups separately, each group being seen by one therapist for the first two weeks and by the other for the next two weeks. Twelve mutual acquaintances of both therapists were interviewed and unanimously judged one as achieving better social relationships than the other. Each therapist described all patients and his ideal patient by sorting a sixty-item Q-sort for each. An independent observer who attended all meetings of the groups judged the relationship established with each patient in the group by the Fiedler Ideal Therapeutic Relationship Q-Sample after the second and fourth week of treatment. These were correlated with the Fiedler Ideal Therapeutic Relationship; the higher the correlation, the better the relationship was considered to be. This relationship score was then related to the measure of the therapist's social relationships and the comparison of the therapist's Q-sort of his ideal patient with his sort for each patient. The investigator found that the therapist who was able to establish better social relationships also established better therapeutic relationships. The therapist who perceived a patient as close to his conception of an ideal patient created a better relationship with that patient. Reservations about this study concern the small and unrepresentative sample and the validity of the instruments used. However, the hypothesis is a potentially useful one and the investigator's attempt to obtain direct measures of the variables is praiseworthy.

Another study by Parloff (1961) attempted to relate patient change to the quality of the therapeutic relationship. Twenty-one primarily psychoneurotic patients were treated in small groups by two therapists for twenty sessions. The quality of the relationship for each group was measured by three trained observers using the array of statements developed by Fiedler. These statements were correlated with those of Fiedler's Ideal Therapeutic Relationship. The criteria of change were measures of discomfort, ineffectiveness, and objectivity or self-understanding. Criteria measures were obtained after the fourth and twentieth sessions. Three of the fourteen correlations between change and the therapeutic relationship were significant. Fourteen patients completed the program. The dropouts had the poorest relationships in contrast to the other members of their group. This extremely detailed study offers support for its hypothesis that patient change is related to the quality of the therapeutic relationship, but the support is greatly limited by the very few patients and therapists and by the questionable validity of the measures of therapeutic relationship.

An attempt to assess the effects of interpersonal relationships upon verbal conditioning was made by Sapolsky (1960). In the first of two experiments, Sapolsky relied upon instructions to create high or low attraction between the experimenter and his subject. In the second study, he used the FIRO-B Scale to establish compatible and incompatible groups in terms of interpersonal needs. The subjects for each study were thirty female college freshmen. The experimenter reinforced sentences beginning with "I" or "we" said by the subject. Subjects who were incompatible or not attracted to the experimenter suppressed the effects of the reinforcement until they were removed from his presence. The author concludes that subtle cues provided by the therapist's "um-hmm" are likely to be effective only if the relationship between him and the patient is positive and compatible and that evaluation of psychotherapeutic effectiveness for a negativistic patient may not be possible at the time therapy is taking place. In another study, Sapolsky (1965) investigated similar hypotheses in a live psychotherapeutic setting. The aspect of relationship studied was compatibility, which proved to be a variable of somewhat limited power to influence outcome.

Pallone and Grande (1965), in an essentially nontherapeutic study, attempted to relate counselor verbal mode to client rapport. Eighty nonpsychopathological secondary students were interviewed. The interviews were analyzed to determine the effects of interrogative, interpretive, reflective, and confrontative verbal behaviors on problem-relevant communications by the clients. It was determined that the client's experience of rapport was not significantly affected by problem focus, verbal mode, or their interaction. The study by Tourney et al. (1966) suggests that similar variables affect different kinds of patients differentially. The categories presented may be useful in a more directly psychotherapeutic study.

A final aspect of this general topic concerns the birth of the psychotherapeutic relationship. What variables determine the establishment of the therapeutic relationship? Wallach (1962a) suggested that independent college students would prefer a therapist who encouraged self-determination and that students who do not make this choice would be more authoritarian. Three paragraphs describing therapists as nurturant (warm, accepting), critic (aware of alternatives, allowing independence), or a model (fine qualities of a model person) were presented to 216 undergraduates. They ranked the order of their preferences, indicated their difficulty in making a choice, and responded to the F Scale and an attitude survey assessing their feelings about obtaining psychiatric help. Thirty-three of the subjects preferred the "nurturant" and five the "model" therapist. Their average F scores were significantly higher than those of the others who preferred the "critic." All this is hypothetical for the students and based upon the assumption that they would behave in the way they indicated if they were in need of help. Certainly no generalization is possible.

Wallach (1962b) also studied the therapist's preference for patients. An unspecified number of residents and fourth-year medical students interviewed 251 outpatients at intake. They rated each patient on a scale of their own willingness to accept him in treatment. Two measures of the patient's degree of disturbance were obtained. These measures were also used to select extreme groups on the dimension "willingness to talk of feelings." The interviewers' ratings of degree of patient disturbance did not correlate significantly with their ratings of patient preference. They did, however, significantly prefer as patients those whom they had rated as least disturbed. The ostensible therapists showed significant preference for those patients who were more willing to talk of their feelings. The interviewers, then, preferred those patients who could be expected to respond best to traditional therapy.

Arbuckle (1956) contributed another "as if" study. Seventy counselor trainees, organized into small groups, were asked toward the end of the semester to list the three people in the class they would consult if they needed a counselor, the three they would be least likely to consult, the three characteristics they most like in a counselor, and the three they least like in a counselor. All the subjects took the MMPI, the Heston Personality Inventory, and the Kuder Preference Record. Those students selected by their peers were significantly higher on the confidence variable of the Heston than those who selected them, and were significantly more normal on a number of the MMPI scales. Those selected were significantly higher on Kuder scores for social service, persuasive, literary, and scientific categories than those who selected them. The clients are not actual clients nor the counselors actual counselors. The crucial comparisons are not between accepted and rejected "counselors" but between "counselors" and their "clients," and the traits measured are not necessarily related to therapeutic function. These and other studies on patient and therapist preferences and expectancies hint that the nature of the relationship that develops may be influenced to some extent by initial attitudes of both parties.

Garetz, Kogl, and Wiener (1959) considered the consequences of failure to select with care therapists for patients who might benefit from the relationship. They evaluated thirteen outpatients referred to a clinical judgment group for assignment and fourteen patients assigned to a random-number group. All patients were referred to two psychiatrists for either drug treatment (fifteen minutes twice a month) or psychotherapy (thirty to fifty minutes a week). The assignments were made for the former by the best judgment of a clinic group, and for the latter by a table of random numbers. After three months of treatment, patients were rated on a five-point scale. Three cases of each group were unimproved, and eleven of the "random" group and ten of the "clinical judgment" group were improved. Unfortunately, the therapists concerned made the ratings of improvement. This study is provocative but leaves us with the need for broader samples of patients and therapists, for more objective judgments of improvement, and for a better understanding of treatment relationships.

Meyer and Tolman (1963) dealt with change in therapeutic relationships because of transfer of the patient. Sixty-eight patients were studied. In forty-two of these cases, treatment was modified in preparation for the change. The therapists reported that there was some reaction, favorable or unfavorable, to the proposed transfer in fifty-nine cases. The patients for whom treatment was modified were significantly more likely to manifest a reaction than those whose treatment was not modified. There was a significant relationship between the therapist's judgment that a patient felt close to him and his judgment that the patient showed a disturbed reaction. The use of an insight approach and the therapist's judgment that the patient felt close to him were significantly associated. Transfer and change is a fairly common situation in psychotherapy. There are many strongly held beliefs about their effects on future therapeutic relationships. This study presents suggestive results, but they would have been more credible if someone other than the therapist made the judgments and elicited the patient's responses to transfer.

Many studies reviewed elsewhere have findings or implications that bear on the therapeutic relationship. Those reviewed here barely explore this universe of variables, some already labeled and some remaining *terra incognita*. We have no systematic knowledge of therapeutic relationships. The few studies that have been done, striking anywhere from the beginning to the end of the therapeutic relationship, provide us with some interesting hypotheses, some useful conceptualizations of therapeutic behavior, and some handy measuring devices. The area is open for many a thoughtful and ingenious investigator.

TRANSFERENCE AND COUNTERTRANSFERENCE

For some therapists transference and countertransference are the keystones of the therapeutic arch. In her research report on transference in group therapy, Chance (1952) defined it as "the patient's tendency to respond to the therapist with feelings, attitudes, and behavior which are stereotypes or clichés of his childhood experience in relationship with the parental figure which had been more important in his development" (p. 41). The experiment was intended to investigate the existence and magnitude of this phenomenon. The proceedings of sixteen group therapy sessions with five men and three women were recorded from memory immediately after each session. The statements taken by these records formed the basic data for the study. Accurate verbatim recording written *after* a group session with eight patients would seem to be a physical impossibility and sufficient grounds to dismiss the results. From these dubious records, 450 statements of feeling relationships were submitted to three judges to rate as hostile, friendly, or ambivalent. The majority ruled when there were disagreements. This is a totally inadequate standard since agreement of at least two out of three judges with three choices can be expected to occur twenty-one out of twenty-seven times by chance alone. Seventy-nine items were selected and submitted to the patients for rating on a nine-point scale from most to least descriptive of the therapist; the rating was then repeated for the more important parent. In each case the rating of the therapist came first, although a counterbalanced order would have been preferable. Correlation between the two measures was taken as the measure of transference. Coefficients ranged from $r = -.25$ to $r = +.63$. It was reported that the correlation coefficients for five of the eight subjects were significant, but one of these, the negative coefficient, is significant in the opposite direction. A second question concerned itself with the degree to which the size of the correlation reflects the intensity of transference. It was reported that the correlations corresponded closely with the therapist's prediction in all but two cases. However, when we compute the rank-difference correlation between the two sets of ranks that were reported, it turns out to be a nonsignificant rho = .33 that reflects no notable relation.

Subotnik (1966a, 1966b) replicated an experiment that had been done with one child on three different children and found support for the hypothesis that the therapist is seen as a parent but not necessarily of the same sex. The technique involved Q-sorts by psychologists of inferred attitudes of the child toward father and mother before and after therapy, and of the therapist's description of attitudes toward him at different points in therapy. These were intercorrelated and factor analyzed to test the hypothesis. Whether similar findings would obtain with other than young children remains to be seen.

Crisp (1964a, 1964b) developed and applied a measure of transference in a series of studies. His test was designed to measure four aspects of transference derived from psychodynamic concepts: idealization, hostility, dependency, and sexual aspects. The Kelly repertory grid technique was applied and found to be sensitive enough. When applied repeatedly over a course of behavior therapy, it was concluded from simple inspection of graphs that changes in transference scores were frequently directionally associated with changes in the clinical state, and in some instances were forerunners of clinical change. Sechrest (1962) gave the Kelly Role Construct Repertory Test early and late in therapy to twenty-eight hospital and seven clinic patients. Of the thirteen stimulus equivalents given, the therapist was found at both points in therapy to be most frequently described as similar to the physician, minister, and liked teacher. Therapist-parent similarity was at chance. The findings offered no support to the transference hypothesis. Instead, similarity was perceived with other life figures based upon such variables as age, role, and title. Sechrest proposed goodness or pleasantness of the relationship as a concept in place of transference. In common usage, transference has come to stand for the therapist-patient relationship in lieu of its strict Freudian meaning.

Rawn (1958) developed a scale of transference and resistance by having raters sophisticated in psychoanalytic thinking do Q-sorts from four taped sessions. A reliable and consistent scale was arrived at in which the terms transference and resistance were given quantitative description. No hypotheses were tested, but the technique has research potential. It would have to be applied to a variety of cases before its utility could be assured. An exploratory study of transference featured the removal of the physical presence of the therapist, who communicated with the patients by microphone from another room (Lowinger & Huston, 1955). Ten neurotic patients were seen from one to three times a week over a twenty-nine-week period. It was concluded that a transference relationship develops and is not dependent upon nonverbal aspects and attributes of the therapist. They maintained that the transference is less intense than it would be if the therapist were in the same room, but there were no data to prove the point. This "confessional" technique is an interesting one, if not new, and is but one step removed from the analyst's sitting out of view of the supine patient.

One phase of Snyder and Snyder's (1961) study of the interpersonal relationship between the therapist and client dealt with transference and countertransference in terms of positive and negative affect within the dyad. It was found that the positive affect of the client tended to increase throughout therapy, whereas the negative affect peaked in the middle of therapy and then declined. Positive affect of the therapist did not vary, but negative affect tended to increase. Fiedler's (1951b) study suggested that negative countertransference, as measured by a quantification method derived from Q-sorts, is greater in less competent therapists. Consistent with this finding, Cutler's (1958) study offered some evidence to support the belief that the appearance in the patient of conflict-relevant behavior for the therapist reduces therapeutic efficiency.

Wolpe (1961) maintained that results in systematic desensitization of phobias are *not* due to transference. As proof, he offered a series of thirty-nine cases in which only the specific phobias for which hierarchies were established and worked on were eliminated. Behavior therapists have been shown to be interchangeable, making transference an unlikely explanation of outcome. Marks and Gelder (1965) reported that a marked attachment for the therapist was observed in five of their patients, but they did not do any better than the rest. Four of the five were women with dependent attachments on the same male therapist.

The concept of transference has been applied beyond the dyadic relationship to the more complex interactions of group therapy. Berzon (1962) hypothesized that the participants in a group initiate interaction with others to the extent that other participants are seen as similar to the parent who is recalled as having been the most threatening. A Perception of Parents' Behavior Questionnaire was administered to adult group members as a measure of current perception of relations with parents when a child. Interaction in the group was observed from a one-way room, and initiation of interaction was recorded. Subjects were also asked to rank group members using the same dimensions on which parents had been rated. No significant relation was found between similarity to parents and predicted or observed interaction rankings, and the hypothesis went unsupported. The dynamics of the immediate group situation, on the other hand, did strongly influence the interaction, as patients initiated interaction in the order they were initiated to. The experiment illustrates the importance of experimentation to test attractive but inaccurate dynamic formulations, emphasizes the importance of "here-and-now" field conditions in contrast to the relative unimportance of the influence of early childhood experiences in determining group interactions, and casts grave doubt upon the naïve "group equals family" formulation.

Some indication of the fact that the group therapist is not acting simply in *loco parentis* can be seen in the research of Harrow et al., who compared thirty-seven variables pertinent to within-group therapy interactions in groups with and without family members present (Harrow, Astrachan, Becker, Detre, & Schwartz, 1967). There was significantly more verbal interaction, less inhibition, more discussion of family issues, more offering of problem solutions, and the introduction of more reality factors. Roles assumed by both patients and therapist probably shift with the composition of the group.

As can be seen, there has been surprisingly little research on this central therapeutic phenomenon. Besides, there are contradictions among the research that does exist. These may stem from diversity of definitions, measuring methods, and variations in transference relations in different types of therapy. The automatic assumption that the therapist stands symbolically for parent is lacking in demonstrated generality. If the concept is expanded to refer to the quality of the relationship, and the stimulus equivalents broadened to include other significant life figures rather than being strictly limited to parents, more consistent support is available.

IDENTIFICATION AND ROLE MODELING

Initial similarity between the therapist and his patient as it affects success of therapy has been examined as an independent variable. A more limited body of research has also been carried out in which patient-therapist similarity has been viewed as a dependent variable. Increased patient-therapist similarity as a consequence of psychotherapy is generally thought of as a one-way affair for good reason. Any dyadic relationship, including the therapeutic one, can theoretically result in mutual influences. By its very nature, however, psychotherapy is structured with the counselor as the influencer who acts upon the counselee with the intention of modifying him in some way. In the process, the counselor is incidentally subject to being influenced. Since the therapist generally has many patients and the patient usually but one therapist, the chances of the therapist becoming more like each of the patients in his caseload is implausible, unless they are all very similar to each other. This may possibly be one of the dangers of an excessively homogeneous caseload, although there are no data on this point. A more realistic matter is what has been termed the "Pygmalion effect," but could more aptly be called the "Jehovah effect," in which the therapist recreates patients into his own image. This could entail intentional or unintentional shaping on the part of the therapist and mechanisms of identification, role modeling, or introjection on the part of the patient. We are not at all concerned here with value judgments about the phenomenon, but only with the issue of whether or not it exists and if so to what degree.

Personality. Using rating scales of patient and therapist personality characteristics, identification, positive rapport, and therapeutic success, Schrier (1953) assessed changes in the direction of similarity with their therapists of nine patients in short-term therapy. Some evidence was presented to support the hypothesis that the patient modifies his perceptions of himself in the direction of his therapist's self-rating. Identification and positive rapport were related to judged success.

Sheehan (1953) investigated Rorschach changes during psychotherapy in relation to the personality of the therapist. Specifically, he was interested in the extent to which the patients' personality shifts were in the direction of becoming more like their therapists. Rorschach tests were administered to the patients at the beginning and at or near the end of therapy. Degree of improvement was separately rated by each therapist. In all, seventeen of the twenty-one college-student patients shifted toward their therapist. The outstanding shifts were in the Rorschach determinants rather than in the presumably more susceptible content areas, particularly in M, m, F%, FC, and Sum C. That the shifts were linked to the therapist was supported by the finding that two groups, who shifted in nearly opposite directions, each shifted toward their respective therapists. The changes were noted to be relatively independent of the theoretical orientation or method of the therapist. Both personality assets and liabilities were adopted. Last, those patients who were rated by their therapists as most improved showed greater shifts toward the therapist. These are rather startling results, particularly with Rorschach determinants. The possibility of a "regression toward the mean" effect cannot be entirely discounted. The finding that patients rated more successful show more shifts in the direction of their therapists suggests the possibility that when a patient becomes more like the therapist, the therapist sees him as improved. It would be worthwhile to look at external criteria of success. The study would bear replication with other than a college sample. In Sechrest's (1962) study, the ascribed similarity between the self and the therapist increased significantly during therapy. Thus, the patients saw themselves as becoming more like their therapists. Whether they actually did was not assessed.

An investigation by Farson (1961) looked into changes in congruence of client and therapist self-descriptions over the course of therapy. The eighteen subjects with mainly neurotic features were seen at the University of Chicago Counseling Center by six attitudinally homogeneous client-centered therapists with two to eight years of experience. Patients described their actual and ideal selves on the Butler-Haigh Q-Sort before therapy, at termination, and six months later. Therapists did an actual-self sort prior to therapy. In addition, the six therapist colleagues ranked each other on psychological adjustment, therapeutic competence, and the likelihood that clients would come to resemble them. Therapists were also ranked for the degree that patients actually came to resemble them. As a control, patients' self-descriptions were compared with those of therapists other than their own. The hypothesis that self-descriptions of a client would tend to become more congruent during therapy with those of his own therapist than with other therapists was not supported. This is not to say that congruence did not increase. Indeed, the degree of congruence between clients as a group and therapists as a group increased at both terminal and follow-up points. The congruence, however, was with therapists as a class rather than as individuals. Judges were able to predict accurately which clients would come to resemble them and which would not. Perhaps the most provocative finding was that therapists who were judged by their colleagues to be most competent and most adjusted were the *least* likely to have their clients tend to resemble them after therapy. The author tentatively concluded that it is not only possible for a patient to achieve an adjustment that is independent of the personality of his therapist but also that the less competent therapist tends to induce conformity to himself in his patients. The reason for Farson's cautiousness in drawing this conclusion is that the sample of both patients and therapists was small and unrepresentative, time intervals were varied and data collection periods separated by several years in some cases, and the meaning of congruence was limited to the type of items that appear in the Q-sample. Therapist constancy in self-description was assumed instead of being determined by the taking of a second measure for therapists as well as for patients. The data about therapist competence were based upon fallible peer judgments that were probably confounded with judgments of the therapist's adjustment level. Nevertheless, the promise here is sufficient to justify more extensive hypothesis testing.

One phase of Cartwright and Lerner's (1963) study bears on the current question. A scale derived from Kelly's Role Construct Repertory Test was administered to twenty-eight patients and their sixteen client-centered therapists after the second interview and after termination. Therapists also rated the patient as he thought the patient would see himself, rated the patient's adjustment on two occasions, and made a final rating of outcome. The actual similarity between the therapist and patient self-descriptions was calculated (real similarity), as was the similarity of the therapist's description of his patient and of himself (assumed similarity). The difference was taken as a measure of distance. On the first occasion, the therapists made the error of reducing the distance with same-sex patients and increasing it with patients of the opposite sex. The initial distancing of improved patients was more extreme than that of unimproved patients. Thus, same-sex patients were seen as more like the therapist, opposite-sex patients as more unlike. Unimproved of the same sex were seen as more different, and of the opposite sex more similar. Inexperienced therapists had significantly more negative distancing errors (thus denying similarity to the patient) than did experienced ones.

Values and Meanings. Wolff's (1954) survey of therapists' opinions revealed that 48 per cent believed that the values of the therapist have a direct influence upon the patient, 24 per cent saw an indirect influence, and 28 per cent saw no influence. The division of expert opinion is apparent when it is noted that Sullivan (1954) thought the social values of the therapist may be of importance whereas Fenichel (1945) and Colby (1951) viewed the therapist's values in terms of countertransference and felt that they had to be kept out of the therapy. Some research has been done on changes in the patient's social and moral values and in his meaning systems in the direction of those of the therapist.

The relation between improvement in psychotherapy and changes in moral values in the direction of the therapist's was the subject of a study at the Henry Phipps Psychiatric Clinic (Rosenthal, 1955). The twelve patients, mean age 29.5, were diagnosed as psychoneurotic or as having personality, psychophysiological, or adjustment disorders. Treatment by psychiatric residents ranged from three weeks to one year with an average of five months. Patients were given the Allport-Vernon-Lindzey Study of Values and a Moral Values Q-Sort at the beginning and end of treatment. Therapists completed the same procedures on a single occasion. The moral values dealt with the areas of sex, aggression, and authority. Benefit from therapy was measured by three judges using a seven-point scale based upon a detailed report of a terminal interview on the effects of therapy. The hypotheses were

(1) that moral values, viewed as the crux of neurotic conflict, do change in psychotherapy despite Mowrer's belief that they are not much subject to the influence of psychotherapy, (2) that the patient learns to accept the moral values of the therapist and that this alleviates psychological stress, (3) that other kinds of values are not systematically influenced by psychotherapy. The therapy referred to here is psychoanalytically oriented. As a test of these hypotheses, the patients were ranked on ratings of improvement and on the degree of difference between initial and final correlations between the patient's and therapist's sortings of moral values. This was repeated for the values reflected in the Allport-Vernon-Lindzey Scale. It was found that ratings of improvement correlated positively (rho = .68) with change in the direction of the moral values of the therapist. Actually, only two patients were rated as more than moderately improved, but those who were unimproved or worse tended to move away from the therapist's value system. The data thus provided information about only the negative side of the relationship, and the values tapped by the Allport-Vernon-Lindzey Scale were not found to be related to the improvement variable.

This study was based upon a total of only twelve patients; many others started in the project but dropped out for various reasons. It is true that one cannot study changes following psychotherapy in those who drop out before receiving it, but when there are many dropouts a residual and biased sample is left and conclusions are limited to the kinds of patients who do remain. This is not a criticism of this particular study, but an unfortunate reality that limits the universality of statements about outcome that can be made from some psychotherapy research. As in several other studies, patients were asked to complete the value survey on two occasions while therapists were spared this second measure on the assumption that *their* values were not apt to change. The assumption is a reasonable one, but the *measure* of their values might change on a second administration. This is a function of the test-retest reliability of the measures, which should be established beforehand. Rosenthal observed that although the changes in moral values in the direction of the therapist were statistically significant by correlational analysis, they were actually small in magnitude. More precise measures of the absolute shifts might not have been very impressive. The study is an intriguing one, but, unfortunately, it was limited to analysis of total movement toward or away from the therapist's values without regard to what these values were. No information is given about the nature of the patients' or therapists' values, nor is it possible to tell if one kind of initial values of patients or therapists facilitates or inhibits improvement more than another. There is also no indication of any differentiation in value shifts in the three content areas—sex, aggression, and authority. All these data were available and their analysis would have greatly added to the scope of the study and increased its value.

Welkowitz et al. hypothesized that therapists and their own patients would have more similar value systems than would therapists randomly paired with patients who were not their own (Welkowitz, Cohen, & Ortmeyer, 1967). They also tested the hypothesis of a direct relation between similarity of patient-therapist values and the therapist's subjective evaluations of improvement in the patient. The data were collected at the William Alanson White Institute and New York University Post-Doctorate Center, both psychoanalytic training institutes. The thirty-eight therapists all had doctorates (Ph.D. or M.D.) and several years of experience. The forty-four patients were mostly in their mid-twenties and of above average intelligence. The Morris Ways to Live and Strong Vocational Interest Blank were administered to patients and therapists alike after the patients had been in therapy from one to nine months. Two weeks later each therapist judged the extent of improvement of each patient on a six-point Improvement Rating Scale, ranging from much worse to marked improvement. The ratings were then collapsed and the patients dichotomized into two groups. Factor analyses were completed for each scale and chi-square tests made of the differences between patients' and therapists' distributions on factors. Various other relevant comparisons were made. Patients and therapists were not found to be differently distributed on the obtained factors. The findings supported the hypothesis that similarity of values between the therapists and their own patients is greater than that between therapists and random patients not their own. Value similarity also tends to increase with the duration of therapy. In addition, there was a significant positive relation between the extent of patient-therapist value similarity and perception by the therapist of improvement in the patient. Thus, on the assumption that patients and therapists were not matched for value similarity at the start, those who were seen by their therapists as improved moved closer to the therapists' values than those seen as not improved. Although the results of this experiment are certainly suggestive, the relevance of the Morris WTL and Strong VIB is open to some question. These conclusions cannot be in terms of values in general but must be restricted at this time to those values that may be tapped by those instruments. The fact that the patients do move closer to the position of their own therapists certainly suggests the specific influence that comes about in unique dyadic relationships. The measure of patient improvement, therapist's rating, may or may not be accurate. It would have been of considerable interest to add one more objective measure to determine if the judgment of improvement by the therapist is biased by the similarity; that is, to find out if therapists see improvement when patients begin to acquire values similar to their own. This is a point of no little importance, as Spohn (1960) demonstrated that congruence of social values is one of the determinants of therapists' clinical judgments about patients.

The congruence between patients' and therapists' evaluations of the importance of topics discussed was studied in two schizophrenic patients, of whom one was unchanged after three and one-half years of intensive individual therapy and the other discharged as recovered after a year and one-half (Parloff, Iflund, & Goldstein, 1960). The unsuccessful patient increased in congruence during the first six weeks but not thereafter. The successful one increased in congruence over the course of therapy but declined over the last fifteen sessions. After eight months, the successful patient was significantly closer to the therapist's values than was the other.

Nawas and Landfield (1963) designed an experiment to study the relation between improvement in psychotherapy and adoption of the therapist's meaning system. They set out to test the hypothesis that improvement is contingent upon adoption by the client of the personal frame of reference of the therapist. Twenty clients in a university setting were seen by six eclectic therapists for from eight to twenty weeks. After the initial session both clients and therapists took a modified version of the Role Construct Repertory Test. The constructs or "personal language dimensions" of each patient-therapist pair were transcribed onto individual cards, shuffled, and given to each to rank for meaningfulness for understanding people. The top 25 per cent of the constructs so ranked by the therapist were compared with those of the patient, and a count was made of the number of therapist constructs that were borrowed by the patient. This procedure was repeated every four weeks, but only the first and last were considered. According to the hypothesis, the most improved patients would show an increase in constructs borrowed from their therapists, and the least improved would show a decrease. Three experienced external judges were brought in to rate improvement in the clients from ten- to thirty-minute pre- and posttherapy typescripts. Patients were dichotomized into most improved ($N = 12$) and least improved ($N = 8$) groups. The results were not statistically significant, but were interpreted as showing a trend in the direction opposite to the hypothesis. The appropriate conclusion from the data should have been no demonstrated relation between improvement and adoption of therapists' values. One could question the validity of improvement ratings based upon short typescripts from initial and terminal interviews. The authors admit that the conclusions are highly tentative, as indeed they must be. Nevertheless, the findings certainly cast doubt on the notion that improvement is *contingent* upon adoption by the client of the therapist's personal meaning system.

This study was extended and modified with somewhat different results (Landfield & Nawas, 1964). The same six therapists were employed, but sixteen patients who had been seen for less than eight weeks were added to the earlier sample, which had been restricted to those seen for at least eight weeks. The procedure was the same as in 1963. Clients and therapists ranked the role-construct statements once a month, rating the self as seen in the present, the ideal self, and the other person (client or therapist) as now seen. Only initial and terminal ratings were used. As in the earlier study, none of the information obtained in interim ratings was analyzed. The information could have added to the scope of the experiment. The hypotheses were: (1) it is essential for improvement that there be a minimal degree of communication within the language dimension of the client between the therapist and client, (2) improvement is accompanied by a shift in the present self of the client toward the therapist's ideal as described within the client's language dimension. These hypotheses may have been more postdiction than prediction since they were made after the 1963 data were analyzed. In addition, the same subjects were used together with some new ones. As a test of the first hypothesis, the five most and least important client constructs were compared with therapist choices, and the frequency of congruence was counted. This was done separately for client and therapist construct dimensions. This yielded two fourfold tables: most improved–least improved, agreed with therapist–no agreement on client's and therapist's constructs. On client language dimensions, agreement with the therapist was achieved in 72 per cent of the most improved patients, but only 39 per cent of the least improved. This finding was of statistical significance. There was no such difference in agreement on therapist constructs. The findings support the hypothesis of the necessity for communication within the client's frame of reference if improvement is to take place.

To test the second hypothesis, thirteen constructs of the client's present self—in both the clients' and therapists' language as described in initial and terminal interviews—were compared with the therapist's ideal ranking. The direction of the shifts toward or away from the ideal was examined. Again there were fourfold tables: most improved–least improved, change toward–change against therapist ideal. When analyzed on the client dimension, a highly significant difference was apparent, with 80 per cent of the most improved shifting toward the therapist's ideal in contrast to 72 per cent of the least improved shifting away from the therapist's ideal. Again, when this is examined in the therapists' language dimension, there was no significant difference between most and least improved.

The scoring system was rather crude and the experiment would be difficult to replicate faithfully as described. Nevertheless, the results are unequivocal. The conclusions and discussion of results appear sound and cogent and somewhat more advanced than the experimental effort. The authors caution that the findings may be restricted to therapists embued with a "psychology of personal constructs" approach. These therapists were active and structuring, and emphasized the present and anticipated the future. The researchers point out that the findings could differ with therapists who teach clients a new set of language dimensions. They speculate that those who serve mainly as cathartic agents would show a move toward independence rather than toward the therapist's language dimensions or ideals, whereas psychoanalytically oriented therapy might be expected to reflect dependency on the therapist at least in the early stages. In short, the school or approach of the therapist was considered crucial in this regard.

As it now stands, there is some evidence that the personality, values, and meaning systems of the patient shift with therapy in the direction of those of the therapist. It is logical that the patient should model himself after his therapist and that he should believe that he has improved as he gets to be more like him. It is just as reasonable that a therapist who sees his job as entailing the re-creation or reconstruction of human beings and their lives should begin to think that a patient has improved when he begins to act and think more and more like him and adopts his value systems. "Mirror mirror on the wall" holds for therapists also; after all is said and done, they are human too. The studies suggest that therapists (except perhaps in behavior therapy) are not interchangeable, since the one whom the patient selects to model himself upon can have considerable bearing upon what the patient becomes. Change, however, is not synonymous with improvement. We need more comprehensive and exhaustive studies of shifts in similarity assessed against objective external measures of outcome, with experience, level of competence, and sex of the therapist controlled and definitive appraisal of the way in which perceived similarity by the patient and the therapist affect the judgment by each of outcome.

17

An Overview of Process Research

Socrates said that the person who asks a question puts the world in danger. The danger is, of course, the doubt raised about the validity of current beliefs. In the case of process studies, neither the questions nor the dangers of change have been very great. Studies of outcome have a central focus; process studies range in a disorganized fashion over the entire field of psychotherapy. The variety of process studies and their lack of unity may be an advantage at the present stage of our knowledge when it is desirable to provide the greatest possible number of explorations of the complex process of psychotherapy. However, this makes it difficult to summarize these studies in a cohesive way. Some problems in carrying out process studies may be due to the difficulties in developing hypotheses, in conceptualizing the variables, and in devising suitable measuring devices. Indeed, many researchers have restricted themselves to highly conventional variables, and others, having devised a way of categorizing behavior in psychotherapy, have reified their device as the process of psychotherapy.

For many investigators, the therapist stands at the center of the process. A conspicuous variable is the professional discipline or membership of the therapist. Very few studies deal with this variable. In those analyzed here, the samples are usually small, and the therapist's behavior is measured by his responses to questionnaires of therapeutic practices, to written statements or sketches of patients, or to films of other therapists' interviews. There is a great deal of overlap between psychologists, psychiatrists, and social workers in their attitudes toward the impersonality and patient-directedness of psychotherapy. The small intergroup differences may reflect therapeutic training or orientation rather than professional discipline. From the available research, there are indications that differences in the therapist's orientation or "school" lead to differences in the way he will conceptualize the therapeutic problem and select techniques for dealing with it. For example, Freudians tend to conceptualize the problem in terms of its childhood referents, to plan therapy, and to control the therapist's spontaneity. Rogerians conceptualize less and stress the therapist's personality and his spontaneity. The studies frequently use large samples of therapists, but their significance is somewhat limited because their data come from questionnaire responses and other indirect measures that are somewhat remote from actual therapeutic behavior. Many therapists express strong convictions concerning one aspect of the "school" issue—the effects of personal analysis or treatment of the therapist upon his behavior in the therapeutic situation. However, there are very few studies, and these yield virtually no meaningful or reliable results.

One potentially important and frequently uncontrolled ingredient, a factor in almost all studies of therapeutic process, is the therapist's experience. In studies that systematically vary experience, investigators sometimes make the assumption that experienced therapists are successful therapists. Therefore, the techniques of the experienced therapists are taken to be those that bring about successful outcomes. Both beliefs are hypotheses to be tested. There are severe limitations upon the knowledge we can draw from the studies reviewed. More than two-thirds of the investigations on this issue obtain their data from simulated interviews and questionnaires, eschewing actual therapeutic behaviors. Criteria of experience vary widely from study to study. Most samples of therapists are drawn from the lower end of the experience continuum: new and advanced graduate students, interns, residents, and recently established practitioners. One wonders if there is any perceptible difference between some of these levels of experience. Neophytes, like college freshmen and white rats, are the most available subjects, but are they the most relevant subjects for the hypotheses studied? Some researchers conclude that experience is not related to differences in techniques and attitudes. Others report that experienced therapists use more diversified techniques, are more critical and less optimistic about their patients, and address themselves more directly and with less anxiety, avoidance, and personal involvement to their patients' needs. Differences and difficulties in experimental arrangements call for additional and more adequate studies of the effect of experience upon the therapist's practices.

A growing body of research deals with those contributions of the therapist that Rogers considers to be the necessary and sufficient conditions for change in the client. These are the therapist's congruence, empathic understanding of, and unconditional positive regard for the client. Client-centered psychotherapists have defined these variables and devised ingenious measures of them, at first questionnaires and later scales of actual therapeutic behavior. It is possible that these variables are fundamental aspects of the psychotherapeutic process. However, many sympathetic researchers have assumed that Rogers' proposal was verified fact, that all that a researcher has to do is to demonstrate that high levels of these therapist-contributed conditions lead to the process of self-exploration in the client. Self-exploration is in turn assumed to be the precursor of improvement. Therefore, in order to induce change, the therapist merely has to establish high levels of these facilitative conditions. Unfortunately, the linkage between self-exploration and improvement has not been clearly demonstrated; indeed, it is challenged by behavior therapists. Several studies have used college students as clients and/or counselors to demonstrate that the ability to establish facilitative conditions is not necessarily a function of professional training or experience. Despite the optimism of this group of researchers, the point has not been established. Certainly, priority should be given to the demonstration, with bona fide patients and therapists, that the "facilitative conditions" lead to desirable process changes in the client and eventually to favorable outcome. Some research suggests that these variables may be differential manifestations of one single general characteristic; other research points to the possibility that patient characteristics also contribute to the necessary and sufficient conditions for patient change. The value of this approach seems to reside in the promise of more exact analyses of process variables and the study of their effects rather than in the claim that they are the validated keystones of effective psychotherapy.

Overwhelmingly, studies of the process of psychotherapy are concerned with the interview. Ways of analyzing the behavior of the participants are as varied as the intentions and ingenuity of the researchers. Naïve empirical approaches to the interview ("let us see what actually happens in the therapeutic interview") have rapidly given way to schemes for conceptualizing even what seem to be the most simple behaviors. The need for establishing and verifying categories that are both meaningful and manageable remains. Most investigators specify the variable of their interest and create scales with which to measure it. For example, there are scales of defensive behavior participation, process, and even a multidimensional scale with which to measure therapist technique. One important issue is that of the size of the units of behavior to which these scales can most suitably be directed. Analyses by problem area and discussion topic have been found to be more useful than analyses by interview sections. However, some investigators find that small segments of the interview, either randomly or systematically selected, serve their purpose best. When this problem has been resolved, the issues of reliability and validity of the measuring device arise. The judgment of experts may not be a very adequate solution, and uninstructed judges may create difficulties. There is an omnipresent need for exact recording and reliable evaluation of data.

Of the verbal techniques discussed, verbal conditioning and reinforcement methods have commanded the greatest recent interest. The research reviewed indicates that the content of a patient's verbalizations can be shaped by verbal reinforcement. A danger suggested by this finding is the possibility that the therapist-researcher may, knowingly or not, accept the verbalizations he has shaped as verification of his hypotheses about psychotherapy. However, reinforcement techniques have not been uniformly successful or unchallenged. For example, schizophrenics seem less responsive to verbal reinforcement than neurotics, and their verbal responses seem more easily extinguished. Some personality characteristics seem to influence the subject's response to conditioning techniques. For example, compliant college students and undergraduates with a need for approval have been shown to perform better than others in conditioning situations. The kind of verbal materials the experimenter chooses to condition seems to be important. In one study, patients who did not usually verbalize their affect did not profit from the reinforcement of affective statements. In another, reinforcement of content, feeling, or both in different groups of students yielded positive results only for the reinforcement of content.

The fate of the expression of dependency in the therapeutic situation is of great interest to psychotherapists. Generally, reinforcement of the expression of dependency leads to more dependency responses, while nonreinforcement leads to a decrease in dependency responses and sometimes to an avoidance of the therapeutic situation. Attempts to obtain extratherapeutic generalization of a variety of reinforced responses have so far not been successful even when experimental arrangements have offered an excellent opportunity for its occurrence. The reinforcement of verbal behavior is not a panacea; its effects are contingent upon the personality of the patient, the nature of the response that is reinforced, and the particular therapeutic situation. Further research with reinforcement techniques may provide the psychotherapist with more specific knowledge of some complex interactions in conventional psychotherapy.

Various aspects of therapist style have been studied with ambiguous results. Degree of lead by the therapist does not appear to be related to client responses of dependency. Therapists vary along a continuum in this respect and may vary their style with different clients. Expectations of influence by the therapist may induce negative client attitudes, but clients may prefer interpretation to passive reflection. It has been demonstrated that structuring by the therapist leads to decline in client self-exploration and nondirection to its continuation. Conflicting results have been obtained on the effect that structuring of the interview has upon anxiety. One research found that direct questioning and "forcing" led to a decrease in understanding. In another investigation clients spoke more to active than to silent counselors; in a third study there was a relation between therapist activity and specificity on the one hand and patient anxiety on the other. Lack of consistency of results may be due to the fact that the samples studied range from college students to hospitalized patients. From one study to another, the variables are cognate but clearly not identical. Therapist activity, directiveness, silence, and friendliness seem to have effects upon patient behavior, effects that must be more closely and specifically pursued in order to be better known.

Interpretation is the psychotherapist's best known and most used tool. How does he know that his interpretations are true? Does he know by the alacrity or apparent sincerity with which the patient accepts the interpretation or by the vehemence with which the patient rejects it? Or, perhaps, is the interpretation held to be true because the therapist's conviction of the validity of the theory influences his interpretation? Does it matter? Noblin's suggestion is that interpretive relevance is not important, that any interpretation will be acceptable. The need may be for any believable cognitive framework that can support a behavioral or attitudinal change. It has also been suggested that an interpretation is more acceptable if it comes from a prestigeful person, but another study indicates that the source of the interpretation may not be important. The "depth" of the interpretation is usually defined as the degree of disparity between the therapist's view and the patient's awareness. There have been some partially successful attempts to quantify the depth of both single statements and entire interviews. To complicate the issue, it has been suggested that depth of interpretation is a multidimensional variable. What of the effects of interpretation upon patients? There are some indications that interpretations that are not particularly disturbing are preferred by subjects. Interpretation, according to Auld and White, does not seem to produce more resistance than other types of intervention. Speisman's work suggests that the level is important, with moderate levels of interpretation evoking less resistance from the patient than deep or superficial ones. More specific interpretations tend to reduce the patient's anxiety. All these statements are important and provocative clues rather than firm conclusions. What knowledge we have of this principal therapeutic tool is based on a scattering of investigations, the best of which are analogue studies.

The therapist and his patient are not limited to speech. Either or both may remain silent. The patient's silence is usually interpreted as resistance and, at least for the instant, as lack of progress. Some studies have demonstrated that the patient's silences are preceded or followed by "resistive" talk or are associated with withheld material. There have been attempts to eliminate this supposedly negative therapeutic behavior by conditioning techniques. However, patient silences have been shown to be associated with long- or short-term gains. Perhaps silence gives the patient time to register, evaluate, review, rehearse, or draw conclusions about psychotherapeutic events. The therapist, too, may remain speechless. His silence has been associated with a succeeding inhibition of the speech of his patient, with less relevant speech, or with the patient's feeling that the therapist is less empathic. Therapist silence may increase as a function of the patient's preceding behavior, such as expressions of hostility. Silence is given meaning by the intentions and motives of the participants. Preconceptions of its significance may easily lead the investigator astray.

Studies of physiological correlates of psychotherapeutic events have usually been limited to very few patients and have been primarily quests for adequate measuring devices. The galvanic skin response has been a favored measure because of its convenience and its supposed correlation with anxiety. It has been used to study patient anxiety during therapy, modes of experiencing, and social interaction. Other measures employed have been heart rate, finger temperature, blood pressure, muscle tension, and eyeblink. A complication is the possibility that some physiological changes may have idiosyncratic meaning. However, the investigation of nonverbal measures of process and change in psychotherapy and of the many somatic correlates of the problems that patients bring to psychotherapy holds the promise of knowledge we should have.

The everyday, moment-by-moment activity of the psychotherapist and patient reflects the interaction within the dyad. These interchanges are so numerous and so complex that the researcher must decide at the beginning which dimensions of interaction he will study. Does he have a hypothesis about the nature of these exchanges or is he seeking some convenient, useful way of categorizing human interactions? Are psychotherapeutic exchanges the same as ordinary social interactions or are they unique to the psychotherapeutic situation? Does the researcher investigate the issue of uniqueness or does his selection of interaction categories hide a hypothesis? What of the problem of generalizing therapeutic behavior to extratherapeutic situations? Bales' system of classifying interactions in small groups has been used directly and in modified form to study therapeutic behavior. This technique has been adapted to show that descriptive behavior declines and evaluative behavior increases during treatment. To explain this change,

Lennard and Bernstein used a larger unit of behavior, the role. They reported that schizophrenics pay less attention to role establishment than do neurotics. Psychotherapists pay a great deal of attention to role induction and are likely to evaluate psychopathology, psychotherapeutic process, change, and potential for change in the light of it. There is need for more specific knowledge. Researchers can contribute greatly by studying patient-role learning and its relations with patient selection, therapeutic process, and outcome.

The Chapple Interaction Chronograph, which measures more formal aspects of verbal exchange, has been found to be highly correlated with the Bales categories. Marked stability of inter-interviewer behavior and intra-interviewer flexibility has been demonstrated. Indications of therapist consistency were shown in one study of counselor constancy of feeling-verbalizations from social to therapeutic situations, and by the discovery that psychiatrists' pauses remain constant from patient to patient. Tentative findings about patients are that less frequent speakers talk longer, are more dominant, and are more oriented toward others. Those who are less active verbally are more submissive and less concerned with interpersonal content.

What general or specific factors on the part of one member of the therapeutic dyad systematically evoke responsive behaviors from the other member? There is some evidence that the therapeutic interaction does not function as a simple information exchange system. It has been reported that counselors utilize similar subroles with different clients and that there are similarities among counselors within one counseling center and differences between those of different counseling centers. However, it has also been found that counselors tend to vary their styles with the particular topic, and their techniques seem to be determined by the particular situation and patient. The limits of therapist consistency and flexibility, as they are determined by client characteristics, have to be demarcated specifically. An example is the effect of client hostility upon therapist response. In one study the hostility of simulated clients evoked anxiety from both experienced and inexperienced therapists. There is also some evidence that the therapist's anxiety is negatively related to his competence and that therapists high in need of approval avoid client hostility, usually by silence or mislabeling. One must bear in mind that these findings are somewhat limited in meaning because of the relative inexperience of some of the therapist samples and because of the frequent use of simulated clients.

Psychotherapy is predominantly a verbal process, and verbal processes have many dimensions. The composition of therapy groups has been considered a determinant of the verbal interactions. The tentative conclusion has been offered that patient-to-patient responses increase with the size of the group and with the greater experience of the therapist. Homogeneity of group membership, generally believed to be an important issue, does not appear to have any great bearing on process or outcome. The degree of participation of patients in the session may be a factor. One investigator found that patients viewed sessions in which they were verbally most active as most helpful to them and to their group. On the other hand, another researcher reported that the most articulate patients did not necessarily change most nor the silent ones least. There is some suggestion that group members prefer individuals high in self-disclosure as comembers but that they may have a greater liking for more reserved persons. In group therapy, content is usually judged to be of secondary importance and feelings of primary importance. However, one study revealed that topics thought by patients to be most helpful (and most disturbing) were considered by psychologists to be more suitable for discussion in intimate settings. Apparently, therapists have more reservations than patients do.

Attempts to develop a taxonomy of group processes are important for future hypothesis formation. Corsini and Rosenberg's categories from the literature included acceptance, intellectualization, reality testing, transference, interaction, spectator therapy, ventilation, altruism, and universalization. Lorr, in contrast, reported factors based on actual patient behavior in groups: hostility, attention-seeking, control, leader role, supportive role, succorance, submissiveness, withdrawal, and disorganized behavior. Categorizations have different purposes. Those based on the actual behavior of the participants seem to provide a more suitable base for the evaluation of change.

Psychologists are not always content to base their conclusions on talk alone. They have long been interested in nonverbal aspects of communication such as acts, gestures, and expressions, and there are a few examples of the application of this work to psychotherapy. There have been attempts to count and classify movements of both therapists and patients during therapeutic sessions and to obtain correlates of various kinds of movements. Upper body "mirror congruent" posture of the participants in the interview has been shown to be indicative of rapport and of interpersonal, positive, and specific content in therapy. Fleeting facial expressions have been related to the patient's verbal blocking and statements of denial. Little has been done to study gestural and expressive behavior in psychotherapy in an era that offers many sophisticated techniques with which to investigate these phenomena.

What the patient and therapist do and say becomes, or grows into, or is a function of the therapeutic relationship. Despite most therapists' overriding interest in the therapeutic relationship and many expressions of opinion, we have little organized knowledge. Some research has stressed the therapist's contribution and suggests that therapists of different schools tend to identify the parameters of the relationships somewhat differently. Efforts have been made to delineate the variables that constitute the relationship, although different studies yield some different factors. There is enough overlap to permit us to isolate and characterize some aspects of the therapeutic relationship for use as variables in future process studies. There have been some attempts to evaluate the psychotherapeutic relationship. In the good therapeutic hour, the patient is reported to be emotionally involved, to have expressed a desire for insight, and to have received, generated, and emitted positive affect. The therapist is reported to be viewed by both participants as friendly and to have believed that the patient desired insight. It has been reported that the therapist's ability to approach Fiedler's ideal therapeutic relationship is associated with his ability to establish better extratherapeutic relationships. Other studies have focused on the facilitative effects of a positive and compatible relationship. Preferences of patients and therapists for particular types of therapeutic partners give some preliminary understanding of the origin and development of relationships. There are sufficient hints of the importance of the therapeutic relationship to stimulate the further exploration of its dimensions and consequences as well as of the conditions for its establishment and techniques of modifying it.

Transference and countertransference are the important dimensions of relationship for some therapists. An attempt to demonstrate the existence and magnitude of transference has led to ambiguous results. Apparently, for some child patients therapists are seen as parental figures, but in other instances patients have reported therapists to be similar to life figures other than parents. One study, dealing with group therapy patients, failed to support the hypothesis that patient interaction was related to similarity of fellow patients to parents. The few studies in this area yield no clear results to support the often fervent belief that transference, in its original Freudian sense, is a central phenomenon in psychotherapy. In some kinds of therapy (systematic desensitization) doubt has been cast upon the importance of transference taken in its broadest sense to be equivalent to a relationship whose determinants lie in the patient's personal life.

Similarity of patient to therapist can be considered a product of therapy. With regard to personality, there is some evidence that the patient modifies his perception of himself in the direction of the therapist's self-rating. It has been reported that ascribed similarity of patient to therapist increases during treatment. One investigator reports, however, that the increased congruence of the patient and therapist is with therapists as a class rather than with the individual therapist. Indeed, congruence appears to be least with those therapists judged by their colleagues to be most competent and best adjusted. A value system is a pervasive variable that many therapists believe to be of central importance in treatment. It has been demonstrated that the patient's values are more similar to those of his own therapist than to those of a randomly selected therapist. Value similarity of patient and therapist tends to increase with duration of therapy. The values of unsuccessful patients are reported to differ increasingly from those of their therapists. Two attempts, however, failed to demonstrate that for successful therapy the patient must adopt the therapist's frame of reference. These studies suggest the need for communication in the client's frame of reference. Patients do seem to absorb certain aspects of the therapist's personality and beliefs. How these effects are related to improvement is still not very clear.

The most striking impression one receives from this survey of process research is the scattering of efforts and results. Studies of outcome present a much more cohesive picture. Perhaps the reason for this disparity lies in the difference of purpose. The preliminary, descriptive, taxonomic, prehypothesis testing phases of process research are merely attempts to find out more about what actually goes on in therapy, which, after all, is exceedingly complex. The ultimate goal is to discover what is therapeutic about psychotherapy and how it comes about. More specific questions lie en route. What are the most effective techniques in modifying personality, behavior, and affect? Are there underlying commonalities shared by all therapeutic methods? Do the various techniques yield differential effects with different kinds of patients and problems? How and when should they be applied? The questions are seemingly endless, and the issues are often far more complex than the single concern with "Is it effective?" There are so many branches of knowledge to pursue that their connections to the main trunk are sometimes lost to view, or perhaps not yet discovered. We do not have the knowledge for present unification of the field. Conversely, attempts to press one experimental model on all problems of process create a procrustean bed. The field is open for all manner of investigations.

Do the questions asked put the world of the psychotherapist in danger? The answers obtained are varied and frequently unclear. Some cherished beliefs derived from major theories receive little or ambiguous support. In many areas, research is sparse but sufficient to indicate that some important phenomenon or relation is present and promising enough to be studied under varying conditions. For psychotherapy, like life, seems to have a multivariate design. A stirring theory might in one sweep offer simple, clear, and definitive directions. The course of verification through research, with all its checks and rechecks, seems painfully slow. The tools themselves often have to be conceived and fabricated before the research work can go forward. The accretion of psychological knowledge through research is a gradual process but nevertheless a potent one. Reviews of research in psychotherapy frequently have caused therapists to wonder about the process of research and researchers to wonder about the process of therapy. Both would do well to consider whether that wonder is translated by researchers into meaningful hypotheses and careful research and by therapists into acceptance and utilization of established research knowledge even when it may run counter to existing beliefs.

References

Abeles, N. Liking for clients—its relationship to therapist's personality: unexpected findings. *Psychotherapy: Theory, Research and Practice,* 1967, *4,* 19–21.

Abse, D. W., & Ewing, J. A. Transference and countertransference in somatic therapies. *J. nerv. ment. Dis.,* 1956, *123,* 32–40.

Adams, Anne, Mallinson, T. J., & Greenland, C. Measuring remotivation. *Psychiatry,* 1962, *25,* 135–146.

Adams, H. B., & Cooper, G. D. Three measures of ego strength and prognosis for psychotherapy, *J. clin. Psychol.,* 1962, *18,* 490–494.

Adams, S. Interaction between individual interview therapy and treatment amenability in Older Youth Authority wards. *Monograph No. 2, Board of Corrections, State of California,* 1961, 27–44.

Affleck, D. C., & Garfield, S. L. Predictive judgments of therapists and duration of stay in psychotherapy. *J. clin. Psychol.,* 1961, *17,* 134–137.

Affleck, D. C., & Mednick, S. A. The use of the Rorschach Test in the prediction of the abrupt terminator in individual psychotherapy. *J. consult. Psychol.,* 1959, *23,* 125–128.

Aidman, T. An objective study of the changing relationship between the present self and wanted self pictures as expressed by the client in client-centered therapy. Unpublished Ph.D. dissertation, University of Chicago, 1951.

Albronda, H. F., Dean, R. L., & Starkweather, J. A. Social class and psychotherapy. *Arch. gen. Psychiat.,* 1964, *10,* 276–283.

Alexik, Mae, & Carkhuff, R. R. The effects of the manipulation of client depth of self-exploration upon high and low functioning counselors. *J. clin. Psychol.,* 1967, *23,* 210-212.

Allen, T. W. Effectiveness of counselor trainees as a function of psychological openness. *J. counsel. Psychol.,* 1967, *14,* 35–40.

Amble, B. R., & Moore, R. The influence of a set on the evaluation of psychotherapy. *Amer. J. Orthopsychiat.,* 1966, *36,* 50–56.

Anderson, R. P. Physiological and verbal behavior during client-centered counseling. *J. counsel. Psychol.,* 1956, *3,* 174–184.

Anker, J. M., & Walsh, R. P. Group psychotherapy, a special activity program, and group structure in the treatment of chronic schizophrenia. *J. consult. Psychol.*, 1961, *25*, 476–481.

Anthony, N. A longitudinal analysis of the effect of experience on the therapeutic approach. *J. clin. Psychol.*, 1967, *23*, 512–516.

Appleby, L. Evaluation of treatment methods for chronic schizophrenia. *Arch. gen. Psychiat.*, 1963, *8*, 8–21

Arbuckle, D. S. Client perception of counselor personality. *J. counsel. Psychol.*, 1956, *3*, 93–96.

Arbuckle, D. S., & Boy, A. V. Client-centered therapy in counseling students with behavior problems. *J. counsel. Psychol.*, 1961, *8*, 136–139.

Aronson, H., & Overall, Betty. Treatment expectations of patients in two social classes. *Soc. Wk.*, 1966, *11*, 35-41.

Aronson, M. A study of the relationships between certain counselor and client characteristics in client-centered therapy. In W. U. Snyder (ed.), *Group report of a program of research in psychotherapy* (mimeographed). University Park, Pa.: Pennsylvania State College, 1953. Pp. 39–54.

Ashby, J. D., Ford, D. H., Guerney, B. G., Jr., & Guerney, Louise F. Effects on clients of a reflective and a leading type of psychotherapy. *Psychol. Monogr.*, 1957, *71*, whole No. 453.

Auld, F., Jr., & Eron, L. D. The use of Rorschach scores to predict whether patients will continue psychotherapy. *J. consult. Psychol.*, 1953, *17*, 104–109.

Auld, F., Jr., & Myers, J. K. Contributions to a theory for selecting psychotherapy patients. *J. clin. Psychol.*, 1954, *10*, 56–60.

Auld, F., Jr., & White, Alice M. Sequential dependencies in psychotherapy. *J. abnorm. soc. Psychol.*, 1959, *58*, 100–104.

Axelrod, J. An evaluation of the effect on progress in therapy of similarities and differences between the personalities of patients and their therapists. Unpublished Ph.D. dissertation, New York University, 1952.

Azima, H., Wittkower, E. D., & Latendresse, J. Object relations therapy in schizophrenic states. *Amer. J. Psychiat.*, 1958, *115*, 60–62.

Baehr, G. O. The comparative effectiveness of individual psychotherapy, group psychotherapy and a combination of these methods. *J. consult. Psychol.*, 1954, *18*, 179–183.

Bailey, M. A., Warshaw, L., & Eichler, R. M. A study of factors related to length of stay in psychotherapy. *J. clin. Psychol.*, 1959, *15*, 442–444.

Bailey, M. A., Warshaw, L., & Eichler, R. M. Patients screened and criteria used for selecting psychotherapy cases in a mental hygiene clinic. *J. nerv. ment. Dis.*, 1960, *130*, 72-77.

Baker, A., & Thorpe, J. Deteriorated psychotic patients—their treatment and its assesment. *J. ment. Sci.*, 1956, *102*, 780–789.

Baker, E. The differential effects of two psychotherapeutic approaches on client perception. *J. counsel. Psychol.*, 1960, *7*, 46–50.

Baker, J. Q., & Wagner, N. W. Social class and treatment in a child psychiatry clinic. *Arch. gen. Psychiat.*, 1966, *14*, 129–133.

Bales, R. F. *Interaction process analysis*. Cambridge, Mass.: Addison-Wesley, 1950.

Bandura, A. Psychotherapist's anxiety level, self-insight, and psychotherapeutic competence. *J. abnorm. soc. Psychol.*, 1956, *52*, 333-337.

Bandura, A., Lipsher, D. H., & Miller, Paula E. Psychotherapists' approach-avoidance reactions to patients' expressions of hostility. *J. consult. Psychol.*, 1960, *24*, 1–8.

Barahal, G. D., Brammer, L. M., & Shostrom, E. L. A client-centered approach to vocational counseling. *J. consult. Psychol.*, 1950, *14*, 256–260.

Barclay, A., & Hilden, A. H. Variables related to duration of individual psychotherapy. *J. proj. Tech.*, 1961, *25*, 268–271.

Bare, Carole E. Relationship of counselor personality and counselor-client similarity to selected counseling success criteria. *J. counsel. Psychol.*, 1967, *14*, 419–425.

Barendregt, J. T. Discussion in H. J. Eysenck, The effects of psychotherapy. *Int. J. Psychiat.*, 1965, *1*, 99–142.

Barendregt, J. T., Bastiaans, J., & Vermeul-Van Mullem, A. W. A Psychological study of the effect of psychoanalysis and psychotherapy. In J. T. Barendregt (ed.), *Research in psychodiagnostics*. The Hague & Paris: Mouton & Co., 1961. Pp. 157–183.

Barrett-Lennard, G. T. Dimensions of therapist response as causal factors in therapeutic change. *Psychol. Monogr.*, 1962, *76*, whole No. 562.

Barrington, B. Changes in psychotherapeutic responses during training in therapy. *J. counsel. Psychol.*, 1958, *5*, 120–124.

Barrington, B. Prediction from counselor behavior of client perception and of case outcome. *J. counsel. Psychol.*, 1961, *8*, 37–42.

Barron, F. Some test correlates of response to psychotherapy. *J. consult. Psychol.*, 1953a, *17*, 235–241.

Barron, F. An ego-strength scale which predicts response to psychotherapy. *J. consult. Psychol.*, 1953b, *17*, 327–333.

Barron, F., & Leary, T. F. Changes in psychoneurotic patients with and without psychotherapy. *J. consult. Psychol.*, 1955, *19*, 239–245.

Bartlett, Marion R. A six month follow-up of the effects of personal adjustment counseling of veterans. *J. consult. Psychol.*, 1950, *14*, 393–394.

Bassin, A., & Smith, A. B. Verbal participation and improvement in group psychotherapy. *Int. J. group Psychother.*, 1962, *12*, 369–373.

Battle, C. C., Imber, S. D., Hoehn-Saric, R., Stone, A. R., Nash, E. R., & Frank, J. D. Target complaints as criteria of improvement. *Amer. J. Psychother.*, 1966, *20*, 184–192.

Baum, O. E., Felzer, S. B., D'Zmura, T. L., & Shumaker, Elaine. Psychotherapy, dropouts and lower socioeconomic patients. *Amer. J. Orthopsychiat.*, 1966, *36*, 629–635.

Beard, J. H., Pitt, R. B., Fisher, S. H., & Goertzel, V. Evaluating the effectiveness of a psychiatric rehabilitation program. *Amer. J. Orthopsychiat.*, 1963, *33*, 701–712.

Beck, J. C., Kantor, D., & Gelineau, V. A. Follow-up study of chronic psychiatric patients "treated" by college case-aide volunteers. *Amer. J. Psychiat.*, 1963, *120,* 269–271.

Behar, Lenore, & Altrocchi, J. Agreement on the concept of the ideal therapist as a function of experience. *J. clin. Psychol.*, 1961, *17,* 66–69.

Bellak, L., Meyer, E. J., Prola, M., Rosenberg, S., & Zuckerman, M. A multiple level study of brief psychotherapy in a trouble shooting clinic. In L. Bellak & L. Small (eds.), *Emergency psychotherapy and brief psychotherapy*. New York: Grune & Stratton, 1965. Pp. 144–163.

Bennett, D. H., & Robertson, J. P. S. The effects of habit training on chronic schizophrenic patients. *J. ment. Sci.*, 1955, *101,* 664–672.

Berenson, B. G., & Carkhuff, R. R. (eds.). *Sources of gain in counseling and psychotherapy*. New York: Holt, Rinehart & Winston, 1967.

Berg, I. A. Ideomotor response set: symbolic sexual gestures in the counseling interview. *J. counsel. Psychol.*, 1954, *1,* 180–183.

Bergin, A. E. The effects of psychotherapy: negative results revisited. *J. counsel. Psychol.*, 1963, *10,* 244–250.

Bergman, D. V. Counseling method and client responses. *J. consult. Psychol.*, 1951, *15,* 216–224.

Berle, Beatrice B., Pinsky, Ruth H., Wolf, S., & Wolff, H. G. Appraisal of the results of treatment in stress disorders. *Res. Publ. Ass. Nerv. Ment. Dis.*, 1953, *31,* 167–177.

Berzon, Betty. Residual parental threat and selective interaction in group psychotherapy. *Int. J. group Psychother.*, 1962, *12,* 347–354.

Berzon, Betty, & Solomon, L. N. The self-directed therapeutic group: an exploratory study. *Int. J. group Psychother.*, 1964, *14,* 366–369.

Betz, Barbara J. Differential success rates of psychotherapists with "process" and "non-process" schizophrenic patients. *Amer. J. Psychiat.*, 1963, *119,* 1090–1091.

Bixenstine, V. E. A case study of the use of palmar sweating as a measure of psychological tension. *J. abnorm. soc. Psychol.*, 1955, *50,* 138–143.

Blachly, P. H., Pepper, B., Scott, W., & Baganz, P. Group therapy and hospitalization of narcotic addicts. *Arch. gen. Psychiat.*, 1961, *5,* 393–396.

Blake, B. G. The application of behavior therapy to the treatment of alcoholism. *Behav. Res. & Ther.*, 1965, *3,* 75–85.

Blane, H. T., & Meyers, W. R. Social class and establishment of treatment relations by alcoholics. *J. clin. Psychol.*, 1964, *20,* 287–290.

Blau, B. A. A comparison of more improved with less improved clients treated by client-centered methods. In W. U. Snyder (ed.), *Group report of a program of research in psychotherapy* (mimeographed). University Park, Pa.: Pennsylvania State College, 1953. Pp. 120–126.

Blau, T. H. Report on a method of predicting success in psychotherapy. *J. clin. Psychol.*, 1950, *6,* 403–406.

Block, W. E. A preliminary study of achievement motive theory as a basis of patient expectations in psychotherapy. *J. clin. Psychol.*, 1964, *20,* 268–271.

Bloom, B. L. Prognostic significance of the under-productive Rorschach. *J. proj. Tech.*, 1956, *20*, 366–371.

Board, F. A. Patients' and physicians' judgments of outcome of psychotherapy in an outpatient clinic: a questionnaire investigation, *Arch. gen. Psychiat.*, 1959, *1*, 185–196.

Bockoven, J. S. Moral treatment in American psychiatry. *J. nerv. ment. Dis.*, 1956, *124*, 167–194; 292–321.

Boe, E., Gocka, E. F., & Kogan, W. S. The effect of group psychotherapy on interpersonal perceptions of psychiatric patients. *Multivariate Behav. Res.*, 1966, *1*, 177–187.

Bohn, M. J., Jr. Counselor behavior as a function of counselor dominance, counselor experience, and client type. *J. counsel. Psychol.*, 1965, *12*, 346–352.

Bohn, M. J., Jr. Therapist responses to hostility and dependency as a function of training. *J. consult. Psychol.*, 1967, *31*, 195–198.

Bookbinder, L. J., & Gusman, L. J. Social attainment, premorbid adjustment, and participation in inpatient psychiatric treatment. *J. clin. Psychol.*, 1964, *20*, 513–515.

Bookhammer, R. S., Meyers, R. W., Schober, C. C., & Piotrowski, Z. A. A five-year clinical follow-up of schizophrenics treated by Rosen's direct analysis. *Amer. J. Psychiat.*, 1966, *123*, 602–604.

Bowman, P. H. A study of the consistency of current, wish and proper self concepts as a measure of therapeutic progress. Unpublished Ph.D. dissertation, University of Chicago, 1951.

Boyd, R. W., & DiMascio, A. Social behavior and autonomic physiology: a sociophysiologic study. *J. nerv. ment. Dis.*, 1954, *120*, 207-212.

Braaten, L. J. The movement from non-self to self in client-centered psychotherapy. *J. counsel. Psychol.*, 1961, *8*, 20–24.

Bradway, Katherine P., Lion, E. G., & Corrigan, H. G. The use of the Rorschach in a psychiatric study of promiscuous girls. *Ror. Res. Exch.*, 1946, *10*, 105–110.

Brady, J. P., Reznikoff, M., & Zeller, W. W. The relationship of expectation of improvement to actual improvement of hospitalized psychiatric patients. *J. nerv. ment. Dis.*, 1960, *130*, 41–44.

Brams, J. M. Counselor characteristics and effective communication in counseling. *J. counsel. Psychol.*, 1961, *8*, 25–30.

Brandon, M. *Exploring social service discharge plans for mental patients: Parts I & II.* Osawatomie, Kan.: Osawatomie State Hospital, 1961.

Brandt, L. W. Rejection of psychotherapy. *Arch. gen. Psychiatr.*, 1964, *10*, 310–313.

Breger, L., & McGaugh, J. L. Critique and reformulation of "learning theory" approaches to psychotherapy. *Psychol. Bull.*, 1965, *63*, 338–358.

Brill, N. Q., & Beebe, G. W. *A follow-up study of war neuroses.* V.A. Medical Monograph. Washington: Veterans Administration, 1955.

Brill, N. Q., Koegler, R. R., Epstein, L. J., & Forgy, E. W. Controlled study of psychiatric outpatient treatment. *Arch. gen. Psychiat.*, 1964, *10,* 581–595.

Brown, C. C. Changes in avoidance conditioning following psychotherapeutic treatment. *J. nerv. ment. Dis.*, 1957, *125*, 487–489.

Bugental, J. F. T. A method for assessing self and non-self attitudes during the therapeutic series. *J. consult. Psychol.*, 1952, *16*, 435–439.

Burdock, E. I., Cheek, F., & Zubin, J. Predicting success in psychoanalytic training. In P. Hoch & J. Zubin (eds.), *Current approaches to psychoanalysis.* New York: Grune & Stratton, 1960. Pp. 176–191.

Burnham, Catharine A. Reliability and validity of psychologists' evaluation of therapy readiness. *Dissertation Abstr.*, 1952, *12*, 581.

Butler, J. M. *The rank pattern analysis of counseling protocols.* Unpublished manuscript, Counseling Center Library, University of Chicago, 1951.

Butler, J. M. Assessing psychotherapeutic protocols with context coefficients. *J. clin. Psychol.*, 1952, *8*, 199–202.

Butler, J. M., & Haigh, G. Changes in the relation between self-concepts and ideal concepts congruent upon client-centered counseling. In C. R. Rogers & R. F. Dymond (eds.), *Psychotherapy and personality change.* Chicago: University of Chicago Press, 1954. Pp. 55–75.

Cabeen, C. W., & Coleman, J. C. Group therapy with sex offenders: description and evaluation of group therapy program in an institutional setting. *J. clin. Psychol.*, 1961, *17*, 122–129.

Cabeen, C. W., & Coleman, J. C. The selection of sex-offender patients for group psychotherapy. *Int. J. group Psychother.*, 1962, *12*, 326–334.

Cadman, W. H., Misbach, L., & Brown, D. V. An assessment of round-table psychotherapy. *Psychol. Monogr.*, 1954, *68*, whole No. 384.

Calvin A. D. Some misuses of the experimental method in evaluating the effect of client-centered counseling. *J. counsel. Psychol.*, 1954, *1*, 249–251.

Campbell, J. H., & Rosenbaum, C. P. Placebo effect and symptom relief in psychotherapy. *Arch. gen. Psychiat.*, 1967, *16*, 364–368.

Campbell, R. E. Counselor personality and background and his interview subrole behavior. *J. counsel Psychol.*, 1962, *9*, 329–334.

Cappon, D. Results of psychotherapy. *Brit. J. Psychiat.*, 1964, *110*, 35–45.

Caracena, P. F. Elicitation of dependency expressions in the initial stage of psychotherapy. *J. counsel. Psychol.*, 1965, *12*, 268–274.

Carkhuff, R. R., & Truax, C. B. Training in counseling and psychotherapy: an evaluation of an integrated didactic and experiential approach. *J. consult. Psychol.*, 1965a, *29*, 333–336.

Carkhuff, R. R., & Truax, C. B. Lay mental health counseling. The effects of lay group counseling. *J. consult. Psychol.*, 1965b, *29*, 426–431.

Carlson, D. A., Coleman, J. V., Errera, P., & Harrison, R. W. Problems in treating the lower class psychotic. *Arch. gen. Psychiat.*, 1965, *13*, 269–274.

Carr, J. E., & Whittenbaugh, J. Perception of "improvement" and interjudge reliability in therapy-outcome studies. *Proceedings, 73rd Annual Convention, APA*, 1965, 197–198.

Carson, R. C., Harden, Judith A., & Shows, W. D. A-B distinction and behavior in quasi-therapeutic situations. *J. consult. Psychol.*, 1964, *28*, 426–433.

Carson, R. C., & Heine, R. W. Similarity and success in therapeutic dyads. *J. consult. Psychol.*, 1962, *26*, 38–43.

Carson, R. C., & Llewellyn, C. E., Jr. Similarity in therapeutic dyads; A re-evaluation. *J. consult. Psychol.*, 1966, *30*, 458.

Cartwright, D. S. Effectiveness of psychotherapy: a critique of the spontaneous remission argument. *J. counsel. Psychol.*, 1955a, *2*, 290–296.

Cartwright, D. S. Success in psychotherapy as a function of certain actuarial variables. *J. consult. Psychol.*, 1955b, *19*, 357–363.

Cartwright, D. S. Note on "changes in psychoneurotic patients with and without psychotherapy." *J. consult. Psychol.*, 1956a, *20*, 403–404.

Cartwright, D. S. A rapid non-parametric estimate of multi-judge reliability. *Psychometrika*, 1956b, *21*, 17–29.

Cartwright, D. S., & Cartwright, Rosalind D. Faith and improvement in psychotherapy. *J. counsel. Psychol.*, 1958, *5*, 174–177.

Cartwright, D. S., Kirtner, W. L., & Fiske, D. W. Method factors in changes associated with psychotherapy. *J. abnorm. soc. Psychol.*, 1963, *66*, 164–175.

Cartwright, D. S., Robertson, R. J., Fiske, D. W., & Kirtner, W. L. Length of therapy in relation to outcome and change in personal integration. *J. consult. Psychol.*, 1961, *25*, 84–88.

Cartwright, D. S., & Roth, I. Success and satisfaction in psychotherapy. *J. clin. Psychol.*, 1957, *13*, 20–26.

Cartwright, Rosalind D. Effects of psychotherapy on self-consistency. *J. counsel. Psychol.*, 1957, *4*, 15–22.

Cartwright, Rosalind D. Predicting response to client-centered therapy with the Rorschach PR scale. *J. counsel. Psychol.*, 1958, *5*, 11–17.

Cartwright, Rosalind D. A note on the Rorschach prognostic rating scale. *J. counsel. Psychol.*, 1959, *6*, 160–162.

Cartwright, Rosalind D. The effects of psychotherapy on self-consistency: a replication and extension. *J. consult. Psychol.*, 1961, *25*, 376–382.

Cartwright, Rosalind D., & Lerner, Barbara. Empathy, need to change, and improvement with psychotherapy. *J. consult. Psychol.*, 1963, *27*, 138–144.

Cartwright, Rosalind D., & Vogel, J. L. A comparison of changes in psychoneurotic patients during matched periods of therapy and no therapy. *J. consult. Psychol.*, 1960, *24*, 121–127.

Chance, Erika. A study of transference in group psychotherapy. *Int. J. group Psychother.*, 1952, *2*, 40–53.

Chappell, M. N., & Stevenson, T. I. Group psychological training in some organic conditions. *Ment. Hyg.*, 1936, *20*, 588–597.

Charny, E. J. Psychosomatic manifestations of rapport in psychotherapy. *Psychosom. Med.*, 1966, *28*, 305–315.

Chodorkoff, B. Adjustment and the discrepancy between the perceived and ideal self. *J. clin. Psychol.*, 1954, *10*, 266–268.

Clemes, S., & D'Andrea, V. J. Patients' anxiety as a function of expectation and degree of initial interview ambiguity. *J. consult. Psychol.*, 1965, *29*, 397–404.

Cofer, C. N., & Chance, June. The discomfort-relief quotient in published cases of counseling and psychotherapy. *J. Psychol.*, 1950, *29*, 219–224.

Cohen, E., & Cohen, B. D. Verbal reinforcement in schizophrenia. *J. abnorm. soc. Psychol.*, 1960, *60*, 443–446.

Colby, K. M. *A primer for psychotherapists.* New York: Ronald, 1951.

Colby, K. M. On the greater amplifying power of causal-correlative over interrogative inputs on free association in an experimental psychoanalytic situation. *J. nerv. ment. Dis.*, 1961, *133*, 233–239.

Cole, N. J., Branch, C. H., & Allison, R. B. Some relationships between social class and the practice of dynamic psychotherapy. *Amer. J. Psychiat.*, 1962, *118*, 1004–1012.

Collier, R. M. A scale for rating the responses of the psychotherapist. *J. consult. Psychol.*, 1953, *17*, 321–326.

Combs, A. W., & Soper, D. W. The perceptual organization of effective counselors. *J. counsel. Psychol.*, 1963, *10*, 222–226.

Cook, J. J. Silence in psychotherapy. *J. counsel. Psychol.*, 1964, *11*, 42–46.

Cook, T. E. The influence of client-counselor value similarity on change in meaning during brief counseling. *J. counsel. Psychol.*, 1966, *13*, 77–81.

Cooke, G. The efficacy of two desensitization procedures: an analogue study. *Behav. Res. & Ther.*, 1966, *4*, 17–24.

Coolidge, J. C., Brodie, R. D., & Feeney, Barbara. A ten-year follow-up study of sixty-six school-phobic children. *Amer. J. Orthopsychiat.*, 1964, *34*, 675–684.

Coons, W. H. Interaction and insight in group psychotherapy. *Canad. J. Psychol.*, 1957, *11*, 1–8.

Cooper, J. E. A study of behaviour therapy in thirty psychiatric patients. *Lancet*, 1963, *1*, 411–415.

Corsini, R. J., & Rosenberg, B. Mechanisms of group psychotherapy: processes and dynamics. *J. abnorm. soc. Psychol.*, 1955, *51*, 406–411.

Covner, B. J. Studies in phonographic recordings of verbal material: I. The use of phonographic recordings in counseling practice and research. *J. consult. Psychol.*, 1942, *6*, 105–113.

Cowden, R. C., Zax, M., Hague, J. R., & Finney, R. C. Chlorpromazine: alone and as an adjunct to group psychotherapy in the treatment of psychiatric patients. *Amer. J. Psychiat.*, 1956, *112*, 898–902.

Cox, F. N. Sociometric status and individual adjustment before and after play therapy. *J. abnorm. soc. Psychol.*, 1953, *48*, 354–356.

Crisp, A. H. An attempt to measure an aspect of "transference." *Brit. J. Med. Psychol.*, 1964a, *37*, 17–30.

Crisp, A. H. Development and application of a measure of "transference." *J. psychosom. Res.*, 1964b, *8*, 327–335.

Crisp, A. H. "Transference," "symptom emergence," and "social repercussion" in behavior therapy: a study of fifty-four treated patients. *Brit. J. Med. Psychol.*, 1966, *39*, 179–196.

Cronbach, L. J., & Gleser, Goldine C. Assessing similarity between profiles. *Psychol. Bull.*, 1953, *50*, 456–473.

Crowley, R. M. A low-cost psychoanalytic service: first year. *Psychiat. Quart.*, 1950, *24*, 462–482.

Crumpton, Evelyn, Cantor, J. M., & Batiste, C. A factor analytic study of Barron's ego strength scale. *J. clin. Psychol.*, 1960, *16*, 283–291.

Cushing, J. G. N. Report of committee on the evaluation of psychoanalytic therapy. *Bull. Amer. psychoanal. Ass.*, 1950, *6*, 17–19.

Cutler, R. L. Countertransference effects in psychotherapy. *J. consult. Psychol.*, 1958, *22*, 349–356.

Cutler, R. L., Bordin, E. S., Williams, Joan, & Rigler, D. Psychoanalysts as expert observers of the therapy process. *J. consult. Psychol.*, 1958, *22*, 335–340.

Dana, R. The effects of attitudes towards authority on psychotherapy. *J. clin. Psychol.*, 1954, *10*, 350–353.

Danskin, D. G., & Robinson, F. P. Differences in "degree of lead" among experienced counselors. *J. counsel. Psychol.*, 1954, *1*, 78–83.

Davids, A., & Talmadge, M. Utility of the Rorschach in predicting movement in psychiatric casework. *J. consult. Psychol.*, 1964, *28*, 311–316.

Davidson, H. A. Discussion in H. J. Eysenck, The effects of psychotherapy. *Int. J. Psychiat.*, 1965, *1*, 171–173.

Davies, D. L., Shepherd, M., & Myers, E. The two-years' prognosis of 50 alcohol addicts after treatment in hospital. *Quart. J. Stud. Alcohol*, 1956, *17*, 485–502.

DeCharms, R., Levy, J., & Wertheimer, M. A note on attempted evaluations of psychotherapy. *J. clin. Psychol.*, 1954, *10*, 233–235.

DeLeon, G., & Mandell, W. A comparison of conditioning and psychotherapy in the treatment of functional enuresis. *J. clin. Psychol.*, 1966, *22*, 326–330.

Denker, P. G. Results of treatment of psychoneuroses by the general practitioner—a follow-up of 500 cases. *NY State J. Med.*, 1946, *46*, 2164–2166.

Derr, J., & Silver, A. W. Predicting participation and behavior in group therapy from test protocols. *J. clin. Psychol.*, 1962, *18*, 322–325.

Dibner, A. S. Ambiguity and anxiety. *J. abnorm. soc. Psychol.*, 1958, *56*, 165–174.

Dickoff, Hilda, & Lakin, M. Patients' views of group therapy: retrospections and interpretations. *Int. J. group Psychother.*, 1963, *13*, 61–73.

Diener, R. G., & Young, H. H. Factors contributing to requests for mental hygiene treatment by veterans with psychiatric disorders. *J. clin. Psychol.*, 1961, *17*, 397–399.

Dietze, Doris. Relationships between staff and patients in judging criteria for improvement in mental health. *J. clin. Psychol.*, 1967, *23*, 41–46.

DiGiovanni, P. A comparison between orthodox group psychotherapy and activity group therapy in the treatment of chronic hospitalized schizophrenics. Unpublished Ph.D. dissertation, University of Illinois, 1958.

DiMascio, A. A., Boyd, R. W., & Greenblatt, M. Physiological correlates of tension and antagonism during psychotherapy: a study of interpersonal physiology. *Psychosom. Med.*, 1957, *19*, 99–104.

DiMascio, A. A., & Suter, Elsi. Psychological observations in psychiatric interviews. *J. nerv. ment. Dis.*, 1954, *120*, 413–414.

Dinoff, M., Rickard, H. C., Salzberg, H., & Sipprelle, C. N. An experimental analogue of three psychotherapeutic approaches. *J. clin. Psychol.*, 1960, *16*, 70–73.

Dipboye, W. J. Analysis of counselor style by discussion units. *J. counsel. Psychol.*, 1954, *1*, 21–26.

Dittes, J. E. Extinction during psychotherapy or GSR accompanying "embarrassing" statements. *J. abnorm. soc. Psychol.*, 1957a, *54*, 187–191.

Dittes, J. E. Galvanic skin responses as a measure of patient's reaction to therapist's permissiveness. *J. abnorm. soc. Psychol.*, 1957b, *55*, 295–303.

Dittmann, A. T. The interpersonal process in psychotherapy: development of a research method. *J. abnorm. soc. Psychol.*, 1952, *47*, 236–244.

Dittmann, A. T. Psychotherapeutic processes. *Annu. Rev. Psychol.*, 1966, *17*, 51–78.

Dollard, J., & Mowrer, O. H. A method of measuring tension in written documents. *J. abnorm. soc. Psychol.*, 1947, *42*, 3–32.

Dorfman, Elaine. Personality outcomes of client-centered child therapy. *Psychol. Monogr.*, 1958, *72*, whole No. 456.

Draper, F. M. The doctor's personality and social recovery of schizophrenics. *Arch. gen. Psychiat.*, 1967, *16*, 633–639.

Drasgow, J., & Carkhuff, R. R. Kuder neuropsychiatric keys before and after psychotherapy. *J. counsel. Psychol.*, 1964, *11*, 67–69.

Dreiblatt, I. S., & Weatherley, D. A. An evaluation of the efficacy of brief-contact therapy with hospitalized psychiatric patients. *J. consult. Psychol.*, 1965, *29*, 513–519.

Drennen, W. T., & Wiggins, S. L. Manipulation of verbal behavior of chronic hospitalized schizophrenics in a group therapy situation. *Int. J. group Psychother.*, 1964, *14*, 189–193.

Dworin, J., Green, J. A., & Young, H. A follow-up study of relationships between distance from the clinic, degree of disability, and requests for psychiatric treatment. *J. clin. Psychol.*, 1964, *20*, 393–395.

Dymond, Rosalind F. An adjustment score for Q sorts. *J. consult. Psychol.*, 1953, *17*, 339–342.

Dymond, Rosalind F. Adjustment changes over therapy from self-sorts. In C. R. Rogers & Rosalind F. Dymond (eds.), *Psychotherapy and personality change.* Chicago: University of Chicago Press, 1954a. Pp. 76–84.

Dymond, Rosalind F. Adjustment changes over therapy from Thematic Apperception Test ratings. In C. R. Rogers & Rosalind F. Dymond (eds.), *Psychotherapy and personality change.* Chicago: University of Chicago Press, 1954b. Pp. 109–120.

Dymond, Rosalind F. Adjustment changes in the absence of psychotherapy. *J. consult. Psychol.*, 1955, *19*, 103–107.

Dymond, Rosalind F., Grummon, D. L., & Seeman, J. Patterns of perceived inter-personal relations. *Sociometry*, 1956, *19*, 166–177.

D'Zurilla, T. J. Persuasion and praise as techniques for modifying verbal behavior in a "real-life" group setting. *J. abn. Psychol.*, 1966, *71*, 369–376.

Eells, Janet F. Therapists' views and preferences concerning intake cases. *J. consult. Psychol.*, 1964, *28*, 382.

Eisenman, R. Birth order, anxiety, and verbalizations in group psychotherapy. *J. consult. Psychol.*, 1966, *30*, 521–526.

Eldred, S. H., Hamburg, D. A., Inwood, E. R., Salzman, L., Meyersburg, H. A., & Goodrich, Geneva. A procedure for the systematic analysis of psychotherapeutic interviews. *Psychiatry*, 1954, *17*, 337–345.

Eliseo, T. S. Effectiveness of remotivation technique with chronic psychiatric patients. *Psychol. Rep.*, 1964, *14*, 171–178.

Ellis, A. The effectiveness of psychotherapy with individuals who have severe homosexual problems. *J. consult. Psychol.*, 1956, *20*, 191–195.

Ellis, A. Outcome of employing three techniques of psychotherapy. *J. clin. Psychol.*, 1957, *13*, 344–350.

Ellis, A. The private practice of psychotherapy; a clinical psychologist's report. *J. gen. Psychol.*, 1958, *58*, 207–216.

Ellsworth, S. G. The consistency of counselor feeling-verbalization. *J. counsel. Psychol.*, 1963, *10*, 356–361.

Emery, J. R., & Krumboltz, J. D. Standard versus individualized hierarchies in desensitization to reduce test anxiety. *J. counsel. Psychol.*, 1967, *14*, 204–209.

Endicott, N. A., & Endicott, Jean. "Improvement" in untreated psychiatric patients. *Arch. gen. Psychiat.*, 1963, *9*, 575–585.

Endicott, N. A., & Endicott, Jean. Prediction of improvement in treated and untreated patients using the Rorschach prognostic rating scale. *J. consult. Psychol.*, 1964, *28*, 342–348.

Endler, N. S. Changes in meaning during psychotherapy as measured by the Semantic Differential. *J. counsel. Psychol.*, 1961, *8*, 105–111.

Ends, E. J., & Page, C. W. A study of three types of group psychotherapy with hospitalized male inebriates. *Quart. J. Stud. Alcohol*, 1957, *18*, 263–277.

Ends, E. J., & Page, C. W. Group psychotherapy and concomitant psychological change. *Psychol. Monogr.*, 1959, *73*, whole No. 480.

Errera, P., & Coleman, J. V. A long-term follow-up study of neurotic phobic patients in a psychiatric clinic. *J. nerv. ment. Dis.*, 1963, *136*, 267–271.

Eskey, A. Insight and prognosis. *J. clin. Psychol.*, 1958, *14*, 426–429.

Esterson, A., Cooper, D. G., & Laing, R. D. Results of family-oriented therapy with hospitalized schizophrenics. *Brit. med. J.*, 1965, *2*, 1462–1465.

Ewing, T. N. Changes in attitude during counseling. *J. counsel. Psychol.*, 1954, *1*, 232–239.

Ewing, T. N. Changes during counseling appropriate to the client's initial problem. *J. counsel. Psychol.*, 1964, *11*, 146–150.

Exner, J. E., Jr. Therapist attendance as a variable in group psychotherapy. In G. E. Stollak, B. G. Guerney, & M. Rothberg (eds.), *Psychotherapy research*. Chicago: Rand McNally & Co., 1966. Pp. 372–376.

Eysenck, H. J. The effects of psychotherapy: an evaluation. *J. consult. Psychol.*, 1952, *16*, 319–324.

Eysenck, H. J. A reply to Luborsky's note. *Brit. J. Psychol.*, 1954, *45*, 132–133.

Eysenck, H. J. The effects of psychotherapy: A reply. *J. abnorm. soc. Psychol.*, 1955, *50*, 147–148.

Eysenck, H. J. *Handbook of abnormal psychology*. London: Pitman, 1960.

Eysenck, H. J. The outcome problem in psychotherapy: a reply. *Psychotherapy: Theory, Research and Practice*, 1964, *1*, 97–100.

Eysenck, H. J. The effects of psychotherapy. *Int. J. Psychiat.*, 1965, *1*, 99–142.

Eysenck, H. J. New ways in psychotherapy. *Psychology Today*, 1967, *1*, 39–47.

Fairweather, G. *Social psychology in treating mental illness*. New York: John Wiley, 1964.

Fairweather, G., & Simon, R. A further follow-up comparison of psychotherapeutic programs. *J. consult. Psychol.*, 1963, *27*, 186.

Fairweather, G., Simon, R., Gebhard, M., Weingarten, E., Holland, J., Sanders, R., Stone, G., & Reahl, J. Relative effectiveness of psychotherapeutic programs. *Psychol. Monogr.*, 1960, *74*, whole No. 492.

Farquharson, R. F., & Hyland, H. H. Anorexia nervosa: the course of 15 patients treated from 20 to 30 years previously. *Canad. med. Ass. J.*, 1966, *94*, 411–419.

Farson, R. E. Introjection in the psychotherapeutic relationship. *J. counsel. Psychol.*, 1961, *8*, 337–342.

Feder, B. Limited goals in short-term group psychotherapy with institutionalized delinquent adolescent boys. *Int. J. group Psychother.*, 1962, *12*, 503–507.

Feifel, H., & Eells, Janet. Patients and therapists assess the same psychotherapy. *J. consult. Psychol.*, 1963, *27*, 310–318.

Feifel, H., & Schwartz, A. D. Group psychotherapy with acutely disturbed psychotic patients. *J. consult. Psychol.*, 1953, *17*, 113–121.

Feldman, M. P., & MacCulloch, M. The application of anticipatory avoidance learning to the treatment of homosexuality. *Behav. Res. Ther.*, 1965, *2*, 165–172.

Feldman, R., Lorr, M., & Russell, S. B. A mental hygiene clinic case survey. *J. clin. Psychol.*, 1958, *14*, 245–250.

Fenichel, O. *The psychoanalytic theory of neuroses*. New York: W. W. Norton & Co., 1945.

Fey, W. F. Acceptance of self and others, and its relation to therapy-readiness. *J. clin. Psychol.*, 1954, *10*, 269–271.

Fey, W. F. Doctrine and experience: their influence upon the psychotherapist. *J. consult. Psychol.*, 1958, *22*, 403–409.

Fiedler, F. E. An experimental approach to preventive psychotherapy. *J. abnorm. soc. Psychol.*, 1949, *44*, 386–393.

Fiedler, F. E. The concept of an ideal therapeutic relationship. *J. consult. Psychol.*, 1950a, *14*, 239–245.

Fiedler, F. E. A comparison of therapeutic relationships in psychoanalytic, nondirective and Adlerian therapy. *J. consult. Psychol.*, 1950b, *14*, 436–445.

Fiedler, F. E. Factor analyses of psychoanalytic, nondirective, and Adlerian therapeutic relationships. *J. consult. Psychol.*, 1951a, *15*, 32–38.

Fiedler, F. E. A method of objective quantification of certain countertransference attitudes. *J. clin. Psychol.*, 1951b, *7*, 101–107.

Fiedler, F. E., & Senior, K. An exploratory study of unconscious feeling reactions in fifteen patient-therapist pairs. *J. abnorm. soc. Psychol.*, 1952, *47*, 446–453.

Fiedler, F. E., & Siegel, S. M. The Free Drawing Test as a predictor of nonimprovement in psychotherapy. *J. clin. Psychol.*, 1949, *5*, 386–389.

Filmer-Bennett, G. The Rorschach as a means of predicting treatment outcome. *J. consult. Psychol.*, 1955, *19*, 331–334.

Fine, H. J., & Zimet, C. N. Clinical evaluation in psychotherapy. *J. gen. Psychol.*, 1961, *65*, 353–356.

Fisher, S. Plausibility and depth of interpretation. *J. consult. Psychol.*, 1956, *20*, 249–256.

Fisher, S. H. Discussion. *Amer. J. Psychiat.*, 1966, *122*, 805.

Fiske, D. W., Cartwright, D. S., & Kirtner, W. L. Are psychotherapeutic changes predictable? *J. abnorm. soc. Psychol.*, 1964, *69*, 418–426.

Fjeld, S. P., Lucero, R. J., & Rechtschaffen, A. Cross-validation and follow-up of a state hospital total push program for regressed schizophrenics. *J. clin. Psychol.*, 1953, *9*, 394–395.

Ford, D. H., & Urban, H. B. Psychotherapy. *Annu. Rev. Psychol.*, 1967, *18*, 333–372.

Forer, B. R. The fallacy of personal validation: a classroom validation of gullibility. *J. abnorm. soc. Psychol.*, 1949, *44*, 118–123.

Forer, B. R., Farberow, N. L., Feifel, H., Meyer, M. M., Sommers, Vita S., & Tolman, Ruth S. Clinical perception of the therapeutic transaction. *J. consult. Psychol.*, 1961, *25*, 93–101.

Forgy, E. W., & Black, J. D. A follow-up after three years of clients counseled by two methods. *J. counsel. Psychol.*, 1954, *1*, 1–8.

Frank, G. H., & Sweetland, A. A study of the process of psychotherapy: the verbal interaction. *J. consult. Psychol.*, 1962, *26*, 135–138.

Frank, J. D. Discussion in H. J. Eysenck, The effects of psychotherapy. *Int. J. Psychiat.*, 1965, *1*, 150–152.

Frank, J. D., Gliedman, L. H., Imber, S. D., Nash, E. H., Jr., & Stone, A. R. Why patients leave psychotherapy. *Arch. Neurol. Psychiat.*, 1957, *77*, 283–299.

Frank, J. D., Gliedman, L. H., Imber, S. D., Stone, A. R., & Nash, E. H., Jr.

Patients' expectancies and relearning as factors determining improvement in psychotherapy. *Amer. J. Psychiat.*, 1959, *115*, 961–968.

Freeman, T. Psycho-analytical psychotherapy in the National Health Service. *Brit. J. Psychiat.*, 1967, *113*, 321–327.

Fretz, B. R. Postural movements in a counseling dyad. *J. counsel. Psychol.*, 1966a, *13*, 335–343.

Fretz, B. R. Personality correlates of postural movements. *J. counsel. Psychol.*, 1966b, *13*, 344–347.

Friedman, D. E. I., & Silverstone, J. T. Treatment of phobic patients by systematic desensitization. *Lancet*, 1967, *1*, 470–472.

Friedman, H. J. Patient-expectancy and symptom reduction. *Arch. gen. Psychiat.*, 1963, *8*, 61–67.

Friedman, J. H. Short-term psychotherapy of "phobia of travel." *Amer. J. Psychother.*, 1950, *4*, 259–278.

Fuller, Frances F. Influence of sex of counselor and of client on client expressions of feeling. *J. counsel. Psychol.*, 1963, *10*, 34–40.

Galioni, E. Evaluation of a treatment program for chronically ill schizophrenic patients. In L. Appleby, J. Scher, & J. Cumming (eds.), *Chronic schizophrenia: exploration in theory and treatment*. Glencoe, Ill.: The Free Press, 1960.

Galioni, E., Adams, F., & Tallman, F. Intensive treatment of backward patients—a controlled pilot study. *Amer. J. Psychiat.*, 1953, *109*, 576–583.

Gallagher, E. B., & Kanter, S. S. The duration of out-patient psychotherapy. *Psychiat. Quart. Suppl.*, 1961, *35*, 312–331.

Gallagher, E. B., Levinson, D. J., & Erlich, Iza. Some sociopsychological characteristics of patients and their relevance for psychiatric treatment. In M. Greenblatt, D. J. Levinson, & R. Williams (eds.), *The patient and the mental hospital*. New York: The Free Press, 1957. Pp. 357–379.

Gallagher, E. B., Sharaf, M. R., & Levinson, D. J. The influence of patient and therapist in determining the use of psychotherapy in a hospital setting. *Psychiatry*, 1965, *28*, 297–310.

Gallagher, J. J. MMPI changes concomitant with client centered therapy. *J. consult. Psychol.*, 1953, *17*, 334–338.

Gallagher, J. J. Test indications for therapy prognosis. *J. consult. Psychol.*, 1954, *18*, 409–413.

Gamsky, N. R., & Farwell, Gail F. Counselor verbal behavior as a function of client hostility. *J. counsel. Psychol.*, 1966, *13*, 184–190.

Garetz, F. K. A statistical study of treatment oriented behavior. *Arch. gen. Psychiat.*, 1964, *10*, 306–309.

Garetz, F. K., Kogl, R. C., & Wiener, D. A comparison of random and judgmental methods of determining mode of outpatient mental hygiene treatment. *J. clin. Psychol.*, 1959, *15*, 401–402.

Garfield, S. L., & Affleck, D. C. An appraisal of duration of stay in outpatient psychotherapy. *J. nerv. ment. Dis.*, 1959, *129*, 492–498.

Garfield, S. L., & Affleck, D. C. Therapists' judgments concerning patients considered for psychotherapy. *J. consult. Psychol.*, 1961, *25*, 505–509.

Garfield, S. L., Affleck, D. C., & Muffly, R. A study of psychotherapy interaction and continuation of psychotherapy. *J. clin. Psychol.*, 1963, *19*, 473–478.

Garfield, S. L., & Kurz, M. Evaluation of treatment and related procedures in 1,216 cases referred to a mental hygiene clinic. *Psychiat. Quart.*, 1952, *26*, 414–424.

Garfield, S. L., & Wolpin, M. Expectations regarding psychotherapy. *J. nerv. ment. Dis.*, 1963, *137*, 353–362.

Garside, R. F. On change scores and correlation. *J. clin. Psychol.*, 1962, *18*, 92–94.

Gelder, M. G., & Marks, I. M. Severe agoraphobia: a controlled prospective trial of behaviour therapy. *Brit. J. Psychiat.*, 1966, *112*, 309–319.

Gelder, M. G., Marks, I. M., & Wolff, H. Desensitization and psychotherapy in the treatment of phobic states: a controlled inquiry. *Brit. J. Psychiat.*, 1967, *113*, 53–73.

Gendlin, E. T., & Berlin, J. I. Galvanic skin response correlates of different modes of experiencing. *J. clin. Psychol.*, 1961, *17*, 73–77.

Gendlin, E. T., Jenney, R. H. & Shlien, J. M. Counselor ratings of process and outcome in client-centered therapy. *J. clin. Psychol.*, 1960, *16*, 210–213.

Gendlin, E. T. & Shlien, J. M. Immediacy in time attitudes before and after time-limited psychotherapy. *J. clin. Psychol.*, 1961, *17*, 69–72.

Gerler, W. Outcome of psychotherapy as a function of client-counselor similarity. *Dissertation Abstr.*, 1958, *18*, 1864–1865.

Gersten, C. An experimental evaluation of group therapy with juvenile delinquents. *Int. J. group Psychother.*, 1951, *1*, 311–318.

Gerz, H. O. Experience with the logotherapeutic technique of paradoxical intention in the treatment of phobic and obsessive-compulsive patients. *Amer. J. Psychiat.*, 1966, *123*, 548–553.

Getter, H., & Sundland, D. M. The Barron Ego Strength scale and psychotherapeutic outcome. *J. consult. Psychol.*, 1962, *26*, 195.

Gibby, R. G., Stotsky, B. A., Hiler, E. W., & Miller, D. R., Validation of Rorschach criteria for predicting duration of therapy. *J. consult. Psychol.*, 1954, *18*, 185–191.

Gibby, R. G., Stotsky, B. A., Miller, D. R., & Hiler, E. W. Prediction of duration of therapy from the Rorschach test. *J. consult. Psychol.*, 1953, *17*, 348–354.

Gibson, R. L., Snyder, W. U., & Ray, W. S. A factor analysis of change following client-centered therapy. *J. counsel. Psychol.*, 1955, *2*, 83–90.

Gillespie, J. F., Jr. Verbal signs of resistance in client-centered therapy. In W. U. Snyder (ed.), *Group report of a program of research in psychotherapy* (mimeographed). University Park, Pa.: Pennsylvania State College, 1953. Pp. 105–119.

Glad, D. D., Hayne, M. L., Glad, Virginia B., & Ferguson, R. E. Schizophrenic factor reactions to four group psychotherapy methods. *Int. J. group Psychother.*, 1963, *13*, 196–210.

Glatt, M. M. Treatment results in an English mental hospital alcoholic unit. *Acta Psychiat. Scand.*, 1961, *37*, 143–168.

Gliedman, L. H., Nash, E. H., Imber, S. D., Stone, A. R., & Frank, J. D. Reduction of symptoms by pharmacologically inert substances and by short-term psychotherapy. *Arch. Neurol. Psychiat.*, 1958, *79*, 345–351.

Gliedman, L. H., Stone, A. R., Frank, J. D., Nash, E. H., Jr., & Imber, S. D. Incentives for treatment related to remaining or improving in psychotherapy. *Amer. J. Psychother.*, 1957, *11*, 589–598.

Glover, E. Discussion in H. J. Eysenck, The effects of psychotherapy. *Int. J. Psychiat.*, 1965, *1*, 158–161.

Gluck, M. R., Tanner, M. M., Sullivan, Dorothy F., & Erickson, Patricia. Follow-up evaluation of 55 child guidance cases. *Behav. Res. Ther.*, 1964, *2*, 131–134.

Goertzel, V., May, P. R. A., Salkin, Jeri, & Schoop, Trudi. Body-ego technique: an approach to the schizophrenic patient. *J. nerv. ment. Dis.*, 1965, *141*, 53–60.

Goin, Marcia, K., Yamamoto, J., & Silverman, J. Therapy congruent with class-linked expectations. *Arch. gen. Psychiat.*, 1965, *13*, 133–137.

Goldenberg, G. M., & Auld, F., Jr. Equivalence of silence to resistance. *J. consult. Psychol.*, 1964, *28*, 476.

Goldman, Rosaline, & Greenblatt, M. Changes in Thematic Apperception Test stories paralleling changes in clinical status of schizophrenic patients. *J. nerv. ment. Dis.*, 1955, *121*, 243–249.

Goldman-Eisler, Frieda. Individual differences between interviewers and their effect on interviewees' conversational behavior. *J. ment. Sci.*, 1952, *98*, 660–671.

Goldstein, A. P. Therapist and client expectation of personality change in psychotherapy. *J. counsel. Psychol.*, 1960a, *7*, 180–184.

Goldstein, A. P. Patient's expectancies and non-specific therapy as a basis for (un)spontaneous remission. *J. clin. Psychol.*, 1960b, *16*, 399–403.

Goldstein, A. P. *Therapist-patient expectancies in psychotherapy.* New York: Pergamon Press, Inc., 1962.

Goldstein, A. P., & Shipman, W. G. Patient expectancies, symptom reduction and aspects of the initial psychotherapeutic interview. *J. clin. Psychol.*, 1961, *17*, 129–133.

Gonyea, G. G. The "ideal therapeutic relationship" and counseling outcome. *J. clin. Psychol.*, 1963, *19*, 481–487.

Gordon, J. E. Leading and following psychotherapeutic techniques with hypnotically induced repression and hostility. *J. abnorm. soc. Psychol.*, 1957, *54*, 405–410.

Gordon, J. E., Martin, B., & Lundy, R. M. GSRs during repression, suppression, and verbalization in psychotherapeutic interviews. *J. consult. Psychol.*, 1959, *23*, 243–251.

Gordon, T., & Cartwright, D. The effect of psychotherapy upon certain attitudes toward others. In C. R. Rogers & Rosalind F. Dymond (eds.),

Psychotherapy and personality change. Chicago: University of Chicago Press, 1954. Pp. 167–195.

Gottschalk, L. A., Mayerson, P., & Gottlieb, A. A. Prediction and evaluation of outcome in an emergency brief psychotherapy clinic. *J. nerv. ment. Dis.*, 1967, *144*, 77–96.

Grace, W. J., Pinsky, Ruth H., & Wolff, H. G. The treatment of ulcerative colitis: II. *Gastroenterology*, 1954, *26*, 462–468.

Graham, S. R. Patient evaluation of the effectiveness of limited psychoanalytically oriented psychotherapy. *Psychol. Rep.*, 1958, *4*, 231–234.

Graham, S. R. The effects of psychoanalytically oriented psychotherapy on levels of frequency and satisfaction in sexual activity. *J. clin. Psychol.*, 1960, *16*, 94–95

Grant, J. D., & Grant, Marguerite Q. "Therapy readiness" as a research variable. *J. consult. Psychol.*, 1950, *14*, 156–157.

Grater, H. A. Client preferences for affective or cognitive counselor characteristics and first interview behavior. *J. counsel. Psychol.*, 1964, *11*, 248–250.

Greenbaum, R. S. Treatment of school phobias—theory and practice. *Amer. J. Psychother.*, 1964, *28*, 616–634.

Greenfield, N. S. Personality patterns of patients before and after application for psychotherapy. *J. consult. Psychol.*, 1958, *22*, 280.

Greenfield, N. S. & Fey, W. F. Factors influencing utilization of psychotherapeutic services in male college students. *J. clin. Psychol.*, 1956, *12*, 276–279.

Greenwald, A. F. Affective complexity and psychotherapy. *J. proj. Tech.*, 1959, *23*, 429–435.

Grigg, A. E. Client response to counselors at different levels of experience. *J. counsel. Psychol.*, 1961, *8*, 217–233.

Grigg, A. E., & Goodstein, L. D. The use of clients as judges of the counselor's performance. *J. counsel. Psychol.*, 1957, *4*, 31–36.

Grimshaw, L. The outcome of obsessional disorder: a follow-up study of 100 cases. *Brit. J. Psychiat.*, 1965, *111*, 1051–1056.

Groen, J. J., & Pelser, H. E. Experiences with, and results of, group psychotherapy in patients with bronchial asthma. *J. Psychosom. Res.*, 1960, *4*, 191–205.

Gross, W. F., & DeRidder, L. M. Significant movement in comparatively short-term counseling. *J. counsel. Psychol.*, 1966, *13*, 98–99.

Grossman, D. An experimental investigation of the effectiveness, in terms of insight, of reflection of feeling versus interpretation. *Amer. Psychol.*, 1950, *5*, 469–470.

Grossman, D. An experimental investigation of a psychotherapeutic technique. *J. consult. Psychol.*, 1952, *16*, 325–331.

Grosz, H. J., Stern, H., & Wright, C. S. Interactions in therapy groups as a function of differences among therapists and group size. *Psychol. Rep.*, 1965, *17*, 827–834.

Grummon, D. L. An investigation into the use of grammatical and psychogrammatical categories of language for the study of personality and psychotherapy. Unpublished Ph.D. dissertation, University of Chicago, 1950.

Grummon, D. L. Design, procedures, and subjects for the first block. In C. R. Rogers & Rosalind F. Dymond (eds.), *Psychotherapy and personality change.* Chicago: University of Chicago Press, 1954a. pp. 35–52.

Grummon, D. L. Personality changes as a function of time in persons motivated for therapy. In C. R. Rogers & Rosalind F. Dymond (eds.), *Psychotherapy and personality change.* Chicago: University of Chicago Press, 1954b. Pp. 238–255.

Grummon, D. L., & John, Eve S. Changes over client-centered therapy evaluated on psychoanalytically based Thematic Apperception Test scales. In C. R. Rogers & Rosalind F. Dymond (eds.), *Psychotherapy and personality change.* Chicago: University of Chicago Press, 1954. Pp. 121–144.

Gundlach, R. H., & Geller, M. The problem of early termination: is it really the terminee? *J. consult. Psychol.,* 1958, *22,* 410.

Haggard, E. A., Hiken, Julia R., & Isaacs, K. S. Some effects of recording and filming on the psychotherapeutic process. *Psychiatry,* 1965, *28,* 169–191.

Haggard, E. A., & Isaacs, K. S. Micromomentary facial expressions as indicators of ego mechanisms in psychotherapy. In L. A. Gottschalk & A. H. Auerbach (eds.), *Methods of research in psychotherapy.* New York: Appleton-Century-Crofts, 1966. Pp. 154–166.

Haimowitz, N. R. An investigation into some personality changes occurring in individuals undergoing client-centered therapy. Unpublished Ph.D. dissertation, University of Chicago, 1948.

Haimowitz, N. R., & Haimowitz, M. L. Personality changes in client-centered therapy. In W. Wolff & J. A. Precker (eds.), *Success in psychotherapy.* New York: Grune & Stratton, 1952. Pp. 63–93.

Hain, J. D., Butcher, R. H. G., & Stevenson, I. Systematic desensitization therapy: an analysis of results in twenty-seven patients. *Brit. J. Psychiat.,* 1966, *112,* 295–307.

Halkides, Galatia. An investigation of therapeutic success as a function of four therapist variables. Unpublished Ph.D. dissertation, University of Chicago, 1958.

Hamilton, D. M., Varney, H. I., & Wall, J. H. Hospital treatment of patients with psychoneurotic disorders. *Amer. J. Psychiat.,* 1942, *99,* 243–247.

Hamlin, R. M., & Albee, G. W. Muench's tests before and after nondirective therapy: a control group for his subjects. *J. consult. Psychol.,* 1948, *12,* 412–416.

Hannon, J. E., Battle, Carolyn C., & Adams, J. V. Manipulation of direction of speech in a neuropsychiatric group. *J. clin. Psychol.,* 1962, *18,* 428–431.

Hardy, Virginia T. Relation of dominance to non-directiveness in counseling. *J. clin. Psychol.,* 1948, *4,* 300–303.

Hare, A. P., Waxler, Nancy, Saslow, G., & Matarazzo, J. D. Simultaneous recording of Bales and Chapple interaction measures during initial psychiatric interviews. *J. consult. Psychol.*, 1960, *24*, 193.

Hare, Marjorie K. Shortened treatment in a child guidance clinic: the results in 119 cases. *Brit. J. Psychiat.*, 1966, *112*, 613–616.

Harper, R. A., & Hudson, J. W. The use of recordings in marriage counseling: a preliminary empirical investigation. *Marriage fam. Living*, 1952, *14*, 332–334.

Harris, A. A comparative study of results in neurotic patients treated by two different methods. *J. ment. Sci.*, 1954, *100*, 718–721.

Harris, D. H., Firestone, R. W., & Wagner, C. M. Brief psychotherapy and enuresis. *J. consult. Psychol.*, 1955, *19*, 246.

Harris, R. E., & Christiansen, Carole. Prediction of response to brief psychotherapy. *J. Psychol.*, 1946, *21*, 269–284.

Harrow, M., Astrachan, B. M., Becker, R. E., Detre, T., & Schwartz, A. H. An investigation into the nature of the patient-family therapy group. *Amer. J. Orthopsychiat.*, 1967, *37*, 888–899.

Hart, J. T. Unpublished manuscript, University of Wisconsin, 1960.

Harway, N. I. Some factors in psychotherapists' perception of their patients. *J. consult. Psychol.*, 1959, *23*, 379–386.

Harway, N. I., Dittmann, A. T., Raush, H. L., Bordin, E. S., & Rigler, D. The measurement of depth of interpretation. *J. consult. Psychol.*, 1955, *19*, 247–253.

Hastings, D. W. Follow-up results in psychiatric illness. *Amer. J. Psychiat.*, 1958, *114*, 1057–1066.

Hatterer, L. J. Psychiatric treatment of creative work block. *Psychiat. Quart.*, 1960, *34*, 634–647.

Heckel, R. V., Wiggins, S. L., & Salzberg, H. C. Conditioning against silences in group therapy. *J. clin. Psychol.*, 1962, *18*, 216–217.

Heilbrun, A. B., Jr. Male and female personality correlates of early termination in counseling. *J. counsel. Psychol.*, 1961a, *8*, 31–36.

Heilbrun, A. B., Jr. Client personality patterns, counselor dominance, and duration of counseling. *Psychol. Rep.*, 1961b, *9*, 15–25.

Heilbrun, A. B., Jr. Psychological factors related to counseling readiness and implications for counseling behavior. *J. counsel. Psychol.*, 1962, *9*, 353–358.

Heilbrun, A. B., Jr. Further validation of a counseling readiness scale. *J. counsel. Psychol.*, 1964, *11*, 290–292.

Heilbrun, A. B., Jr. & Sullivan, D. J. The prediction of counseling readiness. *Personnel guid. J.*, 1962, *41*, 112–117.

Heilbrunn, G. Results with psychoanalytic therapy and professional commitment. *Amer. J. Psychother.*, 1966, *20*, 89–99.

Heilizer, F. Some cautions concerning the use of change scores. *J. clin. Psychol.*, 1959, *15*, 447–449.

Heine, R. W. An investigation of the relationship between change in personality from psychotherapy as reported by patients and the factors seen by patients as producing change. Unpublished Ph.D. dissertation, University of Chicago, 1950.

Heine, R. W. A comparison of patients' reports on psychotherapeutic experience with psychoanalytic, non-directive and Adlerian therapists. *Amer. J. Psychother.*, 1953, *7*, 16–23.

Heine, R. W., & Trosman, H. Initial expectations of the doctor-patient interaction as a factor in continuance in psychotherapy. *Psychiatry*, 1960, *23*, 275–278.

Heller, K., Davis, J. D., & Myers, R. A. The effects of interviewer style in a standardized interview. *J. consult. Psychol.*, 1966, *30*, 501–508.

Heller, K., & Goldstein, A. P. Client dependency and therapist expectancy as relationship maintaining variables in psychotherapy. *J. consult. Psychol.*, 1961, *25*, 371–375.

Heller, K., Myers, R. A., & Kline, Linda V. Interviewer behavior as a function of standardized client roles. *J. consult. Psychol.*, 1963, *27*, 117–122.

Henderson, K. Objective evaluation of an activity treatment programme for seriously regressed schizophrenic patients. *Canad. Psychiat. Ass. J.*, 1960, *5*, 100–107.

Henry, W. E., & Shlien, J. M. Affective complexity and psychotherapy: some comparisons of time-limited and unlimited treatment. *J. proj. Tech.*, 1958, *22*, 153–162.

Hiler, E. W. An analysis of patient-therapist compatibility. *J. consult. Psychol.*, 1958, *22*, 341–347.

Hiler, E. W. Initial complaints as predictors of continuation in psychotherapy. *J. clin. Psychol.*, 1959a, *15*, 344–345.

Hiler, E. W. The sentence completion test as a predictor of continuation in psychotherapy. *J. consult. Psychol.*, 1959b, *23*, 544–549.

Hoehn-Saric, R., Frank, J. D., Imber, S. D., Nash, E. H., Jr., Stone, A. R., & Battle, Carolyn C. Systematic preparation of patients for psychotherapy: I. Effects on therapy behavior and outcome. *J. Psychiat. Res.*, 1964, *2*, 267–281.

Hoenig, J., & Reed, G. F. The objective assessment of desensitization. *Brit. J. Psychiat.*, 1966, *112*, 1279–1283.

Hoffman, A. E. An analysis of counselor sub-roles. *J. counsel. Psychol.*, 1959, *6*, 61–67.

Hogan, R. A measure of client defensiveness. In W. Wolff & J. A. Precker (eds.), *Success in psychotherapy*. New York: Grune & Stratton, 1952. Pp. 112–142.

Hogan, R., & Kirchner, J. H. Preliminary report of the extinction of learned fears via short-term implosive therapy. *J. abn. Psychol.*, 1967, *72*, 106–109.

Holder, T., Carkhuff, R. R., & Berenson, B. G. Differential effects of the manipulation of therapeutic conditions upon high- and low-functioning clients. *J. counsel. Psychol.*, 1967, *14*, 63–66.

Hollingshead, A. B., & Redlich, F. C. Schizophrenia and social structure. *Amer. J. Psychiat.*, 1954, *110*, 695–701.

Hollon, T. H., & Zolik, E. S. Self-esteem and symptomatic complaints in the initial phase of psychoanalytically oriented psychotherapy. *Amer. J. Psychother.*, 1962, *16*, 83-93.

Holt, R. R., & Luborsky, L. *Personality patterns of psychiatrists*, vols. I & II. New York: Basic Books, 1958.

Horwitz, W. A., Polatin, P., Kolb, L. C., & Hoch, P. H. A study of cases of schizophrenia treated by "direct analysis." *Amer. J. Psychiat.*, 1958, *114*, 780–783.

Howe, E. S. Anxiety-arousal and specificity: rated correlates of the depth of interpretive statements. *J. consult. Psychol.*, 1962, *26*, 178–184.

Howe, E. S. Further data concerning the dimensionality of ratings of the therapist's verbal exploratory behavior. *J. consult. Psychol.*, 1965, *29*, 73–76.

Howe, E. S., & Pope, B. The dimensionality of ratings of therapist verbal responses. *J. consult. Psychol.*, 1961a, *25*, 296–303.

Howe, E. S., & Pope, B. An empirical scale of therapist verbal activity level in the initial interview. *J. consult. Psychol.*, 1961b, *25*, 510–520.

Hyman, M., & Wohl, J. Environmental factors and outpatient clinic intake. *J. consult. Psychol.*, 1958, *22*, 431–432.

Hyman, R., & Breger, L. Discussion in H. J. Eysenck, The effects of psychotherapy. *Int. J. Psychiat.*, 1965, *1*, 317–322.

Imber, S. D., Frank, J. D., Gliedman, L. H., Nash, E. H., Jr., & Stone, A. R. Suggestibility, social class and the acceptance of psychotherapy. *J. clin. Psychol.*, 1956, *12*, 341–344.

Imber, S. D., Frank, J. D., Nash, E. H., Jr., Stone, A. R., & Gliedman, L. H. Improvement and amount of therapeutic contact: an alternative to the use of no-treatment controls in psychotherapy. *J. consult. Psychol.*, 1957, *21*, 309–315.

Imber, S. D., Nash, E. H., Jr., & Stone, A. R. Social class and duration of psychotherapy. *J. clin. Psychol.*, 1955, *11*, 281–284.

Isaacs, K. S., & Haggard, E. A. Some methods used in the study of affect in psychotherapy. In L. A. Gottschalk & A. H. Auerbach (eds.), *Methods of research in psychotherapy*. New York: Appleton-Century-Crofts, 1966. Pp. 226–239.

Jacks, I. Accessibility to group psychotherapy among adolescent offenders in a correctional institution. *Amer. J. Orthopsychiat.*, 1963, *33*, 567–568.

Jenkins, Joan W., Wallach, M. S., & Strupp, H. H. Effects of two methods of response in a quasi-therapeutic situation. *J. clin. Psychol.*, 1962, *18*, 220–223.

Jensen, M. B. Consultation vs. therapy in the psychological treatment of NP hospital patients. *J. clin. Psychol.*, 1961, *17*, 265–268.

Johnson, Elizabeth Z. Klopfer's Prognostic Scale used with Raven's Progressive Matrices in play therapy prognosis. *J. proj. Tech.*, 1953, *17*, 320–326.

Johnson, R. F., & Lee, H. Rehabilitation of chronic schizophrenics. *Arch. gen. Psychiat.*, 1965, *12*, 237–240.

Johnson, R. W. Number of interviews, diagnosis and success of counseling. *J. counsel. Psychol.*, 1965, *12*, 248–251.

Jones, F. D., & Peters, H. N. An experimental evaluation of group psychotherapy. *J. abnorm. soc. Psychol.*, 1952, *47*, 345–353.

Jones, N. F., & Kahn, M. W. Patient attitudes as related to social class and other variables concerned with hospitalization. *J. consult. Psychol.*, 1964, *28*, 403–408.

Jonietz, A. K. A study of changes in perception in relation to psychotherapy. Unpublished Ph.D. dissertation, University of Chicago, 1950.

Kahn, R. L., Pollack, M., & Fink, M. Social factors in the selection of therapy in a voluntary mental hospital. *J. Hillside Hosp.*, 1957, *6*, 216-228.

Kamin, I., & Caughlan, J. Subjective experiences of outpatient psychotherapy. *Amer. J. Psychother.*, 1963, *17*, 660–668.

Kanfer, F. H. Verbal rate, eyeblink, and content in structured psychiatric interviews. *J. abnorm. soc. Psychol.*, 1960, *61*, 341–347.

Kanfer, F. H., & Marston, A. R. Verbal conditioning, ambiguity and psychotherapy. *Psychol. Rep.*, 1961, *9*, 461–475.

Kanfer, F. H., & Marston, A. R. Characteristics of interactional behavior in a psychotherapy analogue. *J. consult. Psychol.*, 1964, *28*, 456–467.

Kanfer, F. H., Phillips, Jeanne S., Matarazzo, J. D., & Saslow, G. Experimental modification of interviewer content in standardized interviews. *J. consult. Psychol.*, 1960, *24*, 528–536.

Kaplan, H. B. Social interaction and GSR activity during group psychotherapy. *Psychosom. Med.*, 1963, *25*, 140–145.

Karson, S., & Wiedershine, L. J. An objective evaluation of dynamically oriented group psychotherapy. *Int. J. group Psychother.*, 1961, *11*, 166–174.

Katahn, M., Strenger, S., & Cherry, Nancy. Group counseling and behavior therapy with test-anxious college students. *J. consult. Psychol.*, 1966, *30*, 544–549.

Katz, J., & Solomon, Rebecca Z. The patient and his experiences in an outpatient clinic. *Arch. Neurol. Psychiat.*, 1958, *80*, 86–92.

Katz, M. M., Lorr, M., & Rubinstein, E. A. Remainer patient attributes and their relation to subsequent improvement in psychotherapy. *J. consult. Psychol.*, 1958, *22*, 411–413.

Kauffman, P. E., & Raimy, V. C. Two methods of assessing therapeutic progress. *J. abnorm. soc. Psychol.*, 1949, *44*, 379–385.

Kaufman, I., Frank, T., Friend, Jeannette, Heims, Lora W., & Weiss, Ruth. Success and failure in the treatment of childhood schizophrenia. *Amer. J. Psychiat.*, 1962, *118*, 909–913.

Kaufmann, P. Changes in the Minnesota Multiphasic Personality Inventory as a function of psychiatric therapy. *J. consult. Psychol.*, 1950, *14*, 458–464.

Kellner, R. Discussion in H. J. Eysenck, the effects of psychotherapy. *Int. J. Psychiat.*, 1965, *1*, 322–327.

Kemp, C. G. Behaviors in group guidance (socio process) and group counseling (psyche process). *J. counsel. Psychol.*, 1963, *10*, 373–377.

Kemp, D. E. Correlates of the Whitehorn-Betz AB scale in a quasi-therapeutic situation. *J. consult. Psychol.*, 1966, *30*, 509–516.

Kenny, D. T. The influence of social desirability on discrepancy measures between real self and ideal-self. *J. consult. Psychol.*, 1956, *20*, 315–318.

Kiesler, D. J. Some myths of psychotherapy research and the search for a paradigm. *Psychol. Bull.*, 1966, *65*, 110–136.

Kiesler, D. J., Mathieu, Philippa L., & Klein, Marjorie H. Sampling from the recorded therapy interview: a comparative study of different segment lengths. *J. consult. Psychol.*, 1964, *28*, 349–357.

Kiesler, D. J., Mathieu, Philippa L., & Klein, Marjorie H. Patient experiencing level and interaction-chronograph variables in therapy interview segments. *J. consult. Psychol.*, 1967, *31*, 224.

King, G. F., Armitage, S. G., & Tilton, J. R. A therapeutic approach to schizophrenics of extreme pathology: an operant-interpersonal method. *J. abnorm. soc. Psychol.*, 1960, *61*, 276–286.

Kirkner, F. J., Wisham, W. W., & Giedt, F. H. A report on the validity of the Rorschach Prognostic Rating Scale. *J. Proj. Tech.*, 1953, *17*, 465–470.

Klein, F. L., McNair, D. M., & Lorr, M. SVIB scores of clinical psychologists, psychiatrists, and social workers. *J. counsel. Psychol.*, 1962, *9*, 176–179.

Klein, Henriette R. A study of changes occurring in patients during and after psychoanalytic treatment. In P. H. Hoch & J. Zubin (eds.), *Current approaches to psychoanalysis.* New York: Grune & Stratton, 1960. Pp. 151–175.

Klopfer, B. Introduction: the development of a prognostic rating scale. *J. proj. Tech.*, 1951, *15*, 421.

Knapp, P. H. Short-term psychoanalytic and psychosomatic predictions. *J. Amer. Psychoanal. Ass.*, 1963, *11*, 245–280.

Knapp, P. H., Levin, S., McCarter, R. H., Wermer, H., & Zetzel, Elizabeth. Suitability for psychoanalysis: a review of one hundred supervised analytic cases. *Psychoanal. Quart.*, 1960, *29*, 459–477.

Knight, R. P. Evaluation of the results of psychoanalytic therapy. *Amer. J. Psychiat.*, 1941, *98*, 434–436.

Knupfer, Genevieve, Jackson, D. D., & Krieger, G. Personality differences between more and less competent psychotherapists as a function of criteria of competence. *J. nerv. ment. Dis.*, 1959, *129*, 375–384.

Koegler, R. R., Brill, N. Q., Epstein, L. J., & Forgy, E. W. A psychiatric clinic evaluates brief-contact therapy. *Ment. Hosp.*, 1964, *15*, 564–570.

Kogan, L. S. The electrical recording of social casework interviews. *Soc. Casewk.*, 1950, *31*, 371–378.

Kotkov, B., & Meadow, A. Rorschach criteria for continuing group therapy. *Int. J. group Psychother.*, 1952, *2*, 324–333.

Kotkov, B., & Meadow, A. Rorschach criteria for predicting continuation in individual psychotherapy. *J. consult. Psychol.*, 1953, *17*, 16–20.

Kratochvil, D., Aspy, D., & Carkhuff, R. R. The differential effects of absolute level and direction of growth in counselor functioning upon client level functioning. *J. clin. Psychol.*, 1967, *23*, 216–217.

Kraus, A. R. Experimental study of the effect of group psychotherapy with chronic psychotic patients. *Int. J. group Psychother.*, 1959, *9*, 293–302.

Krieger, Margery H., & Kogan, W. S. A study of group processes in the small therapeutic group. *Int. J. group Psychother.*, 1964, *14*, 178–188.

Kris, Else. Day hospital treatment versus intramural treatment of mental patients. *Int. J. soc. Psychiat.*, 1964, *Congress Issue*, 29–37.

Krout, Johanna, Krout, M. H., & Dulin, T. J. Rorschach test-retest as a gauge of progress in psychotherapy. *J. clin. Psychol.*, 1952, *8*, 380–384.

Lacey, J. I. The evaluation of autonomic responses: toward a general solution. *Ann. N.Y. Acad. Sci.*, 1956, *67*, 123–164.

Lake, Martha, & Levinger, G. Continuance beyond application interviews at a child guidance clinic. *Soc. Casewk.*, 1960, *41*, 303–309.

Lamb, R., & Mahl, G. F. Manifest reactions of patients and interviewers to the use of sound recording in the psychiatric interview. *Amer. J. Psychiat.*, 1956, *112*, 731–737.

Landfield, A. W., & Nawas, M. M. Psychotherapeutic improvement as a function of communication and adoption of therapist's values. *J. counsel. Psychol.*, 1964, *11*, 336–341.

Landfield, A. W., O'Donovan, D., & Nawas, M. M. Improvement ratings by external judges and psychotherapists. *Psychol. Rep.*, 1962, *11*, 747–748.

Lang, P. J., & Lazovik, A. D. Experimental desensitization of a phobia. *J. abnorm. soc. Psychol.*, 1963, *66*, 519–525.

Lang, P. J., Lazovik, A. D., & Reynolds, D. J. Desensitization, suggestibility, and pseudotherapy. *J. abnorm. Psychol.*, 1965, *70*, 395–402.

Lanyon, R. I. Verbal conditioning: transfer of training in a therapy-like situation. *J. abnorm. Psychol.*, 1967, *72*, 30–34.

Lazarus, A. A. Group therapy of phobic disorders by systematic desensitization. *J. abnorm. soc. Psychol.*, 1961, *63*, 504–510.

Lazarus, A. A. The results of behaviour therapy in 126 cases of severe neurosis. *Behav. Res. Ther.*, 1963, *1*, 69–79.

Lazarus, A. A. Behaviour rehearsal vs. non-directive therapy vs. advice in effecting behaviour change. *Behav. Res. Ther.*, 1966, *4*, 209–212.

Leary, T. F., & Harvey, Joan S. A methodology for measuring personality changes in psychotherapy. *J. clin. Psychol.*, 1956, *12*, 123–132.

Lennard, H. L., & Bernstein, A. *The anatomy of psychotherapy: systems of communication and expectation.* New York: Columbia University Press, 1960.

Lennard, H. L., & Bernstein, A. Role learning in psychotherapy. *Psychotherapy: Theory, Research, and Practice,* 1967, *4*, 1–6.

Lesser, W. M. The relationship between counseling progress and empathic understanding. *J. counsel. Psychol.*, 1961, *8*, 330–336.

Lessing, Elise E. Prognostic value of the Rorschach in a child guidance clinic. *J. proj. Tech.*, 1960, *24*, 310–321.

Lessler, K. J., & Strupp, H. H. Outcome evaluations and affective response of psychotherapists to patients in treatment. *Psychotherapy: Theory, Research, and Practice*, 1967, *4*, 103–106.

Levine, D., Marks, H. K., & Hall, R. Differential effect of factors in an activity therapy program. *Amer. J. Psychiat.*, 1957, *114*, 532–535.

Levis, D. J., & Carrera, R. Effects of ten hours of implosive therapy in the treatment of outpatients. *J. abnorm. Psychol.*, 1967, *72*, 504–508.

Levitt, E. E. The results of psychotherapy with children: an evaluation. *J. consult. Psychol.*, 1957a, *21*, 189–196.

Levitt, E. E. A comparison of "remainers" and "defectors" among child clinic patients. *J. consult. Psychol.*, 1957b, *21*, 316.

Levitt, E. E. A comparative judgmental study of "defection" from treatment at a child guidance clinic. *J. clin. Psychol.*, 1958, *14*, 429–432.

Levitt, E. E., Beiser, Helen R., & Robertson, R. E. A follow-up evaluation of cases treated at a community child guidance clinic. *Amer. J. Orthopsychiat.*, 1959, *29*, 337–349.

Levy, L. H. The meaning and generality of perceived actual-ideal discrepancies. *J consult. Psychol.*, 1956, *20*, 396–398.

Lewinsohn, P. M., & Nichols, R. C. Dimensions of change in mental hospital patients. *J. clin. Psychol.*, 1967, *23*, 498–503.

Libo, L. M. The projective expression of patient-therapist attraction. *J. clin. Psychol.*, 1957, *13*, 33–36.

Lichtenstein, E. Personality similarity and therapeutic success: a failure to replicate. *J. consult. Psychol.*, 1966, *30*, 282.

Lieberman, D., & Siegel, B. A program for "sexual psychopaths" in a state mental hospital. *Amer. J. Psychiat.*, 1957, *113*, 801–807.

Lief, H. I., Lief, V. F., Warren, C. O., & Heath, R. G. Low dropout rate in a psychiatric clinic. *Arch. gen. Psychiat.*, 1961, *5*, 200–211.

Lindsay, J. S. B. The length of treatment. *Brit. J. soc. & clin. Psychol.*, 1965, *4*, 117–123.

Lipkin, S. Clients' feelings and attitudes in relation to the outcome of client-centered therapy. *Psychol. Monogr.*, 1954, *68*, whole No. 372.

Lipton, E., & Ceres, Mildred. Correlation of clinical improvement of intensively treated psychoneurotics with changes in consecutive Rorschach tests. *Psychiat. Quart. Suppl.*, 1952, *26*, 103–117.

Loevinger, Jane, & Ossorio, A. Evaluation of therapy by self-report: a paradox. *J. abnorm. soc. Psychol.*, 1959, *58*, 392–394.

Lord, F. M. Further problems in the measurement of growth. *Educ. Psychol. Measmt.*, 1958, *18*, 437–451.

Lord, F. M. Elementary models for measuring change. In C. W. Harris (ed.), *Problems in measuring change.* Madison: University of Wisconsin Press, 1963. Pp. 21–38.

Lorr, M. Client perceptions of therapists: a study of the therapeutic relation. *J. consult. Psychol.*, 1965, *29*, 146–149.

Lorr, M. Dimensions of interaction in group therapy. *Multivariate Behav. Res.*, 1966, *1*, 67–73.

Lorr, M., Katz, M. M., & Rubinstein, E. A. The prediction of length of stay in psychotherapy. *J. consult. Psychol.*, 1958, *22*, 321–327.

Lorr, M., & McNair, D. M. Correlates of length of psychotherapy. *J. clin. Psychol.*, 1964a, *20*, 497–504.

Lorr, M., & McNair, D. M. The interview relationship in therapy. *J. nerv. ment. Dis.*, 1964b, *139*, 328–331.

Lorr, M., McNair, D. M., Michaux, W. W., & Raskin, A. Frequency of treatment and change in psychotherapy. *J. abnorm. soc. Psychol.*, 1962, *64*, 281–292.

Lowinger, P., & Dobie, Shirley. Attitudes and emotions of the psychiatrist in the initial interview. *Amer. J. Psychother.*, 1966, *20*, 17–34.

Lowinger, P. L., & Huston, P. E. Transference and the physical presence of the physician. *J. nerv. ment. Dis.*, 1955, *121*, 250–256.

Luborsky, L. A note on Eysenck's article "The effects of psychotherapy: an evaluation." *Brit. J. Psychol.*, 1954, *45*, 129–131.

Luff, Mary C., & Garrod, Marjorie. The after-results of psychotherapy in 500 adult cases. *Brit. med. J.*, 1935, *2*, 54–59.

Lundy, B. Temporal factors of interaction in psychotherapy. Unpublished Ph.D. dissertation, University of Chicago, 1955.

Luria, Zella. A semantic analysis of a normal and a neurotic therapy group. *J. abnorm. soc. Psychol.*, 1959, *58*, 216–220.

MacCulloch, M. J., Feldman, M. P., Orford, J. F., & MacCulloch, M. L. Anticipatory avoidance learning in the treatment of alcoholism: a record of therapeutic failure. *Behav. Res. Ther.*, 1966, *4*, 187–196.

MacDonald, W. S., Blochberger, C. W., & Maynard, H. M. Group therapy; a comparison of patient-led and staff-led groups on an open hospital ward. *Psychiat. Quart. Suppl.*, 1964, *38*, 290–303.

Maher-Loughnan, G. P., MacDonald, N., Mason, A. A., & Fry, L. Controlled trial of hypnosis in the symptomatic treatment of asthma. *Brit. med. J.*, 1962, *2*, 371–376.

Mahl, G. F. Disturbances and silences in the patient's speech in psychotherapy. *J. abnorm. soc. Psychol.*, 1956, *53*, 1–15.

Mainord, W. A., Burk, H. W., & Collins, L. G. Confrontation versus diversion in group therapy with chronic schizophrenics as measured by a "positive incident" criterion. *J. clin. Psychol.*, 1965, *21*, 222–225.

Malan, D. H. *A study of brief psychotherapy*. Springfield, Ill.: Charles C Thomas, 1963.

Marks, I. M., & Gelder, H. G. A controlled retrospective study of behavior therapy in phobic patients. *Brit. J. Psychiat.*, 1965, *111*, 561–573.

Marks, I. M., & Sartorius, N. H. A contribution to the measurement of sexual attitude. *J. nerv. ment. Dis.*, 1967, *145*, 441–447.

Marlowe, D. Need for social approval and the operant conditioning of meaningful verbal behavior. *J. consult. Psychol.*, 1962, *26*, 79–83.

Martin, B., Lundy, R. M., & Lewin, M. H. Verbal and GSR responses in experimental interviews as a function of three degrees of "therapist" communication. *J. abnorm. soc. Psychol.*, 1960, *60*, 234–240.

Martin, J. C., Carkhuff, R. R., & Berenson, B. G. Process variables in counseling and psychotherapy: a study of counseling and friendship. *J. counsel. Psychol.*, 1966, *13*, 356–359.

Massimo, J. L., & Shore, M. F. The effectiveness of a comprehensive vocationally oriented psychotherapeutic program for adolescent delinquent boys. *Amer. J. Orthopsychiat.*, 1963, *33*, 634–642.

Matarazzo, J. D., Saslow, G., & Guze, S. B. Stability of interaction patterns during interviews: A replication. *J. consult. Psychol.*, 1956, *20*, 267–274.

Matarazzo, J. D., Weitman, M., & Saslow, G. Interview content and interviewee speech durations. *J. clin. Psychol.*, 1963, *19*, 463–472.

May, A. Changes of social environment: their effect on mentally deteriorated patients. *Lancet*, 1956, *1*, 500–502.

May, A. An attempt to counter "institutionalisation" in chronic schizophrenic patients. *Lancet*, 1957, *1*, 1294–1295.

May, A., & Robertson, J. The efficacy of habit training in chronic schizophrenia. *J. clin. Psychol.*, 1960, *16*, 359–362.

May, P. R. A., & Tuma, A. H. The effect of psychotherapy and stelazine on length of hospital stay, release rate and supplemental treatment of schizophrenic patients. *J. nerv. ment. Dis.*, 1964, *139*, 362–369.

May, P. R. A., & Tuma, A. H. Treatment of schizophrenia: an experimental study of five treatment methods. *Brit. J. Psychiat.*, 1965, *111*, 503–510.

McCue, Miriam C. Patient cancellations following a sudden cancellation by the therapist. *J. consult. Psychol.*, 1954, *18*, 176–178.

McCue, Miriam C., Goodman, M., & Rosenthal, M. Failure to return for treatment in tested and non-tested patients. *J. consult. Psychol.*, 1954, *18*, 280.

McGinnis, C. A. The effect of group-therapy on the Ego-Strength Scale scores of alcoholic patients. *J. clin. Psychol.*, 1963, *19*, 346–347.

McHugh, R. B. On Heilizer's treatment of change scores. *J. clin. Psychol.*, 1961, *17*, 206–207.

McNair, D. M., Callahan, D. M., & Lorr, M. Therapist "type" and patient response to psychotherapy. *J. consult. Psychol.*, 1962, *26*, 425–429.

McNair, D. M., & Lorr, M. Therapists' judgments of appropriateness of psychotherapy frequency schedules. *J. consult. Psychol.*, 1960, *24*, 500–506.

McNair, D. M., & Lorr, M. An analysis of professed psychotherapeutic techniques. *J. consult. Psychol.*, 1964a, *28*, 265–271.

McNair, D. M., & Lorr, M. Three kinds of psychotherapy goals. *J. clin. Psychol.*, 1964b, *20*, 390–393.

McNair, D. M., Lorr, M., & Callahan, D. M. Patient and therapist influences on quitting psychotherapy. *J. consult. Psychol.*, 1963, *27*, 10–17.

McNair, D.M., Lorr, M., Young, H. H., Roth, I., & Boyd, R. W. A three-year follow-up of psychotherapy patients. *J. clin. Psychol.*, 1964, *20*, 258–264.

McNemar, Q. On growth measurement. *Educ. psychol. Measmt.*, 1958, *18*, 47–55.

McPherson, F. M., & Walton, H. J. Changes in communications of patients treated in a closed therapeutic group. *Sixth Int. Congr. Psychother., London, 1964; Selected Lectures 91–97*. Basel & New York: S. Karger, 1965.

Meehl, P. E. Discussion in H. J. Eysenck, The effects of psychotherapy. *Int. J. Psychiat.*, 1965, *1*, 156–157.

Meltzoff, J., & Blumenthal, R. L. *The day treatment center: principles, application and evaluation.* Springfield, Ill.: Charles C Thomas, 1966.

Mendel, W. M., & Rapport, S. Outpatient treatment for chronic schizophrenic patients: therapeutic consequences of an existential view. *Arch. gen. Psychiat.*, 1963, *8*, 190–196.

Mendelsohn, G. A. Effects of client personality and client-counselor similarity on the duration of counseling: a replication and extension. *J. counsel. Psychol.*, 1966, *13*, 228–234.

Mendelsohn, G. A., & Geller, M. H. Effects of counselor-client similarity on the outcome of counseling. *J. counsel. Psychol.*, 1963, *10*, 71–77.

Mendelsohn, G. A., & Geller, M. H. Structure of client attitudes toward counseling and their relation to client-counselor similarity. *J. consult. Psychol.*, 1965, *29*, 63–72.

Mendelsohn, G. A., & Geller, M. H. Similarity, missed sessions, and early termination. *J. counsel. Psychol.*, 1967, *14*, 210–215.

Mensh, I. N., & Watson, R. I. Psychiatric opinions on personality factors in psychotherapy. *J. clin. Psychol.*, 1950, *6*, 237–242.

Merry, J. An experiment in a chronic psychotic ward. *Brit. J. med. Psychol.*, 1956, *28*, 287–294.

Meyer, E., Spiro, H. R., Slaughter, Regina, Pollack, I. W., Weingartner, H., & Novey, S. Contractually time-limited psychotherapy in an outpatient psychosomatic clinic. *Amer. J. Psychiat.*, 1967, *124*, *Suppl.* 57–66.

Meyer, M. M., & Tolman, Ruth S. The reactions of patients to enforced changes of therapists. *J. clin. Psychol.*, 1963, *19*, 241–243.

Meyer, V., & Crisp, H. Some problems in behavior therapy. *Brit. J. Psychiat.*, 1966, *112*, 367–381.

Michaux, W. W., & Lorr, M. Psychotherapists' treatment goals. *J. counsel. Psychol.*, 1961, *8*, 250–254.

Miles, H. H. W., Barrabee, Edna L., & Finesinger, J. E. Evaluation of psychotherapy. *Psychosom. Med.*, 1951, *13*, 83–105.

Miller, D., & Clancy, J. An approach to the social rehabilitation of chronic psychotic patients. *Psychiatry*, 1952, *15*, 435–443.

Miller, D., Clancy, J., & Cumming, E. A method of evaluating progress in patients suffering from chronic schizophrenia. *Psychiat. Quart.*, 1953, *27*, 439–451.

Mills, D. H., & Abeles, N. Counselor needs for affiliation and nurturance as related to liking for clients and counseling process. *J. counsel. Psychol.*, 1965, *12*, 353–358.

Mills, D. H., & Zytowski, D. G. Helping relationship: a structural analysis. *J. counsel. Psychol.*, 1967, *14*, 193–197.

Milton, G. A. Changes in essential hypertension over time: a factor analytic case study. *J. clin. Psychol.*, 1961, *17*, 322–326.

Mindess, H. Predicting patients' responses to psychotherapy: a preliminary study designed to investigate the validity of the "Rorschach Prognostic Rating Scale." *J. proj. Tech.*, 1953, *17*, 327–334.

Mintz, Elizabeth E., Schmeidler, Gertrude R., & Bristol, Marjorie. Rorschach changes during psychoanalysis. *J. proj. Tech.*, 1956, *20*, 414-417.

Moore, F. J., Chernell, E., & West, M. J. Television as a therapeutic tool. *Arch. gen. Psychiat.*, 1965, *12*, 217–220.

Moore, R. A., Benedek, Elissa P., & Wallace, J. G. Social class, schizophrenia and the psychiatrist. *Amer. J. Psychiat.*, 1963, *120*, 149–154.

Moore, R. A., & Ramseur, Freida. Effects of psychotherapy in an open-ward hospital on patients with alcoholism. *Quart. J. Stud. Alcohol*, 1960, *21*, 233–252.

Moos, R. H. The retention and generalization of operant conditioning effects in an interview situation. *J. abnorm. soc. Psychol.*, 1963, *66*, 52–58.

Moos, R. H., & Clemes, S. R. Multivariate study of the patient-therapist system. *J. consult. Psychol.*, 1967, *31*, 119–130.

Morgenstern, F. S., Pearce, J. F., & Rees, W. L. Predicting the outcome of behaviour therapy by psychological tests. *Behav. Res. Ther.*, 1965, *2*, 191–200.

Morton, R. B. An experiment in brief psychotherapy. *Psychol. Monogr.*, 1955, *69*, whole No. 386.

Mosak, H. Evaluation in psychotherapy: a study of some current measures. Unpublished Ph.D. dissertation, University of Chicago, 1950.

Mowrer, O. H. *Psychotherapy: theory and research.* New York: Ronald, 1953.

Mowrer, O. H., Hunt. J. McV., & Kogan, L. S. Further studies in utilizing the discomfort-relief quotient. In O. H. Mowrer, *Psychotherapy: theory and research.* New York: Ronald, 1953. Pp. 257–295.

Muench, G. A. An evaluation of non-directive psychotherapy by means of the Rorschach and other tests. *Appl. Psychol. Monogr.*, 1947, *13*, 1–163.

Muench, G. A. An investigation of the efficacy of time-limited psychotherapy. *J. counsel. Psychol.*, 1965, *12*, 294 299.

Mundy, Lydia. Therapy with physically and mentally handicapped children in a mental deficiency hospital. *J. clin. Psychol.*, 1957, *13*, 3–9.

Munzer, Jean. The effect on analytic therapy groups of the experimental introduction of special "warm-up" procedures during the first five sessions. *Int. J. group Psychother.*, 1964, *14*, 60–71.

Murphy, I. C. Extinction of an incapacitating fear of earthworms. *J. clin. Psychol.*, 1964, *20*, 396–398.

Murray, E. J., Auld, F., Jr., & White, Alice M. A psychotherapy case showing progress but no decrease in the Discomfort-Relief Quotient. *J. consult. Psychol.*, 1954, *18*, 349–353.

Muthard, J. E. The relative effectiveness of larger units used in interview analysis. *J. consult. Psychol.*, 1953, *17*, 184–188.

Myers, J. K., & Auld, F., Jr. Some variables related to outcome of psychotherapy. *J. clin. Psychol.*, 1955, *11*, 51–54.

Myers, J. K., & Schaffer, L. Social stratification and psychiatric practice: a study of an outpatient clinic. *Amer. sociol. Rev.*, 1954, *19*, 307–310.

Nachand, D. W. A factorial study of client-centered therapy; the case of Miss Bime. Unpublished M.A. thesis, University of Chicago, 1952.

Nagel, E. Methodological issues in psychoanalytic theory. In S. Hook (ed.), *Psychoanalysis, scientific method, and philosophy.* New York: New York University Press, 1959. Pp. 38–56.

Nahinsky, I. D. The self-ideal correlation as a measure of generalized self-satisfaction. *Psychol. Rec.*, 1966, *16*, 55–64.

Nawas, M. M., & Landfield, A. W. Improvement in psychotherapy and adoption of the therapist's meaning system. *Psychol. Rep.*, 1963, *13*, 97–98.

Newburger, H. M. Psychotherapy and anxiety: a sociometric study. *Group Psychother.*, 1963, *16*, 1–7.

Newburger, H. M., & Schauer, G. Sociometric evaluation of group psychotherapy. *Group Psychother.*, 1953, *6*, 7–20.

Nichols, R. C., & Beck, K. W. Factors in psychotherapy change. *J. consult. Psychol.*, 1960, *24*, 388–399.

Noblin, C. D., Timmons, E. O., & Reynard, Marian C. Psychoanalytic interpretations as verbal reinforcers: importance of interpretation content. *J. clin. Psychol.*, 1963, *19*, 479–481.

Novick, J. I. Comparison between short-term group and individual psychotherapy in effecting change in nondesirable behavior in children. *Int. J. group Psychother.*, 1965, *15*, 366–373.

Nunnally, J. C. A systematic approach to the construction of hypotheses about the process of psychotherapy. *J. consult. Psychol.*, 1955, *19*, 17–20.

O'Connor, J. F., Daniels, G., Flood, C., Karush, A., Moses, L., & Stern, Lenore O. An evaluation of the effectiveness of psychotherapy in the treatment of ulcerative colitis. *Ann. intern. Med.*, 1964, *60*, 587–602.

Orlinsky, D. E., & Howard, K. I. The good therapy hour. *Arch. gen. Psychiat.*, 1967, *16*, 621–632.

Overall, Betty, & Aronson, H. Expectations of psychotherapy in patients of lower socioeconomic class. *Amer. J. Orthopsychiat.*, 1963, *33*, 421–430.

Pace, R. Situational therapy. *J. Pers.*, 1957, *25*, 578–588.

Pack, G. T., & Davis, A. H. *Burns: types, pathology, and management.* Philadelphia: J. B. Lippincott, 1930.

Page, H. A. An assessment of the predictive value of certain language measures in psychotherapeutic counseling. In W. U. Snyder (ed.), *Group report of a program of research in psychotherapy* (mimeographed). University Park, Pa.: Pennsylvania State College, 1953. Pp. 88–93.

Pallone, N. J., & Grande, P. P. Counselor verbal mode, problem relevant communication, and client rapport. *J. counsel. Psychol.*, 1965, *12*, 359–365.

Panek, D. M., & Martin, B. The relationship between GSR and speech disturbances in psychotherapy. *J. abnorm. soc. Psychol.*, 1959, *58*, 402–405.

Parloff, M. B. Some factors affecting the quality of therapeutic relationships. *J. abnorm. soc. Psychol.*, 1956, *52*, 5–10.

Parloff, M. B. Therapist-patient relationships and outcome of psychotherapy. *J. consult. Psychol.*, 1961, *25*, 29–38.

Parloff, M. B., Iflund, B., & Goldstein, N. Communication of "therapy values" between therapist and schizophrenic patients. *J. nerv. ment. Dis.*, 1960, *130*, 193–199.

Parloff, M. B., Kelman, H. C., & Frank, J. D. Comfort, effectiveness and self-awareness as criteria of improvement in psychotherapy. *Amer. J. Psychiat.*, 1954, *111*, 343–352.

Pascal, G. R., & Zax, M. Psychotherapeutics: success or failure. *J. consult. Psychol.*, 1956, *20*, 325–331.

Paul, G. L. *Insight vs. desensitization in psychotherapy*. Stanford, Calif.: Stanford University Press, 1966.

Paul, G. L. Strategy of outcome research in psychotherapy. *J. consult. Psychol.*, 1967, *31*, 109–118.

Paul, G. L., & Shannon, D. T. Treatment of anxiety through systematic desensitization in therapy groups. *J. abnorm. Psychol.*, 1966, *71*, 124–135.

Peck, R. E. Comparison of adjunct group therapy with individual psychotherapy. *Arch. Neurol. Psychiat.*, 1949, *62*, 173–177.

Pepinsky, H. B., Siegel, L., & Vanatta, E. L. The criterion in counseling: a group participation scale. *J. abnorm. soc. Psychol.*, 1952, *47*, 415–419.

Persons, R. W. Psychotherapy with sociopathic offenders: an empirical evaluation. *J. clin. Psychol.*, 1965, *21*, 205–207.

Persons, R. W. Psychological and behavioral change in delinquents following psychotherapy. *J. clin. Psychol.*, 1966, *22*, 337–340.

Persons, R. W. Relationship between psychotherapy with institutionalized boys and subsequent community adjustment. *J. consult. Psychol.*, 1967, *31*, 137–141.

Peters, H. N., & Jones, F. D. Evaluation of group psychotherapy by means of performance tests. *J. consult. Psychol.*, 1951, *15*, 363–367.

Peterson, A. O. D. A comparative study of Rorschach scoring methods in evaluating personality changes resulting from psychotherapy. *J. clin. Psychol.*, 1954, *10*, 190–192.

Peterson, A. O. D., Snyder, W. U., Guthrie, G. M., & Ray, W. S. Therapist factors: an exploratory investigation of therapeutic biases. *J. counsel. Psychol.*, 1958, *5*, 169–173.

Peyman, D. A. R. An investigation of the effects of group psychotherapy on chronic schizophrenic patients. *Group Psychother.*, 1956, *9*, 35–39.

Phillips, E. L., & Agnew, J. W. A study of Rogers' "reflection" hypothesis. *J. clin. Psychol.*, 1953, *9*, 281–284.

Phillips, E. L., & Johnston, M. S. H. Theoretical and clinical aspects of short-term parent-child psychotherapy. *Psychiatry*, 1954, *17*, 267–275.

Phillips, Jeanne S., Matarazzo, Ruth G., Matarazzo, J. D., Saslow, G., &

Kanfer, F. Relationships between descriptive content and interaction behavior in interviews. *J. consult. Psychol.*, 1961, *25*, 260–266.

Phillipson, H. The assessment of progress after at least two years of group psychotherapy. *Brit. J. med. Psychol.*, 1958, *31*, 32–42.

Pierce, W. D., & Mosher, D. L. Perceived empathy, interviewer behavior, and interviewee anxiety. *J. consult. Psychol.*, 1967, *31*, 101.

Piotrowski, Z. A. A defense attitude associated with improvement in schizophrenia and measurable with a modified Rorschach Test. *J. nerv. ment. Dis.*, 1955, *122*, 36–41.

Piotrowski, Z. A., & Bricklin, B. A long-term prognostic criterion for schizophrenics based on Rorschach data. *Psychiat. Quart. Suppl.*, 1958, *32*, 315–329.

Piotrowski, Z. A., & Bricklin, B. A second validation of a long-term Rorschach prognostic index for schizophrenic patients. *J. consult. Psychol.*, 1961, *25*, 123–128.

Piotrowski, Z. A., & Lewis, N. D. C. An experimental criterion for the prognostication of the status of schizophrenics after a three-year interval based on Rorschach data. In P. Hoch & J. Zubin (eds.), *Relation of psychological tests to psychiatry*. New York: Grune & Stratton, 1952. Pp. 51–72.

Pollack, I. W., & Kiev, A. Spatial orientations and psychotherapy: an experimental study of perception. *J. nerv. ment. Dis.*, 1963, *137*, 93–97.

Pope, B., & Siegman, A. W. The effect of therapist verbal activity level and specificity on patient productivity and speech disturbance in the initial interview. *J. consult. Psychol.*, 1962, *26*, 489.

Poser, E. G. The effect of therapists' training on group therapeutic outcome. *J. consult. Psychol.*, 1966, *30*, 283–289.

Pruit, W. A. Satiation effect in vocationally oriented group therapy as determined by the Palo Alto Group Psychotherapy Scale. *Group Psychother.*, 1963, *16*, 55–58.

Pumroy, D. K. Some counseling behavior correlates of the Social Desirability Scale. *J. counsel. Psychol.*, 1961, *8*, 49–53.

Quay, H. The effect of verbal reinforcement on the recall of early memories. *J. abnorm. soc. Psychol.*, 1959, *59*, 254–257.

Query, Joy M. N., & Query, W. T., Jr. Prognosis and progress: a five-year study of forty-eight schizophrenic men. *J. consult. Psychol.*, 1964, *28*, 501–505.

Query, W. T., Jr. Self-disclosure as a variable in group psychotherapy. *Int. J. group Psychother.*, 1964, *14*, 107–115.

Rabkin, L. Y., & Lytle, Carlah. Further information on the ecology of service. *J. consult. Psychol.*, 1966, *30*, 146–150.

Rachman, S. Spontaneous remission and latent learning. *Behav. Res Ther.*, 1963, *1*, 133–137.

Rachman, S. Studies in desensitization: I. The separate effects of relaxation and desensitization. *Behav. Res. Ther.*, 1965, *3*, 245–251.

Rachman, S. Studies in desensitization: II. Flooding. *Behav. Res. Ther.*, 1966, *4*, 1–6.

Raimy, V. C. Self-reference in counseling interviews. *J. consult. Psychol.*, 1948, *12*, 153–163.

Rakusin, J. M. The role of Rorschach variability in the prediction of client behavior during psychotherapy. In W. U. Snyder (ed.), *Group report of a program of research in psychotherapy* (mimeographed). University Park, Pa.: Pennsylvania State College, 1953. Pp. 60–74.

Ramsay, R. W., Barends, J., Breuker, J., & Kruseman, A. Massed versus spaced desensitization of fear. *Behav. Res. Ther.*, 1966, *4*, 205–207.

Raskin, A. Factors therapists associate with motivation to enter psychotherapy. *J. clin. Psychol.*, 1961, *17*, 62–65.

Raskin, A. Observable signs of anxiety or distress during psychotherapy. *J. consult. Psychol.*, 1962, *26*, 389.

Raskin, N. J. An analysis of six parallel studies of the therapeutic process. *J. consult. Psychol.*, 1949, *13*, 206–220.

Raskin, N. J. The psychotherapy research project of the American Academy of Psychotherapists. *Proc. 73rd Annual Convention APA*, 1965, 253–254.

Rathod, N. H., Gregory, E., Blows, D., & Thomas, G. H. A two-year follow-up study of alcoholic patients. *Brit. J. Psychiat.*, 1966, *112*, 683–692.

Raush, H. L., Sperber, Z., Rigler, D., Williams, J., Harway, N. I., Bordin, E. S., Dittmann, A. T., & Hays, W. L. A dimensional analysis of depth of interpretation. *J. consult. Psychol.*, 1956, *20*, 43–48.

Rawn, M. L. An experimental study of transference and resistance phenomena in psychoanalytically oriented psychotherapy. *J. clin. Psychol.*, 1958, *14*, 418–425.

Redlich, F. C., Hollingshead, A. B., & Bellis, Elizabeth. Social class differences in attitudes toward psychiatry. *Amer. J. Orthopsychiat.*, 1955, *25*, 60–70.

Redlich, F. C., Hollingshead, A. B., Roberts, B. H., Robinson, H. A., Freedman, L. Z., & Myers, J. K. Social structure and psychiatric disorders. *Amer. J. Psychiat.*, 1953, *109*, 729–734.

Renneker, R. E. The use of the sound recorder in psychoanalytic therapy. Paper read at meeting of American Psychoanalytic Association, May 6, 1960.

Rice, Laura N. Therapist's style of participation and case outcome. *J. consult. Psychol.*, 1965, *29*, 155–160.

Riess, B. F. Changes in patient income concomitant with psychotherapy. *J. consult. Psychol.*, 1967, *31*, 430.

Rigler, D. Some determinants of therapist behavior. Unpublished Ph.D. dissertation, University of Michigan, 1957.

Rioch, Margaret J. The use of the Rorschach test in the assessment of change in patients under psychotherapy. *Psychiatry*, 1949, *12*, 427–434.

Rioch, Margaret J., Elkes, C., Flint, A. A., Usdansky, B. S., Newman, R. G.,

& Silber, E. National Institute of Mental Health pilot study in training mental health counselors. *Amer. J. Orthopsychiat.*, 1963, *33*, 678–689.

Rioch, Margaret J., & Lubin, A. Prognosis of social adjustment for mental hospital patients under psychotherapy. *J. consult. Psychol.*, 1959, *23*, 313–318.

Roberts, A. H. Housebound housewives—a follow-up study of a phobic anxiety state. *Brit. J. Psychiat.*, 1964, *110*, 191–197.

Roberts, L. K. The failure of some Rorschach indices to predict the outcome of psychotherapy. *J. consult. Psychol.*, 1954, *18*, 96–98.

Roberts, R. R., Jr., & Renzaglia, G. A. The influence of tape recording on counseling. *J. counsel. Psychol.*, 1965, *12*, 10–16.

Robertson, M. H. A comparison of client and therapist ratings on two psychotherapeutic variables. *J. consult. Psychol.*, 1957, *21*, 110.

Robinson, H. A., Redlich, F. C., & Myers, J. K. Social structure and psychiatric treatment. *Amer. J. Orthopsychiat.*, 1954, *24*, 307–316.

Rodriguez, A., Rodriguez, Maria, & Eisenberg, L. The outcome of school phobia: a follow-up study based on 41 cases. *Amer. J. Psychiat.*, 1959, *116*, 540–544.

Rogers, C. R. Changes in the maturity of behavior as related to therapy. in C. R. Roger & Rosalind F. Dymond (eds.), *Psychotherapy and personality change.* Chicago: University of Chicago Press, 1954. Pp. 215–237.

Rogers, C. R. The necessary and sufficient conditions of therapeutic personality change. *J. consult. Psychol.*, 1957, *21*, 95–103.

Rogers, C. R. Psychotherapy today, or where do we go from here? *Amer. J. Psychother.*, 1963, *17*, 5–16.

Rogers, C. R., & Dymond, Rosalind F. (eds.). *Psychotherapy and personality change.* Chicago: University of Chicago Press, 1954.

Rogers, J. M. Operant conditioning in a quasi-therapy setting. *J. abnorm. soc. Psychol.*, 1960, *60*, 247–252.

Rogers, L. S. Drop-out rates and results of psychotherapy in government aided mental hygiene clinics. *J. clin. Psychol.*, 1960, *16*, 89–92.

Rogers, L. S., & Hammond, K. R. Prediction of the results of therapy by means of the Rorschach Test. *J. consult. Psychol.*, 1953, *17*, 8–15.

Rogers, L. S., Knauss, Joanne, & Hammond, K. R. Predicting continuation in therapy by means of the Rorschach test. *J. consult. Psychol.*, 1951, *15*, 368–371.

Roos, P., Hayes, R. L., Marion, R. R., & England, B. C. Evaluation of remotivation with institutionalized psychotics. *J. clin. Psychol.*, 1963, *19*, 341–343.

Rosen, J. N. The treatment of schizophrenic psychosis by direct analytic therapy. *Psychiat. Quart.*, 1947, *21*, 3–37, 117–119.

Rosen, J. N. *Direct anclysis: selected papers.* New York: Grune & Stratton, 1953.

Rosenbaum, M., Friedlander, Jane, & Kaplan, S. M. Evaluation of results of psychotherapy. *Psychosom. Med.*, 1956, *18*, 113–132.

Rosenberg, S. The relationship of certain personality factors to prognosis in psychotherapy. *J. clin. Psychol.*, 1954, *10*, 341–345.

Rosenman, S. Changes in the representations of self, other, and interrelationship in client-centered therapy. *J. counsel. Psychol.*, 1955, *2*, 271–277.

Rosenthal, D. Changes in some moral values following psychotherapy. *J. consult. Psychol.*, 1955, *19*, 431–436.

Rosenthal, D., & Frank, J. D. Psychotherapy and the placebo effect. *Psychol. Bull.*, 1956, *53*, 294–302.

Rosenthal, D., & Frank, J. D. The fate of psychiatric clinic outpatients assigned to psychotherapy. *J. nerv. ment. Dis.*, 1958, *127*, 330–343.

Rosenzweig, S. A transvaluation of therapy—a reply to Hans Eysenck. *J. abnorm. soc. Psychol.*, 1954, *49*, 298–304.

Roshal, Jean J. G. The type-token ratio as a measure of changes in behavior variability during psychotherapy. In W. U. Snyder (ed.), *Group report of a program of research in psychotherapy* (mimeographed). University Park, Pa.: Pennsylvania State College, 1953. Pp. 94–104.

Ross, A. O., & Lacey, H. M. Characteristics of terminators and remainers in child guidance treatment. *J. consult. Psychol.*, 1961, *25*, 420–424.

Ross, M., & Mendelsohn, F. Homosexuality in college. *Arch. Neurol. Psychiat.*, 1958, *80*, 253–263.

Rothaus, P., Johnson, D. L., Hanson, P. G., Brown, J. B., & Lyle, F. A. Sentence-completion test prediction of autonomous and therapist-led group behavior. *J. counsel. Psychol.*, 1967, *14*, 28–34.

Rothaus, P., Johnson, D. L., Hanson, P. G., & Lyle, F. A. Participation and sociometry in autonomous and trainer-led patient groups. *J. counsel. Psychol.*, 1966, *13*, 68–76.

Rottschafer, R. H., & Renzaglia, G. A. The relationship of dependent-like verbal behaviors to counselor style and induced set. *J. consult. Psychol.*, 1962, *26*, 172–177.

Rubinstein, E. A., & Lorr, M. A comparison of terminators and remainers in outpatient psychotherapy. *J. clin. Psychol.*, 1956, *12*, 345–349.

Rubinstein, E. A., & Lorr, M. Self and peer personality ratings of psychotherapists. *J. clin. Psychol.*, 1957, *13*, 295–298.

Rudikoff, Esselyn C. A comparative study of the changes in the concepts of the self, the ordinary person, and the ideal, in eight cases. In C. R. Rogers & Rosalind F. Dymond (eds.), *Psychotherapy and personality change*. Chicago: University of Chicago Press, 1954. Pp. 85–98.

Russell, P. D., & Snyder, W. U. Counselor anxiety in relation to amount of clinical experience and quality of affect demonstrated by clients. *J. consult. Psychol.*, 1963, *27*, 358–363.

Sacks, J. M., & Berger, S. Group therapy techniques with hospitalized chronic schizophrenic patients. *J. consult. Psychol.*, 1954, *18*, 297–302.

Salzberg, H. C. Effects of silence and redirection on verbal responses in group psychotherapy. *Psychol. Rep.*, 1962, *11*, 455–461.

Salzberg, H. C. Verbal behavior in group psychotherapy with and without a therapist. *J. counsel. Psychol.*, 1967, *14*, 24–27.

Salzinger, K., & Pisoni, Stephanie. Reinforcement of verbal affect responses of normal subjects during the interview. *J. abnorm. soc. Psychol.*, 1960, *60*, 127–130.

Sanders, R. The therapeutic value of psychosocial treatment. Paper read at American Psychological Association, Philadelphia, 1963.

Sanders, R., Weinman, B., Smith, R., Smith, A., Kenny, J., & Fitzgerald, B. Social treatment of the male chronic mental patient. *J. nerv. ment. Dis.*, 1962, *134*, 244–255.

Sanford, R. N. Clinical methods: psychotherapy. *Annu. Rev. Psychol.*, 1953, *4*, 317–342.

Sapolsky, A. Effect of interpersonal relationships upon verbal conditioning. *J. abnorm. soc. Psychol.*, 1960, *60*, 241–246.

Sapolsky, A. Relationship between patient-doctor compatibility, mutual perception, and outcome of treatment. *J. abnorm. Psychol.*, 1965, *70*, 70–76.

Sarason, I. G. Interrelationships among individual difference variables, behavior in psychotherapy, and verbal conditioning. *J. abnorm. soc. Psychol.*, 1958, *56*, 339–344.

Saslow, G., Matarazzo, J. D., & Guze, S. B. The stability of interaction chronograph patterns in psychiatric interviews. *J. consult. Psychol.*, 1955, *19*, 417–430.

Saslow, G., & Peters, Ann D. A follow-up study of "untreated" patients with various behavior disorders. *Psychiat. Quart.*, 1956, *30*, 283–302.

Satz, P., & Baraff, A. S. Changes in the relation between self-concepts and ideal-concepts of psychotics consequent upon therapy. *J. gen. Psychol.*, 1962, *67*, 291–298.

Schaefer, H. H., & Martin, P. L. Behavioral therapy for "apathy" of hospitalized schizophrenics. *Psychol. Rep.*, 1966, *19*, 1147–1158.

Schaffer, L., & Myers, J. K. Psychotherapy and social stratification. *Psychiatry,* 1954, *17*, 83–93.

Scher, Maryonda, & Johnson, M. H. Attendance fluctuations in an after-care group. *Int. J. group Psychother.*, 1964, *14*, 223–224.

Schjelderup, H. Lasting effects of psychoanalytic treatment. *Psychiatry,* 1955, *18*, 109–133.

Schmidt, Elsa, Castell, D., & Brown, P. A retrospective study of 42 cases of behaviour therapy. *Behav. Res. Ther.*, 1965, *3*, 9–19.

Schnore, M. Re-evaluation of an activity treatment programme with regressed schizophrenics. *Canad. Psychiat. Ass. J.*, 1961, *6*, 158–162.

Schoenberg, B., & Carr, A. C. An investigation of criteria for brief psychotherapy of neurodermatitis. *Psychosom. Med.*, 1963, *25*, 253–263.

Schofield, W. Changes in responses to the Minnesota Multiphasic Inventory following certain therapies. *Psychol. Monogr.*, 1950, *64*, whole No. 311.

Schopler, J. H. The relation of patient-therapist personality similarity to the outcome of psychotherapy. Unpublished Ph.D. dissertation, University of Colorado, 1958.

Schreiber, Leona E. Evaluation of family group treatment in a family agency. *Fam. Process*, 1966, *5*, 21–29.

Schrier, H. The significance of identification in therapy. *Amer. J. Orthopsychiat.*, 1953, *23*, 585-604.

Schroeder, Pearl. Client acceptance of responsibility and difficulty of therapy. *J. consult. Psychol.*, 1960, *24*, 467-471.

Schuldt, W. J. Psychotherapists' approach-avoidance responses and clients' expressions of dependency. *J. counsel. Psychol.*, 1966, *13*, 178-183.

Schulman, R. E. Use of the Rorschach Prognostic Rating Scale in predicting movement in counseling. *J. counsel. Psychol.*, 1963, *10*, 198-199.

Schwartz, A. M., & Hawkins, H. L. Patient models and affect statements in group therapy. *Proc. 73rd Annual Convention APA*, 1965, 265-266.

Schwitzgebel, R., & Kolb, D. A. Inducing behaviour change in adolescent delinquents. *Behav. Res. Ther.*, 1964, *1*, 297-304.

Sechrest, L. Stimulus equivalents of the psychotherapist. *J. indiv. Psychol.*, 1962, *18*, 172-176.

Sechrest, L., & Barger, B. Verbal participation and perceived benefit from group psychotherapy. *Int. J. group Psychother.*, 1961, *11*, 49-59.

Seeman, J. A study of the process of nondirective therapy. *J. consult. Psychol.*, 1949, *13*, 157-168.

Seeman, J. Counselor judgments of therapeutic process and outcome. In C. R. Rogers & Rosalind F. Dymond (eds.), *Psychotherapy and personality change.* Chicago: University of Chicago Press, 1954. Pp. 99-108.

Seeman, J. Psychotherapy and perceptual behavior. *J. clin. Psychol.*, 1962, *18*, 34-37.

Seeman, J., Barry, Edyth, & Ellinwood, Charlotte. Interpersonal assessment of play therapy outcome. *Psychotherapy: Theory, Research, and Practice,* 1964, *1*, 64-66.

Seeman, W. Clinical opinion on the role of the therapist adjustment in psychotherapy. *J. consult. Psychol.*, 1950, *14*, 49-52.

Seidel, Claudene. The relationship between Klopfer's Rorschach Prognostic Rating Scale and Phillips' Case History Prognostic Rating Scale. *J. consult. Psychol.*, 1960, *24*, 46-49.

Sells, S. B. Problems of criteria and validity in diagnosis and therapy. *J. clin. Psychol.*, 1952, *8*, 23-28.

Semon, R. G., & Goldstein, N. The effectiveness of group psychotherapy with chronic schizophrenic patients and an evaluation of different therapeutic methods. *J. consult. Psychol.*, 1957, *21*, 317-322.

Severinsen, K. N. Client expectation and perception of the counselor's role and their relationship to client satisfaction. *J. counsel. Psychol.*, 1966, *13*, 109-112.

Shagass, C., & Malmo, R. B. Psychodynamic themes and localized muscular tension during psychotherapy. *Psychosom. Med.*, 1954, *16*, 295-314.

Shanan, J., & Moses, R. The readiness to offer psychotherapy: its relationship to social background and formulation of complaint. *Arch. gen. Psychiat.*, 1961, *4*, 202-212.

Shattan, S. P., Dcamp, L., Fujii, E., Fross, G. G., & Wolff, R. J. Group treatment of conditionally discharged patients in a mental health clinic. *Amer. J. Psychiat.*, 1966, *122*, 798–805.

Sheehan, J. G. Rorschach changes during psychotherapy in relation to personality of the therapist. *Amer. Psychologist*, 1953, *8*, 434–435.

Sheehan, J. G., Frederick, C. J., Rosevear, W. H., & Spiegelman, M. A validity study of the Rorschach Prognostic Rating Scale. *J. proj. Tech.*, 1954, *18*, 233–239.

Sheerer, Elizabeth T. An analysis of the relationship between acceptance of and respect for self and acceptance of and respect for others in ten counseling cases. *J. consult. Psychol.*, 1949, *13*, 169–175.

Sheldon, A. An evaluation of psychiatric after-care. *Brit. J. Psychiat.*, 1964, *110*, 662–667.

Shelley, E. L. V., & Johnson, W. F., Jr. Evaluating an organized counseling service for youthful offenders. *J. counsel. Psychol.*, 1961, *8*, 351–354.

Shlien, J. M., Mosak, H. H., & Dreikurs, R. Effect of time limits: a comparison of two psychotherapies. *J. counsel. Psychol.*, 1962, *9*, 31–34.

Shore, M. F., & Massimo, J. L. Comprehensive vocationally oriented psychotherapy for adolescent delinquent boys: a follow-up study. *Amer. J. Orthopsychiat.*, 1966, *36*, 609–615.

Shore, M. F., Massimo, J. L., & Mack, R. Changes in the perception of interpersonal relationships in successfully treated adolescent delinquent boys. *J. consult. Psychol.*, 1965, *29*, 213–217.

Shore, M. F., Massimo, J. L., & Ricks, D. F. A factor analytic study of psychotherapeutic change in delinquent boys. *J. clin. Psychol.*, 1965, *21*, 208–212.

Shostrom, E. L., & Knapp, R. R. The relationship of a measure of self-actualization (POI) to a measure of pathology (MMPI) and to therapeutic growth. *Amer. J. Psychother.*, 1966, *20*, 193–202.

Shouksmith, G., & Taylor, J. W. The effect of counseling on the achievement of high ability pupils. *Brit. J. educ. Psychol.*, 1964, *1*, 51–57.

Shows, W. D., & Carson, R. C. The A-B therapist "type" distinction and spatial orientation: replication and extension. *J. nerv. ment. Dis.*, 1965, *141*, 455–462.

Simmons, W. L., & Tyler, F. B. A comparison of patient and staff conceptions of psychotherapists. *J. clin. Psychol.*, 1964, *20*, 508–512.

Sinclair-Gieben, A. H. C., & Chalmers, D. Evaluation of treatment of warts by hypnosis. *Lancet*, 1959, *2*, 480–482.

Sines, J., Lucero, R., & Kamman, G. A state hospital total push program for regressed schizophrenics. *J. clin. Psychol.*, 1952, *8*, 189–193.

Sines, L. K., Silver, R. J., & Lucero, R. J. The effect of therapeutic intervention by untrained "therapists." *J. clin. Psychol.*, 1961, *17*, 394–396.

Skinner, Kathryn, & Anderson, G. V. Personality and attitude characteristics associated with "therapy readiness." *Amer. Psychologist*, 1959, *14*, 376–377.

Slawson, P. F. Psychodrama as a treatment for hospitalized patients: a controlled study. *Amer. J. Psychiat.*, 1965, *122*, 530–533.

Slechta, Joan, Gwynn, W., & Peoples, C. Verbal conditioning of schizophrenics and normals in a situation resembling psychotherapy. *J. consult. Psychol.*, 1963, *27*, 223–227.

Smith, A. B., Bassin, A., & Froehlich, A. Change in attitudes and degree of verbal participation in group therapy with adult offenders. *J. consult. Psychol.*, 1960, *24*, 247–249.

Smith, G. J. W., & Johnson. G. The influence of psychiatric treatment upon the process of reality construction: an investigation utilizing the results of a serial tachistoscopic experiment. *J. consult. Psychol.*, 1962, *26*, 520–526.

Snyder, R., & Sechrest, L. B. An experimental study of directive group therapy with defective delinquents. *Amer. J. ment. Defic.*, 1959, *63*, 117–123.

Snyder, W. U. (ed.). *Group report of a program of research in psychotherapy* (mimeographed). University Park, Pa.: Pennsylvania State College, 1953.

Snyder, W. U., & Snyder, B. June. *The psychotherapy relationship.* New York: Macmillan, 1961.

Sobel, R. The private practice of child psychiatry. A ten-year study. *Amer. J. Psychother.*, 1962, *16*, 567–579.

Sommer, G. R., Mazo, B., & Lehner, G. F. J. An empirical investigation of therapeutic "listening." *J. clin. Psychol.*, 1955, *11*, 132–136.

Spear, F. G. Deterioration in schizophrenic control groups. *Brit. J. med. Psychol.*, 1960, *33*, 143–148.

Speisman, J. C. Depth of interpretation and verbal resistance in psychotherapy. *J. consult. Psychol.*, 1959, *23*, 93–99.

Spohn, H. E. The influence of social values upon the clinical judgments of psychotherapists. In J. G. Peatman & E. L. Hartley (eds.), *Festschrift for Gardner Murphy.* New York: Harper, 1960. Pp. 274–290.

Standal, S. W., & van der Veen, F. Length of therapy in relation to counselor estimates of personal integration and other case variables. *J. consult. Psychol.*, 1957, *21*, 1–9.

Stephens, J. H., & Astrup, C. Treatment outcome in "process" and "nonprocess" schizophrenics treated by "A" and "B" types of therapists. *J. nerv. ment. Dis.*, 1965, *140*, 449–456.

Sternberg, Rae S., Chapman, Jean, & Shakow, D. Psychotherapy research and the problem of intrusions on privacy. *Psychiatry*, 1958, *21*, 195–203.

Stieper, D. R., & Wiener, D. N. The problem of interminability in outpatient psychotherapy. *J. consult. Psychol.*, 1959, *23*, 237–242.

Stieper, D. R., & Wiener, D. N. *Dimensions of psychotherapy: an experimental and clinical approach.* Chicago: Aldine, 1965.

Stoler, N. Client likability: a variable in the study of psychotherapy. *J. consult. Psychol.*, 1963, *27*, 175–178.

Stollak, G. E., & Guerney, B., Jr. Exploration of personal problems by juvenile delinquents under conditions of minimal reinforcement. *J. clin. Psychol.*, 1964, *20*, 279–283.

Stoller, R. J., & Geertsma, R. H. The consistency of psychiatrists' clinical judgments. *J. nerv. ment. Dis.*, 1963, *137*, 58–66.

Stone, A. R., Frank, J. D., Nash, E. H., Jr., & Imber, S. D. An intensive five-year follow-up study of treated psychiatric patients. *J. nerv. ment. Dis.*, 1961, *133*, 410–422.

Storrow, H. A. The measurement of outcome in psychotherapy. *Arch. gen. Psychiat.*, 1960, *2*, 142–146.

Stotsky, B. A., Daston, P. G., & Vardolk, C. N. An evaluation of the counseling of chronic schizophrenics. *J. counsel. Psychol.*, 1955, *2*, 248–255.

Straight, E. M. Evaluation of group therapy by follow-up study of formerly hospitalized patients. *Group Psychother.*, 1960, *13*, 110–118.

Streitfeld, J. W. Expressed acceptance of self and others by psychotherapists. *J. consult. Psychol.*, 1959, *23*, 435–441.

Strickland, Bonnie R., & Crowne, D. P. Need for approval and the premature termination of psychotherapy. *J. consult. Psychol.*, 1963, *27*, 95–101.

Strupp, H. H. An empirical study of certain psychotherapeutic operations: an exploration of the verbal response techniques of psychiatrists, psychologists and psychiatric social workers. Unpublished Ph.D. dissertation, George Washington University, 1954.

Strupp, H. H. An objective comparison of Rogerian and psychoanalytic techniques. *J. consult. Psychol.*, 1955a, *19*, 1–7.

Strupp, H. H. Psychotherapeutic technique, professional affiliation, and experience level. *J. consult. Psychol.*, 1955b, *19*, 97–102.

Strupp, H. H. The effect of the psychotherapist's personal analysis upon his techniques. *J. consult. Psychol.*, 1955c, *19*, 197–204.

Strupp, H. H. A multidimensional system for analyzing psychotherapeutic techniques. *Psychiatry*, 1957a, *20*, 293–306.

Strupp, H. H. A multidimensional analysis of technique in brief psychotherapy. *Psychiatry*, 1957b, *20*, 387–397.

Strupp, H. H. A multidimensional comparison of therapist activity in analytic and client-centered therapy. *J. consult. Psychol.*, 1957c, *21*, 301–308.

Strupp, H. H. The performance of psychiatrists and psychologists in a therapeutic interview. *J. clin. Psychol.*, 1958a, *14*, 219–226.

Strupp, H. H. The performance of psychoanalytic and client-centered therapists in an initial interview. *J. consult. Psychol.*, 1958b, *22*, 265–274.

Strupp, H. H. The psychotherapist's contribution to the treatment process. *Behav. Sci.*, 1958c, *3*, 34–67.

Strupp, H. H. The outcome problem in psychotherapy revisited. *Psychotherapy: Theory, Research, and Practice*, 1963, *1*, 1–13.

Strupp, H. H., Wallach, M. S., Wogan, M., & Jenkins, Joan W. Psychotherapists' assessment of former patients. *J. nerv. ment. Dis.*, 1963, *137*, 222–230.

Subotnik, L. Transference in client-centered play therapy. *Psychology*, 1966a, *3*, 2–17.

Subotnik, L. Transference in child therapy: a third replication. *Psychol. Rec.*, 1966*b*, *16*, 265–277.

Sullivan, H. S. *The psychiatric interview.* New York: Norton, 1954.

Sullivan, P. L., Miller, C., & Smelser, W. Factors in length of stay and progress in psychotherapy. *J. consult. Psychol.*, 1958, *22*, 1–9.

Sundland, D. M. & Barker, E. N. The orientations of psychotherapists. *J. consult. Psychol.*, 1962, *26*, 201–212.

Swensen, C. H. Psychotherapy as a special case of dyadic interaction: some suggestions for theory and research. *Psychotherapy: Theory, Research, and Practice*, 1967, *4*, 7–13.

Swensen, C. H., Jr., & Pascal, G. R. Prognostic significance of type of onset of mental illness. *J. consult. Psychol.*, 1954a, *18*, 127–130.

Swensen, C. H., Jr., & Pascal, G. R. Duration of illness as a prognostic indicator in mental illness. *J. consult. Psychol.*, 1954b, *18*, 363–365.

Taffel, C. Anxiety and the conditioning of verbal behavior. *J. abnorm. soc. Psychol.*, 1955, *51*, 496–501.

Talland, G. A., & Clark, D. H. Evaluation of topics in therapy group discussion. *J. clin. Psychol.*, 1954, *10*, 131–137.

Taulbee, E. S. Relationship between certain personality variables and continuation in psychotherapy. *J consult. Psychol.*, 1958, *22*, 83–89.

Taylor, J. W. Relationship of success and length of psychotherapy. *J. consult. Psychol.*, 1956, *20*, 332.

Teuber, H. L., & Powers, E. Evaluating therapy in a delinquency prevention program. *Psychiatric Treatment*, 1953, *21*, 138–147.

Thomson, G. H. An alternate formula for the true correlation of initial values with gains. *J. exp. Psychol.*, 1925, *8*, 323–324.

Thorley, A. S., & Craske, N. Comparison and estimate of group and individual methods of treatment. *Brit. med. J.*, 1950, *1*, 97–100.

Thorndike, E. L. The influence of the chance imperfections of measures upon the relation of initial score to gain or loss. *J. exp. Psychol.*, 1924, *7*, 225–232.

Tindall, R. H., & Robinson, F. P. The use of silence as a technique in counseling. *J. clin. Psychol.*, 1947, *3*, 136–141.

Titchener, J. L., Sheldon, M. B., & Ross, W. D. Changes in blood pressure of hypertensive patients with and without group psychotherapy. *J. psychosom. Res.*, 1959, *4*, 10–12.

Todd, W. B., & Ewing, T. N. Changes in self-reference during counseling. *J. counsel. Psychol.*, 1961, *8*, 112–115.

Tolman, Ruth S., & Meyer, M. M. Who returns to the clinic for more therapy? *Ment. Hyg.*, 1957, *41*, 497–506.

Tolor, A., & Kissinger, R. D. The role of the therapist's interventions in a simulated therapy situation. *J. clin. Psychol.*, 1965, *21*, 442–445.

Toman, W. Pause analysis as a short interviewing technique. *J. consult. Psychol.*, 1953, *17*, 1–7.

Tomlinson, T. M., & Hart, J. T., Jr. A validation study of the Process Scale. *J. consult. Psychol.*, 1962, *26*, 74–78.

Tomlinson, T. M., & Stoler, N. The relationship between affective evaluation and ratings of therapy process and outcome with schizophrenics. *Psychotherapy: Theory, Research, and Practice*, 1967, *4*, 14–18.

Tougas, R. R. Ethnocentrism as a limiting factor in verbal therapy. In C. R. Rogers & Rosalind F. Dymond (eds.), *Psychotherapy and personality change*. Chicago: University of Chicago Press, 1954. Pp. 196–214.

Tourney, G. Bloom, V., Lowinger, P. L., Schorer, C., Auld, F., & Gusell, J. A study of psychotherapeutic variables in psychoneurotic and schizophrenic patients. *Amer. J. Psychother.*, 1966, *20*, 112–124.

Tourney, G., Senf, Rita, Dunham, W., Glen, R., & Gottlieb, J. The effect of resocialization techniques on chronic schizophrenic patients. *Amer. J. Psychiat.*, 1960, *116*, 993–1000.

Truax, C. B. Effective ingredients in psychotherapy: an approach to unraveling the patient-therapist interaction. *J. counsel. Psychol.*, 1963, *10*, 256–263.

Truax, C. B. Therapist empathy, warmth, and genuineness, and patient personality change in group psychotherapy: a comparison between interaction unit measures, time sample measures, patient perception measures. *J. clin. Psychol.*, 1966a, *22*, 225–229.

Truax, C. B. Reinforcement and nonreinforcement in Rogerian psychotherapy. *J. abnorm. Psychol.*, 1966b, *71*, 1–9.

Truax, C. B., & Carkhuff, R. R. Concreteness: a neglected variable in research in psychotherapy. *J. clin. Psychol.*, 1964, *20*, 264–267.

Truax, C. B., & Carkhuff, R. R. Personality change in hospitalized mental patients during group psychotherapy as a function of the use of alternate sessions and vicarious therapy pretraining. *J. clin. Psychol.*, 1965a, *21*, 225–228.

Truax, C. B., & Carkhuff, R. R. Experimental manipulation of therapeutic conditions. *J. consult. Psychol.*, 1965b, *29*, 119–124.

Truax, C. B., & Carkhuff, R. R. *Toward effective counseling and psychotherapy*. Chicago: Aldine, 1967.

Truax, C. B., Carkhuff, R. R., & Kodman, F. Relationships between therapist-offered conditions and patient change in group psychotherapy. *J. clin. Psychol.*, 1965, *21*, 327–329.

Truax, C. B., Wargo, D. G., Frank, J. D., Imber, S. D., Battle, Carolyn C., Hoehn-Saric, R., Nash, E. H., & Stone, A. R. The therapist's contribution to accurate empathy, non-possessive warmth, and genuineness in psychotherapy. *J. clin. Psychol.*, 1966a, *22*, 331–334.

Truax, C. B., Wargo, D. G., Frank, J. D., Imber, S. D., Battle, Carolyn C., Hoehn-Saric, R., Nash, E. H., & Stone, A. R. Therapist empathy, genuineness, and warmth and patient therapeutic outcome. *J. consult. Psychol.*, 1966b, *30*, 395–401.

Truax, C. B., Wargo, D. G., & Silber, L. D. Effects of group psychotherapy with high accurate empathy and nonpossessive warmth upon female institutionalized delinquents. *J. abnorm. Psychol.*, 1966, *71*, 267–274.

Tucker, J. E. Measuring client progress in client-centered psychotherapy.

In W. U. Snyder (ed.), *Group report of a program of research in psychotherapy* (mimeographed). University Park, Pa.: Pennsylvania State College, 1953. Pp. 55–59.

Tucker, J. E. Group psychotherapy with chronic psychotic soiling patients. *J. consult. Psychol.*, 1956, *20*, 430.

Tuckman, J., & Lavell, Martha. Social status and clinic contact. *J. clin. Psychol.*, 1959, *15*, 345–348.

Tuma, A. H., & Gustad, J. W. The effects of client and counselor personality characteristics on client learning in counseling. *J. counsel. Psychol.*, 1957, *4*, 136–141.

Tyler, F. B., & Simmons, W. L. Patients' conceptions of therapists. *J. clin. Psychol.*, 1964, *20*, 122–133.

Ullmann, L. P., Forsman, R. G., Kenny, J. W., McInnis, T. L., Jr., Unikel, I. P., & Zeisset, R. M. Selective reinforcement of schizophrenics' interview responses. *Behav. Res. Ther.*, 1965, *2*, 205–212.

Ullmann, L. P., Krasner, L., & Collins, Beverly J. Modification of behavior through verbal conditioning: effects in group therapy. *J. abnorm. soc. Psychol.*, 1961, *62*, 128–132.

Ulrich, R. E., Stachnik, T. J., & Stainton, N. R. Student acceptance of generalized personality interpretations. *Psychol. Rep.*, 1963, *13*, 831–834.

van der Veen, F. Dimensions of client and therapist behavior in relation to outcome. *Proc. 73rd Annual Convention, APA*, 1965a, 279–280.

van der Veen, F. Effects of the therapist and the patient on each other's therapeutic behavior. *J. consult. Psychol.*, 1965b, *29*, 19–26.

Vargas, M. J. Changes in self-awareness during client-centered therapy. In C. R. Rogers & Rosalind F. Dymond (eds.), *Psychotherapy and personality change*. Chicago: University of Chicago Press, 1954. Pp. 145–166.

Vaught, G. M., & Rosenbaum, G. A note on the Ego-Strength Scale and sex differences in college students. *Psychol. Rec.*, 1966, *16*, 87–89.

Vitale, J., & Steinbach, M. The prevention of relapse of chronic mental patients. *Int. J. soc. Psychiat.*, 1965, *10*, 85–95.

Voegtlin, W. L. Treatment of alcoholism by establishing a conditioned reflex. *Amer. J. med. Sci.*, 1940, *199*, 802–810.

Vogel, J. L. Authoritarianism in the therapeutic relationship. *J. consult. Psychol.*, 1961, *25*, 102–108.

Volsky, T., Jr., Magoon, T. M., Norman, W. T., & Hoyt, D. P. *The outcomes of counseling and psychotherapy. Theory and research.* Minneapolis: University of Minnesota Press, 1965.

Walker, A. M., Rablen, R. A., & Rogers, C. R. Development of a scale to measure process changes in psychotherapy. *J. clin. Psychol.*, 1960, *16*, 79–85.

Walker, R. G., & Kelley, F. E. Shortterm psychotherapy with hospitalized schizophrenic patients. *Acta. psychiat. Scand.*, 1960, *35*, 34–56.

Walker, R. G., & Kelley, F. E. Shortterm psychotherapy with schizophrenic patients evaluated over a three-year follow-up period. *J. nerv. ment. Dis.*, 1963, *137*, 349–352.

Wallace, H. E. R., & Whyte, M. B. H. Natural history of the psychoneuroses. *Brit. med. J.*, 1959, *1*, 144–149.

Wallach, M. S. Authoritarianism and therapist preference. *J. clin. Psychol.*, 1962a, *18*, 325–327.

Wallach, M. S. Therapists' patient preferences and their relationship to two patient variables. *J. clin. Psychol.*, 1962b, *18*, 497–501.

Wallach, M. S. Judgments of motivation for psychotherapy: some further explorations. *J. consult. Psychol.*, 1963, *27*, 185.

Wallach, M. S., & Strupp, H. H. Dimensions of psychotherapists' activity. *J. consult. Psychol.*, 1964, *28*, 120–125.

Walton, H. J., & McPherson, F. M. Clinicians as observers of psychological events. *J. psychosom. Res.*, 1964, *8*, 319–325.

Warne, Merna M., Canter, A. H., & Wizma, B. Analysis and follow-up of patients with psychiatric disorders. *Amer. J. Psychother.*, 1953, *7*, 278–288.

Warren, W. A study of adolescent psychiatric in-patients and the outcome six or more years later: II. The follow-up study. *J. child Psychol. Psychiat.*, 1965, *6*, 141–160.

Waskow, Irene E. Reinforcement in a therapy-like situation through selective responding to feelings or content. *J. consult. Psychol.*, 1962, *26*, 11–19.

Waskow, Irene E. Counselor attitudes and client behavior. *J. consult. Psychol.*, 1963, *27*, 405–412.

Watkins, J. G. Evaluating success in psychotherapy. *Amer. Psychologist*, 1949, *4*, 396.

Watson, P. D., & Kanter, S. S. Some influences of an experimental situation on the psychotherapeutic process. *J. nerv. ment. Dis.*, 1954, *120*, 414.

Watson, P. D., & Kanter, S. S. Some influences of an experimental situation on the psychotherapeutic process. *Psychosom. Med.*, 1956, *18*, 457–470.

Weber, J. J., Elinson, J., & Moss, L. Psychoanalysis and change: A study of psychoanalytic clinic records utilizing electronic data processing techniques. *Arch. gen. Psychiat.*, 1967, *17*, 687–709.

Welkowitz, Joan, Cohen, J., & Ortmeyer, D. Value system similarity: investigation of patient-therapist dyads. *J. consult. Psychol.*, 1967, *31*, 48–55.

Wenar, C., Ruttenberg, B. A., Dratman, M. L., & Wolf, Enid G. Changing autistic behavior: the effectiveness of three milieus. *Arch. gen. Psychiat.*, 1967, *17*, 26–35.

White, Alice M., Fichtenbaum, L., & Dollard, J. Measure for predicting dropping out of psychotherapy. *J. consult. Psychol.*, 1964, *28*, 326–332.

White, Alice M., Fichtenbaum, L., Cooper, L., & Dollard, J. Physiological focus in psychiatric interviews. *J. consult. Psychol.*, 1966, *30*, 363.

Whitehorn, J. C., & Betz, Barbara J. A study of psychotherapeutic relationships between physicians and schizophrenic patients. *Amer. J. Psychiat.*, 1954, *111*, 321–331.

Whitehorn, J. C., & Betz, Barbara J. A comparison of psychotherapeutic relationships between physicians and schizophrenic patients when insulin is combined with psychotherapy and when psychotherapy is used alone. *Amer. J. Psychiat.*, 1957, *113*, 901–910.

Whitehorn, J. C., & Betz, Barbara J. Further studies of the doctor as a crucial variable in the outcome of treatment with schizophrenic patients. *Amer. J. Psychiat.*, 1960, *117*, 215–223.

Wiener, D. N. The effect of arbitrary termination on return to psychotherapy. *J. clin. Psychol.*, 1959, *15*, 335–338.

Wiener, M. The effects of two experimental counseling techniques on performances impaired by induced stress. *J. abnorm. soc. Psychol.*, 1955, *51*, 565–572.

Wilcox, G. T., & Guthrie, G. M. Changes in adjustment of institutionalized female defectives following group psychotherapy. *J. clin. Psychol.*, 1957, *13*, 9–13.

Williams, M., McGee, T., Kittleson, S., & Halperin, L. An evaluation of an intensive group living program with schizophrenic patients. *Psychol. Monogr.*, 1962, *76*, whole No. 543.

Williams, R., & Pollack, R. H. Some non-psychological variables in therapy defection in a child-guidance clinic. *J. Psychol.*, 1964, *58*, 145–155.

Wimsatt, W. R., & Vestre, N. D. Extraexperimental effects in verbal conditioning. *J. consult. Psychol.*, 1963, *27*, 400–404.

Winder, A. E., & Hersko, M. The effect of social class on the length and type of psychotherapy in a Veterans Administration mental hygiene clinic. *J. clin. Psychol.*, 1955, *11*, 77–79.

Winder, C. L., Ahmad, F. Z., Bandura, A., & Rau, Lucy C. Dependency of patients, psychotherapists' responses, and aspects of psychotherapy. *J. consult. Psychol.*, 1962, *26*, 129–134.

Winkler, R. C., & Myers, R. A. Some concomitants of self-ideal discrepancy measures of self-acceptance. *J. counsel. Psychol.*, 1963, *10*, 83–86.

Wispé, L. G., & Parloff, M. B. Impact of psychotherapy on the productivity of psychologists. *J. abnorm. Psychol.*, 1965, *70*, 188–193.

Wolff, W. Fact and value in psychotherapy. *Amer. J. Psychother.*, 1954, *8*, 466–486.

Wolk, R. L. The relationship of group psychotherapy to institutional adjustment. *Group Psychother.*, 1963, *16*, 141–144.

Wolpe, J. The systematic desensitization treatment of neuroses. *J. nerv. ment. Dis.*, 1961, *132*, 189–203.

Wolpin, M., & Raines, J. Visual imagery, expected roles and extinction as possible factors in reducing fear and avoidance behavior. *Behav. Res. Ther.*, 1966, *4*, 25–37.

Wrenn, R. L. Counselor orientation: theoretical or situational? *J. counsel. Psychol.*, 1960, *7*, 40–45.

Yalom, I. D. A study of group therapy dropouts. *Arch. gen. Psychiat.*, 1966, *14*, 393–414.

Yalom, I. D., Houts, P. S., Newell, G., & Rand, K. H. Preparation of patients for group therapy. *Arch. gen. Psychiat.*, 1967, *17*, 416–427.

Yalom, I. D., Houts, P. S., Zimerberg, S. M., & Rand, K. H. Prediction of improvement in group therapy. *Arch. gen. Psychiat.*, 1967, *17*, 159–168.

Yamamoto, J., & Goin, Marcia K. On the treatment of the poor. *Amer. J. Psychiat.*, 1965, *122*, 267–271.

Yoder, D. A socialization program in the treatment of dementia praecox. *Occup. Ther. Rehab.*, 1938, *17*, 107–114.

Yonge, K. A., & O'Connor, N. Measurable effects of group psychotherapy with defective delinquents. *J. ment. Sci.*, 1954, *100*, 944–952.

Zhukov, I. A. Hypnotherapy of dermatoses in resort treatment. In R. B. Winn (ed.), *Psychotherapy in the Soviet Union.* New York: Philosophical Library, 1961. Pp. 178–181.

Zielonka, W. A. The effects of external therapeutic environment on patient behavior. Unpublished Ph. D. dissertation, University of Chicago, 1951.

Zieve, L. Note on the correlation of initial scores with gains. *J. educ. Psychol.*, 1940, *31*, 391–394.

Zimmer, J. M., & Park, P. Factor analysis of counselor communications. *J. counsel. Psychol.*, 1967, *14*, 198–203.

Zirkle, G. A. Five-minute psychotherapy. *Amer. J. Psychiat.*, 1961, *118*, 544–546.

Name Index

Subject Index